SAS Publishing

Step-by-Step Programming with
Base SAS® Software

The Power to Know™

D1089391

The correct bibliographic citation for this manual is as follows: SAS Institute Inc., *Step-by-Step Programming with Base SAS® Software*, Cary, NC: SAS Institute Inc., 2001.

Step-by-Step Programming with Base SAS® Software

SAS Publishing provides a complete selection of books and electronic products to help customers use SAS software to its fullest potential. For more information about our e-books, CD-ROM, hard copy books, and Web-based training, visit the SAS Publishing Web site at www.sas.com/pubs or call 1-800-727–3228.

Contents

P A R T *1*

Introduction to the SAS System

CHAPTER

1

What Is the SAS System?

Introduction

SAS is an integrated system of software solutions that enables you to perform

- □ data entry, retrieval, and management
- □ report writing and graphics design
- □ statistical and mathematical analysis
- □ business forecasting and decision support
- □ operations research and project management
- □ applications development.

How you use SAS depends on what you want to accomplish. Some people use many of the capabilities of the SAS System, and others use only a few.

At the core of the SAS System is base SAS software, the software product you learn to use in this book. This chapter presents an overview of base SAS software. It introduces the capabilities of base SAS software, addresses methods of running SAS, and outlines various types of output.

Components of Base SAS Software

Overview

Base SAS software contains

- □ a data management facility
- □ a programming language
- □ data analysis and reporting utilities.

Learning to use base SAS software enables you to work with these features of SAS. It also prepares you to learn other SAS software products, because all SAS software products follow the same basic rules.

Data Management Facility

SAS organizes data into a rectangular form or table that is called a *SAS data set*. The following figure shows a SAS data set. The data describes participants in a 16-week weight program at a health and fitness club. The data for each participant includes an identification number, name, team name, and weight (in U.S. pounds) at the beginning and end of the program.

Figure 1.1 Rectangular Form of a SAS Data Set

variable

	IdNumber	Name	Team	StartWeight	EndWeight	
1	1023	David Shaw	red	189	165	
2	1049	Amelia Serrano	yellow	145	124	observation
3	1219	Alan Nance	red	210	192	
4	1246	Ravi Sinha	yellow	194	177	— data value
5	1078	Ashley McKnight	red	127	118	

data value

In a SAS data set, each row represents information about an individual entity and is called an *observation*. Each column represents the same type of information and is called a *variable*. Each separate piece of information is a *data value*. In a SAS data set, an observation contains all the data values for an entity; a variable contains the same type of data value for all entities.

To build a SAS data set with base SAS software, you write a program that uses statements in the SAS programming language. A SAS program that begins with a DATA statement and typically creates a SAS data set or a report is called a *DATA step*.

The following SAS program creates a SAS data set named WEIGHT_CLUB from the health club data:

```
data weight_club; ❶
    input IdNumber 1-4 Name $ 6-24 Team $ StartWeight EndWeight; ❷
    Loss=StartWeight-EndWeight; ❸
    datalines; ❹
1023 David Shaw           red 189 165 ❺
1049 Amelia Serrano       yellow 145 124 ❺
1219 Alan Nance           red 210 192 ❺
1246 Ravi Sinha           yellow 194 177 ❺
1078 Ashley McKnight      red 127 118 ❺
; ❻
```

The following list corresponds to the numbered items in the preceding program:

❶ The DATA statement tells SAS to begin building a SAS data set named WEIGHT_CLUB.

❷ The INPUT statement identifies the fields to be read from the input data and names the SAS variables to be created from them (IdNumber, Name, Team, StartWeight, and EndWeight).

❸ The third statement is an assignment statement. It calculates the weight each person lost and assigns the result to a new variable, Loss.

❹ The DATALINES statement indicates that data lines follow.

❺ The data lines follow the DATALINES statement. This approach to processing raw data is useful when you have only a few lines of data. (Later chapters show ways to access larger amounts of data that are stored in files.)

❻ The semicolon signals the end of the raw data, and is a step boundary. It tells SAS that the preceding statements are ready for execution.

Note: By default, the data set WEIGHT_CLUB is temporary; that is, it exists only for the current job or session. For information about how to create a permanent SAS data set, see Chapter 2, "Introduction to DATA Step Processing," on page 19. △

Programming Language

Elements of the SAS Language

The statements that created the data set WEIGHT_CLUB are part of the SAS programming language. The SAS language contains statements, expressions, functions and CALL routines, options, formats, and informats – elements that many programming languages share. However, the way you use the elements of the SAS language depends on certain programming rules. The most important rules are listed in the next two sections.

Rules for SAS Statements

The conventions that are shown in the programs in this book, such as indention of subordinate statements and extra spacing and blank lines, are for the purpose of clarity and ease of use. They are not required by SAS. There are only a few rules for writing SAS statements:

- □ SAS statements end with a semicolon.
- □ You can enter SAS statements in lowercase, uppercase, or a mixture of the two.
- □ You can begin SAS statements in any column of a line and write several statements on the same line.
- □ You can begin a statement on one line and continue it on another line, but you cannot split a word between two lines.
- □ Words in SAS statements are separated by blanks or by special characters (such as the equal sign and the minus sign in the calculation of the Loss variable in the WEIGHT_CLUB example).

Rules for Most SAS Names

SAS names are used for SAS data set names, variable names, and other items. The following rules apply:

- □ A SAS name can contain from one to 32 characters.
- □ The first character must be a letter or an underscore (_).
- □ Subsequent characters must be letters, numbers, or underscores.
- □ Blanks cannot appear in SAS names.

Special Rules for Variable Names

For variable names only, SAS remembers the combination of uppercase and lowercase letters that you use when you create the variable name. Internally, the case of letters does not matter. "CAT," "cat," and "Cat" all represent the same variable. But for presentation purposes, SAS remembers the initial case of each letter and uses it to represent the variable name when printing it.

Data Analysis and Reporting Utilities

The SAS programming language is both powerful and flexible. You can program any number of analyses and reports with it. SAS can also simplify programming for you with its library of built-in programs known as *SAS procedures*. SAS procedures use data values from SAS data sets to produce preprogrammed reports, requiring minimal effort from you.

For example, the following SAS program produces a report that displays the values of the variables in the SAS data set WEIGHT_CLUB. Weight values are presented in U.S. pounds.

```
options linesize=80 pagesize=60 pageno=1 nodate;

proc print data=weight_club;
    title 'Health Club Data';
run;
```

This procedure, known as the PRINT procedure, displays the variables in a simple, organized form. The following output shows the results:

Output 1.1 Displaying the Values in a SAS Data Set

```
                                Health Club Data                             1

            Id                                      Start     End
   Obs    Number    Name              Team          Weight   Weight    Loss

    1      1023     David Shaw        red            189      165       24
    2      1049     Amelia Serrano    yellow         145      124       21
    3      1219     Alan Nance        red            210      192       18
    4      1246     Ravi Sinha        yellow         194      177       17
    5      1078     Ashley McKnight   red            127      118        9
```

To produce a table showing mean starting weight, ending weight, and weight loss for each team, use the TABULATE procedure.

```
options linesize=80 pagesize=60 pageno=1 nodate;

proc tabulate data=weight_club;
   class team;
   var StartWeight EndWeight Loss;
   table team, mean*(StartWeight EndWeight Loss);
   title 'Mean Starting Weight, Ending Weight,';
   title2 'and Weight Loss';
run;
```

The following output shows the results:

Output 1.2 Table of Mean Values for Each Team

```
                   Mean Starting Weight, Ending Weight,                      1
                             and Weight Loss


        -----------------------------------------------------------
        |                 |                   Mean                 |
        |                 |-----------------------------------------|
        |                 |StartWeight | EndWeight  |    Loss       |
        |-----------------+------------+------------+------------|
        |Team             |            |            |            |
        |-----------------|            |            |            |
        |red              |     175.33 |     158.33 |      17.00 |
        |-----------------+------------+------------+------------|
        |yellow           |     169.50 |     150.50 |      19.00 |
        -----------------------------------------------------------
```

A portion of a SAS program that begins with a PROC (procedure) statement and ends with a RUN statement (or is ended by another PROC or DATA statement) is called a *PROC step*. Both of the PROC steps that create the previous two outputs comprise the following elements:

☐ a PROC statement, which includes the word PROC, the name of the procedure you want to use, and the name of the SAS data set that contains the values. (If you omit the DATA= option and data set name, the procedure uses the SAS data set that was most recently created in the program.)

☐ additional statements that give SAS more information about what you want to do, for example, the CLASS, VAR, TABLE, and TITLE statements.

□ a RUN statement, which indicates that the preceding group of statements is ready
   to be executed.

Output Produced by the SAS System

Traditional Output

A SAS program can produce some or all of the following kinds of output:

a SAS data set
   contains data values that are stored as a table of observations and variables. It
   also stores descriptive information about the data set, such as the names and
   arrangement of variables, the number of observations, and the creation date of the
   data set. A SAS data set can be temporary or permanent. The examples in this
   chapter create the temporary data set WEIGHT_CLUB.

the SAS log
   is a record of the SAS statements that you entered and of messages from SAS
   about the execution of your program. It can appear as a file on disk, a display on
   your monitor, or a hardcopy listing. The exact appearance of the SAS log varies
   according to your operating environment and your site. The output in Output 1.3
   on page 9 shows a typical SAS log for the program in this chapter.

a report or simple listing
   ranges from a simple listing of data values to a subset of a large data set or a
   complex summary report that groups and summarizes data and displays statistics.
   The appearance of procedure output varies according to your site and the options
   that you specify in the program, but the output in Output 1.1 on page 7 and
   Output 1.2 on page 7 illustrate typical procedure output. You can also use a DATA
   step to produce a completely customized report (see "Creating Customized
   Reports" on page 387).

other SAS files such as catalogs
   contain information that cannot be represented as tables of data values. Examples
   of items that can be stored in SAS catalogs include function key settings, letters
   that are produced by SAS/FSP software, and displays that are produced by
   SAS/GRAPH software.

external files or entries in other databases
   can be created and updated by SAS programs. SAS/ACCESS software enables you
   to create and update files that are stored in databases such as Oracle.

Output 1.3 Traditional Output: A SAS Log

```
NOTE: PROCEDURE PRINTTO used:
      real time           0.02 seconds
      cpu time            0.01 seconds

22
23   options pagesize=60 linesize=80 pageno=1 nodate;
24
25   data weight_club;
26      input IdNumber 1-4 Name $ 6-24 Team $ StartWeight EndWeight;
27      Loss=StartWeight-EndWeight;
28      datalines;
NOTE: The data set WORK.WEIGHT_CLUB has 5 observations and 6 variables.
NOTE: DATA statement used:
      real time           0.14 seconds
      cpu time            0.07 seconds

34   ;
35
36
37   proc tabulate data=weight_club;
38      class team;
39      var StartWeight EndWeight Loss;
40      table team, mean*(StartWeight EndWeight Loss);
41      title 'Mean Starting Weight, Ending Weight,';
42      title2 'and Weight Loss';
43   run;
NOTE: There were 5 observations read from the data set WORK.WEIGHT_CLUB.
NOTE: PROCEDURE TABULATE used:
      real time           0.18 seconds
      cpu time            0.09 seconds

44   proc printto; run;
```

Output from the Output Delivery System (ODS)

The Output Delivery System (ODS) enables you to produce output in a variety of formats, such as

- □ an HTML file
- □ a traditional SAS Listing (monospace)
- □ a PostScript file
- □ an RTF file (for use with Microsoft Word)
- □ an output data set.

The following figure illustrates the concept of output for SAS Version 8.

Figure 1.2   Model of the Production of ODS Output

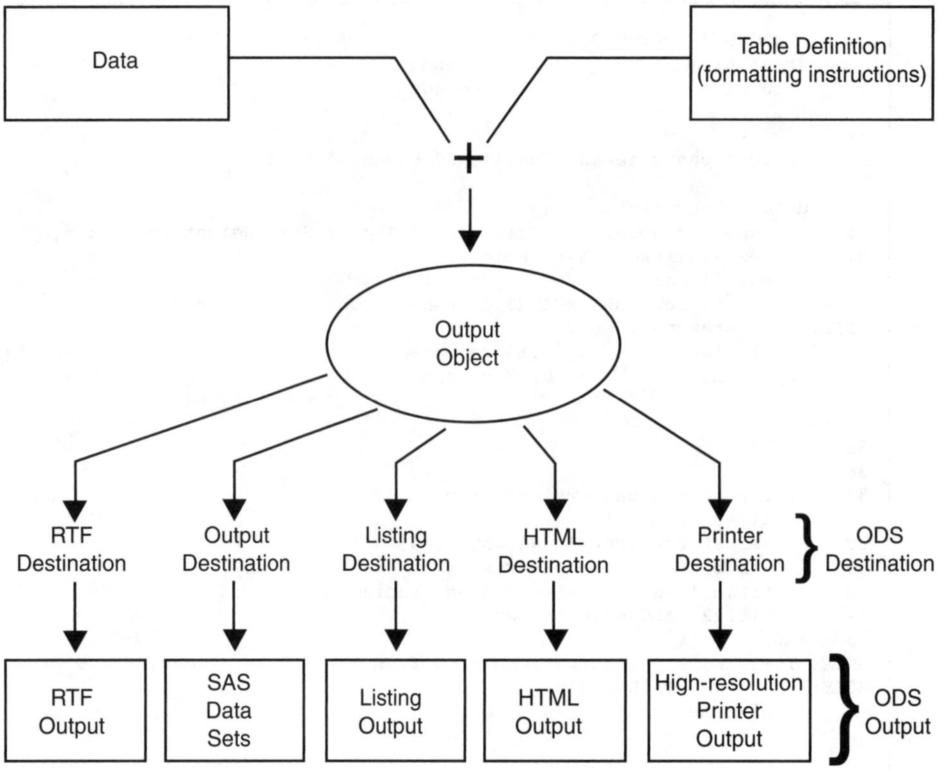

The following definitions describe the terms in the preceding figure:

data
> Each procedure that supports ODS and each DATA step produces data, which contains the results (numbers and characters) of the step in a form similar to a SAS data set.

table definition
> The table definition is a set of instructions that describes how to format the data. This description includes but is not limited to

> □ the order of the columns

> □ text and order of column headings

> □ formats for data

> □ font sizes and font faces.

output object
> ODS combines formatting instructions with the data to produce an output object. The output object, therefore, contains both the results of the procedure or DATA step and information about how to format the results. An output object has a name, a label, and a path.

> *Note:*   Although many output objects include formatting instructions, not all do. In some cases the output object consists of only the data. △

ODS destinations
> An ODS destination specifies a specific type of output. ODS supports a number of destinations, which include the following:

RTF
> produces output that is formatted for use with Microsoft Word.

Output
> produces a SAS data set.

Listing
> produces traditional SAS output (monospace format).

HTML
> produces output that is formatted in Hyper Text Markup Language (HTML). You can access the output on the web with your web browser.

Printer
> produces output that is formatted for a high-resolution printer. An example of this type of output is a PostScript file.

ODS output
> ODS output consists of formatted output from any of the ODS destinations.

For more information about ODS output, see Chapter 23, "Directing SAS Output and the SAS Log," on page 347 and Chapter 32, "Understanding and Customizing SAS Output: The Output Delivery System (ODS)," on page 561.

For complete information about ODS, see *The Complete Guide to the SAS Output Delivery System*.

Ways to Run SAS Programs

Selecting an Approach

There are several ways to run SAS programs. They differ in the speed with which they run, the amount of computer resources that are required, and the amount of interaction that you have with the program (that is, the kinds of changes you can make while the program is running).

The examples in this book produce the same results, regardless of the way you run the programs. However, in a few cases, the way that you run a program determines the appearance of output. The following sections briefly introduce different ways to run SAS programs.

SAS Windowing Environment

The SAS windowing environment enables you to interact with SAS directly through a series of windows. You can use these windows to perform common tasks, such as locating and organizing files, entering and editing programs, reviewing log information, viewing procedure output, setting options, and more. If needed, you can issue operating system commands from within this environment. Or, you can suspend the current SAS windowing environment session, enter operating system commands, and then resume the SAS windowing environment session at a later time.

Using the SAS windowing environment is a quick and convenient way to program in SAS. It is especially useful for learning SAS and developing programs on small test files. Although it uses more computer resources than other techniques, using the SAS windowing environment can save a lot of program development time.

For more information about the SAS windowing environment, see Chapter 39, "Using the SAS Windowing Environment," on page 651.

SAS/ASSIST Software

One important feature of SAS is the availability of SAS/ASSIST software. SAS/ASSIST provides a point-and-click interface that enables you to select the tasks that you want to perform. SAS then submits the SAS statements to accomplish those tasks. You do not need to know how to program in the SAS language in order to use SAS/ASSIST.

SAS/ASSIST works by submitting SAS statements just like the ones shown earlier in this chapter. In that way, it provides a number of features, but it does not represent the total functionality of SAS software. If you want to perform tasks other than those that are available in SAS/ASSIST, you need to learn to program in SAS as described in this book.

Noninteractive Mode

In noninteractive mode, you prepare a file that contains SAS statements and any system statements that are required by your operating environment, and submit the program. The program runs immediately and occupies your current workstation session. You cannot continue to work in that session while the program is running,* and you usually cannot interact with the program.** The log and procedure output go to prespecified destinations, and you usually do not see them until the program ends. To modify the program or correct errors, you must edit and resubmit the program.

Noninteractive execution may be faster than batch execution because the computer system runs the program immediately rather than waiting to schedule your program among other programs.

Batch Mode

To run a program in batch mode, you prepare a file that contains SAS statements and any system statements that are required by your operating environment, and then you submit the program.

You can then work on another task at your workstation. While you are working, the operating environment schedules your job for execution (along with jobs submitted by other people) and runs it. When execution is complete, you can look at the log and the procedure output.

The central feature of batch execution is that it is completely separate from other activities at your workstation. You do not see the program while it is running, and you cannot correct errors at the time they occur. The log and procedure output go to prespecified destinations; you can look at them only after the program has finished running. To modify the SAS program, you edit the program with the editor that is supported by your operating environment and submit a new batch job.

When sites charge for computer resources, batch processing is a relatively inexpensive way to execute programs. It is particularly useful for large programs or when you need to use your workstation for other tasks while the program is executing. However, for learning SAS or developing and testing new programs, using batch mode might not be efficient.

---

*   In a workstation environment, you can switch to another window and continue working.
** Limited ways of interaction are available. You can, for example, use the asterisk (*) option in a %INCLUDE statement in your program.

Interactive Line Mode

In an interactive line-mode session, you enter one line of a SAS program at a time, and SAS executes each DATA or PROC step automatically as soon as it recognizes the end of the step. You usually see procedure output immediately on your display monitor. Depending on your site's computer system and on your workstation, you may be able to scroll backward and forward to see different parts of your log and procedure output, or you may lose them when they scroll off the top of your screen. There are limited facilities for modifying programs and correcting errors.

Interactive line-mode sessions use fewer computer resources than a windowing environment. If you use line mode, you should familiarize yourself with the %INCLUDE, %LIST, and RUN statements in *SAS Language Reference: Dictionary*.

Running Programs in the SAS Windowing Environment

You can run most programs in this book by using any of the methods that are described in the previous sections. This book uses the SAS windowing environment (as it appears on Windows and UNIX operating environments) when it is necessary to show programming within a SAS session. The SAS windowing environment appears differently depending on the operating environment that you use. For more information about the SAS windowing environment, see Chapter 39, "Using the SAS Windowing Environment," on page 651.

The following example gives a brief overview of a SAS session that uses the SAS windowing environment. When you invoke SAS, the following windows appear.

Display 1.1 SAS Windowing Environment

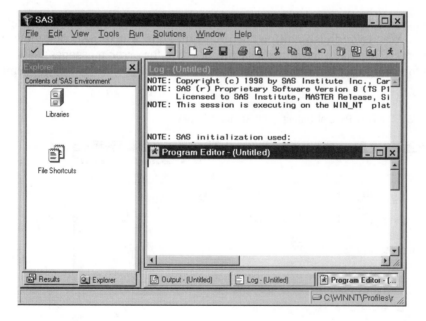

The specific window placement, display colors, messages, and some other details vary according to your site, your monitor, and your operating environment. The window on the left side of the display is the SAS Explorer window, which you can use to assign and locate SAS libraries, files, and other items. The window at the top right is the Log window; it contains the SAS log for the session. The window at the bottom right is the Program Editor window. This window provides an editor in which you edit your SAS programs.

To create the program for the health and fitness club, type the statements in the Program Editor window. You can turn line numbers on or off to facilitate program creation. The following display shows the beginning of the program.

Display 1.2 Editing a Program in the Program Editor Window

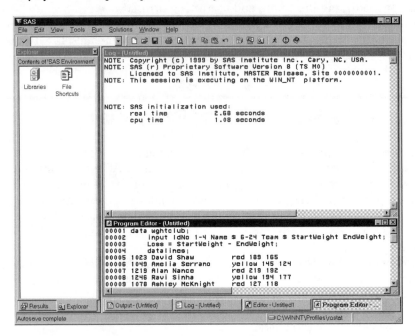

When you fill the Program Editor window, scroll down to continue typing the program. When you finish editing the program, submit it to SAS and view the output. (If SAS does not create output, check the SAS log for error messages.)

The following displays show the first and second pages of the Output window.

Display 1.3 The First Page of Output in the Output Window

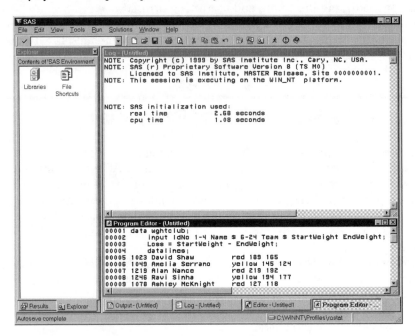

Display 1.4 The Second Page of Output in the Output Window

After you finish viewing the output, you can return to the Program Editor window to begin creating a new program.

By default, the output from all submissions remains in the Output window, and all statements that you submit remain in memory until the end of your session. You can view the output at any time, and you can recall previously submitted statements for editing and resubmitting. You can also clear a window of its contents.

All the commands that you use to move through the SAS windowing environment can be executed as words or as function keys. You can also customize the SAS windowing environment by determining which windows appear, as well as by assigning commands to function keys. For more information about customizing the SAS windowing environment, see Chapter 40, "Customizing the SAS Environment," on page 691.

Review of SAS Tools

Statements

DATA *SAS-data-set*;
> begins a DATA step and tells SAS to begin creating a SAS data set. *SAS-data-set* names the data set that is being created.

%INCLUDE *source(s)* </<SOURCE2> <S2=*length*> <*host-options*>>;
> brings SAS programming statements, data lines, or both into a current SAS program.

RUN;
> tells SAS to begin executing the preceding group of SAS statements.

For more information, see Statements in *SAS Language Reference: Dictionary*.

Procedures

PROC *procedure* <DATA=*SAS-data-set*>;
> begins a PROC step and tells SAS to invoke a particular SAS procedure to process the SAS data set that is specified in the DATA= option. If you omit the DATA= option, then the procedure processes the most recently created SAS data set in the program.

For more information about using procedures, see the *SAS Procedures Guide*.

Learning More

Basic SAS usage
> For an entry-level introduction to basic SAS programming language, see *The Little SAS Book: A Primer, Second Edition*.

DATA step
> For more information about how to create SAS data sets, see Chapter 2, "Introduction to DATA Step Processing," on page 19.

DATA step processing
> For more information about DATA step processing, see Chapter 6, "Understanding DATA Step Processing," on page 97.

> For information about how to easily use the SAS environment, see *Getting Started with the SAS System*.

P A R T *2*

Getting Your Data into Shape

Introduction to DATA Step Processing

Introduction

Purpose

The DATA step is one of the basic building blocks of SAS programming. It creates the data sets that are used in a SAS program's analysis and reporting procedures. Understanding the basic structure, functioning, and components of the DATA step is fundamental to learning how to create your own SAS data sets. In this chapter, you will learn

- □ what a SAS data set is and why it is needed
- □ how the DATA step works
- □ what information you have to supply to SAS so that it can construct a SAS data set for you.

Prerequisites

You should understand the concepts introduced in Chapter 1, "What Is the SAS System?," on page 3 before continuing.

The SAS Data Set: Your Key to the SAS System

Understanding the Function of the SAS Data Set

SAS enables you to solve problems by providing methods to analyze or to process your data in some way. You need to first get the data into a form that SAS can recognize and process. After the data is in that form, you can analyze it and generate reports. The following figure shows this process in the simplest case.

Figure 2.1 From Raw Data to Final Analysis

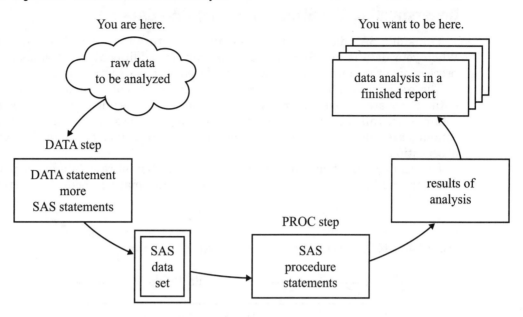

You begin with *raw data*, that is, a collection of data that has not yet been processed by SAS. You use a set of statements known as a *DATA step* to get your data into a SAS data set. Then you can further process your data with additional DATA step programming or with SAS procedures.

In its simplest form, the DATA step can be represented by the three components that are shown in the following figure.

Figure 2.2 From Raw Data to a SAS Data Set

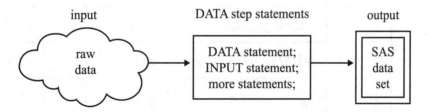

SAS processes input in the form of raw data and creates a SAS data set.

When you have a SAS data set, you can use it as input to other DATA steps. The following figure shows the SAS statements that you can use to create a new SAS data set.

Figure 2.3 Using One SAS Data Set to Create Another

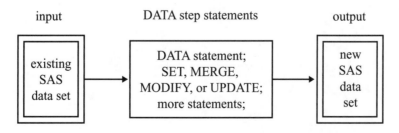

Understanding the Structure of the SAS Data Set

Think of a SAS data set as a rectangular structure that identifies and stores data. When your data is in a SAS data set, you can use additional DATA steps for further processing, or perform many types of analyses with SAS procedures.

The rectangular structure of a SAS data set consists of rows and columns in which data values are stored. The rows in a SAS data set are called *observations*, and the columns are called *variables*. In a raw data file, the rows are called *records* and the columns are called *fields*. Variables contain the data values for all of the items in an observation.

For example, the following figure shows a collection of raw data about participants in a health and fitness club. Each record contains information about one participant.

Figure 2.4   Raw Data from the Health and Fitness Club

data fields

Health and Fitness Club Data

raw data

Id	Name	Team	Starting Weight	Ending Weight
1023	David Shaw	red	189	165
1049	Amelia Serrano	yellow	145	124
1219	Alan Nance	red	210	192
1246	Ravi Sinha	yellow	194	177
1078	Ashley McKnight	red	127	118
1221	Jim Brown	yellow	220	—

The following figure shows how easily the health club records can be translated into parts of a SAS data set. Each record becomes an observation. In this case, each observation represents a participant in the program. Each field in the record becomes a variable. The variables represent each participant's identification number, name, team name, and weight at the beginning and end of a 16-week program.

Figure 2.5 How Data Fits into a SAS Data Set

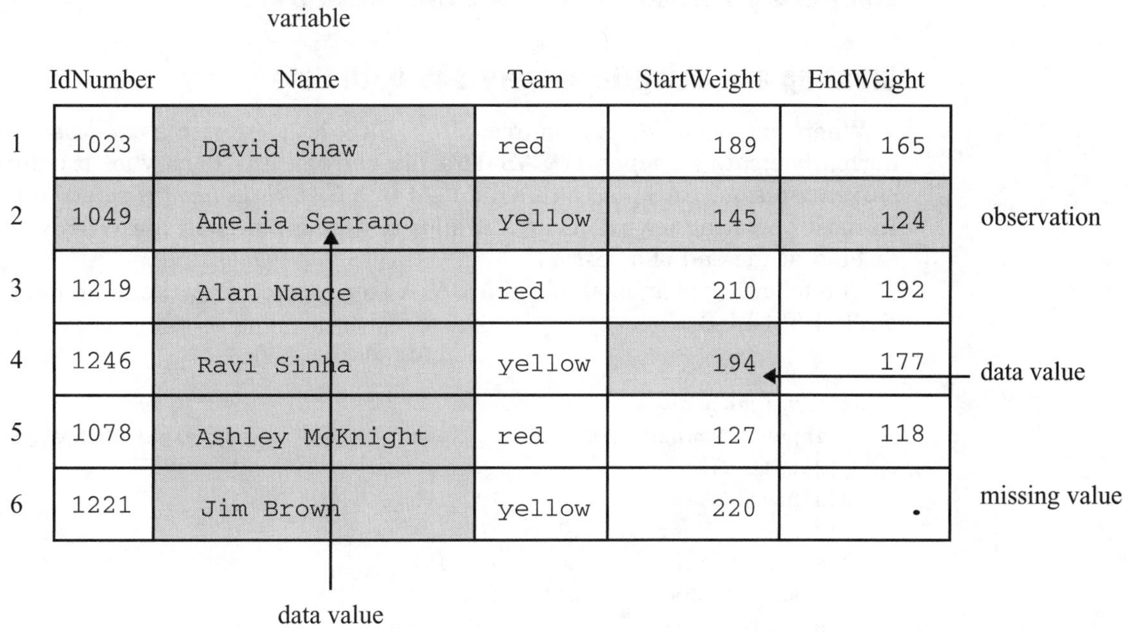

variable

	IdNumber	Name	Team	StartWeight	EndWeight	
1	1023	David Shaw	red	189	165	
2	1049	Amelia Serrano	yellow	145	124	observation
3	1219	Alan Nance	red	210	192	
4	1246	Ravi Sinha	yellow	194	177	data value
5	1078	Ashley McKnight	red	127	118	
6	1221	Jim Brown	yellow	220	.	missing value

data value

In a SAS data set, every variable exists for every observation. What if you do not have all the data for each observation? If the raw data is incomplete because a value for the numeric variable EndWeight was not recorded for one observation, then this *missing value* is represented by a period that serves as a placeholder, as shown in observation 6 in the previous figure. (Missing values for character variables are represented by blanks. Character and numeric variables are discussed later in this chapter.) By coding a value as missing, you can add an observation to the data set for which the data is incomplete and still retain the rectangular shape necessary for a SAS data set.

Along with data values, each SAS data set contains a descriptor portion, as illustrated in the following figure:

Figure 2.6 Parts of a SAS Data Set

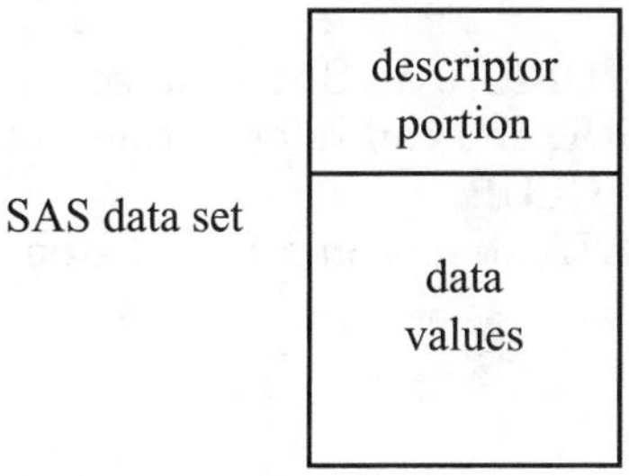

SAS data set

| descriptor portion |
| data values |

The descriptor portion consists of details that SAS records about a data set, such as the names and attributes of all the variables, the number of observations in the data set, and the date and time that the data set was created and updated.

Operating Environment Information: Depending on your operating environment and the engine used to write the SAS data set, SAS may store additional information about a SAS data set in its descriptor portion. For more information, refer to the SAS documentation for your operating environment. △

Temporary versus Permanent SAS Data Sets

Creating and Using Temporary SAS Data Sets

When you use a DATA step to create a SAS data set with a *one-level name*, you normally create a *temporary* SAS data set, one that exists only for the duration of your current session. SAS places this data set in a *SAS data library* referred to as WORK. In most operating environments, all files that SAS stores in the WORK library are deleted at the end of a session.

The following is an example of a DATA step that creates the temporary data set WEIGHT_CLUB.

```
data weight_club;
   input IdNumber Name $ 6--20 Team $ 22--27 StartWeight EndWeight;
   datalines;
1023 David Shaw       red    189 165
1049 Amelia Serrano   yellow 145 124
1219 Alan Nance       red    210 192
1246 Ravi Sinha       yellow 194 177
1078 Ashley McKnight  red    127 118
1221 Jim Brown        yellow 220 .
;
```

The preceding program code refers to the temporary data set as WEIGHT_CLUB. SAS. However, it assigns the first-level name WORK to all temporary data sets, and refers to the WEIGHT_CLUB data set with its two-level name, WORK.WEIGHT_CLUB. The following output from the SAS log shows the name of the temporary data set.

Output 2.1   SAS Log: The WORK.WEIGHT_CLUB Temporary Data Set

```
162   data weight_club;
163      input IdNumber Name $ 6-20 Team $ 22-27 StartWeight EndWeight;
164      datalines;
NOTE: The data set WORK.WEIGHT_CLUB has 6 observations and 5 variables.
```

Because SAS assigns the first-level name WORK to all SAS data sets that have only a one-level name, you do not need to use WORK. You can refer to these temporary data sets with a one-level name, such as WEIGHT_CLUB.

To reference this SAS data set in a later DATA step or in a PROC step, you can use a one-level name:

```
proc print data = weight_club;
run;
```

Creating and Using Permanent SAS Data Sets

To create a *permanent* SAS data set, you must indicate a SAS data library other than WORK. (WORK is a reserved libref that SAS automatically assigns to a temporary SAS data library.) Use a LIBNAME statement to assign a *libref* to a SAS data library on your operating environment's file system. The libref functions as a shorthand way of referring to a SAS data library. Here is the form of the LIBNAME statement.

LIBNAME *libref 'your-data-library'*;

where

libref
> is a shortcut name to where your SAS files are stored. *libref* must be a valid SAS name. It must begin with a letter or an underscore, and it can contain uppercase and lowercase letters, numbers, or underscores. A libref has a maximum length of 8 characters.

'your-data-library'
> must be the physical name for your SAS data library. The physical name is the name that is recognized by the operating environment.

Operating Environment Information: Additional restrictions can apply to librefs and physical file names under some operating environments. For more information, refer to the SAS documentation for your operating environment. △

The following is an example of the LIBNAME statement that is used with a DATA step:

```
libname saveit 'your-data-library';  ❶
data saveit.weight_club;  ❷
   ...more SAS statements...
;

proc print data = saveit.weight_club;  ❸
run;
```

The following list corresponds to the numbered items:

❶ The LIBNAME statement associates the libref SAVEIT with *your-data-library*, where *your-data-library* is your operating environment's name for a SAS data library.

❷ To create a new permanent SAS data set and store it in this SAS data library, you must use the two-level name SAVEIT.WEIGHT_CLUB in the DATA statement.

❸ To reference this SAS data set in a later DATA step or in a PROC step, you must use the two-level name SAVEIT.WEIGHT_CLUB in the PROC step.

For more information, see Chapter 33, "Understanding SAS Data Libraries," on page 591.

Conventions That Are Used in This Book

Data sets that are used in examples are usually shown as temporary data sets specified with a one-level name:

```
data fitness;
```

In rare cases in this book, data sets are created as permanent SAS data sets. These data sets are specified with a two-level name, and a LIBNAME statement precedes each DATA step in which a permanent SAS data set is created:

```
libname saveit 'your-data-library';
data saveit.weight_club;
```

How the DATA Step Works: A Basic Introduction

Overview

The DATA step consists of a group of SAS statements that begins with a DATA statement. The DATA statement begins the process of building a SAS data set and names the data set. The statements that make up the DATA step are compiled, and the syntax is checked. If the syntax is correct, then the statements are executed. In its simplest form, the DATA step is a loop with an automatic output and return action. The following figure illustrates the flow of action in a typical DATA step.

Figure 2.7 Flow of Action in a Typical DATA Step

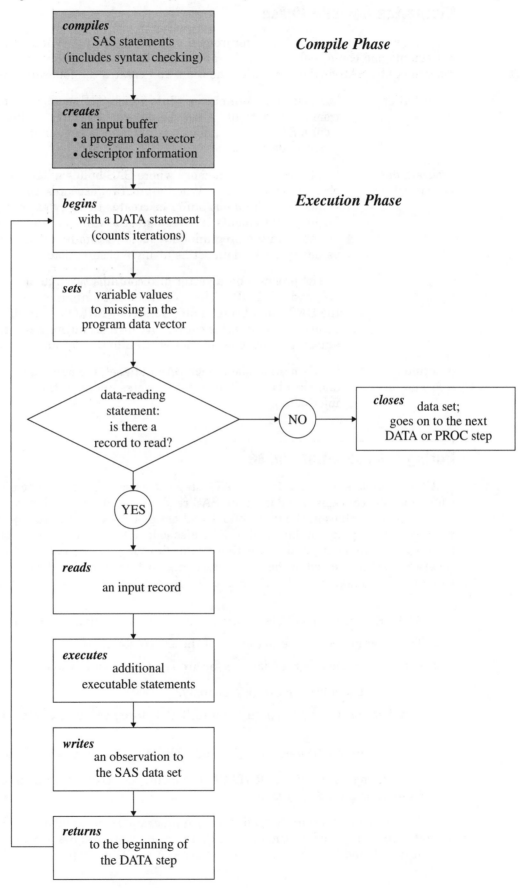

During the Compile Phase

When you submit a DATA step for execution, SAS checks the syntax of the SAS statements and compiles them, that is, automatically translates the statements into machine code. SAS further processes the code, and creates the following three items:

input buffer	is a logical area in memory into which SAS reads each record of data from a raw data file when the program executes. (When SAS reads from a SAS data set, however, the data is written directly to the program data vector.)
program data vector	is a logical area of memory where SAS builds a data set, one observation at a time. When a program executes, SAS reads data values from the input buffer or creates them by executing SAS language statements. SAS assigns the values to the appropriate variables in the program data vector. From here, SAS writes the values to a SAS data set as a single observation.
	The program data vector also contains two automatic variables, _N_ and _ERROR_. The _N_ variable counts the number of times the DATA step begins to iterate. The _ERROR_ variable signals the occurrence of an error caused by the data during execution. These automatic variables are not written to the output data set.
descriptor information	is information about each SAS data set, including data set attributes and variable attributes. SAS creates and maintains the descriptor information.

During the Execution Phase

All executable statements in the DATA step are executed once for each iteration. If your input file contains raw data, then SAS reads a record into the input buffer. SAS then reads the values in the input buffer and assigns the values to the appropriate variables in the program data vector. SAS also calculates values for variables created by program statements, and writes these values to the program data vector. When the program reaches the end of the DATA step, three actions occur by default that make using the SAS language different from using most other programming languages:

1 SAS writes the current observation from the program data vector to the data set.

2 The program loops back to the top of the DATA step.

3 Variables in the program data vector are reset to missing values.

Note: The following exceptions apply:

□ Variables that you specify in a RETAIN statement are not reset to missing values.

□ The automatic variables _N_ and _ERROR_ are not reset to missing.

For information about the RETAIN statement, see "Using a Value in a Later Observation" on page 196. △

If there is another record to read, then the program executes again. SAS builds the second observation, and continues until there are no more records to read. The data set is then closed, and SAS goes on to the next DATA or PROC step.

Example of a DATA Step

The DATA Step

The following simple DATA step produces a SAS data set from the data collected for a health and fitness club. As discussed earlier, the input data contains each participant's identification number, name, team name, and weight at the beginning and end of a 16-week weight program:

```
data weight_club; ❶
    input IdNumber 1-4 Name $ 6-24 Team $ StartWeight EndWeight; ❷
    Loss = StartWeight - EndWeight; ❸

    datalines; ❹
1023 David Shaw         red    189 165
1049 Amelia Serrano     yellow 145 124
1219 Alan Nance         red    210 192
1246 Ravi Sinha         yellow 194 177
1078 Ashley McKnight    red    127 118
1221 Jim Brown          yellow 220  .
1095 Susan Stewart      blue   135 127
1157 Rosa Gomez         green  155 141
1331 Jason Schock       blue   187 172
1067 Kanoko Nagasaka    green  135 122
1251 Richard Rose       blue   181 166
1333 Li-Hwa Lee         green  141 129
1192 Charlene Armstrong yellow 152 139
1352 Bette Long         green  156 137
1262 Yao Chen           blue   196 180
1087 Kim Sikorski       red    148 135
1124 Adrienne Fink      green  156 142
1197 Lynne Overby       red    138 125
1133 John VanMeter      blue   180 167
1036 Becky Redding      green  135 123
1057 Margie Vanhoy      yellow 146 132
1328 Hisashi Ito        red    155 142
1243 Deanna Hicks       blue   134 122
1177 Holly Choate       red    141 130
1259 Raoul Sanchez      green  189 172
1017 Jennifer Brooks    blue   138 127
1099 Asha Garg          yellow 148 132
1329 Larry Goss         yellow 188 174
; ❹
```

The Statements

The following list corresponds to the numbered items in the preceding program:

❶ The DATA statement begins the DATA step and names the data set that is being created.

② The INPUT statement creates five variables, indicates how SAS reads the values from the input buffer, and assigns the values to variables in the program data vector.

③ The assignment statement creates an additional variable called Loss, calculates the value of Loss during each iteration of the DATA step, and writes the value to the program data vector.

④ The DATALINES statement marks the beginning of the input data. The single semicolon marks the end of the input data and the DATA step.

Note: A DATA step that does not contain a DATALINES statement must end with a RUN statement. △

The Process

When you submit a DATA step for execution, SAS automatically compiles the DATA step and then executes it. At compile time, SAS creates the input buffer, program data vector, and descriptor information for the data set WEIGHT_CLUB. As the following figure shows, the program data vector contains the variables that are named in the INPUT statement, as well as the variable Loss. All variable values, except _N_ and _ERROR_, are initially set to missing. Note that missing numeric values are represented by a period, and missing character values are represented by a blank.

Figure 2.8 Variable Values Initially Set to Missing

Input Buffer

```
----+----1----+----2----+----3----+----4----+----5----+----6----+----7
```

Program Data Vector

IdNumber	Name	Team	StartWeight	EndWeight	Loss
.			.	.	.

The syntax is correct, so the DATA step executes. As the following figure illustrates, the INPUT statement causes SAS to read the first record of raw data into the input buffer. Then, according to the instructions in the INPUT statement, SAS reads the data values in the input buffer and assigns them to variables in the program data vector.

Figure 2.9 Values Assigned to Variables by the INPUT Statement

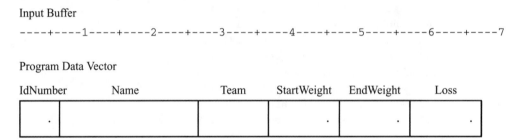

Input Buffer

```
----+----1----+----2----+----3----+----4----+----5----+----6----+----7
1023 David Shaw        red     189 165
```

Program Data Vector

IdNumber	Name	Team	StartWeight	EndWeight	Loss
1023	David Shaw	red	189	165	.

When SAS assigns values to all variables that are listed in the INPUT statement, SAS executes the next statement in the program:

```
Loss = StartWeight - EndWeight;
```

This assignment statement calculates the value for the variable Loss and writes that value to the program data vector, as the following figure shows.

Figure 2.10   Value Computed and Assigned to the Variable Loss

Input Buffer
```
----+----1----+----2----+----3----+----4----+----5----+----6----+----7
1023 David Shaw        red     189 165
```

Program Data Vector

IdNumber	Name	Team	StartWeight	EndWeight	Loss
1023	David Shaw	red	189	165	24

SAS has now reached the end of the DATA step, and the program automatically

1 writes the first observation to the data set
2 loops back to the top of the DATA step to begin the next iteration
3 sets all values in the program data vector to missing values, as the following figure shows.

Figure 2.11   Values Set to Missing

Input Buffer
```
----+----1----+----2----+----3----+----4----+----5----+----6----+----7
1023 David Shaw        red     189 165
```

Program Data Vector

IdNumber	Name	Team	StartWeight	EndWeight	Loss
.			.	.	.

Execution continues. The INPUT statement looks for another record to read. If there are no more records, then SAS closes the data set and the system goes on to the next DATA or PROC step. In this example, however, more records exist and the INPUT statement reads the second record into the input buffer, as the following figure shows.

Figure 2.12   Second Record Is Read into the Input Buffer

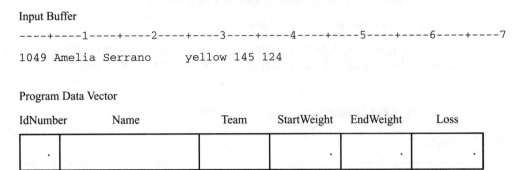

The following figure shows that SAS assigned values to the variables in the program data vector and calculated the value for the variable Loss, building the second observation just as it did the first one.

Figure 2.13   Results of Second Iteration of the DATA Step

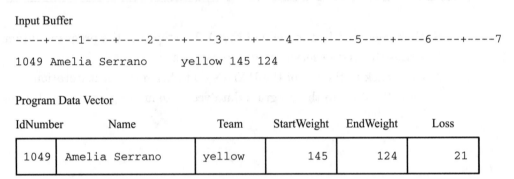

This entire process continues until SAS detects the end of the file. The DATA step iterates as many times as there are records to read. Then SAS closes the data set WEIGHT_CLUB, and SAS looks for the beginning of the next DATA or PROC step.

Now that SAS has transformed the collected data from raw data into a SAS data set, it can be processed by a SAS procedure. The following output, produced with the PRINT procedure, shows the data set that has just been created.

```
proc print data=weight_club;
    title 'Fitness Center Weight Club';
run;
```

Output 2.2 PROC PRINT Output of the WEIGHT_CLUB Data Set

```
                         Fitness Center Weight Club                              1

              Id                                    Start      End
      Obs    Number    Name              Team      Weight    Weight    Loss

       1      1023     David Shaw        red         189       165      24
       2      1049     Amelia Serrano    yellow      145       124      21
       3      1219     Alan Nance        red         210       192      18
       4      1246     Ravi Sinha        yellow      194       177      17
       5      1078     Ashley McKnight   red         127       118       9
       6      1221     Jim Brown         yellow      220         .       .
       7      1095     Susan Stewart     blue        135       127       8
       8      1157     Rosa Gomez        green       155       141      14
       9      1331     Jason Schock      blue        187       172      15
      10      1067     Kanoko Nagasaka   green       135       122      13
      11      1251     Richard Rose      blue        181       166      15
      12      1333     Li-Hwa Lee        green       141       129      12
      13      1192     Charlene Armstrong yellow     152       139      13
      14      1352     Bette Long        green       156       137      19
      15      1262     Yao Chen          blue        196       180      16
      16      1087     Kim Sikorski      red         148       135      13
      17      1124     Adrienne Fink     green       156       142      14
      18      1197     Lynne Overby      red         138       125      13
      19      1133     John VanMeter     blue        180       167      13
      20      1036     Becky Redding     green       135       123      12
      21      1057     Margie Vanhoy     yellow      146       132      14
      22      1328     Hisashi Ito       red         155       142      13
      23      1243     Deanna Hicks      blue        134       122      12
      24      1177     Holly Choate      red         141       130      11
      25      1259     Raoul Sanchez     green       189       172      17
      26      1017     Jennifer Brooks   blue        138       127      11
      27      1099     Asha Garg         yellow      148       132      16
      28      1329     Larry Goss        yellow      188       174      14
```

Supplying Information to Create a SAS Data Set

Overview

You supply SAS with specific information for reading raw data so that you can create a SAS data set from the raw data. You can use the data set for further processing, data analysis, or report writing. To process raw data in a DATA step, you must

□ use an INPUT statement to tell SAS how to read the data

□ define the variables and indicate whether they are character or numeric

□ specify the location of the raw data.

Telling SAS How to Read the Data: Styles of Input

SAS provides many tools for reading raw data into a SAS data set. These tools include three basic input styles as well as various format modifiers and pointer controls.

List input is used when each field in the raw data is separated by at least one space and does not contain embedded spaces. The INPUT statement simply contains a list of the variable names. List input, however, places numerous restrictions on your data. These restrictions are discussed in detail in Chapter 3, "Starting with Raw Data: The Basics," on page 43. The following example shows list input. Note that there is at least one blank space between each data value.

```
data scores;
   input Name $ Test_1 Test_2 Test_3;
   datalines;
Bill 187 97 103
Carlos 156 76 74
Monique 99 102 129
;
```

Column input enables you to read the same data if it is located in fixed columns:

```
data scores;
   input Name $ 1-7 Test_1 9-11 Test_2 13-15 Test_3 17-19;
   datalines;
Bill    187  97 103
Carlos  156  76  74
Monique  99 102 129
;
```

Formatted input enables you to supply special instructions in the INPUT statement for reading data. For example, to read numeric data that contains special symbols, you need to supply SAS with special instructions so that it can read the data correctly. These instructions, called *informats*, are discussed in more detail in Chapter 3, "Starting with Raw Data: The Basics," on page 43. In the INPUT statement, you can specify an informat to be used to read a data value, as in the example that follows:

```
data total_sales;
   input Date mmddyy10. +2 Amount comma5.;
   datalines;
09/05/2000  1,382
10/19/2000  1,235
11/30/2000  2,391
;
```

In this example, the MMDDYY10. informat for the variable Date tells SAS to interpret the raw data as a month, day, and year, ignoring the slashes. The COMMA5. informat for the variable Amount tells SAS to interpret the raw data as a number, ignoring the comma. The +2 is a *pointer control* that tells SAS where to look for the next item. For more information about pointer controls, see Chapter 3, "Starting with Raw Data: The Basics," on page 43.

SAS also enables you to mix these styles of input as required by the way values are arranged in the data records. Chapter 3, "Starting with Raw Data: The Basics," on page 43 discusses in detail input styles (including their rules and restrictions), as well as additional data-reading tools.

Reading Dates with Two-Digit and Four-Digit Year Values

In the previous example, the year values in the dates in the raw data had four digits:

```
09/05/2000
10/19/2000
11/30/2000
```

However, SAS is also capable of reading two-digit year values (for example, 09/05/99). In this example, use the MMDDYY8. informat for the variable Date.

How does SAS know to which century a two-digit year belongs? SAS uses the value of the YEARCUTOFF= SAS system option. In Version 7 and later of SAS, the default value of the YEARCUTOFF= option is 1920. This means that two-digit years from 00 to

19 are assumed to be in the twenty-first century, that is, 2000 to 2019. Two-digit years from 20 to 99 are assumed to be in the twentieth century, that is, 1920 to 1999.

Note: The YEARCUTOFF= option and the default setting may be different at your site. △

To avoid confusion, you should use four-digit year values in your raw data wherever possible. For more information, see the Dates, Times, and Intervals section of *SAS Language Reference: Concepts*.

Defining Variables in SAS

So far you have seen that the INPUT statement instructs SAS on how to read raw data lines. At the same time that the INPUT statement provides instructions for reading data, it defines the variables for the data set that come from the raw data. By assuming default values for variable attributes, the INPUT statement does much of the work for you. Later in this book, you will learn other statements that enable you to define variables and assign attributes to variables, but this chapter and Chapter 3, "Starting with Raw Data: The Basics," on page 43 concentrate on the use of the INPUT statement.

SAS variables can have these attributes:

- □ name
- □ type
- □ length
- □ informat
- □ format
- □ label
- □ position in observation
- □ index type

See the SAS Variables section of *SAS Language Reference: Concepts* for more information about variable attributes.

In an INPUT statement, you must supply each variable name. Unless you also supply an informat, the type is assumed to be numeric, and its length is assumed to be eight bytes. The following INPUT statement creates four numeric variables, each with a length of eight bytes, without requiring you to specify either type or length. The table summarizes this information.

```
input IdNumber Test_1 Test_2 Test_3;
```

Variable name	Type	Length
IdNumber	numeric	8
Test_1	numeric	8
Test_2	numeric	8
Test_3	numeric	8

The values of numeric variables can contain only numbers. To store values that contain alphabetic or special characters, you must create a character variable. By following a variable name in an INPUT statement with a dollar sign ($), you create a character variable. The default length of a character variable is also eight bytes. The following statement creates a data set that contains one character variable and four numeric variables, all with a default length of eight bytes. The table summarizes this information.

```
input IdNumber Name $ Test_1 Test_2 Test_3;
```

Variable name	Type	Length
IdNumber	numeric	8
Name	character	8
Test_1	numeric	8
Test_2	numeric	8
Test_3	numeric	8

In addition to specifying the types of variables in the INPUT statement, you can also specify the lengths of character variables. Character variables can be up to 32,767 bytes in length. To specify the length of a character variable in an INPUT statement, you need to supply an informat or use column numbers. For example, following a variable name in the INPUT statement with the informat $20., or with column specifications such as 1-20, creates a character variable that is 20 bytes long.

Note that the length of numeric variables is not affected by informats or column specifications in an INPUT statement. See *SAS Language Reference: Concepts* for more information about numeric variables and lengths.

Two other variable attributes, format and label, affect how variable values and names are represented when they are printed or displayed. These attributes are assigned with different statements that you will learn about later.

Indicating the Location of Your Data

Data Locations

To create a SAS data set, you can read data from one of four locations:

- □ raw data in the data (job) stream, that is, following a DATALINES statement
- □ raw data in a file that you specify with an INFILE statement
- □ data from an existing SAS data set
- □ data in a database management system (DBMS) file.

Raw Data in the Job Stream

You can place data directly in the job stream with the programming statements that make up the DATA step. The DATALINES statement tells SAS that raw data follows. The single semicolon that follows the last line of data marks the end of the data. The DATALINES statement and data lines must occur last in the DATA step statements:

```
data weight_club;
    input IdNumber 1-4 Name $ 6-24 Team $ StartWeight EndWeight;
```

```
    Loss = StartWeight - EndWeight;
    datalines;
1023 David Shaw          red      189 165
1049 Amelia Serrano      yellow 145 124
1219 Alan Nance          red      210 192
1246 Ravi Sinha          yellow 194 177
1078 Ashley McKnight     red      127 118
;
```

Data in an External File

If your raw data is already stored in a file, then you do not have to bring that file into the data stream. Use an INFILE statement to specify the file containing the raw data. (See "Using External Files in Your SAS Job" on page 38 for details about INFILE, FILE, and FILENAME statements.) The statements in the code that follows demonstrate the same example, this time showing that the raw data is stored in an external file:

```
data weight_club;
   infile 'your-input-file';
   input IdNumber $ 1-4 Name $ 6-23 StartWeight 24-26
         EndWeight 28-30;
   Loss=StartWeight-EndWeight;
run;
```

Data in a SAS Data Set

You can also use data that is already stored in a SAS data set as input to a new data set. To read data from an existing SAS data set, you must specify the existing data set's name in one of these statements:

- □ SET statement
- □ MERGE statement
- □ MODIFY statement
- □ UPDATE statement

For example, the statements that follow create a new SAS data set named RED that adds the variable LossPercent:

```
data red;
   set weight_club;
   LossPercent = Loss / StartWeight * 100;
run;
```

The SET statement indicates that the input data is already in the structure of a SAS data set and gives the name of the SAS data set to be read. In this example, the SET statement tells SAS to read the WEIGHT_CLUB data set in the WORK library.

Data in a DBMS File

If you have data that is stored in another vendor's database management system (DBMS) files, then you can use SAS/ACCESS software to bring this data into a SAS data set. SAS/ACCESS software enables you to assign a libref to a library containing the DBMS file. In this example, a libref is declared, and points to a library containing Oracle data. SAS reads data from an Oracle file into a SAS data set:

```
libname dblib oracle user=scott password=tiger path='hrdept_002';
data employees;
   set dblib.employees;
run;
```

See *SAS/ACCESS Software for Relational Databases: Reference* for more information about using SAS/ACCESS software to access DBMS files.

Using External Files in Your SAS Job

Your SAS programs often need to read raw data from a file, or write data or reports to a file that is not a SAS data set. To use a file that is not a SAS data set in a SAS program, you need to tell SAS where to find it. You can

□ identify the file directly in the INFILE, FILE, or other SAS statement that uses the file

□ set up a *fileref* for the file by using the FILENAME statement, and then use the fileref in the INFILE, FILE, or other SAS statement

□ use operating environment commands to set up a fileref, and then use the fileref in the INFILE, FILE, or other SAS statement.

The first two methods are described here. The third method depends on the operating environment that you use.

Operating Environment Information: For more information, refer to the SAS documentation for your operating environment. △

Identifying an External File Directly

The simplest method for referring to an external file is to use the name of the file in the INFILE, FILE, or other SAS statement that needs to refer to the file. For example, if your raw data is stored in a file in your operating environment, and you want to read the data using a SAS DATA step, you can tell SAS where to find the raw data by putting the name of the file in the INFILE statement:

```
data temp;
   infile 'your-input-file';
   input IdNumber $ 1-4 Name $ 6-23 StartWeight 24-26
         EndWeight 28-30;
run;
```

The INFILE statement for this example may appear as follows for various operating environments:

Table 2.1 Example INFILE Statements for Various Operating Environments

Operating environment	INFILE statement example
OS/390	`infile 'fitness.weight.rawdata(club1)';`
CMS	`infile 'club1 weight a';`
OpenVMS	`infile '[fitness.weight.rawdata]club1.dat';`

UNIX	`infile '/usr/local/fitness/club1.dat';`
Windows	`infile 'c:\fitness\club1.dat';`

Operating Environment Information: For more information, refer to the SAS documentation for your operating environment. △

Referencing an External File with a Fileref

An alternate method for referencing an external file is to use the FILENAME statement to set up a *fileref* for a file. The fileref functions as a shorthand way of referring to an external file. You then use the fileref in later SAS statements that reference the file, such as the FILE or INFILE statement. The advantage of this method is that if the program contains many references to the same external file and the external filename changes, then the program needs to be modified in only one place, rather than in every place where the file is referenced.

Here is the form of the FILENAME statement:

FILENAME *fileref 'your-input-or-output-file'*;

The *fileref* must be a valid SAS name, that is, it must
- □ begin with a letter or an underscore
- □ contain only letters, numbers, or underscores
- □ have no more than 8 characters.

Operating Environment Information: Additional restrictions may apply under some operating environments. For more information, refer to the SAS documentation for your operating environment. △

For example, you can reference the raw data that is stored in a file in your operating environment by first using the FILENAME statement to specify the name of the file and its fileref, and then using the INFILE statement with the same fileref to reference the file.

```
filename fitclub 'your-input-file';

data temp;
   infile fitclub;
   input IdNumber $ 1-4 Name $ 6-23 StartWeight 24-26 EndWeight 28-30;
run;
```

In this example, the INFILE statement stays the same for all operating environments. The FILENAME statement, however, can appear differently in different operating environments, as the following table shows:

Table 2.2   Example FILENAME Statements for Various Operating Environments

Operating environment	FILENAME statement example
OS/390	`filename fitclub 'fitness.weight.rawdata(club1)';`
CMS	`filename fitclub 'club1 weight a';`
OpenVMS	`filename fitclub '[fitness.weight.rawdata]club1.dat';`

UNIX	`filename fitclub '/usr/local/fitness/club1.dat';`
Windows	`filename fitclub 'c:\fitness\club1.dat';`

If you need to use several files or members from the same directory, partitioned data set (PDS), or MACLIB, then you can use the FILENAME statement to create a fileref that identifies the name of the directory, PDS, or MACLIB. Then you can use the fileref in the INFILE statement and enclose the name of the file, PDS member, or MACLIB member in parentheses immediately after the fileref, as in this example:

```
filename fitclub 'directory-or-PDS-or-MACLIB';
```

```
data temp;
   infile fitclub(club1);
   input IdNumber $ 1-4 Name $ 6-23 StartWeight 24-26 EndWeight 28-30;
run;

data temp2;
   infile fitclub(club2);
   input IdNumber $ 1-4 Name $ 6-23 StartWeight 24-26 EndWeight 28-30;
run;
```

In this case, the INFILE statements stay the same for all operating environments. The FILENAME statement, however, can appear differently for different operating environments, as the following table shows:

Table 2.3 Referencing Directories, PDSs, and MACLIBs in Various Operating Environments

Operating environment	FILENAME statement example
OS/390	`filename fitclub 'fitness.weight.rawdata';`
CMS	`filename fitclub 'use1 maclib';`[1]
OpenVMS	`filename fitclub '[fitness.weight.rawdata]';`
UNIX	`filename fitclub '/usr/local/fitness';`
Windows	`filename fitclub 'c:\fitness';`

1 Under CMS, the external file must be a CMS MACLIB, a CMS TXTLIB, or an OS/390 PDS.

Review of SAS Tools

Statements

DATA <*libref.*>*SAS-data-set*;
    tells SAS to begin creating a SAS data set. If you omit the *libref*, then SAS creates a temporary SAS data set. (SAS attaches the libref WORK for its internal processing.) If you give a previously defined *libref* as the first level of the name, then SAS stores the data set permanently in the library referenced by the libref. A

SAS program or a portion of a program that begins with a DATA statement and ends with a RUN statement, another DATA statement, or a PROC statement is called a DATA step.

FILENAME *fileref 'your-input-or-output-file'*;
associates a *fileref* with an external file. Enclose the name of the external file in quotation marks.

INFILE *fileref | 'your-input-file'*;
identifies an external file to be read by an INPUT statement. Specify a *fileref* that has been assigned with a FILENAME statement or with an appropriate operating environment command, or specify the actual name of the external file.

INPUT *variable <$>*;
reads raw data using list input. At least one blank must occur between any two data values. The $ denotes a character variable.

INPUT *variable<$>column-range*;
reads raw data that is aligned in columns. The $ denotes a character variable.

INPUT *variable informat*;
reads raw data using formatted input. An informat supplies special instructions for reading the data.

LIBNAME *libref 'your-SAS-data-library'*;
associates a *libref* with a SAS data library. Enclose the name of the library in quotation marks. SAS locates a permanent SAS data set by matching the libref in a two-level SAS data set name with the library associated with that libref in a LIBNAME statement. The rules for creating a SAS data library depend on your operating environment.

Learning More

ATTRIBUTE statement
For information about how the ATTRIBUTE statement enables you to assign attributes to variables, see *SAS Language Reference: Dictionary*.

DBMS access
This book explains how to use SAS for reading files of raw data and SAS data sets and writing to SAS data sets. However, SAS documentation for SAS/ACCESS software provides complete information about using SAS to read and write information stored in several types of database management system (DBMS) files.

Informats
For a discussion about informats that you use with dates, see Chapter 14, "Working with Dates in the SAS System," on page 211.

Length of variables
For more information about how a variable's length affects the values you can store in the variable, see Chapter 7, "Working with Numeric Variables," on page 107 and Chapter 8, "Working with Character Variables," on page 119.

LINESIZE= option
For information about how to use the LINESIZE= option in an INPUT statement to limit how much of each data line the INPUT statement reads, see *SAS Language Reference: Dictionary*.

MERGE, MODIFY, or UPDATE statements
In addition to the SET statement, you can read a SAS data set with the MERGE, MODIFY, or UPDATE statements. For more information, see Chapter 18, "Merging SAS Data Sets," on page 269 and Chapter 19, "Updating SAS Data Sets," on page 293.

SET statement
For information about the SET statement, see Chapter 5, "Starting with SAS Data Sets," on page 81.

USER= SAS system option
You can specify the USER= SAS system option to use one-level names to point to permanent SAS files. (If you specify USER=WORK, then SAS assumes that files referenced with one-level names refer to temporary work files.) See the SAS System Options section in *SAS Language Reference: Dictionary* for details.

CHAPTER

3

Starting with Raw Data: The Basics

Introduction

Purpose

To create a SAS data set from raw data, you must examine the data records first to determine how the data values that you want to read are arranged. Then you can look at the styles of reading input that are available in the INPUT statement. SAS provides three basic input styles:

- □ list
- □ column
- □ formatted.

You can use these styles individually, in combination with each other, or in conjunction with various line-hold specifiers, line-pointer controls, and column-pointer controls. This chapter demonstrates various ways of using the INPUT statement to turn your raw data into SAS data sets.

You can enter the data directly in a DATA step or use an existing file of raw data. If your data is machine readable, then you need to learn how to use those tools that enable SAS to read them. If your data is not yet entered, then you can choose the input style that enables you to enter the data most easily.

Prerequisites

You should understand the concepts presented in Chapter 1, "What Is the SAS System?," on page 3 and Chapter 2, "Introduction to DATA Step Processing," on page 19 before continuing.

Examine the Structure of the Raw Data: Factors to Consider

Before you can select the appropriate style of input, examine the structure of the raw data that you want to read. Some of the factors you need to consider are

- □ how the data is arranged in the input records (For example, are data fields aligned in columns or unaligned? Are they separated by blanks or by other characters?)
- □ whether character values contain embedded blanks
- □ whether numeric values contain non-numeric characters such as commas
- □ whether the data contains time or date values
- □ whether each input record contains data for more than one observation
- □ whether data for a single observation is spread over multiple input records.

Reading Unaligned Data

Understanding List Input

The simplest form of the INPUT statement uses *list input*. List input is used to read data values that are separated by a delimiter character (by default, a blank space). With list input, SAS reads a data value until it encounters a blank space. SAS assumes the value has ended and assigns the data to the appropriate variable in the program data vector. SAS continues to scan the record until it reaches a nonblank character again. SAS reads a data value until it encounters a blank space or the end of the input record.

Program: Basic List Input

This program uses the health and fitness club data from Chapter 2, "Introduction to DATA Step Processing," on page 19 to illustrate a DATA step that uses list input in an INPUT statement.

```
data club1;
   input IdNumber Name $ Team $ StartWeight EndWeight; ❸
   datalines; ❶
1023 David red 189 165 ❷
1049 Amelia yellow 145 124
1219 Alan red 210 192
1246 Ravi yellow 194 177
1078 Ashley red 127 118
1221 Jim yellow 220 . ❷
; ❶

proc print data=club1;
   title 'Weight of Club Members';
run;
```

The following list corresponds to the numbered items in the preceding program:

❶ The DATALINES statement marks the beginning of the data lines. The semicolon that follows the data lines marks the end of the data lines and the end of the DATA step.

❷ Each data value in the raw data record is separated from the next by at least one blank space. The last record contains a missing value, represented by a period, for the value of EndWeight.

❸ The variable names in the INPUT statement are specified in exactly the same order as the fields in the raw data records.

The output that follows shows the resulting data set. The PROC PRINT statement that follows the DATA step produces this listing.

Output 3.1 Data Set Created with List Input

```
                       Weight of Club Members                           1

                Id                          Start     End
       Obs    Number    Name      Team      Weight    Weight

        1      1023     David     red        189       165
        2      1049     Amelia    yellow     145       124
        3      1219     Alan      red        210       192
        4      1246     Ravi      yellow     194       177
        5      1078     Ashley    red        127       118
        6      1221     Jim       yellow     220        .
```

Program: When the Data Is Delimited by Characters, Not Blanks

This program also uses the health and fitness club data but notice that here the data is delimited by a comma instead of a blank space, the default delimiter.

```
options pagesize=60 linesize=80 pageno=1 nodate;
data club1;
    infile datalines❷ dlm=','❸;
    input IdNumber Name $ Team $ StartWeight EndWeight;
    datalines;
1023,David,red,189,165❶
1049,Amelia,yellow,145,124
1219,Alan,red,210,192
1246,Ravi,yellow,194,177
1078,Ashley,red,127,118
1221,Jim,yellow,220,.
;
proc print data=club1;
    title 'Weight of Club Members';
run;
```

The following list corresponds to the numbered items in the preceding output:

❶ These data values are separated by commas instead of blanks.

❷ List input, by default, scans the input records, looking for blank spaces to delimit each data value. The DLM= option enables list input to recognize a character, here a comma, as the delimiter.

❸ This example required the DLM= option, which is available only in the INFILE statement. Usually this statement is used only when the input data resides in an external file. The DATALINES specification, however, enables you to take advantage of INFILE statement options, when you are reading data records from the job stream.

Output 3.2   Reading Data Delimited by Commas

```
                     Weight of Club Members                        1

             Id                          Start     End
    Obs    Number     Name     Team      Weight    Weight

     1      1023      David     red        189       165
     2      1049      Amelia    yellow     145       124
     3      1219      Alan      red        210       192
     4      1246      Ravi      yellow     194       177
     5      1078      Ashley    red        127       118
     6      1221      Jim       yellow     220         .
```

List Input: Points to Remember

The points to remember when you use list input are

- □ Use list input when each field is separated by at least one blank space or delimiter.
- □ Specify each field in the order that they appear in the records of raw data.

□ Represent missing values by a placeholder such as a period. (Under the default behavior, a blank field causes the variable names and values to become mismatched.)

□ Character values cannot contain embedded blanks.

□ The default length of character variables is eight bytes. SAS truncates a longer value when it writes the value to the program data vector. (To read a character variable that contains more than eight characters with list input, use a LENGTH statement. See "Defining Enough Storage Space for Variables" on page 103.)

□ Data must be in standard character or numeric format (that is, it can be read without an informat).

Note: List input requires the fewest specifications in the INPUT statement. However, the restrictions that are placed on the data may require that you learn to use other styles of input to read your data. For example, column input, which is discussed in the next section, is less restrictive. This section has introduced only simple list input. See "Understanding How to Make List Input More Flexible" on page 53 to learn about modified list input. △

Reading Data That Is Aligned in Columns

Understanding Column Input

With *column input*, data values occupy the same fields within each data record. When you use column input in the INPUT statement, list the variable names and specify column positions that identify the location of the corresponding data fields. You can use column input when your raw data is in fixed columns and does not require the use of informats to be read.

Program: Reading Data Aligned in Columns

The following program also uses the health and fitness club data, but now two more data values are missing. The data is aligned in columns and SAS reads the data with column input:

```
data club1;
   input IdNumber 1-4 Name $ 6-11 Team $ 13-18 StartWeight 20-22
         EndWeight 24-26;
   datalines;
1023 David  red    189 165
1049 Amelia yellow 145
1219 Alan   red    210 192
1246 Ravi   yellow     177
1078 Ashley red    127 118
1221 Jim    yellow 220
;

proc print data=club1;
   title 'Weight Club Members';
run;
```

The specification that follows each variable name indicates the beginning and ending columns in which the variable value will be found. Note that with column input you are not required to indicate missing values with a placeholder such as a period.

The following output shows the resulting data set. Missing numeric values occur three times in the data set, and are indicated by periods.

Output 3.3   Data Set Created with Column Input

```
                        Weight Club Members                                1

                  Id                           Start      End
      Obs       Number     Name      Team      Weight    Weight

       1         1023     David      red        189        165
       2         1049     Amelia     yellow     145         .
       3         1219     Alan       red        210        192
       4         1246     Ravi       yellow      .         177
       5         1078     Ashley     red        127        118
       6         1221     Jim        yellow     220         .
```

Understanding Some Advantages of Column Input over Simple List Input

Here are several advantages of using column input:

☐ With column input, character variables can contain embedded blanks.

☐ Column input also enables the creation of variables that are longer than eight bytes. In the preceding example, the variable Name in the data set CLUB1 contains only the members' first names. By using column input, you can read the first and last names as a single value. These differences between input styles are possible for two reasons:

  ☐ Column input uses the columns that you specify to determine the length of character variables.

  ☐ Column input, unlike list input, reads data until it reaches the last specified column, not until it reaches a blank space.

☐ Column input enables you to skip some data fields when reading records of raw data. It also enables you to read the data fields in any order and reread some fields or parts of fields.

Reading Embedded Blanks and Creating Longer Variables

This DATA step uses column input to create a new data set named CLUB2. The program still uses the health and fitness club weight data. However, the data has been modified to include members' first and last names. Now the second data field in each record or raw data contains an embedded blank and is 18 bytes long.

```
data club2;
    input IdNumber 1-4 Name $ 6-23 Team $ 25-30 StartWeight 32-34
          EndWeight 36-38;
    datalines;
1023 David Shaw       red       189 165
```

```
1049 Amelia Serrano      yellow 145 124
1219 Alan Nance          red    210 192
1246 Ravi Sinha          yellow 194 177
1078 Ashley McKnight     red    127 118
1221 Jim Brown           yellow 220
;

proc print data=club2;
   title 'Weight Club Members';
run;
```

The following output shows the resulting data set.

Output 3.4 Data Set Created with Column Input (Embedded Blanks)

```
                       Weight Club Members                              1

              Id                              Start     End
    Obs     Number     Name         Team      Weight   Weight

     1       1023      David Shaw    red        189      165
     2       1049      Amelia Serrano yellow    145      124
     3       1219      Alan Nance    red        210      192
     4       1246      Ravi Sinha    yellow     194      177
     5       1078      Ashley McKnight red      127      118
     6       1221      Jim Brown     yellow     220       .
```

Program: Skipping Fields When Reading Data Records

Column input also enables you to skip over fields or to read the fields in any order. This example uses column input to read the same health and fitness club data, but it reads the value for the variable Team first and omits the variable IdNumber altogether.

You can read or reread part of a value when using column input. For example, because the team names begin with different letters, this program saves storage space by reading only the first character in the field that contains the team name. Note the INPUT statement:

```
data club2;
   input Team $ 25 Name $ 6-23 StartWeight 32-34 EndWeight 36-38;
   datalines;
1023 David Shaw         red    189 165
1049 Amelia Serrano     yellow 145 124
1219 Alan Nance         red    210 192
1246 Ravi Sinha         yellow 194 177
1078 Ashley McKnight    red    127 118
1221 Jim Brown          yellow 220
;

proc print data=club2;
   title 'Weight Club Members';
run;
```

The following output shows the resulting data set. The variable that contains the identification number is no longer in the data set. Instead, Team is the first variable in the new data set, and it contains only one character to represent the team value.

Output 3.5 Data Set Created with Column Input (Skipping Fields)

```
                        Weight Club Members                         1

                                        Start    End
        Obs    Team    Name            Weight   Weight

         1      r      David Shaw        189      165
         2      y      Amelia Serrano    145      124
         3      r      Alan Nance        210      192
         4      y      Ravi Sinha        194      177
         5      r      Ashley McKnight   127      118
         6      y      Jim Brown         220       .
```

Column Input: Points to Remember

Remember the following rules when you use column input:

☐ Character variables can be up to 32,767 bytes (32KB) in length and are not limited to the default length of eight bytes.

☐ Character variables can contain embedded blanks.

☐ You can read fields in any order.

☐ A placeholder is not required to indicate a missing data value. A blank field is read as missing and does not cause other values to be read incorrectly.

☐ You can skip over part of the data in the data record.

☐ You can reread fields or parts of fields.

☐ You can read standard character and numeric data only. Informats are ignored.

Reading Data That Requires Special Instructions

Understanding Formatted Input

Sometimes the INPUT statement requires special instructions to read the data correctly. For example, SAS can read numeric data that is in special formats such as binary, packed decimal, or date/time. SAS can also read numeric values that contain special characters such as commas and currency symbols. In these situations, use formatted input. *Formatted input* combines the features of column input with the ability to read nonstandard numeric or character values, for example:

☐ 1,262

☐ $55.64

☐ 02JAN2002

Program: Reading Data That Requires Special Instructions

The data in this program includes numeric values that contain a comma, which is an invalid character for a numeric variable:

```
data january_sales;
   input Item $ 1-16 Amount comma5.;
   datalines;
```

```
trucks          1,382
vans            1,235
sedans          2,391
;


proc print data=january_sales;
   title 'January Sales in Thousands';
run;
```

The INPUT statement cannot read the values for the variable Amount as valid numeric values without the additional instructions provided by an informat. The informat COMMA5. enables the INPUT statement to read and store this data as a valid numeric value.

The following figure shows that the informat COMMA5. instructs the program to read five characters of data (the comma counts as part of the length of the data), to remove the comma from the data, and to write the resulting numeric value to the program data vector. Note that the name of an informat always ends in a period (.).

Figure 3.1   Reading a Value with an Informat

The following figure shows that the data values are read into the input buffer exactly as they occur in the raw data records, but they are written to the program data vector (and then to the data set as an observation) as valid numeric values without any special characters.

Figure 3.2   Input Value Compared to Variable Value

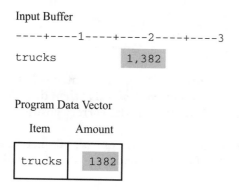

The following output shows the resulting data set. The values for Amount contain only numbers. Note that the commas are removed.

Output 3.6   Data Set Created with Column and Formatted Input

```
                       January Sales in Thousands                        1

                     Obs     Item     Amount

                      1     trucks     1382
                      2     vans       1235
                      3     sedans     2391
```

In a report, you might want to include the comma in numeric values to improve readability. Just as the informat gives instructions on how to read a value and to remove the comma, a format gives instructions to add characters to variable values in the output. See "Writing Output without Creating a Data Set" on page 518 for an example.

Understanding How to Control the Position of the Pointer

As the INPUT statement reads data values, it uses an *input pointer* to keep track of the position of the data in the input buffer. *Column-pointer controls* provide additional control over pointer movement and are especially useful with formatted input. Column-pointer controls tell how far to advance the pointer before SAS reads the next value. In this example, SAS reads data lines with a combination of column and formatted input:

```
data january_sales;
   input Item $ 1-16 Amount comma5.;
   datalines;
trucks          1,382
vans            1,235
sedans          2,391
;
```

In the next example, SAS reads data lines by using formatted input with a column-pointer control:

```
data january_sales;
   input Item $10. @17 Amount comma5.;
   datalines;
trucks          1,382
vans            1,235
sedans          2,391
;
```

After SAS reads the first value for the variable Item, the pointer is left in the next position, column 11. The *absolute column-pointer control*, @17, then directs the pointer to move to column 17 in the input buffer. Now, it is in the correct position to read a value for the variable Amount.

In the following program, the *relative column-pointer control*, +6, instructs the pointer to move six columns to the right before SAS reads the next data value.

```
data january_sales;
   input Item $10. +6 Amount comma5.;
   datalines;
trucks          1,382
vans            1,235
sedans          2,391
```

```
;
```

The data in these two programs is aligned in columns. As with column input, you instruct the pointer to move from field to field. With column input you use column specifications; with formatted input you use the length that is specified in the informat together with pointer controls.

Formatted Input: Points to Remember

Remember the following rules when you use formatted input:

☐ SAS reads formatted input data until it has read the number of columns that the informat indicates. This method of reading the data is different from list input, which reads until a blank space (or other defined delimiter character) is reached.

☐ You can position the pointer to read the next value by using pointer controls.

☐ You can read data stored in nonstandard form such as packed decimal, or data that contains commas.

☐ You have the flexibility of using informats with all the features of column input, as described in "Column Input: Points to Remember" on page 50.

Reading Unaligned Data with More Flexibility

Understanding How to Make List Input More Flexible

While list input is the simplest to code, remember that it places restrictions on your data. By using format modifiers, you can take advantage of the simplicity of list input without the inconvenience of the usual restrictions. For example, you can use *modified list input* to

☐ create character variables that are longer than the default length of eight bytes

☐ read numeric data with special characters like commas, dashes, and currency symbols

☐ read character data that contains embedded blanks

☐ read data values that can be stored as SAS date variables.

Creating Longer Variables and Reading Numeric Data That Contains Special Characters

By simply modifying list input with the *colon format modifier* (:) you can read

☐ character data that contains more than eight characters

☐ numeric data that contains special characters.

To use the colon format modifier with list input, place the colon between the variable name and the informat. As in simple list input, at least one blank (or other defined delimiter character) must separate each value from the next, and character values cannot contain embedded blanks (or other defined delimiter characters). Consider this DATA step:

```
data january_sales;
   input Item : $12. Amount : comma5.;
   datalines;
Trucks 1,382
```

```
Vans 1,235
Sedans 2,391
SportUtility 987
;


proc print data=january_sales;
    title 'January Sales in Thousands';
run;
```

The variable Item has a length of 12, and the variable Amount requires an informat (in this case, COMMA5.) that removes commas from numbers so that they are read as valid numeric values. The data values are not aligned in columns as was required in the last example, which used formatted input to read the data.

The following output shows the resulting data set.

Output 3.7   Data Set Created with Modified List Input (: comma5.)

```
                        January Sales in Thousands                    1

                  Obs     Item          Amount

                   1      Trucks          1382
                   2      Vans            1235
                   3      Sedans          2391
                   4      SportUtility     987
```

Reading Character Data That Contains Embedded Blanks

Because list input uses a blank space to determine where one value ends and the next one begins, values normally cannot contain blanks. However, with the *ampersand format modifier* (&) you can use list input to read data that contains single embedded blanks. The only restriction is that at least two blanks must divide each value from the next data value in the record.

To use the ampersand format modifier with list input, place the ampersand between the variable name and the informat. The following DATA step uses the ampersand format modifier with list input to create the data set CLUB2. Note that the data is not in fixed columns; therefore, column input is not appropriate.

```
data club2;
    input IdNumber Name & $18. Team $ StartWeight EndWeight;
    datalines;
1023 David Shaw    red 189 165
1049 Amelia Serrano  yellow 145 124
1219 Alan Nance   red 210 192
1246 Ravi Sinha   yellow 194 177
1078 Ashley McKnight   red 127 118
1221 Jim Brown   yellow 220 .
;


proc print data=club2;
    title 'Weight Club Members';
run;
```

The character variable Name, with a length of 18, contains members' first and last names separated by one blank space. The data lines must have two blank spaces between the values for the variable Name and the variable Team for the INPUT statement to correctly read the data.

The following output shows the resulting data set.

Output 3.8 Data Set Created with Modified List Input (& $18.)

```
                           Weight Club Members                              1

                 Id                               Start      End
     Obs       Number     Name            Team    Weight    Weight

      1         1023      David Shaw       red      189       165
      2         1049      Amelia Serrano   yellow   145       124
      3         1219      Alan Nance       red      210       192
      4         1246      Ravi Sinha       yellow   194       177
      5         1078      Ashley McKnight  red      127       118
      6         1221      Jim Brown        yellow   220        .
```

Mixing Styles of Input

An Example of Mixed Input

When you begin an INPUT statement in a particular style (list, column, or formatted), you are not restricted to using that style alone. You can mix input styles in a single INPUT statement as long as you mix them in a way that appropriately describes the raw data records. For example, this DATA step uses all three input styles:

```
data club1;
   input IdNumber ❶
         Name $18. ❷
         Team $ 25-30 ❸
         StartWeight EndWeight; ❶
   datalines;
1023 David Shaw        red     189 165
1049 Amelia Serrano    yellow 145 124
1219 Alan Nance        red     210 192
1246 Ravi Sinha        yellow 194 177
1078 Ashley McKnight   red     127 118
1221 Jim Brown         yellow 220   .
;

proc print data=club1;
   title 'Weight Club Members';
run;
```

The following list corresponds to the numbered items in the preceding program:

❶ The variables IdNumber, StartWeight, and EndWeight are read with list input.

❷ The variable Name is read with formatted input.

❸ The variable Team is read with column input.

The following output demonstrates that the data is read correctly.

Output 3.9   Data Set Created with Mixed Styles of Input

```
                           Weight Club Members                                    1

                   Id                                  Start       End
         Obs      Number    Name              Team     Weight    Weight

          1        1023     David Shaw        red        189       165
          2        1049     Amelia Serrano    yellow     145       124
          3        1219     Alan Nance        red        210       192
          4        1246     Ravi Sinha        yellow     194       177
          5        1078     Ashley McKnight   red        127       118
          6        1221     Jim Brown         yellow     220         .
```

Understanding the Effect of Input Style on Pointer Location

Why You Can Get into Trouble by Mixing Input Styles

CAUTION:

When you mix styles of input in a single INPUT statement, you can get unexpected results if you do not understand where the input pointer is positioned after SAS reads a value in the input buffer. As the INPUT statement reads data values from the record in the input buffer, it uses a *pointer* to keep track of its position. Read the following sections so that you understand how the pointer movement differs between input styles before mixing multiple input styles in a single INPUT statement △

Pointer Location with Column and Formatted Input

With column and formatted input, you supply the instructions that determine the exact pointer location. With column input, SAS reads the columns that you specify in the INPUT statement. With formatted input, SAS reads the exact length that you specify with the informat. In both cases, the pointer moves as far as you instruct it and stops. The pointer is left in the column that immediately follows the last column that is read.

Here are two examples of input followed by an explanation of the pointer location. The first DATA step shows column input:

```
data scores;
   input Team $ 1-6 Score 12-13;
   datalines;
red        59
blue       95
yellow     63
green      76
;
```

The second DATA step uses the same data to show formatted input:

```
data scores;
   input Team $6. +5 Score 2.;
   datalines;
red        59
blue       95
yellow     63
green      76
```

;

The following figure shows that the pointer is located in column 7 after the first value is read with either of the two previous INPUT statements.

Figure 3.3   Pointer Position: Column and Formatted Input

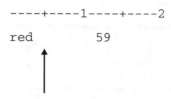

```
----+----1----+----2
red         59
```

Unlike list input, column and formatted input rely totally on your instructions to move the pointer and read the value for the second variable, Score. Column input uses column specifications to move the pointer to each data field. Formatted input uses informats and pointer controls to control the position of the pointer.

This INPUT statement uses column input with the column specifications 12-13 to move the pointer to column 12 and read the value for the variable Score:

```
input Team $ 1-6 Score 12-13;
```

This INPUT statement uses formatted input with the +5 column-pointer control to move the pointer to column 12. Then the value for the variable Score is read with the 2. numeric informat.

```
input Team $6. +5 Score 2.;
```

Without the use of a pointer control, which moves the pointer to the column where the value begins, this INPUT statement would attempt to read the value for Score in columns 7 and 8, which are blank.

Pointer Location with List Input

List input, on the other hand, uses a scanning method to determine the pointer location. With list input, the pointer reads until a blank is reached and then stops in the next column. To read the next variable value, the pointer moves automatically to the first nonblank column, discarding any leading blanks it encounters. Here is the same data that is read with list input:

```
data scores;
   input Team $ Score;
   datalines;
red        59
blue       95
yellow     63
green      76
;
```

The following figure shows that the pointer is located in column 5 after the value **red** is read. Because Score, the next variable, is read with list input, the pointer scans for the next nonblank space before it begins to read a value for Score. Unlike column and formatted input, you do not have to explicitly move the pointer to the beginning of the next field in list input.

Figure 3.4   Pointer Position: List Input

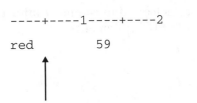

```
----+----1----+----2
red         59
```

Review of SAS Tools

Statements

DATALINES;
> indicates that data lines immediately follow the DATALINES statement. A
> semicolon in the line that immediately follows the last data line indicates the end
> of the data and causes the DATA step to compile and execute.

INFILE DATALINES DLM=*'character'*;
> identifies the source of the input records as data lines in the job stream rather
> than as an external file. When your program contains the input data, the data
> lines directly follow the DATALINES statement. Because you can specify
> DATALINES in the INFILE statement, you can take advantage of many
> data-reading options that are available only through the INFILE statement.
>
> The DLM= option specifies the character that is used to separate data values in
> the input records. By default, a blank space denotes the end of a data value. This
> option is useful when you want to use list input to read data records in which a
> character other than a blank separates data values.

INPUT *variable* <&> <$>;
> reads the input data record using list input. The & (ampersand format modifier)
> enables character values to contain embedded blanks. When you use the
> ampersand format modifier, two blanks are required to signal the end of a data
> value. The $ indicates a character variable.

INPUT *variable start-column <– end-column>*;
> reads the input data record using column input. You can omit *end-column* if the
> data is only 1 byte long. This style of input enables you to skip columns of data
> that you want to omit.

INPUT *variable* : *informat*;
INPUT *variable* & *informat*;
> read the input data record using modified list input. The : (colon format modifier)
> instructs SAS to use the informat that follows to read the data value. The &
> (ampersand format modifier) instructs SAS to use the informat that follows to read
> the data value. When you use the ampersand format modifier, two blanks are
> required to signal the end of a data value.

INPUT *<pointer-control> variable informat*;
> reads raw data using formatted input. The *informat* supplies special instructions
> to read the data. You can also use a *pointer-control* to direct SAS to start reading
> at a particular column.

The syntax given above for the three styles of input shows only one *variable*.
Subsequent variables in the INPUT statement may or may not be described in the

same input style as the first one. You may use any of the three styles of input (list, column, and formatted) in a single INPUT statement.

Column-Pointer Controls

@*n*
> moves the pointer to the *n*th column in the input buffer.

+*n*
> moves the pointer forward *n* columns in the input buffer.

/
> moves the pointer to the next line in the input buffer.

#*n*
> moves the pointer to the *n*th line in the input buffer.

Learning More

Advanced features
> For a few more advanced data-reading features, see the following chapter, Chapter 4, "Starting with Raw Data: Beyond the Basics," on page 61.

Character-delimited data
> For more information about reading data that is delimited by a character other than a blank space, see the DELIMITER= option in the INFILE statement in *SAS Language Reference: Dictionary* .

Pointer controls
> For a complete discussion and listing of column-pointer controls, line-pointer controls, and line-hold specifiers, see *SAS Language Reference: Dictionary*.

Types of input
> For more information about the INPUT statement, see the "Statements" chapter in *SAS Language Reference: Dictionary*. See also "INPUT, List"; "INPUT, Column"; "INPUT, Formatted"; and "INPUT, Named."

CHAPTER

4

Starting with Raw Data: Beyond the Basics

Introduction

Purpose

To create a SAS data set from raw data, you often need more than the most basic features. In this chapter you will learn advanced features for reading raw data that include

- □ how to understand and then control what happens when a value is unexpectedly missing in an input record
- □ how to read a record more than once so that you may test a condition before taking action on the current record
- □ how to create multiple observations from a single input record
- □ how to read multiple observations to create a single record.

Prerequisites

You should understand the concepts presented in Chapter 1, "What Is the SAS System?," on page 3 and Chapter 2, "Introduction to DATA Step Processing," on page 19 before continuing.

Testing a Condition before Creating an Observation

Sometimes you need to read a record, and hold that record in the input buffer while you test for a specified condition before a decision can be made about further processing. As an example, the ability to hold a record so that you can read from it again, if necessary, is useful when you need to test for a condition before SAS creates an observation from a data record. To do this, you can use the trailing at-sign (@).

For example, to create a SAS data set that is a subset of a larger group of records, you might need to test for a condition to decide if a particular record will be used to create an observation. The trailing at-sign placed before the semicolon at the end of an INPUT statement instructs SAS to hold the current data line in the input buffer. This makes the data line available for a subsequent INPUT statement. Otherwise, the next INPUT statement causes SAS to read a new record into the input buffer.

You can set up the process to read each record twice by following these steps:

1 Use an INPUT statement to read a portion of the record.

2 Use a trailing @ at the end of the INPUT statement to hold the record in the input buffer for the execution of the next INPUT statement.

3 Use an IF statement on the portion that is read in to test for a condition.

4 If the condition is met, use another INPUT statement to read the remainder of the record to create an observation.

5 If the condition is not met, the record is released and control passes back to the top of the DATA step.

To read from a record twice, you must prevent SAS from automatically placing a new record into the input buffer when the next INPUT statement executes. Use of a trailing @ in the first INPUT statement serves this purpose. The trailing @ is one of two line-hold specifiers that enable you to hold a record in the input buffer for further processing.

For example, the health and fitness club data contains information about all members. This DATA step creates a SAS data set that contains only members of the red team:

```
data red_team;
   input Team $ 13-18 @;    ❶
   if Team='red';    ❷
   input IdNumber 1-4 StartWeight 20-22 EndWeight 24-26;    ❸
   datalines;
1023 David   red      189 165
1049 Amelia  yellow   145 124
1219 Alan    red      210 192
1246 Ravi    yellow   194 177
1078 Ashley  red      127 118
1221 Jim     yellow   220   .
;    ❹

proc print data=red_team;
```

```
    title 'Red Team';
run;
```

In this DATA step, these actions occur:

❶ The INPUT statement reads a record into the input buffer, reads a data value from columns 13 through 18, and assigns that value to the variable Team in the program data vector. The single trailing @ holds the record in the input buffer.

❷ The IF statement enables the current iteration of the DATA step to continue only when the value for Team is **red**. When the value is not red, the current iteration stops and SAS returns to the top of the DATA step, resets values in the program data vector to missing, and releases the held record from the input buffer.

❸ The INPUT statement executes only when the value of Team is **red**. It reads the remaining data values from the record held in the input buffer and assigns values to the variables IdNumber, StartWeight, and EndWeight.

❹ The record is released from the input buffer when the program returns to the top of the DATA step.

The following output shows the resulting data set:

Output 4.1   Subset Data Set Created with Trailing @

```
                            Red Team                                    1

                       Id        Start      End
       Obs    Team    Number    Weight    Weight

        1     red      1023       189       165
        2     red      1219       210       192
        3     red      1078       127       118
```

Creating Multiple Observations from a Single Record

Using the Double Trailing @ Line-Hold Specifier

Sometimes you may need to create multiple observations from a single record of raw data. One way to tell SAS how to read such a record is to use the other line-hold specifier, the double trailing at-sign (@@ or "double trailing @"). The double trailing @ not only prevents SAS from reading a new record into the input buffer when a new INPUT statement is encountered, but it also prevents the record from being released when the program returns to the top of the DATA step. (Remember that the trailing @ does not hold a record in the input buffer across iterations of the DATA step.)

For example, this DATA step uses the double trailing @ in the INPUT statement:

```
data body_fat;
   input Gender $ PercentFat @@;
   datalines;
m 13.3 f 22
m 22    f 23.2
m 16    m 12
;

proc print data=body_fat;
```

```
    title 'Results of Body Fat Testing';
run;
```

The following output shows the resulting data set:

Output 4.2   Data Set Created with Double Trailing @

```
                    Results of Body Fat Testing                          1

                                   Percent
              Obs     Gender        Fat

               1        m           13.3
               2        f           22.0
               3        m           22.0
               4        f           23.2
               5        m           16.0
               6        m           12.0
```

Understanding How the Double Trailing @ Affects DATA Step Execution

To understand how the data records in the previous example were read, look at the data lines that were used in the previous DATA step:

```
m 13.3 f 22
m 22    f 23.2
m 16    m 12
```

Each record contains the raw data for two observations instead of one. Consider this example in terms of the flow of the DATA step, as explained in Chapter 2, "Introduction to DATA Step Processing," on page 19.

When SAS reaches the end of the DATA step, it returns to the top of the program and begins the next iteration, executing until there are no more records to read. Each time it returns to the top of the DATA step and executes the INPUT statement, it automatically reads a new record into the input buffer. The second set of data values in each record, therefore, would never be read:

```
m 13.3 f 22
m 22    f 23.2
m 16    m 12
```

To allow the second set of data values in each record to be read, the double trailing @ tells SAS to hold the record in the input buffer. Each record is held in the input buffer until the end of the record is reached. The program does not automatically place the next record into the input buffer each time the INPUT statement is executed, and the current record is not automatically released when it returns to the top of the DATA step. As a result, the pointer location is maintained on the current record which enables the program to read each value in that record. Each time the DATA step completes an iteration, an observation is written to the data set.

The next five figures demonstrate what happens in the input buffer when a double trailing @ appears in the INPUT statement, as in this example:

```
input Gender $ PercentFat @@;
```

The first figure shows that all values in the program data vector are set to missing. The INPUT statement reads the first record into the input buffer. The program begins to read values from the current pointer location, which is the beginning of the input buffer.

Figure 4.1 First Iteration: First Record Is Read

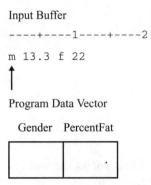

The following figure shows that the value **m** is written to the program data vector. When the pointer reaches the blank space that follows 13.3, the complete value for the variable PercentFat has been read. The pointer stops in the next column, and the value 13.3 is written to the program data vector.

Figure 4.2 First Observation Is Created

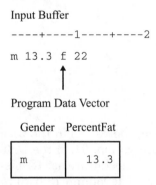

There are no other variables in the INPUT statement and no more statements in the DATA step, so three actions take place:

1 The first observation is written to the data set.
2 The DATA step begins its next iteration.
3 The values in the program data vector are set to missing.

The following figure shows the current position of the pointer. SAS is ready to read the next piece of data in the same record.

Figure 4.3   Second Iteration: First Record Remains in the Input Buffer

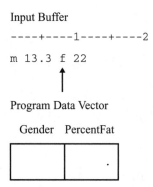

The following figure shows that the INPUT statement reads the next two values from the input buffer and writes them to the program data vector.

Figure 4.4   Second Observation Is Created

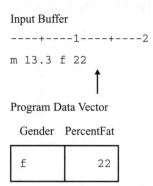

When the DATA step completes the second iteration, the values in the program data vector are written to the data set as the second observation. Then the DATA step begins its third iteration. Values in the program data vector are set to missing, and the INPUT statement executes. The pointer, which is now at column 13 (two columns to the right of the last data value that was read), continues reading. Because this is list input, the pointer scans for the next nonblank character to begin reading the next value. When the pointer reaches the end of the input buffer and fails to find a nonblank character, SAS reads a new record into the input buffer.

The final figure shows that values for the third observation are read from the beginning of the second record.

Figure 4.5 Third Iteration: Second Record Is Read into the Input Buffer

Input Buffer

```
----+----1----+----2
m 22   f 23.2
```
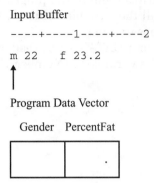

Program Data Vector

Gender PercentFat

	.

The process continues until SAS reads all the records. The resulting SAS data set contains six observations instead of three.

Note: Although this program successfully reads all of the data in the input records, SAS writes a message to the log noting that the program had to go to a new line. △

Reading Multiple Records to Create a Single Observation

How the Data Records Are Structured

An earlier example (see "Reading Character Data That Contains Embedded Blanks" on page 54) shows data for several observations that are contained in a single record of raw data:

```
1023 David Shaw      red 189 165
```

This INPUT statement reads all the data values arranged across a single record:

```
input IdNumber 1-4 Name $ 6-23 Team $ StartWeight EndWeight;
```

Now, consider the opposite situation: when information for a single observation is not contained in a single record of raw data but is scattered across several records. For example, the health and fitness club data could be constructed in such a way that the information about a single member is spread across several records instead of in a single record:

```
1023 David Shaw
red
189 165
```

Method 1: Using Multiple Input Statements

Multiple INPUT statements, one for each record, can read each record into a single observation, as in this example:

```
input IdNumber 1-4 Name $ 6-23;
input Team $ 1-6;
input StartWeight 1-3 EndWeight 5-7;
```

To understand how to use multiple INPUT statements, consider what happens as a DATA step executes. Remember that one record is read into the INPUT buffer automatically as each INPUT statement is encountered during each iteration. SAS reads the data values from the input buffer and writes them to the program data vector as variable values. At the end of the DATA step, all the variable values in the program data vector are written automatically as a single observation.

This example uses multiple INPUT statements in a DATA step to read only selected data fields and create a data set containing only the variables IdNumber, StartWeight, and EndWeight.

```
data club2;
   input IdNumber 1-4;   ❶
   input;   ❷
   input StartWeight 1-3 EndWeight 5-7;   ❸
   datalines;
1023 David Shaw
red
189 165
1049 Amelia Serrano
yellow
145 124
1219 Alan Nance
red
210 192
1246 Ravi Sinha
yellow
194 177
1078 Ashley McKnight
red
127 118
1221 Jim Brown
yellow
220  .
;

proc print data=club2;
   title 'Weight Club Members';
run;
```

The following list corresponds to the numbered items in the preceding program:

❶ The first INPUT statement reads only one data field in the first record and assigns a value to the variable IdNumber.

❷ The second INPUT statement, without arguments, is a null INPUT statement that reads the second record into the input buffer. However, it does not assign a value to a variable.

❸ The third INPUT statement reads the third record into the input buffer and assigns values to the variables StartWeight and EndWeight.

The following output shows the resulting data set:

Output 4.3 Data Set Created with Multiple INPUT Statements

```
                    Weight Club Members                              1

                     Id      Start     End
             Obs    Number   Weight   Weight

              1     1023      189      165
              2     1049      145      124
              3     1219      210      192
              4     1246      194      177
              5     1078      127      118
              6     1221      220       .
```

Method 2: Using the / Line-Pointer Control

Writing a separate INPUT statement for each record is not the only way to create a single observation. You can write a single INPUT statement and use the slash (/) line-pointer control. The *slash line-pointer control* forces a new record into the input buffer and positions the pointer at the beginning of that record.

This example uses only one INPUT statement to read multiple records:

```
data club2;
   input IdNumber 1-4 / / StartWeight 1-3 EndWeight 5-7;
   datalines;
1023 David Shaw
red
189 165
1049 Amelia Serrano
yellow
145 124
1219 Alan Nance
red
210 192
1246 Ravi Sinha
yellow
194 177
1078 Ashley McKnight
red
127 118
1221 Jim Brown
yellow
220   .
;

proc print data=club2;
   title 'Weight Club Members';
run;
```

The / line-pointer control appears exactly where a new INPUT statement begins in the previous example (see "Method 1: Using Multiple Input Statements" on page 67). The sequence of events in the input buffer and the program data vector as this DATA step executes is identical to the previous example in method 1. The / is the signal to read a new record into the input buffer, which happens automatically when the DATA step encounters a new INPUT statement. The preceding example shows two slashes

(/ /), indicating that SAS skips a record. SAS reads the first record, skips the second record, and reads the third record.

The following output shows the resulting data set:

Output 4.4   Data Set Created with the / Line-Pointer Control

```
                        Weight Club Members                              1

                          Id      Start     End
              Obs       Number    Weight    Weight

               1         1023      189       165
               2         1049      145       124
               3         1219      210       192
               4         1246      194       177
               5         1078      127       118
               6         1221      220        .
```

Reading Variables from Multiple Records in Any Order

You can also read multiple records to create a single observation by pointing to a specific record in a set of input records with the #*n* line-pointer control. As you saw in the last section, the advantage of using the / line-pointer control over multiple INPUT statements is that it requires fewer statements. However, using the #*n* line-pointer control enables you to read the variables in any order, no matter which record contains the data values. It is also useful if you want to skip data lines.

This example uses one INPUT statement to read multiple data lines in a different order:

```
data club2;
   input #2 Team $ 1-6 #1 Name $ 6-23 IdNumber 1-4
         #3 StartWeight 1-3 EndWeight 5-7;
   datalines;
1023 David Shaw
red
189 165
1049 Amelia Serrano
yellow
145 124
1219 Alan Nance
red
210 192
1246 Ravi Sinha
yellow
194 177
1078 Ashley McKnight
red
127 118
1221 Jim Brown
yellow
220   .
;

proc print data=club2;
```

```
      title 'Weight Club Members';
   run;
```

The following output shows the resulting data set:

Output 4.5 Data Set Created with the *#n* Line-Pointer Control

```
                         Weight Club Members                                  1

                                          Id      Start    End
         Obs    Team     Name           Number    Weight   Weight

          1     red      David Shaw       1023      189      165
          2     yellow   Amelia Serrano   1049      145      124
          3     red      Alan Nance       1219      210      192
          4     yellow   Ravi Sinha       1246      194      177
          5     red      Ashley McKnight  1078      127      118
          6     yellow   Jim Brown        1221      220        .
```

The order of the observations is the same as in the raw records (). However, the order of the variables in the data set differs from the order of the variables in the raw input data records. This occurs because the order of the variables in the INPUT statements corresponds with their order in the resulting data sets.

Understanding How the *#n* Line-Pointer Control Affects DATA Step Execution

To understand the importance of the *#n* line-pointer control, remember the sequence of events in the DATA steps that demonstrate the / line-pointer control and multiple INPUT statements. Each record is read into the input buffer sequentially. The data is read, and then a / or a new INPUT statement causes the program to read the next record into the input buffer. It is impossible for the program to read a value from the first record after a value from the second record is read because the data in the first record is no longer available in the input buffer.

To solve this problem, use the *#n* line-pointer control. The *#n* line-pointer control signals the program to create a multiple-line input buffer so that all the data for a single observation is available while the observation is being built in the program data vector. The *#n* line-pointer control also identifies the record in which data for each variable appears. To use the *#n* line-pointer control, the raw data must have the same number of records for each observation; for example, it cannot have three records for one observation and two for the next.

When the program compiles and builds the input buffer, it looks at the INPUT statement and creates an input buffer with as many lines as are necessary to contain the number of records it needs to read for a single observation. In this example, the highest number of records specified is three, so the input buffer is built to contain three records at one time. The following figures demonstrate the flow of the DATA step in this example.

This figure shows that the values are set to missing in the program data vector and that the INPUT statement reads the first three records into the input buffer.

Figure 4.6 Three Records Are Read into the Input Buffer as a Single Observation

Input Buffer

```
----+----1----+----2----+----3----+----4----+----5----+----6
1023 David Shaw


----+----1----+----2----+----3----+----4----+----5----+----6
red


----+----1----+----2----+----3----+----4----+----5----+----6
189 165
```

Program Data Vector

Team	Name	IdNumber	StartWeight	EndWeight
		.	.	.

The INPUT statement for this example is as follows:

```
input #2 Team $ 1-6
      #1 Name $ 6-23 IdNumber 1-4
      #3 StartWeight 1-3 EndWeight 5-7;
```

The first variable is preceded by #2 to indicate that the value in the second record is assigned to the variable Team. The following figure shows that the pointer advances to the second line in the input buffer, reads the value, and writes it to the program data vector.

Figure 4.7 Reading from the Second Record First

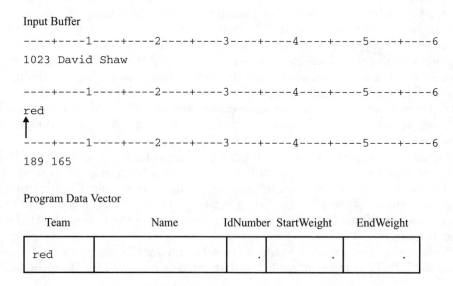

Input Buffer

```
----+----1----+----2----+----3----+----4----+----5----+----6
1023 David Shaw


----+----1----+----2----+----3----+----4----+----5----+----6
red

----+----1----+----2----+----3----+----4----+----5----+----6
189 165
```

Program Data Vector

Team	Name	IdNumber	StartWeight	EndWeight
red		.	.	.

The following figure shows that the pointer then moves to the sixth column in the first record, reads a value, and assigns it to the variable Name in the program data vector. It then moves to the first column to read the id number, and assigns it to the variable IdNumber.

Figure 4.8 Reading from the First Record

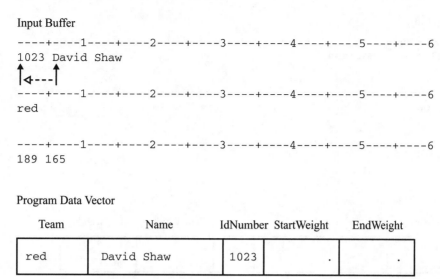

Program Data Vector

Team	Name	IdNumber	StartWeight	EndWeight
red	David Shaw	1023	.	.

The following figure shows that the process continues with the pointer moving to the third record in the first observation. Values are read and assigned to StartWeight and EndWeight, the last variable that is listed.

Figure 4.9 Reading from the Third Record

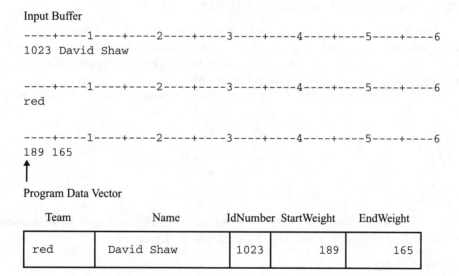

Program Data Vector

Team	Name	IdNumber	StartWeight	EndWeight
red	David Shaw	1023	189	165

When the bottom of the DATA step is reached, variable values in the program data vector are written as an observation to the data set. The DATA step returns to the top, and values in the program data vector are set to missing. The INPUT statement executes again. The final figure shows that the next three records are read into the input buffer, ready to create the second observation.

Figure 4.10   Reading the Next Three Records into the Input Buffer

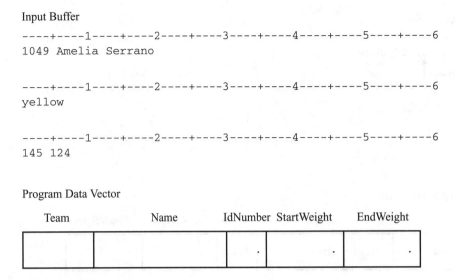

Input Buffer

```
----+----1----+----2----+----3----+----4----+----5----+----6
1049 Amelia Serrano


----+----1----+----2----+----3----+----4----+----5----+----6
yellow


----+----1----+----2----+----3----+----4----+----5----+----6
145 124
```

Program Data Vector

Team	Name	IdNumber	StartWeight	EndWeight
		.	.	.

Problem Solving: When an Input Record Unexpectedly Does Not Have Enough Values

Understanding the Default Behavior

When a DATA step reads raw data from an external file, problems can occur when SAS encounters the end of an input line before reading in data for all variables specified in the input statement. This problem can occur when reading variable-length records and/or records containing missing values.

The following is an example of an external file that contains variable-length records:

```
----+-----1-----+-----2


22
333
4444
55555
```

This DATA step uses the numeric informat 5. to read a single field in each record of raw data and to assign values to the variable TestNumber:

```
data numbers;
   infile 'your-external-file';
   input TestNumber 5.;
run;


proc print data=numbers;
   title 'Test DATA Step';
run;
```

The DATA step reads the first value (22). Because the value is shorter than the 5 characters expected by the informat, the DATA step attempts to finish filling the value with the next record (333). This value is entered into the PDV and becomes the value of the TestNumber variable for the first observation. The DATA step then goes to the next record, but encounters the same problem because the value (4444) is shorter than the value that is expected by the informat. Again, the DATA step goes to the next record, reads the value (55555), and assigns that value to the TestNumber variable for the second observation.

The following output shows the results. After this program runs, the SAS log contains a note to indicate the places where SAS went to the next record to search for data values.

Output 4.6   Reading Raw Data Past the End of a Line: Default Behavior

```
                              Test DATA Step                                 1

                                  Test
                       Obs      Number

                        1          333
                        2        55555
```

Methods of Control: Your Options

Four Options: FLOWOVER, STOPOVER, MISSOVER, and TRUNCOVER

To control how SAS behaves after it attempts to read past the end of a data line, you can use the following options in the INFILE statement:

`infile 'your-external-file' `**`flowover`**`;`
is the default behavior. The DATA step simply reads the next record into the input buffer, attempting to find values to assign to the rest of the variable names in the INPUT statement.

`infile 'your-external-file' `**`stopover`**`;`
causes the DATA step to stop processing if an INPUT statement reaches the end of the current record without finding values for all variables in the statement. Use this option if you expect all of the data in the external file to conform to a given standard and if you want the DATA step to stop when it encounters a data record that does not conform to the standard.

`infile 'your-external-file' `**`missover`**`;`
prevents the DATA step from going to the next line if it does not find values in the current record for all of the variables in the INPUT statement. Instead, the DATA step assigns a missing value for all variables that do not have values.

`infile 'your-external-file' `**`truncover`**`;`
causes the DATA step to assign the raw data value to the variable even if the value is shorter than expected by the INPUT statement. If, when the DATA step encounters the end of an input record, there are variables without values, the variables are assigned missing values for that observation.

You can also use these options even when your data lines are in the program itself, that is, when they follow the DATALINES statement. Simply use **`datalines`** instead of a reference to an external file to indicate that the data records are in the DATA step itself:

□ `infile datalines flowover;`

□ `infile datalines stopover;`

□ `infile datalines missover;`

□ `infile datalines truncover;`

Note: The examples in this section show the use of the MISSOVER and
TRUNCOVER options with formatted input. You can also use these options with list
input and column input. △

Understanding the MISSOVER Option

The MISSOVER option prevents the DATA step from going to the next line if it does
not find values in the current record for all of the variables in the INPUT statement.
Instead, the DATA step assigns a missing value for all variables that do not have
complete values according to any specified informats. The input file contains the
following raw data:

```
----+-----1-----+-----2


22
333
4444
55555
```

The following example uses the MISSOVER option:

```
data numbers;
    infile 'your-external-file' missover;
    input TestNumber 5.;
run;


proc print data=numbers;
    title 'Test DATA Step';
run;
```

Output 4.7   Output from the MISSOVER Option

```
                        Test DATA Step                              1

                           Test
                 Obs      Number

                  1          .
                  2          .
                  3          .
                  4        55555
```

Because the fourth record is the only one whose value matches the informat, it is the
only record whose value is assigned to the TestNumber variable. The other observations
receive missing values. This result is probably not the desired outcome for this
example, but the MISSOVER option can sometimes be valuable. For an example, see
"Updating a Data Set" on page 295.

Note: If there is a blank line at the end of the last record, the DATA step attempts
to load another record into the input buffer. Because there are no more records, the
MISSOVER option instructs the DATA step to assign missing values to all variables,
and an extra observation is added to the data set. To prevent this situation from

occurring, make sure that your input data does not have a blank line at the end of the last record. △

Understanding the TRUNCOVER Option

The TRUNCOVER option causes the DATA step to assign the raw data value to the variable even if the value is shorter than the length that is expected by the INPUT statement. If, when the DATA step encounters the end of an input record, there are variables without values, the variables are assigned missing values for that observation. The following example demonstrates the use of the TRUNCOVER statement:

```
data numbers;
    infile 'your-external-file' truncover;
    input TestNumber 5.;
run;


proc print data=numbers;
    title 'Test DATA Step';
run;
```

Output 4.8   Output from the TRUNCOVER Option

```
                          Test DATA Step                            1

                               Test
                  Obs         Number

                   1              22
                   2             333
                   3            4444
                   4           55555
```

This result shows that all of the values were assigned to the TestNumber variable, despite the fact that three of them did not match the informat. For another example using the TRUNCOVER option, see "Input SAS Data Set for Examples" on page 140.

Review of SAS Tools

Column-Pointer Controls

@ *n*
> moves the pointer to the *n* column in the input buffer.

+*n*
> moves the pointer forward *n* columns in the input buffer.

/
> moves the pointer to the next line in the input buffer.

#*n*
> moves the pointer to the *n*th line in the input buffer.

Line-Hold Specifiers

@

(trailing @) prevents SAS from automatically reading a new data record into the input buffer when a new INPUT statement is executed within the same iteration of the DATA step. When used, the trailing @ must be the last item in the INPUT statement.

@@

(double trailing @) prevents SAS from automatically reading a new data record into the input buffer when the next INPUT statement is executed, even if the DATA step returns to the top for another iteration. When used, the double trailing @ must be the last item in the INPUT statement.

Statements

DATALINES;

indicates that data lines immediately follow. A semicolon in the line that immediately follows the last data line indicates the end of the data and causes the DATA step to compile and execute.

INFILE *fileref*< FLOWOVER | STOPOVER | MISSOVER | TRUNCOVER>;
INFILE *'external-file'* <FLOWOVER | STOPOVER | MISSOVER | TRUNCOVER>;

identifies an external file to be read by an INPUT statement. Specify a *fileref* that has been assigned with a FILENAME statement or with an appropriate operating environment command. Or you can specify the actual name of the external file.

These options give you control over how SAS behaves if the end of a data record is encountered before all of the variables are assigned values. You can use these options with list, modified list, formatted, and column input.

FLOWOVER

is the default behavior. It causes the DATA step to look in the next record if the end of the current record is encountered before all of the variables are assigned values

MISSOVER

causes the DATA step to assign missing values to any variables that do not have values when the end of a data record is encountered. The DATA step continues processing.

STOPOVER

causes the DATA step to stop execution immediately and write a note to the SAS log.

TRUNCOVER

causes the DATA step to assign values to variables, even if the values are shorter than expected by the INPUT statement, and to assign missing values to any variables that do not have values when the end of a record is encountered.

INPUT *variable <&> <$>*;

reads the input data record using list input. The & (ampersand format modifier) allows character values to contain embedded blanks. When you use the ampersand format modifier, two blanks are required to signal the end of a data value. The $ indicates a character variable.

INPUT *variable start-column<end-column>*;

    reads the input data record using column input. You can omit *end-column* if the data is only 1 byte long. This style of input enables you to skip columns of data that you want to omit.

INPUT *variable : informat*;
INPUT *variable & informat*;

    reads the input data record using modified list input. The : (colon format modifier) instructs SAS to use the informat that follows to read the data value. The & (ampersand format modifier) instructs SAS to use the informat that follows to read the data value. When you use the ampersand format modifier, two blanks are required to signal the end of a data value.

INPUT *<pointer-control> variable informat*;

    reads raw data using formatted input. The *informat* supplies special instructions to read the data. You can also use a *pointer-control* to direct SAS to start reading at a particular column.

The syntax given above for the three styles of input shows only one *variable*. Subsequent variables in the INPUT statement may or may not be described in the same input style as the first one. You may use any of the three styles of input (list, column, and formatted) in a single INPUT statement.

Learning More

Handling missing data values

    For complete details about the FLOWOVER, STOPOVER, MISSOVER, and TRUNCOVER options in the INFILE statement, see *SAS Language Reference: Dictionary*.

Reading multiple input records

Testing a condition

    ☐ For more information about performing conditional processing with the IF statement, see Chapter 9, "Acting on Selected Observations," on page 139 and Chapter 10, "Creating Subsets of Observations," on page 159.

    ☐ For a complete discussion and listing of line-pointer controls and line-hold specifiers, see *SAS Language Reference: Dictionary*.

CHAPTER

5

Starting with SAS Data Sets

Introduction

Purpose

Using the techniques presented in this chapter, you will learn how to

□ display information about a SAS data set

□ create a new SAS data set from an existing SAS data set rather than creating it from raw data records.

Reading a SAS data set in a DATA step is simpler than reading raw data because the work of describing the data to SAS has already been done.

Prerequisites

You should understand the concepts presented in Chapter 1, "What Is the SAS System?," on page 3 and Chapter 2, "Introduction to DATA Step Processing," on page 19 before continuing with this chapter.

Understanding the Basics

When you use a SAS data set as input into a DATA step, the description of the data set is available to SAS. In your DATA step, use a SET, MERGE, MODIFY, or UPDATE statement to read the SAS data set. Use SAS programming statements to process the data and create an output SAS data set.

In a DATA step, you can create a new data set that is a subset of the original data set. For example, if you have a large data set of personnel data, you might want to look at a subset of observations that meet certain conditions, such as observations for employees hired after a certain date. Alternatively, you might want to see all observations but only a few variables, such as the number of years of education or years of service to the company.

When you use existing SAS data sets, as well as with subsets created from SAS data sets, you can make more efficient use of computer resources than if you use raw data or if you are working with large data sets. Reading fewer variables means that SAS creates a smaller program data vector, and reading fewer observations means that fewer iterations of the DATA step occur. Reading data directly from a SAS data set is more efficient than reading the raw data again, because the work of describing and converting the data has already been done.

One way of looking at a SAS data set is to produce a listing of the data in a SAS data set by using the PRINT procedure. Another way to look at a SAS data set is to display information that describes its structure rather than its data values. To display information about the structure of a data set, use the DATASETS procedure with the CONTENTS statement. If you need to work with a SAS data set that is unfamiliar to you, the CONTENTS statement in the DATASETS procedure displays valuable information such as the name, type, and length of all the variables in the data set. An example that shows the CONTENTS statement in the DATASETS procedure is shown in "Input SAS Data Set for Examples" on page 82.

Input SAS Data Set for Examples

The examples in this chapter use a SAS data set named CITY, which contains information about expenditures for a small city. It reports total city expenditures for the years 1980 through 2000 and divides the expenses into two major categories: services and administration. (To see the program that creates the CITY data set, see "DATA Step to Create the Data Set CITY" on page 712.)

The following example uses the DATASETS procedure with the NOLIST option to display the CITY data set. The NOLIST option prevents the DATASETS procedure from listing other data sets that are also located in the WORK library:

```
proc datasets library=work nolist;
   contents data=city;
run;
```

Output 5.1 The Structure of CITY as Shown by PROC DATASETS

```
                              The SAS System                              1

                           The DATASETS Procedure

Data Set Name: WORK.CITY                      Observations:          21 ❶
Member Type:   DATA                           Variables:             10 ❶
Engine:        V8                             Indexes:               0
Created:       9:54 Wednesday, October 6, 1999 Observation Length:   80
Last Modified: 9:54 Wednesday, October 6, 1999 Deleted Observations: 0
Protection:                                   Compressed:            NO
Data Set Type:                                Sorted:                NO
Label:



                   -----Engine/Host Dependent Information-----   ❷

Data Set Page Size:        8192
Number of Data Set Pages:  1
First Data Page:           1
Max Obs per Page:          101
Obs in First Data Page:    21
Number of Data Set Repairs: 0
File Name:                 /usr/tmp/code_editor_saswork/SAS_
                           work63ED00006E98/city.sas7bdat
Release Created:           8.0001M0
Host Created:              HP-UX
Inode Number:              62403
Access Permission:         rw-r--r--
Owner Name:                abcdef
File Size (bytes):         16384


               -----Alphabetic List of Variables and Attributes-----

❸ #    Variable           Type   Len   Pos ❹ Label
   ----------------------------------------------------------------------
    5   AdminLabor          Num    8     32   Administration: Labor
    6   AdminSupplies       Num    8     40   Administration: Supplies
    9   AdminTotal          Num    8     64   Administration: Total
    7   AdminUtilities      Num    8     48   Administration: Utilities
    3   ServicesFire        Num    8     16   Services: Fire
    2   ServicesPolice      Num    8     8    Services: Police
    8   ServicesTotal       Num    8     56   Services: Total
    4   ServicesWater_Sewer Num    8     24   Services: Water & Sewer
   10   Total               Num    8     72   Total Outlays
    1   Year                Num    8     0
```

The following list corresponds to the numbered items in the previous SAS output:

❶ The Observations and the Variables fields identify the number of observations and the number of variables.

❷ The Engine/Host Dependent Information section lists detailed information about the data set. This information is generated by the *engine*, which is the mechanism for reading from and writing to files.

Operating Environment Information: The output in this section may differ, depending on your operating environment. For more information, refer to the SAS documentation for your operating environment. △

❸ The Alphabetic List of Variables and Attributes lists the name, type, length, and position of each variable.

❹ The Label lists the format, informat, and label for each variable, if they exist.

Reading Selected Observations

If you are interested in only part of a large data set, you can use data set options to create a subset of your data. Data set options specify which observations you want the new data set to include. In Chapter 10, "Creating Subsets of Observations," on page 159 you learn how to use the subsetting IF statement to create a subset of a large SAS data set. In this section, you learn how to use the FIRSTOBS= and OBS= data set options to create subsets of a larger data set.

For example, you might not want to read the observations at the beginning of the data set. You can use the FIRSTOBS= data set option to define which observation should be the first one that is processed. For the data set CITY, this example creates a data set that excludes observations that contain data prior to 1991 by specifying FIRSTOBS=12. As a result, SAS does not read the first 11 observations, which contain data prior to 1991. (To see the program that creates the CITY data set, see "DATA Step to Create the Data Set CITY" on page 712.)

The following program creates the data set CITY2, which contains the same number of variables but fewer observations than CITY.

```
data city2;
   set city(firstobs=12);
run;

proc print;
   title 'City Expenditures';
   title2 '1991 - 2000';
run;
```

The following output shows the results:

Output 5.2 Subsetting a Data Set by Observations

```
                                   City Expenditures                          1
                                      1991 - 2000

                                        S
                                        e
                                        r
                                        v
                                        i
                          S             c                 A
                          e             e         A       d
                          r       S     s         d       m
                          v       e     W         m       i           S
                          i       r     a         i       n           e
                          c       v     t     A   n       U           r           A
                          e       i     e     d   S       t           v           d
                          s       c     r     m   u       i           i           m
                          P       e     _     i   p       l           c           i
                          o       s     S     n   p       i           e           n
                  Y       l       F     e     L   l       t           T           T
          O       e       i       i     w     a   i       i           o           o
          b       a       c       r     e     b   e       e           t           t
          s       r       e       e     r     o   s       s           a           a
                                              r                       l           l

          1      1991    2195    1002   643   256  24      55         3840        335        4175
          2      1992    2204     964   692   256  28      70         3860        354        4214
          3      1993    2175    1144   735   241  19      83         4054        343        4397
          4      1994    2556    1341   813   238  25      97         4710        360        5070
          5      1995    2026    1380   868   226  24      97         4274        347        4621
          6      1996    2526    1454   946   317  13      89         4926        419        5345
          7      1997    2027    1486  1043   226   .      82         4556         .           .
          8      1998    2037    1667  1152   244  20      88         4856        352        5208
          9      1999    2852    1834  1318   270  23      74         6004        367        6371
         10      2000    2787    1701  1317   307  26      66         5805        399        6204
```

You can also specify the last observation you want to include in a new data set with the OBS= data set option. For example, the next program creates a SAS data set containing only the observations for 1989 (the 10th observation) through 1994 (the 15th observation).

```
data city3;
   set city (firstobs=10 obs=15);
run;
```

Reading Selected Variables

Overview

You can create a subset of a larger data set not only by excluding observations but also by specifying which variables you want the new data set to contain. In a DATA step you can use the SET statement and the KEEP= or DROP= data set options (or the DROP and KEEP statements) to create a subset from a larger data set by specifying which variables you want the new data set to include.

Keeping Selected Variables

This example uses the KEEP= data set option in the SET statement to read only the variables that represent the services-related expenditures of the data set CITY.

```
data services;
   set city (keep=Year ServicesTotal ServicesPolice ServicesFire
            ServicesWater_Sewer);
run;


proc print data=services;
   title 'City Services-Related Expenditures';
run;
```

The following output shows the resulting data set. Note that the data set SERVICES contains only those variables that are specified in the KEEP= option.

Output 5.3 Selecting Variables with the KEEP= Option

```
                     City Services-Related Expenditures                    1

                                             Services
                       Services    Services    Water_     Services
        Obs    Year     Police       Fire      Sewer       Total

         1     1980      2819        1120        422        4361
         2     1981      2477        1160        500        4137
         3     1982      2028        1061        510        3599
         4     1983      2754         893        540        4187
         5     1984      2195         963        541        3699
         6     1985      1877         926        535        3338
         7     1986      1727        1111        535        3373
         8     1987      1532        1220        519        3271
         9     1988      1448        1156        577        3181
        10     1989      1500        1076        606        3182
        11     1990      1934         969        646        3549
        12     1991      2195        1002        643        3840
        13     1992      2204         964        692        3860
        14     1993      2175        1144        735        4054
        15     1994      2556        1341        813        4710
        16     1995      2026        1380        868        4274
        17     1996      2526        1454        946        4926
        18     1997      2027        1486       1043        4556
        19     1998      2037        1667       1152        4856
        20     1999      2852        1834       1318        6004
        21     2000      2787        1701       1317        5805
```

The following example uses the KEEP statement instead of the KEEP= data set option to read all of the variables from the CITY data set. The KEEP statement creates a new data set (SERVICES) that contains only the variables listed in the KEEP statement. The following program gives results that are identical to those in the previous example:

```
data services;
   set city;
   keep Year ServicesTotal ServicesPolice ServicesFire
        ServicesWater_Sewer;
run;
```

The following example has the same effect as using the KEEP= data set option in the DATA statement. All of the variables are read into the program data vector, but only the specified variables are written to the SERVICES data set:

```
data services (keep=Year ServicesTotal ServicesPolice ServicesFire
          ServicesWater_Sewer);
   set city;
run;
```

Dropping Selected Variables

Use the DROP= option to create a subset of a larger data set when you want to specify which variables are being excluded rather than which ones are being included. The following DATA step reads all of the variables from the data set CITY except for those that are specified with the DROP= option, and then creates a data set named SERVICES2:

```
data services2;
   set city (drop=Total AdminTotal AdminLabor AdminSupplies
          AdminUtilities);
run;

proc print data=services2;
   title 'City Services-Related Expenditures';
run;
```

The following output shows the resulting data set:

Output 5.4 Excluding Variables with the DROP= Option

```
                      City Services-Related Expenditures                        1

                                              Services
                       Services    Services    Water_      Services
          Obs   Year    Police      Fire       Sewer        Total

           1    1980     2819       1120        422          4361
           2    1981     2477       1160        500          4137
           3    1982     2028       1061        510          3599
           4    1983     2754        893        540          4187
           5    1984     2195        963        541          3699
           6    1985     1877        926        535          3338
           7    1986     1727       1111        535          3373
           8    1987     1532       1220        519          3271
           9    1988     1448       1156        577          3181
          10    1989     1500       1076        606          3182
          11    1990     1934        969        646          3549
          12    1991     2195       1002        643          3840
          13    1992     2204        964        692          3860
          14    1993     2175       1144        735          4054
          15    1994     2556       1341        813          4710
          16    1995     2026       1380        868          4274
          17    1996     2526       1454        946          4926
          18    1997     2027       1486       1043          4556
          19    1998     2037       1667       1152          4856
          20    1999     2852       1834       1318          6004
          21    2000     2787       1701       1317          5805
```

The following example uses the DROP statement instead of the DROP= data set option to read all of the variables from the CITY data set and to exclude the variables that are listed in the DROP statement from being written to the new data set. The results are identical to those in the previous example:

```
data services2;
   set city;
   drop Total AdminTotal AdminLabor AdminSupplies AdminUtilities;
run;
proc print data=services2;
run;
```

Choosing between Data Set Options and Statements

When you create only one data set in the DATA step, the data set options to drop and keep variables have the same effect on the output data set as the statements to drop and keep variables. When you want to control which variables are read into the program data vector, using the data set options in the statement (such as a SET statement) that reads the SAS data set is generally more efficient than using the statements. Later sections in this chapter show that you can use the data set options in some cases where the statements will not work.

Choosing between the DROP= and KEEP= Data Set Option

In a simple case, you might decide to use the DROP= or KEEP= option, depending on which method enables you to specify fewer variables. If you work with large jobs that read data sets, and you expect that variables might be added between the times your batch jobs run, you may want to use the KEEP= option to specify which variables are included in the subset data set.

The following figure shows two data sets named SMALL. They have different contents because the new variable F was added to data set BIG before the DATA step ran on Tuesday. The DATA step uses the DROP= option to keep variables D and E from being written to the output data set. The result is that the data sets contain different contents: the second SMALL data set has an extra variable, F. If the DATA step used the KEEP= option to specify A, B, and C, then both of the SMALL data sets would have the same variables (A, B, and C). The addition of variable F to the original data set BIG would have no effect on the creation of the SMALL data set.

Figure 5.1   Using the DROP= Option

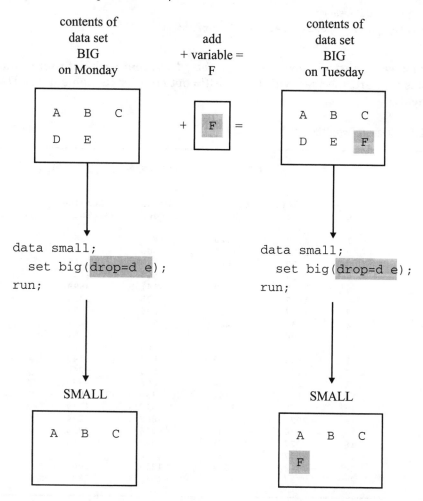

Creating More Than One Data Set in a Single DATA Step

You can use a single DATA step to create more than one data set at a time. You can create data sets with different contents by using the KEEP= or DROP= data set options. For example, the following DATA step creates two SAS data sets: SERVICES contains variables that show services-related expenditures, and ADMIN contains variables that represent the administration-related expenditures. Use the KEEP= option after each data set name in the DATA statement to determine which variables are written to each SAS data set being created.

```
data services(keep=ServicesTotal ServicesPolice ServicesFire
            ServicesWater_Sewer)
     admin(keep=AdminTotal AdminLabor AdminSupplies
            AdminUtilities);
   set city;
run;

proc print data=services;
   title 'City Expenditures: Services';
run;
```

```
proc print data=admin;
    title 'City Expenditures: Administration';
run;
```

The following output shows both data sets. Note that each data set contains only the variables that are specified with the KEEP= option after its name in the DATA statement.

Output 5.5 Creating Two Data Sets in One DATA Step

```
                    City Expenditures: Services                           1

                                  Services
                 Services   Services   Water_    Services
        Obs      Police     Fire       Sewer     Total

         1        2819       1120        422       4361
         2        2477       1160        500       4137
         3        2028       1061        510       3599
         4        2754        893        540       4187
         5        2195        963        541       3699
         6        1877        926        535       3338
         7        1727       1111        535       3373
         8        1532       1220        519       3271
         9        1448       1156        577       3181
        10        1500       1076        606       3182
        11        1934        969        646       3549
        12        2195       1002        643       3840
        13        2204        964        692       3860
        14        2175       1144        735       4054
        15        2556       1341        813       4710
        16        2026       1380        868       4274
        17        2526       1454        946       4926
        18        2027       1486       1043       4556
        19        2037       1667       1152       4856
        20        2852       1834       1318       6004
        21        2787       1701       1317       5805
```

```
              City Expenditures: Administration                    2

                Admin      Admin      Admin      Admin
       Obs      Labor    Supplies   Utilities    Total

        1        391        63         98         552
        2        172        47         70         289
        3        269        29         79         377
        4        227        21         67         315
        5        214        21         59         294
        6        198        16         80         294
        7        213        27         70         310
        8        195        11         69         275
        9        225        12         58         295
       10        235        19         62         316
       11        266        11         63         340
       12        256        24         55         335
       13        256        28         70         354
       14        241        19         83         343
       15        238        25         97         360
       16        226        24         97         347
       17        317        13         89         419
       18        226         .         82          .
       19        244        20         88         352
       20        270        23         74         367
       21        307        26         66         399
```

Note: In this case, using the KEEP= data set option is necessary, because when you use the KEEP statement, all data sets that are created in the DATA step contain the same variables. △

Using the DROP= and KEEP= Data Set Options for Efficiency

The DROP= and KEEP= data set options are valid in both the DATA statement and the SET statement. However, you can write a more efficient DATA step if you understand the consequences of using these options in the DATA statement rather than the SET statement.

In the DATA statement, these options affect which variables SAS writes from the program data vector to the resulting SAS data set. In the SET statement, these options determine which variables SAS reads from the input SAS data set. Therefore, they determine how the program data vector is built.

When you specify the DROP= or KEEP= option in the SET statement, SAS does not read the excluded variables into the program data vector. If you work with a large data set (perhaps one containing thousands or millions of observations), you can construct a more efficient DATA step by not reading unneeded variables from the input data set.

Note also that if you use a variable from the input data set to perform a calculation, the variable must be read into the program data vector. If you do not want that variable to appear in the new data set, however, use the DROP= option in the DATA statement to exclude it.

The following DATA step creates the same two data sets as the DATA step in the previous example, but it does not read the variable Total into the program data vector. Compare the SET statement here to the one in "Creating More Than One Data Set in a Single DATA Step" on page 89.

```
data services (keep=ServicesTotal ServicesPolice ServicesFire
       ServicesWater_Sewer)
```

```
      admin (keep=AdminTotal AdminLabor AdminSupplies
             AdminUtilities);
   set city(drop=Total);
run;

proc print data=services;
   title 'City Expenditures: Services';
run;

proc print data=admin;
   title 'City Expenditures: Administration';
run;
```

In contrast with previous examples, the data set options in this example appear in both the DATA and SET statements. In the SET statement, the DROP= option determines which variables are omitted from the program data vector. In the DATA statement, the KEEP= option controls which variables are written from the program data vector to each data set being created.

Note: Using a DROP or KEEP statement is comparable to using a DROP= or KEEP= option in the DATA statement. All variables are included in the program data vector; they are excluded when the observation is written from the program data vector to the new data set. When you create more than one data set in a single DATA step, using the data set options enables you to drop or keep different variables in each of the new data sets. A DROP or KEEP statement, on the other hand, affects all of the data sets that are created. △

Review of SAS Tools

Data Set Options

DROP=*variable(s)*
:   specifies the variables to be excluded.

    Used in the SET statement, DROP= specifies the variables that are not to be read from the existing SAS data set into the program data vector. Used in the DATA statement, DROP= specifies the variables to be excluded from the data set that is being created.

FIRSTOBS=*n*
:   specifies the first observation to be read from the SAS data set that you specify in the SET statement.

KEEP=*variable(s)*
:   specifies the variables to be included.

    Used in the SET statement, KEEP= specifies the variables to be read from the existing SAS data set into the program data vector. Used in the DATA statement, KEEP= specifies which variables in the program data vector are to be written to the data set being created.

OBS=*n*
:   specifies the last observation to be read from the SAS data set that you specify in the SET statement.

Procedures

PROC DATASETS <LIBRARY=*SAS-data-library*>;
CONTENTS <DATA=*SAS-data set*>;
 describes the structure of a SAS data set, including the name, type, and length of all variables in the data set.

Statements

DATA *SAS-data-set<(data-set-options)>*;
 begins a DATA step and names the SAS data set or data sets that are being created. You can specify the DROP= or KEEP= data set options in parentheses after each data set name to control which variables are written to the output data set from the program data vector.

DROP *variable(s)*;
 specifies the variables to be excluded from the data set that is being created. See also the DROP= data set option.

KEEP *variable(s)*
 specifies the variables to be written to the data set that is being created. See also the KEEP= data set option.

SET *SAS-data-set(data-set-options)*;
 reads observations from a SAS data set rather than records of raw data. You can specify the DROP= or KEEP= data set options in parentheses after a data set name to control which variables are read into the program data vector from the input data set.

Learning More

Creating SAS data sets
 For a general discussion about creating SAS data sets from other SAS data sets by merging, concatenating, interleaving, and updating, see Chapter 15, "Methods of Combining SAS Data Sets," on page 233.

Data set options
 See the "Data Set Options" section of *SAS Language Reference: Dictionary*, and the SAS documentation for your operating environment.

DROP and KEEP statements
 See the "Statements" section of *SAS Language Reference: Dictionary*.

Engines
 see the "SAS Data Libraries" chapter in *SAS Language Reference: Concepts*.

Subsetting IF statement
 You can use the subsetting IF statement and conditional (IF-THEN) logic when creating a new SAS data set from an existing one. For more information, see Chapter 9, "Acting on Selected Observations," on page 139 and Chapter 10, "Creating Subsets of Observations," on page 159.

P A R T *3*

Basic Programming

CHAPTER

6

Understanding DATA Step Processing

Introduction

Purpose

To add, modify, and delete information in a SAS data set, you use a DATA step. In this chapter, you will learn how the DATA step works, the general form of the statements, and some programming techniques.

Prerequisites

You should understand the concepts presented in Chapter 2, "Introduction to DATA Step Processing," on page 19 and Chapter 3, "Starting with Raw Data: The Basics," on page 43 before proceeding with this chapter.

Input SAS Data Set for Examples

Tradewinds Travel Inc. has an external file that they use to manipulate and store data about their tours. The external file contains the following information:

❶ **❷❸ ❹ ❺**
France 8 793 575 Major

```
Spain 10 805 510 Hispania
India 10   . 489 Royal
Peru   7 722 590 Mundial
```

The numbered fields represent

❶ the name of the country toured
❷ the number of nights on the tour
❸ the airfare in US dollars
❹ the cost of the land package in US dollars
❺ the name of the company that offers the tour.

Notice that the cost of the airfare for the tour to India has a missing value, which is indicated by a period.

The following DATA step creates a permanent SAS data set named MYLIB.INTERNATIONALTOURS:

```
options pagesize=60 linesize=80 pageno=1 nodate;
libname mylib 'permanent-data-library';

data mylib.internationaltours;
    infile 'input-file';
    input Country $ Nights AirCost LandCost Vendor $;

proc print data = mylib.internationaltours;
    title 'Data Set MYLIB.INTERNATIONALTOURS';
run;
```

The PROC PRINT statement that follows the DATA step produces this display of the MYLIB.INTERNATIONALTOURS data set:

Output 6.1   Creating a Permanent SAS Data Set

```
              Data Set MYLIB.INTERNATIONALTOURS                        1

                               Air    Land
     Obs    Country    Nights  Cost   Cost   Vendor

      1     France       8     793    575    Major
      2     Spain       10     805    510    Hispania
      3     India       10      .     489    Royal
      4     Peru         7     722    590    Mundial
```

Adding Information to a SAS Data Set

Understanding the Assignment Statement

One of the most common reasons for using program statements in the DATA step is to produce new information from the original information or to change the information read by the INPUT or SET/MERGE/MODIFY/UPDATE statement. How do you add information to observations with a DATA step?

The basic method of adding information to a SAS data set is to create a new variable in a DATA step with an *assignment statement*. An assignment statement has the form:

variable=expression;

The *variable* receives the new information; the *expression* creates the new information. You specify the calculation necessary to produce the information and write the calculation as the expression. When the expression contains character data, you must enclose the data in quotation marks. SAS evaluates the expression and stores the new information in the variable that you name. It is important to remember that if you need to add the information to only one or two observations out of many, SAS creates that variable for all observations. The SAS data set that is being created must have information in every observation and every variable.

Making Uniform Changes to Data by Creating a Variable

Sometimes you want to make a particular change to every observation. For example, at Tradewinds Travel the airfare must be increased for every tour by $10 because of a new tax. One way to do this is to write an assignment statement that creates a new variable that calculates the new airfare:

```
NewAirCost = AirCost+10;
```

This statement directs SAS to read the value of AirCost, add 10 to it, and assign the result to the new variable, NewAirCost.

When this assignment statement is included in a DATA step, the DATA step looks like this:

```
options pagesize=60 linesize=80 pageno=1 nodate;
data newair;
   set mylib.internationaltours;
   NewAirCost = AirCost + 10;

proc print data=newair;
   var Country AirCost NewAirCost;
   title 'Increasing the Air Fare by $10 for All Tours';
run;
```

Note: In this example, the VAR statement in the PROC PRINT step determines which variables are displayed in the output. △

The following output shows the resulting SAS data set, NEWAIR:

Output 6.2 Adding Information to All Observations by Using a New Variable

```
              Increasing the Air Fare by $10 for All Tours                 1

                                            New ❶
                                    Air     Air
              Obs    Country        Cost    Cost

               1     France         793     803
               2     Spain          805     815
               3     India           .       . ❷
               4     Peru           722     732
```

Notice in this data set that

❶ because SAS carries out each statement in the DATA step for every observation, NewAirCost is calculated during each iteration of the DATA step.

❷ the observation for India contains a missing value for AirCost; SAS therefore assigns a missing value to NewAirCost for that observation.

The SAS data set has information in every observation and every variable.

Adding Information to Some Observations but Not Others

Often you need to add information to some observations but not to others. For example, some tour operators award bonus points to travel agencies for booking particular tours. Two companies, Hispania and Mundial, are offering bonus points this year.

IF-THEN/ELSE statements can cause assignment statements to be carried out only when a condition is met. In the following DATA step, the IF statements check the value of the variable Vendor. If the value is either Hispania or Mundial, information about the bonus points is added to those observations.

```
options pagesize=60 linesize=80 pageno=1 nodate;
data bonus;
   set mylib.internationaltours;
   if Vendor = 'Hispania' then BonusPoints = 'For 10+ people';
   else if Vendor = 'Mundial' then BonusPoints = 'Yes';
run;

proc print data=bonus;
   var Country Vendor BonusPoints;
   title1 'Adding Information to Observations for';
   title2 'Vendors Who Award Bonus Points';
run;
```

The following output displays the results:

Output 6.3 Specifying Values for Specific Observations by Using a New Variable

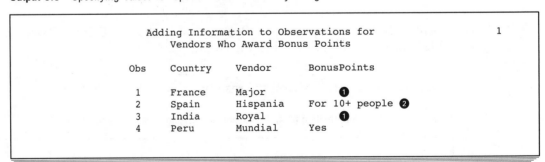

```
                 Adding Information to Observations for                 1
                    Vendors Who Award Bonus Points

      Obs    Country    Vendor       BonusPoints

       1     France     Major            ❶
       2     Spain      Hispania     For 10+ people ❷
       3     India      Royal            ❶
       4     Peru       Mundial      Yes
```

The new variable BonusPoints has the following information:

❶ In the two observations that are not assigned a value for BonusPoints, SAS assigns a missing value, represented by a blank in this case, to indicate the absence of a character value.

❷ The first value that SAS encounters for BonusPoints contains 14 characters; therefore, SAS sets aside 14 bytes of storage in each observation for BonusPoints, regardless of the length of the value for that observation.

Making Uniform Changes to Data Without Creating Variables

Sometimes you want to change the value of existing variables without adding new variables. For example, in one DATA step a new variable, NewAirCost, was created to contain the value of the airfare plus the new $10 tax:

```
NewAirCost = AirCost + 10;
```

You can also decide to change the value of an existing variable rather than create a new variable. Following the example, AirCost is changed as follows:

```
AirCost = AirCost + 10;
```

SAS processes this statement just as it does other assignment statements. It evaluates the expression on the right side of the equal sign and assigns the result to the variable on the left side of the equal sign. The fact that the same variable appears on the right and left sides of the equal sign does not matter. SAS evaluates the expression on the right side of the equal sign before looking at the variable on the left side.

The following program contains the new assignment statement:

```
options pagesize=60 linesize=80 pageno=1 nodate;
data newair2;
   set mylib.internationaltours;
   AirCost = AirCost + 10;

proc print data=newair2;
   var Country AirCost;
   title 'Adding Tax to the Air Cost Without Adding a New Variable';
run;
```

The following output displays the results:

Output 6.4   Changing the Information in a Variable

```
          Adding Tax to the Air Cost Without Adding a New Variable           1

                                      Air
                    Obs    Country    Cost

                     1     France      803
                     2     Spain       815
                     3     India         .
                     4     Peru        732
```

When you change the kind of information that a variable contains, you change the meaning of that variable. In this case, you are changing the meaning of AirCost from *airfare without tax* to *airfare with tax*. If you remember the current meaning and if you know that you do not need the original information, then changing a variable's values is useful. However, for many programmers, having separate variables is easier than recalling one variable whose definition changes.

Using Variables Efficiently

Variables that contain information that applies to only one or two observations use more storage space than necessary. When possible, create fewer variables that apply to more observations in the data set, and allow the different values in different observations to supply the information.

For example, the Major company offers discounts, not bonus points, for groups of 30 or more people. An inefficient program would create separate variables for bonus points and discounts, as follows:

```
/* inefficient use of variables */
options pagesize=60 linesize=80 pageno=1 nodate;
data tourinfo;
   set mylib.internationaltours;
   if Vendor = 'Hispania' then BonusPoints = 'For 10+ people';
   else if Vendor = 'Mundial' then BonusPoints = 'Yes';
        else if Vendor = 'Major' then Discount = 'For 30+ people';
run;

proc print data=tourinfo;
   var Country Vendor BonusPoints Discount;
   title 'Information About Vendors';
run;
```

The following output displays the results:

Output 6.5   Inefficient: Using Variables That Scatter Information Across Multiple Variables

```
                     Information About Vendors                          1

        Obs    Country    Vendor      BonusPoints         Discount

         1     France     Major                          For 30+ people
         2     Spain      Hispania    For 10+ people
         3     India      Royal
         4     Peru       Mundial     Yes
```

As you can see, storage space is used inefficiently. Both BonusPoints and Discount have a significant number of missing values.

With a little planning, you can make the SAS data set much more efficient. In the following DATA step, the variable Remarks contains information about bonus points, discounts, and any other special features of any tour.

```
/* efficient use of variables */
options pagesize=60 linesize=80 pageno=1 nodate;
data newinfo;
   set mylib.internationaltours;
   if Vendor = 'Hispania' then Remarks = 'Bonus for 10+ people';
   else if Vendor = 'Mundial' then Remarks = 'Bonus points';
        else if Vendor = 'Major' then Remarks = 'Discount: 30+ people';
run;

proc print data=newinfo;
   var Country Vendor Remarks;
   title 'Information About Vendors';
run;
```

The following output displays a more efficient use of variables:

Output 6.6 Efficient: Using Variables to Contain Maximum Information

```
                      Information About Vendors                              1

            Obs    Country    Vendor    Remarks

             1     France     Major     Discount: 30+ people
             2     Spain      Hispania  Bonus for 10+ people
             3     India      Royal
             4     Peru       Mundial   Bonus points
```

Remarks has fewer missing values and contains all the information that is used by BonusPoints and Discount in the inefficient example. Using variables efficiently can save storage space and optimize your SAS data set.

Defining Enough Storage Space for Variables

The first time that a value is assigned to a variable, SAS enables as many bytes of storage space for the variable as there are characters in the first value assigned to it. At times, you may need to specify the amount of storage space that a variable requires. For example, as shown in the preceding example, the variable Remarks contains miscellaneous information about tours:

```
if Vendor = 'Hispania' then Remarks = 'Bonus for 10+ people';
```

In this assignment statement, SAS enables 20 bytes of storage space for Remarks as there are 20 characters in the first value assigned to it. The longest value may not be the first one assigned, so you specify a more appropriate length for the variable before the first value is assigned to it:

```
length Remarks $ 30;
```

This statement, called a LENGTH statement, applies to the entire data set. It defines the number of bytes of storage that is used for the variable Remarks in every observation. SAS uses the LENGTH statement during compilation, not when it is processing statements on individual observations. The following DATA step shows the use of the LENGTH statement:

```
options pagesize=60 linesize=80 pageno=1 nodate;
data newlength;
   set mylib.internationaltours;
   length Remarks $ 30;
   if Vendor = 'Hispania' then Remarks = 'Bonus for 10+ people';
   else if Vendor = 'Mundial' then Remarks = 'Bonus points';
       else if Vendor = 'Major' then Remarks = 'Discount for 30+ people';
run;

proc print data=newlength;
   var Country Vendor Remarks;
   title 'Information About Vendors';
run;
```

The following output displays the NEWLENGTH data set:

Output 6.7   Using a LENGTH Statement

```
                         Information About Vendors                          1

          Obs     Country     Vendor       Remarks

           1      France      Major        Discount for 30+ people
           2      Spain       Hispania     Bonus for 10+ people
           3      India       Royal
           4      Peru        Mundial      Bonus points
```

Because the LENGTH statement affects variable storage, not the spacing of columns in printed output, the Remarks variable appears the same in Output 6.6 on page 103 and Output 6.7 on page 104. To show the effect of the LENGTH statement on variable storage using the DATASETS procedures, see Chapter 35, "Getting Information about Your SAS Data Sets," on page 603.

Conditionally Deleting an Observation

If you do not want the program data vector to write to a data set based on a condition, use the DELETE statement in the DATA step. For example, if the tour to Peru has been discontinued, it is no longer necessary to include the observation for Peru in the data set that is being created. The following example uses the DELETE statement to prevent SAS from writing that observation to the output data set:

```
options pagesize=60 linesize=80 pageno=1 nodate;
data subset;
   set mylib.internationaltours;
   if Country = 'Peru' then delete;
run;

proc print data=subset;
   title 'Omitting a Discontinued Tour';
run;
```

The following output displays the results:

Output 6.8   Deleting an Observation

```
                       Omitting a Discontinued Tour                         1

                                    Air     Land
          Obs     Country    Nights Cost    Cost    Vendor

           1      France       8     793     575    Major
           2      Spain       10     805     510    Hispania
           3      India       10      .      489    Royal
```

The observation for Peru has been deleted from the data set.

Review of SAS Tools

Statements

DELETE;
> prevents SAS from writing a particular observation to the output data set. It usually appears as part of an IF-THEN/ELSE statement.

If *condition* THEN *action* ELSE *action*;
> tests whether the *condition* is true. When the condition is true, the THEN statement specifies the *action* to take. When the *condition* is false, the ELSE statement provides an alternative *action*. The *action* can be one or more statements, including assignment statements.

LENGTH *variable* <$> *length*;
> assigns the number of bytes of storage (*length*) for a *variable*. Include a dollar sign ($) if the variable is character. The LENGTH statement must appear before the first use of the variable.

variable=expression;
> is an assignment statement. It causes SAS to evaluate the *expression* on the right side of the equal sign and assign the result to the *variable* on the left. You must select the name of the variable and create the proper expression for calculating its value. The same variable name can appear on the left and right sides of the equal sign because SAS evaluates the right side before assigning the result to the variable on the left side.

Learning More

Character variables
> For information about expressions involving alphabetic and special characters as well as numbers, see Chapter 8, "Working with Character Variables," on page 119.

DATA step
> For general DATA step information, see Chapter 2, "Introduction to DATA Step Processing," on page 19. Complete information about the DATA step can be found in the "DATA Step Concepts" section of *SAS Language Reference: Concepts*.

IF-THEN/ELSE statements
> The IF-THEN/ELSE statements are discussed in Chapter 9, "Acting on Selected Observations," on page 139.

LENGTH statement
> Additional information about the LENGTH statement can be found in Chapter 7, "Working with Numeric Variables," on page 107 and Chapter 8, "Working with Character Variables," on page 119. To show the effect of the LENGTH statement on variable storage using the DATASETS procedures, see Chapter 35, "Getting Information about Your SAS Data Sets," on page 603.

Missing values
> For more information about missing values, see the in Chapter 7, "Working with Numeric Variables," on page 107 and Chapter 8, "Working with Character Variables," on page 119.

Numeric variables
Information about working with numeric variables and expressions can be found in Chapter 7, "Working with Numeric Variables," on page 107.

SAS statements
For complete reference information about the IF-THEN/ELSE, LENGTH, DELETE, assignment, and comment statements, see *SAS Language Reference: Dictionary*.

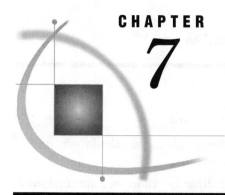

CHAPTER

7

Working with Numeric Variables

Introduction

Purpose

In this chapter, you will learn

☐ how to perform arithmetic calculations in SAS using arithmetic operators and the SAS functions ROUND and SUM

☐ how to compare numeric variables using logical operators

☐ how to store numeric variables efficiently when disk space is limited.

Prerequisites

Before proceeding with this chapter, you should understand the concepts presented in

☐ Part 1, "Introduction to the SAS System"

□ Part 2, "Getting Your Data into Shape"

□ Chapter 6, "Understanding DATA Step Processing," on page 97.

About Numeric Variables in SAS

A *numeric variable* is a variable whose values are numbers.

Note: SAS uses double-precision floating point representation for calculations and, by default, for storing numeric variables in SAS data sets. △

SAS accepts numbers in many forms, for example, scientific notation, hexadecimal, and so on. For more information, see the discussion on the types of numbers that SAS can read from data lines in the "SAS Variables" chapter of *SAS Language Reference: Concepts*. For simplicity, this book concentrates on numbers in standard representation, as shown here:

```
1254
 336.05
-243
```

You can use SAS to perform all kinds of mathematical operations. To perform a calculation in a DATA step, you can write an assignment statement in which the expression contains arithmetic operators, SAS functions, or a combination of the two. To compare numeric variables, you can write an IF-THEN/ELSE statement using logical operators. For more information on numeric functions, see the discussion in the "Functions and CALL Routines" chapter in *SAS Language Reference: Dictionary*.

Input SAS Data Set for Examples

Tradewinds Travel Inc. has an *external* file that contains information about their most popular tours:

❶	**❷**	**❸**	**❹**	**❺**
Japan	8	982	1020	Express
Greece	12	.	748	Express
New Zealand	16	1368	1539	Southsea
Ireland	7	787	628	Express
Venezuela	9	426	505	Mundial
Italy	8	852	598	Express
Russia	14	1106	1024	A-B-C
Switzerland	9	816	834	Tour2000
Australia	12	1299	1169	Southsea
Brazil	8	682	610	Almeida

The numbered fields represent

❶ the name of the country toured

❷ the number of nights on the tour

❸ the airfare in US dollars

❹ the cost of the land package in US dollars

❺ the name of the company that offers the tour.

The following program creates a permanent SAS data set named MYLIB.POPULARTOURS:

```
options pagesize=60 linesize=80 pageno=1 nodate;
libname mylib 'permanent-data-library';

data mylib.populartours;
   infile 'input-file';
   input Country $ 1-11 Nights AirCost LandCost Vendor $;
run;

proc print data=mylib.populartours;
   title 'Data Set MYLIB.POPULARTOURS';
run;
```

The following output shows the data set:

Output 7.1   Data Set MYLIB.POPULARTOURS

```
                      Data Set MYLIB.POPULARTOURS                        1

                                      Air    Land
          Obs    Country    Nights    Cost   Cost   Vendor

           1     Japan         8       982    1020   Express
           2     Greece       12        .      748   Express
           3     New Zealand  16      1368    1539   Southsea
           4     Ireland       7       787     628   Express
           5     Venezuela     9       426     505   Mundial
           6     Italy         8       852     598   Express
           7     Russia       14      1106    1024   A-B-C
           8     Switzerland   9       816     834   Tour2000
           9     Australia    12      1299    1169   Southsea
          10     Brazil        8       682     610   Almeida
```

In MYLIB.POPULARTOURS, the variables Nights, AirCost, and LandCost contain numbers and are stored as numeric variables. For comparison, variables Country and Vendor contain alphabetic and special characters as well as numbers; they are stored as character variables.

Calculating with Numeric Variables

Using Arithmetic Operators in Assignment Statements

One way to perform calculations on numeric variables is to write an assignment statement using arithmetic operators. Arithmetic operators indicate addition, subtraction, multiplication, division, and exponentiation (raising to a power). For more information on arithmetic expressions, see the discussion in *SAS Language Reference: Concepts*. The following table shows operators that you can use in arithmetic expressions.

Table 7.1   Operators in Arithmetic Expressions

Operation	Symbol	Example
addition	+	x = y + z;
subtraction	–	x = y - z;
multiplication	*	x = y * z
division	/	x = y / z
exponentiation	**	x = y ** z

The following examples show some typical calculations using the Tradewinds Travel sample data.

Table 7.2   Examples of Using Arithmetic Operators

Action	SAS Statement
Add the airfare and land cost to produce the total cost.	TotalCost = AirCost + Landcost;
Calculate the peak season airfares by increasing the basic fare by 10% and adding an $8 departure tax.	PeakAir = (AirCost * 1.10) + 8;
Show the cost per night of each land package.	NightCost = LandCost / Nights;

In each case, the variable on the left side of the equal sign receives the calculated value from the numeric expression on the right side of the equal sign. Including these statements in the following DATA step produces data set NEWTOUR:

```
options pagesize=60 linesize=80 pageno=1 nodate;
data newtour;
   set mylib.populartours;
   TotalCost = AirCost + LandCost;
   PeakAir = (AirCost * 1.10) + 8;
   NightCost = LandCost / Nights;
run;

proc print data=newtour;
   var Country Nights AirCost LandCost TotalCost PeakAir NightCost;
   title 'Costs for Tours';
run;
```

The VAR statement in the PROC PRINT step causes only the variables listed in the statement to be displayed in the output.

Output 7.2 Creating New Variables by Using Arithmetic Expressions

```
                           Costs for Tours                              1

                              Air     Land    Total    Peak    Night
     Obs    Country   Nights  Cost    Cost    Cost     Air     Cost

       1    Japan        8     982    1020    2002    1088.2   127.500
       2    Greece      12       .     748       .        .     62.333
       3    New Zealand 16    1368    1539    2907    1512.8    96.188
       4    Ireland      7     787     628    1415     873.7    89.714
       5    Venezuela    9     426     505     931     476.6    56.111
       6    Italy        8     852     598    1450     945.2    74.750
       7    Russia      14    1106    1024    2130    1224.6    73.143
       8    Switzerland  9     816     834    1650     905.6    92.667
       9    Australia   12    1299    1169    2468    1436.9    97.417
      10    Brazil       8     682     610    1292     758.2    76.250
```

Understanding Numeric Expressions and Assignment Statements

Numeric expressions in SAS share some features with mathematical expressions:

☐ When an expression contains more than one operator, the operations have the same order of precedence as in a mathematical expression: exponentiation is done first, then multiplication and division, and finally addition and subtraction.

☐ When operators of equal precedence appear, the operations are performed from left to right (except exponentiation, which is performed right to left).

☐ Parentheses are used to group parts of an expression; as in mathematical expressions, operations in parentheses are performed first.

Note: The equal sign in an assignment statement does not perform the same function as the equal sign in a mathematical equation. The sequence *variable=* in an assignment statement defines the statement, and the variable must appear on the left side of the equal sign. You cannot switch the positions of the result variable and the expression as you can in a mathematical equation. △

Understanding How SAS Handles Missing Values

Why SAS Assigns Missing Values

What if an observation lacks a value for a particular numeric variable? For example, in the data set MYLIB.POPULARTOURS, as shown in Output 7.2 on page 111, the observation for Greece has no value for the variable AirCost. To maintain the rectangular structure of a SAS data set, SAS assigns a missing value to the variable in that observation. A missing value indicates that no information is present for the variable in that observation.

Rules for Missing Values

The following rules describe missing values in several situations:

☐ In data lines, a missing numeric value is represented by a period, for example,

```
Greece      8 12   .   748 Express
```

By default, SAS interprets a single period in a numeric field as a missing value. (If the INPUT statement reads the value from particular columns, as in column input, a field that contains only blanks also produces a missing value.)

□ In an expression, a missing numeric value is represented by a period, for example,

```
if AirCost= . then Status = 'Need air cost';
```

□ In a comparison and in sorting, a missing numeric value is a lower value than any other numeric value.

□ In procedure output, SAS by default represents a missing numeric value with a period.

□ Some procedures eliminate missing values from their analyses; others do not. Documentation for individual procedures describes how each procedure handles missing values.

Propagating Missing Values

When you use a missing value in an arithmetic expression, SAS sets the result of the expression to missing. If you use that result in another expression, the next result is also missing. In SAS, this method of treating missing values is called *propagation of missing values*. For example, Output 7.2 on page 111 shows that in the data set NEWTOUR, the values for TOTALCOST and PEAKAIR are also missing in the observation for Greece.

Note: SAS enables you to distinguish between various kinds of numeric missing values. See "Missing Values" chapter of *SAS Language Reference: Concepts*. The SAS language contains 27 special missing values based on the letters A–Z and the underscore (_). △

Calculating Numbers Using SAS Functions

Rounding Values

In the example data that lists costs of the different tours (Output 7.1 on page 109), some of the tours have odd prices: $748 instead of $750, $1299 instead of $1300, and so on. Rounded numbers, created by rounding the tour prices to the nearest $10, would be easier to work with.

Programming a rounding calculation with only the arithmetic operators is a lengthy process. However, SAS contains around 280 built-in numeric expressions called *functions*. You can use them in expressions just as you do the arithmetic operators. For example, the following assignment statement rounds the value of AirCost to the nearest $50:

```
RoundAir = round(AirCost,50);
```

The following statement calculates the total cost of each tour, rounded to the nearest $100:

```
TotalCostR = round(AirCost + LandCost,100);
```

Calculating a Cost When There Are Missing Values

As another example, the travel agent can calculate a total cost for the tours based on all nonmissing costs. Therefore, when the airfare is missing (as it is for Greece) the total cost represents the land cost, not a missing value. (Of course, you must decide whether skipping missing values in a particular calculation is a good idea.) The SUM function calculates the sum of its arguments, ignoring missing values. This example illustrates the SUM function:

```
SumCost = sum(AirCost,LandCost);
```

Combining Functions

It is possible for you to combine functions. The ROUND function rounds the quantity given in the first argument to the nearest unit given in the second argument. The SUM function adds any number of arguments, ignoring missing values. The calculation in the following assignment statement rounds the sum of all nonmissing airfares and land costs to the nearest $100 and assigns the value to RoundSum:

```
RoundSum = round(sum(AirCost,LandCost),100);
```

Using the ROUND and SUM functions in the following DATA step creates the data set MORETOUR:

```
options pagesize=60 linesize=80 pageno=1 nodate;
data moretour;
   set mylib.populartours;
   RoundAir = round(AirCost,50);
   TotalCostR = round(AirCost + LandCost,100);
   CostSum = sum(AirCost,LandCost);
   RoundSum = round(sum(AirCost,LandCost),100);
run;

proc print data=moretour;
   var Country AirCost LandCost RoundAir TotalCostR CostSum RoundSum;
   title 'Rounding and Summing Values';
run;
```

The following output displays the results:

Output 7.3 Creating New Variables with ROUND and SUM Functions

```
                      Rounding and Summing Values                        1

                 Air    Land   Round   Total   Cost   Round
   Obs  Country   Cost    Cost    Air    CostR    Sum    Sum

    1   Japan      982    1020   1000    2000    2002   2000
    2   Greece       .     748      .       .     748    700
    3   New Zealand 1368   1539   1350    2900    2907   2900
    4   Ireland     787     628    800    1400    1415   1400
    5   Venezuela   426     505    450     900     931    900
    6   Italy       852     598    850    1500    1450   1500
    7   Russia     1106    1024   1100    2100    2130   2100
    8   Switzerland  816     834    800    1700    1650   1700
    9   Australia  1299    1169   1300    2500    2468   2500
   10   Brazil      682     610    700    1300    1292   1300
```

Comparing Numeric Variables

Often in a program you need to know if variables are equal to each other, or if they are greater than or less than each other. To compare two numeric variables, you can write an IF-THEN/ELSE statement using logical operators. The following table lists some of the logical operators you can use for variable comparisons.

Table 7.3 Logical Operators

Symbol	Mnemonic Equivalent	Logical Operation
=	eq	equal
¬=, ^=, ~=	ne	not equal to (the ¬=, ^=, or ~= symbol, depending on your keyboard)
>	gt	greater than
>=	ge	greater than or equal to
<	lt	less than
<=	le	less than or equal to

In this example, the total cost of each tour in the POPULARTOURS data set is compared to 2000 using the greater-than logical operator (gt). If the total cost of the tour is greater than 2000, the tour is excluded from the data set. The resulting data set TOURSUNDER2K contains tours that are $2000 or less.

```
options pagesize=60 linesize=80 pageno=1 nodate;
data toursunder2K;
   set mylib.populartours;
   TotalCost = AirCost + LandCost;
   if TotalCost gt 2000 then delete;
run;
proc print data=toursunder2K;
   var Country Nights AirCost Landcost TotalCost Vendor;
   title 'Tours $2000 or Less';
run;
```

The following output shows the tours that are less than $2000 in total cost:

Output 7.4 Comparing Numeric Variables

```
                           Tours $2000 or Less                             1

                                       Air     Land    Total
      Obs    Country      Nights       Cost    Cost    Cost      Vendor

       1     Greece         12            .     748       .      Express
       2     Ireland         7          787     628     1415     Express
       3     Venezuela       9          426     505      931     Mundial
       4     Italy           8          852     598     1450     Express
       5     Switzerland     9          816     834     1650     Tour2000
       6     Brazil          8          682     610     1292     Almeida
```

The TotalCost value for Greece is a missing value because any calculation that includes a missing value results in a missing value. In a comparison, missing numeric values are lower than any other numeric value.

If you need to compare a variable to more than one value, you can include multiple comparisons in a *condition*. To eliminate tours with missing values, a second comparison is added:

```
options pagesize=60 linesize=80 pageno=1 nodate;
data toursunder2K2;
   set mylib.populartours;
   TotalCost = AirCost + LandCost;
   if TotalCost gt 2000 or Totalcost = . then delete;
run;


proc print data=toursunder2K2;
   var Country Nights TotalCost Vendor;
   title 'Tours $2000 or Less';
run;
```

The following output displays the results:

Output 7.5 Multiple Comparisons in a Condition

```
                        Tours $2000 or Less                           1

                                          Total
            Obs    Country      Nights     Cost      Vendor

             1     Ireland         7       1415      Express
             2     Venezuela       9        931      Mundial
             3     Italy           8       1450      Express
             4     Switzerland     9       1650      Tour2000
             5     Brazil          8       1292      Almeida
```

Notice that Greece is no longer included in the tours for under $2000.

Storing Numeric Variables Efficiently

The data sets shown in this chapter are very small, but data sets are often very large. If you have a large data set, you may need to think about the storage space that your data set occupies. There are ways to save space when you store numeric variables in SAS data sets.

Note: The SAS documentation for your operating environment provides information about storing numeric variables whose values are limited to 1 or 0 in the minimum number of bytes used by SAS (either 2 or 3 bytes, depending on your operating environment). △

By default, SAS uses 8 bytes of storage in a data set for each numeric variable. Therefore, storing the variables for each observation in the earlier data set MORETOUR requires 75 bytes:

```
56 bytes for numeric variables
   (8 bytes per variable * 7 numeric variables)
11 bytes for Country
```

```
8 bytes for Vendor
```

```
75 bytes for all variables
```

When numeric variables contain only integers (whole numbers), you can often shorten them in the data set being created. For example, a length of 4 bytes accurately stores all integers up to at least 2,000,000.

Note: Under some operating environments, the maximum number of bytes is much greater. For more information, refer to the documentation provided by the vendor for your operating environment. △

To change the number of bytes used for each variable, use a LENGTH statement.

A LENGTH statement contains the names of the variables followed by the number of bytes to be used for their storage. For numeric variables, the LENGTH statement affects only the data set being created; it does not affect the program data vector. The following program changes the storage space for all numeric variables that are in the data set SHORTER:

```
options pagesize=60 linesize=80 pageno=1 nodate;
data shorter;
   set mylib.populartours;
   length Nights AirCost LandCost RoundAir TotalCostR
          Costsum RoundSum 4;
   RoundAir = round(AirCost,50);
   TotalCostR = round(AirCost + LandCost,100);
   CostSum = sum(AirCost,LandCost);
   RoundSum = round(sum(AirCost,LandCost),100);
run;
```

By calculating the storage space that is needed for the variables in each observation of SHORTER, you can see how the LENGTH statement changes the amount of storage space used:

```
28 bytes for numeric variables
    (4 bytes per variable in the LENGTH statement X 7 numeric variables)
11 bytes for Country
 8 bytes for Vendor
```

```
47 bytes for all variables
```

Because of the 7 variables in SHORTER are shortened by the LENGTH statement, the storage space for the variables in each observation is reduced by almost half.

CAUTION:

Be careful in shortening the length of numeric variables if your variable values are not integers. Fractional numbers lose precision permanently if they are truncated. In general, use the LENGTH statement to truncate values only when disk space is limited. Use the default length of 8 bytes to store variables containing fractions. △

Review of SAS Tools

Functions

ROUND (*expression, round-off-unit*)
rounds the quantity in *expression* to the figure given in *round-off-unit*. The
expression can be a numeric variable name, a numeric constant, or an arithmetic
expression. Separate *round-off-unit* from *expression* with a comma.

SUM (*expression-1<, . . . expression-n>*)
produces the sum of all *expressions* that you specify in the parentheses. The SUM
function ignores missing values as it calculates the sum of the *expressions*. Each
expression can be a numeric variable, a numeric constant, another arithmetic
expression, or another numeric function.

Statements

LENGTH *variable-list number-of-bytes*;
indicates that the variables in the *variable-list* are to be stored in the data set
according to the *number-of-bytes* that you specify. Numeric variables are not
affected while they are in the program data vector. The default length for a
numeric variable is 8 bytes. In general, the minimum you should use is 4 bytes for
variables that contain integers and 8 bytes for variables that contain fractions.
You can assign lengths to both numeric and character variables (discussed in the
next chapter) in a single LENGTH statement.

variable=expression;
is an assignment statement. It causes SAS to calculate the value of the *expression*
on the right side of the equal sign and assign the result to the *variable* on the left.
When *variable* is numeric, the expression can be an arithmetic calculation, a
numeric constant, or a numeric function.

Learning More

Abbreviating lists of variables
Ways to abbreviate lists of variables in function arguments is documented in the
"SAS Variables" chapter of *SAS Language Reference: Concepts*. Many functions,
including the SUM function, accept abbreviated lists of variables as arguments.

DEFAULT= option
Information about using the DEFAULT= option in the LENGTH statement to
assign a default storage length to all newly created numeric variables can be found
in *SAS Language Reference: Dictionary*.

Logical expressions
Additional information about the use of logical expressions can be found in *SAS
Language Reference: Concepts*.

Numeric precision
For a discussion about numeric precision, see the "SAS Variables" chapter in *SAS
Language Reference: Concepts*. Because the computer's hardware determines the
way that a computer stores numbers, the precision with which SAS can store

numbers depends on the hardware of the computer system on which it is installed. Specific limits for hardware are discussed in the SAS documentation for each operating environment.

Saving space

For information about how you can save space by treating some numeric values as character values see Chapter 8, "Working with Character Variables," on page 119.

Working with Character Variables

Introduction

Purpose

In this chapter, you will learn how to

☐ identify character variables

☐ set the length of character variables

☐ align character values within character variables

☐ handle missing values of character variables

☐ work with character variables, character constants, and character expressions in SAS program statements

☐ instruct SAS to read fields that contain numbers as character variables in order to save space.

Prerequisites

Before proceeding with this chapter, you should understand the concepts presented in

☐ Part 1, "Introduction to SAS"

☐ Part 2, "Getting Your Data into Shape"

☐ Chapter 6, "Understanding DATA Step Processing," on page 97.

Character Variables in SAS

A *character variable* is a variable whose value contains letters, numbers, and special characters, and whose length can be from 1 to 32,767 characters long. Character variables can be used in declarative statements, comparison statements, or assignment statements where they can be manipulated to create new character variables.

Input SAS Data Set for Examples

Tradewinds Travel has an external file with data on flight schedules for tours. The following DATA step reads the information and stores it in a data set named AIR.DEPARTURES:

```
options pagesize=60 linesize=80 pageno=1 nodate;
libname mylib 'permanent-data-library';

data mylib.departures;
   input Country $ 1-9 CitiesInTour 11-12 USGate $ 14-26
         ArrivalDepartureGates $ 28-48;
   datalines;
❶          ❷ ❸             ❹
Japan       5 San Francisco    Tokyo, Osaka
Italy       8 New York          Rome, Naples
Australia  12 Honolulu        Sydney, Brisbane
Venezuela   4 Miami          Caracas, Maracaibo
Brazil      4                Rio de Janeiro, Belem
;
proc print data=mylib.departures;
   title 'Data Set AIR.DEPARTURES';
run;
```

The numbered fields represent

❶ the name of the country toured

❷ the number of cities in the tour

❸ the city from which the tour leaves the United States (the gateway city)

❹ the cities of arrival and departure in the destination country.

The PROC PRINT statement that follows the DATA step produces this display of the AIR.DEPARTURES data set:

Output 8.1   Data Set AIR.DEPARTURES

```
                            Data Set AIR.DEPARTURES                              1

                         Cities
        Obs    Country    InTour     USGate           ArrivalDepartureGates

         1     Japan        5        San Francisco    Tokyo, Osaka
         2     Italy        8        New York         Rome, Naples
         3     Australia   12        Honolulu         Sydney, Brisbane
         4     Venezuela    4        Miami            Caracas, Maracaibo
         5     Brazil       4                         Rio de Janeiro, Belem
```

In AIR.DEPARTURES, the variables Country, USGate, and ArrivalDepartureGates contain information other than numbers, so they must be stored as character variables. The variable CitiesInTour contains only numbers; therefore, it can be created and stored as either a character or numeric variable.

Identifying Character Variables and Expressing Character Values

To store character values in a SAS data set, you need to create a character value. One way to create a character variable is to define it in an input statement. Simply place a dollar sign after the variable name in the INPUT statement, as shown in the DATA step that created AIR.DEPARTURES:

```
input Country $ 1-9 CitiesInTour 11-12 USGate $ 14-26
      ArrivalDepartureGates $ 28-48;
```

You can also create a character variable and assign a value to it in an assignment statement. Simply enclose the value in quotation marks:

```
Schedule = '3-4 tours per season';
```

Either single quotation marks (apostrophes) or double quotation marks are acceptable. If the value itself contains a single quote, then surround the value with double quotation marks, as in

```
Remarks = "See last year's schedule";
```

Note: Matching quotation marks properly is important. Missing or extraneous quotation marks cause SAS to misread both the erroneous statement and the statements following it. △

When you specify a character value in an expression, you must also enclose the value in quotation marks. For example, the following statement compares the value of USGate to San Francisco and, when a match occurs, assigns the airport code SFO to the variable Airport:

```
if USGate = 'San Francisco' then Airport = 'SFO';
```

In character values, SAS distinguishes uppercase letters from lowercase letters. For example, in the data set AIR.DEPARTURES, the value of USGate in the observation for Australia is **Honolulu**. The following IF condition is true; therefore, SAS assigns to Airport the value HNL:

```
else if USGate = 'Honolulu' then Airport = 'HNL';
```

However, the following condition is false:

```
if USGate = 'HONOLULU' then Airport = 'HNL';
```

SAS does not select that observation because the characters in Honolulu and HONOLULU are not equivalent.

The following program places these shaded statements in a DATA step:

```
options pagesize=60 linesize=80 pageno=1 nodate;

data charvars;
   set mylib.departures;
   Schedule = '3-4 tours per season';
   Remarks = "See last year's schedule";
   if USGate = 'San Francisco' then Airport = 'SFO';
     else if USGate = 'Honolulu' then Airport = 'HNL';
run;

proc print data=charvars noobs❶;
   var Country Schedule Remarks USGate Airport;
   title 'Tours By City of Departure';
run;
```

❶The NOOBS option in the PROC PRINT statement suppresses the display of observation numbers in the output.

The following output displays the character variables in the data set CHARVARS:

Output 8.2   Examples of Character Variables

```
                        Tours By City of Departure                      1

Country        Schedule              Remarks           USGate      Airport

Japan      3-4 tours per season See last year's schedule San Francisco SFO
Italy      3-4 tours per season See last year's schedule New York
Australia  3-4 tours per season See last year's schedule Honolulu      HNL
Venezuela  3-4 tours per season See last year's schedule Miami
Brazil     3-4 tours per season See last year's schedule
```

Setting the Length of Character Variables

This example illustrates why you may want to specify a length for a character variable, rather than let the first assigned value determine the length. Because New York City has two airports, both the abbreviations for John F. Kennedy International Airport and La Guardia Airport can be assigned to the Airport variable as in the DATA step.

Note: When you create character variables, SAS determines the length of the variable from its first occurrence in the DATA step. Therefore, you must allow for the longest possible value in the first statement that mentions the variable. If you do not assign the longest value the first time the variable is assigned, then data can be truncated. △

```
    /* first attempt */
options pagesize=60 linesize=80 pageno=1 nodate;
data aircode;
   set mylib.departures;
   if USGate = 'San Francisco' then Airport = 'SFO';
   else if USGate = 'Honolulu' then Airport = 'HNL';
       else if USGate = 'New York' then Airport = 'JFK or LGA';
run;

proc print data=aircode;
   var Country USGate Airport;
   title 'Country by US Point of Departure';
run;
```

The following output displays the results:

Output 8.3 Truncation of Character Values

```
              Country by US Point of Departure                    1

         Obs     Country      USGate         Airport

          1      Japan        San Francisco  SFO
          2      Italy        New York       JFK
          3      Australia    Honolulu       HNL
          4      Venezuela    Miami
          5      Brazil
```

Only the characters JFK appear in the observation for New York. SAS first encounters Airport in the statement that assigns the value SFO. Therefore, SAS creates Airport with a length of three bytes and uses only the first three characters in the New York observation.

To allow space to write JFK or LGA, use a LENGTH statement as the first reference to Airport. The LENGTH statement is a *declarative statement* and has the form

LENGTH *variable-list* $ *number-of-bytes*;

where *variable-list* is the variable or variables to which you are assigning the length *number-of-bytes*. The dollar sign ($) indicates that the variable is a character variable. The LENGTH statement determines the length of a *character* variable in both the program data vector and the data set that are being created. (In contrast, a LENGTH statement determines the length of a *numeric* variable only in the data set that is being created.) The maximum length of any character value in SAS is 32,767 bytes.

This LENGTH statement assigns a length of 10 to the character variable Airport:

```
length Airport $ 10;
```

Note: If you use a LENGTH statement to assign a length to a character variable, then it must be the first reference to the character variables in the DATA step. Therefore, the best position in the DATA step for a LENGTH statement is immediately after the DATA statement. △

The following DATA step includes the LENGTH statement for Airport. Remember that you can use the DATASETS procedure to display the length of variables in a SAS data set.

```
                     /* correct method */
        options pagesize=60 linesize=80 pageno=1 nodate;
        data aircode2;
           length Airport $ 10;
           set mylib.departures;
           if USGate = 'San Francisco' then Airport = 'SFO';
           else if USGate = 'Honolulu' then Airport = 'HNL';
                 else if USGate = 'New York' then Airport = 'JFK or LGA';
                       else if USGate = 'Miami' then Airport = 'MIA';
        run;

        proc print data=aircode2;
           var Country USGate Airport;
           title 'Country by US Point of Departure';
        run;
```

The following output displays the results:

Output 8.4   Using a LENGTH Statement to Capture Complete Variable Information

```
                    Country by US Point of Departure                      1

          Obs    Country      USGate          Airport

           1     Japan        San Francisco   SFO
           2     Italy        New York        JFK or LGA
           3     Australia    Honolulu        HNL
           4     Venezuela    Miami           MIA
           5     Brazil
```

Handling Missing Values

Reading Missing Values

SAS uses a blank to represent a missing value of a character variable. For example, the data line for Brazil lacks the departure city from the United States:

```
Japan       5 San Francisco      Tokyo, Osaka
Italy       8 New York           Rome, Naples
Australia  12 Honolulu        Sydney, Brisbane
Venezuela   4 Miami          Caracas, Maracaibo
Brazil      4              Rio de Janeiro, Belem
```

As Output 8.1 on page 121 shows, when the INPUT statement reads the data line for Brazil and determines that the value for USGate in columns 14-26 is missing, SAS assigns a missing value to USGate for that observation. The missing value is represented by a blank when printing.

One special case occurs when you read character data values with list input. In that case, you must use a period to represent a missing value in data lines. (Blanks in list input separate values; therefore, SAS interprets blanks as a signal to keep searching for the value, not as a missing value.) In the following DATA step, the TourGuide information for Venezuela is missing and is represented with a period:

```
options pagesize=60 linesize=80 pageno=1 nodate;

data missingval;
   length Country $ 10 TourGuide $ 10;
   input Country TourGuide;
   datalines;
Japan Yamada
Italy Militello
Australia Edney
Venezuela .
Brazil Cardoso
;

proc print data=missingval;
   title 'Missing Values for Character List Input Data';
run;
```

The following output displays the results:

Output 8.5 Using a Period in List Input for Missing Character Data

```
              Missing Values for Character List Data                   1

              Obs     Country      TourGuide

               1      Japan        Yamada
               2      Italy        Militello
               3      Australia    Edney
               4      Venezuela
               5      Brazil       Cardoso
```

SAS recognized the period as a missing value in the fourth data line; therefore, it recorded a missing value for the character variable TourGuide in the resulting data set.

Checking for Missing Character Values

When you want to check for missing character values, compare the character variable to a blank surrounded by quotation marks:

```
if USGate = ' ' then GateInformation = 'Missing';
```

The following DATA step includes this statement to check USGate for missing information. The results are recorded in GateInformation:

```
options pagesize=60 linesize=80 pageno=1 nodate;

data checkgate;
   length GateInformation $ 15;
   set mylib.departures;
   if USGate = ' ' then GateInformation = 'Missing';
   else GateInformation = 'Available';
run;
proc print data=checkgate;
```

```
      var Country CitiesIntour USGate ArrivalDepartureGates GateInformation;
      title 'Checking For Missing Gate Information';
run;
```

The following output displays the results:

Output 8.6   Checking for Missing Character Values

```
                    Checking For Missing Gate Information                        1

                    Cities                                        Gate
    Obs   Country   InTour   USGate         ArrivalDepartureGates  Information

     1    Japan        5     San Francisco  Tokyo, Osaka           Available
     2    Italy        8     New York       Rome, Naples           Available
     3    Australia   12     Honolulu       Sydney, Brisbane       Available
     4    Venezuela    4     Miami          Caracas, Maracaibo     Available
     5    Brazil       4                    Rio de Janeiro, Belem  Missing
```

Setting a Character Variable Value to Missing

You can assign missing character values in assignment statements by setting the character variable to a blank surrounded by quotation marks. For example, the following statement sets the day of departure based on the number of days in the tour. If the number of cities in the tour is a week or less, then the day of departure is a Sunday. Otherwise, the day of departure is not known and is set to a missing value.

```
if Cities <=7 then DayOfDeparture = 'Sunday';
else DayOfDeparture = ' ';
```

The following DATA step includes these statements:

```
options pagesize=60 linesize=80 pageno=1 nodate;
data departuredays;
   set mylib.departures;
   length DayOfDeparture $ 8;
   if CitiesInTour <=7 then DayOfDeparture = 'Sunday';
   else DayOfDeparture = ' ';
run;

proc print data=departuredays;
   var Country CitiesInTour DayOfDeparture;
   title 'Departure Day is Sunday or Missing';
run;
```

The following output displays the results:

Output 8.7 Assigning Missing Character Values

```
                    Departure Day is Sunday or Missing                    1

                                  Cities      DayOf
            Obs     Country       InTour    Departure

             1      Japan           5        Sunday
             2      Italy           8
             3      Australia      12
             4      Venezuela       4        Sunday
             5      Brazil          4        Sunday
```

Creating New Character Values

Extracting a Portion of a Character Value

Understanding the SCAN Function

Some character values may contain multiple pieces of information that need to be isolated and assigned to separate character variables. For example, the value of ArrivalDepartureGates contains two cities: the city of arrival and the city of departure. How can the individual values be isolated so that separate variables can be created for the two cities?

The SCAN function returns a character string when it is given the source string, the position of the desired character string, and a character delimiter:

> **SCAN** (*source,n<,list-of-delimiters>*)

The *source* is the value that you want to examine. It can be any kind of character expression, including character variables, character constants, and so on. The *n* is the position of the term to be selected from the source. The *list-of-delimiters* can list one, multiple, or no delimiters. If you specify more than one delimiter, then SAS uses any of them; if you omit the delimiter, then SAS divides words according to a default list of delimiters (including the blank and some special characters).

For example, to select the first term in the value of ArrivalDepartureGates and assign it to a new variable named ArrivalGate, write

```
ArrivalGate = scan(ArrivalDepartureGates,1,',');
```

The SCAN function examines the value of ArrivalDepartureGates and selects the first string as identified by a comma.

Although default values can be used for the delimiter, it is a good idea to specify the delimiter to be used. If the default delimiter is used in the SCAN function when the observation for Brazil is processed, then SAS recognizes a blank space as the delimiter and selects **Rio** rather than **Rio de Janeiro** as the first term. Specifying the delimiter enables you to control where the division of the term occurs.

To select the second term from ArrivalDepartureGates and assign it to a new variable term named DEPARTUREGATE, write

```
DepartureGate = scan(ArrivalDepartureGates,2,',');
```

Note: The default length of a target variable where the expression contains the SCAN function is 200 bytes. △

Aligning New Values

Remember that SAS maintains the existing alignment of a character value used in an expression; it does not perform any automatic realignment. This example creates the values for a new variable DepartureGate from the values of ArrivalDepartureGates. The value of ArrivalDepartureGates contains a comma and a blank between the two city names as shown in the following output:

Output 8.8 Dividing Values into Separate Words Using the SCAN Function

```
                      Data Set AIR.DEPARTURES                         1

                    Cities
    Obs    Country  InTour    USGate         ArrivalDepartureGates

     1     Japan       5      San Francisco  Tokyo, Osaka
     2     Italy       8      New York       Rome, Naples
     3     Australia  12      Honolulu       Sydney, Brisbane
     4     Venezuela   4      Miami          Caracas, Maracaibo
     5     Brazil      4                     Rio de Janeiro, Belem
```

When the SCAN function divides the names at the comma, the second term begins with a blank; therefore, all the values that are assigned to DepartureGate begin with a blank.

To left-align the values, use the LEFT function:

LEFT (*source*)

The LEFT function produces a value that has all leading blanks in the *source* moved to the right side of the value; therefore, the result is left aligned. The source can be any kind of character expression, including a character variable, a character constant enclosed in quotation marks, or another character function.

This example uses the LEFT function in the second assignment statement:

```
DepartureGate = scan(ArrivalDepartureGates,2,',');
DepartureGate = left(DepartureGate);
```

You can also nest the two functions:

```
DepartureGate = left(scan(ArrivalDepartureGates,2,','));
```

When you nest functions, SAS performs the action in the innermost function first. It uses the result of that function as the argument of the next function, and so on.

The following DATA step creates separate variables for the arrival gates and the departure gates:

```
options pagesize=60 linesize=80 pageno=1 nodate;

data gates;
   set mylib.departures;
   ArrivalGate = scan(ArrivalDepartureGates,1,',');
   DepartureGate = left(scan(ArrivalDepartureGates,2,','));
run;

proc print data=gates;
   var Country ArrivalDepartureGates ArrivalGate DepartureGate;
   title 'Arrival and Departure Gates';
run;
```

The following output displays the results:

Output 8.9 Dividing Values into Separate Words with the SCAN Function

```
                          Arrival and Departure Gates                        1

                                                              Departure
      Obs    Country     ArrivalDepartureGates    ArrivalGate     Gate

       1     Japan       Tokyo, Osaka             Tokyo        Osaka
       2     Italy       Rome, Naples             Rome         Naples
       3     Australia   Sydney, Brisbane         Sydney       Brisbane
       4     Venezuela   Caracas, Maracaibo       Caracas      Maracaibo
       5     Brazil      Rio de Janeiro, Belem    Rio de Janeiro  Belem
```

Saving Storage Space When Using the SCAN Function

The SCAN function causes SAS to assign a length of 200 bytes to the target variable in an assignment statement. Most of the other character functions cause the target to have the same length as the original value. In the data set GATELENGTH, the variable ArrivalGate has a length of 200 because the SCAN function creates it. The variable DepartureGate also has a length of 200 because the argument of the LEFT function contains the SCAN function.

Setting the lengths of ArrivalGate and DepartureGate to the needed values rather than to the default length saves a lot of storage space. Because SAS sets the length of a character variable the first time SAS encounters it, the LENGTH statement must appear before the assignment statements that create values for the variables:

```
data gatelength;
   length ArrivalGate $ 14 DepartureGate $ 9;
   set mylib.departures;
   ArrivalGate = scan(ArrivalDepartureGate,1,',');
   DepartureGate = left(scan(ArrivalDepartureGate,2,','));
run;
```

Combining Character Values: Using Concatenation

Understanding Concatenation of Variable Values

SAS enables you to combine character values into longer ones using an operation known as *concatenation*. Concatenation combines character values by placing them one after the other and assigning them to a variable. In SAS programming, the concatenation operator is a pair of vertical bars (||). If your keyboard does not have a solid vertical bar, use two broken vertical bars (¦¦) or two exclamation points (!!). The length of the new variable is the sum of the lengths of the pieces or number of characters that is specified in a LENGTH statement for the new variable. Concatenation is illustrated in the following figure:

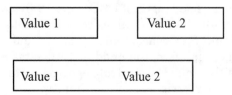

Performing a Simple Concatenation

The following statement combines all the cities named as gateways into a single variable named AllGates:

```
AllGates = USGate || ArrivalDepartureGates;
```

SAS attaches the beginning of each value of ArrivalDepartureGates to the end of each value of USGate and assigns the results to AllGates. The following DATA step includes this statement:

```
   /* first try */
options pagesize=60 linesize=80 pageno=1 nodate;
data all;
   set mylib.departures;
   AllGates = USGate || ArrivalDepartureGates;
run;

proc print data=all;
   var Country USGate ArrivalDepartureGates AllGates;
   title 'All Tour Gates';
run;
```

The following output displays the results:

Output 8.10   Simple Concatenation: Interior Blanks Not Removed

```
                           All Tour Gates                                1

           Obs     Country      USGate           ArrivalDepartureGates

            1      Japan        San Francisco    Tokyo, Osaka
            2      Italy        New York         Rome, Naples
            3      Australia    Honolulu         Sydney, Brisbane
            4      Venezuela    Miami            Caracas, Maracaibo
            5      Brazil                        Rio de Janeiro, Belem

           Obs                  AllGates

            1      San FranciscoTokyo, Osaka
            2      New York     Rome, Naples
            3      Honolulu  ❶  Sydney, Brisbane
            4      Miami        Caracas, Maracaibo
            5         ❷         Rio de Janeiro, Belem
```

Removing Interior Blanks

Why, in the previous output, does

❶ the middle of AllGates contain blanks?

❷ the beginning of AllGates in the Brazil observation contain blanks?

When a character value is shorter than the length of the variable to which it belongs, SAS pads the value with trailing blanks. The length of USGate is 13 bytes, but only San Francisco uses all of them. Therefore, the other values contain blanks at the end, and the value for Brazil is entirely blank. SAS concatenates USGate and ArrivalDepartureGates without change; therefore, the middle of AllGates contains blanks for most observations. Most of the values of ArrivalDepartureGates also contain trailing blanks. If you concatenate another variable such as Country to

ArrivalDepartureGates, you will see the trailing blanks in ArrivalDepartureGates. To eliminate trailing blanks, use the TRIM function:

TRIM (*source*)

The TRIM function produces a value without the trailing blanks in the *source*.

Note: Other rules about trailing blanks in SAS still apply. If the trimmed result is shorter than the length of the variable to which the result is assigned, SAS pads the result with new blanks as it makes the assignment. △

To eliminate the trailing blanks in USGate from AllGates, add the TRIM function to the expression:

```
AllGate2 = trim(USGate) || ArrivalDepartureGates;
```

The following program adds this statement to the DATA step:

```
    /* removing interior blanks */
options pagesize=60 linesize=80 pageno=1 nodate;
data all2;
   set mylib.departures;
   AllGate2 = trim(USGate) || ArrivalDepartureGates;
run;

proc print data=all2;
   var Country USGate ArrivalDepartureGates AllGate2;
   title 'All Tour Gates';
run;
```

The following output displays the results:

Output 8.11   Removing Blanks with the TRIM Function

```
                               All Tour Gates                               1

 Obs   Country    USGate        ArrivalDepartureGates        AllGate2

  1    Japan      San Francisco Tokyo, Osaka            San FranciscoTokyo, Osaka
  2    Italy      New York      Rome, Naples            New YorkRome, Naples
  3    Australia  Honolulu      Sydney, Brisbane        HonoluluSydney, Brisbane
  4    Venezuela  Miami         Caracas, Maracaibo      MiamiCaracas, Maracaibo
  5    Brazil                   Rio de Janeiro, Belem    Rio de Janeiro, Belem
                                                           ❶
```

Notice at ❶ that the AllGate2 value for Brazil has a blank space before Rio de Janeiro, Belem. When the TRIM function encounters a missing value in the argument, one blank space is returned. In this observation, USGate has a missing value; therefore, one blank space is concatenated with Rio de Janeiro, Belem.

Adding Additional Characters

Data set ALL2 shows that removing the trailing blanks from USGate causes all the values of ArrivalDepartureGates to appear immediately after the corresponding values of USGate. To make the result easier to read, you can concatenate a comma and blank between the trimmed value of USGate and the value of ArrivalDepartureGates. Also, to align the AllGate3 value for Brazil with all other values of AllGate3, use an IF-THEN statement to equate the value of AllGate3 with the value of ArrivalDepartureGates in that observation.

```
AllGate3 = trim(USGate)||', '||ArrivalDepartureGates;
if Country = 'Brazil' then AllGate3 = ArrivalDepartureGates;
```

This DATA step includes these statements:

```
    /* final version */
options pagesize=60 linesize=80 pageno=1 nodate;
data all3;
   set mylib.departures;
   AllGate3 = trim(USGate)||', '||ArrivalDepartureGates;
   if Country = 'Brazil' then AllGate3 = ArrivalDepartureGates;
run;

proc print data=all3;
   var Country USGate ArrivalDepartureGates AllGate3;
   title 'All Tour Gates';
run;
```

The following output displays the results:

Output 8.12   Concatenating Additional Characters for Readability

```
                              All Tour Gates                                 1

Obs Country    USGate         ArrivalDepartureGates         AllGate3

  1 Japan      San Francisco Tokyo, Osaka        San Francisco, Tokyo, Osaka
  2 Italy      New York       Rome, Naples        New York, Rome, Naples
  3 Australia  Honolulu       Sydney, Brisbane    Honolulu, Sydney, Brisbane
  4 Venezuela  Miami          Caracas, Maracaibo  Miami, Caracas, Maracaibo
  5 Brazil                    Rio de Janeiro, Belem Rio de Janeiro, Belem
```

Troubleshooting: When New Variables Appear Truncated

When you concatenate variables, you might see the apparent loss of part of a concatenated value. Earlier in this chapter, ArrivalDepartureGates was divided into two new variables, ArrivalGate and DepartureGate, each with a default length of 200 bytes. (Remember that when a variable is created by an expression that uses the SCAN function, the variable length is 200 bytes.) For reference, this example re-creates the DATA step:

```
options pagesize=60 linesize=80 pageno=1 nodate;
data gates;
   set mylib.departures;
   ArrivalGate = scan(ArrivalDepartureGates,1,',');
   DepartureGate = left(scan(ArrivalDepartureGates,2,','));
run;
```

If the variables ArrivalGate and DepartureGate are concatenated, as they are in the next DATA step, then the length of the resulting concatenation is 402 bytes: 200 bytes for each variable and 1 byte each for the comma and the blank space. This example uses the VLENGTH function to show the length of ADGates.

```
    /* accidentally omitting the TRIM function */
options pagesize=60 linesize=80 pageno=1 nodate;
data gates2;
   set gates;
```

```
   ADGates = ArrivalGate||', '||DepartureGate;;
   ADLength = vlength(ADGates);
run;

proc print data=gates2;
   var Country ArrivalDepartureGates ADGates ADLength;
   title 'All Tour Gates';
run;
```

The following output displays the results:

Output 8.13 Losing Part of a Concatenated Value

```
            All Tour Gates           1

Obs  Country       ArrivalDepartureGates

 1   Japan         Tokyo, Osaka
 2   Italy         Rome, Naples
 3   Australia     Sydney, Brisbane
 4   Venezuela     Caracas, Maracaibo
 5   Brazil        Rio de Janeiro, Belem

Obs                                      ADGates

 1   Tokyo
 2   Rome
 3   Sydney
 4   Caracas
 5   Rio de Janeiro

Obs ADLength

 1     402
 2     402
 3     402
 4     402
 5     402
```

The concatenated value from DepartureGate appears to be truncated in the output. It has been concatenated after the trailing blanks of ArrivalGate, and it does not appear because the output does not display 402 bytes.

There is a two-step solution to the problem.

1 The TRIM function can trim the trailing blanks from ArrivalGate, as shown in the preceding section. The significant characters from all three pieces that are assigned to ADGates can then fit in the output.

2 The length of ADGates remains 402 bytes. The LENGTH statement can assign to the variable a length that is shorter but large enough to contain the significant pieces.

The following DATA step uses the TRIM function and the LENGTH statement to remove interior blanks from the concatenation:

```
options pagesize=60 linesize=80 pageno=1 nodate;
data gates3;
   length ADGates $ 30;
   set gates;
   ADGates = trim(ArrivalGate)||', '||DepartureGate;
run;
```

```
proc print data=gates3;
   var country ArrivalDepartureGates ADGates;
   title 'All Tour Gates';
run;
```

The following output displays the results:

Output 8.14 Showing All of a Newly Concatenated Value

```
                        All Tour Gates                                     1

    Obs    Country     ArrivalDepartureGates    ADGates

     1     Japan       Tokyo, Osaka             Tokyo, Osaka
     2     Italy       Rome, Naples             Rome, Naples
     3     Australia   Sydney, Brisbane         Sydney, Brisbane
     4     Venezuela   Caracas, Maracaibo       Caracas, Maracaibo
     5     Brazil      Rio de Janeiro, Belem    Rio de Janeiro, Belem
```

Saving Storage Space by Treating Numbers as Characters

Remember that SAS uses eight bytes of storage for every numeric value in the DATA step; by default, SAS also uses eight bytes of storage for each numeric value in an output data set. However, a character value can contain a minimum of one character; in that case, SAS uses one byte for the character variable, both in the program data vector and in the output data set. In addition, SAS treats the digits 0 through 9 in a character value like any other character. When you are not going to perform calculations on a variable, you can save storage space by treating a value that contains digits as a character value.

For example, some tours offer various prices, depending on the quality of the hotel room. The brochures rank the rooms as two stars, three stars, and so on. In this case the values 2, 3, and 4 are really the names of categories, and arithmetic operations are not expected to be performed on them. Therefore, the values can be read into a character variable. The following DATA step reads HotelRank as a character variable and assigns it a length of one byte:

```
data hotels;
   input Country $ 1-9 HotelRank $ 11 LandCost;
   datalines;
Italy     2   498
Italy     4   698
Australia 2   915
Australia 3  1169
Australia 4  1399
;

proc print data=hotels;
   title 'Hotel Rankings';
run;
```

In the previous example, the INPUT statement assigns HotelRank a length of one byte because the INPUT statement reads one column to find the value (shown by the use of column input). If you are using list input, place a LENGTH statement before the INPUT statement to set the length to one byte.

If you read a number as a character value and then discover that you need to use it in a numeric expression, then you can do so without making changes in your program. SAS automatically produces a numeric value from the character value for use in the expression; it also issues a note in the log that the conversion occurred. (Of course, the conversion causes the DATA step to use slightly more computer resources.) The original variable remains unchanged.

The following output displays the results:

Output 8.15 Saving Storage Space by Creating a Character Variable

```
                 Hotel Rankings                  1

                                    Hotel    Land
              Obs    Country        Rank     Cost

               1     Italy           2        498
               2     Italy           4        698
               3     Australia       2        915
               4     Australia       3       1169
               5     Australia       4       1399
```

Note: Note that the width of the column is not the default width of eight. △

Review of SAS Tools

Functions

LEFT (*source*)
: left-aligns the *source* by moving any leading blanks to the end of the value. The *source* can be any kind of character expression, including a character variable, a character constant enclosed in quotation marks, or another character function. Because any blanks removed from the left are added to the right, the length of the result matches the length of the source.

SCAN (*source,n<,list-of-delimiters>*)
: selects the *n*th term from the *source*. The source can be any kind of character expression, including a character variable, a character constant enclosed in quotation marks, or another character function. To choose the character that divides the terms, use a *delimiter*; if you omit the *delimiter*, then SAS divides the terms using a default list of delimiters (the blank and some special characters).

TRIM (*source*)
: trims trailing blanks from the *source*. The *source* can be any kind of character expression, including a character variable, a character constant enclosed in quotation marks, or another character function. The TRIM function does not affect the way a variable is stored. If you use the TRIM function to remove trailing blanks and assign the trimmed value to a variable that is longer than that value,

then SAS pads the value with new trailing blanks to make the value match the length of the new variable.

Statements

LENGTH *variable-list* $ *number-of-bytes*;

assigns a length that you specify in *number-of-bytes* to the character variable or variables in *variable-list*. You can assign any number of lengths in a single LENGTH statement, and you can assign lengths to both character and numeric variables in the same statement. Place a dollar sign ($) before the length of any character variable.

Learning More

Character values

This chapter illustrates the flexibility that SAS provides for manipulating character values. In addition to the functions that are described in this chapter, these character functions are also frequently used:

COMPBL

removes multiple blanks from a character string.

COMPRESS

removes specified character(s) from the source.

INDEX

searches the source data for a pattern of characters.

LOWCASE

converts all letters in an argument to lowercase.

RIGHT

right-aligns the source.

SUBSTR

extracts a group of characters.

TRANSLATE

replaces specific characters in a character expression.

UPCASE

returns the source data in uppercase.

The INDEX and UPCASE functions are discussed in Chapter 9, "Acting on Selected Observations," on page 139. Complete descriptions of all character functions appear in *SAS Language Reference: Dictionary*.

Character variables

Detailed information about character variables is found in the "SAS Variables" chapter of *SAS Language Reference: Concepts*.

Additional information about aligning character variables is explained in the TEMPLATE procedure, which is documented in *The Complete Guide to the SAS Output Delivery System*, and in the REPORT procedure, which is documented in *SAS Procedures Guide*.

Comparing uppercase and lowercase characters
How to compare uppercase and lowercase characters is shown in Chapter 9, "Acting on Selected Observations," on page 139.

Concatenation operator
Information about the concatenation operator can be found in the "Expressions" chapter of *SAS Language Reference: Concepts*.

DATASETS procedure
Using the DATASETS procedure to display the length of variables in a SAS data set is explained in Chapter 35, "Getting Information about Your SAS Data Sets," on page 603.

IF-THEN statements
A detailed explanation of the IF-THEN statements can be found in Chapter 9, "Acting on Selected Observations," on page 139.

Informats and formats
Complete information about the SAS System's numerous informats and formats for reading and writing character variables is found in *SAS Language Reference: Dictionary*.

Missing values
Detailed information about missing values is found in the "Missing Values" chapter of *SAS Language Reference: Concepts*.

VLENGTH function
The VLENGTH function is explained in detail in *SAS Language Reference: Dictionary*.

CHAPTER

9

Acting on Selected Observations

Introduction

Purpose

One of the most useful features of SAS is its ability to perform an action on only the observations that you have selected. In this chapter you will learn

☐ how the selection process works

☐ how to write statements that select observations based on a condition

□ some special points about selecting numeric and character variables.

Prerequisites

You should understand the concepts presented in all previous chapters before proceeding with this chapter.

Input SAS Data Set for Examples

Tradewinds Travel offers tours to art museums and galleries in various cities. The company has decided that in order to make its process more efficient, additional information is needed. For example, if the tour covers too many museums and galleries within a time period, then the number of museums visited must be decreased or the number of days for the tour needs to change. If the guide who is assigned to the tour is not available, then another guide must be assigned. Most of the process involves selecting observations that meet or that do not meet various criteria and then taking the required action.

The Tradewinds Travel tour data is stored in an external file that contains the following information:

```
❶          ❷  ❸  ❹ ❺              ❻         ❼
Rome       3  750 7 4 M, 3 G       D'Amico   Torres
Paris      8 1680 6 5 M, 1 other   Lucas     Lucas
London     6 1230 5 3 M, 2 G       Wilson    Lucas
New York   6   . 8 5 M, 1 G, 2 other Lucas   D'Amico
Madrid     3  370 5 3 M, 2 other    Torres   D'Amico
Amsterdam 4  580 6 3 M, 3 G                   Vandever
```

The numbered fields represent

❶ the name of the city

❷ the number of nights in the city

❸ the cost of the land package (not airfare) in US dollars

❹ the number of events the trip offers (such as visits to museums and galleries)

❺ a brief description of the events (where **M** indicates a museum; **G**, a gallery; and **other**, another kind of event)

❻ the name of the tour guide

❼ the name of the backup tour guide.

The following DATA step creates MYLIB.ARTTOURS:

```
options pagesize=60 linesize=80 pageno=1 nodate;
libname mylib 'permanent-data-library';

data mylib.arttours;
   infile 'input-file' truncover;
   input City $ 1-9 Nights 11 LandCost 13-16 NumberOfEvents 18
         EventDescription $ 20-36 TourGuide $ 38-45
         BackUpGuide $ 47-54;
run;

proc print data=mylib.arttours;
   title 'Data Set MYLIB.ARTTOURS';
run;
```

Note: When the TRUNCOVER option is specified in the INFILE statement, and when the record is shorter than what the INPUT statement expects, SAS will read a variable length record. △

The PROC PRINT statement that follows the DATA step produces this display of the MYLIB.ARTTOURS data set:

Output 9.1 Data Set MYLIB.ARTTOURS

```
                       Data Set MYLIB.ARTTOURS                           1
                                                          ❸        ❹
                      Land   Number ❶        ❷          Tour     BackUp
   Obs   City    Nights  Cost  OfEvents  EventDescription  Guide    Guide

    1    Rome       3    750      7      4 M, 3 G         D'Amico  Torres
    2    Paris      8   1680      6      5 M, 1 other     Lucas    Lucas
    3    London     6   1230      5      3 M, 2 G         Wilson   Lucas
    4    New York   6      .      8      5 M, 1 G, 2 other Lucas   D'Amico
    5    Madrid     3    370      5      3 M, 2 other     Torres   D'Amico
    6    Amsterdam  4    580      6      3 M, 3 G                  Vandever
```

The following list corresponds to the numbered items in the preceding output:

❶ the variable NumberOfEvents contains the number of attractions visited during the tour

❷ EventDescription lists the number of museums (**M**), art galleries (**G**), and other attractions (**other**) visited

❸ TourGuide lists the name of the tour guide assigned to the tour

❹ BackUpGuide lists the alternate tour guide in case the original tour guide is unavailable.

Selecting Observations

Understanding the Selection Process

The most common way that SAS selects observations for action in a DATA step is through the IF-THEN statement:

IF *condition* **THEN** *action*;

The *condition* is one or more comparisons, for example,

☐ `City = 'Rome'`

☐ `NumberOfEvents > Nights`

☐ `TourGuide = 'Lucas' and Nights > 7`

(The symbol > stands for greater than. You will see how to use symbols as comparison operators in "Understanding Construct Conditions" on page 145.)

For a given observation, a comparison is either true or false. In the first example, the value of City is either **Rome** or it is not. In the second example, the value of NumberOfEvents in the current observation is either greater than the value of Nights in the same observation or it is not. If the condition contains more than one comparison, as in the third example, then SAS evaluates all of them according to its rules (discussed later) and declares the entire condition to be true or false.

When the condition is true, SAS takes the action in the THEN clause. The action must be expressed as a SAS statement that can be executed in an individual iteration of the DATA step. Such statements are called *executable statements*. The most common executable statements are assignment statements, such as

☐ `LandCost = LandCost + 30;`

☐ `Calendar = 'Check schedule';`

☐ `TourGuide = 'Torres';`

This chapter concentrates on assignment statements in the THEN clause, but examples in other chapters show other types of statements that are used with the THEN clause.

Statements that provide information about a data set are not executable. Such statements are called *declarative statements*. For example, the LENGTH statement affects a variable as a whole, not how the variable is treated in a particular observation. Therefore, you cannot use a LENGTH statement in a THEN clause.

When the condition is false, SAS ignores the THEN clause and proceeds to the next statement in the DATA step.

Selecting Observations Based on a Simple Condition

The following DATA step uses the previous example conditions and actions in IF-THEN statements:

```
options pagesize=60 linesize=80 pageno=1 nodate;
data revise;
   set mylib.arttours;
   if City = 'Rome' then LandCost = LandCost + 30;
   if NumberOfEvents > Nights then Calendar = 'Check schedule';
   if TourGuide = 'Lucas' and Nights > 7 then TourGuide = 'Torres';
run;

proc print data=revise;
   var City Nights LandCost NumberOfEvents TourGuide Calendar;
   title 'Tour Information';
run;
```

The following output displays the results:

Output 9.2   Selecting Observations with IF-THEN Statements

```
                          Tour Information                                1

                          Land     Number    Tour
   Obs    City    Nights   Cost    OfEvents   Guide        Calendar ❷

    1     Rome       3      780 ❶     7       D'Amico      Check schedule
    2     Paris      8     1680       6       Torres ❸
    3     London     6     1230       5       Wilson
    4     New York   6       .        8       Lucas        Check schedule
    5     Madrid     3      370       5       Torres       Check schedule
    6     Amsterdam  4      580       6                    Check schedule
```

You can see in the output that

❶ the land cost was increased by \$30 in the observation for Rome

❷ four observations have a greater number of events than they do number of days in the tour

❸ the tour guide for Paris is replaced by Torres because the original tour guide is Lucas and the number of nights in the tour is greater than 7.

Providing an Alternative Action

Remember that SAS creates a variable in all observations, even if you do not assign the variable a value in all observations. In the previous output, the value of Calendar is blank in two observations. A second IF-THEN statement can assign a different value, as in these examples:

```
if NumberOfEvents > Nights then Calendar = 'Check schedule';
if NumberOfEvents <= Nights then Calendar = 'No problems';
```

(The symbol <= means less than or equal to.) In this case, SAS compares the values of Events and Nights twice, once in each IF condition. A more efficient way to provide an alternative action is to use an ELSE statement:

ELSE *action*;

An ELSE statement names an alternative action to be taken when the IF condition is false. It must immediately follow the corresponding IF-THEN statement, as shown here:

```
if NumberOfEvents > Nights then Calendar = 'Check schedule';
else Calendar = 'No problems';
```

The REVISE2 DATA step adds the preceding ELSE statement to the previous DATA step:

```
options pagesize=60 linesize=80 pageno=1 nodate;
data revise2;
   set mylib.arttours;
   if City = 'Rome' then LandCost = LandCost + 30;
   if NumberOfEvents > Nights then Calendar = 'Check schedule';
   else Calendar = 'No problems';
   if TourGuide = 'Lucas' and Nights > 7 then TourGuide = 'Torres';
run;

proc print data=revise2;
   var City Nights LandCost NumberOfEvents TourGuide Calendar;
   title 'Tour Information';
run;
```

The following output displays the results:

Output 9.3   Providing an Alternative Action with the ELSE Statement

```
                         Tour Information                              1

                     Land    Number     Tour
    Obs   City      Nights   Cost    OfEvents   Guide      Calendar

     1    Rome         3      780        7      D'Amico   Check schedule
     2    Paris        8     1680        6      Torres    No problems
     3    London       6     1230        5      Wilson    No problems
     4    New York     6        .       8      Lucas     Check schedule
     5    Madrid       3      370        5      Torres    Check schedule
     6    Amsterdam    4      580        6                Check schedule
```

Creating a Series of Mutually Exclusive Conditions

Using an ELSE statement after an IF-THEN statement provides one alternative action when the IF condition is false. However, many cases involve a series of mutually exclusive conditions, each of which requires a separate action. In this example, tour prices can be classified as high, medium, or low. A series of IF-THEN and ELSE statements classifies the tour prices appropriately:

```
if LandCost >= 1500 then Price = 'High  ';
else if LandCost >= 700 then Price = 'Medium';
     else Price = 'Low';
```

(The symbol >= is greater than or equal to.) To see how SAS executes this series of statements, consider two observations: Amsterdam, whose value of LandCost is 580, and Paris, whose value is 1680.

When the value of LandCost is 580:

1 SAS tests whether 580 is equal to or greater than 1500, determines that the comparison is false, ignores the THEN clause, and proceeds to the ELSE statement.

2 The action in the ELSE statement is to evaluate another condition. SAS tests whether 580 is equal to or greater than 700, determines that the comparison is false, ignores the THEN clause, and proceeds to the accompanying ELSE statement.

3 SAS executes the action in the ELSE statement and assigns Price the value **Low**.

When the value of LandCost is 1680:

1 SAS tests whether 1680 is greater than or equal to 1500, determines that the comparison is true, and executes the action in the THEN clause. The value of Price becomes **High**.

2 SAS ignores the ELSE statement. Because the entire remaining series is part of the first ELSE statement, SAS skips all remaining actions in the series.

A simple way to think of these actions is to remember that when an observation satisfies one condition in a series of mutually exclusive IF-THEN/ELSE statements, SAS processes that THEN action and skips the rest of the statements. (Therefore, you can increase the efficiency of a program by ordering the IF-THEN/ELSE statements so that the most common conditions appear first.)

The following DATA step includes the preceding series of statements:

```
options pagesize=60 linesize=80 pageno=1 nodate;
data prices;
```

```
       set mylib.arttours;
       if LandCost >= 1500 then Price = 'High   ';
       else if LandCost >= 700 then Price = 'Medium';
             else Price = 'Low';
    run;

    proc print data=prices;
       var City LandCost Price;
       title 'Tour Prices';
    run;
```

The following output displays the results:

Output 9.4 Assigning Mutually Exclusive Values with IF-THEN/ELSE Statements

```
                          Tour Prices                           1

                                    Land
                  Obs    City       Cost    Price

                   1     Rome        750    Medium
                   2     Paris      1680    High
                   3     London     1230    Medium
                   4     New York      .    Low
                   5     Madrid      370    Low
                   6     Amsterdam   580    Low
```

Note the value of Price in the fourth observation. The Price value is **Low** because the LandCost value for the New York trip is a missing value. Remember that a missing value is the lowest possible numeric value.

Constructing Conditions

Understanding Construct Conditions

When you use an IF-THEN statement, you ask SAS to make a comparison. SAS must determine whether a value is equal to another value, greater than another value, and so on. SAS has six main comparison operators:

Table 9.1 Comparison Operators

Symbol	Mnemonic Operator	Meaning
=	EQ	equal to
¬=, ^= , ~=	NE	not equal to (the ¬, ^, or ~ symbol, depending on your keyboard)
>	GT	greater than
<	LT	less than

Symbol	Mnemonic Operator	Meaning
>=	GE	greater than or equal to
<=	LE	less than or equal to

The symbols in the table are based on mathematical symbols; the letter abbreviations, known as *mnemonic operators*, have the same effect. Use the form that you prefer, but remember that you can use the mnemonic operators only in comparisons. For example, the equal sign in an assignment statement must be represented by the symbol =, not the mnemonic operator. Both of the following statements compare the number of nights in the tour to six:

- `if Nights >= 6 then Stay = 'Week+';`

- `if Nights ge 6 then Stay = 'Week+';`

The terms on each side of the comparison operator can be variables, expressions, or constants. The side a particular term appears on does not matter, as long as you use the correct operator. All of the following comparisons are constructed correctly for use in SAS statements:

- `Guide = ' '`

- `LandCost ne .`

- `LandCost lt 600`

- `600 ge LandCost`

- `NumberOfEvents / Nights > 2`

- `2 <= NumberOfEvents / Nights`

Selecting an Observation Based on Simple Conditions

The following DATA step illustrates some of these conditions:

```
options pagesize=60 linesize=80 pageno=1 nodate;
data changes;
    set mylib.arttours;
    if Nights >= 6 then Stay = 'Week+';
    else Stay = 'Days';
    if LandCost ne . then Remarks = 'OK   ';
    else Remarks = 'Redo';
    if LandCost lt 600 then Budget = 'Low    ';
    else Budget = 'Medium';
    if NumberOfEvents / Nights > 2 then Pace = 'Too fast';
    else Pace = 'OK';
run;

proc print data=changes;
    var City Nights LandCost NumberOfEvents Stay Remarks Budget Pace;
    title 'Tour Information';
run;
```

The following output displays the results:

Output 9.5 Assigning Values to Variables According to Specific Conditions

```
                              Tour Information                            1

                         Land    Number
   Obs   City    Nights   Cost   OfEvents   Stay    Remarks   Budget   Pace

    1    Rome       3      750       7      Days     OK       Medium   Too fast
    2    Paris      8     1680       6      Week+    OK       Medium   OK
    3    London     6     1230       5      Week+    OK       Medium   OK
    4    New York   6       .        8      Week+    Redo     Low      OK
    5    Madrid     3      370       5      Days     OK       Low      OK
    6    Amsterdam  4      580       6      Days     OK       Low      OK
```

Using More Than One Comparison in a Condition

Specifying Multiple Comparisons

You can specify more than one comparison in a condition with these operators:

☐ **&** or **AND**

☐ **|** or **OR**

A condition can contain any number of ANDs, ORs, or both.

Making Comparisons When All of the Conditions Must Be True

When comparisons are connected by AND, all of the comparisons must be true for the condition to be true. Consider this example:

```
if City = 'Paris' and TourGuide = 'Lucas' then Remarks = 'Bilingual';
```

The comparison is true for observations in which the value of City is **Paris** and the value of TourGuide is **Lucas**.

A common comparison is to determine whether a value is between two quantities, greater than one quantity and less than another quantity. For example, to select observations in which the value of LandCost is greater than or equal to 1000, and less than or equal to 1500, you can write a comparison with AND:

```
if LandCost >= 1000 and LandCost <= 1500 then Price = '1000-1500';
```

A simpler way to write this comparison is

```
if 1000 <= LandCost <= 1500 then Price = '1000-1500';
```

This comparison has the same meaning as the previous one. You can use any of the operators <, <=, >, >=, or their mnemonic equivalents in this way.

The following DATA step includes these multiple comparison statements:

```
options pagesize=60 linesize=80 pageno=1 nodate;
data showand;
   set mylib.arttours;
   if City = 'Paris' and TourGuide = 'Lucas' then Remarks = 'Bilingual';
   if 1000 <= LandCost <= 1500 then Price = '1000-1500';
run;

proc print data=showand;
   var City LandCost TourGuide Remarks Price;
```

```
      title 'Tour Information';
run;
```

The following output displays the results:

Output 9.6 Using AND When Making Multiple Comparisons

```
                        Tour Information                            1

                     Land    Tour
      Obs   City     Cost    Guide      Remarks        Price

       1    Rome      750    D'Amico
       2    Paris    1680    Lucas      Bilingual
       3    London   1230    Wilson                    1000-1500
       4    New York    .    Lucas
       5    Madrid    370    Torres
       6    Amsterdam 580
```

When Only One Condition Must Be True

When comparisons are connected by OR, only one of the comparisons needs to be true for the condition to be true. Consider the following example:

```
if LandCost gt 1500 or LandCost / Nights gt 200 then Level = 'Deluxe';
```

Any observation in which the land cost is over $1500, the cost per night is over $200, or both, satisfies the condition. The following DATA step shows this condition:

```
options pagesize=60 linesize=80 pageno=1 nodate;
data showor;
   set mylib.arttours;
   if LandCost gt 1500 or LandCost / Nights gt 200 then Level = 'Deluxe';
run;
proc print data=showor;
   var City LandCost Nights Level;
   title 'Tour Information';
run;
```

The following output displays the results:

Output 9.7 Using OR When Making Multiple Comparisons

```
                          Tour Information                          1

                          Land
           Obs   City     Cost    Nights   Level

            1    Rome      750      3      Deluxe
            2    Paris    1680      8      Deluxe
            3    London   1230      6      Deluxe
            4    New York    .      6
            5    Madrid    370      3
            6    Amsterdam 580      4
```

Using Negative Operators with AND or OR

Be careful when you combine negative operators with OR. Often, the operator that you really need is AND. For example, the variable TourGuide contains some problems with the data. In the observation for Paris, the tour guide and the backup tour guide are both Lucas; in the observation for Amsterdam, the name of the tour guide is missing. You want to label the observations that have no problems with TourGuide as OK. Should you write the IF condition with OR or with AND?

The following DATA step shows both conditions:

```
options pagesize=60 linesize=80 pageno=1 nodate;
data test;
    set mylib.arttours;
    if TourGuide ne BackUpGuide or TourGuide ne ' ' then GuideCheckUsingOR = 'OK';
    else GuideCheckUsingOR = 'No';
    if TourGuide ne BackUpGuide and TourGuide ne ' ' then GuideCheckUsingAND = 'OK';
    else GuideCheckUsingAND = 'No';
run;

proc print data = test;
    var City TourGuide BackUpGuide GuideCheckUsingOR GuideCheckUsingAND;
    title 'Negative Operators with OR and AND';
run;
```

The following output displays the results:

Output 9.8 Using Negative Operators When Making Comparisons

```
                     Negative Operators with OR and AND                        1

                                                   Guide         Guide
                               Tour      BackUp    Check         Check
        Obs    City            Guide     Guide     UsingOR       UsingAND

         1     Rome            D'Amico   Torres    OK            OK
         2     Paris           Lucas     Lucas     OK    ❶       No
         3     London          Wilson    Lucas     OK            OK
         4     New York        Lucas     D'Amico   OK            OK
         5     Madrid          Torres    D'Amico   OK            OK
         6     Amsterdam                 Vandever  OK    ❷       No
```

In the IF-THEN/ELSE statements that create GuideCheckUsingOR, only one comparison needs to be true to make the condition true. Note that for the Paris and Amsterdam observations in the data set MYLIB.ARTTOURS,

❶ in the observation for Paris, TourGuide does not have a missing value and the comparison **TourGuide NE** ' ' is true.

❷ for Amsterdam, the comparison **TourGuide NE BackUpGuide** is true.

Because one OR comparison is true in each observation, GuideCheckUsingOR is labeled OK for all observations. The IF-THEN/ELSE statements that create GuideCheckUsingAND achieve better results. That is, the AND operator selects the observations in which the value of TourGuide is not the same as BackUpGuide and is not missing.

Using Complex Comparisons That Require AND and OR

A condition can contain both ANDs and ORs. When it does, SAS evaluates the ANDs before the ORs. The following example specifies a list of cities and a list of guides:

```
   /* first attempt */
if City = 'Paris' or City = 'Rome' and TourGuide = 'Lucas' or
   TourGuide = "D'Amico" then Topic = 'Art history';
```

SAS first joins the items that are connected by AND:

```
City = 'Rome' and TourGuide = 'Lucas'
```

Then SAS makes the following OR comparisons:

```
City = 'Paris'
     or
City = 'Rome' and TourGuide = 'Lucas'
     or
TourGuide = "D'Amico"
```

To group the City comparisons and the TourGuide comparisons, use parentheses:

```
   /* correct method */
if (City = 'Paris' or City = 'Rome') and
   (TourGuide = 'Lucas' or TourGuide = "D'Amico") then
   Topic = 'Art history';
```

SAS evaluates the comparisons within parentheses first and uses the results as the terms of the larger comparison. You can use parentheses in any condition to control the grouping of comparisons or to make the condition easier to read.

The following DATA step illustrates these conditions:

```
options pagesize=60 linesize=80 pageno=1 nodate;
data combine;
   set mylib.arttours;
   if (City = 'Paris' or City = 'Rome') and
      (TourGuide = 'Lucas' or TourGuide = "D'Amico") then
      Topic = 'Art history';
run;

proc print data=combine;
   var City TourGuide Topic;
   title 'Tour Information';
run;
```

The following output displays the results:

Output 9.9 Using Parentheses to Combine Comparisons with AND and OR

```
                      Tour Information                              1

                               Tour
          Obs    City          Guide        Topic

           1     Rome          D'Amico      Art history
           2     Paris         Lucas        Art history
           3     London        Wilson
           4     New York      Lucas
           5     Madrid        Torres
           6     Amsterdam
```

Abbreviating Numeric Comparisons

Two points about numeric comparisons are especially helpful to know:

☐ An abbreviated form of comparison is possible.

☐ Abbreviated comparisons with OR require you to use caution.

In computing terms, a value of TRUE is 1 and a value of FALSE is 0. In SAS,

☐ any numeric value other than 0 or missing is true.

☐ a value of 0 or missing is false.

Therefore, a numeric variable or expression can stand alone in a condition. If its value is a number other than 0 or if the value is missing, then the condition is true; if its value is 0 or missing, then the condition is false.

The following example assigns a value to the variable Remarks only if the value of LandCost is present for a given observation:

```
if LandCost then Remarks = 'Ready to budget';
```

This statement is equivalent to

```
if LandCost ne . and LandCost ne 0 then Remarks = 'Ready to budget';
```

Be careful when you abbreviate comparisons with OR; it is easy to produce unexpected results. For example, this IF-THEN statement selects tours that last six or eight nights:

```
   /* first try */
if Nights = 6 or 8 then Stay = 'Medium';
```

SAS treats the condition as the following comparisons:

```
Nights=6
   or
   8
```

The second comparison does not use the values of Nights; it is simply the number 8 standing alone. Because the number 8 is neither 0 nor a missing value, it always has the value TRUE. Because only one comparison in a series of OR comparisons needs to be true to make the condition true, this condition is true for all observations.

The following comparisons correctly select observations that have six or eight nights:

```
   /* correct way */
if Nights = 6 or Nights = 8 then Stay = 'Medium';
```

The following DATA step includes these IF-THEN statements:

```
options pagesize=60 linesize=80 pageno=1 nodate;
data morecomp;
   set mylib.arttours;
   if LandCost then Remarks = 'Ready to budget';
   else Remarks = 'Need land cost';
   if Nights = 6 or Nights = 8 then Stay = 'Medium';
   else Stay = 'Short';
run;

proc print data=morecomp;
   var City Nights LandCost Remarks Stay;
   title 'Tour Information';
run;
```

The following output displays the results:

Output 9.10   Abbreviating Numeric Comparisons

```
                              Tour Information                                1

                                      Land
          Obs    City        Nights   Cost       Remarks         Stay

           1     Rome           3      750     Ready to budget   Short
           2     Paris          8     1680     Ready to budget   Medium
           3     London         6     1230     Ready to budget   Medium
           4     New York       6        .     Need land cost    Medium
           5     Madrid         3      370     Ready to budget   Short
           6     Amsterdam      4      580     Ready to budget   Short
```

Comparing Characters

Types of Character Comparisons

Some special situations occur when you make character comparisons. You may need to

- □ compare uppercase and lowercase characters
- □ select all values beginning with a particular group of characters
- □ select all values beginning with a particular range of characters
- □ find a particular value anywhere within another character value.

Comparing Uppercase and Lowercase Characters

SAS distinguishes between uppercase and lowercase letters in comparisons. For example, the values **Madrid** and **MADRID** are not equivalent. To compare values that may occur in different cases, use the UPCASE function to produce an uppercase value; then make the comparison between two uppercase values, as shown here:

```
options pagesize=60 linesize=80 pageno=1 nodate;
data newguide;
   set mylib.arttours;
   if upcase(City) = 'MADRID' then TourGuide = 'Balarezo';
run;

proc print data=newguide;
   var City TourGuide;
   title 'Tour Guides';
run;
```

Within the comparison, SAS produces an uppercase version of the value of City and compares it to the uppercase constant MADRID. The value of City in the observation remains in its original case. The following output displays the results:

Output 9.11 Data Set Produced by an Uppercase Comparison

```
                          Tour Guides                              1

                                  Tour
              Obs   City          Guide

               1    Rome          D'Amico
               2    Paris         Lucas
               3    London        Wilson
               4    New York      Lucas
               5    Madrid        Balarezo
               6    Amsterdam
```

Now Balarezo is assigned as the tour guide for Madrid because the UPCASE function compares the uppercase value of Madrid with the value MADRID. The UPCASE function enables SAS to read the two values as equal.

Selecting All Values That Begin with the Same Group of Characters

Sometimes you need to select a group of character values, such as all tour guides whose names begin with the letter D.

By default, SAS compares values of different lengths by adding blanks to the end of the shorter value and testing the result against the longer value. In this example,

```
    /* first attempt */
if Tourguide = 'D' then Chosen = 'Yes';
else Chosen = 'No';
```

SAS interprets the comparison as

```
TourGuide = 'D       '
```

where **D** is followed by seven blanks (because TourGuide, a character variable created by column input, has a length of eight bytes). Because the value of TourGuide never consists of the single letter D, the comparison is never true.

To compare a long value to a shorter standard, put a colon (:) after the operator, as in this example:

```
    /* correct method */
if TourGuide =: 'D' then Chosen = 'Yes';
else Chosen = 'No';
```

The colon causes SAS to compare the same number of characters in the shorter value and the longer value. In this case, the shorter string contains one character; therefore, SAS tests only the first character from the longer value. All names beginning with a D make the comparison true. (If you are not sure that all the values of TourGuide begin with a capital letter, then use the UPCASE function.) The following DATA step selects names beginning with D:

```
options pagesize=60 linesize=80 pageno=1 nodate;
data dguide;
   set mylib.arttours;
   if TourGuide =: 'D' then Chosen = 'Yes';
   else Chosen = 'No';
run;

proc print data=dguide;
```

```
      var City TourGuide Chosen;
      title 'Guides Whose Names Begin with D';
run;
```

The following output displays the results:

Output 9.12   Selecting All Values That Begin with a Particular String

```
              Guides Whose Names Begin with D                    1

                             Tour
        Obs    City          Guide      Chosen

         1     Rome          D'Amico     Yes
         2     Paris         Lucas       No
         3     London        Wilson      No
         4     New York      Lucas       No
         5     Madrid        Torres      No
         6     Amsterdam                 No
```

Selecting a Range of Character Values

You may want to select values beginning with a range of characters, such as all names beginning with A through L or M through Z. To select a range of character values, you need to understand the following points:

☐ In computer processing, letters have magnitude. A is the smallest letter in the alphabet and Z is the largest. Therefore, the comparison A<B is true; so is the comparison D>C.*

☐ A blank is smaller than any letter.

The following statements divide the names of the guides into two groups beginning with A-L and M-Z by combining the comparison operator with the colon:

```
if TourGuide <=: 'L' then TourGuideGroup = 'A-L';
   else TourGuideGroup = 'M-Z';
```

The following DATA step creates the groups:

```
options pagesize=60 linesize=80 pageno=1 nodate;
data guidegrp;
   set mylib.arttours;
   if TourGuide <=: 'L' then TourGuideGroup = 'A-L';
   else TourGuideGroup = 'M-Z';
run;

proc print data=guidegrp;
   var City TourGuide TourGuideGroup;
   title 'Tour Guide Groups';
run;
```

The following output displays the results:

---

* The magnitude of letters in the alphabet is true for all operating environments under which SAS runs. Other points, such as whether uppercase or lowercase letters are larger and how to treat numbers in character values, depend on your operating system. See Chapter 10, "Working with Grouped or Sorted Observations," for more information about how character values are sorted under various operating environments.

Output 9.13 Selecting All Values Beginning with a Range of Characters

```
                      Tour Guide Groups                              1

                                       Tour
                                Tour   Guide
             Obs    City       Guide   Group

              1     Rome       D'Amico  A-L
              2     Paris      Lucas    A-L
              3     London     Wilson   M-Z
              4     New York   Lucas    A-L
              5     Madrid     Torres   M-Z
              6     Amsterdam           A-L
```

All names beginning with A through L, as well as the missing value, go into group A-L. The missing value goes into that group because a blank is smaller than any letter.

Finding a Value Anywhere within Another Character Value

A data set is needed that lists tours that visit other attractions in addition to museums and galleries. In the data set MYLIB.ARTTOURS, the variable **EventDescription** refers to those events as **other**. However, the position of the word **other** varies in different observations. How can it be determined that **other** exists anywhere in the value of **EventDescription** for a given observation?

The INDEX function determines whether a specified character string (the excerpt) is present within a particular character value (the source):

INDEX (*source,excerpt*)

Both *source* and *excerpt* can be any kind of character expression, including character strings enclosed in quotation marks, character variables, and other character functions. If *excerpt* does occur within *source*, then the function returns the position of the first character of *excerpt*, which is a positive number. If it does not, then the function returns a 0. By testing for a value greater than 0, you can determine whether a particular character string is present in another character value.

The following statements select observations containing the string **other**:

```
if index(EventDescription,'other') > 0 then OtherEvents = 'Yes';
else OtherEvents = 'No';
```

You can also write the condition as

```
if index(EventDescription,'other') then OtherEvents = 'Yes';
else OtherEvents = 'No';
```

The second example uses the fact that any value other than 0 or missing makes the condition true. This statement is included in the following DATA step:

```
options pagesize=60 linesize=80 pageno=1 nodate;
data otherevent;
   set mylib.arttours;
   if index(EventDescription,'other') then OtherEvents = 'Yes';
   else OtherEvents = 'No';
run;

proc print data=otherevent;
   var City EventDescription OtherEvents;
```

```
              title 'Tour Events';
run;
```

The following output displays the results:

Output 9.14 Finding a Character String within Another Value

```
                          Tour Events                              1

                                            Other
        Obs    City        EventDescription  Events

         1     Rome        4 M, 3 G          No
         2     Paris       5 M, 1 other      Yes
         3     London      3 M, 2 G          No
         4     New York    5 M, 1 G, 2 other Yes
         5     Madrid      3 M, 2 other      Yes
         6     Amsterdam   3 M, 3 G          No
```

In the observations for Paris and Madrid, the INDEX function returns the value 8 because the string **other** is found in the eighth field of the variable (**5 M, 1 other** for Paris and **3 M, 2 other** for Madrid). For New York, it returns the value 13 because the string **other** is found in the thirteenth field of the variable (**5 M, 1 G, 2 other**). In the remaining observations, the function does not find the string **other** and returns a 0.

Review of SAS Tools

Statements

IF *condition* THEN *action*;
<ELSE *action*;>

tests whether the *condition* is true; if so, the *action* in the THEN clause is carried out. If the *condition* is false and an ELSE statement is present, then the ELSE *action* is carried out. If the *condition* is false and no ELSE statement is present, then the next statement in the DATA step is processed. The *condition* is one or more numeric or character comparisons. The *action* must be an executable statement; that is, one that can be processed in an individual iteration of the DATA step. (Statements that affect the entire DATA step, such as LENGTH, are not executable.)

In SAS processing, any numeric value other than 0 or missing is true; 0 and missing are false. Therefore, a numeric value can stand alone in a comparison. If its value is 0 or missing, then the comparison is false; otherwise, the comparison is true.

Functions

INDEX(*source,excerpt*)

searches the *source* for the string given in *excerpt*. Both the *source* and *excerpt* can be any kind of character expression, such as character variables, character strings enclosed in quotation marks, other character functions, and so on. When *excerpt* is present in *source*, the function returns the position of the first character of *excerpt* (a positive number). When *excerpt* is not present, the function returns a 0.

UPCASE(*argument*)
>produces an uppercase value of *argument*, which can be any kind of character expression, such as character variables, character strings enclosed in quotation marks, other character functions, and so on.

Learning More

Base SAS functions
>Base SAS functions are documented in *SAS Language Reference: Dictionary*.

Comparison and logical operators
>Complete information about comparison and logical operators is provided in the "Expressions" chapter of *SAS Language Reference: Concepts*.

Executable statements
>You can issue only executable statements in IF-THEN/ELSE statements. For a complete list of executable and nonexecutable statements, see the "Statements" chapter in *SAS Language Reference: Dictionary*.

IF-THEN and ELSE statement and clauses
>The IF-THEN and ELSE statement and clauses are documented in *SAS Language Reference: Dictionary*.

IN operator
>Information about the IN operator can be found in the "Where-Expression Processing" chapter of *SAS Language Reference: Concepts*. You can use the IN operator to shorten a comparison when you are comparing a value to a series of numeric or character constants (not variables or expressions).

SELECT statement
>The SELECT statement, which selects observations based on a condition, is documented in *SAS Language Reference: Dictionary*. Its action is equivalent to a series of IF-THEN/ELSE statements. If you have a long series of conditions and actions, then the DATA step may be easier to read if you write them in a SELECT group.

TRUNCOVER option
>The TRUNCOVER option in the INFILE statement is described in Chapter 3, "Starting with Raw Data: The Basics," on page 43 .

CHAPTER

10

Creating Subsets of Observations

Introduction

Purpose

In this chapter, you will learn to select specific observations from existing SAS data sets in order to create

☐ a new SAS data set that includes only some of the observations from the input data source

☐ several new SAS data sets by writing observations from an input data source, using a single DATA step.

Prerequisites

Before proceeding with this chapter, you should understand the concepts presented in

☐ "Introduction to the SAS System"

☐ Part 2, "Getting Your Data into Shape"

☐ Chapter 6, "Understanding DATA Step Processing," on page 97.

Input SAS Data Set for Examples

Tradewinds Travel has a schedule for tours to various art museums and galleries. It would be convenient to keep different SAS data sets that contain different information about the tours. The tour data is stored in an external file that contains the following information:

❶   ❷ ❸   ❹   ❺
```
Rome         3   750 Medium D'Amico
Paris        8  1680 High   Lucas
London       6  1230 High   Wilson
New York     6     .        Lucas
Madrid       3   370 Low    Torres
Amsterdam    4   580 Low
```

The numbered fields represent

❶ the name of the destination city

❷ the number of nights on the tour

❸ the cost of the land package in US dollars

❹ a rating of the budget

❺ the name of the tour guide.

The following program creates a permanent SAS data set named MYLIB.ARTS:

```
options pagesize=60 linesize=80 pageno=1 nodate;
libname mylib 'permanent-data-library';

data mylib.arts;
   infile 'input-file' truncover;
   input City $ 1-9 Nights 11 LandCost 13-16 Budget $ 18-23
         TourGuide $ 25-32;
;

proc print data=mylib.arts;
   title 'Data Set MYLIB.ARTS';
run;
```

The PROC PRINT statement that follows the DATA step produces this display of the MYLIB.ARTS data set:

Output 10.1   Data Set MYLIB.ARTS

```
                    Data Set MYLIB.ARTS                          1

                                 Land         Tour
        Obs   City      Nights   Cost  Budget Guide

         1    Rome         3      750  Medium D'Amico
         2    Paris        8     1680  High   Lucas
         3    London       6     1230  High   Wilson
         4    New York     6       .          Lucas
         5    Madrid       3      370  Low    Torres
         6    Amsterdam    4      580  Low
```

Selecting Observations for a New SAS Data Set

Deleting Observations Based on a Condition

There are two ways to select specific observations in a SAS data set when creating a new SAS data set:

1 Delete the observations that do not meet a condition, keeping only the ones that you want.

2 Accept only the observations that meet a condition.

To delete an observation, first identify it with an IF condition; then use a DELETE statement in the THEN clause:

IF *condition* **THEN DELETE**

Processing the DELETE statement for an observation causes SAS to return immediately to the beginning of the DATA step for a new observation without writing the current observation to the output DATA set. The DELETE statement does not include the observation in the output data set, but it does not delete the observation from the input data set. For example, the following statement deletes observations that contain a missing value for LandCost:

```
if LandCost = . then delete;
```

The following DATA step includes this statement:

```
options pagesize=60 linesize=80 pageno=1 nodate;
data remove;
   set mylib.arts;
   if LandCost = . then delete;
;

proc print data=remove;
   title 'Tours With Complete Land Costs';
run;
```

The following output displays the results:

Output 10.2   Deleting Observations That Have a Particular Value

```
                 Tours With Complete Land Costs                        1

                              Land           Tour
      Obs    City      Nights  Cost   Budget  Guide

       1     Rome        3      750   Medium  D'Amico
       2     Paris       8     1680   High    Lucas
       3     London      6     1230   High    Wilson
       4     Madrid      3      370   Low     Torres
       5     Amsterdam   4      580   Low
```

New York, the observation that is missing a value for LandCost, is not included in the resulting data set, REMOVE.

You can also delete observations as you enter data from an external file. The following DATA step produces the same SAS data set as the REMOVE data set:

```
options pagesize=60 linesize=80 pageno=1 nodate;
data remove2;
   infile 'input-file' truncover;
   input City $ 1-9 Nights 11 LandCost 13-16 Budget $ 18-23
         TourGuide $ 25-32;
   if LandCost = . then delete;
;

proc print data=remove2;
   title 'Tours With Complete Land Costs';
run;
```

The following output displays the results:

Output 10.3   Deleting Observations While Reading from an External File

```
                       Tours With Complete Land Costs                        1

                                     Land            Tour
          Obs   City        Nights   Cost   Budget   Guide

           1    Rome           3      750   Medium   D'Amico
           2    Paris          8     1680   High     Lucas
           3    London         6     1230   High     Wilson
           4    Madrid         3      370   Low      Torres
           5    Amsterdam      4      580   Low
```

Accepting Observations Based on a Condition

One data set that is needed by the travel agency contains observations for tours that last only six nights. One way to make the selection is to delete observations in which the value of Nights is not equal to 6:

```
if Nights ne 6 then delete;
```

A more straightforward way is to select only observations meeting the criterion. The *subsetting IF statement* selects the observations that you specify. It contains only a condition:

IF *condition*;

The implicit action in a subsetting IF statement is always the same: if the condition is true, then continue processing the observation; if it is false, then stop processing the observation and return to the top of the DATA step for a new observation. The statement is called subsetting because the result is a subset of the original observations. For example, if you want to select only observations in which the value of Nights is equal to 6, then you specify the following statement:

```
if Nights = 6;
```

The following DATA step includes the subsetting IF:

```
options pagesize=60 linesize=80 pageno=1 nodate;
data subset6;
   set mylib.arts;
   if nights=6;
;
```

```
proc print data=subset6;
   title 'Six-Night Tours';
run;
```

The following output displays the results:

Output 10.4 Selecting Observations with a Subsetting IF Statement

```
                           Six-Night Tours                                1

                                  Land              Tour
          Obs     City    Nights   Cost   Budget   Guide

           1     London      6     1230    High    Wilson
           2     New York    6      .              Lucas
```

Two observations met the criteria for a six-night tour.

Comparing the DELETE and Subsetting IF Statements

The main reasons for choosing between a DELETE statement and a subsetting IF statement are that

- □ it is usually easier to choose the statement that requires the fewest comparisons to identify the condition.
- □ it is usually easier to think in positive terms than negative ones (this favors the subsetting IF).

One additional situation favors the subsetting IF: it is the safer method if your data has missing or misspelled values. Consider the following situation.

Tradewinds Travel needs a SAS data set of low- to medium-priced tours. Knowing that the values of Budget are **Low**, **Medium**, and **High**, a first thought would be to delete observations with a value of **High**. The following program creates a SAS data set by deleting observations that have a Budget value of HIGH:

```
   /* first attempt */
options pagesize=60 linesize=80 pageno=1 nodate;
data lowmed;
   set mylib.arts;
   if upcase(Budget) = 'HIGH' then delete;
;

proc print data=lowmed;
   title 'Medium and Low Priced Tours';
run;
```

The following output displays the results:

Output 10.5 Producing a Subset by Deletion

```
                        Medium and Low Priced Tours                      1

                                        Land              Tour
           Obs    City         Nights   Cost    Budget    Guide

            1     Rome            3       750    Medium    D'Amico
            2     New York        6        .               Lucas
            3     Madrid          3       370    Low       Torres
            4     Amsterdam       4       580    Low
```

The data set LOWMED contains both the tours that you want and the tour to New York. The inclusion of the tour to New York is erroneous because the value of Budget for the New York observation is missing. Using a subsetting IF statement ensures that the data set contains exactly the observations you want. This DATA step creates the subset with a subsetting IF statement:

```
    /* a safer method */
options pagesize=60 linesize=80 pageno=1 nodate;
data lowmed2;
   set mylib.arts;
   if upcase(Budget) = 'MEDIUM' or upcase(Budget) = 'LOW';
;

proc print data=lowmed2;
   title 'Medium and Low Priced Tours';
run;
```

The following output displays the results:

Output 10.6 Producing an Exact Subset with Subsetting IF

```
                        Medium and Low Priced Tours                      1

                                        Land              Tour
          Obs    City         Nights    Cost    Budget    Guide

           1     Rome            3        750    Medium    D'Amico
           2     Madrid          3        370    Low       Torres
           3     Amsterdam       4        580    Low
```

The result is a SAS data set with no missing values for Budget.

Conditionally Writing Observations to One or More SAS Data Sets

Understanding the OUTPUT Statement

SAS enables you to create multiple SAS data sets in a single DATA step using an OUTPUT statement:

OUTPUT <*SAS-data-set(s)*>;

When you use an OUTPUT statement without specifying a data set name, SAS writes the current observation to all data sets named in the DATA statement. If you want to write observations to a selected data set, then you specify that data set name directly in the OUTPUT statement. Any data set name appearing in the OUTPUT statement must also appear in the DATA statement.

Example for Conditionally Writing Observations to Multiple Data Sets

One of the SAS data sets contains tours that are guided by the tour guide Lucas and the other contains tours led by other guides. Writing to multiple data sets is accomplished by

1 naming both data sets in the DATA statement.

2 selecting the observations using an IF condition.

3 using an OUTPUT statement in the THEN and ELSE clauses to output the observations to the appropriate data sets.

The following DATA step shows these steps:

```
options pagesize=60 linesize=80 pageno=1 nodate;
data lucastour othertours;
    set mylib.arts;
    if TourGuide = 'Lucas' then output lucastour;
    else output othertours;
;

proc print data=lucastour;
    title "Data Set with TourGuide = 'Lucas'";
;

proc print data=othertours;
    title "Data Set with Other Guides";
run;
```

The following output displays the results:

Output 10.7   Creating Two Data Sets wth One DATA Step

```
                   Data Set with TourGuide = 'Lucas'                       1

                                      Land            Tour
           Obs    City      Nights    Cost   Budget   Guide

            1     Paris        8      1680    High    Lucas
            2     New York     6       .              Lucas
```

```
                   Data Set with Other Guides                             2

                                      Land            Tour
           Obs    City      Nights    Cost   Budget   Guide

            1     Rome         3       750   Medium   D'Amico
            2     London       6      1230   High     Wilson
            3     Madrid       3       370   Low      Torres
            4     Amsterdam    4       580   Low
```

A Common Mistake When Writing to Multiple Data Sets

If you use an OUTPUT statement, then you supress the automatic output of observations at the end of the DATA step. Therefore, if you plan to use any OUTPUT statements in a DATA step, then you must program *all* output for that step with OUTPUT statements. For example, in the previous DATA step you sent output to both LUCASTOUR and OTHERTOURS. For comparison, the following program shows what would happen if you omit the ELSE statement in the DATA step:

```
options pagesize=60 linesize=80 pageno=1 nodate;
data lucastour2 othertour2;
   set mylib.arts;
   if TourGuide = 'Lucas' then output lucastour2;
run;

proc print data=lucastour2;
   title "Data Set with Guide = 'Lucas'";
run;

proc print data=othertour2;
   title "Data Set with Other Guides";
run;
```

The following output displays the results:

Output 10.8 Failing to Direct Output to a Second Data Set

```
                    Data Set with Guide = 'Lucas'                        1

                                      Land            Tour
          Obs   City       Nights     Cost    Budget  Guide

           1    Paris         8       1680     High   Lucas
           2    New York      6        .              Lucas
```

No observations are written to OTHERTOUR2 because output was not directed to it.

Understanding Why the Placement of the OUTPUT Statement Is Important

By default SAS writes an observation to the output data set at the end of each iteration. When you use an OUTPUT statement, you override the automatic output feature. Where you place the OUTPUT statement, therefore, is very important. For example, if a variable value is calculated after the OUTPUT statement executes, then that value is not available when the observation is written to the output data set.

For example, in the following DATA step, an assignment statement is placed after the IF-THEN/ELSE group:

```
/* first attempt to combine assignment and OUTPUT statements */
options pagesize=60 linesize=80 pageno=1 nodate;
data lucasdays otherdays;
   set mylib.arts;
   if TourGuide = 'Lucas' then output lucasdays;
   else output otherdays;
```

```
      Days = Nights+1;
run;


proc print data=lucasdays;
   title "Number of Days in Lucas's Tours";
run;


proc print data=otherdays;
   title "Number of Days in Other Guides' Tours";
run;
```

Output 10.9 Unintended Results: Outputting Observations *before* Assigning Values

```
                    Number of Days in Lucas's Tours                        1

                                 Land           Tour
          Obs    City      Nights Cost  Budget  Guide   Days

           1     Paris        8    1680  High    Lucas    .
           2     New York     6     .            Lucas    .
```

```
                 Number of Days in Other Guides' Tours                     2

                              Land           Tour
          Obs    City    Nights Cost  Budget  Guide    Days

           1    Rome        3    750   Medium  D'Amico   .
           2    London      6   1230   High    Wilson    .
           3    Madrid      3    370   Low     Torres    .
           4    Amsterdam   4    580   Low               .
```

The value of DAYS is missing in all observations because the OUTPUT statement writes the observation to the SAS data sets before the assignment statement is processed. If you want the value of DAY to appear in the data sets, then use the assignment statement before you use the OUTPUT statement. The following program shows the correct position:

```
   /* correct position of assignment statement */
options pagesize=60 linesize=80 pageno=1 nodate;
data lucasdays2 otherdays2;
   set mylib.arts;
   Days = Nights + 1;
   if TourGuide = 'Lucas' then output lucasdays2;
   else output otherdays2;
run;


proc print data=lucasdays2;
   title "Number of Days in Lucas's Tours";
run;
proc print data=otherdays2;
```

```
      title "Number of Days in Other Guides' Tours";
   run;
```

Output 10.10   Intended Results: Assigning Values *after* Outputting Observations

```
                     Number of Days in Lucas's Tours                            1

                                   Land              Tour
          Obs     City     Nights  Cost   Budget     Guide    Days

           1      Paris       8     1680   High       Lucas     9
           2      New York    6      .                Lucas     7
```

```
                  Number of Days in Other Guides' Tours                         2

                                 Land            Tour
        Obs     City     Nights  Cost   Budget   Guide    Days

         1      Rome        3     750    Medium   D'Amico   4
         2      London      6     1230   High     Wilson    7
         3      Madrid      3     370    Low      Torres    4
         4      Amsterdam   4     580    Low                5
```

Writing an Observation Multiple Times to One or More Data Sets

After SAS processes an OUTPUT statement, the observation remains in the program data vector and you can continue programming with it. You can even output it again to the same SAS data set or to a different one. The following example creates two pairs of data sets, one pair based on the name of the tour guide and one pair based on the number of nights.

```
options pagesize=60 linesize=80 pageno=1 nodate;
data lucastour othertour weektour daytour;
   set mylib.arts;
   if TourGuide = 'Lucas' then output lucastour;
   else output othertour;
   if nights >= 6 then output weektour;
   else output daytour;
run;

proc print data=lucastour;
   title "Lucas's Tours";
run;

proc print data=othertour;
   title "Other Guides' Tours";
run;
proc print data=weektour;
```

```
        title 'Tours Lasting a Week or More';
run;


proc print data=daytour;
        title 'Tours Lasting Less Than a Week';
run;
```

The following output displays the results:

Output 10.11   Assigning Observations to More Than One Data Set

```
                          Lucas's Tours                                1

                                  Land              Tour
        Obs     City      Nights  Cost    Budget    Guide

         1      Paris        8     1680    High      Lucas
         2      New York     6       .               Lucas
```

```
                       Other Guides' Tours                             2

                                  Land              Tour
        Obs     City      Nights  Cost    Budget    Guide

         1      Rome         3     750     Medium    D'Amico
         2      London       6     1230    High      Wilson
         3      Madrid       3     370     Low       Torres
         4      Amsterdam    4     580     Low
```

```
                    Tours Lasting a Week or More                       3

                                  Land              Tour
        Obs     City      Nights  Cost    Budget    Guide

         1      Paris        8     1680    High      Lucas
         2      London       6     1230    High      Wilson
         3      New York     6       .               Lucas
```

```
                  Tours Lasting Less Than a Week                       4

                                  Land              Tour
        Obs     City      Nights  Cost    Budget    Guide

         1      Rome         3     750     Medium    D'Amico
         2      Madrid       3     370     Low       Torres
         3      Amsterdam    4     580     Low
```

The first IF-THEN/ELSE group outputs all observations to either data set
LUCASTOUR or OTHERTOUR. The second IF-THEN/ELSE group outputs the same
observations to a different pair of data sets, WEEKTOUR and DAYTOUR. This
repetition is possible because each observation remains in the program data vector after
the first OUTPUT statement is processed and can be output again.

Review of SAS Tools

Statements

DATA *<libref-1.>SAS-data-set-1< . . .<libref-n.>SAS-data-set-n>*;
names the *SAS data set(s)* to be created in the DATA step.

DELETE;
deletes the current observation. The DELETE statement is usually used as part of an IF-THEN/ELSE group.

IF *condition*;
tests whether the *condition* is true. If it is true, then SAS continues processing the current observation; if it is not true, then SAS stops processing the observation, does not add it to the SAS data set, and returns to the top of the DATA step. The *conditions* used are the same as in the IF-THEN/ELSE statements. This type of IF statement is called a subsetting IF statement because it produces a subset of the original observations.

OUTPUT *<SAS data set>*;
immediately writes the current observation to the *SAS data set*. The observation remains in the program data vector, and you can continue programming with it, including outputting it again if you desire. When an OUTPUT statement appears in a DATA step, SAS does not automatically output observations to the SAS data set; you must specify the destination for all output in the DATA step with OUTPUT statements. Any SAS data set that you specify in an OUTPUT statement must also appear in the DATA statement.

Learning More

Comparison and logical operators
See Chapter 9, "Acting on Selected Observations," on page 139 and the "Expressions" chapter of *SAS Language Reference: Concepts*.

DROP= and KEEP= data set options
Using the DROP= and KEEP= data set options to output a subset of variables to a SAS data set are discussed in Chapter 5, "Starting with SAS Data Sets," on page 81.

FIRSTOBS= and OBS= data set options
Using these data set options to select observations from the beginning, middle, or end of a SAS data set are discussed in Chapter 5, "Starting with SAS Data Sets," on page 81. They are documented completely in *SAS Language Reference: Dictionary*.

IF-THEN/ELSE, DELETE, and OUTPUT statements
The IF-THEN/ELSE, DELETE, and OUTPUT statements are completely documented in *SAS Language Reference: Dictionary*.

WHERE statement
See Chapter 25, "Producing Detail Reports with the PRINT Procedure," on page 367. The WHERE statement selects observations based on a condition. Its action is similar to that of a subsetting IF statement. The WHERE statement is

extremely useful in PROC steps, and it can also be useful in some DATA steps. The WHERE statement selects observations before they enter the program data vector (in contrast to the subsetting IF statement, which selects observations already in the program data vector).

Note: In some cases, the same condition in a WHERE statement in the DATA step and in a subsetting IF statement produces different subsets. The difference is described in the discussion of the WHERE statement in *SAS Language Reference: Dictionary*. Be sure you understand the difference before you use the WHERE statement in the DATA step. With that caution in mind, a WHERE statement can increase the efficiency of the DATA step considerably. △

Working with Grouped or Sorted Observations

Introduction

Purpose

Sometimes you need to create reports where observations are grouped according to the values of a particular variable, or where observations are sorted alphabetically. In this chapter you will learn

- ☐ how to group observations by variables and how to work with grouped observations
- ☐ how to sort the observations and how to work with sorted observations.

Prerequisites

Before proceeding with this chapter, you should understand the concepts presented in

- ☐ Part 1, "Introduction to the SAS System"
- ☐ Part 2, "Getting Your Data into Shape"

□ Chapter 6, "Understanding DATA Step Processing," on page 97.

Input SAS Data Set for Examples

Tradewinds Travel has an external file that contains data about tours that emphasize either architecture or scenery. After the data is created in a SAS data set and the observations for those tours are grouped together, SAS can produce reports on each group separately. In addition, if the observations need to be alphabetized by country, SAS can sort them. The external file looks like this:

```
❶             ❷           ❸   ❹   ❺
Spain         architecture  10   510 World
Japan         architecture   8   720 Express
Switzerland   scenery        9   734 World
France        architecture   8   575 World
Ireland       scenery        7   558 Express
New Zealand   scenery       16  1489 Southsea
Italy         architecture   8   468 Express
Greece        scenery       12   698 Express
```

The numbered fields represent

❶ the name of the destination country

❷ the tour's area of emphasis

❸ the number of nights on the tour

❹ the cost of the land package in US dollars

❺ the name of the tour vendor.

The following DATA step creates the permanent SAS data set MYLIB.ARCH_OR_SCEN:

```
options pagesize=60 linesize=80 pageno=1 nodate;


libname mylib 'permanent-data-library';
data mylib.arch_or_scen;
   infile 'input-file' truncover;
   input Country $ 1-11 TourType $ 13-24 Nights LandCost Vendor $;
run;

proc print data=mylib.arch_or_scen;
   title 'Data Set MYLIB.ARCH_OR_SCEN';
run;
```

The PROC PRINT statement that follows the DATA step produces this display of the MYLIB.ARCH_OR_SCEN data set:

Output 11.1 Data Set MYLIB.ARCH_OR_SCEN

```
                      Data Set MYLIB.ARCH_OR_SCEN                          1

                                                 Land
         Obs    Country       TourType      Nights   Cost    Vendor

          1     Spain         architecture    10     510     World
          2     Japan         architecture     8     720     Express
          3     Switzerland   scenery          9     734     World
          4     France        architecture     8     575     World
          5     Ireland       scenery          7     558     Express
          6     New Zealand   scenery         16    1489     Southsea
          7     Italy         architecture     8     468     Express
          8     Greece        scenery         12     698     Express
```

Working with Grouped Data

Understanding the Basics of Grouping Data

The basic method for grouping data is to use a BY statement:

BY *list-of-variables*;

The BY statement can be used in a DATA step with a SET, MERGE, MODIFY, or UPDATE statement, or it can be used in SAS procedures.

To work with grouped data using the SET, MERGE, MODIFY, or UPDATE statements, the data must meet these conditions:

☐ The observations must be in a SAS data set, not an external file.

☐ The variables that define the groups must appear in the BY statement.

☐ All observations in the input data set must be in ascending or descending numeric or character order, or grouped in some way, such as by calendar month or a formatted value, according to the variables that will be specified in the BY statement.

> *Note:* If you use the MODIFY statement, the input data does not need to be in any order. However, ordering the data can improve performance. △

If the third condition is not met, the data are in a SAS data set but are not arranged in the groups you want, you can order the data using the SORT procedure (discussed in the next section).

Once the SAS data set is arranged in some order, you can use the BY statement to group values of one or more common variables.

Grouping Observations with the SORT Procedure

All observations in the input data set must be in a particular order. To meet this condition, the observations in MYLIB.ARCH_OR_SCEN can be ordered by the values of TourType, **architecture** and **scenery**:

```
proc sort data=mylib.arch_or_scen out=tourorder;
   by TourType;
run;
```

The SORT procedure sorts the data set MYLIB.ARCH_OR_SCEN alphabetically according to the values of TourType. The sorted observations go into a new data set specified by the OUT= option. In this example, TOURORDER is the sorted data set. If the OUT= option is omitted, the sorted version of the data set replaces the data set MYLIB.ARCH_OR_SCEN.

The SORT procedure does not produce output other than the sorted data set. A message in the SAS log says that the SORT procedure was executed:

Output 11.2   Message That the SORT Procedure Has Executed Successfully

```
2    proc sort data=mylib.arch_or_scen out=tourorder;
3       by TourType;
4    run;
NOTE: There were 8 observations read from the data set MYLIB.ARCH_OR_SCEN.
NOTE: The data set WORK.TOURORDER has 8 observations and 5 variables.
NOTE: PROCEDURE SORT used:
```

To see the sorted data set, add a PROC PRINT step to the program:

```
options pagesize=60 linesize=80 pageno=1 nodate;
proc sort data=mylib.arch_or_scen out=tourorder;
   by TourType;
run;

proc print data=tourorder;
   var TourType Country Nights LandCost Vendor;
   title 'Tours Sorted by Architecture or Scenic Tours';
run;
```

The following output displays the results:

Output 11.3   Displaying the Sorted Output

```
                 Tours Sorted by Architecture or Scenic Tours                1

                                                    Land
       Obs    TourType       Country       Nights   Cost    Vendor

        1     architecture   Spain           10      510    World
        2     architecture   Japan            8      720    Express
        3     architecture   France           8      575    World
        4     architecture   Italy            8      468    Express
        5     scenery        Switzerland      9      734    World
        6     scenery        Ireland          7      558    Express
        7     scenery        New Zealand     16     1489    Southsea
        8     scenery        Greece          12      698    Express
```

By default, SAS arranges groups in ascending order of the BY values, smallest to largest. Sorting a data set does not change the order of the variables within it. However, most examples in this chapter use a VAR statement in the PRINT procedure to display the BY variable in the first column. (The PRINT procedure and other procedures used in this book can also produce a separate report for each BY group.)

Grouping by More Than One Variable

You can group observations by as many variables as you want. This example groups observations by TourType, Vendor, and LandCost:

```
options pagesize=60 linesize=80 pageno=1 nodate;
proc sort data=mylib.arch_or_scen out=tourorder2;
   by TourType Vendor Landcost;
run;

proc print data=tourorder2;
   var TourType Vendor Landcost Country Nights;
   title 'Tours Grouped by Type of Tour, Vendor, and Price';
run;
```

The following output displays the results:

Output 11.4 *Grouping by Several Variables*

```
          Tours Grouped by Type of Tour, Vendor, and Price             1

                                 Land
     Obs   TourType      Vendor   Cost   Country        Nights

      1    architecture  Express   468   Italy            8
      2    architecture  Express   720   Japan            8
      3    architecture  World     510   Spain           10
      4    architecture  World     575   France           8
      5    scenery       Express   558   Ireland          7
      6    scenery       Express   698   Greece          12
      7    scenery       Southsea 1489   New Zealand     16
      8    scenery       World     734   Switzerland      9
```

As this example shows, SAS groups the observations by the first variable that is named within those groups, by the second variable named; and so on. The groups defined by all variables contain only one observation each. In this example, no two variables have the same values for all observations. In other words, this example does not have any duplicate entries.

Arranging Groups in Descending Order

In the data sets that are grouped by TourType, the group for **architecture** comes before the group for **scenery** because **architecture** begins with an "a"; "a" is smaller than "s" in computer processing. (The order of characters, known as their *collating sequence*, is discussed later in this chapter.) To produce a descending order for a particular variable, place the DESCENDING option before the name of the variable in the BY statement of the SORT procedure. In the next example, the observations are grouped in descending order by TourType, but in ascending order by Vendor and LandCost:

```
options pagesize=60 linesize=80 pageno=1 nodate;
proc sort data=mylib.arch_or_scen out=tourorder3;
   by descending TourType Vendor LandCost;
run;
```

```
proc print data=tourorder3;
   var TourType Vendor LandCost Country Nights;
   title 'Descending Order of TourType';
run;
```

The following output displays the results:

Output 11.5   Combining Descending and Ascending Sorted Observations

```
                       Descending Order of TourType                       1

                                    Land
        Obs    TourType      Vendor    Cost   Country      Nights

         1     scenery       Express    558   Ireland         7
         2     scenery       Express    698   Greece         12
         3     scenery       Southsea  1489   New Zealand    16
         4     scenery       World      734   Switzerland     9
         5     architecture  Express    468   Italy           8
         6     architecture  Express    720   Japan           8
         7     architecture  World      510   Spain          10
         8     architecture  World      575   France          8
```

Finding the First or Last Observation in a Group

If you do not want to display the entire data set, how can you create a data set containing only the least expensive tour that features architecture, and the least expensive tour that features scenery?

First, sort the data set by TourType and LandCost:

```
options pagesize=60 linesize=80 pageno=1 nodate;
proc sort data=mylib.arch_or_scen out=tourorder4;
   by TourType LandCost;
run;

proc print data=tourorder4;
   var TourType LandCost Country Nights Vendor;
   title 'Tours Arranged by TourType and LandCost';
run;
```

The following output displays the results:

Output 11.6   Sorting to Find the Least Expensive Tours

```
                    Tours Arranged by TourType and LandCost                    1

                        Land
        Obs    TourType   Cost   Country        Nights   Vendor

         1    architecture   468   Italy            8    Express
         2    architecture   510   Spain           10    World
         3    architecture   575   France           8    World
         4    architecture   720   Japan            8    Express
         5    scenery        558   Ireland          7    Express
         6    scenery        698   Greece          12    Express
         7    scenery        734   Switzerland      9    World
         8    scenery       1489   New Zealand     16    Southsea
```

You sorted LandCost in ascending order, so the first observation in each value of
TourType has the lowest value of LandCost. If you can locate the first observation in
each BY group in a DATA step, you can use a subsetting IF statement to select that
observation. But how can you locate the first observation with each value of TourType?

When you use a BY statement in a DATA step, SAS automatically creates two
additional variables for each variable in the BY statement. One is named
FIRST.*variable*, where *variable* is the name of the BY variable, and the other is named
LAST.*variable*. Their values are either 1 or 0. They exist in the program data vector
and are available for DATA step programming, but SAS does not add them to the SAS
data set being created. For example, the DATA step begins with these statements:

```
data lowcost;
   set tourorder4;
   by TourType;
   ...more SAS statements...
run;
```

The BY statement causes SAS to create one variable called FIRST.TOURTYPE and
another variable called LAST.TOURTYPE. When SAS processes the first observation
with the value **architecture**, the value of FIRST.TOURTYPE is 1; in other
observations with the value **architecture**, it is 0. Similarly, when SAS processes the
last observation with the value **architecture**, the value of LAST.TOURTYPE is 1; in
other **architecture** observations, it is 0. The same result occurs in the **scenery** group
with the observations.

SAS does not write FIRST. and LAST. variables to the output data set, so you can not
display their values with the PRINT procedure. Therefore, the simplest method of
displaying the values of FIRST. and LAST. variables is to assign their values to other
variables. This example assigns the value of FIRST.TOURTYPE to a variable named
FirstTour and the value of LAST.TOURTYPE to a variable named LastTour:

```
options pagesize=60 linesize=80 pageno=1 nodate;
data temp;
   set tourorder4;
   by TourType;
   FirstTour = first.TourType;
   LastTour = last.TourType;
run;
proc print data=temp;
```

```
      var Country Tourtype FirstTour LastTour;
      title 'Specifying FIRST.TOURTYPE and LAST.TOURTYPE';
   run;
```

The following output displays the results:

Output 11.7 Demonstrating FIRST. and LAST. Values

```
                Specifying FIRST.TOURTYPE and LAST.TOURTYPE                 1

                                                   First    Last
           Obs     Country       TourType          Tour     Tour

            1      Italy         architecture        1        0
            2      Spain         architecture        0        0
            3      France        architecture        0        0
            4      Japan         architecture        0        1
            5      Ireland       scenery             1        0
            6      Greece        scenery             0        0
            7      Switzerland   scenery             0        0
            8      New Zealand   scenery             0        1
```

In this data set, Italy is the first observation with the value **architecture**; for that observation, the value of FIRST.TOURTYPE is 1. Italy is not the last observation with the value **architecture**, so its value of LAST.TOURTYPE is 0. The observations for Spain and France are neither the first nor the last with the value **architecture**; both FIRST.TOURTYPE and LAST.TOURTYPE are 0 for them. Japan is the last with the value **architecture**; the value of LAST.TOURTYPE is 1. The same rules apply to observations in the **scenery** group.

Now you're ready to use FIRST.TOURTYPE in a subsetting IF statement. When the data are sorted by TourType and LandCost, selecting the first observation in each type of tour gives you the lowest price of any tour in that category:

```
options pagesize=60 linesize=80 pageno=1 nodate;
proc sort data=mylib.arch_or_scen out=tourorder4;
   by TourType LandCost;
run;

data lowcost;
   set tourorder4;
   by TourType;
   if first.TourType;
run;

proc print data=lowcost;
   title 'Least Expensive Tour for Each Type of Tour';
run;
```

The following output displays the results:

Output 11.8   Selecting One Observation from Each BY Group

```
                 Least Expensive Tour for Each Type of Tour                    1

                                                 Land
            Obs    Country    TourType      Nights    Cost    Vendor

             1     Italy      architecture      8      468    Express
             2     Ireland    scenery           7      558    Express
```

Working with Sorted Data

Understanding Sorted Data

By default, groups appear in ascending order of the BY values. In some cases you want to emphasize the order in which the observations are sorted, not the fact that they can be grouped. For example, you may want to alphabetize the tours by country.

To sort your data in a particular order, use the SORT procedure just as you do for grouped data. When the sorted order is more important than the grouping, you usually want only one observation with a given BY value in the resulting data set. Therefore, you may need to remove duplicate observations.

Operating Environment Information: The SORT procedure accesses either a sorting utility that is supplied as part of SAS, or a sorting utility supplied by the host operating system. All examples in this book use the SAS sorting utility. Some operating system utilities do not accept particular options, including the NODUPRECS option described later in this chapter. The default sorting utility is set by your site. For more information about the utilities available to you, see the documentation for your operating system. △

Sorting Data

The following example sorts data set MYLIB.ARCH_OR_SCEN by COUNTRY:

```
options pagesize=60 linesize=80 pageno=1 nodate;
proc sort data=mylib.arch_or_scen out=bycountry;
   by Country;
run;

proc print data=bycountry;
   title 'Tours in Alphabetical Order by Country';
run;
```

The following output displays the results:

Output 11.9 Sorting Data

```
                      Tours in Alphabetical Order by Country                1

                                                      Land
          Obs     Country      TourType      Nights   Cost    Vendor

           1      France       architecture     8     575     World
           2      Greece       scenery         12     698     Express
           3      Ireland      scenery          7     558     Express
           4      Italy        architecture     8     468     Express
           5      Japan        architecture     8     720     Express
           6      New Zealand  scenery         16    1489     Southsea
           7      Spain        architecture    10     510     World
           8      Switzerland  scenery          9     734     World
```

Deleting Duplicate Observations

You can eliminate duplicate observations in a SAS data set by using the NODUPRECS option with the SORT procedure. The following programs show you how to create a SAS data set and then remove duplicate observations.

The external file shown below contains a duplicate observation for Switzerland:

```
Spain        architecture   10   510 World
Japan        architecture    8   720 Express
Switzerland  scenery         9   734 World
France       architecture    8   575 World
Switzerland  scenery         9   734 World
Ireland      scenery         7   558 Express
New Zealand  scenery        16  1489 Southsea
Italy        architecture    8   468 Express
Greece       scenery        12   698 Express
```

The following DATA step creates a permanent SAS data set named MYLIB.ARCH_OR_SCEN2.

```
options pagesize=60 linesize=80 pageno=1 nodate;

libname mylib 'SAS-data-library';
data mylib.arch_or_scen2;
   infile 'input-file';
   input Country $ 1--11 TourType $ 13--24 Nights LandCost Vendor $;
run;

proc print data=mylib.arch_or_scen2;
   title 'Data Set MYLIB.ARCH_OR_SCEN2';
run;
```

The following output shows that this data set contains a duplicate observation for Switzerland:

Output 11.10 Data Set MYLIB.ARCH_OR_SCEN2

```
                      Data Set MYLIB.ARCH_OR_SCEN2                        1

                                                    Land
         Obs    Country        TourType      Nights  Cost   Vendor

          1     Spain          architecture    10    510    World
          2     Japan          architecture     8    720    Express
          3     Switzerland    scenery          9    734    World
          4     France         architecture     8    575    World
          5     Switzerland    scenery          9    734    World
          6     Ireland        scenery          7    558    Express
          7     New Zealand    scenery         16   1489    Southsea
          8     Italy          architecture     8    468    Express
          9     Greece         scenery         12    698    Express
```

The following program uses the NODUPRECS option in the SORT procedure to delete duplicate observations. The program creates a new data set called FIXED.

```
options pagesize=60 linesize=80 pageno=1 nodate;
proc sort data=mylib.arch_or_scen out=fixed noduprecs;
    by Country;
run;

proc print data=fixed;
    title 'Data Set FIXED: MYLIB.ARCH_OR_SCEN2 With Duplicates Removed';
run;
```

The following output displays messages that appear in the SAS log:

Output 11.11 Partial SAS Log Indicating Duplicate Observations Deleted

```
311  options pagesize=60 linesize=80 pageno=1 nodate;
312  proc sort data=mylib.arch_or_scen out=fixed noduprecs;
313      by Country;
314  run;
NOTE: 1 duplicate observations were deleted.
NOTE: There were 9 observations read from the data set MYLIB.ARCH_OR_SCEN.
NOTE: The data set WORK.FIXED has 8 observations and 5 variables.
315
316  proc print data=fixed;
317      title 'Data Set FIXED: MYLIB.ARCH_OR_SCEN2 With Duplicates Removed';
318  run;
NOTE: There were 8 observations read from the data set WORK.FIXED.
```

The following output shows the results of the NODUPRECS option:

Output 11.12   Data Set FIXED with No Duplicate Observations

```
          Data Set FIXED: MYLIB.ARCH_OR_SCEN2 With Duplicates Removed        1

                                               Land
   Obs     Country       TourType      Nights  Cost   Vendor

    1      France        architecture     8    575    World
    2      Greece        scenery         12    698    Express
    3      Ireland       scenery          7    558    Express
    4      Italy         architecture     8    468    Express
    5      Japan         architecture     8    720    Express
    6      New Zealand   scenery         16   1489    Southsea
    7      Spain         architecture    10    510    World
    8      Switzerland   scenery          9    734    World
```

Understanding Collating Sequences

Both numeric and character variables can be sorted into ascending or descending order. For numeric variables, ascending or descending order is easy to understand, but what about the order of characters? Character values include uppercase and lowercase letters, special characters, and the digits 0 through 9 when they are treated as characters rather than as numbers. How does SAS sort these characters?

The order in which characters sort is called a *collating sequence*. By default, SAS sorts characters in one of two sequences: EBCDIC or ASCII, depending on the operating environment under which SAS is running. For reference, both sequences are displayed here.

As long as you work under a single operating system, you seldom need to think about the details of collating sequences. However, when you transfer files from an operating system using EBCDIC to an operating system using ASCII or vice versa, character values that are sorted on one operating system are not necessarily in the correct order for the other operating system. The simplest solution to the problem is to re-sort character data (not numeric data) on the destination operating system. For detailed information about collating sequences, see the documentation for your operating environment.

ASCII Collating Sequence

The following operating systems use the ASCII collating sequence:

Macintosh

MS-DOS

OpenVMS

OS/2

PC DOS

UNIX and its derivatives

Windows

From the smallest to the largest displayable character, the English-language ASCII sequence is

blank!"#$%&'()*+,– ./0123456789:;<=>?@

ABCDEFGHIJKLMNOPQRSTUVWXYZ [\ ]^_

abcdefghijklmnopqrstuvwxyz{}~

The main features of the ASCII sequence are that digits are smaller than uppercase letters and uppercase letters are smaller than lowercase ones. The blank is the smallest displayable character, followed by the other types of characters:

blank < digits < uppercase letters < lowercase letters

EBCDIC Collating Sequence

The following operating systems use the EBCDIC collating sequence:

CMS

OS/390

From the smallest to largest displayable character, the English-language EBCDIC sequence is

blank.<(+|&!$*);¬ – /,%_>?:#@'="

abcdefghijklmnopqr~stuvwxyz

{ABCDEFGHI}JKLMNOPQR\ STUVWXYZ

0123456789

The main features of the EBCDIC sequence are that lowercase letters are smaller than uppercase letters and uppercase letters are smaller than digits. The blank is the smallest displayable character, followed by the other types of characters:

blank < lowercase letters < uppercase letters < digits

Review of SAS Tools

Procedures

PROC SORT <DATA=*SAS-data-set*> <OUT=*SAS-data-set*> <NODUPRECS>;
sorts a SAS data set by the values of variables listed in the BY statement. If you specify the OUT= option, the sorted data are stored in a different SAS data set than the input data. The NODUPRECS option tells PROC SORT to eliminate identical observations.

Statements

BY <DESCENDING> *variable-1* < . . . <DESCENDING> *variable-n*>;
in a DATA step causes SAS to create FIRST. and LAST. variables for each variable named in the statement. The value of FIRST.*variable-1* is 1 for the first observation with a given BY value and 0 for other observations. Similarly, the value of LAST.*variable-1* is 1 for the last observation for a given BY value and 0 for other observations. The BY statement can follow a SET, MERGE, MODIFY, or UPDATE statement in the DATA step; it can not be used with an INPUT statement. By default, SAS assumes that data being read with a BY statement are in ascending order of the BY values. The DESCENDING option indicates that values of the variable that follow are in the opposite order, that is, largest to smallest.

Learning More

Alternative to sorting observations
Information about an alternative to sorting observations: creating an index that identifies the observations with particular values of a variable, can be found in the "SAS Data Files" chapter of *SAS Language Reference: Concepts.*

BY statement and BY-group processing
See *SAS Language Reference: Dictionary* and *SAS Language Reference: Concepts.*

Interleaving, merging, and updating SAS data sets
See Chapter 17, "Interleaving SAS Data Sets," on page 263, Chapter 18, "Merging SAS Data Sets," on page 269, and Chapter 19, "Updating SAS Data Sets," on page 293. These operations depend on the BY statement in the DATA step. *Interleaving* combines data sets in sorted order (Chapter 17, "Interleaving SAS Data Sets," on page 263); *match-merging* joins observations identified by the value of a BY variable (Chapter 18, "Merging SAS Data Sets," on page 269); and *updating* uses a data set containing transactions to change values in a master file Chapter 19, "Updating SAS Data Sets," on page 293).

NOTSORTED option
The NOTSORTED option can be used in both DATA and PROC steps, except for the SORT procedure. Information about the NOTSORTED option can be found in Chapter 30, "Writing Lines to the SAS Log or to an Output File," on page 517. The NOTSORTED option is useful when data are grouped according to the values of a variable, but the groups are not in ascending or descending order. Using the NOTSORTED option in the BY statement enables SAS to process them.

SORT procedure
The SORT procedure and the role of the BY statement in it is documented in *SAS Procedures Guide.* It also describes how to specify different sorting utilities.

□ When you work with large data sets, plan your work so that you sort the data set as few times as possible. For example, if you need to sort a data set by STATE at the beginning of a program and by CITY within STATE later, sort the data set by STATE and CITY at the beginning of the program.

□ To eliminate observations whose BY values duplicate BY values in other observations (but not necessarily values of other variables), use the NODUPKEY option in the SORT procedure.

□ SAS can sort data in sequences other than English-language EBCDIC or ASCII. Examples include the Danish-Norwegian and Finnish/Swedish sequences.

The SAS documentation for your operating system presents operating system-specific information about the SORT procedure. In general, many points about sorting data depend on the operating system and other local conditions at your site (such as whether various operating system utilities are available).

12

Using More Than One Observation in a Calculation

Introduction

Purpose

In this chapter you will learn about calculations that require more than one observation. Examples of those calculations include:

- □ accumulating a total across a data set or a BY group
- □ saving a value from one observation in order to compare it to a value in a later observation.

Prerequisites

Before proceeding with this chapter, you should understand the concepts presented in

- □ Chapter 6, "Understanding DATA Step Processing," on page 97
- □ Chapter 11, "Working with Grouped or Sorted Observations," on page 173.

Input File and SAS Data Set for Examples

Tradewinds Travel needs to know how much business the company did with various tour vendors during the peak season. The data that the copmany wants to look at is the total number of people that are booked on tours with various vendors, and the total value of the tours that are booked.

The following external file contains data about Tradewinds Travel tours:

```
    ❶               ❷   ❸      ❹
    France          575 Express   10
    Spain           510 World     12
    Brazil          540 World      6
    India           489 Express    .
    Japan           720 Express   10
    Greece          698 Express   20
    New Zealand    1489 Southsea   6
    Venezuela       425 World      8
    Italy           468 Express    9
    USSR            924 World      6
    Switzerland     734 World     20
    Australia      1079 Southsea  10
    Ireland         558 Express    9
```

The numbered fields represent

❶ the destination country for the tour

❷ the cost of the land package in US dollars

❸ the name of the vendor

❹ the number of people that were booked on that tour.

The first step is to create a permanent SAS data set. The following program creates the data set MYLIB.TOURREVENUE:

```
options pagesize=60 linesize=80 pageno=1 nodate;
libname mylib 'permanent-data-library';


data mylib.tourrevenue;
   infile 'input-file' truncover;
   input Country $ 1-11 LandCost Vendor $ NumberOfBookings;
run;

proc print data=mylib.tourrevenue;
   title 'SAS Data Set MYLIB.TOURREVENUE';
run;
```

The PROC PRINT statement that follows the DATA step produces this display of the MYLIB.TOURREVENUE data set:

Output 12.1 Data Set MYLIB.TOURREVENUE

```
                      SAS Data Set MYLIB.TOURREVENUE                       1

                                             Number
                                  Land        Of
              Obs    Country      Cost  Vendor    Bookings

               1    France        575  Express      10
               2    Spain         510  World        12
               3    Brazil        540  World         6
               4    India         489  Express       .
               5    Japan         720  Express      10
               6    Greece        698  Express      20
               7    New Zealand  1489  Southsea      6
               8    Venezuela     425  World         8
               9    Italy         468  Express       9
              10    USSR          924  World         6
              11    Switzerland   734  World        20
              12    Australia    1079  Southsea     10
              13    Ireland       558  Express       9
```

Each observation in the data set MYLIB.TOURREVENUE contains the cost of a tour and the number of people who booked that tour. The tasks of Tradewinds Travel are

□ to determine how much money was spent with each vendor and with all vendors together

□ to store the totals in a SAS data set that is separate from the individual vendors' records

□ to find the tour that produced the most revenue, which is determined by the land cost times the number of people who booked the tour.

Accumulating a Total for an Entire Data Set

Creating a Running Total

The first task in performing calculations on the data set MYLIB.TOURREVENUE is to find out the total number of people who booked tours with Tradewinds Travel. Therefore, a variable is needed whose value starts at 0 and increases by the number of bookings in each observation. The sum statement gives you that capability:

variable + expression

In a sum statement, the value of the *variable* on the left side of the plus sign is 0 before the statement is processed for the first time. Processing the statement adds the value of the *expression* on the right side of the plus sign to the initial value; the sum variable retains the new value until the next processing of the statement. The sum statement ignores a missing value for the expression; the previous total remains unchanged.

The following statement creates the total number of bookings :

```
TotalBookings + NumberOfBookings;
```

The following DATA step includes the sum statement above:

```
options pagesize=60 linesize=80 pageno=1 nodate;
data total;
    set mylib.tourrevenue;
```

```
    TotalBookings + NumberOfBookings;
run;

proc print data=total;
   var Country NumberOfBookings TotalBookings;
   title 'Total Tours Booked';
run;
```

The following output displays the results:

Output 12.2   Accumulating a Total for a Data Set

```
                        Total Tours Booked                              1

                              Number
                                Of         Total
             Obs   Country    Bookings    Bookings

              1    France        10          10
              2    Spain         12          22
              3    Brazil         6          28
              4    India          .          28
              5    Japan         10          38
              6    Greece        20          58
              7    New Zealand    6          64
              8    Venezuela      8          72
              9    Italy          9          81
             10    USSR           6          87
             11    Switzerland   20         107
             12    Australia     10         117
             13    Ireland        9         126
```

The TotalBookings variable in the last observation of the TOTAL data set contains the total number of bookings for the year.

Printing Only the Total

If the total is the only information that is needed from the data set, a data set that contains only one observation and one variable (the TotalBookings variable) can be created by writing a DATA step that does all of the following:

☐ specifies the END= option in the SET statement to determine if the current observation is the last observation

☐ uses a subsetting IF to write only the last observation to the SAS data set

☐ specifies the KEEP= option in the DATA step to keep only the variable that totals the bookings.

When the END= option in the SET statement is specified, the variable that is named in the END= option is set to 1 when the DATA step is processing the last observation; the variable that is named in the END= option is set to 0 for other observations:

SET *SAS-data-set* <END=*variable*>;

SAS does not add the END= variable to the data set that is being created. By testing the value of the END= variable, you can determine which observation is the last observation.

The following program selects the last observation with a subsetting IF statement and uses a KEEP= data set option to keep only the variable TotalBookings in the data set:

```
options pagesize=60 linesize=80 pageno=1 nodate;
data total2(keep=TotalBookings);
   set mylib.tourrevenue end=Lastobs;
   TotalBookings + NumberOfBookings;
   if Lastobs;
run;


proc print data=total2;
   title 'Total Number of Tours Booked';
run;
```

The following output displays the results:

Output 12.3   Selecting the Last Observation in a Data Set

```
                    Total Number of Tours Booked                        1

                                  Total
                  Obs           Bookings

                   1              126
```

The condition in the subsetting IF statement is true when Lastobs has a value of 1. When SAS is processing the last observation from MYLIB.TOURREVENUE, it assigns to Lastobs the value 1. Therefore, the subsetting IF statement accepts only the last observation from MYLIB.TOURREVENUE, and SAS writes the last observation to the data set TOTAL2.

Obtaining a Total for Each BY Group

An additional requirement of Tradewinds Travel is to determine the number of tours that are booked with each vendor. In order to accomplish this task, a program must group the data by a variable; that is, the program must organize the data set into groups of observations, with one group for each vendor. In this case, the program must group the data by the Vendor variable. Each group is known generically as a *BY group*; the variable that is used to determine the groupings is called a *BY variable*.

In order to group the data by the Vendor variable, the program must

□ include a PROC SORT step to group the observations by the Vendor variable

□ use a BY statement in the DATA step

□ use a sum statement to total the bookings

□ reset the sum variable to 0 at the beginning of each group of observations.

The following program sorts the data set by Vendor and sums the total bookings for each vendor.

```
options pagesize=60 linesize=80 pageno=1 nodate;
proc sort  data=mylib.tourrevenue out=mylib.sorttour;
   by Vendor;
run;
```

```
data totalby;
   set mylib.sorttour;
   by Vendor;
   if First.Vendor then VendorBookings = 0;
   VendorBookings + NumberOfBookings;
   run;

   proc print data=totalby;
      title 'Summary of Bookings by Vendor';
   run;
```

In the preceding program, the FIRST.Vendor variable is used in an IF-THEN statement to set the sum variable (VendorBookings) to 0 in the first observation of each BY group. (For more information on the FIRST.*variable* and LAST.*variable* temporary variables, see "Finding the First or Last Observation in a Group" on page 178.)

The following output displays the results.

Output 12.4   Creating Totals for BY Groups

```
                       Summary of Bookings by Vendor                        1

                                              Number
                             Land               Of        Vendor
       Obs    Country        Cost   Vendor    Bookings    Bookings

        1     France          575   Express      10          10
        2     India           489   Express       .          10
        3     Japan           720   Express      10          20
        4     Greece          698   Express      20          40
        5     Italy           468   Express       9          49
        6     Ireland         558   Express       9          58
        7     New Zealand    1489   Southsea      6           6
        8     Australia      1079   Southsea     10          16
        9     Spain           510   World        12          12
       10     Brazil          540   World         6          18
       11     Venezuela       425   World         8          26
       12     USSR            924   World         6          32
       13     Switzerland     734   World        20          52
```

Notice that while this output does in fact include the total number of bookings for each vendor, it also includes a great deal of extraneous information. Reporting the total bookings for each vendor requires only the variables Vendor and VendorBookings from the last observation for each vendor. Therefore, the program can

□ use the DROP= or KEEP= data set options to eliminate the variables Country, LandCost, and NumberOfBookings from the output data set

□ use the LAST.Vendor variable in a subsetting IF statement to write only the last observation in each group to the data set TOTALBY.

The following program creates data set TOTALBY:

```
options pagesize=60 linesize=80 pageno=1 nodate;
proc sort data=mylib.tourrevenue out=mylib.sorttour;
   by Vendor;
run;

data totalby(drop=country landcost);
```

```
    set mylib.sorttour;
    by Vendor;
    if First.Vendor then VendorBookings = 0;
    VendorBookings + NumberOfBookings;
    if Last.Vendor;
run;

proc print data=totalby;
    title 'Total Bookings by Vendor';
run;
```

The following output displays the results:

Output 12.5 Putting Totals for Each BY Group in a New Data Set

```
                    Total Bookings by Vendor                        1

                                        Vendor
                    Obs    Vendor      Bookings

                     1     Express        58
                     2     Southsea       16
                     3     World          52
```

Writing to Separate Data Sets

Writing Observations to Separate Data Sets

Tradewinds Travel wants overall information about the tours that were conducted this year. One SAS data set is needed to contain detailed information about each tour, including the total money that was spent on that tour. Another SAS data set is needed to contain the total number of bookings with each vendor and the total money spent with that vendor. Both of these data sets can be created using the techniques that you have learned so far.

Begin the program by creating two SAS data sets from the SAS data set MYLIB.SORTTOUR using the following DATA and SET statements:

```
data tourdetails vendordetails;
    set mylib.sorttour;
```

The data set TOURDETAILS will contain the individual records, and VENDORDETAILS will contain the information about vendors. The observations do not need to be grouped for TOURDETAILS, but they need to be grouped by Vendor for VENDORDETAILS.

If the data are not already grouped by Vendor, first use the SORT procedure. Add a BY statement to the DATA step for use with VENDORDETAILS.

```
proc sort   data=mylib.tourrevenue out=mylib.sorttour;
    by Vendor;
run;

data tourdetails vendordetails;
```

```
   set mylib.sorttour;
   by Vendor;
run;
```

The only calculation that is needed for the individual tours is the amount of money that was spent on each tour. Therefore, calculate the amount in an assignment statement and write the record to TOURDETAILS.

```
Money = LandCost * NumberOfBookings;
output tourdetails;
```

The portion of the DATA step that builds TOURDETAILS is now complete.

Writing Totals to Separate Data Sets

Because observations remain in the program data vector after an OUTPUT statement executes, you can continue using them in programming statements. The rest of the DATA step creates information for the VENDORDETAILS data set.

Use the FIRST.Vendor variable to determine when SAS is processing the first observation in each group.

Then set the sum variables VendorBookings and VendorMoney to 0 in that observation. VendorBookings totals the bookings for each vendor, and VendorMoney totals the costs. Add the following statements to the DATA step:

```
if First.Vendor then
   do;
      VendorBookings = 0;
      VendorMoney = 0;
   end;
 VendorBookings + NumberOfBookings;
 VendorMoney + Money;
```

Note: The program uses a DO group. Using DO groups enables the program to evaluate a condition once and take more than one action as a result. For more information on DO groups, see "Performing More Than One Action in an IF-THEN Statement" on page 202. △

The last observation in each BY group contains the totals for that vendor; therefore, use the following statement to output the last observation to the data set VENDORDETAILS:

```
if Last.Vendor then output vendordetails;
```

As a final step, use KEEP= and DROP= data set options to remove extraneous variables from the two data sets so that each data set has just the variables that are wanted.

```
data tourdetails(drop=VendorBookings VendorMoney)
     vendordetails(keep=Vendor VendorBookings VendorMoney);
```

The Program

The following is the complete program that creates the VENDORDETAILS and TOURDETAILS data sets:

```
options pagesize=60 linesize=80 pageno=1 nodate;
```

```
proc sort data=mylib.tourrevenue out=mylib.sorttour;
   by Vendor;
run;

data tourdetails(drop=VendorBookings VendorMoney)
     vendordetails(keep=Vendor VendorBookings VendorMoney);
   set mylib.sorttour;
   by Vendor;
   Money = LandCost * NumberOfBookings;
   output tourdetails;
   if First.Vendor then
      do;
         VendorBookings = 0;
         VendorMoney = 0;
      end;
   VendorBookings + NumberOfBookings;
   VendorMoney + Money;
   if Last.Vendor then output vendordetails;
run;

proc print data=tourdetails;
   title 'Detail Records: Dollars Spent on Individual Tours';
run;

proc print data=vendordetails;
   title 'Vendor Totals: Dollars Spent and Bookings by Vendor';
run;
```

The following output displays the results:

Output 12.6   Detail Tour Records in One SAS Data Set and Vendor Totals in Another

```
                Detail Records: Dollars Spent on Individual Tours                1

                                            Number
                              Land            Of
        Obs    Country        Cost   Vendor   Bookings   Money

          1    France          575   Express      10      5750
          2    India           489   Express       .         .
          3    Japan           720   Express      10      7200
          4    Greece          698   Express      20     13960
          5    Italy           468   Express       9      4212
          6    Ireland         558   Express       9      5022
          7    New Zealand    1489   Southsea      6      8934
          8    Australia      1079   Southsea     10     10790
          9    Spain           510   World        12      6120
         10    Brazil          540   World         6      3240
         11    Venezuela       425   World         8      3400
         12    USSR            924   World         6      5544
         13    Switzerland     734   World        20     14680
```

```
            Vendor Totals: Dollars Spent and Bookings by Vendor            2

                                  Vendor      Vendor
                 Obs    Vendor    Bookings    Money

                  1     Express      58        36144
                  2     Southsea     16        19724
                  3     World        52        32984
```

Using a Value in a Later Observation

A further requirement of Tradewinds Travel is a separate SAS data set that contains the tour that generated the most revenue. (The revenue total comes from the price of the tour multiplied by the number of bookings.) One method of creating the new data set might be to follow these three steps:

1 Calculate the revenue in a DATA step.

2 Sort the data set in descending order by the revenue.

3 Use another DATA step with the OBS= data set option to write that observation.

A more efficient method compares the revenue from all observations in a single DATA step. SAS can retain a value from the current observation to use in future observations. When the processing of the DATA step reaches the next observation, the held value represents information from the previous observation.

The RETAIN statement causes a variable that is created in the DATA step to retain its value from the current observation into the next observation rather than being set to missing at the beginning of each iteration of the DATA step. It is a declarative statement, not an executable statement. This statement has the following form:

RETAIN *variable-1 < . . . variable-n>*;

To compare the Revenue value in one observation to the Revenue value in the next observation, create a retained variable named HoldRevenue and assign the value of the current Revenue variable to it. In the next observation, the HoldRevenue variable contains the Revenue value from the previous observation, and its value can be compared to that of Revenue in the current observation.

To see how the RETAIN statement works, look at the next example. The following DATA step outputs observations to data set TEMP before SAS assigns the current revenue to HoldRevenue:

```
options pagesize=60 linesize=80 pageno=1 nodate;
data temp;
   set mylib.tourrevenue;
   retain HoldRevenue;
   Revenue = LandCost * NumberOfBookings;
   output;
   HoldRevenue = Revenue;
run;

proc print data=temp;
   var Country LandCost NumberOfBookings Revenue HoldRevenue;
   title 'Tour Revenue';
run;
```

The following output displays the results:

Output 12.7 Retaining a Value By Using the Retain Statement

```
                              Tour Revenue                                1

                                   Number
                            Land      Of              Hold
        Obs    Country      Cost   Bookings  Revenue  Revenue

         1     France       575      10       5750       .
         2     Spain        510      12       6120      5750
         3     Brazil       540       6       3240      6120
         4     India        489       .         .       3240
         5     Japan        720      10       7200       .
         6     Greece       698      20      13960      7200
         7     New Zealand 1489       6       8934     13960
         8     Venezuela    425       8       3400      8934
         9     Italy        468       9       4212      3400
        10     USSR         924       6       5544      4212
        11     Switzerland  734      20      14680      5544
        12     Australia   1079      10      10790     14680
        13     Ireland      558       9       5022     10790
```

The value of HoldRevenue is missing at the beginning of the first observation; it is still missing when the OUTPUT statement writes the first observation to TEMP. After the OUTPUT statement, an assignment statement assigns the value of Revenue to HoldRevenue. Because HoldRevenue is retained, that value is present at the beginning of the next iteration of the DATA step. When the OUTPUT statement executes again, the value of HoldRevenue still contains that value.

To find the largest value of Revenue, assign the value of Revenue to HoldRevenue only when Revenue is larger than HoldRevenue, as shown in the following program:

```
options pagesize=60 linesize=80 pageno=1 nodate;
data mostrevenue;
   set mylib.tourrevenue;
   retain HoldRevenue;
   Revenue = LandCost * NumberOfBookings;
   if Revenue > HoldRevenue then HoldRevenue = Revenue;
run;

proc print data=mostrevenue;
   var Country LandCost NumberOfBookings Revenue HoldRevenue;
   title 'Tour Revenue';
run;
```

The following output displays the results:

Output 12.8   Holding the Largest Value in a Retained Variable

```
                            Tour Revenue                               1

                            Number
                   Land       Of                   Hold
    Obs   Country  Cost    Bookings    Revenue    Revenue

     1    France    575       10        5750       5750
     2    Spain     510       12        6120       6120
     3    Brazil    540        6        3240       6120
     4    India     489        .          .        6120
     5    Japan     720       10        7200       7200
     6    Greece    698       20       13960      13960
     7    New Zealand 1489     6        8934      13960
     8    Venezuela 425        8        3400      13960
     9    Italy     468        9        4212      13960
    10    USSR      924        6        5544      13960
    11    Switzerland 734     20       14680      14680
    12    Australia 1079      10       10790      14680
    13    Ireland   558        9        5022      14680
```

The value of HoldRevenue in the last observation represents the largest revenue that is generated by any tour. To determine which observation the value came from, create a variable named HoldCountry to hold the name of the country from the observations with the largest revenue. Include HoldCountry in the RETAIN statement to retain its value until explicitly changed. Then use the END= data set option to select the last observation, and use the KEEP= data set option to keep only HoldRevenue and HoldCountry in MOSTREVENUE.

```
options pagesize=60 linesize=80 pageno=1 nodate;
data mostrevenue (keep=HoldCountry HoldRevenue);
   set mylib.tourrevenue  end=LastOne;
   retain HoldRevenue HoldCountry;
   Revenue = LandCost * NumberOfBookings;
   if Revenue > HoldRevenue then
      do;
         HoldRevenue = Revenue;
         HoldCountry = Country;
      end;
   if LastOne;
run;
proc print data=mostrevenue;
   title 'Country with the Largest Value of Revenue';
run;
```

Note: The program uses a DO group. Using DO groups enables the program to evaluate a condition once and take more than one action as a result. For more information on DO groups, see "Performing More Than One Action in an IF-THEN Statement" on page 202. △

The following output displays the results:

Output 12.9 Selecting a New Data Set Using RETAIN and Subsetting IF Statements

```
                   Country with the Largest Value of Revenue                    1

                              Hold
                   Obs       Revenue     HoldCountry

                    1        14680       Switzerland
```

Review of SAS Tools

Statements

RETAIN *variable-1 < . . . variable-n>*;
> retains the value of the *variable* for use in a subsequent observation. The RETAIN statement prevents the value of the variable from being reinitialized to missing when control returns to the top of the DATA step.
>
> The RETAIN statement affects variables that are created in the current DATA step (for example, variables that are created with an INPUT or assignment statement). Variables that are read with a SET, MERGE, or UPDATE statement are retained automatically; naming them in a RETAIN statement has no effect.
>
> The RETAIN statement can assign an initial value to a variable. If you need a variable to have the same value in all observations of a DATA step, it is more efficient to put the value in a RETAIN statement rather than in an assignment statement. SAS assigns the value in the RETAIN statement when it is compiling the DATA step, but it carries out the assignment statement during each execution of the DATA step.
>
> The plus sign is required in the sum statement; to subtract successive values from a starting value, add negative values to the sum variable.

SET *SAS-data-set <END=variable>*;
> reads from the *SAS-data-set* specified. The *variable* specified in the END= option has the value 0 until SAS is processing the last observation in the data set. Then the variable has the value 1. SAS does not include the END= variable in the data set that is being created.

variable + expression;
> is called a sum statement; it adds the result of the *expression* on the right side of the plus sign to the *variable* on the left side of the plus sign and holds the new value of *variable* for use in subsequent observations. The expression can be a numeric variable or expression. The value of *variable* is retained. If the expression is a missing value, the variable maintains its previous value. Before the sum statement is executed for the first time, the default value of the variable is 0.
>
> The plus sign is required in the sum statement; to subtract successive values from a starting value, add negative values to the sum variable.

Learning More

Automatic variable _N_
  The automatic variable _N_, which provides a way to count the number of times
  SAS executes a DATA step, is discussed in Chapter 30, "Writing Lines to the SAS
  Log or to an Output File," on page 517. Using _N_ is more efficient than using a
  sum statement. SAS creates _N_ in each DATA step. The first time SAS begins to
  execute the DATA step, the value of _N_ is 1; the second time, 2; and so on. SAS
  does not add _N_ to the output data set.

DO groups
  information about DO groups can be found in Chapter 13, "Finding Shortcuts in
  Programming," on page 201.

END= option
  Another example of using the END= option in the SET statement is presented in
  Chapter 21, "Conditionally Processing Observations from Multiple SAS Data Sets,"
  on page 321.

KEEP= and DROP= data set options
  see Chapter 5, "Starting with SAS Data Sets," on page 81.

LAG family of functions
  See *SAS Language Reference: Dictionary*. LAG functions provide another way to
  retain a value from one observation for use in a subsequent observation. LAG
  functions can retain a value for up to 100 observations.

RETAIN, SUM, and SET statements
  See *SAS Language Reference: Dictionary*.

SUM and SUMBY statements
  The SUM and SUMBY statements in the PRINT procedure are discussed in
  Chapter 25, "Producing Detail Reports with the PRINT Procedure," on page 367.
  The SUM and SUMBY statements can be used in the PRINT procedure if the only
  purpose in getting a total is to display it in a report.

SUMMARY and MEANS procedures
  The SUMMARY and MEANS procedures, which can also be used to compute totals
  are documented in *SAS Procedures Guide*.

CHAPTER

13

Finding Shortcuts in Programming

Introduction

Purpose

In this chapter you will learn two DATA step programming techniques that make the code easier to write and read. They are

□ using a DO group to perform more than one action after evaluating an IF condition

□ using arrays to perform the same action on more than one variable with a single group of statements.

Prerequisites

You should understand the topics presented in Chapter 6, "Understanding DATA Step Processing," on page 97 and Chapter 9, "Acting on Selected Observations," on page 139 before proceeding with this chapter.

Input File and SAS Data Set

In the following example, Tradewinds Travel is making adjustments to their data about tours to art museums and galleries. The data for the tours is as follows:

❶   **❷ ❸❹ ❺**   **❻**
Rome   4 3 . D'Amico 2

```
Paris       5 . 1 Lucas    5
London      3 2 . Wilson   3
New York    5 1 2 Lucas    5
Madrid      . . 5 Torres   4
Amsterdam 3 3 .            .
```

The numbered fields represent

❶ the name of the city

❷ the number of museums to be visited

❸ the number of art galleries in the tour

❹ the number of other attractions to be toured

❺ the last name of the tour guide

❻ the number of years of experience the guide has.

The following program creates the permanent SAS data set MYLIB.ATTRACTIONS:

```
options pagesize=60 linesize=80 pageno=1 nodate;
libname mylib 'permanent-data-library';


data mylib.attractions;
   infile 'input-file';
   input City $ 1-9 Museums 11 Galleries 13
         Other 15 TourGuide $ 17-24 YearsExperience 26;
run;


proc print data=mylib.attractions;
   title 'Data Set MYLIB.ATTRACTIONS';
run;
```

The PROC PRINT statement that follows the DATA step produces this report of the MYLIB.ATTRACTIONS data set:

Output 13.1   Data Set MYLIB.ATTRACTIONS

```
                    Data Set MYLIB.ATTRACTIONS                         1

                                                   Tour      Years
     Obs    City      Museums   Galleries   Other  Guide     Experience

      1     Rome         4          3         .    D'Amico      2
      2     Paris        5          .         1    Lucas        5
      3     London       3          2         .    Wilson       3
      4     New York     5          1         2    Lucas        5
      5     Madrid       .          .         5    Torres       4
      6     Amsterdam    3          3         .                 .
```

Performing More Than One Action in an IF-THEN Statement

Several changes are needed in the observations for Madrid and Amsterdam. One way to select those observations is to evaluate an IF condition in a series of IF-THEN statements, as follows:

```
    /* multiple actions based on the same condition */
data updatedattractions;
   set mylib.attractions;
   if City = 'Madrid' then Museums = 3;
   if City = 'Madrid' then Other = 2;
   if City = 'Amsterdam' then TourGuide = 'Vandever';
   if City = 'Amsterdam' then YearsExperience = 4;
run;
```

To avoid writing the IF condition twice for each city, use a DO group in the THEN clause, for example:

IF *condition* THEN

    DO;

        ...more SAS statements...

    END;

The DO statement causes all statements following it to be treated as a unit until a matching END statement appears. A group of SAS statements that begin with DO and end with END is called a *DO group*.

The following DATA step replaces the multiple IF-THEN statements with DO groups:

```
options pagesize=60 linesize=80 pageno=1 nodate;
    /* a more efficient method */
data updatedattractions2;
   set mylib.attractions;
   if City = 'Madrid' then
      do;
         Museums = 3;
         Other = 2;
      end;
   else if City = 'Amsterdam' then
      do;
         TourGuide = 'Vandever';
         YearsExperience = 4;
      end;
run;


proc print data=updatedattractions2;
   title 'Data Set MYLIB.UPDATEDATTRACTIONS';
run;
```

Output 13.2   Using DO Groups to Produce a Data Set

```
                    Data Set MYLIB.UPDATEDATTRACTIONS                      1

                                                  Tour           Years
    Obs    City       Museums    Galleries    Other    Guide        Experience

     1     Rome          4          3           .      D'Amico          2
     2     Paris         5          .           1      Lucas            5
     3     London        3          2           .      Wilson           3
     4     New York      5          1           2      Lucas            5
     5     Madrid        3          .           2      Torres           4
     6     Amsterdam     3          3           .      Vandever         4
```

Using DO groups makes the program faster to write and easier to read. It also makes the program more efficient for SAS in two ways:

1 The IF condition is evaluated fewer times. (Although there are more statements in this DATA step than in the preceding one, the DO and END statements require very few computer resources.)

2 The conditions `City = 'Madrid'` and `City = 'Amsterdam'` are mutually exclusive, as condensing the multiple IF-THEN statements into two statements reveals. You can make the second IF-THEN statement part of an ELSE statement; therefore, the second IF condition is not evaluated when the first IF condition is true.

Performing the Same Action for a Series of Variables

Using a Series of IF-THEN statements

In the data set MYLIB.ATTRACTIONS, the variables Museums, Galleries, and Other contain missing values when the tour does not feature that kind of attraction. To change the missing values to 0, you can write a series of IF-THEN statements with assignment statements, as the following program illustrates:

```
    /* same action for different variables */
data changes;
    set mylib.attractions;
    if Museums = . then Museums = 0;
    if Galleries = . then Galleries = 0;
    if Other = . then Other = 0;
run;
```

The pattern of action is the same in the three IF-THEN statements; only the variable name is different. To make the program easier to read, you can write SAS statements that perform the same action several times, changing only the variable that is affected. This technique is called *array processing*, and consists of the following three steps:

1 grouping variables into arrays

2 repeating the action

3 selecting the current variable to be acted upon.

Grouping Variables into Arrays

In DATA step programming you can put variables into a temporary group called an *array*. To define an array, use an ARRAY statement. A simple ARRAY statement has the following form:

ARRAY *array-name{number-of-variables}* variable-1 < . . . variable-n>;

The *array-name* is a SAS name that you choose to identify the group of variables. The *number-of-variables*, enclosed in braces, tells SAS how many variables you are grouping, and *variable-1< . . . variable-n>* lists their names.

Note: If you have worked with arrays in other programming languages, note that arrays in SAS are different from those in many other languages. In SAS, an array is simply a convenient way of temporarily identifying a group of variables by assigning an alias to them. It is not a permanent data structure; it exists only for the duration of the DATA step. The *array-name* identifies the array and distinguishes it from any other arrays in the same DATA step; it is not a variable. △

The following ARRAY statement lists the three variables Museums, Galleries, and Other:

```
array changelist{3} Museums Galleries Other;
```

This statement tells SAS to

□ make a group named CHANGELIST for the duration of this DATA step

□ put three variable names in CHANGELIST: Museums, Galleries, and Other.

In addition, by listing a variable in an ARRAY statement, you assign the variable an extra name with the form *array-name {position}*, where *position* is the position of the variable in the list (1, 2, or 3 in this case). The position can be a number, or the name of a variable whose value is the number. This additional name is called an *array reference*, and the position is called the *subscript*. The previous ARRAY statement assigns to Museums the array reference CHANGELIST{1}; Galleries, CHANGELIST{2}; and Other, CHANGELIST{3}. From that point in the DATA step, you can refer to the variable by either its original name or by its array reference. For example, the names Museums and CHANGELIST{1} are equivalent.

Repeating the Action

To tell SAS to perform the same action several times, use an iterative DO loop of the following form:

DO *index-variable*=1 TO *number-of-variables-in-array*;

   ...SAS statements...

END;

An iterative DO loop begins with an iterative DO statement, contains other SAS statements, and ends with an END statement. The loop is processed repeatedly (iterated) according to the directions in the iterative DO statement. The iterative DO statement contains an *index-variable* whose name you choose and whose value changes in each iteration of the loop. In array processing, you usually want the loop to execute as many times as there are variables in the array; therefore, you specify that the values of *index-variable* are 1 TO *number-of-variables-in-array*. By default, SAS increases the value of *index-variable* by 1 before each new iteration of the loop. When the value becomes greater than *number-of-variables-in-array*, SAS stops processing the loop. By default, SAS adds the index variable to the data set that is being created.

An iterative DO loop that processes three times and has an index variable named Count looks like this:

```
do Count = 1 to 3;
   SAS statements
end;
```

The first time the loop is processed, the value of Count is 1; the second time, the value is 2; and the third time, the value is 3. At the beginning of the fourth execution, the value of Count is 4, exceeding the specified range of 1 TO 3. SAS stops processing the loop.

Selecting the Current Variable

Now that you have grouped the variables and you know how many times the loop will be processed, you must tell SAS which variable in the array to use in each iteration of the loop. Recall that variables in an array can be identified by their array references, and that the subscript of the reference can be a variable name as well as a number. Therefore, you can write programming statements in which the index variable of the DO loop is the subscript of the array reference:

array-name {index-variable}

When the value of the index variable changes, the subscript of the array reference (and, therefore, the variable that is referenced) also changes.

The following statement uses the index variable Count as the subscript of array references:

```
if changelist{Count} = . then changelist{Count} = 0;
```

You can place this statement inside an iterative DO loop. When the value of Count is 1, SAS reads the array reference as CHANGELIST{1} and processes the IF-THEN statement on CHANGELIST{1}, that is, Museums. When Count has the value 2 or 3, SAS processes the statement on CHANGELIST{2}, Galleries, or CHANGELIST{3}, Other. The complete iterative DO loop with array references looks like this:

```
do Count = 1 to 3;
    if changelist{Count} = . then changelist{Count} = 0;
end;
```

These statements tell SAS to

□ perform the actions in the loop three times

□ replace the array subscript Count with the current value of Count for each iteration of the IF-THEN statement

□ locate the variable with that array reference and process the IF-THEN statement on that variable.

The following DATA step uses the ARRAY statement and iterative DO loop:

```
options pagesize=60 linesize=80 pageno=1 nodate;
data changes;
    set mylib.attractions;
    array changelist{3} Museums Galleries Other;
    do Count = 1 to 3;
        if changelist{Count} = . then changelist{Count} = 0;
    end;
run;

proc print data=changes;
    title 'Tour Attractions';
run;
```

The following output displays the results:

Output 13.3   Using an Array and an Iterative DO Loop to Produce a Data Set

```
                              Tour Attractions                                    1

                                                    Tour        Years
        Obs   City       Museums   Galleries  Other  Guide    Experience  Count

         1    Rome          4          3        0   D'Amico        2         4
         2    Paris         5          0        1   Lucas          5         4
         3    London        3          2        0   Wilson         3         4
         4    New York      5          1        2   Lucas          5         4
         5    Madrid        0          0        5   Torres         4         4
         6    Amsterdam     3          3        0                  .         4
```

The data set CHANGES shows that the missing values for the variables Museums, Galleries, and Other are now zero. In addition, the data set contains the variable Count with the value 4 (the value that caused processing of the loop to cease in each observation). To exclude Count from the data set, use a DROP= data set option:

```
options pagesize=60 linesize=80 pageno=1 nodate;
data changes2 (drop=Count);
   set mylib.attractions;
   array changelist{3} Museums Galleries Other;
   do Count = 1 to 3;
      if changelist{Count} = . then changelist{count} = 0;
   end;
run;


proc print data=changes2;
   title 'Tour Attractions';
run;
```

The following output displays the results:

Output 13.4   Dropping the Index Variable from a Data Set

```
                              Tour Attractions                                    1

                                                    Tour        Years
        Obs   City       Museums   Galleries  Other  Guide    Experience

         1    Rome          4          3        0   D'Amico        2
         2    Paris         5          0        1   Lucas          5
         3    London        3          2        0   Wilson         3
         4    New York      5          1        2   Lucas          5
         5    Madrid        0          0        5   Torres         4
         6    Amsterdam     3          3        0                  .
```

Review of SAS Tools

Statements

ARRAY *array-name{number-of-variables}* variable-1 < . . . variable-n>;

creates a named, ordered list of variables that exists for processing of the current DATA step. The *array-name* must be a valid SAS name. Each *variable* is the name of a variable to be included in the array. *Number-of-variables* is the number of variables listed.

When you place a variable in an array, the variable can also be accessed by *array-name {position}*, where *position* is the position of the variable in the list (from 1 to *number-of-variables*). This way of accessing the variable is called an *array reference*, and the *position* is known as the subscript of the array reference. After you list a variable in an ARRAY statement, programming statements in the same DATA step can use either the original name of the variable or the array reference.

This book uses curly braces around the subscript. Parentheses ( ) are also acceptable, and square brackets [ ] are acceptable on operating environments that support those characters. Refer to the documentation provided by the vendor for your operating environment to determine the supported characters.

DO;
...*SAS statements*...
END;

treats the enclosed *SAS statements* as a unit. A group of statements beginning with DO and ending with END is called a DO group. DO groups usually appear in THEN clauses or ELSE statements.

DO *index-variable*=1 **TO** *number-of-variables-in-array*;
... *SAS statements*...
END;

is known as an iterative DO loop. In each execution of the DATA step, an iterative DO loop is processed repeatedly (is iterated) based on the value of *index-variable*. To create an index variable, simply use a SAS variable name in an iterative DO statement.

When you use iterative DO loops for array processing, the value of *index-variable* usually starts at 1 and increases by 1 before each iteration of the loop. When the value becomes greater than the *number-of-variables-in-array* (usually the number of variables in the array being processed), SAS stops processing the loop and proceeds to the next statement in the DATA step.

In array processing, the SAS statements in an iterative DO loop usually contain array references whose subscript is the name of the index variable (as in *array-name {index-variable}*). In each iteration of the loop, SAS replaces the subscript in the reference with the index variable's current value. Therefore, successive iterations of the loop cause SAS to process the statements on the first variable in the array, then on the second variable, and so on.

Learning More

Arrays
Detailed information about using arrays can be found in *SAS Language Reference: Concepts*. Arrays can be single or multidimensional.

DO groups
information about DO groups and iterative DO loops can be found in *SAS Language Reference: Dictionary*.

Iterative DO statements are flexible and powerful; they are useful in many situations other than array processing. The range of the index variable can start and stop with any number, and the increment can be any positive or negative number. The range of the index variable can be given as starting and stopping values; the values of the DIM, LBOUND, and HBOUND functions; a list of values separated by commas; or a combination of these. A range can also contain a WHILE or UNTIL clause. The index variable can also be a character variable (in that case, the range must be given as a list of character values). The DIM, LBOUND, and HBOUND functions are documented in *SAS Language Reference: Dictionary*.

DO WHILE and DO UNTIL statements
A DO WHILE statement processes a loop as long as a condition is true; a DO UNTIL statement processes a loop until a condition is true. (A DO UNTIL loop always processes at least once; a DO WHILE loop is not processed at all if the condition is initially false.) For more information, see *SAS Language Reference: Dictionary*.

Working with Dates in the SAS System

Introduction

Purpose

SAS stores dates as single, unique numbers so that they can be used in programs like any other numeric variable. In this chapter you will learn how to

☐ make SAS read dates in raw data files and store them as SAS date values

□ indicate which calendar form SAS should use to display SAS date values

□ calculate with dates, that is, determine the number of days between dates, find the day of the week on which a date falls, and use today's date in calculations.

Prerequisites

You should understand the following topics before proceeding with this chapter:

□ Chapter 6, "Understanding DATA Step Processing," on page 97

□ Chapter 10, "Creating Subsets of Observations," on page 159

□ Chapter 11, "Working with Grouped or Sorted Observations," on page 173.

Understanding How SAS Handles Dates

How SAS Stores Date Values

Dates are written in many different ways. Some dates contain only numbers, while others contain various combinations of numbers, letters, and characters. For example, all the following forms represent the date July 26, 2000:

072600	26JUL00	002607
7/26/00	26JUL2000	July 26, 2000

With so many different forms of dates, there must be some common ground, a way to store dates and use them in calculations, regardless of how dates are entered or displayed.

The common ground that SAS uses to represent dates is called a *SAS date value*. No matter which form you use to write a date, SAS can convert and store that date as the number of days between January 1, 1960, and the date that you enter. The following figure shows some dates written in calendar form and as SAS date values:

Figure 14.1   Comparing Calendar Dates to SAS Date Values

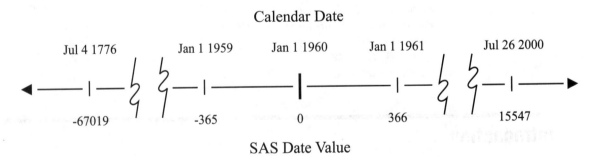

In SAS, every date is a unique number on a number line. Dates before January 1, 1960, are negative numbers; those after January 1, 1960, are positive. Because SAS date values are numeric variables, you can sort them easily, determine time intervals, and use dates as constants, as arguments in SAS functions, or in calculations.

Note: SAS date values are valid for dates based on the Gregorian calendar from A.D. 1582 through A.D. 19,900. Use caution when working with historical dates. Although the Gregorian calendar was used throughout most of Europe from 1582, Great Britain and the American colonies did not adopt the calendar until 1752. △

Determining the Century for Dates with Two-Digit Years

If dates in your external data sources or SAS program statements contain two-digit years, then you can determine which century prefix should be assigned to them by using the YEARCUTOFF= system option. The YEARCUTOFF= system option specifies the first year of the 100-year span that is used to determine the century of a two-digit year. Before you use the YEARCUTOFF= system option, examine the dates in your data:

☐ If the dates in your data fall within a 100-year span, then you can use the YEARCUTOFF= system option.

☐ If the dates in your data do not fall within a 100-year span, then you must either convert the two-digit years to four-digit years or use a DATA step with conditional logic to assign the proper century prefix.

After you have determined that the YEARCUTOFF= system option is appropriate for your range of data, you can determine the setting to use. The best setting for YEARCUTOFF= is the year before the lowest year in your data. For example, if you have data in a range from 1921 to 2001, then set YEARCUTOFF= to 1920, if that is not already your system default. The result of setting YEARCUTOFF= to 1920 is that

☐ SAS interprets all two-digit dates in the range of 20 through 99 as 1920 through 1999.

☐ SAS interprets all two-digit dates in the range of 00 through 19 as 2000 through 2019.

With YEARCUTOFF= set to 1920, a two-digit year of 10 would be interpreted as 2010 and a two-digit year of 22 would be interpreted as 1922.

Input File and SAS Data Set for Examples

In the travel industry, some of the most important data about a tour includes dates, when the tour leaves and returns, when payments are due, when refunds are allowed, and so on. Tradewinds Travel has data that contains dates of past and upcoming popular tours as well as the number of nights spent on the tour. The raw data is stored in an external file that looks like this:

```
❶              ❷        ❸
Japan          13may2000 8
Greece         17oct99   12
New Zealand    03feb2001 16
Brazil         28feb2001 8
Venezuela      10nov00   9
Italy          25apr2001 8
USSR           03jun1997 14
Switzerland    14jan2001 9
Australia      24oct98   12
Ireland        27aug2000 7
```

The numbered fields represent

❶ the name of the country toured

❷ the departure date

❸ the number of nights on the tour.

Entering Dates

Understanding Informats for Date Values

In order for SAS to read a value as a SAS date value, you must give it a set of directions called an *informat*. By default, SAS reads numeric variables with a standard numeric informat that does not include letters or special characters. When a field that contains data does not match the standard patterns, you specify the appropriate informat in the INPUT statement.

SAS provides many informats. Four informats that are commonly used to read date values are

MMDDYY8.   reads dates written as *mm/dd/yy*.

MMDDYY10.   reads dates written as *mm/dd/yyyy*.

DATE7.   reads dates in the form *ddMMMyy*.

DATE9.   reads dates in the form *ddMMMyyyy*.

Note that each informat name ends with a period and contains a width specification that tells SAS how many columns to read.

Reading a Date Value

To create a SAS data set for the Tradewinds Travel data, the DATE9. informat is used in the INPUT statement to read the variable DepartureDate.

```
input Country $ 1-11 @13 DepartureDate date9. Nights;
```

Using an informat in the INPUT statement is called *formatted input*. The formatted input in this example contains the following items:

☐ a pointer to indicate the column in which the value begins (@13)

☐ the name of the variable to be read (DepartureDate)

☐ the name of the informat to use (DATE9.).

The following DATA step creates MYLIB.TOURDATES using the DATE9. informat to create SAS date values:

```
options yearcutoff=1920 pagesize=60 linesize=80 pageno=1 nodate;
libname mylib 'permanent-data-library';

data mylib.tourdates;
   infile 'input-file';
   input Country $ 1-11 @13 DepartureDate date9. Nights;
run;

proc print data=mylib.tourdates;
   title 'Tour Departure Dates as SAS Date Values';
run;
```

The following output displays the results:

Output 14.1 Creating SAS Date Values from Calendar Dates

```
                   Tour Departure Dates as SAS Date Values                    1

                                       Departure
                Obs    Country           Date       Nights

                 1     Japan            14743          8
                 2     Greece           14534         12
                 3     New Zealand      15009         16
                 4     Brazil           15034          8
                 5     Venezuela        14924          9
                 6     Italy            15090          8
                 7     Russia           13668         14
                 8     Switzerland      14989          9
                 9     Australia        14176         12
                10     Ireland          14849          7
```

Compare the SAS values of the variable DepartureDate with the values of the raw data shown in the previous section. The data set MYLIB.TOURDATES shows that SAS read the departure dates and created SAS date values. Now you need a way to display the dates in a recognizable form.

Using Good Programming Practices to Read Dates

When reading dates, it is good programming practice to always use the DATE9. or MMDDYY10. informats to be sure that the data is read correctly. If you use the DATE7. or MMDDYY8. informat, then SAS reads only the first two digits of the year. If the data contains four-digit years, then SAS reads the century and not the year.

Consider the Tradewinds Travel external file with both two-digit years and four-digit years:

```
Japan       13may2000  8
Greece      17oct99   12
New Zealand 03feb2001 16
Brazil      28feb2001  8
Venezuela   10nov00    9
Italy       25apr2001  8
USSR        03jun1997 14
Switzerland 14jan2001  9
Australia   24oct98   12
Ireland     27aug2000  7
```

The following DATA step creates a SAS data set MYLIB.TOURDATES7 by using the DATE7. informat:

```
options yearcutoff=1920 pagesize=60 linesize=80 pageno=1 nodate;

data mylib.tourdates7;
   infile 'input-file';
   input Country $ 1-11 @13 DepartureDate date7. Nights;
run;

proc print data=mylib.tourdates7;
   title 'Tour Departure Dates Using the DATE7. Informat';
```

```
      title2 'Displayed as Two-Digit Calendar Dates';
      format DepartureDate date7.;
   run;


   proc print data=mylib.tourdates7;
      title 'Tour Departure Dates Using the DATE7. Informat';
      title2 'Displayed as Four-Digit Calendar Dates';
      format DepartureDate date9.;
   run;
```

The PRINT procedures format DepartureDate using two-digit year (DATE7.) and four-digit year (DATE9.) calendar dates. The following output displays the results:

Output 14.2   Using the Wrong Informat Can Produce Invalid SAS Data Sets

```
                  Tour Departure Dates Using the DATE7. Informat              1
                      Displayed as Two-Digit Calendar Dates


                                         Departure
                  Obs    Country           Date        Nights
                                            ❶            ❷
                   1     Japan            13MAY20         0
                   2     Greece           17OCT99        12
                   3     New Zealand      03FEB20         1
                   4     Brazil           28FEB20         1
                   5     Venezuela        10NOV00         9
                   6     Italy            25APR20         1
                   7     Russia           03JUN19        97
                   8     Switzerland      14JAN20         1
                   9     Australia        24OCT98        12
                  10     Ireland          27AUG20         0
```

```
                  Tour Departure Dates Using the DATE7. Informat              2
                     Displayed as Four-Digit Calendar Dates


                                         Departure
                  Obs    Country           Date        Nights
                                            ❸
                   1     Japan            13MAY1920       0
                   2     Greece           17OCT1999      12
                   3     New Zealand      03FEB1920       1
                   4     Brazil           28FEB1920       1
                   5     Venezuela        10NOV2000       9
                   6     Italy            25APR1920       1
                   7     Russia           03JUN2019      97
                   8     Switzerland      14JAN1920       1
                   9     Australia        24OCT1998      12
                  10     Ireland          27AUG1920       0
```

Notice that the four-digit years in the input file do not match the years in MYLIB.TOURDATES7 for observations 1, 3, 4, 6, 7, 8, and 10:

❶ SAS stopped reading the date after seven characters; it read the first two digits, the century, and not the complete four-digit year.

❷ To read the data for the next variable, SAS moved the pointer one column and read the next two numeric characters (the years 00, 01, and 97) as the value for the variable Nights. The data for Nights in the input file was ignored.

❸ When the dates were formatted for four-digit calendar dates, SAS used the YEARCUTOFF= 1920 system option to determine the century for the two-digit year. What was originally 1997 in observation 7 became 2019, and what was originally 2000 and 2001 in observations 1, 3, 4, 6, 8, and 10 became 1920.

Using Dates as Constants

If the tour of Switzerland leaves on January 21, 2001 instead of January 14, then you can use the following assignment statement to make the update:

```
if Country = 'Switzerland' then DepartureDate = '21jan2001'd;
```

The value '21jan2001'D is a *SAS date constant*. To write a SAS date constant, enclose a date in quotation marks in the standard SAS form *ddMMMyyyy* and immediately follow the final quotation mark with the letter D. The D suffix tells SAS to convert the calendar date to a SAS date value. The following DATA step includes the use of the SAS date constant:

```
options pagesize=60 linesize=80 pageno=1 nodate;
data correctdates;
   set mylib.tourdates;
   if Country = 'Switzerland' then DepartureDate = '21jan2001'd;
run;

proc print data=correctdates;
   title 'Corrected Departure Date for Switzerland';
   format DepartureDate date9.;
run;
```

The following output displays the results:

Output 14.3 Changing a Date by Using a SAS Date Constant

```
                  Corrected Departure Date for Switzerland                    1

                                 Departure
          Obs    Country          Date      Nights

           1     Japan          13MAY2000       8
           2     Greece         17OCT1999      12
           3     New Zealand    03FEB2001      16
           4     Brazil         28FEB2001       8
           5     Venezuela      10NOV2000       9
           6     Italy          25APR2001       8
           7     Russia         03JUN1997      14
           8     Switzerland    21JAN2001       9
           9     Australia      24OCT1998      12
          10     Ireland        27AUG2000       7
```

Displaying Dates

Understanding How SAS Displays Values

To understand how to display the departure dates, you need to understand how SAS displays values in general. SAS displays all data values with a set of directions called a *format*. By default, SAS uses a standard numeric format with no commas, letters, or other special notation to display the values of numeric variables. Output 14.1 on page 214 shows that printing SAS date values with the standard numeric format produces numbers that are difficult to recognize. To display these numbers as calendar dates, you need to specify a SAS date format for the variable.

SAS date formats are available for the most common ways of writing calendar dates. The DATE9. format represents dates in the form *ddMMMyyyy*. If you want the month, day, and year to be spelled out, then use the WORDDATE18. format. The WEEKDATE29. format includes the day of the week. There are also formats available for number representations such as the format MMDDYY8., which displays the calendar date in the form *mm/dd/yy*, or the format MMDDYY10., which displays the calendar date in the form *mm/dd/yyyy*. Like informat names, each format name ends with a period and contains a width specification that tells SAS how many columns to use when displaying the date value.

Formatting a Date Value

You tell SAS which format to use by specifying the variable and the format name in a FORMAT statement. The following FORMAT statement assigns the MMDDYY10. format to the variable DepartureDate:

```
format DepartureDate mmddyy10.;
```

In this example, the FORMAT statement contains the following items:

☐ the name of the variable (DepartureDate)

☐ the name of the format to be used (MMDDYY10.)

The following PRINT procedures format the variable DepartureDate in both the two-digit year calendar format and the four-digit year calendar format:

```
options pagesize=60 linesize=80 pageno=1 nodate;
proc print data=mylib.tourdates;
    title 'Departure Dates in Two-Digit Calendar Format';
    format DepartureDate mmddyy8.;
run;

proc print data=mylib.tourdates;
    title 'Departure Dates in Four-Digit Calendar Format';
    format DepartureDate mmddyy10.;
run;
```

The following output displays the results:

Output 14.4 Displaying a Formatted Date Value

```
          Departure Dates in Two-Digit Calendar Format            1

                            Departure
        Obs    Country        Date      Nights

          1    Japan        05/13/00       8
          2    Greece       10/17/99      12
          3    New Zealand  02/03/01      16
          4    Brazil       02/28/01       8
          5    Venezuela    11/10/00       9
          6    Italy        04/25/01       8
          7    Russia       06/03/97      14
          8    Switzerland  01/14/01       9
          9    Australia    10/24/98      12
         10    Ireland      08/27/00       7
```

```
                    Departure Dates in Four-Digit Calendar Format                 2

                                    Departure
            Obs     Country             Date      Nights

              1     Japan           05/13/2000        8
              2     Greece          10/17/1999       12
              3     New Zealand     02/03/2001       16
              4     Brazil          02/28/2001        8
              5     Venezuela       11/10/2000        9
              6     Italy           04/25/2001        8
              7     Russia          06/03/1997       14
              8     Switzerland     01/14/2001        9
              9     Australia       10/24/1998       12
             10     Ireland         08/27/2000        7
```

Placing a FORMAT statement in a PROC step associates the format with the variable only for that step. To associate a format with a variable permanently, use the FORMAT statement in a DATA step.

Assigning Permanent Date Formats to Variables

The next example creates a new permanent SAS data set and assigns the DATE9. format in the DATA step. Now all subsequent procedures and DATA steps that use the variable DepartureDate will use the DATE9. format by default. The PROC CONTENTS step displays the characteristics of the data set MYLIB.TOURDATE.

```
options yearcutoff=1920 pagesize=60 linesize=80 pageno=1 nodate;

data mylib.fmttourdate;
   set mylib.tourdates;
   format DepartureDate date9.;
run;

proc contents data=mylib.fmttourdate nodetails;
run;
```

The following output shows that the DATE9. format is permanently associated with DepartureDate:

Output 14.5   Assigning a Format in a DATA Step

```
                              The SAS System                               1

                            The CONTENTS Procedure

Data Set Name: MYLIB.FMTTOURDATE              Observations:          10
Member Type:   DATA                           Variables:             3
Engine:        V8                             Indexes:               0
Created:       14:15 Friday, November 19, 1999  Observation Length:  32
Last Modified: 14:15 Friday, November 19, 1999  Deleted Observations: 0
Protection:                                   Compressed:            NO
Data Set Type:                                Sorted:                NO
Label:


                    -----Engine/Host Dependent Information-----

Data Set Page Size:        8192
Number of Data Set Pages:  1
First Data Page:           1
Max Obs per Page:          254
Obs in First Data Page:    10
Number of Data Set Repairs: 0
filename:                  /SAS_DATA_LIBRARY/fmttourdate.sas7bdat
Release Created:           8.0001M0
Host Created:              HP-UX
Inode Number:              1498874206
Access Permission:         rw-r--r--
Owner Name:                user01
File Size (bytes):         16384


              -----Alphabetic List of Variables and Attributes-----

          #   Variable        Type    Len    Pos    Format
          ---------------------------------------------------
          1   Country         Char     11     16
          2   DepartureDate   Num       8      0    DATE9.
          3   Nights          Num       8      8
```

Changing Formats Temporarily

If you are preparing a report that requires the date in a different format, then you can override the permanent format by using a FORMAT statement in a PROC step. For example, to display the value for DepartureDate in the data set MYLIB.TOURDATES in the form of *month-name dd, yyyy*, you can issue a FORMAT statement in a PROC PRINT step. The following program specifies the WORDDATE18. format for the variable DepartureDate:

```
options pagesize=60 linesize=80 pageno=1 nodate;
proc print data=mylib.tourdates;
   title 'Tour Departure Dates';
   format DepartureDate worddate18.;
run;
```

The following output displays the results:

Output 14.6 Overriding a Previously Specified Format

```
                           Tour Departure Dates                            1

              Obs    Country           DepartureDate    Nights

               1     Japan              May 13, 2000       8
               2     Greece             October 17, 1999  12
               3     New Zealand        February 3, 2001  16
               4     Brazil             February 28, 2001  8
               5     Venezuela          November 10, 2000  9
               6     Italy              April 25, 2001     8
               7     Russia             June 3, 1997      14
               8     Switzerland        January 14, 2001   9
               9     Australia          October 24, 1998  12
              10     Ireland            August 27, 2000    7
```

The format DATE9. is still permanently assigned to DepartureDate. Calendar dates in the remaining examples are in the form *ddMMMyyyy* unless a FORMAT statement is included in the PROC PRINT step.

Using Dates in Calculations

Sorting Dates

Because SAS date values are numeric variables, you can sort them and use them in calculations. The following example uses the data set MYLIB.TOURDATES to extract other information about the Tradewinds Travel data.

To help determine how frequently tours are scheduled, you can print a report with the tours listed in chronological order. The first step is to specify the following BY statement in a PROC SORT step to tell SAS to arrange the observations in ascending order of the date variable DepartureDate:

```
by DepartureDate;
```

By using a VAR statement in the following PROC PRINT step, you can list the departure date as the first column in the report:

```
options pagesize=60 linesize=80 pageno=1 nodate;
proc sort data=mylib.fmttourdate out=sortdate;
   by DepartureDate;
run;

proc print data=sortdate;
   var DepartureDate Country Nights;
   title 'Departure Dates Listed in Chronological Order';
run;
```

The following output displays the results:

Output 14.7   Sorting by SAS Date Values

```
              Departure Dates Listed in Chronological Order              1

                    Departure
              Obs      Date       Country        Nights

               1     03JUN1997   Russia           14
               2     24OCT1998   Australia        12
               3     17OCT1999   Greece           12
               4     13MAY2000   Japan             8
               5     27AUG2000   Ireland           7
               6     10NOV2000   Venezuela         9
               7     14JAN2001   Switzerland       9
               8     03FEB2001   New Zealand      16
               9     28FEB2001   Brazil            8
              10     25APR2001   Italy             8
```

The observations in the data set SORTDATE are now arranged in chronological order. Note that there are no FORMAT statements in this example, so the dates are displayed in the DATE9. format you assigned to DepartureDate when you created the data set MYLIB.FMTTOURDATE.

Creating New Date Variables

Because you know the departure date and the number of nights spent on each tour, you can calculate the return date for each tour. To start, create a new variable by adding the number of nights to the departure date, as follows:

```
Return = DepartureDate + Nights;
```

The result is a SAS date value for the return date that you can display by assigning it the DATE9. format, as follows:

```
options yearcutoff=1920 pagesize=60 linesize=80 pageno=1 nodate;
data home;
   set mylib.tourdates;
   Return = DepartureDate + Nights;
   format Return date9.;
run;

proc print data=home;
   title 'Dates of Departure and Return';
run;
```

Output 14.8   Adding Days to a Date Value

```
                    Dates of Departure and Return                    1

                        Departure
       Obs   Country       Date     Nights      Return

        1    Japan         14743       8       21MAY2000
        2    Greece        14534      12       29OCT1999
        3    New Zealand   15009      16       19FEB2001
        4    Brazil        15034       8       08MAR2001
        5    Venezuela     14924       9       19NOV2000
        6    Italy         15090       8       03MAY2001
        7    Russia        13668      14       17JUN1997
        8    Switzerland   14989       9       23JAN2001
        9    Australia     14176      12       05NOV1998
       10    Ireland       14849       7       03SEP2000
```

Note that because the variable DepartureDate in the data set MYLIB.TOURDATES has no permanent format, you see a numeric value instead of a readable calendar date for that variable.

Using SAS Date Functions

Finding the Day of the Week

SAS has various functions that produce calendar dates from SAS date values. SAS date functions enable you to do such things as derive partial date information or use the current date in calculations.

If the final payment for a tour is due 30 days before the tour leaves, then the final payment date can be calculated using subtraction; however, Tradewinds Travel is closed on Sundays. If the payment is due on a Sunday, then an additional day must be subtracted to make the payment due on Saturday. The WEEKDAY function, which returns the day of the week as a number from 1 through 7 (Sunday through Saturday) can be used to determine if the return day is a Sunday.

The following statements determine the final payment date by

□ subtracting 30 from the departure date

□ checking the value returned by the WEEKDAY function

□ subtracting an additional day if necessary.

```
DueDate = DepartureDate - 30;
if Weekday(DueDate) = 1 then DueDate = DueDate - 1;
```

Constructing a data set with these statements produces a list of payment due dates. The following program includes these statements and assigns the format WEEKDATE29. to the new variable DueDate:

```
options yearcutoff=1920 pagesize=60 linesize=80 pageno=1 nodate;
data pay;
   set mylib.tourdates;
   DueDate = DepartureDate - 30;
   if Weekday(DueDate) = 1 then DueDate = DueDate - 1;
```

```
        format DueDate weekdate29.;
run;


proc print data=pay;
   var Country DueDate;
   title 'Date and Day of Week Payment Is Due';
run;
```

Output 14.9   Using the WEEKDAY Function

```
                   Date and Day of Week Payment Is Due                        1

        Obs    Country                         DueDate

         1     Japan              Thursday, April 13, 2000
         2     Greece           Friday, September 17, 1999
         3     New Zealand       Thursday, January 4, 2001
         4     Brazil              Monday, January 29, 2001
         5     Venezuela       Wednesday, October 11, 2000
         6     Italy                Monday, March 26, 2001
         7     Russia                 Saturday, May 3, 1997
         8     Switzerland     Friday, December 15, 2000
         9     Australia       Thursday, September 24, 1998
        10     Ireland              Friday, July 28, 2000
```

Calculating a Date from Today

Tradewinds Travel occasionally gets the opportunity to do special advertising promotions. In general, tours that depart more than 90 days from today's date, but less than 180 days from today's date, are advertised. The following figure illustrates the time frame for advertising:

Figure 14.2   Optimum Interval for Advertising Tours Based on Today's Date

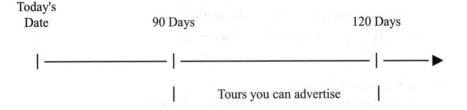

A program is needed that determines which tours leave between 90 and 180 days from the date the program is run, regardless of when you run the program.

The TODAY function produces a SAS date value that corresponds to the date when the program is run. The following statements determine which tours depart at least 90 days from today's date but not more than 180 days from now:

```
Now = today();
if Now + 90 <= DepartureDate <= Now + 180;
```

To print the value that is returned by the TODAY function, this example creates a variable that is equal to the value returned by the TODAY function. This step is not necessary but is used here to clarify the program. You can also use the function as part of the program statement.

```
if today() + 90 <= DepartureDate <= today() + 180;
```

The following program uses the TODAY function to determine which tours to advertise:

```
options yearcutoff=1920 pagesize=60 linesize=80 pageno=1 nodate;
data ads;
   set mylib.tourdates;
   Now = today();
   if Now + 90 <= DepartureDate <= Now + 180;
run;

proc print data=ads;
   title 'Tours Departing between 90 and 180 Days from Today';
   format DepartureDate Now date9.;
run;
```

The following output displays the results:

Output 14.10   Using the Current Date as a SAS Date Value

```
              Tours Departing between 90 and 180 Days from Today              1

                          Departure
        Obs    Country      Date       Nights        Now

         1     Japan      13MAY2000       8        23NOV1999
```

Note that the PROC PRINT step contains a FORMAT statement that temporarily assigns the format DATE9. to the variables DepartureDate and Now.

Comparing Durations and SAS Date Values

You can use SAS date values to find the units of time between dates. Tradewinds Travel was founded on February 8, 1982. On November 23, 1999, you decide to find out how old Tradewinds Travel is, and you write the following program:

```
options yearcutoff=1920 pagesize=60 linesize=80 pageno=1 nodate;
   /* Calculating a duration in days */
data ttage;
   Start = '08feb82'd;
   RightNow = today();
   Age = RightNow - Start;
   format Start RightNow date9.;
run;

proc print data=ttage;
   title 'Age of Tradewinds Travel';
run;
```

Output 14.11   Calculating a Duration in Days

```
                        Age of Tradewinds Travel                        1

               Obs       Start      RightNow      Age

                1      08FEB1982    23NOV1999      6497
```

The value of Age is 6497, a number that looks like an unformatted SAS date value. However, Age is actually the difference between February 8, 1982, and November 23, 1999, and represents a duration in days, not a SAS date value. To make the value of Age more understandable, divide the number of days by 365 (more precisely, 365.25) to produce a duration in years. The following DATA step calculates the age of Tradewinds Travel in years:

```
options yearcutoff=1920 pagesize=60 linesize=80 pageno=1 nodate;
   /* Calculating a duration in years */
data ttage2;
   Start = '08feb82'd;
   RightNow = today();
   AgeInDays = RightNow - Start;
   AgeInYears = AgeInDays / 365.25;
   format AgeInYears 4.1 Start RightNow date9.;
run;

proc print data=ttage2;
   title 'Age in Years of Tradewinds Travel';
 run;
```

The following output displays the results:

Output 14.12   Calculating a Duration in Years

```
                  Age in Years of Tradewinds Travel                       1

                                             Age      Age
                                              In       In
                Obs       Start    RightNow   Days    Years

                 1     08FEB1982   23NOV1999   6497    17.8
```

To show a portion of a year, the value for AgeInYears is assigned a numeric format of 4.1 in the FORMAT statement of the DATA step. The 4 tells SAS that the number contains up to four characters. The 1 tells SAS that the number includes one digit after the decimal point.

Review of SAS Tools

Statements

date-variable='ddMMMyy'D;
> is an assignment statement that tells SAS to convert the date in quotation marks to a SAS date value and assign it to *date-variable*. The SAS date constant *'ddMMMyy'D* specifies a particular date, for example, '23NOV00'D, and can be used in many SAS statements and expressions, not only assignment statements.

FORMAT *date-variable date-format*;
> tells SAS to format the values of the *date-variable* using the *date-format*. A FORMAT statement within a DATA step permanently associates a format with a *date-variable*.

INPUT *date-variable date-informat*;
> tells SAS how to read the values for the *date-variable* from an external file. The *date-informat* is an instruction that tells SAS the form of the date in the external file.

Formats and Informats for Dates

DATE9.
> the form of the *date-variable* is *ddMMMyyyy*, for example 23NOV2000.

DATE7.
> the form of the *date-variable* is *ddMMMyy*, for example 23NOV00.

MMDDYY10.
> the form of the *date-variable* is mm/dd/yyyy, for example, 11/23/2000.

MMDDYY8.
> the form of the *date-variable* is mm/dd/yy, for example, 11/23/00.

WORDDATE18.
> the form of the *date-variable* is *month-name dd, yyyy*, for example, November 23, 2000.

WEEKDATE29.
> the form of the *date-variable* is *day-of-the-week, month-name dd, yyyy*, for example, Thursday, November 23, 2000.

Functions

WEEKDAY (*SAS-date-value*)
> is a function that returns the day of the week on which the *SAS-date-value* falls as a number 1 through 7, with Sunday assigned the value 1.

TODAY()
> is a function that returns a SAS date value corresponding to the date on which the SAS program is initiated.

System Options

YEARCUTOFF=
specifies the first year of a 100-year span that is used by informats and functions to read two-digit years, and used by formats to display two-digit years. The value that is specified in YEARCUTOFF= can result in a range of years that span two centuries. If YEARCUTOFF=1950, then any two-digit value between 50 and 99 inclusive refers to the first half of the 100-year span, which is in the 1900s. Any two-digit value between 00 and 49 inclusive refers to the second half of the 100-year span, which is in the 2000s. YEARCUTOFF= has no effect on existing SAS dates or dates that are read from input data that include a four-digit year.

Learning More

ATTRIB statement
Information about using the ATTRIB statement to assign or change a permanent format can be found in *SAS Language Reference: Dictionary*.

DATASETS procedure
To assign or change a variable to a permanent format see the DATASETS procedure in Chapter 34, "Managing SAS Data Libraries," on page 599.

PUT and INPUT functions
The PUT and INPUT functions can be used for correcting two common errors in working with SAS dates: treating date values that contain letters or symbols as character variables or storing dates written as numbers as ordinary numeric variables. Neither method enables you to use dates in calculations. Information about these functions can be found in *SAS Language Reference: Dictionary*.

SAS date values
Documentation on informats, formats, and functions for working with SAS date values, *SAS time*, and *SAS datetime values* can be found in *SAS Language Reference: Concepts*. This documentation includes the following date and time information:

□ SAS stores a time as the number of seconds since midnight of the current day. For example, 9:30 am. is 34200. A number of this type is known as a SAS time value. A SAS time value is independent of the date; the count begins at 0 each midnight.

□ When a date and a time are both present, SAS stores the value as the number of seconds since midnight, January 1, 1960. For example, 9:30 am, November 23, 2000, is 1290591000. This type of number is known as a SAS datetime value.

□ SAS date and time informats read fields of different widths. SAS date and time formats can display date variables in different ways according to the widths that you specify in the format name. The number at the end of the format or informat name indicates the number of columns that SAS can use. For example, the DATE9. informat reads up to nine columns (as in 23NOV2000). The WEEKDATE8. format displays eight columns, as in

Thursday, and WEEKDATE27. displays 27 columns, as in Thursday, November 23, 2000.

□ SAS provides date, time, and datetime intervals for counting different periods of elapsed time, such as MONTH, which represents an interval from the beginning of one month to the next, not a period of 30 or 31 days.

□ International date, time, and datetime formats.

SYSDATE9

To include the current date in a title, you can use the macro variable SYSDATE9, which is explained in Chapter 25, "Producing Detail Reports with the PRINT Procedure," on page 367.

PART 4

Combining SAS Data Sets

CHAPTER

15

Methods of Combining SAS Data Sets

Introduction

Purpose

SAS provides several different methods for combining SAS data sets. In this chapter, you will be introduced to five methods of combining data sets:

- concatenating
- interleaving
- merging
- updating
- modifying

Subsequent chapters teach you how to use these methods.

Prerequisites

Before continuing with this chapter, you should understand the concepts presented in

- Chapter 2, "Introduction to DATA Step Processing," on page 19
- Chapter 5, "Starting with SAS Data Sets," on page 81
- Chapter 6, "Understanding DATA Step Processing," on page 97.

Definition of Concatenating

Concatenating combines two or more SAS data sets, one after the other, into a single SAS data set. You concatenate data sets using either the SET statement in a DATA step or the APPEND procedure. The following figure shows the results of concatenating two SAS data sets, and the DATA step that produces the results.

Figure 15.1   Concatenating Two SAS Data Sets

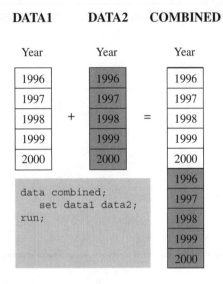

Definition of Interleaving

Interleaving combines individual, sorted SAS data sets into one sorted SAS data set. For each observation, the following figure shows the value of the variable by which the data sets are sorted. (In this example, the data sets are sorted by the variable Year.) You interleave data sets using a SET statement along with a BY statement.

Figure 15.2 Interleaving SAS Data Sets

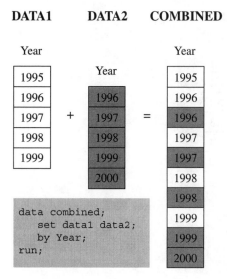

DATA1   DATA2   COMBINED

Definition of Merging

Merging combines observations from two or more SAS data sets into a single observation in a new data set.

A *one-to-one merge*, shown in the following figure, combines observations based on their position in the data sets. You use the MERGE statement for one-to-one merging.

Figure 15.3 One-to-One Merging

DATA1   **DATA2**   **COMBINED**

VarX		VarY		VarX	VarY
X1		Y1		X1	Y1
X2		Y2		X2	Y2
X3	+	Y3	=	X3	Y3
X4		Y4		X4	Y4
X5		Y5		X5	Y5

```
data combined;
   merge data1 data2;
run;
```

A *match-merge*, shown in the following figure, combines observations based on the values of one or more common variables. If you are performing a match-merge, then use the MERGE statement along with a BY statement. (In this example, two data sets are match-merged by the value of the variable Year.)

Figure 15.4   Match-Merging Two SAS Data Sets

DATA1		DATA2		COMBINED		
Year	VarX	Year	VarY	Year	VarX	VarY
1996	X1	1996	Y1	1996	X1	Y1
1997	X2	1996	Y2	1996	X1	Y2
1998	X3	1998	Y3	1997	X2	.
1999	X4	1999	Y4	1998	X3	Y3
2000	X5	2000	Y5	1999	X4	Y4
				2000	X5	Y5

```
data combined;
   merge data1 data2;
   by Year;
run;
```

Definition of Updating

Updating a SAS data set replaces the values of variables in one data set (the master data set) with values from another data set (the transaction data set). If the UPDATEMODE= option in the UPDATE statement is set to MISSINGCHECK, then missing values in a transaction data set do not replace existing values in a master data set. If the UPDATEMODE= option is set to NOMISSINGCHECK, then missing values in a transaction data set replace existing values in a master data set. The default setting is MISSINGCHECK.

You update a data set by using the UPDATE statement along with a BY statement. Both of the input data sets must be sorted by the variable that you use in the BY statement. The following figure shows the results of updating a SAS data set.

Figure 15.5 Updating a Master Data Set

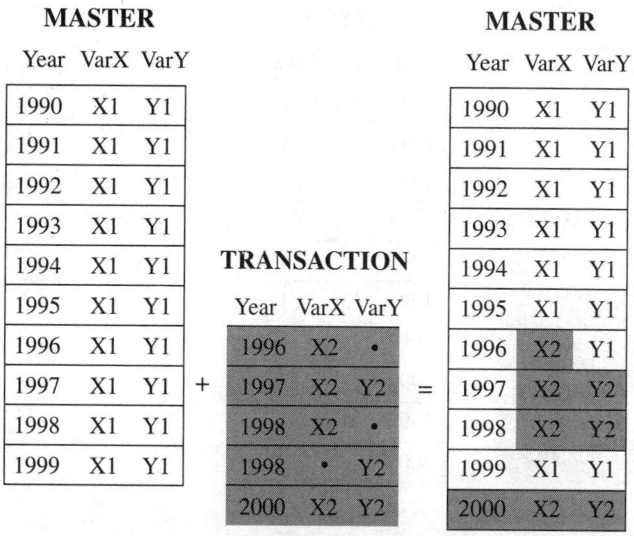

MASTER				TRANSACTION				MASTER		
Year	VarX	VarY		Year	VarX	VarY		Year	VarX	VarY
1990	X1	Y1						1990	X1	Y1
1991	X1	Y1						1991	X1	Y1
1992	X1	Y1						1992	X1	Y1
1993	X1	Y1						1993	X1	Y1
1994	X1	Y1						1994	X1	Y1
1995	X1	Y1						1995	X1	Y1
1996	X1	Y1		1996	X2	•		1996	X2	Y1
1997	X1	Y1	+	1997	X2	Y2	=	1997	X2	Y2
1998	X1	Y1		1998	X2	•		1998	X2	Y2
1999	X1	Y1		1998	•	Y2		1999	X1	Y1
				2000	X2	Y2		2000	X2	Y2

```
data master;
   update master transaction;
   by Year;
run;
```

Definition of Modifying

Modifying a SAS data set replaces, deletes, or appends observations in an existing data set. Modifying a SAS data set is similar to updating a SAS data set, but the following differences exist:

□ Modifying cannot create a new data set, while updating can.

□ Unlike updating, modifying does not require that the master data set or the transaction data set be sorted.

You change an existing file by using the MODIFY statement along with a BY statement. The following figure shows the results.

Figure 15.6   Modifying a Data Set

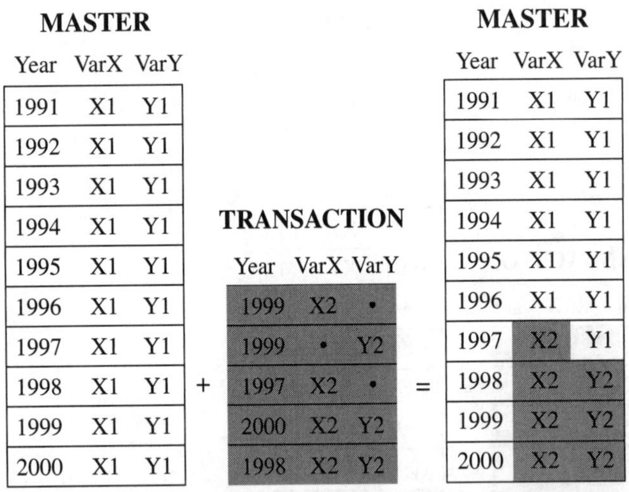

MASTER

Year	VarX	VarY
1991	X1	Y1
1992	X1	Y1
1993	X1	Y1
1994	X1	Y1
1995	X1	Y1
1996	X1	Y1
1997	X1	Y1
1998	X1	Y1
1999	X1	Y1
2000	X1	Y1

TRANSACTION

Year	VarX	VarY
1999	X2	.
1999	.	Y2
1997	X2	.
2000	X2	Y2
1998	X2	Y2

MASTER

Year	VarX	VarY
1991	X1	Y1
1992	X1	Y1
1993	X1	Y1
1994	X1	Y1
1995	X1	Y1
1996	X1	Y1
1997	X2	Y1
1998	X2	Y2
1999	X2	Y2
2000	X2	Y2

```
data master;
   modify master transaction;
   by Year;
run;
```

Comparing Modifying, Merging, and Updating Data Sets

The table that follows summarizes several differences among the MERGE, UPDATE, and MODIFY statements.

Criterion	MERGE	UPDATE	MODIFY
Data sets must be sorted or indexed	Match-merge: Yes One-to-one merge: No	Yes	No
BY values must be unique	No	Master data set: Yes Transaction data set: No	No
Can create or delete variables	Yes	Yes	No

Criterion	MERGE	UPDATE	MODIFY
Number of data sets combined	Any number	2	2
Processing missing values	Overwrites nonmissing values from first data set with missing values from second data set	Default behavior: missing values in the transaction data set do not replace values in the master data set	Depends on the value of the UPDATEMODE= option (see "Handling Missing Values" on page 317) Default: MISSINGCHECK

Learning More

Concatenating data sets
    For more information about concatenating data sets, see Chapter 16, "Concatenating SAS Data Sets," on page 241.

Interleaving data sets
    For more information about interleaving data sets, see Chapter 17, "Interleaving SAS Data Sets," on page 263.

Manipulating data sets
    You can manipulate data sets as you combine them. For example, you can select certain observations from each data set and determine which data set an observation came from. For more information, see Chapter 21, "Conditionally Processing Observations from Multiple SAS Data Sets," on page 321.

MERGE, MODIFY, and UPDATE statements
    For more information about these statements, see the Statements section of *SAS Language Reference: Dictionary*, and the Reading, Combining, and Modifying SAS Data Sets section of *SAS Language Reference: Concepts*.

Merging data sets
    For more information about merging data sets, see Chapter 18, "Merging SAS Data Sets," on page 269.

Modifying data sets
    For more information about modifying data sets, see Chapter 20, "Modifying SAS Data Sets," on page 309, and Chapter 21, "Conditionally Processing Observations from Multiple SAS Data Sets," on page 321.

Updating data sets
    For more information about updating data sets, see Chapter 19, "Updating SAS Data Sets," on page 293.

CHAPTER

16

Concatenating SAS Data Sets

Introduction

Purpose

Concatenating combines two or more SAS data sets, one after the other, into a single data set. The number of observations in the new data set is the sum of the number of observations in the original data sets.

You can concatenate SAS data sets by using

☐ the SET statement in a DATA step

☐ the APPEND procedure.

If the data sets that you concatenate contain the same variables, and each variable has the same attributes in all data sets, then the results of the SET statement and PROC

APPEND are the same. In other cases, the results differ. In this chapter you will learn both of these methods and their differences so that you can decide which one to use.

Prerequisites

Before continuing with this chapter, you should be familiar with the concepts presented in Chapter 5, "Starting with SAS Data Sets," on page 81 through Chapter 8, "Working with Character Variables," on page 119.

Concatenating Data Sets with the SET Statement

Understanding the SET Statement

The SET statement reads observations from one or more SAS data sets and uses them to build a new data set.

The SET statement for concatenating data sets has the following form:

SET *SAS-data-set(s)*;

where

SAS-data-set

is two or more SAS data sets to concatenate. The observations from the first data set that you name in the SET statement appear first in the new data set. The observations from the second data set follow those from the first data set, and so on. The list can contain any number of data sets.

Using the SET Statement: The Simplest Case

In the simplest situation, the data sets that you concatenate contain the same variables (variables with the same name). In addition, the type, length, informat, format, and label of each variable match across all data sets. In this case, SAS copies all observations from the first data set into the new data set, then copies all observations from the second data set into the new data set, and so on. Each observation is an exact copy of the original.

In the following example, a company that uses SAS to maintain personnel records for six separate departments decided to combine all personnel records. Two departments, Sales and Customer Support, store their data in the same form. Each observation in both data sets contains values for these variables:

EmployeeID	is a character variable that contains the employee's identification number.
Name	is a character variable that contains the employee's name in the form last name, comma, first name.
HireDate	is a numeric variable that contains the date the employee was hired. This variable has a format of DATE9.
Salary	is a numeric variable that contains the employee's annual salary in US dollars.
HomePhone	is a character variable that contains the employee's home telephone number.

The following program creates the SAS data sets SALES and CUSTOMER_SUPPORT:

```
options pagesize=60 linesize=80 pageno=1 nodate;

data sales;
   input EmployeeID $ 1-9 Name $ 11-29 @30 HireDate date9.
        Salary HomePhone $;
   format HireDate date9.;
   datalines;
429685482 Martin, Virginia    09aug1990 34800 493-0824
244967839 Singleton, MaryAnn  24apr1995 27900 929-2623
996740216 Leighton, Maurice   16dec1993 32600 933-6908
675443925 Freuler, Carl       15feb1998 29900 493-3993
845729308 Cage, Merce         19oct1992 39800 286-0519
;

proc print data=sales;
   title 'Sales Department Employees';
run;

data customer_support;
    input EmployeeID $ 1-9 Name $ 11-29 @30 HireDate date9.
        Salary HomePhone $;
   format HireDate date9.;
   datalines;
324987451 Sayre, Jay        15nov1994 44800 933-2998
596771321 Tolson, Andrew    18mar1998 41200 929-4800
477562122 Jensen, Helga     01feb1991 47400 286-2816
894724859 Kulenic, Marie    24jun1993 41400 493-1472
988427431 Zweerink, Anna    07jul1995 43700 929-3885
;

proc print data=customer_support;
   title 'Customer Support Department Employees';
run;
```

The following output shows the results of both DATA steps:

Output 16.1 The SALES and the CUSTOMER_SUPPORT Data Sets

```
                          Sales Department Employees                        1

           Employee                                              Home
   Obs        ID        Name              HireDate    Salary    Phone

    1      429685482   Martin, Virginia    09AUG1990   34800   493-0824
    2      244967839   Singleton, MaryAnn  24APR1995   27900   929-2623
    3      996740216   Leighton, Maurice   16DEC1993   32600   933-6908
    4      675443925   Freuler, Carl       15FEB1998   29900   493-3993
    5      845729308   Cage, Merce         19OCT1992   39800   286-0519
```

```
                    Customer Support Department Employees                 2

          Employee                                            Home
   Obs       ID           Name         HireDate    Salary     Phone

    1      324987451    Sayre, Jay      15NOV1994    44800    933-2998
    2      596771321    Tolson, Andrew  18MAR1998    41200    929-4800
    3      477562122    Jensen, Helga   01FEB1991    47400    286-2816
    4      894724859    Kulenic, Marie  24JUN1993    41400    493-1472
    5      988427431    Zweerink, Anna  07JUL1995    43700    929-3885
```

To concatenate the two data sets, list them in the SET statement. Use the PRINT procedure to display the resulting DEPT1_2 data set.

```
options pagesize=60 linesize=80 pageno=1 nodate;

data dept1_2;
   set sales customer_support;
run;

proc print data=dept1_2;
   title 'Employees in Sales and Customer Support Departments';
run;
```

The following output shows the new DEPT1_2 data set. The data set contains all observations from SALES followed by all observations from CUSTOMER_SUPPORT:

Output 16.2   The Concatenated DEPT1_2 Data Set

```
             Employees in Sales and Customer Support Departments       1

          Employee                                            Home
   Obs       ID           Name          HireDate    Salary    Phone

    1      429685482    Martin, Virginia    09AUG1990    34800    493-0824
    2      244967839    Singleton, MaryAnn  24APR1995    27900    929-2623
    3      996740216    Leighton, Maurice   16DEC1993    32600    933-6908
    4      675443925    Freuler, Carl       15FEB1998    29900    493-3993
    5      845729308    Cage, Merce         19OCT1992    39800    286-0519
    6      324987451    Sayre, Jay          15NOV1994    44800    933-2998
    7      596771321    Tolson, Andrew      18MAR1998    41200    929-4800
    8      477562122    Jensen, Helga       01FEB1991    47400    286-2816
    9      894724859    Kulenic, Marie      24JUN1993    41400    493-1472
   10      988427431    Zweerink, Anna      07JUL1995    43700    929-3885
```

Using the SET Statement When Data Sets Contain Different Variables

The two data sets in the previous example contain the same variables, and each variable is defined the same way in both data sets. However, you might want to concatenate data sets when not all variables are common to the data sets that are named in the SET statement. In this case, each observation in the new data set includes all variables from the SAS data sets that are named in the SET statement.

The examples in this section show the SECURITY data set, and the concatenation of this data set to the SALES and the CUSTOMER_SUPPORT data sets. Not all variables are common to the three data sets. The personnel records for the Security department do not include the variable HomePhone, and do include the new variable Gender, which does not appear in the SALES or the CUSTOMER_SUPPORT data sets.

The following program creates the SECURITY data set:

```
options pagesize=60 linesize=80 pageno=1 nodate;

data security;
   input EmployeeID $ 1-9 Name $ 11-29 Gender $ 30
         @32 HireDate date9. Salary;
   format HireDate date9.;
   datalines;
744289612 Saparilas, Theresa F 09may1998 33400
824904032 Brosnihan, Dylan   M 04jan1992 38200
242779184 Chao, Daeyong      M 28sep1995 37500
544382887 Slifkin, Leah      F 24jul1994 45000
933476520 Perry, Marguerite  F 19apr1992 39900
;


proc print data=security;
   title 'Security Department Employees';
run;
```

The following output shows the results:

Output 16.3   The SECURITY Data Set

```
                        Security Department Employees                          1

             Employee
    Obs         ID                Name           Gender    HireDate    Salary

     1       744289612     Saparilas, Theresa       F      09MAY1998    33400
     2       824904032     Brosnihan, Dylan         M      04JAN1992    38200
     3       242779184     Chao, Daeyong            M      28SEP1995    37500
     4       544382887     Slifkin, Leah            F      24JUL1994    45000
     5       933476520     Perry, Marguerite        F      19APR1992    39900
```

The following program concatenates the SALES, CUSTOMER_SUPPORT, and SECURITY data sets, and creates the new data set, DEPT1_3:

```
options pagesize=60 linesize=80 pageno=1 nodate;

data dept1_3;
   set sales customer_support security;
run;


proc print data=dept1_3;
   title 'Employees in Sales, Customer Support,';
   title2 'and Security Departments';
run;
```

The following output shows the results:

Output 16.4   The Concatenated DEPT1_3 Data Set

```
                        Employees in Sales, Customer Support,                    1
                              and Security Departments

           Employee                                            Home
     Obs       ID       Name              HireDate   Salary    Phone      Gender

      1    429685482    Martin, Virginia  09AUG1990   34800   493-0824
      2    244967839    Singleton, MaryAnn 24APR1995  27900   929-2623
      3    996740216    Leighton, Maurice  16DEC1993  32600   933-6908
      4    675443925    Freuler, Carl      15FEB1998  29900   493-3993
      5    845729308    Cage, Merce        19OCT1992  39800   286-0519
      6    324987451    Sayre, Jay         15NOV1994  44800   933-2998
      7    596771321    Tolson, Andrew     18MAR1998  41200   929-4800
      8    477562122    Jensen, Helga      01FEB1991  47400   286-2816
      9    894724859    Kulenic, Marie     24JUN1993  41400   493-1472
     10    988427431    Zweerink, Anna     07JUL1995  43700   929-3885
     11    744289612    Saparilas, Theresa 09MAY1998  33400             F
     12    824904032    Brosnihan, Dylan   04JAN1992  38200             M
     13    242779184    Chao, Daeyong      28SEP1995  37500             M
     14    544382887    Slifkin, Leah      24JUL1994  45000             F
     15    933476520    Perry, Marguerite  19APR1992  39900             F
```

All observations in the data set DEPT1_3 have values for both the variable Gender and the variable HomePhone. Observations from data sets SALES and CUSTOMER_SUPPORT, the data sets that do not contain the variable Gender, have missing values for Gender (indicated by blanks under the variable name). Observations from SECURITY, the data set that does not contain the variable HomePhone, have missing values for HomePhone (indicated by blanks under the variable name).

Using the SET Statement When Variables Have Different Attributes

Understanding Attributes

Each variable in a SAS data set can have as many as six attributes that are associated with it. These attributes are

name
: identifies a variable. That is, when SAS looks at two or more data sets, it considers variables with the same name to be the same variable.

type
: identifies a variable as character or numeric.

length
: refers to the number of bytes that SAS uses to store each of the variable's values in a SAS data set. Length is an especially important consideration when you use character variables, because the default length of character variables is eight bytes. If your data values are greater than eight bytes, then you can use a LENGTH statement to specify the number of bytes of storage that you need so that your data is not truncated.

informat
: refers to the instructions that SAS uses when reading data values. These instructions specify the form of an input value.

format
: refers to the instructions that SAS uses when writing data values. These instructions specify the form of an output value.

label
: refers to descriptive text that is associated with a specific variable.

If the data sets that you name in the SET statement contain variables with the same names and types, then you can concatenate the data sets without modification. However, if variable types differ, then you must modify one or more data sets before concatenating them. When lengths, formats, informats, or labels differ, you might want to modify one or more data sets before proceeding.

Using the SET Statement When Variables Have Different Types

If a variable is defined as a character variable in one data set that is named in the SET statement, and as a numeric variable in another, then SAS issues an error message and does not concatenate the data sets.

In the following example, the Accounting department in the company treats the employee identification number (EmployeeID) as a numeric variable, whereas all other departments treat it as a character variable.

The following program creates the ACCOUNTING data set:

```
options pagesize=60 linesize=80 pageno=1 nodate;

data accounting;
    input EmployeeID 1-9 Name $ 11-29 Gender $ 30
          @32 HireDate date9. Salary;
    format HireDate date9.;
    datalines;
634875680 Gardinski, Barbara F 29may1998 49800
824576630 Robertson, Hannah  F 14mar1995 52700
744826703 Gresham, Jean      F 28apr1992 54000
824447605 Kruize, Ronald     M 23may1994 49200
988674342 Linzer, Fritz      M 23jul1992 50400
;

proc print data=accounting;
    title 'Accounting Department Employees';
run;
```

The following output shows the results:

Output 16.5 The ACCOUNTING Data Set

```
                    Accounting Department Employees                    1

        Employee
 Obs       ID          Name          Gender   HireDate    Salary

  1     634875680   Gardinski, Barbara   F    29MAY1998    49800
  2     824576630   Robertson, Hannah    F    14MAR1995    52700
  3     744826703   Gresham, Jean        F    28APR1992    54000
  4     824447605   Kruize, Ronald       M    23MAY1994    49200
  5     988674342   Linzer, Fritz        M    23JUL1992    50400
```

The following program attempts to concatenate the data sets for all four departments:

```
data dept1_4;
    set sales customer_support security accounting;
run;
```

The program fails because of the difference in variable type among the four departments, and SAS writes the following error message to the log:

```
ERROR: Variable EmployeeID has been defined as both character
       and numeric.
```

Changing the Type of a Variable

One way to correct the error in the previous example is to change the type of the variable EmployeeID in ACCOUNTING from numeric to character. Because performing calculations on employee identification numbers is unlikely, EmployeeID can be a character variable.

To change the type of the variable EmployeeID, you can

- □ re-create the data set, changing the INPUT statement so that it identifies EmployeeID as a character variable
- □ use the PUT function to create a new variable, and data set options to rename and drop variables.

The following program uses the PUT function and data set options to change the variable type of EmployeeID from numeric to character:

```
options pagesize=60 linesize=80 pageno=1 nodate;

data new_accounting (rename=(TempVar=EmployeeID)drop=EmployeeID); ❶
   set accounting; ❷
   TempVar=put(EmployeeID, 9.); ❸
run;

proc datasets library=work; ❹
   contents data=new_accounting;
run;
```

The following list corresponds to the numbered items in the preceding program:

❶ The RENAME= data set option renames the variable TempVar to EmployeeID when SAS writes an observation to the output data set. The DROP= data set option is applied before the RENAME= option. The result is a change in the variable type for EmployeeID from numeric to character.

Note: Although this example creates a new data set called NEW_ACCOUNTING, you can create a data set that has the same name as the data set that is listed on the SET statement. If you do this, then the type attribute for EmployeeID will be permanently altered in the ACCOUNTING data set. △

❷ The SET statement reads observations from the ACCOUNTING data set.

❸ The PUT function converts a numeric value to a character value, and applies a format to the variable EmployeeID. The assignment statement assigns the result of the PUT function to the variable TempVar.

❹ The DATASETS procedure enables you to verify the new attribute type for EmployeeID.

The following output shows a partial listing from PROC DATASETS:

Output 16.6 PROC DATASETS Output for the NEW_ACCOUNTING Data Set

```
         -----Alphabetic List of Variables and Attributes-----

         #     Variable     Type    Len    Pos    Format
         ------------------------------------------------
         5     EmployeeID   Char      9     36
         2     Gender       Char      1     35
         3     HireDate     Num       8      0    DATE9.
         1     Name         Char     19     16
         4     Salary       Num       8      8
```

Now that the types of all variables match, you can easily concatenate all four data sets using the following program:

```
options pagesize=60 linesize=80 pageno=1 nodate;

data dept1_4;
   set sales customer_support security new_accounting;
run;

proc print data=dept1_4;
   title 'Employees in Sales, Customer Support, Security,';
   title2 'and Accounting Departments';
run;
```

The following output shows the results:

Output 16.7 The Concatenated DEPT1_4 Data Set

```
             Employees in Sales, Customer Support, Security,              1
                      and Accounting Departments

        Employee                                            Home
Obs        ID       Name           HireDate   Salary       Phone      Gender

  1     429685482   Martin, Virginia   09AUG1990   34800   493-0824
  2     244967839   Singleton, MaryAnn 24APR1995   27900   929-2623
  3     996740216   Leighton, Maurice  16DEC1993   32600   933-6908
  4     675443925   Freuler, Carl      15FEB1998   29900   493-3993
  5     845729308   Cage, Merce        19OCT1992   39800   286-0519
  6     324987451   Sayre, Jay         15NOV1994   44800   933-2998
  7     596771321   Tolson, Andrew     18MAR1998   41200   929-4800
  8     477562122   Jensen, Helga      01FEB1991   47400   286-2816
  9     894724859   Kulenic, Marie     24JUN1993   41400   493-1472
 10     988427431   Zweerink, Anna     07JUL1995   43700   929-3885
 11     744289612   Saparilas, Theresa 09MAY1998   33400                F
 12     824904032   Brosnihan, Dylan   04JAN1992   38200                M
 13     242779184   Chao, Daeyong      28SEP1995   37500                M
 14     544382887   Slifkin, Leah      24JUL1994   45000                F
 15     933476520   Perry, Marguerite  19APR1992   39900                F
 16     634875680   Gardinski, Barbara 29MAY1998   49800                F
 17     824576630   Robertson, Hannah  14MAR1995   52700                F
 18     744826703   Gresham, Jean      28APR1992   54000                F
 19     824447605   Kruize, Ronald     23MAY1994   49200                M
 20     988674342   Linzer, Fritz      23JUL1992   50400                M
```

Using the SET Statement When Variables Have Different Formats, Informats, or Labels

When you concatenate data sets with the SET statement, the following rules determine which formats, informats, and labels are associated with variables in the new data set.

□ An explicitly defined format, informat, or label overrides a default, regardless of the position of the data sets in the SET statement.

□ If two or more data sets explicitly define different formats, informats, or labels for the same variable, then the variable in the new data set assumes the attribute from the first data set in the SET statement that explicitly defines that attribute.

Returning to the examples, you may have noticed that the DATA steps that created the SALES, CUSTOMER_SUPPORT, SECURITY, and ACCOUNTING data sets use a FORMAT statement to explicitly assign a format of DATE9. to the variable HireDate. Therefore, although HireDate is a numeric variable, it appears in all displays as DDMMMYYYY (for example, 13DEC2000). The SHIPPING data set that is created in the following example, however, uses a format of DATE7. for HireDate. The DATE7. format displays as DDMMMYY (for example, 13DEC00).

In addition, the SALES, CUSTOMER_SUPPORT, SECURITY, and ACCOUNTING data sets contain a default format for Salary, whereas the SHIPPING data set contains an explicitly defined format, COMMA6., for the same variable. The COMMA6. format inserts a comma in the appropriate place when SAS displays the numeric variable Salary.

The following program creates the data set for the Shipping department:

```
options pagesize=60 linesize=80 pageno=1 nodate;


data shipping;
    input employeeID $ 1-9 Name $ 11-29 Gender $ 30
          @32 HireDate date9.
          @42 Salary;
    format HireDate date7.
           Salary comma6.;
    datalines;
688774609 Carlton, Susan      F 28jan1995 29200
922448328 Hoffmann, Gerald    M 12oct1997 27600
544909752 DePuis, David       M 23aug1994 32900
745609821 Hahn, Kenneth       M 23aug1994 33300
634774295 Landau, Jennifer    F 30apr1996 32900
;


proc print data=shipping;
    title 'Shipping Department Employees';
run;
```

The following output shows the results:

Output 16.8 The SHIPPING Data Set

```
                         Shipping Department Employees                          1

              employee                                    Hire
      Obs        ID            Name         Gender         Date      Salary

       1      688774609    Carlton, Susan     F          28JAN95     29,200
       2      922448328    Hoffmann, Gerald   M          12OCT97     27,600
       3      544909752    DePuis, David      M          23AUG94     32,900
       4      745609821    Hahn, Kenneth      M          23AUG94     33,300
       5      634774295    Landau, Jennifer   F          30APR96     32,900
```

Now consider what happens when you concatenate SHIPPING with the previous four data sets.

```
options pagesize=60 linesize=80 pageno=1 nodate;

data dept1_5;
   set sales customer_support security new_accounting shipping;
run;


proc print data=dept1_5;
   title 'Employees in Sales, Customer Support, Security,';
   title2 'Accounting, and Shipping Departments';
run;
```

The following output shows the results:

Output 16.9 The DEPT1_5 Data Set: Concatenation of Five Data Sets

```
                   Employees in Sales, Customer Support, Security,                    1
                         Accounting, and Shipping Departments

           Employee                                           Home
   Obs        ID       Name             HireDate   Salary     Phone      Gender

     1     429685482   Martin, Virginia   09AUG1990  34,800   493-0824
     2     244967839   Singleton, MaryAnn 24APR1995  27,900   929-2623
     3     996740216   Leighton, Maurice  16DEC1993  32,600   933-6908
     4     675443925   Freuler, Carl      15FEB1998  29,900   493-3993
     5     845729308   Cage, Merce        19OCT1992  39,800   286-0519
     6     324987451   Sayre, Jay         15NOV1994  44,800   933-2998
     7     596771321   Tolson, Andrew     18MAR1998  41,200   929-4800
     8     477562122   Jensen, Helga      01FEB1991  47,400   286-2816
     9     894724859   Kulenic, Marie     24JUN1993  41,400   493-1472
    10     988427431   Zweerink, Anna     07JUL1995  43,700   929-3885
    11     744289612   Saparilas, Theresa 09MAY1998  33,400              F
    12     824904032   Brosnihan, Dylan   04JAN1992  38,200              M
    13     242779184   Chao, Daeyong      28SEP1995  37,500              M
    14     544382887   Slifkin, Leah      24JUL1994  45,000              F
    15     933476520   Perry, Marguerite  19APR1992  39,900              F
    16     634875680   Gardinski, Barbara 29MAY1998  49,800              F
    17     824576630   Robertson, Hannah  14MAR1995  52,700              F
    18     744826703   Gresham, Jean      28APR1992  54,000              F
    19     824447605   Kruize, Ronald     23MAY1994  49,200              M
    20     988674342   Linzer, Fritz      23JUL1992  50,400              M
    21     688774609   Carlton, Susan     28JAN1995  29,200              F
    22     922448328   Hoffmann, Gerald   12OCT1997  27,600              M
    23     544909752   DePuis, David      23AUG1994  32,900              M
    24     745609821   Hahn, Kenneth      23AUG1994  33,300              M
    25     634774295   Landau, Jennifer   30APR1996  32,900              F
```

In this concatenation, the input data sets contain the variable HireDate, which was explicitly defined using two different formats. The data sets also contain the variable Salary, which has both a default and an explicit format. You can see from the output that SAS creates the new data set according to the rules mentioned earlier:

- □ In the case of HireDate, SAS uses the format that is defined in the first data set that is named in the SET statement (DATE9. in SALES).
- □ In the case of Salary, SAS uses the explicit format (COMMA6.) that is defined in the SHIPPING data set. In this case, SAS does not use the default format.

Notice the difference if you perform a similar concatenation but reverse the order of the data sets in the SET statement.

```
options pagesize=60 linesize=80 pageno=1 nodate;

data dept5_1;
   set shipping new_accounting security customer_support sales;
run;


proc print data=dept5_1;
   title 'Employees in Shipping, Accounting, Security,';
   title2 'Customer Support, and Sales Departments';
run;
```

The following output shows the results:

Output 16.10   The DEPT5_1 Data Set: Changing the Order of Concatenation

```
                      Employees in Shipping, Accounting, Security,              1
                         Customer Support, and Sales Departments

            employee                                   Hire               Home
    Obs        ID      Name              Gender         Date    Salary     Phone

     1     688774609   Carlton, Susan       F         28JAN95   29,200
     2     922448328   Hoffmann, Gerald     M         12OCT97   27,600
     3     544909752   DePuis, David        M         23AUG94   32,900
     4     745609821   Hahn, Kenneth        M         23AUG94   33,300
     5     634774295   Landau, Jennifer     F         30APR96   32,900
     6     634875680   Gardinski, Barbara   F         29MAY98   49,800
     7     824576630   Robertson, Hannah    F         14MAR95   52,700
     8     744826703   Gresham, Jean        F         28APR92   54,000
     9     824447605   Kruize, Ronald       M         23MAY94   49,200
    10     988674342   Linzer, Fritz        M         23JUL92   50,400
    11     744289612   Saparilas, Theresa   F         09MAY98   33,400
    12     824904032   Brosnihan, Dylan     M         04JAN92   38,200
    13     242779184   Chao, Daeyong        M         28SEP95   37,500
    14     544382887   Slifkin, Leah        F         24JUL94   45,000
    15     933476520   Perry, Marguerite    F         19APR92   39,900
    16     324987451   Sayre, Jay                     15NOV94   44,800   933-2998
    17     596771321   Tolson, Andrew                 18MAR98   41,200   929-4800
    18     477562122   Jensen, Helga                  01FEB91   47,400   286-2816
    19     894724859   Kulenic, Marie                 24JUN93   41,400   493-1472
    20     988427431   Zweerink, Anna                 07JUL95   43,700   929-3885
    21     429685482   Martin, Virginia               09AUG90   34,800   493-0824
    22     244967839   Singleton, MaryAnn             24APR95   27,900   929-2623
    23     996740216   Leighton, Maurice              16DEC93   32,600   933-6908
    24     675443925   Freuler, Carl                  15FEB98   29,900   493-3993
    25     845729308   Cage, Merce                    19OCT92   39,800   286-0519
```

Compared with the output in Output 16.9 on page 252, this example shows that not only does the order of the observations change, but in the case of HireDate, the DATE7. format specified in SHIPPING now prevails because that data set now appears first in the SET statement. The COMMA6. format prevails for the variable Salary because SHIPPING is the only data set that explicitly specifies a format for the variable.

Using the SET Statement When Variables Have Different Lengths

If you use the SET statement to concatenate data sets in which the same variable has different lengths, then the outcome of the concatenation depends on whether the variable is character or numeric. The SET statement determines the length of variables as follows:

- □ For a character or numeric variable, an explicitly defined length overrides a default, regardless of the position of the data sets in the SET statement.
- □ If two or more data sets explicitly define different lengths for the same numeric variable, then the variable in the new data set has the same length as the variable in the data set that appears first in the SET statement.
- □ If the length of a character variable differs among data sets, whether or not the differences are explicit, then the variable in the new data set has the same length as the variable in the data set that appears first in the SET statement.

The following program creates the RESEARCH data set for the sixth department, Research. Notice that the INPUT statement for this data set creates the variable Name with a length of 27; in all other data sets, Name has a length of 19.

```
options pagesize=60 linesize=80 pageno=1 nodate;
```

```
data research;
   input EmployeeID $ 1-9 Name $ 11-37 Gender $ 38
         @40 HireDate date9. Salary;
   format HireDate date9.;
   datalines;
922854076 Schoenberg, Marguerite     F 19nov1994 39800
770434994 Addison-Hardy, Jonathon    M 23feb1992 41400
242784883 McNaughton, Elizabeth      F 24jul1993 45000
377882806 Tharrington, Catherine     F 28sep1994 38600
292450691 Frangipani, Christopher    M 12aug1990 43900
;
```

```
proc print data=research;
   title 'Research Department Employees';
run;
```

The following output shows the results:

Output 16.11   The RESEARCH Data Set

```
                     Research Department Employees                         1

        Employee
 Obs       ID             Name           Gender   HireDate   Salary

  1     922854076   Schoenberg, Marguerite    F    19NOV1994   39800
  2     770434994   Addison-Hardy, Jonathon   M    23FEB1992   41400
  3     242784883   McNaughton, Elizabeth     F    24JUL1993   45000
  4     377882806   Tharrington, Catherine    F    28SEP1994   38600
  5     292450691   Frangipani, Christopher   M    12AUG1990   43900
```

If you concatenate all six data sets, naming RESEARCH in any position except the first in the SET statement, then SAS defines Name with a length of 19.

If you want your program to use the Name variable that has a length of 27, then you have two options. You can

☐ change the order of data sets in the SET statement

☐ change the length of Name in the new data set.

In the first case, list the data set (RESEARCH) that uses the longer length first:

```
data dept6_1;
   set research shipping new_accounting
       security customer_support sales;
run;
```

In the second case, include a LENGTH statement in the DATA step that creates the new data set. If you change the length of a numeric variable, then the LENGTH statement can appear anywhere in the DATA step. However, if you change the length of a character variable, then the LENGTH statement must precede the SET statement.

The following program creates the data set DEPT1_6A. The LENGTH statement gives the character variable Name a length of 27, even though the first data set in the SET statement (SALES) assigns it a length of 19.

```
options pagesize=60 linesize=80 pageno=1 nodate;
```

```
data dept1_6a;
   length Name $ 27;
   set sales customer_support security
      new_accounting shipping research;
run;


proc print data=dept1_6a;
   title 'Employees in All Departments';
run;
```

The following output shows that all values of Name are complete. Note that the order of the variables in the new data set changes because Name is the first variable encountered in the DATA step.

Output 16.12   The DEPT1_6A Data Set: Effects of Using a LENGTH Statement

```
                        Employees in All Departments                        1

                          Employee                      Home
    Obs   Name               ID      HireDate  Salary    Phone     Gender

     1    Martin, Virginia        429685482  09AUG1990  34,800   493-0824
     2    Singleton, MaryAnn      244967839  24APR1995  27,900   929-2623
     3    Leighton, Maurice       996740216  16DEC1993  32,600   933-6908
     4    Freuler, Carl           675443925  15FEB1998  29,900   493-3993
     5    Cage, Merce             845729308  19OCT1992  39,800   286-0519
     6    Sayre, Jay              324987451  15NOV1994  44,800   933-2998
     7    Tolson, Andrew          596771321  18MAR1998  41,200   929-4800
     8    Jensen, Helga           477562122  01FEB1991  47,400   286-2816
     9    Kulenic, Marie          894724859  24JUN1993  41,400   493-1472
    10    Zweerink, Anna          988427431  07JUL1995  43,700   929-3885
    11    Saparilas, Theresa      744289612  09MAY1998  33,400              F
    12    Brosnihan, Dylan        824904032  04JAN1992  38,200              M
    13    Chao, Daeyong           242779184  28SEP1995  37,500              M
    14    Slifkin, Leah           544382887  24JUL1994  45,000              F
    15    Perry, Marguerite       933476520  19APR1992  39,900              F
    16    Gardinski, Barbara      634875680  29MAY1998  49,800              F
    17    Robertson, Hannah       824576630  14MAR1995  52,700              F
    18    Gresham, Jean           744826703  28APR1992  54,000              F
    19    Kruize, Ronald          824447605  23MAY1994  49,200              M
    20    Linzer, Fritz           988674342  23JUL1992  50,400              M
    21    Carlton, Susan          688774609  28JAN1995  29,200              F
    22    Hoffmann, Gerald        922448328  12OCT1997  27,600              M
    23    DePuis, David           544909752  23AUG1994  32,900              M
    24    Hahn, Kenneth           745609821  23AUG1994  33,300              M
    25    Landau, Jennifer        634774295  30APR1996  32,900              F
    26    Schoenberg, Marguerite  922854076  19NOV1994  39,800              F
    27    Addison-Hardy, Jonathon 770434994  23FEB1992  41,400              M
    28    McNaughton, Elizabeth   242784883  24JUL1993  45,000              F
    29    Tharrington, Catherine  377882806  28SEP1994  38,600              F
    30    Frangipani, Christopher 292450691  12AUG1990  43,900              M
```

Concatenating Data Sets Using the APPEND Procedure

Understanding the APPEND Procedure

The APPEND procedure adds the observations from one SAS data set to the end of another SAS data set. PROC APPEND does not process the observations in the first data set. It adds the observations in the second data set directly to the end of the original data set.

The APPEND procedure has the following form:

PROC APPEND BASE=*base-SAS-data-set* <DATA=*SAS-data-set-to-append*>
    <FORCE>;

where

base-SAS-data-set
    names the SAS data set to which you want to append the observations. If this data set does not exist, then SAS creates it. At the completion of PROC APPEND, the value of *base-SAS-data-set* becomes the current (most recently created) SAS data set.

SAS-data-set-to-append
    names the SAS data set that contains the observations to add to the end of the base data set. If you omit this option, then PROC APPEND adds the observations in the current SAS data set to the end of the base data set.

FORCE
    forces PROC APPEND to concatenate the files in some situations in which the procedure would normally fail.

Using the APPEND Procedure: The Simplest Case

The following program appends the data set CUSTOMER_SUPPORT to the data set SALES. Both data sets contain the same variables and each variable has the same attributes in both data sets.

```
options pagesize=60 linesize=80 pageno=1 nodate;

proc append base=sales data=customer_support;
run;

proc print data=sales;
    title 'Employees in Sales and Customer Support Departments';
run;
```

The following output shows the results:

Output 16.13 Output from PROC APPEND

```
            Employees in Sales and Customer Support Departments           1

         Employee                                              Home
 Obs       ID        Name              HireDate    Salary     Phone

   1    429685482    Martin, Virginia   09AUG1990    34800    493-0824
   2    244967839    Singleton, MaryAnn 24APR1995    27900    929-2623
   3    996740216    Leighton, Maurice  16DEC1993    32600    933-6908
   4    675443925    Freuler, Carl      15FEB1998    29900    493-3993
   5    845729308    Cage, Merce        19OCT1992    39800    286-0519
   6    324987451    Sayre, Jay         15NOV1994    44800    933-2998
   7    596771321    Tolson, Andrew     18MAR1998    41200    929-4800
   8    477562122    Jensen, Helga      01FEB1991    47400    286-2816
   9    894724859    Kulenic, Marie     24JUN1993    41400    493-1472
  10    988427431    Zweerink, Anna     07JUL1995    43700    929-3885
```

The resulting data set is identical to the data set that was created by naming SALES and CUSTOMER_SUPPORT in the SET statement (see Output 16.2 on page 244). It is important to realize that PROC APPEND permanently alters the SALES data set, which is the data set for the BASE= option. SALES now contains observations from both the Sales and the Customer Support departments.

Using the APPEND Procedure When Data Sets Contain Different Variables

Recall that the SECURITY data set contains the variable Gender, which is not in the SALES data set, and lacks the variable HomePhone, which is present in the SALES data set. What happens if you try to use PROC APPEND to concatenate data sets that contain different variables?

If you try to append SECURITY to SALES using the following program, then the concatenation fails:

```
proc append base=sales data=security;
run;
```

SAS writes the following messages to the log:

Output 16.14   SAS Log: PROC APPEND Error

```
2    proc append base=sales data=security;
3        run;
NOTE: Appending WORK.SECURITY to WORK.SALES.
WARNING: Variable Gender was not found on BASE file.
WARNING: Variable HomePhone was not found on DATA file.
ERROR: No appending done because of anomalies listed above.
      Use FORCE option to append these files.
NOTE: 0 observations added.
NOTE: The data set WORK.SALES has 5 observations and 5 variables.
NOTE: Statements not processed because of errors noted above.
NOTE: The SAS System stopped processing this step because of errors.
```

You must use the FORCE option with PROC APPEND when the DATA= data set contains a variable that is not in the BASE= data set. If you modify the program to include the FORCE option, then it successfully concatenates the files.

```
options pagesize=60 linesize=80 pageno=1 nodate;

proc append base=sales data=security force;
run;

proc print data=sales;
    title 'Employees in the Sales and the Security Departments';
run;
```

The following output shows the results:

Output 16.15   The SALES Data Set: Using FORCE with PROC APPEND

```
                 Employees in the Sales and the Security Departments              1

             Employee                                                    Home
      Obs       ID          Name                HireDate     Salary      Phone

       1     429685482    Martin, Virginia      09AUG1990    34800     493-0824
       2     244967839    Singleton, MaryAnn    24APR1995    27900     929-2623
       3     996740216    Leighton, Maurice     16DEC1993    32600     933-6908
       4     675443925    Freuler, Carl         15FEB1998    29900     493-3993
       5     845729308    Cage, Merce           19OCT1992    39800     286-0519
       6     744289612    Saparilas, Theresa    09MAY1998    33400
       7     824904032    Brosnihan, Dylan      04JAN1992    38200
       8     242779184    Chao, Daeyong         28SEP1995    37500
       9     544382887    Slifkin, Leah         24JUL1994    45000
      10     933476520    Perry, Marguerite     19APR1992    39900
```

This output illustrates two important points about using PROC APPEND to concatenate data sets with different variables:

- □ If the BASE= data set contains a variable that is not in the DATA= data set (for example, HomePhone), then PROC APPEND concatenates the data sets and assigns a missing value to that variable in the observations that are taken from the DATA= data set.

- □ If the DATA= data set contains a variable that is not in the BASE= data set (for example, Gender), then the FORCE option in PROC APPEND forces the procedure to concatenate the two data sets. But because that variable is not in the descriptor portion of the BASE= data set, the procedure cannot include it in the concatenated data set.

Note: In the current example, each data set contains a variable that is not in the other. It is only the case of a variable in the DATA= data set that is not in the BASE= data set that requires the use of the FORCE option. However, both cases display a warning in the log. △

Using the APPEND Procedure When Variables Have Different Attributes

When you use PROC APPEND with variables that have different attributes, the following applies:

- □ If a variable has different attributes in the BASE= data set than it does in the DATA= data set, then the attributes in the BASE= data set prevail. In the cases of differing formats, informats, and labels, the concatenation succeeds.

- □ If the length of a variable is longer in the BASE= data set than in the DATA= data set, then the concatenation succeeds.

- □ If the length of a variable is longer in the DATA= data set than in the BASE= data set, or if the same variable is a character variable in one data set and a numeric variable in the other, then PROC APPEND fails to concatenate the files unless you specify the FORCE option.

Using the FORCE option has these consequences:

- □ The length that is specified in the BASE= data set prevails. Therefore, SAS truncates values from the DATA= data set to fit them into the length that is specified in the BASE= data set.

□ The type that is specified in the BASE= data set prevails. The procedure replaces values of the wrong type (all values for the variable in the DATA= data set) with missing values.

Choosing between the SET Statement and the APPEND Procedure

If two data sets contain the same variables and the variables possess the same attributes, then the file that results from concatenating them with the SET statement is the same as the file that results from concatenating them with the APPEND procedure. The APPEND procedure concatenates much faster than the SET statement, particularly when the BASE= data set is large, because the APPEND procedure does not process the observations from the BASE= data set. However, the two methods of concatenating are sufficiently different when the variables or their attributes differ between data sets. In this case, you must consider the differences in behavior before you decide which method to use.

The following table summarizes the major differences between using the SET statement and using the APPEND procedure to concatenate files.

Table 16.1   Differences between the SET Statement and the APPEND Procedure

Criterion	SET statement	APPEND procedure
Number of data sets that you can concatenate	Uses any number of data sets.	Uses two data sets.
Handling of data sets that contain different variables	Uses all variables and assigns missing values where appropriate.	Uses all variables in the BASE= data set and assigns missing values to observations from the DATA= data set where appropriate. Requires the FORCE option to concatenate data sets if the DATA= data set contains variables that are not in the BASE= data set. Cannot include variables found only in the DATA= data set when concatenating the data sets.
Handling of different formats, informats, or labels	Uses explicitly defined formats, informats, and labels rather than defaults. If two or more data sets explicitly define the format, informat, or label, then SAS uses the definition from the data set you name first in the SET statement.	Uses formats, informats, and labels from the BASE= data set.

Criterion	SET statement	APPEND procedure
Handling of different variable lengths	If the same variable has a different length in two or more data sets, then SAS uses the length from the data set you name first in the SET statement.	Requires the FORCE option if the length of a variable is longer in the DATA= data set. Truncates the values of the variable to match the length in the BASE= data set.
Handling of different variable types	Does not concatenate the data sets.	Requires the FORCE option to concatenate data sets. Uses the type attribute from the BASE= data set and assigns missing values to the variable in observations from the DATA= data set.

Review of SAS Tools

Statements

LENGTH *variable(s)* <$> *length*;
  specifies the number of bytes that are used for storing variables.

SET *SAS-data-set(s)*;
  reads one or more SAS data sets and creates a single SAS data set that you specify in the DATA statement.

Procedures

PROC APPEND BASE=*base-SAS-data-set* <DATA=*SAS-data-set-to-append*> <FORCE>;
  appends the DATA= data set to the BASE= data set. *base-SAS-data-set* names the SAS data set to which you want to append the observations. If this data set does not exist, then SAS creates it. At the completion of PROC APPEND the base data set becomes the current (most recently created) SAS data set.
  SAS-data-set-to-append names the SAS data set that contains the observations to add to the end of the base data set. If you omit this option, then PROC APPEND adds the observations in the current SAS data set to the end of the base data set. The FORCE option forces PROC APPEND to concatenate the files in situations in which the procedure would otherwise fail.

Learning More

CONTENTS statement
  The CONTENTS statement in the DATASETS procedure displays information about a data set, including the names and attributes of all variables. This

information reveals any problems that you might have when you try to concatenate data sets, and helps you decide whether to use the SET statement or PROC APPEND. For more information about using the CONTENTS statement in the DATASETS procedure, see Chapter 33, "Understanding SAS Data Libraries," on page 591.

END= statement option

enables you to determine when SAS is processing the last observation in the DATA step. For more information about using the END= option in the SET statement, see Chapter 21, "Conditionally Processing Observations from Multiple SAS Data Sets," on page 321.

IN= data set option

enables you to process observations from each data set differently. For more information about using the IN= option in the SET statement, see Chapter 21, "Conditionally Processing Observations from Multiple SAS Data Sets," on page 321.

Variable attributes

For more information about variable attributes, see *SAS Language Reference: Dictionary*.

CHAPTER

17

Interleaving SAS Data Sets

Introduction

Purpose

Interleaving combines individual sorted SAS data sets into one sorted data set. You interleave data sets using a SET statement and a BY statement in a DATA step. The number of observations in the new data set is the sum of the number of observations in the original data sets.

In this chapter, you will learn how to use the BY statement, how to sort data sets to prepare for interleaving, and how to use the SET and BY statements together to interleave observations.

Prerequisites

Before continuing with this chapter, you should be familiar with the concepts presented in Chapter 3, "Starting with Raw Data: The Basics," on page 43 and Chapter 5, "Starting with SAS Data Sets," on page 81.

Understanding BY-Group Processing Concepts

The BY statement specifies the variable or variables by which you want to interleave the data sets. In order to understand interleaving, you must understand BY variables, BY values, and BY groups.

BY variable

is a variable that is named in a BY statement and by which the data is sorted or needs to be sorted.

BY value

is the value of a BY variable.

BY group

is the set of all observations with the same value for a BY variable (when only one BY variable is specified). If you use more than one variable in a BY statement, then a BY group is a group of observations with a unique combination of values for those variables. In discussions of interleaving, BY groups commonly span more than one data set.

Interleaving Data Sets

Preparing to Interleave Data Sets

Before you can interleave data sets, the data must be sorted by the same variable or variables you will use with the BY statement that accompanies your SET statement.

For example, the Research and Development division and the Publications division of a company both maintain data sets containing information about each project currently under way. Each data set includes these variables:

Project   is a unique code that identifies the project.

Department   is the name of a department involved in the project.

Manager   is the last name of the manager from Department.

StaffCount   is the number of people working for Manager on this project.

Senior management for the company wants to combine the data sets by Project so that the new data set shows the resources that both divisions are devoting to each project. Both data sets must be sorted by Project before they can be interleaved.

The program that follows creates and displays the data set RESEARCH_DEVELOPMENT. See Output 17.1 on page 265. Note that the input data is already sorted by Project.

```
data research_development;
   length Department Manager $ 10;
   input Project $ Department $ Manager $ StaffCount;
   datalines;
MP971 Designing Daugherty 10
MP971 Coding Newton 8
MP971 Testing Miller 7
SL827 Designing Ramirez 8
SL827 Coding Cho 10
SL827 Testing Baker 7
WP057 Designing Hascal 11
WP057 Coding Constant 13
WP057 Testing Slivko 10
;
run;
```

```
proc print data=research_development;
   title 'Research and Development Project Staffing';
run;
```

Output 17.1 The RESEARCH_DEVELOPMENT Data Set

```
                  Research and Development Project Staffing                    1

                                                     Staff
            Obs    Department    Manager    Project   Count

             1     Designing     Daugherty   MP971     10
             2     Coding        Newton      MP971      8
             3     Testing       Miller      MP971      7
             4     Designing     Ramirez     SL827      8
             5     Coding        Cho         SL827     10
             6     Testing       Baker       SL827      7
             7     Designing     Hascal      WP057     11
             8     Coding        Constant    WP057     13
             9     Testing       Slivko      WP057     10
```

The following program creates, sorts, and displays the second data set,
PUBLICATIONS. Output 17.2 on page 266 shows the data set sorted by Project.

```
data publications;
   length Department Manager $ 10;
   input Manager $ Department $ Project $ StaffCount;
   datalines;
Cook Writing WP057 5
Deakins Writing SL827 7
Franscombe Editing MP971 4
Henry Editing WP057 3
King Production SL827 5
Krysonski Production WP057 3
Lassiter Graphics SL827 3
Miedema Editing SL827 5
Morard Writing MP971 6
Posey Production MP971 4
Spackle Graphics WP057 2
;
run;
proc sort data=publications;
   by Project;
run;


proc print data=publications;
   title 'Publications Project Staffing';
run;
```

Output 17.2   The PUBLICATIONS Data Set

```
                  Publications Project Staffing                      1
                                                 Staff
          Obs    Department    Manager    Project    Count

           1     Editing       Franscombe   MP971      4
           2     Writing       Morard       MP971      6
           3     Production    Posey        MP971      4
           4     Writing       Deakins      SL827      7
           5     Production    King         SL827      5
           6     Graphics      Lassiter     SL827      3
           7     Editing       Miedema      SL827      5
           8     Writing       Cook         WP057      5
           9     Editing       Henry        WP057      3
          10     Production    Krysonski    WP057      3
          11     Graphics      Spackle      WP057      2
```

Understanding the Interleaving Process

When interleaving, SAS creates a new data set as follows:

1 Before executing the SET statement, SAS reads the descriptor portion of each data set that you name in the SET statement. Then SAS creates a program data vector that, by default, contains all the variables from all data sets as well as any variables created by the DATA step. It sets the value of each variable to missing.

2 It looks at the first BY group in each data set in the SET statement in order to determine which BY group should appear first in the new data set.

3 It copies to the new data set all observations in that BY group from each data set that contains observations in the BY group. It copies from the data sets in the same order as they appear in the SET statement.

4 It looks at the next BY group in each data set to determine which BY group should appear next in the new data set.

5 It sets the value of each variable in the program data vector to missing.

6 It repeats steps 3 through 5 until it has copied all observations to the new data set.

Using the Interleaving Process

The following program uses the SET and BY statements to interleave the data sets RESEARCH_DEVELOPMENT and PUBLICATIONS. Output 17.3 on page 266 shows the new data set.

```
data rnd_pubs;
   set research_development publications;
   by Project;
run;

proc print data=rnd_pubs;
   title 'Project Participation by Research and Development';
   title2 'and Publications Departments';
   title3 'Sorted by Project'
run;
```

Output 17.3 Interleaving the Data Sets

```
            Project Participation by Research and Development          1
                   and Publications Departments
                        Sorted by Project


                                             Staff
         Obs    Department    Manager      Project   Count

          1     Designing     Daugherty     MP971     10
          2     Coding        Newton        MP971      8
          3     Testing       Miller        MP971      7
          4     Editing       Franscombe    MP971      4
          5     Writing       Morard        MP971      6
          6     Production    Posey         MP971      4
          7     Designing     Ramirez       SL827      8
          8     Coding        Cho           SL827     10
          9     Testing       Baker         SL827      7
         10     Writing       Deakins       SL827      7
         11     Production    King          SL827      5
         12     Graphics      Lassiter      SL827      3
         13     Editing       Miedema       SL827      5
         14     Designing     Hascal        WP057     11
         15     Coding        Constant      WP057     13
         16     Testing       Slivko        WP057     10
         17     Writing       Cook          WP057      5
         18     Editing       Henry         WP057      3
         19     Production    Krysonski     WP057      3
         20     Graphics      Spackle       WP057      2
```

The new data set RND_PUBS includes all observations from both data sets. Each BY group in the new data set contains observations from RESEARCH_DEVELOPMENT followed by observations from PUBLICATIONS.

Review of SAS Tools

Statements

SET *SAS-data-set-list*;
BY *variable-list*;
   read multiple sorted SAS data sets and create one sorted SAS data set.
   SAS-data-set-list is a list of the SAS data sets to interleave; *variable-list* contains the names of one or more variables (BY variables) by which to interleave the data sets. All of the data sets must be sorted by the same variable(s) before you can interleave them.

Learning More

Indexes
   You do not need to sort unordered data sets before interleaving them if the data sets have an index on the variable or variables by which you want to interleave.

For more information about indexes, see *SAS Language Reference: Concepts* and the *SAS Procedures Guide*.

Interleaving data sets

For information about interleaving data sets when they contain different variables or when the same variables have different attributes, see Chapter 16, "Concatenating SAS Data Sets," on page 241. The same rules apply to interleaving data sets as to concatenating them.

SORT procedure and the BY statement

See Chapter 11, "Working with Grouped or Sorted Observations," on page 173.

CHAPTER

18

Merging SAS Data Sets

Introduction

Purpose

Merging combines observations from two or more SAS data sets into a single observation in a new SAS data set. The new data set contains all variables from all the original data sets unless you specify otherwise.

In this chapter, you will learn about two types of merging: one-to-one merging and match merging. In *one-to-one merging*, you do not use a BY statement. Observations are combined based on their positions in the input data sets. In *match merging*, you use a BY statement to combine observations from the input data sets based on common values of the variable by which you merge the data sets.

Prerequisites

Before continuing with this chapter, you should be familiar with the concepts presented in Chapter 3, "Starting with Raw Data: The Basics," on page 43 and Chapter 5, "Starting with SAS Data Sets," on page 81.

Understanding the MERGE Statement

You merge data sets using the MERGE statement in a DATA step. The form of the MERGE statement that is used in this chapter is

MERGE *SAS-data-set-list*;

BY *variable-list*;

where

SAS-data-set-list	is the names of two or more SAS data sets to merge. The list may contain any number of data sets.
variable-list	is one or more variables by which to merge the data sets. If you use a BY statement, then the data sets must be sorted by the same BY variables before you can merge them.

One-to-One Merging

Definition

When you use the MERGE statement without a BY statement, SAS combines the first observation in all data sets you name in the MERGE statement into the first observation in the new data set, the second observation in all data sets into the second observation in the new data set, and so on. In a one-to-one merge, the number of observations in the new data set is equal to the number of observations in the largest data set you name in the MERGE statement.

Performing a Simple One-to-One Merge

Input SAS Data Set for Examples

For example, the instructor of a college acting class wants to schedule a conference with each student. One data set, CLASS, contains these variables:

Name is the student's name.

Year is the student's year: first, second, third, or fourth.

Major is the student's area of specialization. This value is always missing for first-year and second-year students, who have not selected a major subject yet.

The following program creates and displays the data set CLASS:

```
data class;
   input Name $ 1-25 Year $ 26-34 Major $ 36-50;
   datalines;
Abbott, Jennifer          first
Carter, Tom               third     Theater
Kirby, Elissa             fourth    Mathematics
Tucker, Rachel            first
Uhl, Roland               second
Wacenske, Maurice         third     Theater
;


proc print data=class;
   title 'Acting Class Roster';
run;
```

The following output displays the data set CLASS:

Output 18.1   The CLASS Data Set

```
                        Acting Class Roster                          1

        Obs    Name                    Year        Major

         1     Abbott, Jennifer        first
         2     Carter, Tom             third       Theater
         3     Kirby, Elissa           fourth      Mathematics
         4     Tucker, Rachel          first
         5     Uhl, Roland             second
         6     Wacenske, Maurice       third       Theater
```

A second data set contains a list of the dates and times the instructor has scheduled conferences and the rooms in which the conferences are to take place. The following program creates and displays the data set TIME_SLOT. Note the use of the date format and informat.

```
data time_slot;
   input Date date9.  @12 Time $ @19 Room $;
   format date date9.;
   datalines;
```

```
14sep2000   10:00   103
14sep2000   10:30   103
14sep2000   11:00   207
15sep2000   10:00   105
15sep2000   10:30   105
17sep2000   11:00   207
;
```

```
proc print data=time_slot;
   title 'Dates, Times, and Locations of Conferences';
run;
```

The following output displays the data set TIME_SLOT:

Output 18.2   The TIME_SLOT Data Set

```
            Dates, Times, and Locations of Conferences                1

            Obs        Date      Time     Room

             1      14SEP2000   10:00     103
             2      14SEP2000   10:30     103
             3      14SEP2000   11:00     207
             4      15SEP2000   10:00     105
             5      15SEP2000   10:30     105
             6      17SEP2000   11:00     207
```

The Program

The following program performs a one-to-one merge of these data sets, assigning a time slot for a conference to each student in the class.

```
data schedule;
   merge class time_slot;
run;
```

```
proc print data=schedule;
   title 'Student Conference Assignments';
run;
```

The following output displays the conference schedule data set:

Output 18.3   One-to-One Merge

```
                    Student Conference Assignments                      1

  Obs   Name              Year       Major           Date     Time   Room

   1   Abbott, Jennifer   first                    14SEP2000  10:00   103
   2   Carter, Tom        third      Theater       14SEP2000  10:30   103
   3   Kirby, Elissa      fourth     Mathematics   14SEP2000  11:00   207
   4   Tucker, Rachel     first                    15SEP2000  10:00   105
   5   Uhl, Roland        second                   15SEP2000  10:30   105
   6   Wacenske, Maurice  third      Theater       17SEP2000  11:00   207
```

Explanation

Output 18.3 on page 272 shows that the new data set combines the first observation from CLASS with the first observation from TIME_SLOT, the second observation from CLASS with the second observation from TIME_SLOT, and so on.

Performing a One-to-One Merge on Data Sets with the Same Variables

Input SAS Data Set for Examples

The previous example illustrates the simplest case of a one-to-one merge: the data sets contain the same number of observations, all variables have unique names, and you want to keep all variables from both data sets in the new data set. This example merges data sets that contain variables with the same names. Also, the second data set in this example contains one more observation than the first data set. Each data set contains data on a separate acting class.

In addition to the data set CLASS, the instructor also uses the data set CLASS2, which contains the same variables as CLASS but one more observation. The following program creates and displays the data set CLASS2:

```
data class2;
   input Name $ 1-25 Year $ 26-34 Major $ 36-50;
   datalines;
Hitchcock-Tyler, Erin     second
Keil, Deborah             third      Theater
Nacewicz, Chester         third      Theater
Norgaard, Rolf            second
Prism, Lindsay            fourth     Anthropology
Singh, Rajiv              second
Wittich, Stefan           third      Physics
;


proc print data=class2;
   title 'Acting Class Roster';
   title2 '(second section)';
run;
```

The following output displays the data set CLASS2:

Output 18.4 The CLASS2 Data Set

```
                        Acting Class Roster                        1
                          (second section)

        Obs    Name                   Year       Major

          1    Hitchcock-Tyler, Erin  second
          2    Keil, Deborah          third      Theater
          3    Nacewicz, Chester      third      Theater
          4    Norgaard, Rolf         second
          5    Prism, Lindsay         fourth     Anthropology
          6    Singh, Rajiv           second
          7    Wittich, Stefan        third      Physics
```

The Program

Instead of scheduling conferences for one class, the instructor wants to schedule acting exercises for pairs of students, one student from each class. The instructor wants to create a data set in which each observation contains the name of one student from each class and the date, time, and location of the exercise. The variables Year and Major should not be in the new data set.

This new data set can be created by merging the data sets CLASS, CLASS2, and TIME_SLOT. Because Year and Major are not wanted in the new data set, the DROP= data set option can be used to drop them. Notice that the data sets CLASS and CLASS2 both contain the variable Name, but the values for Name are different in each data set. To preserve both sets of values, the RENAME= data set option must be used to rename the variable in one of the data sets.

The following program uses these data set options to merge the three data sets:

```
data exercise;
   merge class (drop=Year Major)
         class2 (drop=Year Major rename=(Name=Name2))
         time_slot;
run;

proc print data=exercise;
   title 'Acting Class Exercise Schedule';
run;
```

The following output displays the new data set:

Output 18.5   Merging Three Data Sets

```
                    Acting Class Exercise Schedule                       1

Obs    Name                  Name2                 Date       Time    Room

 1     Abbott, Jennifer      Hitchcock-Tyler, Erin  14SEP2000   10:00   103
 2     Carter, Tom           Keil, Deborah          14SEP2000   10:30   103
 3     Kirby, Elissa         Nacewicz, Chester      14SEP2000   11:00   207
 4     Tucker, Rachel        Norgaard, Rolf         15SEP2000   10:00   105
 5     Uhl, Roland           Prism, Lindsay         15SEP2000   10:30   105
 6     Wacenske, Maurice     Singh, Rajiv           17SEP2000   11:00   207
 7                           Wittich, Stefan            .
```

Explanation

The following steps describe how SAS merges the data sets:

1 Before executing the DATA step, SAS reads the descriptor portion of each data set that you name in the MERGE statement. Then SAS creates a program data vector for the new data set that, by default, contains all the variables from all data sets, as well as variables created by the DATA step. In this case, however, the DROP= data set option excludes the variables Year and Major from the program data vector. The RENAME= data set option adds the variable Name2 to the program data vector. Therefore, the program data vector contains the variables Name, Name2, Date, Time, and Room.

2 SAS sets the value of each variable in the program data vector to missing, as the next figure illustrates.

Figure 18.1 Program Data Vector before Reading from Data Sets

Name	Name2	Date	Time	Room
		.		

3 Next, SAS reads and copies the first observation from each data set into the program data vector (reading the data sets in the same order they appear in the MERGE statement), as the next figure illustrates.

Figure 18.2 Program Data Vector after Reading from Each Data Set

Name	Name2	Date	Time	Room
Abbott, Jennifer		.		

Name	Name2	Date	Time	Room
Abbott, Jennifer	Hitchcock-Tyler, Erin	.		

Name	Name2	Date	Time	Room
Abbott, Jennifer	Hitchcock-Tyler, Erin	14SEP2000	10:00	103

4 After processing the first observation from the last data set and executing any other statements in the DATA step, SAS writes the contents of the program data vector to the new data set. If the DATA step attempts to read past the end of a data set, then the values of all variables from that data set in the program data vector are set to missing.

This behavior has two important consequences:

□ If a variable exists in more than one data set, then the value from the last data set SAS reads is the value that goes into the new data set, even if that value is missing. If you want to keep all the values for like-named variables from different data sets, then you must rename one or more of the variables with the RENAME= data set option so that each variable has a unique name.

□ After SAS processes all observations in a data set, the program data vector and all subsequent observations in the new data set have missing values for the variables unique to that data set. So, as the next figure shows, the program data vector for the last observation in the new data set contains missing values for all variables except Name2.

Figure 18.3 Program Data Vector for the Last Observation

Name	Name2	Date	Time	Room
	Wittich, Stefan	.		

5 SAS continues to merge observations until it has copied all observations from all data sets.

Match-Merging

Definitions

Merging with a BY statement enables you to match observations according to the values of the BY variables that you specify. Before you can perform a match-merge, all data sets must be sorted by the variables that you want to use for the merge.

In order to understand match-merging, you must understand three key concepts:

BY *variable*   is a variable named in a BY statement.

BY *value*   is the value of a BY variable.

BY *group*   is the set of all observations with the same value for the BY variable (if there is only one BY variable). If you use more than one variable in a BY statement, then a BY group is the set of observations with a unique combination of values for those variables. In discussions of match-merging, BY groups commonly span more than one data set.

Input SAS Data Set for Examples

For example, the director of a small repertory theater company, the Little Theatre, maintains company records in two SAS data sets, COMPANY and FINANCE.

Data Set	Variable	Description
COMPANY	Name	player's name
	Age	player's age
	Gender	player's gender
FINANCE	Name	player's name
	IdNumber	player's employee ID number
	Salary	player's annual salary

The following program creates, sorts, and displays COMPANY and FINANCE:

```
data company;
   input Name $ 1-25 Age 27-28 Gender $ 30;
   datalines;
Vincent, Martina          34 F
Phillipon, Marie-Odile    28 F
Gunter, Thomas            27 M
Harbinger, Nicholas       36 M
Benito, Gisela            32 F
Rudelich, Herbert         39 M
```

```
Sirignano, Emily          12 F
Morrison, Michael         32 M
;

proc sort data=company;
   by Name;
run;

data finance;
      input IdNumber $ 1-11 Name $ 13-40 Salary;
   datalines;
074-53-9892 Vincent, Martina         35000
776-84-5391 Phillipon, Marie-Odile   29750
929-75-0218 Gunter, Thomas           27500
446-93-2122 Harbinger, Nicholas      33900
228-88-9649 Benito, Gisela           28000
029-46-9261 Rudelich, Herbert        35000
442-21-8075 Sirignano, Emily         5000
;
proc sort data=finance;
   by Name;
run;


proc print data=company;
   title 'Little Theatre Company Roster';
run;


proc print data=finance;
   title 'Little Theatre Employee Information';
run;
```

The following output displays the data sets. Notice that the FINANCE data set does not contain an observation for Michael Morrison.

Output 18.6   The COMPANY and FINANCE Data Sets

```
                        Little Theatre Company Roster                        1

            Obs    Name                    Age    Gender

             1     Benito, Gisela           32      F
             2     Gunter, Thomas           27      M
             3     Harbinger, Nicholas      36      M
             4     Morrison, Michael        32      M
             5     Phillipon, Marie-Odile   28      F
             6     Rudelich, Herbert        39      M
             7     Sirignano, Emily         12      F
             8     Vincent, Martina         34      F
```

```
                    Little Theatre Employee Information                    2

             Obs      IdNumber      Name                    Salary

              1      228-88-9649   Benito, Gisela           28000
              2      929-75-0218   Gunter, Thomas           27500
              3      446-93-2122   Harbinger, Nicholas      33900
              4      776-84-5391   Phillipon, Marie-Odile   29750
              5      029-46-9261   Rudelich, Herbert        35000
              6      442-21-8075   Sirignano, Emily          5000
              7      074-53-9892   Vincent, Martina         35000
```

The Program

To avoid having to maintain two separate data sets, the director wants to merge the records for each player from both data sets into a new data set that contains all the variables. The variable that is common to both data sets is Name. Therefore, Name is the appropriate BY variable.

The data sets are already sorted by NAME, so no further sorting is required. The following program merges them by NAME:

```
data employee_info;
   merge company finance;
   by name;
run;

proc print data=employee_info;
   title 'Little Theatre Employee Information';
   title2 '(including personal and financial information)';
run;
```

The following output displays the merged data set:

Output 18.7   Match-Merging

```
                    Little Theatre Employee Information                    1
                 (including personal and financial information)

     Obs   Name                     Age   Gender    IdNumber      Salary

      1    Benito, Gisela            32      F      228-88-9649    28000
      2    Gunter, Thomas            27      M      929-75-0218    27500
      3    Harbinger, Nicholas       36      M      446-93-2122    33900
      4    Morrison, Michael         32      M                         .
      5    Phillipon, Marie-Odile    28      F      776-84-5391    29750
      6    Rudelich, Herbert         39      M      029-46-9261    35000
      7    Sirignano, Emily          12      F      442-21-8075     5000
      8    Vincent, Martina          34      F      074-53-9892    35000
```

Explanation

The new data set contains one observation for each player in the company. Each observation contains all the variables from both data sets. Notice in particular the fourth observation. The data set FINANCE does not have an observation for Michael

Morrison. In this case, the values of the variables that are unique to FINANCE (IdNumber and Salary) are missing.

Match-Merging Data Sets with Multiple Observations in a BY Group

Input SAS Data Set for Examples

The Little Theatre has a third data set, REPERTORY, that tracks the casting assignments in each of the season's plays. REPERTORY contains these variables:

Play   is the name of one of the plays in the repertory.

Role   is the name of a character in Play.

IdNumber   is the employee ID number of the player playing Role.

The following program creates and displays REPERTORY:

```
data repertory;
    input Play $ 1-23 Role $ 25-48 IdNumber $ 50-60;
    datalines;
No Exit                 Estelle                   074-53-9892
No Exit                 Inez                      776-84-5391
No Exit                 Valet                     929-75-0218
No Exit                 Garcin                    446-93-2122
Happy Days              Winnie                    074-53-9892
Happy Days              Willie                    446-93-2122
The Glass Menagerie     Amanda Wingfield          228-88-9649
The Glass Menagerie     Laura Wingfield           776-84-5391
The Glass Menagerie     Tom Wingfield             929-75-0218
The Glass Menagerie     Jim O'Connor              029-46-9261
The Dear Departed       Mrs. Slater               228-88-9649
The Dear Departed       Mrs. Jordan               074-53-9892
The Dear Departed       Henry Slater              029-46-9261
The Dear Departed       Ben Jordan                446-93-2122
The Dear Departed       Victoria Slater           442-21-8075
The Dear Departed       Abel Merryweather         929-75-0218
;


proc print data=repertory;
    title 'Little Theater Season Casting Assignments';
run;
```

The following output displays the REPERTORY data set:

Output 18.8   The REPERTORY Data Set

```
                   Little Theater Season Casting Assignments                    1

          Obs    Play                  Role                  IdNumber

           1     No Exit               Estelle               074-53-9892
           2     No Exit               Inez                  776-84-5391
           3     No Exit               Valet                 929-75-0218
           4     No Exit               Garcin                446-93-2122
           5     Happy Days            Winnie                074-53-9892
           6     Happy Days            Willie                446-93-2122
           7     The Glass Menagerie   Amanda Wingfield      228-88-9649
           8     The Glass Menagerie   Laura Wingfield       776-84-5391
           9     The Glass Menagerie   Tom Wingfield         929-75-0218
          10     The Glass Menagerie   Jim O'Connor          029-46-9261
          11     The Dear Departed     Mrs. Slater           228-88-9649
          12     The Dear Departed     Mrs. Jordan           074-53-9892
          13     The Dear Departed     Henry Slater          029-46-9261
          14     The Dear Departed     Ben Jordan            446-93-2122
          15     The Dear Departed     Victoria Slater       442-21-8075
          16     The Dear Departed     Abel Merryweather     929-75-0218
```

To maintain confidentiality during preliminary casting, this data set identifies players by employee ID number. However, casting decisions are now final, and the manager wants to replace each employee ID number with the player's name. Of course, it is possible to re-create the data set, entering each player's name instead of the employee ID number in the raw data. However, it is more efficient to make use of the data set FINANCE, which already contains the name and employee ID number of all players (see Output 18.6 on page 277). When the data sets are merged, SAS takes care of adding the players' names to the data set.

Of course, before you can merge the data sets, you must sort them by IdNumber.

```
proc sort data=finance;
   by IdNumber;
run;


proc sort data=repertory;
   by IdNumber;
run;



proc print data=finance;
   title 'Little Theatre Employee Information';
   title2 '(sorted by employee ID number)';
run;

proc print data=repertory;
   title 'Little Theatre Season Casting Assignments';
   title2 '(sorted by employee ID number)';
run;
```

The following output displays the FINANCE and REPERTORY data sets, sorted by IdNumber:

Output 18.9 Sorting the FINANCE and REPERTORY Data Sets by IdNumber

```
                      Little Theatre Employee Information                    1
                         (sorted by employee ID number)

          Obs      IdNumber      Name                    Salary

           1      029-46-9261   Rudelich, Herbert         35000
           2      074-53-9892   Vincent, Martina          35000
           3      228-88-9649   Benito, Gisela            28000
           4      442-21-8075   Sirignano, Emily           5000
           5      446-93-2122   Harbinger, Nicholas       33900
           6      776-84-5391   Phillipon, Marie-Odile    29750
           7      929-75-0218   Gunter, Thomas            27500
```

```
                   Little Theatre Season Casting Assignments               2
                         (sorted by employee ID number)

        Obs    Play                  Role                IdNumber

          1    The Glass Menagerie   Jim O'Connor        029-46-9261
          2    The Dear Departed     Henry Slater        029-46-9261
          3    No Exit               Estelle             074-53-9892
          4    Happy Days            Winnie              074-53-9892
          5    The Dear Departed     Mrs. Jordan         074-53-9892
          6    The Glass Menagerie   Amanda Wingfield    228-88-9649
          7    The Dear Departed     Mrs. Slater         228-88-9649
          8    The Dear Departed     Victoria Slater     442-21-8075
          9    No Exit               Garcin              446-93-2122
         10    Happy Days            Willie              446-93-2122
         11    The Dear Departed     Ben Jordan          446-93-2122
         12    No Exit               Inez                776-84-5391
         13    The Glass Menagerie   Laura Wingfield     776-84-5391
         14    No Exit               Valet               929-75-0218
         15    The Glass Menagerie   Tom Wingfield       929-75-0218
         16    The Dear Departed     Abel Merryweather   929-75-0218
```

These two data sets contain seven BY groups; that is, among the 23 observations are seven different values for the BY variable, IdNumber. The first BY group has a value of 029-46-9261 for IdNumber. FINANCE has one observation in this BY group; REPERTORY has two. The last BY group has a value of 929-75-0218 for IdNumber. FINANCE has one observation in this BY group; REPERTORY has three.

The Program

The following program merges the data sets FINANCE and REPERTORY and illustrates what happens when a BY group in one data set has more observations in it than the same BY group in the other data set.

The resulting data set contains all variables from both data sets.

```
options linesize=120;

data repertory_name;
   merge finance repertory;
   by IdNumber;
run;

proc print data=repertory_name;
```

```
                title 'Little Theatre Season Casting Assignments';
                title2 'with employee financial information';
        run;
```

Note: The OPTIONS statement extends the line size to 120 so that PROC PRINT can display all variables on one line. Most output in this chapter is created with line size set to 76 in the OPTIONS statement. An OPTIONS statement appears only in examples using a different line size. When you set the LINESIZE= option, it remains in effect until you reset it or end the SAS session. △

The following output displays the merged data set:

Output 18.10   Match-Merge with Multiple Observations in a BY Group

```
                        Little Theatre Season Casting Assignments                          1
                           with employee financial information

   Obs     IdNumber      Name               Salary   Play                 Role

     1    029-46-9261    Rudelich, Herbert   35000   The Glass Menagerie   Jim O'Connor
     2    029-46-9261    Rudelich, Herbert   35000   The Dear Departed     Henry Slater
     3    074-53-9892    Vincent, Martina    35000   No Exit               Estelle
     4    074-53-9892    Vincent, Martina    35000   Happy Days            Winnie
     5    074-53-9892    Vincent, Martina    35000   The Dear Departed     Mrs. Jordan
     6    228-88-9649    Benito, Gisela      28000   The Glass Menagerie   Amanda Wingfield
     7    228-88-9649    Benito, Gisela      28000   The Dear Departed     Mrs. Slater
     8    442-21-8075    Sirignano, Emily     5000   The Dear Departed     Victoria Slater
     9    446-93-2122    Harbinger, Nicholas 33900   No Exit               Garcin
    10    446-93-2122    Harbinger, Nicholas 33900   Happy Days            Willie
    11    446-93-2122    Harbinger, Nicholas 33900   The Dear Departed     Ben Jordan
    12    776-84-5391    Phillipon, Marie-Odile 29750 No Exit              Inez
    13    776-84-5391    Phillipon, Marie-Odile 29750 The Glass Menagerie  Laura Wingfield
    14    929-75-0218    Gunter, Thomas      27500   No Exit               Valet
    15    929-75-0218    Gunter, Thomas      27500   The Glass Menagerie   Tom Wingfield
    16    929-75-0218    Gunter, Thomas      27500   The Dear Departed     Abel Merryweather
```

Explanation

Carefully examine the first few observations in the new data set and consider how SAS creates them.

1 Before executing the DATA step, SAS reads the descriptor portion of the two data sets and creates a program data vector that contains all variables from both data sets:

□ IdNumber, Name, and Salary from FINANCE

□ Play and Role from REPERTORY.

IdNumber is already in the program data vector because it is in FINANCE. SAS sets the values of all variables to missing, as the following figure illustrates.

Figure 18.4   Program Data Vector before Reading from Data Sets

IdNumber	Name	Salary	Play	Role
		.		

2 SAS looks at the first BY group in each data set to determine which BY group should appear first. In this case, the first BY group, observations with the value 029-46-9261 for IdNumber, is the same in both data sets.

3 SAS reads and copies the first observation from FINANCE into the program data vector, as the next figure illustrates.

Figure 18.5   Program Data Vector after Reading FINANCE Data Set

IdNumber	Name	Salary	Play	Role
029-46-9261	Rudelich, Herbert	35000		

4 SAS reads and copies the first observation from REPERTORY into the program data vector, as the next figure illustrates. If a data set does not have any observations in a BY group, then the program data vector contains missing values for the variables that are unique to that data set.

Figure 18.6   Program Data Vector after Reading REPERTORY Data Set

IdNumber	Name	Salary	Play	Role
029-46-9261	Rudelich, Herbert	35000		

5 SAS writes the observation to the new data set and retains the values in the program data vector. (If the program data vector contained variables created by the DATA step, then SAS would set them to missing after writing to the new data set.)

6 SAS looks for a second observation in the BY group in each data set. REPERTORY has one; FINANCE does not. The MERGE statement reads the second observation in the BY group from REPERTORY. Because FINANCE has only one observation in the BY group, the statement uses the values of Name (**Rudelich , Herbert**) and Salary (**35000**) retained in the program data vector for the second observation in the new data set. The next figure illustrates this behavior.

Figure 18.7   Program Data Vector with Second Observation in the BY Group

IdNumber	Name	Salary	Play	Role
029-46-9261	Rudelich, Herbert	35000	The Dear Departed	Henry Slater

7 SAS writes the observation to the new data set. Neither data set contains any more observations in this BY group. Therefore, as the final figure illustrates, SAS sets all values in the program data vector to missing and begins processing the next BY group. It continues processing observations until it exhausts all observations in both data sets.

Figure 18.8   Program Data Vector before New BY Groups

IdNumber	Name	Salary	Play	Role
		.		

Match-Merging Data Sets with Dropped Variables

Now that casting decisions are final, the director wants to post the casting list, but does not want to include salary or employee ID information. As the next program illustrates, Salary and IdNumber can be eliminated by using the DROP= data set option when creating the new data set.

```
data newrep (drop=IdNumber);
   merge finance (drop=Salary) repertory;
   by IdNumber;
run;

proc print data=newrep;
   title 'Final Little Theatre Season Casting Assignments';
run;
```

Note: The difference in placement of the two DROP= data set options is crucial. Dropping IdNumber in the DATA statement means that the variable is available to the MERGE and BY statements (to which it is essential) but that it does not go into the new data set. Dropping Salary in the MERGE statement means that the MERGE statement does not even read this variable, so Salary is unavailable to the program statements. Because the variable Salary is not needed for processing, it is more efficient to prevent it from being read into the PDV in the first place. △

The following output displays the merged data set without the IdNumber and Salary variables:

Output 18.11   Match-Merging Data Sets with Dropped Variables

```
             Final Little Theatre Season Casting Assignments               1

   Obs    Name                   Play                  Role

    1     Rudelich, Herbert      The Glass Menagerie   Jim O'Connor
    2     Rudelich, Herbert      The Dear Departed     Henry Slater
    3     Vincent, Martina       No Exit               Estelle
    4     Vincent, Martina       Happy Days            Winnie
    5     Vincent, Martina       The Dear Departed     Mrs. Jordan
    6     Benito, Gisela         The Glass Menagerie   Amanda Wingfield
    7     Benito, Gisela         The Dear Departed     Mrs. Slater
    8     Sirignano, Emily       The Dear Departed     Victoria Slater
    9     Harbinger, Nicholas    No Exit               Garcin
   10     Harbinger, Nicholas    Happy Days            Willie
   11     Harbinger, Nicholas    The Dear Departed     Ben Jordan
   12     Phillipon, Marie-Odile No Exit               Inez
   13     Phillipon, Marie-Odile The Glass Menagerie   Laura Wingfield
   14     Gunter, Thomas         No Exit               Valet
   15     Gunter, Thomas         The Glass Menagerie   Tom Wingfield
   16     Gunter, Thomas         The Dear Departed     Abel Merryweather
```

Match-Merging Data Sets with the Same Variables

You can match-merge data sets that contain the same variables (variables with the same name) by using the RENAME= data set option, just as you would when performing a one-to-one merge (see "Performing a One-to-One Merge on Data Sets with the Same Variables" on page 273).

If you do not use the RENAME= option and a variable exists in more than one data set, then the value of that variable in the last data set read is the value that goes into the new data set.

Match-Merging Data Sets That Lack a Common Variable

You can name any number of data sets in the MERGE statement. However, if you are match-merging the data sets, then you must be sure they all have a common variable and are sorted by that variable. If the data sets do not have a common variable, then you might be able to use another data set that has variables common to the original data sets to merge them.

For instance, consider the data sets that are used in the match-merge examples. The table that follows shows the names of the data sets and the names of the variables in each data set.

Data Set	Variables
COMPANY	Name, Age, Gender
FINANCE	Name, IdNumber, Salary
REPERTORY	Play, Role, IdNumber

These data sets do not share a common variable. However, COMPANY and FINANCE share the variable Name. Similarly, FINANCE and REPERTORY share the variable IdNumber. Therefore, as the next program shows, you can merge the data sets into one with two separate DATA steps. As usual, you must sort the data sets by the appropriate BY variable. (REPERTORY is already sorted by IdNumber.)

```
options linesize=120;
   /* Sort FINANCE and COMPANY by Name */
proc sort data=finance;
   by Name;
run;

proc sort data=company;
   by Name;
run;

   /* Merge COMPANY and FINANCE into a */
   /* temporary data set.             */
data temp;
   merge company finance;
   by Name;
run;

proc sort data=temp;
   by IdNumber;
run;

   /* Merge the temporary data set with REPERTORY */
data all;
```

```
merge temp repertory;
by IdNumber;
run;

proc print data=all;
    title 'Little Theatre Complete Casting Information';
run;
```

In order to merge the three data sets, this program

□ sorts FINANCE and COMPANY by Name

□ merges COMPANY and FINANCE into a temporary data set, TEMP

□ sorts TEMP by IdNumber

□ merges TEMP and REPERTORY by IdNumber.

The following ouput displays the resulting data set, ALL:

Output 18.12   Match-Merging Data Sets That Lack a Common Variable

```
                        Little Theatre Complete Casting Information                              1

Obs   Name                   Age   Gender   IdNumber     Salary   Play                  Role

  1   Morrison, Michael       32     M                        .
  2   Rudelich, Herbert       39     M      029-46-9261    35000   The Glass Menagerie   Jim O'Connor
  3   Rudelich, Herbert       39     M      029-46-9261    35000   The Dear Departed     Henry Slater
  4   Vincent, Martina        34     F      074-53-9892    35000   No Exit               Estelle
  5   Vincent, Martina        34     F      074-53-9892    35000   Happy Days            Winnie
  6   Vincent, Martina        34     F      074-53-9892    35000   The Dear Departed     Mrs. Jordan
  7   Benito, Gisela          32     F      228-88-9649    28000   The Glass Menagerie   Amanda Wingfield
  8   Benito, Gisela          32     F      228-88-9649    28000   The Dear Departed     Mrs. Slater
  9   Sirignano, Emily        12     F      442-21-8075     5000   The Dear Departed     Victoria Slater
 10   Harbinger, Nicholas     36     M      446-93-2122    33900   No Exit               Garcin
 11   Harbinger, Nicholas     36     M      446-93-2122    33900   Happy Days            Willie
 12   Harbinger, Nicholas     36     M      446-93-2122    33900   The Dear Departed     Ben Jordan
 13   Phillipon, Marie-Odile  28     F      776-84-5391    29750   No Exit               Inez
 14   Phillipon, Marie-Odile  28     F      776-84-5391    29750   The Glass Menagerie   Laura Wingfield
 15   Gunter, Thomas          27     M      929-75-0218    27500   No Exit               Valet
 16   Gunter, Thomas          27     M      929-75-0218    27500   The Glass Menagerie   Tom Wingfield
 17   Gunter, Thomas          27     M      929-75-0218    27500   The Dear Departed     Abel Merryweather
```

Choosing between One-to-One Merging and Match-Merging

Comparing Match-Merge Methods

Use one-to-one merging when you want to combine one observation from each data set, but it is not important to match observations. For example, when merging an observation that contains a student's name, year, and major with an observation that contains a date, time, and location for a conference, it does not matter which student gets which time slot; therefore, a one-to-one merge is appropriate.

In cases where you must merge certain observations, use a match-merge. For example, when merging employee information from two different data sets, it is crucial that you merge observations that relate to the same employee. Therefore, you must use a match-merge.

Sometimes you might want to merge by a particular variable, but your data is arranged in such a way that you can see that a one-to-one merge will work. The next example illustrates a case when you could use a one-to-one merge for matching observations because you are certain that your data is ordered correctly. However, as a subsequent example shows, it is risky to use a one-to-one merge in such situations.

Input SAS Data Set for Examples

Consider the data set COMPANY2. Each observation in this data set corresponds to an observation with the same value of Name in FINANCE. The program that follows creates and displays COMPANY2; it also displays FINANCE for comparison.

```
data company2;
   input name $ 1-25 age 27-28 gender $ 30;
   datalines;
Benito, Gisela           32 F
Gunter, Thomas           27 M
Harbinger, Nicholas      36 M
Phillipon, Marie-Odile   28 F
Rudelich, Herbert        39 M
Sirignano, Emily         12 F
Vincent, Martina         34 F
;


proc print data=company2;
   title 'Little Theatre Company Roster';
run;

proc print data=finance;
   title 'Little Theatre Employee Information';
run;
```

The following outout displays the two data sets:

Output 18.13   The COMPANY2 and FINANCE Data Sets

```
                   Little Theatre Company Roster                        1

        Obs     name                     age   gender

         1      Benito, Gisela           32     F
         2      Gunter, Thomas           27     M
         3      Harbinger, Nicholas      36     M
         4      Phillipon, Marie-Odile   28     F
         5      Rudelich, Herbert        39     M
         6      Sirignano, Emily         12     F
         7      Vincent, Martina         34     F
```

```
                    Little Theatre Employee Information                    2

            Obs      IdNumber      Name                  Salary

             1      228-88-9649   Benito, Gisela          28000
             2      929-75-0218   Gunter, Thomas          27500
             3      446-93-2122   Harbinger, Nicholas     33900
             4      776-84-5391   Phillipon, Marie-Odile  29750
             5      029-46-9261   Rudelich, Herbert       35000
             6      442-21-8075   Sirignano, Emily         5000
             7      074-53-9892   Vincent, Martina        35000
```

When to Use a One-to-One Merge

The following program shows that because both data sets are sorted by NAME and because each observation in one data set has a corresponding observation in the other data set, a one-to-one merge has the same result as merging by Name.

```
    /* One-to-one merge */
data one_to_one;
    merge company2 finance;
run;


proc print data=one_to_one;
    title 'Using a One-to-One Merge to Combine';
    title2 'COMPANY2 and FINANCE';
run;


    /* Match-merge */
data match;
    merge company2 finance;
    by name;
run;


proc print data=match;
    title 'Using a Match-Merge to Combine';
    title2 'COMPANY2 and FINANCE';
run;
```

The following output displays the results of the two merges. You can see that they are identical.

Output 18.14   Comparing a One-to-One Merge with a Match-Merge When Observations Correspond

```
                   Using a One-to-One Merge to Combine                    1
                          COMPANY2 and FINANCE

        Obs    name                    age  gender    IdNumber      Salary

         1     Benito, Gisela           32     F     228-88-9649     28000
         2     Gunter, Thomas           27     M     929-75-0218     27500
         3     Harbinger, Nicholas      36     M     446-93-2122     33900
         4     Phillipon, Marie-Odile   28     F     776-84-5391     29750
         5     Rudelich, Herbert        39     M     029-46-9261     35000
         6     Sirignano, Emily         12     F     442-21-8075      5000
         7     Vincent, Martina         34     F     074-53-9892     35000
```

```
                 Using a Match-Merge to Combine                2
                     COMPANY2 and FINANCE

     Obs    name                  age  gender   IdNumber    Salary

      1     Benito, Gisela         32    F      228-88-9649   28000
      2     Gunter, Thomas         27    M      929-75-0218   27500
      3     Harbinger, Nicholas    36    M      446-93-2122   33900
      4     Phillipon, Marie-Odile 28    F      776-84-5391   29750
      5     Rudelich, Herbert      39    M      029-46-9261   35000
      6     Sirignano, Emily       12    F      442-21-8075    5000
      7     Vincent, Martina       34    F      074-53-9892   35000
```

Even though the resulting data sets are identical, it is not wise to use a one-to-one merge when it is essential to merge a particular observation from one data set with a particular observation from another data set.

When to Use a Match-Merge

In the previous example, you can easily determine that the data sets contain the same values for Name and that the values appear in the same order. However, if the data sets contained hundreds of observations, then it would be difficult to ascertain that all the values match. If the observations do not match, then serious problems can occur. The next example illustrates why you should not use a one-to-one merge for matching observations.

Consider the original data set, COMPANY, which contains an observation for Michael Morrison (see Output 18.6 on page 277). FINANCE has no corresponding observation. If a programmer did not realize this fact and tried to use the following program to perform a one-to-one merge with FINANCE, then several problems could appear.

```
data badmerge;
   merge company finance;
run;


proc print data=badmerge;
   title 'Using a One-to-One Merge Instead of a Match-Merge';
run;
```

The following output shows the potential problems:

Output 18.15 One-to-One Merge with Unequal Numbers of Observations in Each Data Set

```
            Using a One-to-One Merge Instead of a Match-Merge       1

     Obs    Name                  Age   Gender    IdNumber    Salary

      1     Benito, Gisela         32     F       228-88-9649   28000
      2     Gunter, Thomas         27     M       929-75-0218   27500
      3     Harbinger, Nicholas    36     M       446-93-2122   33900
      4     Phillipon, Marie-Odile 32     M       776-84-5391   29750
      5     Rudelich, Herbert      28     F       029-46-9261   35000
      6     Sirignano, Emily       39     M       442-21-8075    5000
      7     Vincent, Martina       12     F       074-53-9892   35000
      8     Vincent, Martina       34     F                        .
```

The first three observations merge correctly. However, FINANCE does not have an observation for Michael Morrison. A one-to-one merge makes no attempt to match parts of the observations from the different data sets. It simply combines observations based on their positions in the data sets that you name in the MERGE statement. Therefore, the fourth observation in BADMERGE combines the fourth observation in COMPANY (Michael's name, age, and gender) with the fourth observation in FINANCE (Marie-Odile's name, employee ID number, and salary). As SAS combines the observations, Marie-Odile's name overwrites Michael's. After writing this observation to the new data set, SAS processes the next observation in each data set. These observations are similarly mismatched.

This type of mismatch continues until the seventh observation when the MERGE statement exhausts the observations in the smaller data set, FINANCE. After writing the seventh observation to the new data set, SAS begins the next iteration of the DATA step. Because SAS has read all observations in FINANCE, it sets the values for variables from that data set to missing in the program data vector. Then it reads the values for Name, Age, and Gender from COMPANY and writes the contents of the program data vector to the new data set. Therefore, the last observation has the same value for NAME as the previous observation and contains missing values for IdNumber and Salary.

These missing values and the duplication of the value for Name might make you suspect that the observations did not merge as you intended them to. However, if instead of being an additional observation, the observation for Michael Morrison replaced another observation in COMPANY2, then no observations would have missing values, and the problem would not be as easy to spot. Therefore, you are safer using a match-merge in situations that call for it even if you think the data is arranged so that a one-to-one merge will have the same results.

Review of SAS Tools

Statements

MERGE *SAS-data-set-list*;
BY *variable-list*;
   read observations in multiple SAS data sets and combine them into one observation in one new SAS data set. *SAS-data-set-list* is a list of the SAS data sets to merge. The list may contain any number of data sets; *variable-list* is the name of one or more variables by which to merge the data sets. If you use a BY statement, then the data sets must be sorted by the same BY variables before you can merge them. If you do not use a BY statement, then SAS merges observations based on their positions in the original data sets.

Learning More

Indexes
   If a data set has an index on the variable or variables named in the BY statement that accompanies the MERGE statement, then you do not need to sort that data

set. For more information about indexes, see *SAS Language Reference: Concepts* and the *SAS Procedures Guide*.

SAS date and time formats and informats
The examples in this chapter read Time as a character variable, and they read Date with a SAS date informat. You could read Time using special SAS time informats. For more information about SAS date and time formats and informats, see *SAS Language Reference: Dictionary*.

Updating SAS Data Sets

Introduction

Purpose

Updating replaces the values of variables in one data set with nonmissing values from another data set. In this chapter, you will learn about

- □ master data sets and transaction data sets
- □ using the UPDATE statement
- □ how to choose between updating and merging.

Prerequisites

Before using this chapter, you should be familiar with the concepts presented in

- □ Chapter 3, "Starting with Raw Data: The Basics," on page 43
- □ Chapter 5, "Starting with SAS Data Sets," on page 81
- □ Chapter 18, "Merging SAS Data Sets," on page 269.

Understanding the UPDATE Statement

When you update, you work with two SAS data sets. The data set that contains the original information is the *master data set*. The data set that contains the new information is the *transaction data set*. Many applications, such as maintaining mailing lists and inventories, call for periodic updates of information.

In a DATA step, the UPDATE statement reads observations from the transaction data set and updates corresponding observations (observations with the same value of all BY variables) from the master data set. All nonmissing values for variables in the transaction data set replace the corresponding values that are read from the master data set. SAS writes the modified observations to the data set that you name in the DATA statement without modifying either the master or the transaction data set.

The general form of the UPDATE statement is

UPDATE *master-SAS-data-set transaction-SAS-data-set*;

BY *identifier-list*;

where

master-SAS-data-set
   is the SAS data set containing information you want to update.

transaction-SAS-data-set
   is the SAS data set containing information with which you want to update the master data set.

identifier-list
   is the list of BY variables by which you identify corresponding observations.

If the master data set contains an observation that does not correspond to an observation in the transaction data set, the DATA step writes that observation to the new data set without modification. An observation from the transaction data set that does not correspond to any observation in the master data set becomes the basis for a new observation. The new observation may be modified by other observations from the transaction data set before it is written to the new data set.

Understanding How to Select BY Variables

The master data set and the transaction data set must be sorted by the same variable or variables that you specify in the BY statement. Select a variable that meets these criteria:

   □ The value of the variable is unique for each observation in the master data set. If you use more than one BY variable, no two observations in the master data set should have the same values for all BY variables.

   □ The variable or variables never need to be updated.

Some examples of variables that you can use in the BY statement include employee or student identification numbers, stock numbers, and the names of objects in an inventory.

If you are updating a data set, you probably do not want duplicate values of BY variables in the master data set. For example, if you update by NAME, each observation in the master data set should have a unique value of NAME. If you update by NAME and AGE, two or more observations can have the same value for either NAME or AGE but should not have the same values for both. SAS warns you if it finds duplicates but proceeds with the update. It applies all transactions only to the first observation in the BY group in the master data set.

Updating a Data Set

In this example, the circulation department of a magazine maintains a mailing list that contains tens of thousands of names. Each issue of the magazine contains a form for readers to fill out when they change their names or addresses. To simplify the maintenance job, the form requests that readers send only new information. New subscribers can start a subscription by completing the entire form. When a form is received, a data entry operator enters the information on the form into a raw data file. The mailing list is updated once per month from the raw data file.

The mailing list includes these variables for each subscriber:

SubscriberId	is a unique number assigned to the subscriber at the time the subscription begins. A subscriber's SubscriberId never changes.
Name	is the subscriber's name. The last name appears first, followed by a comma and the first name.
StreetAddress	is the subscriber's street address.
City	is the subscriber's city.
StateProv	is the subscriber's state or province. This variable is missing for addresses outside the United States and Canada.
PostalCode	is the subscriber's postal code (zip code for addresses in the United States).
Country	is the subscriber's country.

The following program creates and displays the first part of this data set. The raw data are already sorted by SubscriberId.

```
options pagesize=60 linesize=80 pageno=1 nodate;

data mail_list;
   input SubscriberId 1-8 Name $ 9-27 StreetAddress $ 28-47 City $ 48-62
         StateProv $ 63-64 PostalCode $ 67-73 Country $ ;
   datalines;
1001    Ericson, Jane      111 Clancey Court   Chapel Hill    NC  27514   USA
1002    Dix, Martin        4 Shepherd St.      Vancouver      BC  V6C 3E8 Canada
1003    Gabrielli, Theresa Via Pisanelli, 25   Roma               00196   Italy
1004    Clayton, Aria      14 Bridge St.       San Francisco  CA  94124   USA
1005    Archuleta, Ruby    Box 108             Milagro        NM  87429   USA
1006    Misiewicz, Jeremy  43-C Lakeview Apts. Madison        WI  53704   USA
1007    Ahmadi, Hafez      52 Rue Marston      Paris              75019   France
1008    Jacobson, Becky    1 Lincoln St.       Tallahassee    FL  32312   USA
1009    An, Ing            95 Willow Dr.       Toronto        ON  M5J 2T3 Canada
1010    Slater, Emily      1009 Cherry St.     York           PA  17407   USA

...more data lines...
;

proc print data=mail_list (obs=10);
   title 'Magazine Master Mailing List';
```

```
run;
```

The following output shows the results:

Output 19.1   The MAIL_LIST Data Set

```
                        Magazine Master Mailing List                         1

                       S
          S            t
          u            r
          b            e                                   P
          s            e                           S       o
          c            t                           t       s
          r            A                           a       t       C
          i            d                           t       a       o
          b            d                           e       l       u
          e   N        r                   C       P       C       n
      O   r   a        e                   i       r       o       t
      b   I   m        s                   t       o       d       r
      s   d   e        s                   y       v       e       y

      1  1001 Ericson, Jane      111 Clancey Court   Chapel Hill   NC 27514   USA
      2  1002 Dix, Martin        4 Shepherd St.      Vancouver     BC V6C 3E8 Canada
      3  1003 Gabrielli, Theresa Via Pisanelli, 25   Roma             00196   Italy
      4  1004 Clayton, Aria      14 Bridge St.       San Francisco CA 94124   USA
      5  1005 Archuleta, Ruby    Box 108             Milagro       NM 87429   USA
      6  1006 Misiewicz, Jeremy  43-C Lakeview Apts. Madison       WI 53704   USA
      7  1007 Ahmadi, Hafez      52 Rue Marston      Paris            75019   France
      8  1008 Jacobson, Becky    1 Lincoln St.       Tallahassee   FL 32312   USA
      9  1009 An, Ing            95 Willow Dr.       Toronto       ON M5J 2T3 Canada
     10  1010 Slater, Emily      1009 Cherry St.     York          PA 17407   USA
```

This month the information that follows is received for updating the mailing list:

- Martin Dix changed his name to Martin Dix-Rosen.
- Jane Ericson's postal code changed.
- Jeremy Misiewicz moved to a new street address. His city, state, and postal code remain the same.
- Ing An moved from Toronto, Ontario, to Calgary, Alberta.
- Martin Dix-Rosen, shortly after changing his name, moved from Vancouver, British Columbia, to Seattle, Washington.
- Two new subscribers joined the list. They are given SubscriberID numbers 1011 and 1012.

Each change is entered into the raw data file as soon as it is received. In each case, only the customer's SubscriberId and the new information are entered. The raw data file looks like this:

```
1002      Dix-Rosen, Martin
1001                                                           27516
1006                       932 Webster St.
1009                       2540 Pleasant St.   Calgary      AB T2P 4H2
1011      Mitchell, Wayne  28 Morningside Dr.  New York     NY 10017   USA
1002                       P.O. Box 1850       Seattle      WA 98101   USA
1012      Stavros, Gloria  212 Northampton Rd. South Hadley MA 01075   USA
```

The data is in fixed columns, matching the INPUT statement that created MAIL_LIST.

First, you must transform the raw data into a SAS data set and sort that data set by SubscriberId so that you can use it to update the master list.

```
data mail_trans;
    infile 'your-input-file' missover;
    input SubscriberId 1-8 Name $ 9-27 StreetAddress $ 28-47 City $ 48-62
          StateProv $ 63-64 PostalCode $ 67-73 Country $ 75-80;
run;

proc sort data=mail_trans;
    by SubscriberId;
run;


proc print data=mail_trans;
    title 'Magazine Mailing List Changes';
    title2 '(for current month)';
run;
```

Note the MISSOVER option in the INFILE statement. The MISSOVER option prevents the INPUT statement from going to a new line to search for values for variables which have not received values; instead, any variables that have not received values are set to missing. For example, when the first record is read, the end of the record is encountered before any value has been assigned to the Country variable; instead of going to the next record to search for a value for Country, the Country variable is assigned a missing value. For more information about the MISSOVER option, see Chapter 4, "Starting with Raw Data: Beyond the Basics," on page 61.

The following output shows the sorted data set MAIL_TRANS:

Output 19.2   The MAIL_TRANS Data Set

```
                         Magazine Mailing List Changes                          1
                              (for current month)

                                     S
         S                           t
         u                           r
         b                           e                            P
         s                           e               S            o
         c                           t               t            s
         r                           A               a            t     C
         i                           d               t            a     o
         b                           d               e            l     u
         e          N                r          C    P      C     c     n
    O    r          a                e          i    r      o     o     t
    b    I          m                s          t    o      d     d     r
    s    d          e                s          y    v      e     e     y

    1    1001                                                     27516
    2    1002    Dix-Rosen, Martin
    3    1002                    P.O. Box 1850      Seattle    WA  98101  USA
    4    1006                    932 Webster St.
    5    1009                    2540 Pleasant St.  Calgary    AB  T2P 4H2
    6    1011    Mitchell, Wayne 28 Morningside Dr. New York   NY  10017  USA
    7    1012    Stavros, Gloria 212 Northampton Rd. South Hadley MA 01075 USA
```

Now that the new data are in a sorted SAS data set, the following program updates the mailing list.

```
data mail_newlist;
   update mail_list mail_trans;
   by SubscriberId;
run;

proc print data=mail_newlist;
   title 'Magazine Mailing List';
   title2 '(updated for current month)';
run;
```

The following output shows the resulting data set MAIL_NEWLIST:

Output 19.3   Updating a Data Set

```
                          Magazine Mailing List                              1
                         (updated for current month)

                        S
            S           t
            u           r
            b           e                              P
            s           e                      S       o
            c           t                      t       s
            r           A                      a       t       C
            i           d                      t       a       o
            b           d                      e       l       u
            e   N       r                  C   P       C       n
       O    r   a       e                  i   r       o       t
       b    I   m       s                  t   o       d       r
       s    d   e       s                  y   v       e       y

        1  1001 Ericson, Jane      111 Clancey Court   Chapel Hill   NC 27516     USA
        2  1002 Dix-Rosen, Martin  P.O. Box 1850       Seattle       WA 98101     USA
        3  1003 Gabrielli, Theresa Via Pisanelli, 25   Roma             00196     Italy
        4  1004 Clayton, Aria      14 Bridge St.       San Francisco CA 94124     USA
        5  1005 Archuleta, Ruby    Box 108             Milagro       NM 87429     USA
        6  1006 Misiewicz, Jeremy  932 Webster St.     Madison       WI 53704     USA
        7  1007 Ahmadi, Hafez      52 Rue Marston      Paris            75019     France
        8  1008 Jacobson, Becky    1 Lincoln St.       Tallahassee   FL 32312     USA
        9  1009 An, Ing            2540 Pleasant St.   Calgary       AB T2P 4H2   Canada
       10  1010 Slater, Emily      1009 Cherry St.     York          PA 17407     USA
       11  1011 Mitchell, Wayne    28 Morningside Dr.  New York      NY 10017     USA
       12  1012 Stavros, Gloria    212 Northampton Rd. South Hadley  MA 01075     USA
```

The data for subscriber 1002, who has two update transactions, is used below to show what happens when you update an observation in the master data set with corresponding observations from the transaction data set.

1 Before executing the DATA step, SAS reads the descriptor portion of each data set named in the UPDATE statement and, by default, creates a program data vector that contains all the variables from all data sets. As the following figure illustrates, SAS sets the value of each variable to missing. (Use the DROP= or KEEP= data set option to exclude one or more variables.)

Figure 19.1 Program Data Vector before Execution of the DATA Step

SubscriberId	Name	Street Address	City	StateProv	PostalCode	Country
.						

2 Next, SAS reads the first observation from the master data set and copies it into the program data vector, as the following figure illustrates.

Figure 19.2 Program Data Vector after Reading the First Observation from the Master Data Set

SubscriberId	Name	Street Address	City	StateProv	PostalCode	Country
1002	Dix, Martin	4 Shepherd St.	Vancouver	BC	V6C 3E8	Canada

3 SAS applies the first transaction by copying all nonmissing values (the value of Name) from the first observation in this BY group (ID=1002) into the program data vector, as the following figure illustrates.

Figure 19.3 Program Data Vector after Applying the First Transaction

SubscriberId	Name	Street Address	City	StateProv	PostalCode	Country
1002	Dix-Rosen, Martin	4 Shepherd St.	Vancouver	BC	V6C 3E8	Canada

4 After completing this transaction, SAS looks for another observation in the same BY group in the transaction data set. If it finds a second observation with the same value for ID, then it applies the second transaction too (new values for StreetAddress, City, StateProv, PostalCode, and Country). Now the observation contains the new values from both transactions, as the following figure illustrates.

Figure 19.4 Program Data Vector after Applying the Second Transaction

SubscriberId	Name	Street Address	City	StateProv	Postal Code	Country
1002	Dix-Rosen, Martin	P.O. Box 1850	Seattle	WA	98101	USA

5 After completing the second transaction, SAS looks for a third observation in the same BY group. Because no such observation exists, it writes the observation in its current form to the new data set and sets the values in the program data vector to missing.

As the DATA step iterates, the UPDATE statement continues processing observations in this way until it reaches the end of the master and transaction data sets. The two observations in the transaction data set that describe new subscribers (and therefore have no corresponding observation in the master data set) become observations in the new data set.

Remember that if there are duplicate observations in the master data set, all matching observations in the transaction data set are applied only to the first of the duplicate observations in the master data set.

Updating with Incremental Values

Some applications do not update a data set by overwriting values in the master data set with new values from a transaction data set. Instead, they update a variable by mathematically manipulating its value based on the value of a variable in the transaction data set.

In this example, a bookstore uses SAS to keep track of weekly sales and year-to-date sales. The program that follows creates, sorts by Title, and displays the data set, YEAR_SALES, which contains the year-to-date information.

```
data year_sales;
   input Title $ 1-25 Author $ 27-50 Sales;
   datalines;
The Milagro Beanfield War Nichols, John           303
The Stranger              Camus, Albert           150
Always Coming Home        LeGuin, Ursula           79
Falling through Space     Gilchrist, Ellen        128
Don Quixote               Cervantes, Miguel de     87
The Handmaid's Tale       Atwood, Margaret         64
;

proc sort data=year_sales;
   by title;
run;


proc print data=year_sales (obs=6);
   title 'Bookstore Sales, Year-to-Date';
   title2 'By Title';
run;
```

The following output displays the YEAR_SALES data set:

Output 19.4   The YEAR_SALES Data Set, Sorted by Title

```
                    Bookstore Sales, Year-to-Date                 1
                              By Title

      Obs    Title                    Author              Sales

       1     Always Coming Home       LeGuin, Ursula        79
       2     Don Quixote              Cervantes, Miguel de  87
       3     Falling through Space    Gilchrist, Ellen     128
       4     The Handmaid's Tale      Atwood, Margaret      64
       5     The Milagro Beanfield War Nichols, John       303
       6     The Stranger             Camus, Albert        150
```

Every Saturday a SAS data set is created containing information about all the books that were sold during the past week. The program following creates, sorts by Title, and displays the data set WEEK_SALES, which contains the current week's information.

```
data week_sales;
   input Title $ 1-25 Author $ 27-50 Sales;
   datalines;
The Milagro Beanfield War Nichols, John            32
```

```
The Stranger              Camus, Albert      17
Always Coming Home        LeGuin, Ursula     10
Falling through Space     Gilchrist, Ellen   12
The Accidental Tourist    Tyler, Anne        15
The Handmaid's Tale       Atwood, Margaret    8
;
proc sort data=week_sales;
   by title;
run;


proc print data=week_sales;
   title 'Bookstore Sales for Current Week';
   title2 'By Title';
run;
```

The following output shows the data set, which contains the same variables as the year-to-date data set, but the variable Sales represents sales for only one week:

Output 19.5   The WEEK_SALES Data Set, Sorted by Title

```
                    Bookstore Sales for Current Week                     1
                               By Title

        Obs   Title                      Author          Sales

         1    Always Coming Home         LeGuin, Ursula     10
         2    Falling through Space      Gilchrist, Ellen   12
         3    The Accidental Tourist     Tyler, Anne        15
         4    The Handmaid's Tale        Atwood, Margaret    8
         5    The Milagro Beanfield War  Nichols, John      32
         6    The Stranger               Camus, Albert      17
```

Note: If the transaction data set is updating only titles that are already in YEAR_SALES, it does not need to contain the variable Author. However, because this variable is there, the transaction data set can be used to add complete observations to the master data set. △

The program that follows uses the weekly information to update the year-to-date data set and displays the new data set.

```
data total_sales;
   drop NewSales; ❸
   update year_sales week_sales (rename=(Sales=NewSales)); ❶
   by Title;
   sales=sum(Sales,NewSales); ❷
run;

proc print data=total_sales;
   title 'Updated Year-to-Date Sales';
run;
```

The following list corresponds to the numbered items in the preceding program:

❶ The RENAME= data set option in the UPDATE statement changes the name of the variable Sales in the transaction data set (WEEK_SALES) to NewSales. As a result, these values do not replace the value of Sales that are read from the master data set (YEAR_SALES).

❷ The Sales value that is in the updated data set (TOTAL_SALES) is the sum of the year-to-date sales and the weekly sales.

❸ The program drops the variable NewSales because it is not needed in the new data set.

The following output shows that in addition to updating sales information for the titles already in the master data set, the UPDATE statement has added a new title, **The Accidental Tourist.**

Output 19.6   Updating Year-to-Date Sales with Weekly Sales

```
                       Updated Year-to-Date Sales                          1

      Obs    Title                    Author              Sales

       1     Always Coming Home       LeGuin, Ursula        89
       2     Don Quixote              Cervantes, Miguel de  87
       3     Falling through Space    Gilchrist, Ellen      140
       4     The Accidental Tourist   Tyler, Anne           15
       5     The Handmaid's Tale      Atwood, Margaret      72
       6     The Milagro Beanfield War Nichols, John        335
       7     The Stranger             Camus, Albert         167
```

Understanding the Differences between Updating and Merging

General Comparisons

The MERGE statement and the UPDATE statement both match observations from two SAS data sets; however, the two statements differ significantly. It is important to distinguish between the two processes and to choose the one that is appropriate for your application.

The most straightforward differences are

- ☐ The UPDATE statement uses only two data sets. The number of data sets that the MERGE statement can use is limited only by machine-dependent factors such as memory and disk space.

- ☐ A BY statement must accompany an UPDATE statement. The MERGE statement performs a one-to-one merge if no BY statement follows it.

- ☐ The two statements also process observations differently when a data set contains missing values or multiple observations in a BY group.

To illustrate the differences, compare updating the SAS data set MAIL_LIST with the data set MAIL_TRANS to merging the two data sets. You have already seen the results of updating in the example that created Output 19.3 on page 298. That output appears again in the following output for easy comparison.

Output 19.7 Updating a Data Set

```
                           Magazine Mailing List                         1
                          (updated for current month)

                             S
             S               t
             u               r
             b               e                           P
             s               e                   S       o
             c               t                   t       s
             r               A                   a       t       C
             i               d                   t       a       o
             b               d                   e       l       u
             e   N           r               C   P       C       n
 O   r   a               e               i   r       o       t
 b   I   m           s           t   o       d   r
 s   d   e           s           y           v       e       y

  1 1001 Ericson, Jane     111 Clancey Court  Chapel Hill  NC 27516    USA
  2 1002 Dix-Rosen, Martin P.O. Box 1850      Seattle      WA 98101    USA
  3 1003 Gabrielli, Theresa Via Pisanelli, 25 Roma            00196    Italy
  4 1004 Clayton, Aria     14 Bridge St.      San Francisco CA 94124   USA
  5 1005 Archuleta, Ruby   Box 108            Milagro      NM 87429    USA
  6 1006 Misiewicz, Jeremy 932 Webster St.    Madison      WI 53704    USA
  7 1007 Ahmadi, Hafez     52 Rue Marston     Paris           75019    France
  8 1008 Jacobson, Becky   1 Lincoln St.      Tallahassee  FL 32312    USA
  9 1009 An, Ing           2540 Pleasant St.  Calgary      AB T2P 4H2  Canada
 10 1010 Slater, Emily     1009 Cherry St.    York         PA 17407    USA
 11 1011 Mitchell, Wayne   28 Morningside Dr. New York     NY 10017    USA
 12 1012 Stavros, Gloria   212 Northampton Rd. South Hadley MA 01075   USA
```

In contrast, the following program merges the two data sets.

```
data mail_merged;
   merge mail_list mail_trans;
   by SubscriberId;
run;


proc print data=mail_merged;
   title 'Magazine Mailing List';
run;
```

The following output shows the results of the merge:

Output 19.8   Results of Merging the Master and Transaction Data Sets

```
                           Magazine Mailing List                              1

                       S
         S             t
         u             r
         b             e                                    P
         s             e                          S         o
         c             t                          t         s
         r             A                          a         t      C
         i             d                          t         a      o
         b             d                          e         l      u
         e     N       r                 C        P         C      n
  O      r     a       e                 i        r         o      t
  b      I     m       s                 t        o         d      r
  s      d     e       s                 y        v         e      y

  1  1001                                                 27516
  2  1002  Dix-Rosen, Martin
  3  1002                   P.O. Box 1850      Seattle     WA 98101   USA
  4  1003  Gabrielli, Theresa  Via Pisanelli, 25  Roma        00196     Italy
  5  1004  Clayton, Aria    14 Bridge St.     San Francisco CA 94124   USA
  6  1005  Archuleta, Ruby   Box 108          Milagro     NM 87429   USA
  7  1006                   932 Webster St.
  8  1007  Ahmadi, Hafez    52 Rue Marston    Paris          75019     France
  9  1008  Jacobson, Becky   1 Lincoln St.    Tallahassee FL 32312   USA
 10  1009                   2540 Pleasant St. Calgary     AB T2P 4H2
 11  1010  Slater, Emily    1009 Cherry St.   York        PA 17407   USA
 12  1011  Mitchell, Wayne   28 Morningside Dr. New York    NY 10017   USA
 13  1012  Stavros, Gloria   212 Northampton Rd. South Hadley MA 01075   USA
```

The MERGE statement produces a data set containing 13 observations, whereas UPDATE produces a data set containing 12 observations. In addition, merging the data sets results in several missing values, whereas updating does not. Obviously, using the wrong statement may result in incorrect data. The differences between the merged and updated data sets result from the ways the two statements handle missing values and multiple observations in a BY group.

How the UPDATE and MERGE Statements Process Missing Values Differently

During an update, if a value for a variable is missing in the transaction data set, SAS uses the value from the master data set when it writes the observation to the new data set. When merging the same observations, SAS overwrites the value in the program data vector with the missing value. For example, the following observation exists in data set MAILING.MASTER.

```
1001    ERICSON, JANE    111 CLANCEY COURT    CHAPEL HILL    NC  27514
```

The following corresponding observation exists in MAILING.TRANS.

```
1001                                                        27516
```

Updating combines the two observations and creates the following observation:

```
1001    ERICSON, JANE    111 CLANCEY COURT    CHAPEL HILL    NC  27516
```

Merging combines the two observations and creates this observation:

```
1001                                                        27516
```

How the UPDATE and MERGE Statements Process Multiple Observations in a BY Group Differently

SAS does not write an updated observation to the new data set until it has applied all the transactions in a BY group. When merging data sets, SAS writes one new observation for each observation in the data set with the largest number of observations in the BY group. For example, consider this observation from MAILING.MASTER:

```
1002    DIX, MARTIN        4 SHEPHERD ST.     NORWICH        VT  05055
```

and the corresponding observations from MAILING.TRANS:

```
1002    DIX-ROSEN, MARTIN
1002                       R.R. 2, BOX 1850   HANOVER        NH  03755
```

The UPDATE statement applies both transactions and combines these observations into a single one:

```
1002    DIX-ROSEN, MARTIN  R.R. 2, BOX 1850   HANOVER        NH  03755
```

The MERGE statement, on the other hand, first merges the observation from MAILING.MASTER with the first observation in the corresponding BY group in MAILING.TRANS. All values of variables from the observation in MAILING.TRANS are used, even if they are missing. Then SAS writes the observation to the new data set:

```
1002    DIX-ROSEN, MARTIN
```

Next, SAS looks for other observations in the same BY group in each data set. Because more observations are in the BY group in MAILING.TRANS, all the values in the program data vector are retained. SAS merges them with the second observation in the BY group from MAILING.TRANS and writes the result to the new data set:

```
1002                       R.R. 2, BOX 1850   HANOVER        NH  03755
```

Therefore, merging creates two observations for the new data set, whereas updating creates only one.

Handling Missing Values

If a transaction data set has an observation with a missing value for NewStock, how would the MODIFY statement handle the missing value? The answer depends on the value that you use with the UPDATEMODE option in the UPDATE statement. UPDATEMODE specifies whether missing values in a transaction data set will replace existing values in a master data set.

The syntax for using the UPDATEMODE option with the UPDATE statement is

UPDATE *master-SAS-data-set transaction-SAS-data-set*
   <UPDATEMODE=MISSINGCHECK | NOMISSINGCHECK>;

BY *by-variable*;

The MISSINGCHECK value in the UPDATEMODE option prevents missing values in a transaction data set from replacing values in a master data set. This is the default. The NOMISSINGCHECK value in the UPDATEMODE option enables missing values in a transaction data set to replace values in a master data set by preventing the check for missing data from being performed.

```
options pagesize=60 linesize=80 pageno=1 nodate;

data inventory;
   input PartNumber $ Description $ InStock @17
         ReceivedDate date9. @27 Price;
   format  ReceivedDate date9.;
   datalines;
K89R seal   34  27jul1998 245.00
M4J7 sander 98  20jun1998 45.88
LK43 filter 121 19may1999 10.99
MN21 brace 43   10aug1999 27.87
BC85 clamp 80   16aug1999 9.55
NCF3 valve 198  20mar1999 24.50
KJ66 cutter 6   18jun1999 19.77
UYN7 rod   211  09sep1999 11.55
JD03 switch 383 09jan2000 13.99
BV1E timer 26   03aug2000 34.50
;


proc print data=inventory;
   title 'Tool Warehouse Inventory';
run;
```

The following output shows the results:

Output 19.9 The INVENTORY Data Set

```
                     Tool Warehouse Inventory                        1

              Part                    In     Received
     Obs     Number   Description   Stock      Date      Price

       1     K89R     seal           34     27JUL1998   245.00
       2     M4J7     sander         98     20JUN1998    45.88
       3     LK43     filter        121     19MAY1999    10.99
       4     MN21     brace          43     10AUG1999    27.87
       5     BC85     clamp          80     16AUG1999     9.55
       6     NCF3     valve         198     20MAR1999    24.50
       7     KJ66     cutter          6     18JUN1999    19.77
       8     UYN7     rod           211     09SEP1999    11.55
       9     JD03     switch        383     09JAN2000    13.99
      10     BV1E     timer          26     03AUG2000    34.50
```

The following program creates the transaction data set ADD_INVENTORY_4 . The second and fourth records contain missing values.

```
data add_inventory_4;
   input PartNumber $ 1-4 NewStock 6-8;
   datalines;
BC85 57
NCF3
KJ66 2
MN21
UYN7 108
JD03 55
;
```

The following program updates the master data set INVENTORY (Output 20.1 on page 311). The UPDATE statement uses the NOMISSINGCHECK value of the UPDATEMODE= option. Note that observations four and six are updated with missing values because the data is missing in the transaction data set.

```
options pagesize=60 linesize=80 pageno=1 nodate;

data inventory;
   update inventory add_inventory_4 updatemode=nomissingcheck;
   by PartNumber;
   ReceivedDate=today();
   InStock=InStock+NewStock;
run;

proc print data=inventory;
   title 'Tool Warehouse Inventory';
run;
```

Review of SAS Tools

Statements

UPDATE *master-SAS-data-set transaction-SAS-data-set*;
BY *identifier-list*;
   replace the values of variables in one SAS data set with nonmissing values from another SAS data set. *Master-SAS-data-set* is the SAS data set containing information that you want to update; *transaction-SAS-data-set* is the SAS data set containing information with which you want to update the master data set; *identifier-list* is the list of BY variables by which you identify corresponding observations.

Learning More

DATASETS procedure
   When you update a data set, you create a new data set containing the updated information. Typically, you want to use PROC DATASETS to delete the old master data set and rename the new one so that you can use the same program the next time you update the information. For more information about the DATASETS procedure, see Chapter 34, "Managing SAS Data Libraries," on page 599 of this book.

Indexes
   If a data set has an index on the variable or variables named in the BY statement that accompanies the UPDATE statement, you do not need to sort that data set. For more information about indexes, see the *SAS Language Reference: Dictionary* and the *SAS Language Reference: Concepts*.

Merge statement
   See Chapter 18, "Merging SAS Data Sets," on page 269.

CHAPTER

20

Modifying SAS Data Sets

Introduction

Purpose

In this chapter, you will learn how to use the MODIFY statement in a DATA step to
- replace values in a data set
- replace values in a *master data set* with values from a *transaction data set*
- append observations to an existing SAS data set
- delete observations from an existing SAS data set.

The MODIFY statement modifies observations directly in the original master file. It does not create a copy of the file.

Prerequisites

Before continuing with this chapter, you should be familiar with the concepts presented in
- Chapter 3, "Starting with Raw Data: The Basics," on page 43
- Chapter 5, "Starting with SAS Data Sets," on page 81

□ Chapter 18, "Merging SAS Data Sets," on page 269
□ Chapter 19, "Updating SAS Data Sets," on page 293.

Input SAS Data Set for Examples

In this chapter you will look at examples from an inventory tracking system that is used by a tool vendor. The examples use the SAS data set INVENTORY as input. The data set contains these variables:

PartNumber   is a character variable that contains a unique value that identifies each item.

Description   is a character variable that contains the text description of each item.

InStock   is a numeric variable that contains a value that describes how many units of each tool the warehouse has in stock.

ReceivedDate is a numeric variable that contains the SAS date value that is the day for which InStock values are current.

Price   is a numeric variable that contains the price of each item.

The following program creates and displays the INVENTORY data set:

```
options pagesize=60 linesize=80 pageno=1 nodate;

data inventory;
    input PartNumber $ Description $ InStock @17
          ReceivedDate date9. @27 Price;
    format ReceivedDate date9.;
    datalines;
K89R seal    34   27jul1998 245.00
M4J7 sander 98   20jun1998 45.88
LK43 filter 121  19may1999 10.99
MN21 brace 43    10aug1999 27.87
BC85 clamp 80    16aug1999 9.55
NCF3 valve 198   20mar1999 24.50
KJ66 cutter 6    18jun1999 19.77
UYN7 rod   211   09sep1999 11.55
JD03 switch 383  09jan2000 13.99
BV1E timer 26    03aug2000 34.50
;


proc print data=inventory;
    title 'Tool Warehouse Inventory';
run;
```

The following output shows the results:

Output 20.1 The INVENTORY Data Set

```
                       Tool Warehouse Inventory                        1

             Part                   In      Received
    Obs     Number   Description   Stock      Date      Price

     1      K89R      seal          34      27JUL1998   245.00
     2      M4J7      sander        98      20JUN1998    45.88
     3      LK43      filter       121      19MAY1999    10.99
     4      MN21      brace         43      10AUG1999    27.87
     5      BC85      clamp         80      16AUG1999     9.55
     6      NCF3      valve        198      20MAR1999    24.50
     7      KJ66      cutter         6      18JUN1999    19.77
     8      UYN7      rod          211      09SEP1999    11.55
     9      JD03      switch       383      09JAN2000    13.99
    10      BV1E      timer         26      03AUG2000    34.50
```

Modifying a SAS Data Set: The Simplest Case

You can use the MODIFY statement to replace all values for a specific variable or variables in a data set. The syntax for using the MODIFY statement for this purpose is

MODIFY *SAS-data-set*;

In the following program, the price of each part in the inventory is increased by 15%. The new values for PRICE replace the old values on all records in the original INVENTORY data set. The FORMAT statement in the print procedure writes the price of each item with two-digit decimal precision.

```
data inventory;
   modify inventory;
   price=price+(price*.15);
run;

proc print data=inventory;
   title 'Tool Warehouse Inventory';
   title2 '(Price reflects 15% increase)';
   format price 8.2;
run;
```

The following output shows the results:

Output 20.2   The INVENTORY Data Set with Updated Prices

```
                            Tool Warehouse Inventory                        1
                            (Price reflects 15% increase)

                  Part                    In      Received
        Obs      Number    Description   Stock      Date        Price

         1       K89R        seal         34      27JUL1998     281.75
         2       M4J7        sander       98      20JUN1998      52.76
         3       LK43        filter      121      19MAY1999      12.64
         4       MN21        brace        43      10AUG1999      32.05
         5       BC85        clamp        80      16AUG1999      10.98
         6       NCF3        valve       198      20MAR1999      28.18
         7       KJ66        cutter        6      18JUN1999      22.74
         8       UYN7        rod         211      09SEP1999      13.28
         9       JD03        switch      383      09JAN2000      16.09
        10       BV1E        timer        26      03AUG2000      39.68
```

Modifying a Master Data Set with Observations from a Transaction Data Set

Understanding the MODIFY Statement

The MODIFY statement replaces data in a master data set with data from a transaction data set, and makes the changes in the original master data set. You can use a BY statement to match observations from the transaction data set with observations in the master data set. The syntax for using the MODIFY statement and the BY statement is

MODIFY *master-SAS-data-set transaction-SAS-data-set*;

BY *by-variable*;

The *master-SAS-data-set* specifies the SAS data set that you want to modify. The *transaction-SAS-data-set* specifies the SAS data set that provides the values for updating the master data set. The *by-variable* specifies one or more variables by which you identify corresponding observations.

When you use a BY statement with the MODIFY statement, the DATA step uses dynamic WHERE processing to find observations in the master data set. Neither the master data set nor the transaction data set needs to be sorted. For large data sets, however, sorting the data before you modify it can enhance performance significantly.

Adding New Observations to the Master Data Set

You can use the MODIFY statement to add observations to an existing master data set. If the transaction data set contains an observation that does not match an observation in the master data set, then SAS enables you to write a new observation to the master data set if you use an explicit OUTPUT statement in your program. When you specify an explicit OUTPUT statement, you must also specify a REPLACE statement if you want to replace observations in place. All new observations append to the end of the master data set.

Checking for Program Errors

You can use the _IORC_ automatic variable for error checking in your DATA step program. The _IORC_ automatic variable contains the return code for each I/O operation that the MODIFY statement attempts to perform.

The best way to test the values of _IORC_ is with the mnemonic codes that are provided by the SYSRC autocall macro. Each mnemonic code describes one condition. The mnemonics provide an easy method for testing problems in a DATA step program. The following is a partial list of codes:

_DSENMR

    specifies that the transaction data set observation does not exist in the master data set (used only with MODIFY and BY statements). If consecutive observations with different BY values do not find a match in the master data set, then both of them return _DSENMR.

_DSEMTR

    specifies that multiple transaction data set observations with a given BY value do not exist in the master data set (used only with MODIFY and BY statements). If consecutive observations with the same BY values do not find a match in the master data set, then the first observation returns _DSENMR and the subsequent observations return _DSEMTR.

_SOK

    specifies that the observation was located in the master data set.

For a complete list of mnemonic codes, see the MODIFY statement in *SAS Language Reference: Dictionary*.

The Program

The program in this section updates values in a master data set with values from a transaction data set. If a transaction does not exist in the master data set, then the program adds the transaction to the master data set.

In this example, a warehouse received a shipment of new items, and the INVENTORY master data set must be modified to reflect the changes. The master data set contains a complete list of the inventory items. The transaction data set contains items that are on the master inventory as well as new inventory items.

The following program creates the ADD_INVENTORY transaction data set, which contains items for updating the master data set. The PartNumber variable contains the part number for the item and corresponds to PartNumber in the INVENTORY data set. The Description variable names the item. The NewStock variable contains the number of each item in the current shipment. The NewPrice variable contains the new price of the item.

The program attempts to update the master data set INVENTORY (see Output 20.1 on page 311) according to the values in the transaction data set ADD_INVENTORY. The program uses the _IORC_ automatic variable to detect errors.

```
data add_inventory; ❶
    input PartNumber $ Description $ NewStock @16 NewPrice;
    datalines;
K89R seal   6  247.50
AA11 hammer 55 32.26
BB22 wrench 21 17.35
```

```
              KJ66 cutter 10 24.50
              CC33 socket 7  22.19
              BV1E timer 30  36.50
              ;


       options pagesize=60 linesize=80 pageno=1 nodate;

       data inventory;
          modify inventory add_inventory; ❷
          by PartNumber;
          select (_iorc_); ❸
             /* The observation exists in the master data set. */
             when (%sysrc(_sok)) do; ❹
                 InStock=InStock+NewStock;
                 ReceivedDate=today();
                 Price=NewPrice;
                 replace; ❺
             end;
             /* The observation does not exist in the master data set. */
             when (%sysrc(_dsenmr)) do; ❻
                 InStock=NewStock;
                 ReceivedDate=today();
                 Price=NewPrice;
                 output; ❼
                 _error_=0;
             end;
             otherwise do; ❽
                    put 'An unexpected I/O error has occurred.'/ ❽
                       'Check your data and your program.'; ❽
                 _error_=0;
                 stop;
             end;
          end;


       proc print data=inventory;
          title 'Tool Warehouse Inventory';
       run;
```

The following list corresponds to the numbered items in the preceding program:

❶ The DATA statement creates the transaction data set ADD_INVENTORY.

❷ The MODIFY statement loads the data from the INVENTORY and ADD_INVENTORY data sets.

❸ The _IORC_ automatic variable is used for error checking. The value of _IORC_ is a numeric return code that indicates the status of the most recent I/O operation.

❹ The SYSRC autocall macro checks to see if the value of _IORC_ is _SOK. If the value is _SOK, then an observation in the transaction data set matches an observation in the master data set.

❺ The REPLACE statement updates the master data set INVENTORY by replacing the observation in the master data set with the observation from the transaction data set.

❻ The SYSRC autocall macro checks to see if the value of _IORC_ is _DSENMR. If the value is _DSENMR, then an observation in the transaction data set does not exist in the master data set.

❼ The OUTPUT statement writes the current observation to the end of the master data set.

❽ If neither condition is met, the PUT statement writes a message to the log.

The following output shows the results:

Output 20.3 The Updated INVENTORY Data Set

```
                        Tool Warehouse Inventory                      1

            Part                      In      Received
   Obs     Number    Description    Stock        Date      Price

    1      K89R       seal            40      19JAN2001    247.50
    2      M4J7       sander          98      20JUN1998     45.88
    3      LK43       filter         121      19MAY1999     10.99
    4      MN21       brace           43      10AUG1999     27.87
    5      BC85       clamp           80      16AUG1999      9.55
    6      NCF3       valve          198      20MAR1999     24.50
    7      KJ66       cutter          16      19JAN2001     24.50
    8      UYN7       rod            211      09SEP1999     11.55
    9      JD03       switch         383      09JAN2000     13.99
   10      BV1E       timer           56      19JAN2001     36.50
   11      AA11       hammer          55      19JAN2001     32.26
   12      BB22       wrench          21      19JAN2001     17.35
   13      CC33       socket           7      19JAN2001     22.19
```

SAS writes the following message to the log:

```
NOTE: The data set WORK.INVENTORY has been updated.  There were 3 observations
      rewritten, 3 observations added and 0 observations deleted.
```

CAUTION:
If you execute your program without the OUTPUT and REPLACE statements, then your master file might not update correctly. Using OUTPUT or REPLACE in a DATA step overrides the default replacement of observations. If you use these statements in a DATA step, then you must explicitly program each action that you want to take. △

For more information about the MODIFY, OUTPUT, and REPLACE statements, see the Statements section in *SAS Language Reference: Dictionary*.

Understanding How Duplicate BY Variables Affect File Update

How the DATA Step Processes Duplicate BY Variables

When you use a BY statement with MODIFY, both the master and the transaction data sets can have observations with duplicate values of BY variables. Neither the master nor the transaction data set needs to be sorted, because BY-group processing uses dynamic WHERE processing to find an observation in the master data set.

The DATA step processes duplicate observations in the following ways:

☐ If duplicate BY values exist in the master data set, then MODIFY applies the current transaction to the first occurrence in the master data set.

□ If duplicate BY values exist in the transaction data set, then the observations are applied one on top of another so that the values overwrite each other. The value in the last transaction is the final value in the master data set.

□ If both the master and the transaction data sets contain duplicate BY values, then MODIFY applies each transaction to the first occurrence in the group in the master data set.

The Program

The program in this section updates the master data set INVENTORY_2 with observations from the transaction data set ADD_INVENTORY_2. Both data sets contain consecutive and nonconsecutive duplicate values of the BY variable PartNumber.

The following program creates the master data set INVENTORY_2. Note that the data set contains three observations for PartNumber M4J7.

```
data inventory_2;
   input PartNumber $ Description $ InStock @17
         ReceivedDate date9. @27 Price;
   format  ReceivedDate date9.;
   datalines;
K89R seal    34   27jul1998 245.00
M4J7 sander 98   20jun1998 45.88
M4J7 sander 98   20jun1998 45.88
LK43 filter 121  19may1999 10.99
MN21 brace 43    10aug1999 27.87
M4J7 sander 98   20jun1998 45.88
BC85 clamp 80    16aug1999 9.55
NCF3 valve 198   20mar1999 24.50
KJ66 cutter 6    18jun1999 19.77
;
```

The following program creates the transaction data set ADD_INVENTORY_2, and then modifies the master data set INVENTORY_2. Note that the data set ADD_INVENTORY_2 contains three observations for PartNumber M4J7.

```
options pagesize=60 linesize=80 pageno=1 nodate;

data add_inventory_2;
   input PartNumber $ Description $ NewStock;
   datalines;
K89R abc 17
M4J7 def 72
M4J7 ghi 66
LK43 jkl 311
M4J7 mno 43
BC85 pqr 75
;

data inventory_2;
   modify inventory_2 add_inventory_2;
   by PartNumber;
   ReceivedDate=today();
   InStock=InStock+NewStock;
run;
```

```
proc print data=inventory_2;
   title "Tool Warehouse Inventory";
run;
```

The following output shows the results:

Output 20.4 The Updated INVENTORY_2 Data Set: Duplicate BY Variables

```
                           Tool Warehouse Inventory                           1

                    Part              In      Received
          Obs      Number  Description Stock      Date    Price

           1       K89R    abc          51     22JAN2001  245.00
           2       M4J7    mno         279     22JAN2001   45.88
           3       M4J7    sander       98     20JUN1998   45.88
           4       LK43    jkl         432     22JAN2001   10.99
           5       MN21    brace        43     10AUG1999   27.87
           6       M4J7    sander       98     20JUN1998   45.88
           7       BC85    pqr         155     22JAN2001    9.55
           8       NCF3    valve       198     20MAR1999   24.50
           9       KJ66    cutter        6     18JUN1999   19.77
```

Handling Missing Values

By default, if the transaction data set contains missing values for a variable that is common to both the master and the transaction data sets, then the MODIFY statement does not replace values in the master data set with missing values.

If you want to replace values in the master data set with missing values, then you use the UPDATEMODE= option on the MODIFY statement. UPDATEMODE specifies whether missing values in a transaction data set will replace existing values in a master data set.

The syntax for using the UPDATEMODE= option with the MODIFY statement is

MODIFY *master-SAS-data-set transaction-SAS-data-set*
  <UPDATEMODE=MISSINGCHECK | NOMISSINGCHECK>;

BY *by-variable*;

MISSINGCHECK prevents missing values in a transaction data set from replacing values in a master data set. This is the default. NOMISSINGCHECK enables missing values in a transaction data set to replace values in a master data set by preventing the check for missing data from being performed.

The following example creates the master data set Event_List, which contains the schedule and codes for athletic events. The example then updates Event_List with the transaction data set Event_Change, which contains new information about the schedule. Because the MODIFY statement uses the NOMISSINGCHECK value of the UPDATEMODE= option, values in the master data set are replaced by missing values from the transaction data set.

The following program creates the EVENT_LIST master data set:

```
data Event_List;
   input Event $ 1-10 Weekday $ 12-20 TimeofDay $ 22-30 Fee Code;
   datalines;
Basketball Monday     evening   10 58
Soccer     Tuesday    morning    5 33
Yoga       Wednesday  afternoon 15 92
```

```
Swimming    Wednesday morning    10 63
;
```

The following program creates the EVENT_CHANGE transaction data set:

```
data Event_Change;
   input Event $ 1-10 Weekday $ 12-20 Fee Code;
   datalines;
Basketball Wednesday 10 .
Yoga        Monday    . 63
Swimming              . .
;
```

The following program modifies and prints the master data set:

```
options pagesize=60 linesize=80 pageno=1 nodate;

data Event_List;
    modify Event_List Event_Change updatemode=nomissingcheck;
    by Event;
 run;

proc print data=Event_List;
   title 'Schedule of Athletic Events';
run;
```

The following output shows the results:

Output 20.5   The EVENT_LIST Master Data Set: Missing Values

```
                      Schedule of Athletic Events                           1

        Obs     Event        Weekday       TimeofDay     Fee     Code

         1     Basketball    Wednesday     evening       10       .
         2     Soccer        Tuesday       morning        5       33
         3     Yoga          Monday        afternoon      .       63
         4     Swimming                    morning        .       .
```

Review of SAS Tools

Statements

BY *by-variable*;
   specifies one or more variables to use with the BY statement. You use the BY
   variable to identify corresponding observations in a master data set and a
   transaction data set.

MODIFY *master-SAS-data-set transaction-SAS-data-set*
<UPDATEMODE=MISSINGCHECK|NOMISSINGCHECK>;
   replaces the values of variables in one SAS data set with values from another SAS
   data set. The *master-SAS-data-set* contains data that you want to update. The

transaction-SAS-data-set contains observations with which to update the master data set.

The UPDATEMODE argument determines whether missing values in the transaction data set overwrite values in the master data set. The MISSINGCHECK option prevents missing values in a transaction data set from replacing values in a master data set. This is the default. The NOMISSINGCHECK option enables missing values in a transaction data set to replace values in a master data set by preventing the check for missing data from being performed.

MODIFY *SAS-data-set*;
  replaces the values of variables in a data set with values that you specify in your program.

OUTPUT;
  if a MODIFY statement is present, writes the current observation to the end of the master data set.

REPLACE;
  if a MODIFY statement is present, writes the current observation to the same physical location from which it was read in a data set that is named in the DATA statement.

Learning More

MERGE statement
  See Chapter 18, "Merging SAS Data Sets," on page 269.

MODIFY statement
  For complete information about the various applications of the MODIFY statement, see *SAS Language Reference: Dictionary*.

UPDATE statement
  See Chapter 19, "Updating SAS Data Sets," on page 293.

CHAPTER
21

Conditionally Processing Observations from Multiple SAS Data Sets

Introduction

Purpose

When combining SAS data sets, you can process observations conditionally, based on which data set contributed that observation. You can

- □ determine which data set contributed each observation in the combined data set

- □ create a new data set that includes only selected observations from the data sets that you combine

- □ determine when SAS is processing the last observation in the DATA step so that you can execute conditional operations, such as creating totals.

You have seen some of these concepts in earlier chapters, but in this chapter you will apply them to the processing of multiple data sets. The examples use the SET statement, but you can also use all of the features that are discussed here with the MERGE, MODIFY, and UPDATE statements.

Prerequisites

Before using this chapter, you should understand the concepts presented in

- □ Chapter 3, "Starting with Raw Data: The Basics," on page 43

- □ Chapter 5, "Starting with SAS Data Sets," on page 81

□ Chapter 17, "Interleaving SAS Data Sets," on page 263.

Input SAS Data Sets for Examples

The following program creates two SAS data sets, SOUTHAMERICAN and EUROPEAN. Each data set contains the following variables:

Year
is the year that South American and European countries competed in the World Cup Finals from 1954 to 1998.

Country
is the name of the competing country.

Score
is the final score of the game.

Result
is the result of the game. The value for winners is **won**; the value for losers is **lost**.

```
data southamerican;
    title "South American World Cup Finalists from 1954 to 1998";
    input  Year $  Country $ 9-23 Score $ 25-28 Result $ 32-36;
    datalines;
1998    Brazil          0-3     lost
1994    Brazil          3-2     won
1990    Argentina       0-1     lost
1986    Argentina       3-2     won
1978    Argentina       3-1     won
1970    Brazil          4-1     won
1962    Brazil          3-1     won
1958    Brazil          5-2     won
;


data european;
    title "European World Cup Finalists From 1954 to 1998";
    input  Year $  Country $ 9-23 Score $ 25-28 Result $ 32-36;
    datalines;
1998    France          3-0     won
1994    Italy           2-3     lost
1990    West Germany    1-0     won
1986    West Germany    2-3     lost
1982    Italy           3-1     won
1982    West Germany    1-3     lost
1978    Holland         1-2     lost
1974    West Germany    2-1     won
1974    Holland         1-2     lost
1970    Italy           1-4     lost
1966    England         4-2     won
1966    West Germany    2-4     lost
1962    Czechoslovakia  1-3     lost
1958    Sweden          2-5     lost
1954    West Germany    3-2     won
1954    Hungary         2-3     lost
;

options pagesize=60 linesize=80 pageno=1 nodate;
```

```
proc sort data=southamerican;❶
   by year;❶
run;

proc print data=southamerican;
   title 'World Cup Finalists:';
   title2 'South American Countries';
   title3 'from 1954 to 1998';
run;

proc sort data=european;❶
   by year;❶
run;

proc print data=european;
   title 'World Cup Finalists:';
   title2 'European Countries';
   title3 'from 1954 to 1998';
run;
```

❶ The PROC SORT statement sorts the data set in ascending order according to the BY variable. To create the interleaved data set in the next example, the data must be in ascending order.

Output 21.1 World Cup Finalists by Continent

```
                       World Cup Finalists:                          1
                     South American Countries
                        from 1954 to 1998

          Obs    Year    Country      Score    Result

           1     1958    Brazil       5-2      won
           2     1962    Brazil       3-1      won
           3     1970    Brazil       4-1      won
           4     1978    Argentina    3-1      won
           5     1986    Argentina    3-2      won
           6     1990    Argentina    0-1      lost
           7     1994    Brazil       3-2      won
           8     1998    Brazil       0-3      lost
```

```
                    World Cup Finalists:                          2
                    European Countries
                    from 1954 to 1998

         Obs    Year    Country          Score    Result

          1     1954    West Germany      3-2       won
          2     1954    Hungary           2-3       lost
          3     1958    Sweden            2-5       lost
          4     1962    Czechoslovakia    1-3       lost
          5     1966    England           4-2       won
          6     1966    West Germany      2-4       lost
          7     1970    Italy             1-4       lost
          8     1974    West Germany      2-1       won
          9     1974    Holland           1-2       lost
         10     1978    Holland           1-2       lost
         11     1982    Italy             3-1       won
         12     1982    West Germany      1-3       lost
         13     1986    West Germany      2-3       lost
         14     1990    West Germany      1-0       won
         15     1994    Italy             2-3       lost
         16     1998    France            3-0       won
```

Determining Which Data Set Contributed the Observation

Understanding the IN= Data Set Option

When you create a new data set by combining observations from two or more data sets, knowing which data set an observation came from can be useful. For example, you might want to perform a calculation based on which data set contributed an observation. Otherwise, you might lose important contextual information that you need for later processing. You can determine which data set contributed a particular observation by using the IN= data set option.

The IN= data set option enables you to determine which data sets have contributed to the observation that is currently in the program data vector. The syntax for this option on the SET statement is

SET *SAS-data-set-1* (IN=*variable*) *SAS-data-set-2*;

BY *a-common-variable*;

When you use the IN= option with a data set in a SET, MERGE, MODIFY, or UPDATE statement, SAS creates a temporary *variable* associated with that data set. The value of *variable* is 1 if the data set has contributed to the observation currently in the program data vector. The value is 0 if it has not contributed. You can use the IN= option with any or all the data sets you name in a SET, MERGE, MODIFY, or UPDATE statement, but use a different variable name in each case.

Note: The IN= variable exists during the execution of the DATA step only; it is not written to the output data set that is created. △

The Program

The original data sets, SOUTHAMERICAN and EUROPEAN, do not need a variable that identifies the countries' continent because all observations in SOUTHAMERICAN pertain to the South American continent, and all observations in EUROPEAN pertain to the European continent. However, when you combine the data sets, you lose the context, which in this case is the relevant continent for each observation. The following example uses the SET statement with a BY statement to combine the two data sets into one data set that contains all the observations in chronological order:

```
options pagesize=60 linesize=80 pageno=1 nodate;

data finalists;
   set southamerican european;
   by year;
run;

proc print data=finalists;
   title 'World Cup Finalists';
   title2 'from 1958 to 1998';
run;
```

Output 21.2 World Cup Finalists Grouped by Year

```
                           World Cup Finalists                              1
                           from 1958 to 1998

            Obs     Year    Country          Score     Result

             1      1954    West Germany      3-2       won
             2      1954    Hungary           2-3       lost
             3      1958    Brazil            5-2       won
             4      1958    Sweden            2-5       lost
             5      1962    Brazil            3-1       won
             6      1962    Czechoslovakia    1-3       lost
             7      1966    England           4-2       won
             8      1966    West Germany      2-4       lost
             9      1970    Brazil            4-1       won
            10      1970    Italy             1-4       lost
            11      1974    West Germany      2-1       won
            12      1974    Holland           1-2       lost
            13      1978    Argentina         3-1       won
            14      1978    Holland           1-2       lost
            15      1982    Italy             3-1       won
            16      1982    West Germany      1-3       lost
            17      1986    Argentina         3-2       won
            18      1986    West Germany      2-3       lost
            19      1990    Argentina         0-1       lost
            20      1990    West Germany      1-0       won
            21      1994    Brazil            3-2       won
            22      1994    Italy             2-3       lost
            23      1998    Brazil            0-3       lost
            24      1998    France            3-0       won
```

Notice that this output would be more useful if it showed from which data set each observation originated. To solve this problem, the following program uses the IN= data set option in conjunction with IF-THEN/ELSE statements. By determing which data set contributed an observation, the conditional statement executes and assigns the appropriate value to the variable Continent in each observation in the new data set FINALISTS.

```
options pagesize=60 linesize=80 pageno=1 nodate;

data finalists;
```

```
      set southamerican (in=S) european; ❶
      by Year;
      if S then Continent='South America'; ❷
      else Continent='Europe';
   run;

   proc print data=finalists;
      title 'World Cup Finalists';
      title2 'from 1954 to 1998';
      run;
```

The following list corresponds to the numbered items in the preceding program:

❶ The IN= option in the SET statement tells SAS to create a variable named S.

❷ When the current observation comes from the data set SOUTHAMERICAN, the value of S is 1. Otherwise, the value is 0. The IF-THEN/ELSE statements execute one of two assignment statements, depending on the value of S. If the observation comes from the data set SOUTHAMERICAN, then the value that is assigned to Continent is South America. If the observation comes from the data set EUROPEAN, then the value that is assigned to Continent is Europe.

The following output shows the results:

Output 21.3   World Cup Finalists with Continent

```
                      World Cup Finalists                          1
                        from 1954 to 1998

      Obs    Year    Country        Score    Result    Continent

        1    1954    West Germany     3-2     won       Europe
        2    1954    Hungary          2-3     lost      Europe
        3    1958    Brazil           5-2     won       South America
        4    1958    Sweden           2-5     lost      Europe
        5    1962    Brazil           3-1     won       South America
        6    1962    Czechoslovakia   1-3     lost      Europe
        7    1966    England          4-2     won       Europe
        8    1966    West Germany     2-4     lost      Europe
        9    1970    Brazil           4-1     won       South America
       10    1970    Italy            1-4     lost      Europe
       11    1974    West Germany     2-1     won       Europe
       12    1974    Holland          1-2     lost      Europe
       13    1978    Argentina        3-1     won       South America
       14    1978    Holland          1-2     lost      Europe
       15    1982    Italy            3-1     won       Europe
       16    1982    West Germany     1-3     lost      Europe
       17    1986    Argentina        3-2     won       South America
       18    1986    West Germany     2-3     lost      Europe
       19    1990    Argentina        0-1     lost      South America
       20    1990    West Germany     1-0     won       Europe
       21    1994    Brazil           3-2     won       South America
       22    1994    Italy            2-3     lost      Europe
       23    1998    Brazil           0-3     lost      South America
       24    1998    France           3-0     won       Europe
```

Combining Selected Observations from Multiple Data Sets

To create a data set that contains only the observations that are selected according to a particular criterion, you can use the subsetting IF statement and a SET statement that specifies multiple data sets. The following DATA step reads two input data sets to create a combined data set that lists only the winning teams:

```
data champions(drop=result);①
   set southamerican (in=S) european;②
   by Year;
   if result='won';③
   if S then Continent='South America';④
   else Continent='Europe';
run;

proc print data=champions;
   title 'World Cup Champions from 1954 to 1998';
   title2 'including Countries'' Continent';
run;
```

The following list corresponds to the numbered items in the preceding program:

① The DROP= data set option drops the variable Result from the new data set CHAMPIONS because all values for this variable will be the same.

② The SET statement reads observations from two data sets: SOUTHAMERICAN and EUROPEAN. The S= data option creates the variable S which is set to 1 each time an observation is contributed by the SOUTHAMERICAN data set.

③ A subsetting IF statement writes the observation to the output data set CHAMPIONS only if the value of the Result variable is **won**.

④ When the current observation comes from the data set SOUTHAMERICAN, the value of S is 1. Otherwise, the value is 0. The IF-THEN/ELSE statements execute one of two assignment statements, depending on the value of S. If the observation comes from the data set SOUTHAMERICAN, then the value assigned to Continent is South America. If the observation comes from the data set EUROPEAN, then the value assigned to Continent is Europe.

The following output shows the resulting data set CHAMPIONS:

Output 21.4 Combining Selected Observations

```
               World Cup Champions from 1954 to 1998                   2
                     including Countries' Continent

        Obs    Year    Country       Score    Continent

          1    1954    West Germany   3-2      Europe
          2    1958    Brazil         5-2      South America
          3    1962    Brazil         3-1      South America
          4    1966    England        4-2      Europe
          5    1970    Brazil         4-1      South America
          6    1974    West Germany   2-1      Europe
          7    1978    Argentina      3-1      South America
          8    1982    Italy          3-1      Europe
          9    1986    Argentina      3-2      South America
         10    1990    West Germany   1-0      Europe
         11    1994    Brazil         3-2      South America
         12    1998    France         3-0      Europe
```

Performing a Calculation Based on the Last Observation

Understanding When the Last Observation Is Processed

Many applications require that you determine when the DATA step processes the last observation in the input data set. For example, you might want to perform calculations only on the last observation in a data set, or you might want to write an observation only after the last observation has been processed. For this purpose, you can use the END= option for the SET, MERGE, MODIFY, or UPDATE statement. The syntax for this option is

SET *SAS-data-set-list* END=*variable*;

The END= option defines a temporary *variable* whose value is 1 when the DATA step is processing the last observation. At all other times, the value of *variable* is 0. Although the DATA step can use the END= *variable*, SAS does not add it to the resulting data set.

Note: Chapter 12, "Using More Than One Observation in a Calculation," on page 187 explains how to use the END= option in the SET statement with a single data set. The END= option works the same way with multiple data sets, but it is important to note that END= is set to 1 only when the last observation from all input data sets is being processed. △

The Program

This example uses the data in SOUTHAMERICAN and EUROPEAN to calculate how many years a team from each continent won the World Cup from 1954 to 1998. To perform this calculation, this program must

1 identify on which continent a country is located

2 keep a running total of how many times a team from each continent won the World Cup

3 after processing all observations, multiply the final total for each continent by 4 (the length of time between World Cups) to determine the length of time each continent has been a World Cup champion

4 write only the final observation to the output data set. The variables that contain the totals do not contain the final total until the last observation is processed.

The following DATA step calculates the running totals and produces the output data set that contains only those totals.

```
data timespan (keep=YearsSouthAmerican keep=YearsEuropean);❹
   set southamerican (in=S) european   end=LastYear;❶❸
   by Year;
   if result='won' then
      do;
         if S then SouthAmericanWins+1;❷
         else EuropeanWins+1;❷
      end;
   if lastyear then❸
      do;
         YearsSouthAmerican=SouthAmericanWins*4;
```

```
        YearsEuropean=EuropeanWins*4;
        output;❹
    end;

proc print data=timespan;
    title 'Total Years as Reigning World Cup Champions';
    title2 'from 1954 to 1998';
run;
```

The following list corresponds to the numbered items in the preceding program:

❶ The END= option creates the temporary variable LastYear. The value of LastYear is 0 until the DATA step begins processing the last observation. At that point, the value of LastYear is set to 1.

❷ Two new variables, SouthAmericanWins and EuropeanWins, keep a running total of the number of victories each continent achieves. For each observation in which the value of the variable Result is **won**, a different sum statement executes, based on the data set that the observation came from:

```
    SouthAmericanWins+1;
```

or

```
    EuropeanWins+1;
```

❸ When the DATA step begins processing the last observation, the value of LASTYEAR changes from 0 to 1. When this change occurs, the conditional statement **IF LastYear** becomes true, and the statements that follow it are executed. The assignment statement multiplies the total number of victories for each continent by 4 and assigns the result to the appropriate variable, YearsSouthAmerican or YearsEuropean.

❹ The OUTPUT statement writes the observation to the newly created data set. Remember that the DATA step automatically writes an observation at the end of each iteration. However, the OUTPUT statement turns off this automatic feature. The DATA step writes only the last observation to TIMESPAN. When the DATA step writes the observation from the program data vector to the output data set, it writes only two variables, YearsSouthAmerican and YearsEuropean, as directed by the KEEP= data set option in the DATA statement.

Output 21.5 Using the END= Option to Perform a Calculation Based on the Last Observation in the Data Sets

```
        Total Years as Reigning World Cup Champions              3
                      from 1954 to 1998

                           Years
                           South       Years
                Obs      American     European

                 1          24           24
```

Review of SAS Tools

Statements

IF *condition*;
> tests whether the *condition* is true. If it is true, then SAS continues processing the current observation; if it is false, then SAS stops processing the observation and returns to the beginning of the DATA step. This type of IF statement is called a *subsetting* IF statement because it produces a subset of the original observations.

IF *condition* THEN *action*;
<ELSE *action*;>
> tests whether the *condition* is true; if so, then the *action* in the THEN clause is executed. If the *condition* is false and an ELSE statement is present, then the ELSE *action* is executed. If the *condition* is false and no ELSE statement is present, then execution proceeds to the next statement in the DATA step.

SET *SAS-data-set* (IN=*variable*) *SAS-data-set-list*;
> creates a *variable* that is associated with a SAS data set. The value of *variable* is 1 if the data set has contributed to the observation currently in the program data vector; 0 if it has not. The IN= variable exists only while the DATA step executes; it is not written to the output data set.
>
> You can use the option with any data set that you name in the SET, MERGE, MODIFY, or UPDATE statement, but use a different variable name for each one.

SET *SAS-data-set-list* END=*variable*;
> creates a *variable* whose value is 0 until the DATA step starts to process its last observation. When processing of the last observation begins, the value of *variable* changes to 1. The END= variable exists only while the DATA step executes; it is not written to the output data set.
>
> You can also use the END= option with the MERGE, MODIFY, and UPDATE statements.

Learning More

DATA set options
> For an introduction to data set options, see Chapter 5, "Starting with SAS Data Sets," on page 81.

DO statement
> See Chapter 13, "Finding Shortcuts in Programming," on page 201.

IF statements
> For more information about both the subsetting and conditional IF statements, see Chapter 9, "Acting on Selected Observations," on page 139.

OUTPUT and subsetting IF statement
> See Chapter 10, "Creating Subsets of Observations," on page 159.

SUM statement and END= option
> See Chapter 12, "Using More Than One Observation in a Calculation," on page 187.

PART 5

Understanding Your SAS Session

Analyzing Your SAS Session with the SAS Log

Introduction

Purpose

The SAS log is a useful tool for analyzing your SAS session and programs. In this chapter, you will learn about

- the log in relation to output
- the log structure
- the log's default destination, which depends on the method that you use to run SAS.

You will also learn how to

□ write to the log

□ suppress information to the log.

Prerequisites

You should understand the basic SAS programming concepts that are presented in

□ Chapter 1, "What Is the SAS System?," on page 3

□ Chapter 2, "Introduction to DATA Step Processing," on page 19

□ Chapter 3, "Starting with Raw Data: The Basics," on page 43.

Understanding the SAS Log

Understanding the Role of the SAS Log

The SAS log results from executing a SAS program, and in that sense it is output. The SAS log provides a record of everything that you do in your SAS session or with your SAS program, from the names of the data sets that you have created to the number of observations and variables in those data sets. This record can tell you what statements were executed, how much time the DATA and PROC steps required, and whether your program contains errors.

As with SAS output, the destination of the SAS log varies depending on your method of running SAS and on your operating environment. The content of the SAS log varies according to the DATA and PROC steps that are executed and the options that are used.

The sample log in the following output was generated by a SAS program that contains two PROC steps.* Another typical log is described in detail later in the chapter.

Output 22.1   A Sample SAS Log

```
NOTE: Libref OUT was successfully assigned as follows:
      Engine:        V8
      Physical Name: YOUR-DATA-LIBRARY
57    options linesize=120;
58
59    proc sort data=out.sat_scores;
60       by test;
61    run;
62
63    proc plot data=out.sat_scores;
64       by test;
65       label SATscore='SAT score';
66       plot SATscore*year / haxis= 1972 1975 1978 1981 1984 1987 1990 1993 1996 1999;
67       title1 'SAT Scores by Year, 1972-1999';
68       title3 'Separate statistics by Test Type';
69    run;
NOTE: There were 108 observations read from the data set OUT.SAT_SCORES.
```

---

*   The DATA step that created this data set is shown in the Appendix in "Data Sets for Chapter 20." The data set is stored in a SAS data library referenced by the libref OUT throughout the rest of this chapter. For examples in which raw data is read, the raw data is shown in the Appendix in "Data Sets for Chapters 21 and 23."

Resolving Errors with the Log

The SAS program that generated the log in the previous example ran without errors. If the program had contained errors, then those errors would have been reflected, as part of the session, in the log. SAS generates messages for data errors, syntax errors, and programming errors. You can browse those messages, make necessary changes to your program, and then rerun it successfully.

Locating the SAS Log

The destination of your log depends on the method you are using to start, run, and exit SAS. It also depends on your operating environment and on the setting of SAS system options. The following table shows the default destination for each method of operation:

Method of Operation	Destination of SAS Log
SAS windowing environment (interactive full-screen)	Log window
interactive line mode	on the terminal display, as statements are entered
noninteractive SAS programs	depends on the operating environment
batch jobs	line printer or disk file

Understanding the Log Structure

Detecting a Syntax Error

The following SAS program contains one DATA step and two PROC steps. However, the DATA statement has a syntax error– that is, it does not have a semicolon.

```
/* omitted semicolon */
data out.sat_scores4
   infile 'your-input-file';
   input test $ 1-8 gender $ 18 year 20-23
         score 25-27;
run;

proc sort data = out.sat_scores4;
   by test;
run;

proc print data = out.sat_scores4;
   by test;
run;
```

The following output shows the results. Although some variation occurs across operating environments and among methods of running SAS, the SAS log is a representative sample.

Output 22.2   Analyzing a SAS Log with Error Messages

```
3     /* omitted semicolon */
4        data out.sat_scores4❶
5        infile 'your-input-file';
6        input test $ 1-8 gender $ 18 year 20-23
7              scores 25-27;
8     run;

ERROR: No CARDS or INFILE statement. ❷
ERROR: The value YOUR-INPUT-FILE is not a valid SAS name.
NOTE: The SAS System stopped processing this step because of errors. ❸
WARNING: The data set OUT.SAT_SCORES4 may be incomplete.  When this step was
         stopped there were 0 observations and 4 variables.
WARNING: Data set OUT.SAT_SCORES4 was not replaced because this step was
         stopped.
WARNING: The data set WORK.INFILE may be incomplete.  When this step was
         stopped there were 0 observations and 4 variables.


9
10    proc sort data=out.sat_scores4; ❶
11       by test;
12    run;

NOTE: Input data set is empty.❸
NOTE: The data set OUT.SAT_SCORES4 has 0 observations and 4 variables. ❹


13
14    proc print data=out.sat_scores4; ❶
15       by test;
16    run;

NOTE: No observations in data set OUT.SAT_SCORES4.
```

Examining the Components of a Log

The SAS log provides valuable information, especially if you have questions and need to contact your site's SAS Support Consultant or SAS Technical Support, because the contents of the log will help them diagnose your problem.

The following list corresponds to the numbered items in the preceding log:

❶ SAS statements for the DATA and PROC steps

❷ error messages

❸ notes, which might include warning messages.

❹ notes that contain the number of observations and variables for each data set that is created.

Writing to the SAS Log

Default Output to the SAS Log

The previous sample logs show the information that appears on the log by default. You can also write to the log by using the PUT statement or the LIST statement within a DATA step. These statements can be used to debug your SAS programs.

Using the PUT Statement

The PUT statement enables you to write information that you specify, including text strings and variable values, to the log. Values can be written in column, list, formatted, or named output style.* Used as a screening device, the PUT statement can also be a useful debugging tool. For example, the following statement writes the values of all variables, including the automatic variables _ERROR_ and _N_, that are defined in the current DATA step:

```
put _all_;
```

The following program reads the data set OUT.SAT_SCORES and uses the PUT statement to write to the SAS log the records for which the score is 500 points or more.

The following partial output shows that the records are written to the log immediately after the SAS statements:

```
libname out 'your-data-library';


data _null_;
   set out.sat_scores;
   if SATscore >= 500 then put test gender year;
run;
```

Output 22.3 Writing to the SAS Log with the PUT Statement

```
NOTE: Libref OUT was successfully assigned as follows:
      Engine:        V8
      Physical Name: YOUR-DATA-LIBRARY
123
124  data _null_;
125     set out.sat_scores;
126     if SATscore >= 500 then put test gender year;
127  run;
Math m 1972
Math m 1973
Math m 1974
   .
   .
   .
```

---

* Named output enables you to write a variable's name as well as its value to the SAS log. For more information, see "PUT, Named" in the Statements section of *SAS Language Reference: Dictionary*.

Using the LIST Statement

Use the LIST statement in the DATA step to list on the log the current input record. The following program shows that the LIST statement, like the PUT statement, can be very effective when combined with conditional processing to write selected information to the log:

```
data out.sat_scores3;
   infile 'your-input-file';
   input test $ gender $ year SATscore @@;
   if SATscore < 500 then delete;
   else list;
run;
```

When the LIST statement is executed, SAS causes the current input buffer to be printed following the DATA step. The following partial output shows the results. Note the presence of the columns ruler before the first line. The ruler indicates that input data has been written to the log. It can be used to reference column positions in the input buffer. Also notice that, because two observations are created from each input record, the entire input record is printed whenever either value of the SATscore variable from that input line is at least 500. Finally, note that the LIST statement causes the record length to be printed at the end of each line (in this case, each record has a length of 36). This feature of the LIST statement works only in operating environments that support variable-length (as opposed to fixed-length) input records.

Output 22.4 Writing to the SAS Log with the LIST Statement

```
NOTE: Libref OUT was successfully assigned as follows:
      Engine:        V8
      Physical Name: YOUR-DATA-LIBRARY
248  data out.sat_scores3;
249     infile 'YOUR-DATA-FILE';
250     input test $ gender $ year SATscore @@;
251     if SATscore < 500 then delete;
252     else list;
253  run;
NOTE: The infile
      'YOUR-DATA-FILE' is:

      File
      Name=YOUR-DATA-FILE,
      Owner Name=userid,Group Name=dev,
      Access Permission=rw-r--r--,
      File Size (bytes)=1998

RULE:      ----+----1----+----2----+----3----+----4----+----5----+----6----+----7
1          Verbal m 1972 531  Verbal f 1972 529 36
2          Verbal m 1973 523  Verbal f 1973 521 36
3          Verbal m 1974 524  Verbal f 1974 520 36
   .
   .
   .
53         Math   m 1997 530  Math   f 1997 494 36
54         Math   m 1998 531  Math   f 1998 496 36
NOTE: 54 records were read from the infile
      'YOUR-DATA-FILE'.
      The minimum record length was 36.
      The maximum record length was 36.
NOTE: SAS went to a new line when INPUT statement reached past the end of a
      line.
NOTE: The data set OUT.SAT_SCORES3 has 69 observations and 4 variables.
```

Suppressing Information to the SAS Log

Using SAS System Options to Suppress Log Output

There might be times when you want to prevent some information from being written to the SAS log. You can suppress SAS statements, system messages, and error messages with the NOSOURCE, NONOTES, and ERRORS= SAS system options. You can specify these options when you invoke SAS, in the OPTIONS window, or in an OPTIONS statement. In this chapter, the options are specified in OPTIONS statements.

Note that all SAS system options remain in effect for the duration of your session or until you change them.

Suppressing SAS Statements

If you regularly execute large SAS programs without making changes, then you can use the NOSOURCE system option as follows to suppress the listing of the SAS statements to the log:

```
options nosource;
```

The NOSOURCE option causes only source lines that contain errors to be printed. You can return to the default by specifying the SOURCE system option as follows:

```
options source;
```

The SOURCE option causes all subsequent source lines to be printed.

You can also control whether secondary source statements (from files that are included with a %INCLUDE statement) are printed on the SAS log. Specify the following statement to suppress secondary statements:

```
options nosource2;
```

The following OPTIONS statement causes secondary source statements to print to the log:

```
options source2;
```

Suppressing System Notes

Much of the information that is supplied by the log appears as notes, including

□ copyright information

□ licensing and site information

□ number of observations and variables in the data set.

SAS also issues a note to tell you that it has stopped processing a step because of errors.

If you do not want the notes to appear on the log, then use the NONOTES system option to suppress their printing:

```
options nonotes;
```

All messages starting with NOTE: are suppressed. You can return to the default by specifying the NOTES system option:

```
options notes;
```

Limiting the Number of Error Messages

SAS prints messages for data input errors that appear in your SAS program; the default number is usually 20 but might vary from site to site. Use the ERRORS= system option to specify the maximum number of observations for which error messages are printed.

Note that this option limits only the error messages that are produced for incorrect data. This kind of error is caused primarily by trying to read character values for a variable that the INPUT statement defines as numeric.

If data errors are detected in more observations than the number you specify, then processing continues, but error messages do not print for the additional errors. For example, the following OPTIONS statement specifies printing for a maximum of five observations:

```
options errors=5;
```

However, as discussed in "Suppressing SAS Statements, Notes, and Error Messages" on page 341, it might be dangerous to suppress error messages.

Note: No option is available to eliminate warning messages. △

Suppressing SAS Statements, Notes, and Error Messages

The following SAS program reads the test score data as in the other examples in this chapter, but in this example the character symbol for the variable GENDER is omitted. Also, the data is not sorted before using a BY statement with PROC PRINT. At the same time, for efficiency, SAS statements, notes, and error messages are suppressed.

```
libname out 'your-data-library';
options nosource nonotes errors=0;

data out.sats5;
   infile 'your-input-file';
   input test $ gender year SATscore 25-27;
run;

proc print;
   by test;
run;
```

This program does not generate output. The SAS log that appears is shown in the following output. Because the SAS system option ERRORS=0 is specified, the error limit is reached immediately, and the errors that result from trying to read GENDER as a numeric value are not printed. Also, specifying the NOSOURCE and NONOTES system options causes the log to contain no SAS statements that can be verified and no notes to explain what happened. The log does contain an error message that explains that OUT.SATS5 is not sorted in ascending sequence. This error is not caused by invalid input data, so the ERRORS=0 option has no effect on this error.

Output 22.5 Suppressing Information to the SAS Log

```
NOTE: Libref OUT was successfully assigned as follows:
      Engine:        V8
      Physical Name: YOUR-DATA-LIBRARY
370   options nosource nonotes errors=0;
ERROR: Limit set by ERRORS= option reached.  Further errors of this type will
       not be printed.
ERROR: Data set OUT.SAT_SCORES5 is not sorted in ascending sequence. The
       current by-group has test = Verbal and the next by-group has test = Math.
```

Note: The NOSOURCE, NONOTES, and ERRORS= system options are used to save space. They are most useful with an already-tested program, perhaps one that is run regularly. However, as demonstrated in this section, they are not always appropriate. During development of a new program, the error messages in the log might be essential for debugging, and should not be limited. Similarly, notes should not be suppressed because they can help you pinpoint problems with a program. They are especially important if you seek help in debugging your program from someone not already familiar with it. In short, you should not suppress any information in the log until you have already executed the program without errors. △

The following partial output shows the results if the previous sample SAS code is reexecuted with the SOURCE, NOTES, and ERRORS= options.

Output 22.6   Debugging with the SAS Log

```
412   options source notes errors=20;
413
414   data out.sat_scores5;
415      infile 'YOUR-DATA-FILE';
416      input test $ gender year score @@;
417   run;
NOTE: The infile
      'YOUR-DATA-FILE' is:

      File Name=YOUR-DATA-FILE,
      Owner Name=userid,Group Name=dev,
      Access Permission=rw-r--r--,
      File Size (bytes)=1998

NOTE: Invalid data for gender in line 1 8-8.
RULE:      ----+----1----+----2----+----3----+----4----+----5----+----6----+----7
1          Verbal m 1972 531  Verbal f 1972 529 36
test=Verbal gender=. year=1972 score=531 _ERROR_=1 _N_=1
NOTE: Invalid data for gender in line 1 27-27.
test=Verbal gender=. year=1972 score=529 _ERROR_=1 _N_=2
NOTE: Invalid data for gender in line 2 8-8.
2          Verbal m 1973 523  Verbal f 1973 521 36
test=Verbal gender=. year=1973 score=523 _ERROR_=1 _N_=3
NOTE: Invalid data for gender in line 2 27-27.
test=Verbal gender=. year=1973 score=521 _ERROR_=1 _N_=4
     .
     .
     .
NOTE: Invalid data for gender in line 10 8-8.
10         Verbal m 1981 508  Verbal f 1981 496 36
test=Verbal gender=. year=1981 score=508 _ERROR_=1 _N_=19
NOTE: Invalid data for gender in line 10 27-27.
ERROR: Limit set by ERRORS= option reached.  Further errors of this type will
       not be printed.
test=Verbal gender=. year=1981 score=496 _ERROR_=1 _N_=20
NOTE: 54 records were read from the infile
      'YOUR-DATA-FILE'.
      The minimum record length was 36.
      The maximum record length was 36.
NOTE: SAS went to a new line when INPUT statement reached past the end of a
      line.
NOTE: The data set OUT.SAT_SCORES5 has 108 observations and 4 variables.
418
419   proc print;
420      by test;
421   run;
ERROR: Data set OUT.SAT_SCORES5 is not sorted in ascending sequence. The
       current by-group has test = Verbal and the next by-group has test = Math.
NOTE: The SAS System stopped processing this step because of errors.
NOTE: There were 55 observations read from the data set OUT.SAT_SCORES5.
```

Again, this program does not generate output, but this time the log is a more effective problem-solving tool. The log includes all the SAS statements from the program as well as many informative notes. Specifically, it includes enough messages about the invalid data for the variable GENDER that the problem can be spotted. With this information, the program can be modified and rerun successfully.

Changing the Log's Appearance

Chapter 31, "Understanding and Customizing SAS Output: The Basics," on page 533 shows you how to customize your output. Except in an interactive session, you can also customize the log by using the PAGE and SKIP statements. Use the PAGE statement to move to a new page on the log; use the SKIP statement to skip lines on the log. With the SKIP statement, specify the number of lines that you want to skip; if you do not specify a number, then one line is skipped. If the number that you specify exceeds the number of lines remaining on the page, then SAS treats the SKIP statement like a PAGE statement and skips to the top of the next page. The PAGE and SKIP statements do not appear on the log.

The following output shows the result if a PAGE statement is inserted before the PROC PRINT step in the previous example:

Output 22.7   Using the PAGE Statement

```
456   options source notes errors=20;
457
458   data out.sat_scores5;
459      infile
459! '/dept/pub/doc/802/authoring/TW6025/miscsrc/rawdata/sat_scores.raw';
460      input test $ gender year score @@;
461   run;
NOTE: The infile
      'YOUR-DATA-FILE' is:

      File Name=YOUR-DATA-FILE,
      Owner Name=userid,Group Name=dev,
      Access Permission=rw-r--r--,
      File Size (bytes)=1998

NOTE: Invalid data for gender in line 1 8-8.
RULE:      ----+----1----+----2----+----3----+----4----+----5----+----6----+----7
1          Verbal m 1972 531  Verbal f 1972 529 36
test=Verbal gender=. year=1972 score=531 _ERROR_=1 _N_=1
NOTE: Invalid data for gender in line 1 27-27.
test=Verbal gender=. year=1972 score=529 _ERROR_=1 _N_=2
NOTE: Invalid data for gender in line 2 8-8.
2          Verbal m 1973 523  Verbal f 1973 521 36
test=Verbal gender=. year=1973 score=523 _ERROR_=1 _N_=3
NOTE: Invalid data for gender in line 2 27-27.
test=Verbal gender=. year=1973 score=521 _ERROR_=1 _N_=4

   .
   .
   .

NOTE: Invalid data for gender in line 10 8-8.
10         Verbal m 1981 508  Verbal f 1981 496 36
test=Verbal gender=. year=1981 score=508 _ERROR_=1 _N_=19
NOTE: Invalid data for gender in line 10 27-27.
ERROR: Limit set by ERRORS= option reached.  Further errors of this type will
       not be printed.
test=Verbal gender=. year=1981 score=496 _ERROR_=1 _N_=20
NOTE: 54 records were read from the infile
      '/dept/pub/doc/802/authoring/TW6025/miscsrc/rawdata/sat_scores.raw'.
      The minimum record length was 36.
      The maximum record length was 36.
NOTE: SAS went to a new line when INPUT statement reached past the end of a
      line.
NOTE: The data set OUT.SAT_SCORES5 has 108 observations and 4 variables.
```

```
465   proc print;
466      by test;
467   run;
ERROR: Data set OUT.SAT_SCORES5 is not sorted in ascending sequence. The
       current by-group has test = Verbal and the next by-group has test = Math.
NOTE: The SAS System stopped processing this step because of errors.
NOTE: There were 55 observations read from the data set OUT.SAT_SCORES5.
```

Review of SAS Tools

Statements

The following statements are used to write to the log and to change the log's appearance:

LIST;
> lists on the SAS log the contents of the input buffer for the observation being processed.

PAGE;
> skips to a new page on the log.

PUT <*variable-list*> | <_ALL_>;
> writes lines to the SAS log, the output file, or any file that is specified in a FILE statement. If no FILE statement has been executed in this iteration of the DATA step, then the PUT statement writes to the SAS log. *Variable-list* names the variables whose values are to be written, and _ALL_ signifies that the values of all variables, including _ERROR_ and _N_, are to be written to the log.

SKIP <*n*>;
> on the SAS log, skips the number of lines that you specify with the value *n*. If the number is greater than the number of lines remaining on the page, then SAS treats the SKIP statement like a PAGE statement and skips to the top of the next page.

System Options

The following system options are used to suppress information to the log. In this chapter, they are specified in OPTIONS statements.

ERRORS=*n*
> specifies the maximum number of observations for which error messages about data input errors are printed.

NOTES | NONOTES
> controls whether notes are printed to the log.

SOURCE | NOSOURCE
> controls whether SAS statements are printed to the log.

SOURCE2 | NOSOURCE2
> controls whether secondary SAS statements from files included by %INCLUDE statements are printed to the log.

Learning More

Automatic variables
> Chapter 24, "Diagnosing and Avoiding Errors," on page 355 discusses the automatic variables _N_ and _ERROR_.

FILE and PUT statements
> Chapter 31, "Understanding and Customizing SAS Output: The Basics," on page 533 discusses the FILE and PUT statements.

The Log window
> Chapter 39, "Using the SAS Windowing Environment," on page 651 discusses the Log window.

Operating environment-specific information
> The SAS documentation for your operating environment contains information about the appearance and destination of the SAS log, as well as for routing output.

The SAS environment
> Chapter 38, "Introducing the SAS Environment," on page 639 provides information about methods of operation and on specifying SAS system options when you invoke SAS. It also discusses executing SAS statements automatically.

The SAS log
> *SAS Language Reference: Concepts* provides complete reference information about the SAS log.

SAS statements
> *SAS Language Reference: Dictionary* provides complete reference information about the SAS statements that are discussed in this chapter.

SAS system options
> *SAS Language Reference: Dictionary* provides complete reference information about SAS options that work across all operating environments. Refer to the SAS documentation for your operating environment for information about operating environment-specific options.

Your SAS session
> The other chapters in Part 5 provide more information about your SAS session. See especially Chapter 24, "Diagnosing and Avoiding Errors," on page 355, which contains more information about error messages.

Directing SAS Output and the SAS Log

Introduction

Purpose

The SAS System provides several methods to direct SAS output and the SAS log to different destinations. In this chapter, you will learn how to use the

- PRINTTO procedure from within a program or session to route DATA step output, the SAS log, or procedure output from their default destinations to another destination
- FILE command, in the SAS windowing environment, to store the contents of the Log and Output windows in files
- PRINT= and LOG= system options when you invoke SAS to redefine the destination of the log and output for an entire SAS session.

Prerequisites

Before proceeding with this chapter, you should be familiar with the following features and concepts:

☐ creating DATA step or PROC step output

☐ locating the log and procedure output

☐ referencing external files.

Input File and SAS Data Set for Examples

The examples in this chapter are based on data from a university entrance exam called the Scholastic Aptitude Test, or SAT. The data is provided in one input file that contains the average SAT scores of entering university classes from 1972 to 1998.* The input file has the following structure:

```
Verbal m 1972 531
Verbal f 1972 529
Verbal m 1973 523
Verbal f 1973 521
Verbal m 1974 524
Verbal f 1974 520
Verbal m 1975 515
Verbal f 1975 509
Verbal m 1976 511
Verbal f 1976 508
```

The input file contains the following values from left to right:

☐ type of SAT exam

☐ gender of student

☐ year of the exam

☐ average exam score of the first-year class.

The following program creates the data set that this chapter uses:

```
data sat_scores;
   input Test $ Gender $ Year SATscore @@;
   datalines;
Verbal m 1972 531  Verbal f 1972 529
Verbal m 1973 523  Verbal f 1973 521
Verbal m 1974 524  Verbal f 1974 520

...more data lines...

Math   m 1996 527  Math   f 1996 492
Math   m 1997 530  Math   f 1997 494
Math   m 1998 531  Math   f 1998 496
;
```

---

* See Chapter 31, "Understanding and Customizing SAS Output: The Basics," on page 533 for a complete listing of the input data.

Routing the Output and the SAS Log with PROC PRINTTO

Routing Output to an Alternate Location

You can use the PRINTTO procedure to redirect SAS procedure output from the listing destination to an alternate location. These locations are

□ a permanent file

□ a SAS catalog entry

□ a dummy file, which serves to suppress the output.

After PROC PRINTTO executes, all procedure output is sent to the alternate location until you execute another PROC PRINTTO statement or until your program or session ends.

The default destination for the procedure output depends on how you configure SAS to handle output. For more information, see the discussion of SAS output in Chapter 31, "Understanding and Customizing SAS Output: The Basics," on page 533.

Note: If you used the Output Delivery System (ODS) to close the listing destination, then PROC PRINTTO does not receive any output to redirect. However, the procedure results still go to the destination that you specified with ODS. △

You use the PRINT= option in the PROC PRINTTO statement to specify the name of the file or SAS catalog that will contain the procedure output. If you specify a file, then either use the complete name of the file in quotation marks or use a fileref for the file. (See "Using External Files in Your SAS Job" on page 38 for more information about filerefs and filenames.) You can also specify the NEW option in the PROC PRINTTO statement so that SAS replaces the previous contents of the output file. Otherwise, SAS appends the output to any output that is currently in the file.

To route output to an alternate file, insert a PROC PRINTTO step in the program before the PROC step that generates the procedure output. The following program routes the output from PROC PRINT to an external file:

```
proc printto print='alternate-output-file' new;
run;

proc print data=sat_scores;
    title 'Mean SAT Scores for Entering University Classes';
run;

proc printto;
run;
```

After the PROC PRINT step executes, *alternate-output-file* contains the procedure output. The second PROC PRINTTO step redirects output back to its default destination.

The PRINTTO procedure does not produce the output. Instead it tells SAS to route the results of all subsequent procedures until another PROC PRINTTO statement executes. Therefore, the PROC PRINTTO statement must precede the procedure whose output you want to route.

Figure 23.1 on page 350 shows how SAS uses PROC PRINTTO to route procedure output. You can also use PROC PRINTTO multiple times in a program so that output from different steps of a SAS job is stored in different files.

Figure 23.1 Using PROC PRINTTO Route Output

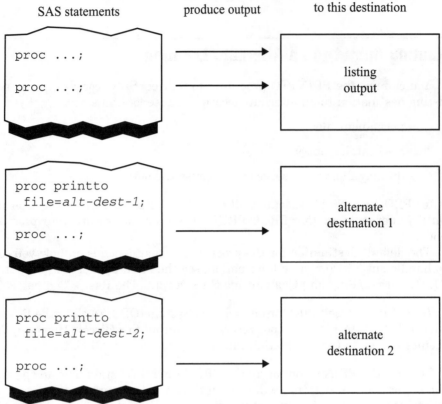

Routing the SAS Log to an Alternate Location

You can use the PRINTTO procedure to redirect the SAS log to an alternate location. The location can be

- □ a permanent file
- □ a SAS catalog entry
- □ a dummy file to suppress the log.

After PROC PRINTTO executes, the log is sent either to a permanent external file or to a SAS catalog entry until you execute another PROC PRINTTO statement, or until your program or session ends.

You use the LOG= option in the PROC PRINTTO statement to specify the name of the file or SAS catalog that will contain the log. If you specify a file, then either use the complete name of the file in quotation marks or use a fileref for the file. You can also specify the NEW option in the PROC PRINTTO statement so that SAS replaces the previous contents of the file. Otherwise, SAS appends the log to any log that is currently in the file.

The following program routes the SAS log to an alternate file:

```
proc printto log='alternate-log-file';
run;
```

After the PROC PRINT step executes, *alternate-log-file* contains the SAS log. The contents of this file are shown in the following output:

Output 23.1   Using the PRINTTO Procedure to Route the SAS Log to an Alternate File

```
8    data sat_scores;
9       input Test $ Gender $ Year SATscore @@;
10      datalines;
NOTE: SAS went to a new line when INPUT statement reached past the end of a line.
NOTE: The data set WORK.SAT_SCORES has 108 observations and 4 variables.
65   ;
66   proc print data=sat_scores;
67      title 'Mean SAT Scores for Entering University Classes';
68   run;
NOTE: There were 108 observations read from the dataset WORK.SAT_SCORES.
69   proc printto; run;
```

Restoring the Default Destination

Specify the PROC PRINTTO statement with no argument when you want to route the log and the output back to their default destinations:

```
proc printto;
run;
```

You might want to return only the log or only the procedure output to its default destination. The following PROC PRINTTO statement routes only the log back to the default destination:

```
proc printto log=log;
run;
```

The following PROC PRINTTO statement routes only the procedure output to the default destination:

```
proc printto print=print;
run;
```

Storing the Output and the SAS Log in the SAS Windowing Environment

Understanding the Default Destination

Within the SAS windowing environment, the default destination for most procedure output is a monospace listing that appears in the Output window. However, you can use the Output Delivery System (ODS) to change which destinations are opened and closed.

Each time you execute a procedure within a single session, SAS appends the output to the existing output. To view the results, you can

☐ scroll the Output window, which contains the output in the order in which you generated it

☐ use the Results window to select a pointer that is a link to the procedure output.

The SAS windowing environment interacts with certain aspects of the ODS to format, control, and manage your output.

In the SAS windowing environment, the default destination for the SAS log messages is the Log window. When you execute a procedure, SAS appends the log messages to the existing log messages in the Log window. You can scroll the Log window to see the results. To print your log messages, execute the PRINT command. To clear the contents of the Log window, execute the CLEAR command. When your session ends, SAS automatically clears the window.

Within the SAS windowing environment, you can use the PRINTTO procedure to route log messages or procedure output to a location other than the default location, just as you can in other methods of operation. For details, see "Routing the Output and the SAS Log with PROC PRINTTO" on page 349. You can also use ODS to change the destination of the procedure output.

For additional information about using ODS, viewing procedure output, and changing the destination of the procedure output, see Chapter 31, "Understanding and Customizing SAS Output: The Basics," on page 533.

Storing the Contents of the Output and Log Windows

If you want to store a copy of the contents of the Output or Log window in a file, then use the FILE command. On the command line, specify the FILE command followed by the name of the file:

file *'file-to-store-contents-of-window'*

SAS has a built-in safeguard that prevents you from accidentally overwriting a file. If you inadvertently specify an existing file, then a *requestor window* appears. The requestor window asks you to choose a course of action, provides you with information, and might prevent you from overwriting the file by mistake. You are asked whether to

☐ replace the contents of the file

☐ append the contents of the file

☐ cancel the FILE command.

Redefining the Default Destination in a Batch or Noninteractive Environment

Determining the Default Destination

Usually, in a batch or noninteractive environment, SAS routes procedure output to the list file and routes the SAS log to a log file. These files are usually defined by your installation and are created automatically when you invoke SAS. Contact your SAS Support Consultant if you have questions pertaining to your site.

Changing the Default Destination

If you want to redefine the default destination for procedure output, then use the PRINT= system option. If you want to redefine the default destination for the SAS log, then use the LOG= system option. You specify these options only at initialization.

Operating Environment Information: The way that you specify output destinations when you use SAS system options depends on your operating environment. For details, see the SAS documentation for your operating environment. △

Options that you must specify at initialization are called *configuration options*. The configuration options affect

☐ the initialization of the SAS System

☐ the hardware interface

□ the operating system interface.

In contrast to other SAS system options, which affect the appearance of output, file handling, use of system variables, or processing of observations, you cannot change configuration options in the middle of a program. You specify configuration options when SAS is invoked, either in the configuration file or in the SAS command.

Understanding the Configuration File

The configuration file is a special file that contains configuration options as well as other SAS system options and their settings. Each time you invoke SAS, the settings of the configuration file are examined. You can specify the options in the configuration file in the same format as they are used in the SAS command for your operating environment. For example, under UNIX this file's contents might include the following:

```
WORK=WORK
SASUSER=SASUSER
EXPLORER
```

SAS automatically sets the options as they appear in the configuration file. If you specify options both in the configuration file and in the SAS command, then the options are concatenated. If you specify the same option in the SAS command and in the configuration file, then the setting in the SAS command overrides the setting in the file. For example, specifying the NOEXPLORER option in the SAS command overrides the EXPLORER option in the configuration file and tells SAS to start your session without displaying the Explorer window.

Review of SAS Tools

PROC PRINTTO Statement Options

PROC PRINTTO <PRINT='*alternate-output-file*'> <LOG='*alternate-log-file*'>
    <NEW>;

LOG='*alternate-log-file*'
    identifies the location and routes the SAS log to this alternate location.

NEW
    specifies that the current log or procedure output writes over the previous contents of the file.

PRINT='*alternate-output-file*'
    identifies the location and routes the procedure output to this alternate location.

SAS Windowing Environment Commands

CLEAR
    clears the contents of a window, as specified.

FILE *<file-to-store-contents-of-window>*
    routes a copy of the contents of a window to the file that you specify; the original contents remain in place.

PRINT
    prints the contents of the window.

SAS System Options

LOG=*system-filename*
    redefines the default destination for the SAS log to the file named *system-filename*.

PRINT=*system-filename*
    redefines the default destination for procedure output to the file named *system-filename*.

Learning More

Output Delivery System
    For complete reference documentation about the Output Delivery System, see *The Complete Guide to the SAS Output Delivery System*.

PROC PRINTTO
    For complete reference documentation about PROC PRINTTO, see *SAS Procedures Guide*.

SAS environment
    For details about the methods of operating SAS and interactive processing in the windowing environment, see Part 10, "Understanding Your SAS Environment."

SAS log
    For complete reference information about the SAS log and procedure output, see *SAS Language Reference: Concepts*.

SAS output
    For more information, see the other chapters in Part 5, "Understanding Your SAS Session."

SAS system options
    For details about SAS system options, including configuration options, see *SAS Language Reference: Dictionary*.
    For operating-specific information about routing output, the PRINT= option, LOG= option, and other SAS system options, see the SAS documentation for your operating environment.

CHAPTER

24

Diagnosing and Avoiding Errors

Introduction

Purpose

In this chapter, you will learn how to diagnose errors in your programs by understanding

- [ ] how the SAS Supervisor checks a program for errors
- [ ] how to distinguish among the types of errors
- [ ] how to interpret the notes, warning messages, and error messages in the log
- [ ] what to check for as you develop a program.

Prerequisites

You should understand the concepts that are presented in

- [ ] Chapter 2, "Introduction to DATA Step Processing," on page 19
- [ ] Chapter 3, "Starting with Raw Data: The Basics," on page 43
- [ ] Chapter 6, "Understanding DATA Step Processing," on page 97
- [ ] Chapter 22, "Analyzing Your SAS Session with the SAS Log," on page 333.

Understanding How the SAS Supervisor Checks a Job

To better understand the errors that you make so that you can avoid others, it is important to understand how the SAS Supervisor checks a job. The SAS Supervisor is the part of SAS that is responsible for executing SAS programs. To check the syntax of a SAS program, the SAS Supervisor

- □ reads the SAS statements and data
- □ translates the program statements into executable machine code or intermediate code
- □ creates data sets
- □ calls SAS procedures, as requested
- □ prints error messages
- □ ends the job.

The SAS Supervisor knows

- □ the forms and types of statements that can be present in a DATA step
- □ the types of statements and the options that can be present in a PROC step.

To process a program, the SAS Supervisor scans all the SAS statements and breaks each statement into words. Each word is processed separately; when all the words in a step are processed, the step is executed. If the SAS Supervisor detects an error, then it flags the error at its location and prints an explanation. The SAS Supervisor assumes that anything it does not recognize is an error.

Understanding How SAS Processes Errors

When SAS detects an error, it usually underlines the error or underlines the point at which it detects the error, identifying the error with a number. Each number is uniquely associated with an error message. Then SAS enters syntax check mode. SAS reads the remaining program statements, checks their syntax, and underlines additional errors if necessary.

In a batch or noninteractive program, an error in a DATA step statement causes SAS to remain in syntax check mode for the rest of the program. It does not execute any more DATA or PROC steps that create external files or SAS data sets. Procedures that read from SAS data sets execute with 0 observations, and procedures that do not read SAS data sets execute normally. A syntax error in a PROC step usually affects only that step. At the end of the step, SAS writes a message in the SAS log for each error that is detected.

Distinguishing Types of Errors

SAS recognizes four kinds of errors:

- □ syntax errors
- □ execution-time errors
- □ data errors
- □ semantic errors.

Syntax errors are errors made in the SAS statements of a program. They include misspelled keywords, missing or invalid punctuation, and invalid statement or data set options. SAS detects syntax errors as it compiles each DATA or PROC step.

Execution-time errors cause a program to fail when it is submitted for execution. Most execution-time errors that are not serious produce notes in the SAS log, but the program is allowed to run to completion. For more serious errors, however, SAS issues error messages and stops all processing.

Data errors are actually a type of execution-time error. They occur when the raw data that you are analyzing with a SAS program contains invalid values. For example, a data error occurs if you specify numeric variables in the INPUT statement for character data. Data errors do not cause a program to stop but instead generate notes in the SAS log.

Semantic errors, another type of execution-time error, occur when the form of a SAS statement is correct, but some elements are not valid in that usage. Examples include

- specifying the wrong number of arguments for a function
- using a numeric variable name where only character variables are valid
- using a libref that has not yet been assigned.

Diagnosing Errors

Examples in This Section

This section uses nationwide test results from the Scholastic Aptitude Test (SAT) for university-bound students from 1972 through 1998* to show what happens when errors occur.

Diagnosing Syntax Errors

The SAS Supervisor detects syntax errors as it compiles each step, and then SAS

- prints the word ERROR
- identifies the error's location
- prints an explanation of the error.

In the following program, the CHART procedure is used to analyze the data. Note that a semicolon in the DATA statement is omitted, and the keyword INFILE is misspelled.

```
/* omitted semicolon and misspelled keyword */
libname out 'your-data-library';

data out.error1
   infill 'your-input-file';
   input test $ gender $ year SATscore @@;
run;

proc chart data = out.error1;
   hbar test / sumvar=SATscore type=mean group=gender discrete;
run;
```

The following output shows the result of the two syntax errors:

---

* See the Appendix for a complete listing of the input data that is used to create the data sets in this chapter.

Output 24.1 Diagnosing Syntax Errors

```
NOTE: Libref OUT was successfully assigned as follows:
      Engine:         V8
      Physical Name: 'YOUR-DATA-LIBRARY'
50   data out.error1
51      infill 'YOUR-INPUT-FILE';
52      input test $ gender $ year SATscore @@;
53   run;
ERROR: No CARDS or INFILE statement.
ERROR: Memtype   field is invalid.
NOTE: The SAS System stopped processing this step because of errors.
WARNING: The data set OUT.ERROR1 may be incomplete.  When this step was stopped
         there were 0 observations and 4 variables.
WARNING: Data set OUT.ERROR1 was not replaced because this step was stopped.
WARNING: The data set WORK.INFILL may be incomplete.  When this step was
         stopped there were 0 observations and 4 variables.
WARNING: Data set WORK.INFILL was not replaced because this step was stopped.
54
55   proc chart data=out.error1;
56      hbar test / sumvar=SATscore type=mean group=gender discrete;
57   run;
NOTE: No observations in data set OUT.ERROR1.
```

As the log indicates, SAS recognizes the keyword DATA and attempts to process the DATA step. Because the DATA statement must end with a semicolon, SAS assumes that INFILL is a data set name and that two data sets are being created: OUT.ERROR1 and WORK.INFILL. Because it considers INFILL the name of a data set, it does not recognize it as part of another statement and, therefore, does not detect the spelling error. Because the quoted string is invalid in a DATA statement, SAS stops processing here and creates no observations for either data set.

SAS attempts to execute the program logically based on the statements that it contains, according to the steps outlined earlier in this chapter. The second syntax error, the misspelled keyword, is never recognized because SAS considers the DATA statement to be in effect until a semicolon ends the statement. The point to remember is that when multiple errors are made in the same program, not all of them might be detected the first time the program is executed, or they might be flagged differently in a group than if they were made alone. You might find that one correction uncovers another error or at least changes its explanation in the log.

To illustrate this point, the previous program is reexecuted with the semicolon added to the DATA statement. An attempt to correct the misspelled keyword simply introduces a different spelling error, as follows.

```
/* misspelled keyword */
 libname out 'your-data-library';

data out.error2;
   unfile 'your-input-file';
   input test $ gender $ year SATscore @@;
run;

proc chart data = out.error1;
   hbar test / sumvar=SATscore type=mean group=gender discrete;
run;
```

The following output shows the results:

Output 24.2 Correcting Syntax and Finding Different Error Messages

```
NOTE: Libref OUT was successfully assigned as follows:
      Engine:        V8
      Physical Name: YOUR-DATA-LIBRARY
70   data out.error2;
71       unfile 'YOUR-INPUT-FILE'
         ------
         180
ERROR 180-322: Statement is not valid or it is used out of proper order.

72       input test $ gender $ year SATscore @@;
73   run;
ERROR: No CARDS or INFILE statement.
NOTE: The SAS System stopped processing this step because of errors.
WARNING: The data set OUT.ERROR2 may be incomplete.  When this step was stopped
         there were 0 observations and 4 variables.
74
75   proc chart data=out.error1;
76       hbar test / sumvar=SATscore type=mean group=gender discrete;
77   run;
NOTE: No observations in data set OUT.ERROR1.
```

With the semicolon added, SAS now attempts to create only one data set. From that point on, SAS reads the SAS statements as it did before and issues many of the same messages. However, this time SAS considers the UNFILE statement invalid or out of proper order, and it creates no observations for the data set.

Diagnosing Execution-Time Errors

Several types of errors are detected at execution time. Execution-time errors include

□ illegal mathematical operations

□ observations out of order for BY-group processing

□ an incorrect reference in an INFILE statement (for example, misspelling or otherwise incorrectly stating the external file).

When the SAS Supervisor encounters an execution-time error, it

□ prints a note, warning, or error message, depending on the seriousness of the error

□ in some cases, lists the values that are stored in the program data vector

□ continues or stops processing, depending on the seriousness of the error.

If the previous program is rerun with the correct spelling for INFILE but with a misspelling of the filename in the INFILE statement, then the error is detected at execution time and the data is not read.

```
/* misspelled file in the INFILE statement */
libname out 'your-data-library';

data out.error3;
    infile 'an-incorrect-filename';
    input test $ gender $ year SATscore @@;
run;

proc chart data = out.error3;
    hbar test / sumvar=SATscore type=mean group=gender discrete;
run;
```

As the SAS log in the following output indicates, SAS cannot find the file. SAS stops processing because of errors and creates no observations in the data set.

Output 24.3 Diagnosing an Error in the INFILE Statement

```
NOTE: Libref OUT was successfully assigned as follows:
      Engine:        V8
      Physical Name: YOUR-DATA-LIBRARY
10   data out.error3;
11       infile 'AN-INCORRECT-FILENAME';
12       input test $ gender $ year SATscore @@;
13   run;
ERROR: Physical file does not exist, AN-INCORRECT-FILENAME
NOTE: The SAS System stopped processing this step because of errors.
WARNING: The data set OUT.ERROR3 may be incomplete.  When this step was stopped
         there were 0 observations and 4 variables.
14
15   proc chart data=out.error3;
16       hbar test / sumvar=SATscore type=mean group=gender discrete;
17   run;
NOTE: No observations in data set OUT.ERROR3.
```

Diagnosing Data Errors

When SAS detects data errors during execution, it continues processing and then

□ prints a note that describes the error

□ lists the values that are stored in the input buffer

□ lists the values that are stored in the program data vector.

Note that the values listed in the program data vector include two variables created automatically by SAS:

_N_   counts the number of times the DATA step iterates.

ERROR   indicates the occurrence of an error during an execution of the DATA step. The value that is assigned to the variable _ERROR_ is 0 when no error is encountered and 1 when an error is encountered.

These automatic variables are assigned temporarily to each observation and are not stored with the data set.

The raw data that is shown here is read by a program that uses formats to determine how variable values are printed:

```
verbal          m 1967 463
 verbal         f 1967 468
 verbal         m 1970 459
 verbal         f 1970 461
 math           m 1967 514
  math           f 1967 467
 math           m 1970 509
 math           f 1970 509
```

However, the data is not aligned correctly in the columns that are described by the INPUT statement. The sixth data line is shifted two spaces to the right, and the rest of the data lines, except for the first, are shifted one space to the right, as shown by a comparison of the raw data with the following program:

```
/* data in wrong columns */
libname out 'your-data-library';
proc format;
```

```
      value xscore . ='accurate scores unavailable';
run;

data out.error4;
   infile 'your--input-file';
   input test $ 1-8 gender $ 18 year 20-23
         score 25-27;
   format score xscore.;
run;

proc print data = out.error4;
   title 'Viewing Incorrect Output';
run;
```

The following output shows the results of the SAS program:

Output 24.4   Detecting Data Errors with Incorrect Output

```
                        Viewing Incorrect Output                              1

       Obs      test     gender    year              score

        1      verbal      m       1967                  463
        2      verbal              196                    46
        3      verbal              197                    45
        4      verbal              197                    46
        5      math                196                    51
        6      math                 .     accurate scores unavailable
        7      math                197                    50
        8      math                197                    50
```

This program generates output, but it is not the expected output. The first observation appears to be correct, but subsequent observations have the following problems:

☐ the values for the variable GENDER are missing

☐ only the first three digits of the value for the variable YEAR are shown except in the sixth observation where a missing value is indicated

☐ the third digit of the value for the variable SCORE is missing, again except in the sixth observation, which does show the assigned value for the missing value.

The SAS log in the following output contains an explanation:

Output 24.5 Diagnosing Data Errors

```
NOTE: Libref OUT was successfully assigned as follows:
      Engine:        V8
      Physical Name: YOUR-DATA-LIBRARY
10   proc format;
NOTE: Format XSCORE has been output.
11      value xscore . ='accurate scores unavailable';
12   run;
13
14   data out.error4;
15      infile 'YOUR--INPUT-FILE';
16      input test $ 1-8 gender $ 18 year 20-23
17            score 25-27;
18      format score xscore.;
19   run;
NOTE: The infile 'YOUR-INPUT-FILE' is:

      File Name=YOUR-INPUT-FILE,
      Owner Name=userid,Group Name=dev,
      Access Permission=rw-r--r--,
      File Size (bytes)=233

NOTE: Invalid data for year in line 6 20-23.
NOTE: Invalid data for score in line 6 25-27.
RULE:      ----+----1----+----2----+----3----+----4----+----5----+----6----+----7
6          math            f 1967 467 29
test=math gender=  year=. score=accurate scores unavailable _ERROR_=1 _N_=6
NOTE: 9 records were read from the infile
      'YOUR-INPUT-FILE'.
      The minimum record length was 0.
      The maximum record length was 29.
NOTE: SAS went to a new line when INPUT statement reached past the end of a
      line.
NOTE: The data set OUT.ERROR4 has 8 observations and 4 variables.
20
21   proc print data=out.error4;
22      title 'Viewing Incorrect Output';
23   run;
NOTE: There were 8 observations read from the data set OUT.ERROR4.
```

The errors are flagged, starting with the first message that line 6 contains invalid data for the variable YEAR. The rule indicates that input data has been written to the log. SAS lists on the log the values that are stored in the program data vector. The following lines from the log indicate that SAS has encountered an error:

```
NOTE: Invalid data for year in line 6 20-23.
NOTE: Invalid data for score in line 6 25-27.
RULE:      ----+----1----+----2----+----3----+----4----+----5----+----6----+----7
6          math            f 1967 467 29
test=math gender=  year=. score=accurate scores unavailable _ERROR_=1 _N_=6
```

Missing values are shown for the variables GENDER and YEAR. The NOTEs in the log indicate that the sixth line of input contained the error.

To debug the program, either the raw data can be repositioned or the INPUT statement can be rewritten, remembering that all the data lines were shifted at least one space to the right. The variable TEST was unaffected, but the variable GENDER was completely removed from its designated field; therefore, SAS reads the variable GENDER as a missing value. In the sixth observation, for which the data was shifted right an additional space, the character value for GENDER occupied part of the field for the numeric variable YEAR. When SAS encounters invalid data, it treats the value as a missing value but also notes on the log that the data is invalid. The important point to remember is that SAS can use only the information that you provide to it, not what you *intend* to provide to it.

Using a Quality Control Checklist

If you follow some basic guidelines as you develop a program, then you can avoid common errors. Use the following checklist to flag and correct common mistakes before you submit your program.

□ *Check the syntax of your program.* In particular, check the following:

□ All SAS statements end with a semicolon; be sure you have not omitted any semicolons or accidentally typed the wrong character.

□ Any starting and ending quotation marks must match; you can use either single or double quotation marks.

□ Most SAS statements begin with a SAS keyword. (Exceptions are assignment statements and sum statements.) Be sure you have not misspelled or omitted any of the keywords.

□ Every DO and SELECT statement must be followed by an END statement.

□ *Check the order of your program.* SAS usually executes the statements in a DATA step one by one, in the order they appear. After executing the DATA step, SAS moves to the next step and continues in the same fashion. Be sure that all the SAS statements appear in order so that SAS can execute them properly. For example, an INFILE statement, if used, must precede an INPUT statement.

Also, be sure to end steps with the RUN statement. This is especially important at the end of your program because the RUN statement causes the previous step to be executed.

□ *Check your INPUT statement and your data.* SAS classifies all variables as either character or numeric. The assignment in the INPUT statement as either character or numeric must correspond to the actual values of variables in your data. Also, SAS allows for list, column, formatted, or named input. The method of input that you specify in the INPUT statement must correspond with the actual arrangement of raw data.

Learning More

INFILE statement options

SAS Language Reference: Dictionary contains information about using the MISSOVER and STOPOVER options in the INFILE statement as debugging tools. The MISSOVER option prevents a SAS program from going past the end of a line to read values with list input if it does not find values in the current line for all INPUT statement variables. Then SAS assigns missing values to variables for which no values appear on the current input line. The STOPOVER option stops processing the DATA step when an INPUT statement using list input reaches the end of the current record without finding values for all variables in the statement. Then SAS sets _ERROR_ to 1, stops building the data set, and prints an incomplete data line.

Program data vector and input buffer

Chapter 2, "Introduction to DATA Step Processing," on page 19 and Chapter 3, "Starting with Raw Data: The Basics," on page 43 contain information about the program data vector and the input buffer.

The SAS log

SAS Language Reference: Concepts contains complete reference information about the SAS log.

SAS output

SAS Language Reference: Concepts contains complete reference information about SAS output.

Your SAS session

The other chapters in Part 5 provide more information about your SAS session. Chapter 23, "Directing SAS Output and the SAS Log," on page 347 discusses warnings, notes, and error messages and presents debugging guidelines.

P A R T *6*

Producing Reports

CHAPTER

25

Producing Detail Reports with the PRINT Procedure

Introduction

Purpose

Detail reports, or simple data listings, contain one row for every observation that is selected for inclusion in the report. A detail report provides information about every record that is processed. For example, a detail report for a sales company includes all the information about every sale made during a particular quarter of the year. The PRINT procedure is one of several report writing tools that you can use to create a variety of detail reports.

In this chapter, you will learn how to

☐ produce simple reports by using a few basic PROC PRINT options and statements

☐ produce enhanced reports by adding additional statements that format values, sum columns, group observations, and compute totals

☐ customize the appearance of reports by adding titles, footnotes, and column labels

☐ substitute text by using macro variables.

Prerequisites

Before proceeding with this chapter, you should be familiar with the following features and concepts:

☐ the assignment statement

☐ the OUTPUT statement

☐ the SORT procedure

☐ the BY statement

☐ the location of the procedure output.

Input File and SAS Data Sets for Examples

The examples in this chapter use one input file* and five SAS data sets. The input file contains sales records for a company, TruBlend Coffee Makers, that distributes the coffee machines. The file has the following structure:

```
01    1    Hollingsworth    Deluxe       260    49.50
01    1    Garcia           Standard      41    30.97
01    1    Hollingsworth    Deluxe       330    49.50
01    1    Jensen           Standard    1110    30.97
01    1    Garcia           Standard     715    30.97
01    1    Jensen           Deluxe       675    49.50
```

---

* See the "Data Set for Chapters 25, 26, and 27" on page 715 for a complete listing of the input data.

```
02       1       Jensen        Standard      45       30.97
02       1       Garcia        Deluxe        10       49.50

...more data lines...

12       4       Hollingsworth Deluxe       125       49.50
12       4       Jensen        Standard    1254       30.97
12       4       Hollingsworth Deluxe       175       49.50
```

The input file contains the following values from left to right:

- □ the month that a sale was made
- □ the quarter of the year that a sale was made
- □ the name of the sales representative
- □ the type of coffee maker sold (standard or deluxe)
- □ the number of units sold
- □ the price of each unit in US dollars.

The first of the five SAS data sets is named YEAR_SALES. This data set contains all the sales data from the input file, and a new variable named AmountSold, which is created by multiplying Units by Price.

The following program creates the five SAS data sets that this chapter uses:

```
data year_sales;
    infile 'your-input-file';
    input Month $ Quarter $ SalesRep $14. Type $ Units Price;
    AmountSold = Units * Price;
```

Creating Simple Reports

Showing All the Variables

By default, the PRINT procedure generates a simple report that shows the values of all the variables and the observations in the data set. For example, the following PROC PRINT step creates a report for the first sales quarter:

```
options linesize=80 pageno=1 nodate;

proc print data=qtr01;
    title 'TruBlend Coffee Makers Quarterly Sales Report';
run;
```

The following output shows the values of all the variables for all the observations in QTR01:

Output 25.1   Showing All Variables and All Observations

```
                  TruBlend Coffee Makers Quarterly Sales Report❷              1

                                                              Amount
     Obs❶   Month   Quarter   SalesRep       Type     Units   Price    Sold

       1    01       1      Hollingsworth   Deluxe      260   49.50   12870.00
       2    01       1      Garcia          Standard     41   30.97    1269.77
       3    01       1      Hollingsworth   Standard    330   30.97   10220.10
       4    01       1      Jensen          Standard    110   30.97    3406.70
       5    01       1      Garcia          Deluxe      715   49.50   35392.50
       6    01       1      Jensen          Standard    675   30.97   20904.75
       7    02       1      Garcia          Standard   2045   30.97   63333.65
       8    02       1      Garcia          Deluxe       10   49.50     495.00
       9    02       1      Garcia          Standard     40   30.97    1238.80
      10    02       1      Hollingsworth   Standard   1030   30.97   31899.10
      11    02       1      Jensen          Standard    153   30.97    4738.41
      12    02       1      Garcia          Standard     98   30.97    3035.06
      13    03       1      Hollingsworth   Standard    125   30.97    3871.25
      14    03       1      Jensen          Standard    154   30.97    4769.38
      15    03       1      Garcia          Standard    118   30.97    3654.46
      16    03       1      Hollingsworth   Standard     25   30.97     774.25
      17    03       1      Jensen          Standard    525   30.97   16259.25
      18    03       1      Garcia          Standard    310   30.97    9600.70
```

The following list corresponds to the numbered items in the preceding output:

❶ The Obs column identifies each observation by a number. By default, SAS automatically displays the observation number at the beginning of each row.

❷ The top of the report has a title and a page number.

The TITLE statement in the PROC PRINT step produces the title. "Creating Customized Reports" on page 387 discusses the TITLE statement in more detail. For now, be aware that all the examples include at least one TITLE statement that produces a descriptive title similar to the one in this example.

The content of the report is very similar to the contents of the original data set QTR01; however, the report is easy to produce and to enhance.

Labeling the Observation Column

A quick way to modify the report is to label the observation number (Obs column). The following SAS program includes the OBS= option in the PROC PRINT statement to change the column label for the Obs column:

```
options linesize=80 pageno=1 nodate;

proc print data=qtr01 obs='Observation Number';
   title 'TruBlend Coffee Makers Quarterly Sales Report';
run;
```

The following output shows the report:

Output 25.2   Labeling the Observation Column

```
                  TruBlend Coffee Makers Quarterly Sales Report                1

Observation                                                        Amount
   Number     Month   Quarter   SalesRep         Type     Units   Price   Sold

      1        01        1      Hollingsworth   Deluxe      260   49.50   12870.00
      2        01        1      Garcia          Standard     41   30.97    1269.77
      3        01        1      Hollingsworth   Standard    330   30.97   10220.10
      4        01        1      Jensen          Standard    110   30.97    3406.70
      5        01        1      Garcia          Deluxe      715   49.50   35392.50
      6        01        1      Jensen          Standard    675   30.97   20904.75
      7        02        1      Garcia          Standard   2045   30.97   63333.65
      8        02        1      Garcia          Deluxe       10   49.50     495.00
      9        02        1      Garcia          Standard     40   30.97    1238.80
     10        02        1      Hollingsworth   Standard   1030   30.97   31899.10
     11        02        1      Jensen          Standard    153   30.97    4738.41
     12        02        1      Garcia          Standard     98   30.97    3035.06
     13        03        1      Hollingsworth   Standard    125   30.97    3871.25
     14        03        1      Jensen          Standard    154   30.97    4769.38
     15        03        1      Garcia          Standard    118   30.97    3654.46
     16        03        1      Hollingsworth   Standard     25   30.97     774.25
     17        03        1      Jensen          Standard    525   30.97   16259.25
     18        03        1      Garcia          Standard    310   30.97    9600.70
```

Suppressing the Observation Column

A quick way to simplify the report is to suppress the observation number (Obs
column). Usually it is unnecessary to identify each observation by number. (In some
cases, you might want to show the observation numbers.) The following SAS program
includes the NOOBS option in the PROC PRINT statement to suppress the Obs column:

```
options linesize=80 pageno=1 nodate;

proc print data=qtr01 noobs;
   title 'TruBlend Coffee Makers Quarterly Sales Report';
run;
```

The following output shows the report:

Output 25.3   Suppressing the Observation Column

```
                  TruBlend Coffee Makers Quarterly Sales Report                1

                                                              Amount
    Month    Quarter    SalesRep         Type       Units    Price     Sold

     01         1       Hollingsworth    Deluxe       260    49.50   12870.00
     01         1       Garcia           Standard      41    30.97    1269.77
     01         1       Hollingsworth    Standard     330    30.97   10220.10
     01         1       Jensen           Standard     110    30.97    3406.70
     01         1       Garcia           Deluxe       715    49.50   35392.50
     01         1       Jensen           Standard     675    30.97   20904.75
     02         1       Garcia           Standard    2045    30.97   63333.65
     02         1       Garcia           Deluxe        10    49.50     495.00
     02         1       Garcia           Standard      40    30.97    1238.80
     02         1       Hollingsworth    Standard    1030    30.97   31899.10
     02         1       Jensen           Standard     153    30.97    4738.41
     02         1       Garcia           Standard      98    30.97    3035.06
     03         1       Hollingsworth    Standard     125    30.97    3871.25
     03         1       Jensen           Standard     154    30.97    4769.38
     03         1       Garcia           Standard     118    30.97    3654.46
     03         1       Hollingsworth    Standard      25    30.97     774.25
     03         1       Jensen           Standard     525    30.97   16259.25
     03         1       Garcia           Standard     310    30.97    9600.70
```

Emphasizing a Key Variable

Understanding the ID Statement

To emphasize a key variable in a data set, you can use the ID statement in the PROC PRINT step. When you identify a variable in the ID statement, PROC PRINT displays the values of this variable in the first column of each row of the report. Highlighting a key variable in this way can help answer questions about your data. For example, the report can answer this question: "For each sales representative, what are the sales figures for the first quarter of the year?" The following two examples demonstrate how to answer this question quickly using data that is unsorted and sorted.

Using an Unsorted Key Variable

To produce a report that emphasizes the sales representative, the PROC PRINT step includes an ID statement that specifies the variable SalesRep. The revised program follows:

```
options linesize=80 pageno=1 nodate;

proc print data=qtr01;
   id SalesRep;
   title 'TruBlend Coffee Makers Quarterly Sales Report';
run;
```

Because the ID statement automatically suppresses the observation numbers, the NOOBS option is not needed in the PROC PRINT statement.

The following output shows the new report:

Output 25.4 Using the ID Statement with an Unsorted Key Variable

```
                  TruBlend Coffee Makers Quarterly Sales Report                 1

                                                              Amount
SalesRep          Month     Quarter      Type       Units     Price     Sold

Hollingsworth      01          1        Deluxe       260      49.50    12870.00
Garcia             01          1        Standard      41      30.97     1269.77
Hollingsworth      01          1        Standard     330      30.97    10220.10
Jensen             01          1        Standard     110      30.97     3406.70
Garcia             01          1        Deluxe       715      49.50    35392.50
Jensen             01          1        Standard     675      30.97    20904.75
Garcia             02          1        Standard    2045      30.97    63333.65
Garcia             02          1        Deluxe        10      49.50      495.00
Garcia             02          1        Standard      40      30.97     1238.80
Hollingsworth      02          1        Standard    1030      30.97    31899.10
Jensen             02          1        Standard     153      30.97     4738.41
Garcia             02          1        Standard      98      30.97     3035.06
Hollingsworth      03          1        Standard     125      30.97     3871.25
Jensen             03          1        Standard     154      30.97     4769.38
Garcia             03          1        Standard     118      30.97     3654.46
Hollingsworth      03          1        Standard      25      30.97      774.25
Jensen             03          1        Standard     525      30.97    16259.25
Garcia             03          1        Standard     310      30.97     9600.70
```

Notice that the names of the sales representatives are not in any particular order. The report will be easier to read when the observations are grouped together in alphabetical order by sales representative.

Using a Sorted Key Variable

If your data is not already ordered by the key variable, then use PROC SORT to sort the observations by this variable. If you do not specify an output data set, then PROC SORT permanently changes the order of the observations in the input data set.

The following program shows how to alphabetically order the observations by sales representative:

```
options linesize=80 pageno=1 nodate;

proc sort data=qtr01;❶
   by SalesRep;❷
run;

proc print data=qtr01;
   id SalesRep;❸
   title 'TruBlend Coffee Makers Quarterly Sales Report';
run;
```

The following list corresponds to the numbered items in the preceding program:

❶ A PROC SORT step precedes the PROC PRINT step. PROC SORT orders the observations in the data set alphabetically by the values of the BY variable and overwrites the input data set.

❷ A BY statement sorts the observations alphabetically by SalesRep.

❸ An ID statement identifies the observations with the value of SalesRep rather than with the observation number. PROC PRINT uses the sorted order of SalesRep to create the report.

The following output shows the report:

Output 25.5   Using the ID Statement with a Sorted Key Variable

```
              TruBlend Coffee Makers Quarterly Sales Report                    1

                                                              Amount
    SalesRep        Month    Quarter    Type      Units    Price    Sold

    Garcia           01        1       Standard     41    30.97    1269.77
    Garcia           01        1       Deluxe      715    49.50   35392.50
    Garcia           02        1       Standard   2045    30.97   63333.65
    Garcia           02        1       Deluxe       10    49.50     495.00
    Garcia           02        1       Standard     40    30.97    1238.80
    Garcia           02        1       Standard     98    30.97    3035.06
    Garcia           03        1       Standard    118    30.97    3654.46
    Garcia           03        1       Standard    310    30.97    9600.70
    Hollingsworth    01        1       Deluxe      260    49.50   12870.00
    Hollingsworth    01        1       Standard    330    30.97   10220.10
    Hollingsworth    02        1       Standard   1030    30.97   31899.10
    Hollingsworth    03        1       Standard    125    30.97    3871.25
    Hollingsworth    03        1       Standard     25    30.97     774.25
    Jensen           01        1       Standard    110    30.97    3406.70
    Jensen           01        1       Standard    675    30.97   20904.75
    Jensen           02        1       Standard    153    30.97    4738.41
    Jensen           03        1       Standard    154    30.97    4769.38
    Jensen           03        1       Standard    525    30.97   16259.25
```

Now, the report clearly shows what each sales representative sold during the first three months of the year.

Reporting the Values of Selected Variables

By default, the PRINT procedure reports the values of all the variables in the data set. However, to control which variables are shown and in what order, add a VAR statement to the PROC PRINT step.

For example, the information for the variables Quarter, Type, and Price is unnecessary. Therefore, the report needs to show only the values of the variables that are specified in the following order:

```
SalesRep  Month  Units  AmountSold
```

The following program adds the VAR statement to create a report that lists the values of the four variables in a specific order:

```
options linesize=80 pageno=1 nodate;

proc print data=qtr01 noobs;
   var SalesRep Month Units AmountSold;
   title 'TruBlend Coffee Makers Quarterly Sales Report';
run;
```

This program does not include the ID statement. It is unnecessary to identify the observations because the variable SalesRep is the first variable that is specified in the VAR statement. The NOOBS option in the PROC PRINT statement suppresses the observation numbers so that the sales representative appears in the first column of the report.

The following output shows the report:

Output 25.6 Showing Selected Variables

```
              TruBlend Coffee Makers Quarterly Sales Report              1

                                             Amount
              SalesRep        Month   Units   Sold

              Hollingsworth    01      260   12870.00
              Garcia           01       41    1269.77
              Hollingsworth    01      330   10220.10
              Jensen           01      110    3406.70
              Garcia           01      715   35392.50
              Jensen           01      675   20904.75
              Garcia           02     2045   63333.65
              Garcia           02       10     495.00
              Garcia           02       40    1238.80
              Hollingsworth    02     1030   31899.10
              Jensen           02      153    4738.41
              Garcia           02       98    3035.06
              Hollingsworth    03      125    3871.25
              Jensen           03      154    4769.38
              Garcia           03      118    3654.46
              Hollingsworth    03       25     774.25
              Jensen           03      525   16259.25
              Garcia           03      310    9600.70
```

The report is concise because it contains only those variables that are specified in the VAR statement. The next example revises the report to show only those observations that satisfy a particular condition.

Selecting Observations

Understanding the WHERE Statement

To select observations that meet a particular condition from a data set, use a WHERE statement. The WHERE statement subsets the input data by specifying certain conditions that each observation must meet before it is available for processing.

The condition that you define in a WHERE statement is an arithmetic or logical expression that generally consists of a sequence of operands and operators.* To compare character values, you must enclose them in single or double quotation marks and the values must match exactly, including capitalization. You can also specify multiple comparisons that are joined by logical operators in the WHERE statement.

Using the WHERE statement might improve the efficiency of your SAS programs because SAS is not required to read all the observations in the input data set.

Making a Single Comparison

You can select observations based on a single comparison by using the WHERE statement. The following program uses a single comparison in a WHERE statement to produce a report that shows the sales activity for a sales representative named Garcia:

```
options linesize=80 pageno=1 nodate;
```

---

* The construction of the WHERE statement is similar to the construction of IF and IF-THEN statements.

```
proc print data=qtr01 noobs;
   var SalesRep Month Units AmountSold;
   where SalesRep='Garcia';
   title 'TruBlend Coffee Makers Quarterly Sales for Garcia';
run;
```

In the WHERE statement, the value **Garcia** is enclosed in quotation marks because SalesRep is a character variable. In addition, the letter G in the value **Garcia** is uppercase so that it matches exactly the value in the data set QTR01.

The following output shows the report:

Output 25.7 Making a Single Comparison

```
              TruBlend Coffee Makers Quarterly Sales for Garcia            1

               Sales                        Amount
               Rep      Month    Units      Sold

               Garcia    01         41     1269.77
               Garcia    01        715    35392.50
               Garcia    02       2045    63333.65
               Garcia    02         10      495.00
               Garcia    02         40     1238.80
               Garcia    02         98     3035.06
               Garcia    03        118     3654.46
               Garcia    03        310     9600.70
```

Making Multiple Comparisons

You can also select observations based on two or more comparisons by using the WHERE statement. However, when you use multiple WHERE statements in a PROC step, then only the last statement is used. You can create a compound comparison by using AND operator. For example, the following WHERE statement selects observations where Garcia sold only the deluxe coffee maker:

where SalesRep = 'Garcia' and Type='Deluxe'

The following program uses two comparisons in a WHERE statement to produce a report that shows sales activities for a sales representative (Garcia) during the first month of the year:

```
options linesize=80 pageno=1 nodate;

proc print data=year_sales noobs;
   var SalesRep Month Units AmountSold;
   where SalesRep='Garcia' and Month='01';
   title 'TruBlend Coffee Makers Monthly Sales for Garcia';
run;
```

The WHERE statement uses the logical AND operator. Therefore, both comparisons must be true for PROC PRINT to include an observation in the report.

The following output shows the report:

Output 25.8 Making Two Comparisons

```
                TruBlend Coffee Makers Monthly Sales for Garcia                1

                 Sales                           Amount
                  Rep        Month     Units      Sold

                 Garcia       01         41      1269.77
                 Garcia       01        715     35392.50
```

You might also want to select observations that meet at least one of several conditions. The following program uses two comparisons in the WHERE statement to create a report that shows every sale during the first quarter of the year that was greater than 500 units or more than $20,000:

```
options linesize=80 pageno=1 nodate;

proc print data=qtr01 noobs;
   var SalesRep Month Units AmountSold;
   where Units>500 or AmountSold>20000;
   title 'Quarterly Report for Sales above 500 Units or $20,000';
run;
```

Notice this WHERE statement uses the logical OR operator. Therefore, only one of the comparisons must be true for PROC PRINT to include an observation in the report.

The following output shows the report:

Output 25.9 Making Comparisons for One Condition or Another

```
            Quarterly Report for Sales above 500 Units or $20,000             1

                                               Amount
               SalesRep        Month    Units   Sold

               Garcia           01        715  35392.50
               Jensen           01        675  20904.75
               Garcia           02       2045  63333.65
               Hollingsworth    02       1030  31899.10
               Jensen           03        525  16259.25
```

Creating Enhanced Reports

Ways to Enhance a Report

With just a few PROC PRINT statements and options, you can produce a variety of detail reports. By using additional statements and options that enhance the reports, you can

- □ format the columns
- □ sum the numeric variables
- □ group the observations based on variable values

□ sum the groups of variable values

□ group the observations on separate pages.

The examples in this section use the SAS data set QTR02, which was created in "Input File and SAS Data Sets for Examples" on page 368.

Specifying Formats for the Variables

Specifying the formats of variables is a simple yet effective way to enhance the readability of your reports. By adding the FORMAT statement to your program, you can specify formats for variables. The format of a variable is a pattern that SAS uses to write the values of the variables. For example, SAS contains formats that add commas to numeric values, that add dollar signs to figures, or that report values as Roman numerals.

Using a format can make the values of the variables Units and AmountSold easier to read than in the previous reports. Specifically, Units can use a COMMA format with a total field width of 7, which includes commas to separate every three digits and omits decimal values. AmountSold can use a DOLLAR format with a total field width of 14, which includes commas to separate every three digits, a decimal point, two decimal places, and a dollar sign.

The following program illustrates how to apply these formats in a FORMAT statement:

```
options linesize=80 pageno=1 nodate;

proc print data=qtr02 noobs;
    var SalesRep Month Units AmountSold;
    where Units>500 or AmountSold>20000;
    format Units comma7. AmountSold dollar14.2;
    title 'Quarterly Report for Sales above 500 Units or $20,000';
run;
```

PROC PRINT applies the COMMA7. format to the values of the variable Units and the DOLLAR14.2 format to the values of the variable AmountSold.

The following output shows the report:

Output 25.10   Formatting Numeric Variables

```
             Quarterly Report for Sales above 500 Units or $20,000          1

        SalesRep         Month     Units      AmountSold

        Hollingsworth     04         530      $16,414.10❶
        Jensen            04       1,110❷     $34,376.70
        Garcia            04       1,715      $53,113.55
        Jensen            04         675      $20,904.75
        Hollingsworth     05       1,120      $34,686.40
        Hollingsworth     05       1,030      $31,899.10
        Garcia            06         512      $15,856.64
        Garcia            06       1,000      $30,970.00
```

The following list corresponds to the numbered items in the preceding output:

❶ AmountSold uses the DOLLAR14.2 format. The maximum column width is 14 spaces. Two spaces are reserved for the decimal part of a value. The remaining 12 spaces include the decimal point, whole numbers, the dollar sign, commas, and a minus sign if a value is negative.

❷ Units uses the COMMA7. format. The maximum column width is seven spaces. The column width includes the numeric value, commas, and a minus sign if a value is negative.

The formats do not affect the internal data values that are stored in the SAS data set. The formats change only how the current PROC step displays the values in the report.

Note: Be sure to specify enough columns in the format to contain the largest value. If the format that you specify is not wide enough to contain the largest value, including special characters such as commas and dollar signs, then SAS applies the most appropriate format. △

Summing Numeric Variables

In addition to reporting the values in a data set, you can add the SUM statement to compute subtotals and totals for the numeric variables. The SUM statement enables you to request totals for one or more variables.

The following program produces a report that shows totals for the two numeric variables Units and AmountSold:

```
options linesize=80 pageno=1 nodate;

proc print data=qtr02 noobs;
   var SalesRep Month Units AmountSold;
   where Units>500 or AmountSold>20000;
   format Units comma7. AmountSold dollar14.2;
   sum Units AmountSold;
   title 'Quarterly Sales Total for Sales above 500 Units or $20,000';
run;
```

The following output shows the report:

Output 25.11   Summing Numeric Variables

```
          Quarterly Sales Totals for Sales above 500 Units or $20,000          1

          SalesRep        Month       Units        AmountSold

          Hollingsworth     04          530         $16,414.10
          Jensen            04        1,110         $34,376.70
          Garcia            04        1,715         $53,113.55
          Jensen            04          675         $20,904.75
          Hollingsworth     05        1,120         $34,686.40
          Hollingsworth     05        1,030         $31,899.10
          Garcia            06          512         $15,856.64
          Garcia            06        1,000         $30,970.00
                                      =======     ==============
                                        7,692       $238,221.24
```

The totals for Units and AmountSold are computed by summing the values for each sale made by all the sales representatives. As the next example shows, the PRINT procedure can also separately compute subtotals for each sales representative.

Grouping Observations by Variable Values

The BY statement enables you to obtain separate analyses on groups of observations. The previous example used the SUM statement to compute totals for the variables

Units and AmountSold. However, the totals were for all three sales representatives as one group. The next two examples show how to use the BY and ID statements as a part of the PROC PRINT step to separate the sales representatives into three groups with three separate subtotals and one grand total.

Computing Group Subtotals

To obtain separate subtotals for specific numeric variables, add a BY statement to the PROC PRINT step. When you use a BY statement, the PRINT procedure expects that you already sorted the data set by using the BY variables. Therefore, if your data is not sorted in the proper order, then you must add a PROC SORT step before the PROC PRINT step.

The BY statement produces a separate section of the report for each BY group. Do not specify in the VAR statement the variable that you use in the BY statement. Otherwise, the values of the BY variable appear twice in the report, as a header across the page and in columns down the page.

The following program uses the BY statement in the PROC PRINT step to obtain separate subtotals of the variables Units and AmountSold for each sales representative:

```
options linesize=80 pageno=1 nodate;

proc sort data=qtr02;
   by SalesRep;❶
run;

proc print data=qtr02 noobs;
   var Month Units AmountSold;❷
   where Units>500 or AmountSold>20000;
   format Units comma7. AmountSold dollar14.2;
   sum Units AmountSold;
   by SalesRep;❷
   title1 'Sales Rep Quarterly Totals for Sales Above 500 Units or $20,000';
run;
```

The following list corresponds to the numbered items in the preceding program:

❶ The BY statement in the PROC SORT step sorts the data.

❷ The variable SalesRep becomes part of the BY statement instead of the VAR statement.

The following output shows the report:

Output 25.12   Grouping Observations with the BY Statement

```
         Sales Rep Quarterly Totals for Sales above 500 Units or $20,000       1
----------------------------- SalesRep=Garcia ---------------------------------❶

                    Month         Units        AmountSold

                    04            1,715         $53,113.55
                    06              512         $15,856.64
                    06            1,000         $30,970.00
                    --------      -------       --------------
                    SalesRep      3,227❷        $99,940.19❷


---------------------------- SalesRep=Hollingsworth ----------------------------

                    Month         Units        AmountSold

                    04              530         $16,414.10
                    05            1,120         $34,686.40
                    05            1,030         $31,899.10
                    --------      -------       --------------
                    SalesRep      2,680         $82,999.60


----------------------------- SalesRep=Jensen ---------------------------------

                    Month         Units        AmountSold

                    04            1,110         $34,376.70
                    04              675         $20,904.75
                    --------      -------       --------------
                    SalesRep      1,785         $55,281.45
                                  =======       ==============
                                  7,692❸        $238,221.24❸
```

The following list corresponds to the numbered items in the preceding report:

❶ The values of the BY variables appear in dashed lines, called BY lines, above the output for the BY group.

❷ The subtotal for the numeric variables is computed for each BY group (the three sales representatives).

❸ A grand total is computed for the numeric variables.

Identifying Group Subtotals

You can use both the BY and ID statements in the PROC PRINT step to modify the appearance of your report. When you specify the same variables in both the BY and ID statements, the PRINT procedure uses the ID variable to identify the start of the BY group.

The following example uses the data set that was sorted in the last example and adds the ID statement to the PROC PRINT step:

```
options linesize=80 pageno=1 nodate;

proc print data=qtr02;
    var Month Units AmountSold;
    where Units>500 or AmountSold>20000;
    format Units comma7. AmountSold dollar14.2;
    sum Units AmountSold;
    by SalesRep;
```

```
id SalesRep;
title1 'Sales Rep Quarterly Totals for Sales above 500 Units or $20,000';
run;
```

The following output shows the report:

Output 25.13   Grouping Observations with the BY and ID Statements

```
        Sales Rep Quarterly Totals for Sales above 500 Units or $20,000          1

            SalesRep          Month      Units     AmountSold

            Garcia              04       1,715      $53,113.55
                                06         512      $15,856.64
                                06       1,000      $30,970.00
            -------------              -------   --------------
            Garcia                       3,227      $99,940.19

            Hollingsworth       04         530      $16,414.10
                                05       1,120      $34,686.40
                                05       1,030      $31,899.10
            -------------              -------   --------------
            Hollingsworth                2,680      $82,999.60

            Jensen              04       1,110      $34,376.70
                                04         675      $20,904.75
            -------------              -------   --------------
            Jensen                       1,785      $55,281.45
                                         =======   ==============
                                         7,692     $238,221.24
```

The report has two distinct features. PROC PRINT separates the report into groups and suppresses the repetitive values of the BY and ID variables. The dashed lines above the BY groups do not appear because the BY and ID statements are used together in the PROC PRINT step.

Remember these general rules about the SUM, BY, and ID statements:

☐ You can specify a variable in the SUM statement while omitting it in the VAR statement. PROC PRINT simply adds the variable to the list of variables in the VAR statement.

☐ You do not specify variables in the SUM statement that you used in the ID or BY statement.

☐ When you use a BY statement and you specify only one BY variable, PROC PRINT subtotals the SUM variable for each BY group that contains more than one observation.

☐ When you use a BY statement and you specify multiple BY variables, PROC PRINT shows a subtotal for a BY variable only when the value changes and when there are multiple observations with that value.

Computing Multiple Group Subtotals

You can also use two or more variables in a BY statement to define groups and subgroups. The following program produces a report that groups observations first by sales representative and then by month:

```
options linesize=80 pageno=1 nodate;
```

```
proc sort data=qtr02;
   by SalesRep Month;❶
run;

proc print data=qtr02 noobs n='Sales Transactions:'❷
                              'Total Sales Transactions:'❷;
   var Units AmountSold;❸
   where Units>500 or AmountSold>20000;
   format Units comma7. AmountSold dollar14.2;
   sum Units AmountSold;
   by SalesRep Month❸;
   title1 'Monthly Sales Rep Totals for Sales above 500 Units or $20,000';
run;
```

The following list corresponds to the numbered items in the preceding program:

❶ The BY statement in the PROC SORT step sorts the data by SalesRep and Month.

❷ The N= option in the PROC PRINT statement reports the number of observations in a BY group and (because of the SUM statement) the overall total number of observations at the end of the report. The first piece of explanatory text that N= provides precedes the number for each BY group. The second piece of explanatory text that N= provides precedes the number for the overall total.

❸ The variables SalesRep and Month are omitted in the VAR statement because the variables are specified in the BY statement. This prevents PROC PRINT from reporting the values for these variables twice.

The following output shows the report:

Output 25.14 Grouping Observations with Multiple BY Variables

```
              Monthly Sales Rep Totals for Sales above 500 Units or $20,000          1
----------------------------- SalesRep=Garcia Month=04 -----------------------------

                         Units          AmountSold

                         1,715         $53,113.55

                         Sales Transactions:1❶


----------------------------- SalesRep=Garcia Month=06 -----------------------------

                         Units          AmountSold

                           512         $15,856.64
                         1,000         $30,970.00
                         -------       --------------
                         1,512❷        $46,826.64❷
                         3,227❸        $99,940.19❸

                         Sales Transactions:2


--------------------------- SalesRep=Hollingsworth Month=04 ------------------------

                         Units          AmountSold

                           530         $16,414.10

                         Sales Transactions:1


--------------------------- SalesRep=Hollingsworth Month=05 ------------------------

                         Units          AmountSold

                         1,120         $34,686.40
                         1,030         $31,899.10
                         -------       --------------
                         2,150         $66,585.50
                         2,680         $82,999.60

                         Sales Transactions:2


----------------------------- SalesRep=Jensen Month=04 -----------------------------

                         Units          AmountSold

                         1,110         $34,376.70
                           675         $20,904.75
                         -------       --------------
                         1,785         $55,281.45
                         1,785         $55,281.45
                         =======       ==============
                         7,692❹       $238,221.24❹

                 Sales Transactions:2❶
           Total Sales Transactions:8❺
```

The following list corresponds to the numbered items in the preceding report:

❶ The number of observations in the BY group is computed. This corresponds to the number of sales transactions for a sales representative in the month.

❷ When the BY group contains two or more observations, then a subtotal is computed for each numeric variable.

❸ When the value of the first variable in the BY group changes, then an overall subtotal is computed for each numeric variable. The values of Units and AmountSold are summed for every month that Garcia had sales transactions because the sales representative changes in the next BY group.

❹ The grand total is computed for the numeric variables.

❺ The number of observations in the whole report is computed. This corresponds to the total number of sales transactions for every sales representative during the second quarter.

Computing Group Totals

When you use multiple BY variables as in the previous example, you can suppress the subtotals every time a change occurs for the value of the BY variables. Use the SUMBY statement to control which BY variable causes subtotals to appear.

You can specify only one SUMBY variable, and this variable must also be specified in the BY statement. PROC PRINT computes sums when a change occurs for

☐ the value of the SUMBY variable

☐ the value of any variable in the BY statement that is specified before the SUMBY variable.

For example, consider the following statements:

```
by Quarter SalesRep Month;
sumby SalesRep;
```

SalesRep is the SUMBY variable. In the BY statement, Quarter comes before SalesRep while Month comes after SalesRep. Therefore, these statements cause PROC PRINT to compute totals when either Quarter or SalesRep changes value, but not when Month changes value.

The following program omits the monthly subtotals for each sales representative by designating SALESREP as the variable to sum by:

```
options linesize=80 pageno=1 nodate;

proc print data=qtr02;
   var Units AmountSold;
   where Units>500 or AmountSold>20000;
   format Units comma7. AmountSold dollar14.2;
   sum Units AmountSold;
   by SalesRep Month;
   id SalesRep Month;
   sumby SalesRep;
   title1 'Sales Rep Quarterly Totals for Sales above 500 Units or $20,000';
run;
```

This program assumes that QTR02 data has been previously sorted by the variables SalesRep and Month.

The following output shows the report:

Output 25.15   Combining Subtotals for Groups of Observations

```
        Sales Rep Quarterly Totals for Sales above 500 Units or $20,000        1

              SalesRep        Month      Units       AmountSold

              Garcia           04         1,715       $53,113.55

              Garcia           06           512       $15,856.64
                                          1,000       $30,970.00
              -------------    -----     -------     --------------
              Garcia                       3,227       $99,940.19

              Hollingsworth    04           530       $16,414.10

              Hollingsworth    05         1,120       $34,686.40
                                          1,030       $31,899.10
              -------------    -----     -------     --------------
              Hollingsworth                2,680       $82,999.60

              Jensen           04         1,110       $34,376.70
                                            675       $20,904.75
              -------------    -----     -------     --------------
              Jensen                       1,785       $55,281.45
                                          =======     ==============
                                          7,692      $238,221.24
```

Grouping Observations on Separate Pages

You can also create a report with multiple sections that appear on separate pages by using the PAGEBY statement with the BY statement. The PAGEBY statement identifies a variable in the BY statement that causes the PRINT procedure to begin the report on a new page when a change occurs for

□ the value of the BY variable

□ the value of any BY variable that precedes it in the BY statement.

The following program uses a PAGEBY statement with the BY statement to create a report with multiple sections:

```
options linesize=80 pageno=1 nodate;

proc print data=qtr02 noobs;
   var Units AmountSold;
   where Units>500 or AmountSold>20000;
   format Units comma7. AmountSold dollar14.2;
   sum Units AmountSold;
   by SalesRep Month;
   id SalesRep Month;
   sumby SalesRep;
   pageby SalesRep;
   title1 'Sales Rep Quarterly Totals for Sales above 500 Units or $20,000';
run;
```

This program assumes that QTR02 data has been previously sorted by the variables SalesRep and Month.

The following output shows the report:

Output 25.16   Grouping Observations on Separate Pages

```
            Sales Rep Quarterly Totals for Sales above 500 Units or $20,000          1

                  SalesRep       Month      Units        AmountSold

                  Garcia          04        1,715        $53,113.55

                  Garcia          06          512        $15,856.64
                                            1,000        $30,970.00
                  -------------   -----    -------     --------------
                  Garcia                    3,227        $99,940.19
```

```
            Sales Rep Quarterly Totals for Sales above 500 Units or $20,000          2

                  SalesRep       Month      Units        AmountSold

                  Hollingsworth   04          530        $16,414.10

                  Hollingsworth   05        1,120        $34,686.40
                                            1,030        $31,899.10
                  -------------   -----    -------     --------------
                  Hollingsworth             2,680        $82,999.60
```

```
            Sales Rep Quarterly Totals for Sales above 500 Units or $20,000          3

                  SalesRep       Month      Units        AmountSold

                  Jensen          04        1,110        $34,376.70
                                              675        $20,904.75
                  -------------   -----    -------     --------------
                  Jensen                    1,785        $55,281.45
                                           =======     ==============
                                            7,692       $238,221.24
```

A page breaks occurs in the report when the value of the variable SalesRep changes from **Garcia** to **Hollingsworth** and from **Hollingsworth** to **Jensen**.

Creating Customized Reports

Ways to Customize a Report

As you have seen from the previous examples, the PRINT procedure produces simple detail reports quickly and easily. With additional statements and options, you can enhance the readability of your reports. For example, you can

□ add descriptive titles and footnotes

□ define and split labels across multiple lines

□ add double spacing

□ ensure that the column widths are uniform across the pages of the report.

Understanding Titles and Footnotes

Adding descriptive titles and footnotes is one of the easiest and most effective ways to improve the appearance of a report. You can use the TITLE statement to include from 1 to 10 lines of text at the top of the report. You can use the FOOTNOTE statement to include from 1 to 10 lines of text at the bottom of the report.

In the TITLE statement, you can specify *n* immediately following the keyword TITLE, to indicate the level of the TITLE statement. *n* is a number from 1 to 10 that specifies the line number of the TITLE. You must enclose the text of each title in single or double quotation marks.

Skipping over some values of *n* indicates that those lines are blank. For example, if you specify TITLE1 and TITLE3 statements but skip TITLE2, then a blank line occurs between the first and third lines.

When you specify a title, SAS uses that title for all subsequent output until you cancel it or define another title for that line. A TITLE statement for a given line cancels the previous TITLE statement for that line and for all lines below it, that is, for those with larger *n* values.

To cancel all existing titles, specify a TITLE statement without the *n* value:

```
title;
```

To suppress the *n*th title and all titles below it, use the following statement:

```
titlen;
```

Footnotes work the same way as titles. In the FOOTNOTE statement, you can specify *n* immediately following the keyword FOOTNOTE, to indicate the level of the FOOTNOTE statement. *n* is a number from 1 to 10 that specifies the line number of the FOOTNOTE. You must enclose the text of each footnote in single or double quotation marks. As with the TITLE statement, skipping over some values of *n* indicates that those lines are blank.

Remember that the footnotes are pushed up from the bottom of the report. In other words, the FOOTNOTE statement with the largest number appears on the bottom line.

When you specify a footnote, SAS uses that footnote for all subsequent output until you cancel it or define another footnote for that line. You cancel and suppress footnotes in the same way that you cancel and suppress titles.

Note: The maximum title length and footnote length that is allowed depends on your operating environment and the value of the LINESIZE= system option. Refer to the SAS documentation for your operating environment for more information.   △

Adding Titles and Footnotes

The following program includes titles and footnotes in a report of second quarter sales during the month of April:

```
options linesize=80 pageno=1 nodate;

proc sort data=qtr02;
   by SalesRep;
run;

proc print data=qtr02 noobs;
   var SalesRep Month Units AmountSold;
   where Month='04';
   format Units comma7. AmountSold dollar14.2;
```

```
    sum Units AmountSold;
    title1 'TruBlend Coffee Makers, Inc.';
    title3 'Quarterly Sales Report';
    footnote1 'April Sales Totals';
    footnote2 'COMPANY CONFIDENTIAL INFORMATION';
run;
```

The report includes three title lines and two footnote lines. The program omits the TITLE2 statement so that the second title line is blank.

The following output shows the report:

Output 25.17   Adding Titles and Footnotes

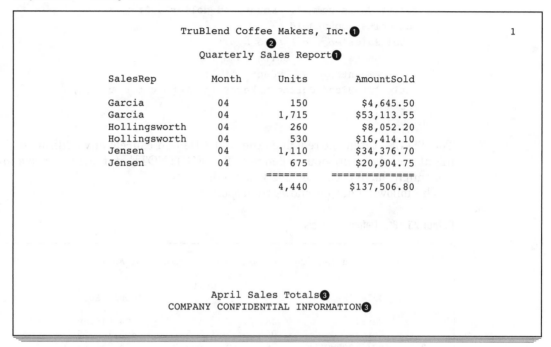

```
                        TruBlend Coffee Makers, Inc.❶                     1
                                     ❷
                            Quarterly Sales Report❶

            SalesRep          Month      Units        AmountSold

            Garcia            04           150         $4,645.50
            Garcia            04         1,715        $53,113.55
            Hollingsworth     04           260         $8,052.20
            Hollingsworth     04           530        $16,414.10
            Jensen            04         1,110        $34,376.70
            Jensen            04           675        $20,904.75
                                       =======    ===============
                                         4,440       $137,506.80




                            April Sales Totals❸
                     COMPANY CONFIDENTIAL INFORMATION❸
```

The following list corresponds to the numbered items in the preceding report:

❶ a descriptive title line that is generated by a TITLE statement

❷ a blank title line that is generated by omitting a TITLE statement for the second line

❸ a descriptive footnote line that is generated by a FOOTNOTE statement.

Defining Labels

By default, SAS uses variable names for column headings. However, to improve the appearance of a report, you can specify your own column headings.

To override the default headings, you need to

☐ add the LABEL option to the PROC PRINT statement

☐ define the labels in the LABEL statement.

The LABEL option causes the report to display labels, instead of variable names, for the column headings. You use the LABEL statement to assign the labels for the specific variables. A label can be up to 256 characters long, including blanks, and must be enclosed in single or double quotation marks. If you assign labels when you created the SAS data set, then you can omit the LABEL statement from the PROC PRINT step.

The following program modifies the previous program and defines labels for the variables SalesRep, Units, and AmountSold:

```
options linesize=80 pageno=1 nodate;

proc sort data=qtr02;
   by SalesRep;
run;

proc print data=qtr02 noobs label;
   var SalesRep Month Units AmountSold;
   where Month='04';
   format Units comma7. AmountSold dollar14.2;
   sum Units AmountSold;
   label SalesRep   = 'Sales Rep.'
         Units      = 'Units Sold'
         AmountSold = 'Amount Sold';
   title 'TruBlend Coffee Maker Sales Report for April';
   footnote;
run;
```

The TITLE statement redefines the first title and cancels any additional titles that might have been previously defined. The FOOTNOTE statement cancels any footnotes that might have been previously defined.

The following output shows the report:

Output 25.18   Defining Labels

```
              TruBlend Coffee Maker Sales Report for April              1

                              Units
        Sales Rep.     Month   Sold      Amount Sold

        Garcia          04      150        $4,645.50
        Garcia          04    1,715       $53,113.55
        Hollingsworth   04      260        $8,052.20
        Hollingsworth   04      530       $16,414.10
        Jensen          04    1,110       $34,376.70
        Jensen          04      675       $20,904.75
                              =======   ==============
                                4,440      $137,506.80
```

The label Units Sold is split between two lines. The PRINT procedure splits the label to conserve space.

Splitting Labels across Two or More Lines

Sometimes labels are too long to fit on one line, or you might want to split a label across two or more lines. By default, SAS automatically splits labels on the basis of column width. You can use the SPLIT= option to control where the labels are separated into multiple lines.

The SPLIT= option replaces the LABEL option in the PROC PRINT statement. (You do not need to use both SPLIT= and LABEL because SPLIT= implies that PROC PRINT use labels.) In the SPLIT= option, you specify an alphanumeric character that indicates where to split labels. To use the SPLIT= option, you need to

□ define the split character as a part of the PROC PRINT statement

□ define the labels with a split character in the LABEL statement.

The following PROC PRINT step defines the slash (/) as the split character and includes slashes in the LABEL statements to split the labels Sales Representative, Units Sold, and Amount Sold into two lines each:

```
options linesize=80 pageno=1 nodate;

proc sort data=qtr02;
   by SalesRep;
run;

proc print data=qtr02 noobs split='/';
   var SalesRep Month Units AmountSold;
   where Month='04';
   format Units comma7. AmountSold dollar14.2;
   sum Units AmountSold;
   title 'TruBlend Coffee Maker Sales Report for April';
   label SalesRep    = 'Sales/Representative'
         Units       = 'Units/Sold'
         AmountSold = 'Amount/Sold';
run;
```

The following output shows the report:

Output 25.19 Reporting: Splitting Labels into Two Lines

```
              TruBlend Coffee Maker Sales Report for April                1

              Sales                Units           Amount
          Representative   Month    Sold             Sold

          Garcia            04       150        $4,645.50
          Garcia            04     1,715       $53,113.55
          Hollingsworth     04       260        $8,052.20
          Hollingsworth     04       530       $16,414.10
          Jensen            04     1,110       $34,376.70
          Jensen            04       675       $20,904.75
                                   =======   ==============
                                     4,440     $137,506.80
```

Adding Double Spacing

You might want to improve the appearance of a report by adding double spaces between the rows of the report. The following program uses the DOUBLE option in the PROC PRINT statement to double-space the report:

```
options linesize=80 pageno=1 nodate;

proc sort data=qtr02;
   by SalesRep;
run;

proc print data=qtr02 noobs split='/' double;
   var SalesRep Month Units AmountSold;
```

```
      where Month='04';
      format Units comma7. AmountSold dollar14.2;
      sum Units AmountSold;
      title 'TruBlend Coffee Maker Sales Report for April';
      label SalesRep    = 'Sales/Representative'
            Units       = 'Units/Sold'
            AmountSold = 'Amount/Sold';
   run;
```

The following output shows the report:

Output 25.20   Adding Double Spacing

```
                 TruBlend Coffee Maker Sales Report for April                  1

                Sales                        Units            Amount
            Representative      Month          Sold             Sold

            Garcia                 04           150         $4,645.50

            Garcia                 04         1,715        $53,113.55

            Hollingsworth          04           260         $8,052.20

            Hollingsworth          04           530        $16,414.10

            Jensen                 04         1,110        $34,376.70

            Jensen                 04           675        $20,904.75

                                           =======   ===============

                                             4,440       $137,506.80
```

Requesting Uniform Column Widths

By default, PROC PRINT uses the width of the formatted variable as the column width. If you do not assign a format to the variable that explicitly specifies a field width, then the column width is the widest value of the variable on that page. This can cause the column widths to vary on different pages of a report.

The WIDTH=UNIFORM option ensures that the columns of data line up from one page to the next. PROC PRINT will use a variable's formatted width or, if no format is assigned, the widest data value as the variable's column width on all pages. Unless you specify this option, PROC PRINT individually constructs each page of output. Each page contains as many variables and observations as possible. As a result, the report might have different numbers of variables or different column widths from one page to the next.

If the sales records for TruBlend Coffee Makers* are sorted by the sales representatives and a report is created without using the WIDTH=UNIFORM option in the PROC PRINT statement, then the columns of values on the first page will not line up with those on the next page. The column shift occurs because of differences in the name length of the sales representatives. PROC PRINT lines up the columns on the first

---

* See "Input File and SAS Data Sets for Examples" on page 368 to examine the sales records.

page of the report, allowing enough space for the longest name, **Hollingsworth**. On the second page the longest name is **Jensen**, so the columns shift relative to the first page.

The following example uses the WIDTH= option in the PROC PRINT statement to prevent the shifting of columns:

```
options pagesize=66 linesize=80 pageno=1 nodate;

proc sort data=qtr03;
   by SalesRep;
run;

proc print data=qtr03 split='/' width=uniform;
   var SalesRep Month Units AmountSold;
   format Units comma7. AmountSold dollar14.2;
   sum Units AmountSold;
   title 'TruBlend Coffee Makers 3rd Quarter Sales Report';
   label SalesRep    = 'Sales/Rep.'
         Units       = 'Units/Sold'
         AmountSold  = 'Amount/Sold';
run;
```

The following output shows the report:

Output 25.21   Reporting: Using Uniform Column Widths

```
                  TruBlend Coffee Makers 3rd Quarter Sales Report                1

             Sales                    Units            Amount
      Obs    Rep.          Month       Sold              Sold

        1    Garcia          07         250          $7,742.50
        2    Garcia          07          90          $2,787.30
        3    Garcia          07          90          $2,787.30
        4    Garcia          07         265          $8,207.05
        5    Garcia          07       1,250         $38,712.50
        6    Garcia          07          90          $2,787.30
        7    Garcia          07          90          $2,787.30
        8    Garcia          07         465         $14,401.05
        9    Garcia          08         110          $5,445.00
       10    Garcia          08         240          $7,432.80
       11    Garcia          08         198          $6,132.06
       12    Garcia          08       1,198         $37,102.06
       13    Garcia          08         110          $5,445.00
       14    Garcia          08         240          $7,432.80
       15    Garcia          08         198          $6,132.06
       16    Garcia          09         118          $3,654.46
       17    Garcia          09         412         $12,759.64
       18    Garcia          09         100          $3,097.00
       19    Garcia          09       1,118         $34,624.46
       20    Garcia          09         412         $12,759.64
       21    Garcia          09         100          $3,097.00
       22    Hollingsworth   07          60          $2,970.00
       23    Hollingsworth   07          30          $1,485.00
       24    Hollingsworth   07         130          $4,026.10
       25    Hollingsworth   07          60          $2,970.00
       26    Hollingsworth   07         330         $10,220.10
       27    Hollingsworth   08         120          $3,716.40
       28    Hollingsworth   08         230          $7,123.10
       29    Hollingsworth   08         230         $11,385.00
       30    Hollingsworth   08         290          $8,981.30
       31    Hollingsworth   08         330         $10,220.10
       32    Hollingsworth   08          50          $2,475.00
       33    Hollingsworth   09         125          $3,871.25
       34    Hollingsworth   09       1,000         $30,970.00
       35    Hollingsworth   09         125          $3,871.25
       36    Hollingsworth   09         175          $5,419.75
       37    Jensen          07         110          $3,406.70
       38    Jensen          07         110          $3,406.70
       39    Jensen          07         275          $8,516.75
       40    Jensen          07         110          $3,406.70
       41    Jensen          07         110          $3,406.70
       42    Jensen          07         675         $20,904.75
       43    Jensen          08         145          $4,490.65
       44    Jensen          08         453         $14,029.41
       45    Jensen          08         453         $14,029.41
       46    Jensen          08          45          $2,227.50
       47    Jensen          08         145          $4,490.65
       48    Jensen          08         453         $14,029.41
       49    Jensen          08         225         $11,137.50
       50    Jensen          09         254          $7,866.38
       51    Jensen          09         284          $8,795.48
       52    Jensen          09         275         $13,612.50
       53    Jensen          09         876         $27,129.72
       54    Jensen          09         254          $7,866.38
       55    Jensen          09         284          $8,795.48
```

```
              TruBlend Coffee Makers 3rd Quarter Sales Report                2

                  Sales                      Units              Amount
            Obs   Rep.          Month        Sold                Sold

             56   Jensen          09          275           $13,612.50
             57   Jensen          09          876           $27,129.72
                                            =======       ===============
                                             17,116          $557,321.62
```

Making Your Reports Easy to Change

Understanding the SAS Macro Facility

Base SAS includes the macro facility as a tool to customize SAS and to reduce the amount of text you must enter to do common tasks. The macro facility enables you to assign a name to character strings or groups of SAS programming statements.

From that point on, you can work with the names rather than with the text itself. When you use a macro facility name in a SAS program, the macro facility generates SAS statements and commands as needed. The rest of SAS receives those statements and uses them in the same way it uses the ones you enter in the standard manner.

The macro facility enables you to create macro variables to substitute text in SAS programs. One of the major advantages of using macro variables is that it enables you to change the value of a variable in one place in your program and then have the change appear in multiple references throughout your program. You can substitute text by using automatic macro variables or by using your own macro variables, which you define and assign values to.

Using Automatic Macro Variables

The SAS macro facility includes many automatic macro variables. Some of the values associated with the automatic macro variables depend on your operating environment. You can use automatic macro variables to provide the time, the day of the week, and the date based on your computer's internal clock as well as other processing information.

To include a second title on a report that displays the text string "Produced on" followed by today's date, add the following TITLE statement to your program:

```
title2 "Produced on &SYSDATE9";
```

Notice the syntax for this statement. First, the ampersand that precedes SYSDATE9 tells the SAS macro facility to replace the reference with its assigned value. In this case, the assigned value is the date the SAS session started and is expressed as *ddmmmyyyy*, where

dd is a two-digit date

mmm is the first three letters of the month name

yyyy is a four-digit year

Second, the text of the TITLE statement is enclosed in double quotation marks because the SAS macro facility resolves macro variable references in the TITLE statement and the FOOTNOTE statement only if they are in double quotation marks.

The following program, which includes a PROC SORT step and the TITLE statement, demonstrates how to use the SYSDATE9. automatic macro variable:

```
options linesize=80 pageno=1 nodate;

proc sort data=qtr04;
   by SalesRep;
run;

proc print data=qtr04 noobs split='/' width=uniform;
   var SalesRep Month Units AmountSold;
   format Units comma7. AmountSold dollar14.2;
   sum Units AmountSold;
   title1 'TruBlend Coffee Maker Quarterly Sales Report';
   title2 "Produced on &SYSDATE9";
   label SalesRep   = 'Sales/Rep.'
         Units      = 'Units/Sold'
         AmountSold = 'Amount/Sold';
run;
```

The following output shows the report:

Output 25.22   Using Automatic Macro Variables

```
                TruBlend Coffee Maker Quarterly Sales Report          1
                       Produced on 30JAN2001

            Sales                     Units            Amount
            Rep.          Month       Sold             Sold

            Garcia          10         250           $7,742.50
            Garcia          10         365          $11,304.05
            Garcia          11         198           $6,132.06
            Garcia          11         120           $3,716.40
            Garcia          12       1,000          $30,970.00
            Hollingsworth   10         530          $16,414.10
            Hollingsworth   10         265           $8,207.05
            Hollingsworth   11       1,230          $38,093.10
            Hollingsworth   11         150           $7,425.00
            Hollingsworth   12         125           $6,187.50
            Hollingsworth   12         175           $5,419.75
            Jensen          10         975          $30,195.75
            Jensen          10          55           $1,703.35
            Jensen          11         453          $14,029.41
            Jensen          11          70           $2,167.90
            Jensen          12         876          $27,129.72
            Jensen          12       1,254          $38,836.38
                                     =======       ==============
                                      8,091        $255,674.02
```

Using Your Own Macro Variables

In addition to using automatic macro variables, you can use the %LET statement to define your own macro variables and refer to them with the ampersand prefix. Defining macro variables at the beginning of your program enables you to change other parts of the program easily. The following example shows how to define two macro variables, Quarter and Year, and how to refer to them in a TITLE statement.

Defining Macro Variables

To use two macro variables that produce flexible report titles, first define the macro variables. The following %LET statements define the two macro variables:

```
%let Quarter=Fourth;
%let Year=2000;
```

The name of the first macro variable is Quarter and it is assigned the value Fourth. The name of the second macro variable is Year and it is assigned the value 2000.

Macro variable names such as these conform to the following rules for SAS names:

□ macro variable names are one to 32 characters long

□ macro variable names begin with a letter or an underscore

□ letters, numbers, and underscores follow the first character.

In these simple situations, do not assign values to macro variables that contain unmatched quotation marks or semicolons. If the values contain leading or trailing blanks, then SAS removes the blanks.

Referring to Macro Variables

To refer to the value of a macro variable, place an ampersand prefix in front of the name of the variable. The following TITLE statement contains references to the values of the macro variables Quarter and Year, which were previously defined in %LET statements:

```
title3 "&Quarter Quarter &Year Sales Totals";
```

The complete program, which includes the two %LET statements and the TITLE3 statement, follows:

```
options linesize=80 pageno=1 nodate;

%let Quarter=Fourth;❶
%let Year=2000;❷

proc sort data=qtr04;
   by SalesRep;
run;
proc print data=qtr04 noobs split='/' width=uniform;
   var SalesRep Month Units AmountSold;
   format Units comma7. AmountSold dollar14.2;
   sum Units AmountSold;
   title1 'TruBlend Coffee Maker Quarterly Sales Report';
   title2 "Produced on &SYSDATE9";
   title3 "&Quarter Quarter &Year Sales Totals";❸
   label SalesRep    = 'Sales/Rep.'
         Units       = 'Units/Sold'
         AmountSold  = 'Amount/Sold';
run;
```

The following list corresponds to the numbered items in the preceding program:

❶ The %LET statement creates a macro variable with the sales quarter. When an ampersand precedes Quarter, the SAS macro facility knows to replace any reference to &Quarter with the assigned value of Fourth.

❷ The %LET statement creates a macro variable with the year. When ampersand precedes Year, the SAS macro facility knows to replace any reference to &Year with the assigned value of 2000.

❸ The text of the TITLE2 and TITLE3 statements are enclosed in double quotation marks so that the SAS macro facility can resolve them.

The following output shows the report:

Output 25.23   Using Your Own Macro Variables

```
                TruBlend Coffee Maker Quarterly Sales Report          1
                         Produced on 12JAN2001
                      Fourth Quarter 2000 Sales Totals

        Sales                        Units              Amount
        Rep.            Month          Sold               Sold

        Garcia            10           250            $7,742.50
        Garcia            10           365           $11,304.05
        Garcia            11           198            $6,132.06
        Garcia            11           120            $3,716.40
        Garcia            12         1,000           $30,970.00
        Hollingsworth     10           530           $16,414.10
        Hollingsworth     10           265            $8,207.05
        Hollingsworth     11         1,230           $38,093.10
        Hollingsworth     11           150            $7,425.00
        Hollingsworth     12           125            $6,187.50
        Hollingsworth     12           175            $5,419.75
        Jensen            10           975           $30,195.75
        Jensen            10            55            $1,703.35
        Jensen            11           453           $14,029.41
        Jensen            11            70            $2,167.90
        Jensen            12           876           $27,129.72
        Jensen            12         1,254           $38,836.38
                                    =======        ==============
                                      8,091          $255,674.02
```

Using macro variables can make your programs easy to modify. For example, if the previous program contained many references to Quarter and Year, then changes in only three places will produce an entirely different report:

- □ the two values in the %LET statements
- □ the data set name in the PROC PRINT statement.

Review of SAS Tools

PROC PRINT Statements

PROC PRINT <DATA=*SAS-data-set*> <*option(s)*>;
   BY *variable(s)*;
   FOOTNOTE<*n*> <*'footnote'*>;
   FORMAT *variable(s) format-name*;
   ID *variable(s)*;
   LABEL *variable='label'*;
   PAGEBY *variable*;
   SUM *variable(s)*;
   SUMBY *variable*;

TITLE<*n*> <*'title'*>;

VAR *variable(s)*;

WHERE *where-expression*;

PROC PRINT <DATA=*SAS-data-set*> <*options*>;
    starts the procedure and, when used alone, shows all variables for all observations in the *SAS-data-set* in the report. Other statements, that are listed below, enable you to control what to report.
    You can specify the following *options* in the PROC PRINT statement:

    DATA=*SAS-data-set*
        names the SAS data set that PROC PRINT uses. If you omit DATA=, then PROC PRINT uses the most recently created data set.

    DOUBLE | D
        writes a blank line between observations.

    LABEL
        uses variable labels instead of variable names as column headings for any variables that have labels defined. Variable labels appear only if you use the LABEL option or the SPLIT= option. You can specify labels in LABEL statements in the DATA step that creates the data set or in the PROC PRINT step. If you do not specify the LABEL option or if there is no label for a variable, then PROC PRINT uses the variable name.

    N<="*string-1*" <"*string-2*">>
        shows the number of observations in the data set, in BY groups, or both and optionally specifies explanatory text to include with the number.

    NOOBS
        suppresses the observation numbers in the output. This option is useful when you omit an ID statement and do not want to show the observation numbers.

    SPLIT='*split-character*'
        specifies the split character, which controls line breaks in column headers. PROC PRINT breaks a column heading when it reaches the split character and continues the header on the next line. The split character is not part of the column heading.
        PROC PRINT uses variable labels only when you use the LABEL option or the SPLIT= option. It is not necessary to use both the LABEL and SPLIT= options because SPLIT= implies to use labels.

    WIDTH=UNIFORM
        uses each variable's formatted width as its column width on all pages. If the variable does not have a format that explicitly specifies a field width, then PROC PRINT uses the widest data value as the column width. Without this option, PROC PRINT fits as many variables and observations on a page as possible. Therefore, the report might contain a different number of columns on each page.

BY *variable(s)*;
    produces a separate section of the report for each BY group. The BY group is made up of the *variables* that you specify. When you use a BY statement, the procedure expects that the input data set is sorted by the *variables*.

FOOTNOTE<*n*> <*'footnote'*>;
    specifies a footnote. The argument *n* is a number from 1 to 10 that immediately follows the word FOOTNOTE, with no intervening blank, and specifies the line

number of the FOOTNOTE. The text of each *footnote* must be enclosed in single or double quotation marks. The maximum footnote length that is allowed depends on your operating environment and the value of the LINESIZE= system option. Refer to the SAS documentation for your operating environment for more information.

FORMAT *variable(s) format-name*;

enables you to report the value of a *variable* using a special pattern that you specify as *format-name*.

ID *variable(s)*;

specifies one or more variables that PROC PRINT uses instead of observation numbers to identify observations in the report.

LABEL *variable='label'*;

specifies to use labels for column headings. *Variable* names the variable to label, and *label* specifies a string of up to 256 characters, which includes blanks. The *label* must be enclosed in single or double quotation marks.

OBS=*'column-header'*

specifies a column header for the column that identifies each observation by number.

PAGEBY *variable*;

causes PROC PRINT to begin a new page when the *variable* that you specify changes value or when any variable that you list before it in the BY statement changes value. You must use a BY statement with the PAGEBY statement.

SUM *variable(s)*;

identifies the numeric variables to total in the report. You can specify a variable in the SUM statement and omit it in the VAR statement because PROC PRINT will add the variable to the VAR list. PROC PRINT ignores requests to total the BY and ID variables. In general, when you also use the BY statement, the SUM statement produces subtotals each time the value of a BY variable changes.

SUMBY *variable*;

limits the number of sums that appear in the report. PROC PRINT reports totals only when *variable* changes value or when any variable that is listed before it in the BY statement changes value. You must use a BY statement with the SUMBY statement.

TITLE<*n*> <*'title'*>;

specifies a title. The argument *n* is a number from 1 to 10 that immediately follows the word TITLE, with no intervening blank, and specifies the level of the TITLE. The text of each *title* must be enclosed in single or double quotation marks. The maximum title length that is allowed depends on your operating environment and the value of the LINESIZE= system option. Refer to the SAS documentation for your operating environment for more information.

VAR *variable(s)*;

identifies one or more variables that appear in the report. The variables appear in the order that you list them in the VAR statement. If you omit the VAR statement, then all the variables appear in the report.

WHERE *where-expression*;

subsets the input data set by identifying certain conditions that each observation must meet before an observation is available for processing. *Where-expression* defines the condition. The condition is a valid arithmetic or logical expression that generally consists of a sequence of operands and operators.

PROC SORT Statements

PROC SORT <DATA=*SAS-data-set*>;
   BY *variable(s)*;

PROC SORT DATA=*SAS-data-set*;
   sorts a SAS data set by the values of variables that you list in the BY statement.

BY *variable(s)*;
   specifies one or more variables by which PROC SORT sorts the observations. By default, PROC SORT arranges the data set by the values in ascending order (smallest value to largest).

SAS Macro Language

%LET *macro-variable=value*;
   is a macro statement that defines a *macro-variable* and assigns it a *value*. The *value* that you define in the %LET statement is substituted for the *macro-variable* in output. To use the *macro-variable* in a program, include an ampersand (&) prefix before it.

SYSDATE9
   is an automatic macro variable that contains the date that a SAS job or session began to execute. SYSDATE9 contains a SAS date value in the DATE9 format (*ddmmmyyyy*). The date displays a two-digit date, the first three letters of the month name, and a four-digit year. To use it in a program, you include an ampersand (&) prefix before SYSDATE9.

Learning More

Data Set Indexes
   For information about indexing data sets, see *SAS Language Reference: Dictionary*. You do not need to sort data sets before using a BY statement in the PRINT procedure if the data sets have an index for the variable or variables that are specified in the BY statement.

PROC PRINT
   For complete documentation, see *SAS Procedures Guide*.

PROC SORT
   For a discussion, see Chapter 11, "Working with Grouped or Sorted Observations," on page 173. For complete reference documentation about the SORT procedure, see *SAS Procedures Guide*.

SAS formats
   For complete documentation, see *SAS Language Reference: Dictionary*. Formats that are available with SAS software include fractions, hexadecimal values, roman

numerals, social security numbers, date and time values, and numbers written as words.

SAS macro facility
For complete reference documentation, see *SAS Macro Language: Reference.*

WHERE statement
For complete reference documentation, see *SAS Language Reference: Dictionary.*
For a complete discussion of WHERE processing, see Chapter 18,
"Where-Expression Processing," in *SAS Language Reference: Concepts.*

CHAPTER
26

Creating Summary Tables with the TABULATE Procedure

Introduction

Purpose

Summary tables display the relationships that exist among the variables in a data set. The variables in the data set form the columns, rows, and pages of summary tables. The data at each intersection of a column and row (that is, each cell) shows a relationship between the variables. The TABULATE procedure enables you to create a variety of summary tables.

In this chapter, you learn how to

- □ produce simple summary tables by using a few basic PROC TABULATE options and statements

- □ produce enhanced summary tables by summarizing more complex relationships between and across variables, applying formats to variables, and calculating statistics for variables

- □ add the finishing touches to tables by using labels, by specifying fonts and colors with the Output Delivery System, and by ordering class variables.

Prerequisites

To understand the examples in this chapter, you should be familiar with the following features and concepts:

- □ summary table design (see the next section)

- □ locating procedure output (see Chapter 31, "Understanding and Customizing SAS Output: The Basics," on page 533)

- □ the TITLE statement (see Chapter 25, "Producing Detail Reports with the PRINT Procedure," on page 367).

Understanding Summary Table Design

If you design your summary table in advance, then you can save time and write simpler SAS code to produce the summary table. The basic steps of summary table design and construction are listed next. For a detailed step-by-step example of the design process, see "Before You Start Writing PROC TABULATE Code" in the book titled *PROC TABULATE by Example*.

Prior to designing a summary table, it is important to understand that the summary table produces summary data wherever values for two or more variables intersect. The point of intersection is a *cell*. When values for two or more variables intersect, the variables are said to be *crossed*. The process of crossing variables to form intersections is called *cross-tabulation*. Variables in columns, rows, and pages can be crossed to produce summary data. The following summary table displays how two variables are crossed by highlighting a single value for each variable:

Display 26.1 Crossing Variables

Crossing Value C with Value Y

	Variable 1			
	value A	value B	value C	value D
Variable 2				
value X				
value Y				
value Z				

Here are the basic steps for designing and constructing a summary table:

1 Start with a question that you want to answer with a summary table.

2 Identify the variables necessary to answer your question.

- □ See if any of the data sets that you are using already use the variables that you identified. If they do not, then you might be able to use the FORMAT procedure to reclassify the variable values in these data sets so that they produce the data that you need.

  For example, you can apply a new format to values for a variable MONTH so that they become values for a variable QUARTER. To do this, assign the values representing the first three months to a value for quarter one, values representing the second set of three months to a value for quarter two, and so on.

- □ If possible, use discrete variables rather than continuous variables for categories or headings. If you must use continuous variables, then it might be helpful to create categories. For example, you can group ages into categories such as ages 15-19, 20-35, 36-55, and 56-higher. This creates four categories rather than a possible 56+ categories. You can use PROC FORMAT to categorize the data.

- □ Choose formats for the variables and the data that you want to display in your summary table. See if the data in your data sets is in a format that you can use. You might need to create new formats with PROC FORMAT, or copy the formats of variables from another data set so that the data will be formatted in the same way.

3 Review the data for anything that might cause discrepancies in your report.

- □ Remove data that does not relate to your needs.

- □ Identify missing data.

- □ Make sure that the data overall seems to make logical sense.

4 Choose statistics that will help answer your question. For a complete list of statistics, see "Statistics Available in PROC TABULATE" in the *SAS Procedures Guide*.

5 Decide on the basic structure of the table. Use the variables that you have identified to determine the headings for the columns, rows, and pages. The values of the variables are the subheadings. Statistics are usually represented as subheadings, but are sometimes represented as headings. Display 26.1 on page 405 is an example of a template for a very basic table.

Understanding the Basics of the TABULATE Procedure

Required Statements for the TABULATE Procedure

The TABULATE procedure requires three statements, usually in the following order:

1 PROC TABULATE statement

2 CLASS statements or VAR statements or both

3 TABLE statements

Note that there can be multiple CLASS statements, VAR statements and TABLE statements.

Begin with the PROC TABULATE Statement

The TABULATE procedure begins with a PROC TABULATE statement. Many options are available with the PROC TABULATE statement; however, most of the examples in this chapter use only two, the DATA= option and the FORMAT= option. The PROC TABULATE statement that follows is used for all of the examples in this chapter:

```
proc tabulate data=year_sales format=comma10.;
```

You can direct PROC TABULATE to use a specific SAS data set with the DATA= option. If you omit the DATA= option in the current job or session, then the TABULATE procedure uses the SAS data set that was created most recently.

You can specify a default format for PROC TABULATE to apply to the value in each cell in the table with the FORMAT= option. You can specify any valid SAS numeric format or user-defined format.

Specify Class Variables with the CLASS Statement

Use the CLASS statement to specify which variables are class variables. *Class variables* (that is, classification variables) contain values that are used to form categories. In summary tables, the categories are used as the column, row, and page headings. The categories are crossed to obtain descriptive statistics. See Display 26.1 on page 405 for an example of crossing categories (variable values).

Class variables can be either character or numeric. The default statistic for class variables is N, which is the frequency or number of observations in the data set for which there are nonmissing variable values.

The following CLASS statement specifies the variables SalesRep and Type as class variables:

```
class SalesRep Type;
```

For important information about how PROC TABULATE behaves when class variables that have missing values are listed in a CLASS statement but are not used in a TABLE statement, see "Identifying Missing Values for Class Variables" on page 407.

Specify Analysis Variables with the VAR Statement

Use the VAR statement to specify which variables are analysis variables. *Analysis variables* contain numeric values for which you want to compute statistics. The default statistic for analysis variables is SUM.

The following VAR statement specifies the variable AmountSold as an analysis variable:

```
var AmountSold;
```

Define the Table Structure with the TABLE Statement

Syntax of a TABLE Statement

Use the TABLE statement to define the structure of the table that you want PROC TABULATE to produce. A TABLE statement consists of one to three dimension expressions, separated by commas. *Dimension expressions* define the columns, rows, and pages of a summary table. Options can follow dimension expressions. You must specify at least one TABLE statement, because there is no default table in a PROC TABULATE step. Here are three variations of the syntax for a basic TABLE statement:

```
TABLE column-expression;
TABLE row-expression, column-expression;
TABLE page-expression, row-expression, column-expression;
```

In this syntax
- □ a column expression is required
- □ a row expression is optional
- □ a page expression is optional
- □ the order of the expressions must be page expression, row expression, and then column expression.

Here is an example of a basic TABLE statement with three dimension expressions:

```
table SalesRep, Type, AmountSold;
```

This TABLE statement defines a three-dimensional summary table that places the values of the variable AmountSold in the column dimension, the values of the variable Type in the row dimension, and the values of the variable SalesRep in the page dimension.

Restrictions on a TABLE Statement

Here are restrictions on the TABLE statement:
- □ A TABLE statement must have a column dimension.
- □ Every variable that is used in a dimension expression in a TABLE statement must appear in either a CLASS statement or a VAR statement, but not both.
- □ All analysis variables must be in the same dimension and cannot be crossed. Therefore, only one dimension of any TABLE statement can contain analysis variables.

Identifying Missing Values for Class Variables

You can identify missing values for class variables with the MISSING option. By default, if an observation contains a missing value for any class variable, that observation will be excluded from all tables even if the variable does not appear in the TABLE statement for one or more tables. Therefore, it is helpful to run your program at least once with the MISSING option to identify missing values.

The MISSING option creates a separate category in the summary table for missing values. It can be used with the PROC TABULATE statement or the CLASS statement. If you specify the MISSING option in the PROC TABULATE statement, the procedure considers missing values as valid levels for all class variables:

```
proc tabulate data=year_sales format=comma10. missing;
   class SalesRep;
   class Month Quarter;
   var AmountSold;
```

Because the MISSING option is in the PROC TABULATE statement in this example, observations with missing values for SalesRep, Month, or Quarter will display in the summary table.

If you specify the MISSING option in a CLASS statement, PROC TABULATE considers missing values as valid levels for the class variable(s) that are specified in that CLASS statement:

```
proc tabulate data=year_sales format=comma10.;
   class SalesRep;
   class Month Quarter / missing;
   var AmountSold;
```

Because the MISSING option is in the second CLASS statement, observations with missing values for Month or Quarter will display in the summary table, but observations with a missing value for SalesRep will not display.

If you have class variables with missing values in your data set, then you must decide whether or not the observations with the missing values should be omitted from every table. If the observations should not be omitted, then you can fill in the missing values where appropriate or continue to run the PROC TABULATE step with the MISSING option. For other options for handling missing values, see "Handling Missing Data" in *PROC TABULATE by Example*. For general information about missing values, see "Missing Values" in *SAS Language Reference: Concepts*.

Input File and SAS Data Set for Examples

The examples in this chapter use one input file* and one SAS data set. The input file contains sales records for a company, TruBlend Coffee Makers, that distributes the coffee machines. The file has the following structure:

```
01      1       Hollingsworth   Deluxe      260     49.50
01      1       Garcia          Standard     41     30.97
01      1       Hollingsworth   Deluxe      330     49.50
01      1       Jensen          Standard   1110     30.97
01      1       Garcia          Standard    715     30.97
01      1       Jensen          Deluxe      675     49.50
02      1       Jensen          Standard     45     30.97
02      1       Garcia          Deluxe       10     49.50

...more data lines...
```

---

* See the "Data Set for Chapters 25, 26, and 27" on page 715 for a complete listing of the input data.

```
12      4      Hollingsworth  Deluxe     125    49.50
12      4      Jensen         Standard  1254    30.97
12      4      Hollingsworth  Deluxe     175    49.50
```

The input file contains the following data from left to right:

- □ the month that a sale was made
- □ the quarter of the year that a sale was made
- □ the name of the sales representative
- □ the type of coffee maker sold (standard or deluxe)
- □ the number of units sold
- □ the price of each unit in US dollars.

The SAS data set is named YEAR_SALES. This data set contains all the sales data from the input file and data from a new variable named AmountSold, which is created by multiplying Units by Price.

The following program creates the SAS data set that is used in this chapter:

```
data year_sales;
   infile 'your-input-file';
   input Month $ Quarter $ SalesRep $14. Type $ Units Price;
   AmountSold = Units * Price;
run;
```

Creating Simple Summary Tables

Creating a Basic One-Dimensional Summary Table

The simplest summary table contains multiple columns but only a single row. It is called a one-dimensional summary table because it has only a column dimension. The PROC TABULATE step that follows creates a one-dimensional summary table that answers the question, "How many times did each sales representative make a sale?"

```
options linesize=84 pageno=1 nodate;
```

```
proc tabulate data=year_sales format=comma10.;
   title1 'TruBlend Coffee Makers, Inc.';
   title2 'Number of Sales by Each Sales Representative';
   class SalesRep;❶
   table SalesRep;❷
run;
```

The numbered items in the previous program correspond to the following:

❶ The variable SalesRep is specified as a class variable in the CLASS statement. A category will be created for each value of SalesRep wherever SalesRep is used in a TABLE statement.

❷ The variable SalesRep is specified in the column dimension of the TABLE statement. A column will be created for each category of SalesRep. Each column will show the number of times (N) that values belonging to the category appear in the data set.

The following summary table displays the results of this program:

Output 26.1   Basic One-Dimensional Summary Table

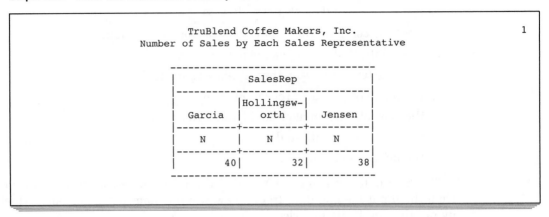

The values 40, 32, and 38 are the frequency with which each sales representative's name (Garcia, Hollingsworth, and Jensen) occurs in the data set. For this data set, each occurrence of the sales representative's name in the data set represents a sale.

Creating a Basic Two-Dimensional Summary Table

The most commonly used form of a summary table has at least one column and multiple rows, and is called a two-dimensional summary table. The PROC TABULATE step that follows creates a two-dimensional summary table that answers the question, "What was the amount that was sold by each sales representative?"

```
options linesize=84 pageno=1 nodate;

proc tabulate data=year_sales format=comma10.;
   title1 'TruBlend Coffee Makers, Inc.';
   title2 'Amount Sold by Each Sales Representative';
   class SalesRep;❶
   var AmountSold;❷
   table SalesRep,❸
         AmountSold;❹;
run;
```

The numbered items in the previous program correspond to the following:

❶ The variable SalesRep is specified as a class variable in the CLASS statement. A category will be created for each value of SalesRep wherever SalesRep is used in a TABLE statement.

❷ The variable AmountSold is specified as an analysis variable in the VAR statement. The values of AmountSold will be used to compute statistics wherever AmountSold is used in a TABLE statement.

❸ The variable SalesRep is in the row dimension of the TABLE statement. A row will be created for each value or category of SalesRep.

❹ The variable AmountSold is in the column dimension of the TABLE statement. The default statistic for analysis variables, SUM, will be used to summarize the values of AmountSold.

The following summary table displays the results of this program:

Output 26.2 Basic Two-Dimensional Summary Table

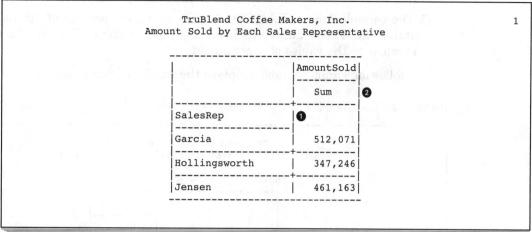

The numbered items in the previous SAS output correspond to the following:

❶ The variable AmountSold has been crossed with the variable SalesRep to produce each data cell of the summary table.

❷ The column heading AmountSold includes the subheading SUM. The values that are displayed in the column dimension are sums of the amount sold by each sales representative.

Creating a Basic Three-Dimensional Summary Table

Three-dimensional summary tables produce the output on separate pages with rows and columns on each page. The PROC TABULATE step that follows creates a three-dimensional summary table that answers the question, "What was the amount that was sold during each quarter of the year by each sales representative?"

```
options linesize=84 pageno=1 nodate;

proc tabulate data=year_sales format=comma10.;
    title1 'TruBlend Coffee Makers, Inc.';
    title2 'Quarterly Sales by Each Sales Representative';
    class SalesRep Quarter;❶
    var AmountSold;❷
    table SalesRep,❸
          Quarter,❹
          AmountSold;❺
run;
```

The numbered items in the previous program correspond to the following:

❶ The variables SalesRep and Quarter are specified as class variables in the CLASS statement. A category will be created for each value of SalesRep wherever SalesRep is used in the TABLE statement. Similarly, a category will be created for each value of Quarter wherever Quarter is used in a TABLE statement.

❷ The variable AmountSold is specified as an analysis variable in the VAR statement. The values of AmountSold will be used to compute statistics wherever AmountSold is used in a TABLE statement.

❸ The variable SalesRep is used in the page dimension of the TABLE statement. A page will be created for each value or category of SalesRep.

❹ The variable Quarter is used in the row dimension of the TABLE statement. A row will be created for each value or category of Quarter.

❺ The variable AmountSold is used in the column dimension of the TABLE statement. The default statistic for analysis variables, SUM, will be used to summarize the values of AmountSold.

The following summary table displays the results of this program:

Output 26.3 Basic Three-Dimensional Summary Table

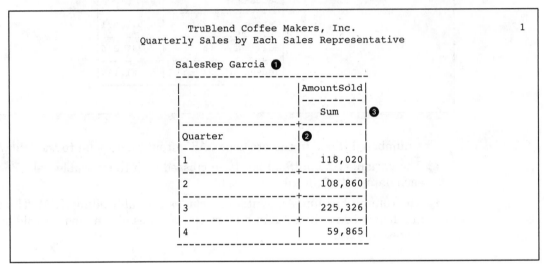

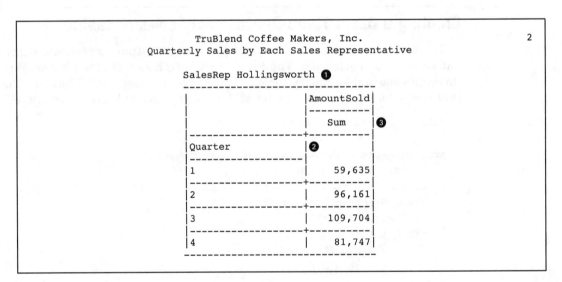

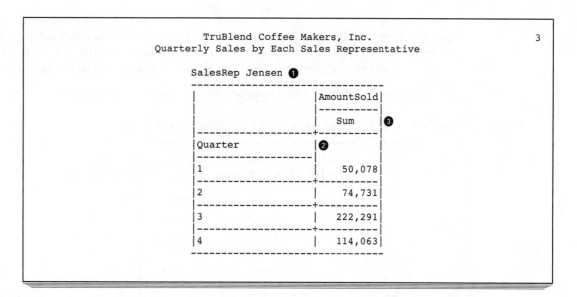

The numbered items in the previous SAS output correspond to the following:

❶ This summary table has a separate page for each sales representative.

❷ For each sales representative, the amount sold is reported for each quarter.

❸ The column heading AmountSold includes the subheading SUM. The values that are displayed in this column indicate the total amount sold in US dollars for each quarter by each sales representative.

Producing Multiple Tables in a Single PROC TABULATE Step

You can produce multiple tables in a single PROC TABULATE step. However, you cannot change the way a variable is used or defined in the middle of the step. In other words, the variables in the CLASS or VAR statements are defined only once for all TABLE statements in the PROC TABULATE step. If you need to change the way a variable is used or defined for different TABLE statements, then you must place the TABLE statements, and define the variables, in multiple PROC TABULATE steps. The program that follows produces three summary tables during one execution of the TABULATE procedure:

```
options linesize=84 pageno=1 nodate;

proc tabulate data=year_sales format=comma10.;
    title1 'TruBlend Coffee Makers, Inc.';
    title2 'Sales of Deluxe Model Versus Standard Model';
    class SalesRep Type;
    var AmountSold Units;
    table Type;❶
    table Type, Units;❷
    table SalesRep, Type, AmountSold;❸
run;
```

The numbered items in the previous program correspond to the following:

❶ The first TABLE statement produces a one-dimensional summary table with the values for the variable Type in the column dimension.

❷ The second TABLE statement produces a two-dimensional summary table with the values for the variable Type in the row dimension and the variable Units in the column dimension.

❸ The third TABLE statement produces a three-dimensional summary table with the values for the variable SalesRep in the page dimension, the values for the variable Type in the row dimension, and the variable AmountSold in the column dimension.

The following summary table displays the results of this program:

Output 26.4 Multiple Tables Produced by a Single PROC TABULATE Step

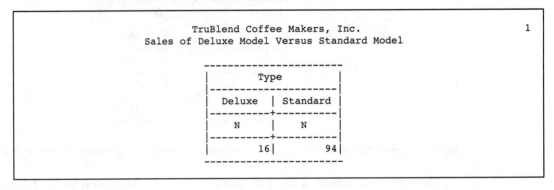

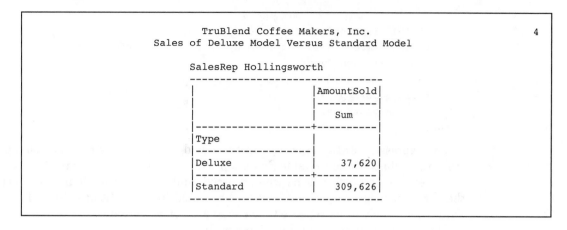

```
                      TruBlend Coffee Makers, Inc.                        4
                Sales of Deluxe Model Versus Standard Model

             SalesRep Hollingsworth
             ---------------------------------
             |                   |AmountSold|
             |                   |----------|
             |                   |   Sum    |
             |-------------------+----------|
             |Type               |          |
             |-------------------|          |
             |Deluxe             |    37,620|
             |-------------------+----------|
             |Standard           |   309,626|
             ---------------------------------
```

```
                      TruBlend Coffee Makers, Inc.                        5
                Sales of Deluxe Model Versus Standard Model

             SalesRep Jensen
             ---------------------------------
             |                   |AmountSold|
             |                   |----------|
             |                   |   Sum    |
             |-------------------+----------|
             |Type               |          |
             |-------------------|          |
             |Deluxe             |    40,590|
             |-------------------+----------|
             |Standard           |   420,573|
             ---------------------------------
```

Creating More Sophisticated Summary Tables

Creating Hierarchical Tables to Report on Subgroups

You can create a hierarchical table to report on subgroups of your data by crossing elements within a dimension. *Crossing* elements is the operation that combines two or more elements, such as class variables, analysis variables, format modifiers, statistics, or styles. Dimensions are automatically crossed. When you cross variables in a single dimension expression, values for one variable are placed within the values for the other variable in the same dimension. This forms a hierarchy of variables and, therefore, a *hierarchical table*. The order in which variables are listed when they are crossed determines the order of the headings in the table. In the column dimension, variables are stacked top to bottom; in the row dimension, left to right; and in the page dimension, front to back. You cross elements in a dimension expression by putting an asterisk between them. Note that two analysis variables cannot be crossed. Also, because dimensions are automatically crossed, all analysis variables must occur in one dimension.

The PROC TABULATE step that follows creates a two-dimensional summary table that crosses two variables and that answers the question, "What was the amount sold of each type of coffee maker by each sales representative?"

```
options linesize=84 pageno=1 nodate;

proc tabulate data=year_sales format=comma10.;
```

```
        title1 'TruBlend Coffee Makers, Inc.';
        title2 'Amount Sold Per Item by Each Sales Representative';
        class SalesRep Type;
        var AmountSold;
        table SalesRep*Type,
              AmountSold;
    run;
```

The expression **SalesRep*Type** in the row dimension uses the asterisk operator to cross the values of the variable SalesRep with the values of the variable Type. Because SalesRep is listed before Type when crossed, and because the elements are crossed in the row dimension, values for Type will be listed to the right of values of SalesRep. Values for Type will be repeated for each value of SalesRep.

The following summary table displays the results:

Output 26.5 Crossing Variables

```
                        TruBlend Coffee Makers, Inc.                        1
              Amount Sold Per Item by Each Sales Representative


                 ---------------------------------------
                 |                   |AmountSold|
                 |                   |----------|
                 |                   |   Sum    |
                 |-------------------+----------|
                 |SalesRep |Type     |          |
                 |---------+---------|          |
                 |Garcia   |Deluxe   |    46,778|
                 |         |---------+----------|
                 |         |Standard |   465,293|
                 |---------+---------+----------|
                 |Hollings-|Deluxe   |    37,620|
                 |worth    |---------+----------|
                 |         |Standard |   309,626|
                 |---------+---------+----------|
                 |Jensen   |Deluxe   |    40,590|
                 |         |---------+----------|
                 |         |Standard |   420,573|
                 ---------------------------------------
```

Notice the hierarchy of values that are created when the values for Type are repeated to the right of each value of SalesRep.

Formatting Output

You can override formats in summary table output by crossing variables with format modifiers. You cross a variable with a format modifier by putting an asterisk between them.

The PROC TABULATE step that follows creates a two-dimensional summary table that crosses a variable with a format modifier and that answers the question, "What was the amount sold of each type of coffee maker by each sales representative?"

```
options linesize=84 pageno=1 nodate;

proc tabulate data=year_sales format=comma10.;
    title1 'TruBlend Coffee Makers, Inc.';
    title2 'Amount Sold Per Item by Each Sales Representative';
    class SalesRep Type;
```

```
      var AmountSold;
      table SalesRep*Type,
            AmountSold*f=dollar16.2;
run;
```

The expression **AmountSold*f=dollar16.2** in the column dimension uses the asterisk operator to cross the values of the variable **AmountSold** with the SAS format modifier **f=dollar16.2**. The values for AmountSold will now display using the DOLLAR16.2 format. The DOLLAR16.2 format is better suited for dollar figures than the COMMA10. format, which is specified as the default in the PROC TABULATE statement.

The following summary table displays the results:

Output 26.6   Crossing Variables with Format Modifiers

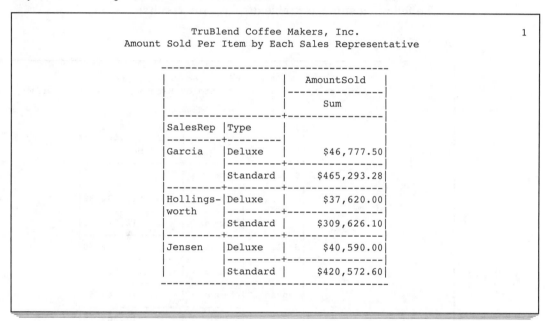

```
                   TruBlend Coffee Makers, Inc.                    1
                Amount Sold Per Item by Each Sales Representative
             -----------------------------------------
             |                     |    AmountSold    |
             |                     |-----------------|
             |                     |      Sum        |
             |-------------------+-----------------|
             |SalesRep |Type      |                 |
             |---------+--------- |                 |
             |Garcia   |Deluxe    |      $46,777.50|
             |         |---------+-----------------|
             |         |Standard  |     $465,293.28|
             |---------+---------+-----------------|
             |Hollings-|Deluxe    |      $37,620.00|
             |worth    |---------+-----------------|
             |         |Standard  |     $309,626.10|
             |---------+---------+-----------------|
             |Jensen   |Deluxe    |      $40,590.00|
             |         |---------+-----------------|
             |         |Standard  |     $420,572.60|
             -----------------------------------------
```

Calculating Descriptive Statistics

You can request descriptive statistics for a variable by crossing that variable with the appropriate statistic keyword. Crossing either a class variable or an analysis variable with a statistic tells PROC TABULATE what type of calculations to perform. Note that two statistics cannot be crossed. Also, because dimensions are automatically crossed, all statistics must occur in one dimension.

The default statistic crossed with a class variable is the N statistic or frequency. Class variables can only be crossed with frequency and percent frequency statistics. The default statistic crossed with an analysis variable is the SUM statistic. Analysis variables can be crossed with any of the many descriptive statistics that are available with PROC TABULATE including commonly used statistics like MIN, MAX, MEAN, STD, and MEDIAN. For a complete list of statistics available for use with analysis variables, see "Statistics Available in PROC TABULATE" in the *SAS Procedures Guide*.

The PROC TABULATE step that follows creates a two-dimensional summary table that crosses elements with a statistic and that answers the question, "What was the average amount per sale of each type of coffee maker by each sales representative?"

```
options linesize=84 pageno=1 nodate;

proc tabulate data=year_sales format=comma10.;
    title1 'TruBlend Coffee Makers, Inc.';
    title2 'Average Amount Sold Per Item by Each Sales Representative';
    class SalesRep Type;
    var AmountSold;
    table SalesRep*Type,
        AmountSold*mean*f=dollar16.2;
run;
```

In this program, the column dimension crosses the variable **AmountSold** with the statistic **mean** and with the format modifier **f=dollar16.2**. The MEAN statistic provides the arithmetic mean for AmountSold.

The following summary table displays the results:

Output 26.7   Crossing a Variable with a Statistic

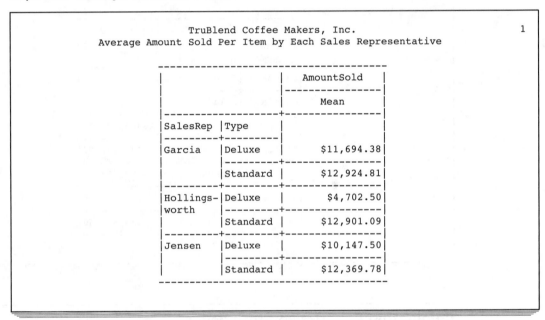

Reporting on Multiple Statistics

You can create summary tables that report on two or more statistics by concatenating variables. *Concatenating* is the operation that joins the information of two or more elements, such as class variables, analysis variables, or statistics, by placing the output of the second and subsequent elements immediately after the output of the first element. You concatenate elements in a dimension expression by putting a blank space between them.

The PROC TABULATE step that follows creates a two-dimensional summary table that uses concatenation and that answers the question, "How many sales were made, and what was the total sales figure for each type of coffee maker sold by each sales representative?"

```
options linesize=84 pageno=1 nodate;

proc tabulate data=year_sales format=comma10.;
```

```
      title1 'TruBlend Coffee Makers, Inc.';
      title2 'Sales Summary by Representative and Product';
      class SalesRep Type;
      var AmountSold;
      table SalesRep*Type,
            AmountSold*n AmountSold*f=dollar16.2;
run;
```

In this program, because the expressions **AmountSold*n** and
AmountSold*f=dollar16.2 in the column dimension are separated by a blank space,
their output will be concatenated.

The following summary table displays the results:

Output 26.8 Concatenating Variables

```
                    TruBlend Coffee Makers, Inc.                        1
               Sales Summary by Representative and Product

                                    ❶              ❷
                    ------------------------------------------------
                    |           |AmountSold|   AmountSold   |
                    |           |----------+----------------|
                    |           |    N     |      Sum        |
                    |-----------+----------+----------------|
                    |SalesRep |Type     |          |                |
                    |---------+---------|          |                |
                    |Garcia   |Deluxe   |        4|      $46,777.50|
                    |         |---------+---------+----------------|
                    |         |Standard |       36|     $465,293.28|
                    |---------+---------+---------+----------------|
                    |Hollings-|Deluxe   |        8|      $37,620.00|
                    |worth    |---------+---------+----------------|
                    |         |Standard |       24|     $309,626.10|
                    |---------+---------+---------+----------------|
                    |Jensen   |Deluxe   |        4|      $40,590.00|
                    |         |---------+---------+----------------|
                    |         |Standard |       34|     $420,572.60|
                    ------------------------------------------------
```

In this summary table the frequency (N) of AmountSold ❶ is shown in the same
table as the SUM of AmountSold ❷.

Reducing Code and Applying a Single Label to Multiple Elements

You can use parentheses to group concatenated elements (variables, formats,
statistics, and so on) that are concatenated or crossed with a common element. This can
reduce the amount of code used and can change how labels are displayed. The PROC
TABULATE step that follows uses parentheses to group elements that are crossed with
AmountSold and answers the question, "How many sales were made, and what was the
total sales figure for each type of coffee maker sold by each sales representative?"

```
options linesize=84 pageno=1 nodate;

proc tabulate data=year_sales format=comma10.;
   title1 'TruBlend Coffee Makers, Inc.';
   title2 'Sales Summary by Representative and Product';
   class SalesRep Type;
   var AmountSold;
```

```
        table SalesRep*Type,
               AmountSold*(n sum*f=dollar16.2);
run;
```

In this program, **AmountSold*(n sum*f=dollar16.2)** takes the place of **AmountSold*n AmountSold*f=dollar16.2**. Notice the default statistic SUM from **AmountSold*f=dollar16.2** must now be included in the expression. This is because the format modifier must be crossed with a variable or a statistic. It cannot be in the expression by itself.

The following summary table displays the results:

Output 26.9   Using Parentheses to Group Elements

```
                         TruBlend Coffee Makers, Inc.                    1
                       Sales Summary by Representative and Product

        ----------------------------------------------------------------
        |                         |            AmountSold              |
        |                         |------------------------------------|
        |                         |     N      |        Sum            |
        |-------------------------+------------+-----------------------|
        |SalesRep  |Type          |            |                       |
        |----------+----------    |            |                       |
        |Garcia    |Deluxe        |        4   |         $46,777.50    |
        |          |----------    +------------+-----------------------|
        |          |Standard      |       36   |        $465,293.28    |
        |----------+----------    +------------+-----------------------|
        |Hollings- |Deluxe        |        8   |         $37,620.00    |
        |worth     |----------    +------------+-----------------------|
        |          |Standard      |       24   |        $309,626.10    |
        |----------+----------    +------------+-----------------------|
        |Jensen    |Deluxe        |        4   |         $40,590.00    |
        |          |----------    +------------+-----------------------|
        |          |Standard      |       34   |        $420,572.60    |
        ----------------------------------------------------------------
```

Note that the label, AmountSold, spans multiple columns rather than appearing twice in the summary table, as it does in Output 26.8 on page 419.

Getting Summaries for All Variables

You can summarize all of the class variables in a dimension with the universal class variable ALL. ALL can be concatenated with each of the three dimensions of the TABLE statement and within groups of elements delimited by parentheses. The PROC TABULATE step that follows creates a two-dimensional summary table with the universal class variable ALL, and answers the question, "For each sales representative and for all of the sales representatives as a group, how many sales were made, what was the average amount per sale, and what was the amount sold?"

```
options linesize=84 pageno=1 nodate;

proc tabulate data=year_sales format=comma10.;
    title1 'TruBlend Coffee Makers, Inc.';
    title2 'Sales Report';
    class SalesRep Type;
    var AmountSold;
    table SalesRep*Type all,
```

```
               AmountSold*(n (mean sum)*f=dollar16.2);
run;
```

In this program, the TABLE statement now includes the universal class variable ALL in the row dimension. SalesRep and Type will be summarized.

The following summary table displays the results:

Output 26.10 Crossing with the Universal Class Variable ALL

```
                         TruBlend Coffee Makers, Inc.                        1
                              Sales Report

     --------------------------------------------------------------------
    |                   |           |       AmountSold                    |
    |                   |           |-------------------------------------|
    |                   |     N     |     Mean      |       Sum           |
    |-------------------+-----------+---------------+---------------------|
    |SalesRep |Type     |           |               |                     |
    |---------+---------|           |               |                     |
    |Garcia   |Deluxe   |         4 |    $11,694.38 |      $46,777.50     |
    |         |---------+-----------+---------------+---------------------|
    |         |Standard |        36 |    $12,924.81 |     $465,293.28     |
    |---------+---------+-----------+---------------+---------------------|
    |Hollings-|Deluxe   |         8 |     $4,702.50 |      $37,620.00     |
    |worth    |---------+-----------+---------------+---------------------|
    |         |Standard |        24 |    $12,901.09 |     $309,626.10     |
    |---------+---------+-----------+---------------+---------------------|
    |Jensen   |Deluxe   |         4 |    $10,147.50 |      $40,590.00     |
    |         |---------+-----------+---------------+---------------------|
    |         |Standard |        34 |    $12,369.78 |     $420,572.60     |
    |-------------------+-----------+---------------+---------------------|
    |All ❶              |       110 |    $12,004.36 |   $1,320,479.48     |
     --------------------------------------------------------------------
```

This summary table reports the frequency (N), the MEAN, and the SUM of AmountSold for each category of SalesRep and Type. This data has been summarized for all categories of SalesRep and Type in the row labeled All ❶.

Defining Labels

You can add your own labels to a summary table or remove headings from a summary table by assigning labels to variables in the TABLE statement. Simply follow the variable with an equal sign (=) followed by either the desired label or by a blank space in quotation marks. A blank space in quotation marks removes the heading from the summary table. The PROC TABULATE step that follows creates a two-dimensional summary table that uses labels in the TABLE statement and that answers the question, "What is the percent of total sales and average amount sold by each sales representative of each type of coffee maker and all coffee makers?"

```
options linesize=84 pageno=1 nodate;

proc tabulate data=year_sales format=comma10.;
   title1 'TruBlend Coffee Makers, Inc.';
   title2 'Sales Performance';
   class SalesRep Type;
   var AmountSold;
   table SalesRep='Sales Representative'❶*
```

```
(Type='Type of Coffee Maker'❶ all) all,
AmountSold=' '❹*
(N='Sales'❷
SUM='Amount'❷*f=dollar16.2
colpctsum='% Sales'❸
mean='Average Sale'❷*f=dollar16.2);
run;
```

The numbered items in the previous program correspond to the following:

❶ The variables SalesRep and Type are assigned labels.

❷ The frequency statistic N, the statistic SUM, and the statistic MEAN are assigned labels.

❸ The statistic COLPCTSUM is used to calculate the percentage of the value in a single table cell in relation to the total of the values in the column and is assigned the label '% Sales'.

❹ The variable AmountSold is assigned a blank label. As a result, the heading for AmountSold does not appear in the summary table.

The following summary table displays the results:

Output 26.11 Using Labels to Customize Summary Tables

```
                        TruBlend Coffee Makers, Inc.                        1
                             Sales Performance
                                     ❶

     -----------------------------------------------------------------------
     |              ❷| Sales   |    Amount      | % Sales |  Average Sale  |
     |-------------+---------+----------------+---------+----------------|
   ❸|Sales        |Type of  |         |                |         |                |
     |Represen-    |Coffee   |         |                |         |                |
     |tative       |Maker    |         |                |         |                |
     |-------------+---------|         |                |         |                |
     |Garcia       |Deluxe   |       4|     $46,777.50|        4|     $11,694.38|
     |             |---------+---------+----------------+---------+----------------|
     |             |Standard |      36|    $465,293.28|       35|     $12,924.81|
     |             |---------+---------+----------------+---------+----------------|
     |             |All      |      40|    $512,070.78|       39|     $12,801.77|
     |-------------+---------+---------+----------------+---------+----------------|
     |Hollings-    |Type of  |         |                |         |                |
     |worth        |Coffee   |         |                |         |                |
     |             |Maker    |         |                |         |                |
     |             |---------|         |                |         |                |
     |             |Deluxe   |       8|     $37,620.00|        3|      $4,702.50|
     |             |---------+---------+----------------+---------+----------------|
     |             |Standard |      24|    $309,626.10|       23|     $12,901.09|
     |             |---------+---------+----------------+---------+----------------|
     |             |All      |      32|    $347,246.10|       26|     $10,851.44|
     |-------------+---------+---------+----------------+---------+----------------|
     |Jensen       |Type of  |         |                |         |                |
     |             |Coffee   |         |                |         |                |
     |             |Maker    |         |                |         |                |
     |             |---------|         |                |         |                |
     |             |Deluxe   |       4|     $40,590.00|        3|     $10,147.50|
     |             |---------+---------+----------------+---------+----------------|
     |             |Standard |      34|    $420,572.60|       32|     $12,369.78|
     |             |---------+---------+----------------+---------+----------------|
     |             |All      |      38|    $461,162.60|       35|     $12,135.86|
     |-------------+---------+---------+----------------+---------+----------------|
     |All          |         |     110|  $1,320,479.48|      100|     $12,004.36|
     -----------------------------------------------------------------------
```

The numbered items in the previous SAS output correspond to the following:

❶ No heading for the variable AmountSold is displayed.

❷ The labels 'Sales', 'Amount', '% Sales', and 'Average Sale' replace the frequency (N), SUM, COLPCTSUM, and MEAN respectively.

❸ labels replace the variables SalesRep and Type.

Using Styles and the Output Delivery System

If you use the Output Delivery System to create output from PROC TABULATE, for any destination other than Listing or Output destinations, then you can

- □ set certain style elements (such as font style, font weight, and color) that the procedure uses for various parts of the table
- □ specify style elements for the labels for variables by adding the option to the CLASS statement
- □ specify style elements for cells in the summary table by crossing the STYLE= option with an element of a dimension expression.

When it is used in a dimension expression, the STYLE= option must be enclosed within square brackets ([and]) or braces ({ and }). The PROC TABULATE step that follows creates a two-dimensional summary table that uses the STYLE= option in a CLASS statement and in the TABLE statement and that answers the question, "What is the percent of total sales and average amount sold by each sales representative of each type of coffee maker and all coffee makers?"

```
options linesize=84 pageno=1 nodate;


ods html file='summary-table.htm';❶
ods printer file='summary-table.ps';❷


proc tabulate data=year_sales format=comma10.;
    title1 'TruBlend Coffee Makers, Inc.';
    title2 'Sales Performance';
    class SalesRep;
    class Type / style=[font_style=italic]❸;
    var AmountSold;
    table SalesRep='Sales Representative'*(Type='Type of Coffee Maker'
        all*[style=[background=yellow font_weight=bold]]❹)
        all*[style=[font_weight=bold]]❺,
        AmountSold=' '*(colpctsum='% Sales' mean='Average Sale'*
        f=dollar16.2);
run;


ods html close;❻
ods printer close;❼
```

The numbered items in the previous program correspond to the following:

❶ The ODS HTML statement opens the HTML destination and creates HTML output. FILE= identifies the file that contains the HTML output. Some browsers require an extension of HTM or HTML on the filename.

❷ The ODS PRINTER statement opens the Printer destination and creates Printer output. FILE= identifies the file that contains the Printer output.

❸ The STYLE= option is specified in the second CLASS statement, which sets the font style of the label for Type to italic. The label for SalesRep is not affected by the STYLE= option because it is in a separate CLASS statement.

④ The universal class variable ALL is crossed with the STYLE= option, which sets the background for the table cells to yellow and the font weight for these cells to bold.

⑤ The universal class variable ALL is crossed with the STYLE= option, which sets the font weight for the table cells to bold.

⑥ The last ODS HTML statement closes the HTML destination and all of the files that are associated with it. You must close the HTML destination before you can view the HTML output with a browser.

⑦ The last ODS PRINTER statement closes the Printer destination. You must close the Printer destination before you can print the output on a physical printer.

The following summary table displays the results:

Display 26.2 Using Style Modifiers and the ODS HTML Statement

TruBlend Coffee Makers, Inc. Sales Performance		% Sales	Average Sale
Sales Representative	*Type of Coffee Maker*		
Garcia	**Deluxe**	4	$11,694.38
	Standard	35	$12,924.81
	All	39	**$12,801.77**
Hollingsworth	*Type of Coffee Maker*		
	Deluxe	3	$4,702.50
	Standard	23	$12,901.09
	All	26	**$10,851.44**
Jensen	*Type of Coffee Maker*		
	Deluxe	3	$10,147.50
	Standard	32	$12,369.78
	All	35	**$12,135.86**
All		**100**	**$12,004.36**

This summary table shows the effects of the three uses of the STYLE= option with the ODS HTML statement in the previous SAS program:

☐ The repeated label, Type of Coffee Maker, is in italics.

☐ The subtotals for each value of sales representative are highlighted in a lighter color (yellow) and are bold.

☐ The totals for all sales representatives are bold.

The following summary table displays the results:

Display 26.3 Using Style Modifiers and the ODS PRINTER Statement

TruBlend Coffee Makers, Inc.
Sales Performance

		% Sales	Average Sale
Sales Representative	*Type of Coffee Maker*		
Garcia	**Deluxe**	4	$11,694.38
	Standard	35	$12,924.81
	All	**39**	**$12,801.77**
Hollingsworth	*Type of Coffee Maker*		
	Deluxe	3	$4,702.50
	Standard	23	$12,901.09
	All	**26**	**$10,851.44**
Jensen	*Type of Coffee Maker*		
	Deluxe	3	$10,147.50
	Standard	32	$12,369.78
	All	**35**	**$12,135.86**
All		**100**	**$12,004.36**

This summary table shows the effects of the three uses of the STYLE= option with the ODS PRINTER statement in the previous SAS program:

☐ The repeated label, Type of Coffee Maker, is in italics.

☐ The subtotals for each value of sales representative are highlighted and are bold.

☐ The totals for all sales representatives are bold.

Ordering Class Variables

You can control the order in which class variable values and their headings display in a summary table with the ORDER= option. You can use the ORDER= option with the PROC TABULATE statement and with individual CLASS statements. The syntax is **ORDER=sort-order**. The four possible sort orders (DATA, FORMATTED, FREQ, and UNFORMATTED) are defined in "Review of SAS Tools" on page 427. The PROC TABULATE step that follows creates a two-dimensional summary table that uses the ORDER= option with the PROC TABULATE statement to order all class variables by frequency, and that answers the question, "Which quarter produced the greatest number of sales, and which sales representative made the most sales overall?"

```
options linesize=84 pageno=1 nodate;

proc tabulate data=year_sales format=comma10. order=freq;
    title1 'TruBlend Coffee Makers, Inc.';
    title2 'Quarterly Sales and Representative Sales by Frequency';
    class SalesRep Quarter;
    table SalesRep all,
          Quarter all;
run;
```

The following summary table displays the results of this program:

Output 26.12 Ordering Class Variables

```
                    TruBlend Coffee Makers, Inc.                        1
              Quarterly Sales and Representative Sales by Frequency


-----------------------------------------------------------------------
|               |                    Quarter               |          |
|               |-------------------------------------------|          |
|               |  3 ❶  |   1    |    2   |   4    |  All   | ❸
|               |-------+--------+--------+--------+--------|
|               |  N    |   N    |    N   |   N    |   N    |
|---------------+-------+--------+--------+--------+--------|
|SalesRep       |       |        |        |        |        |
|---------------|       |        |        |        |        |
|Garcia ❷       |    21 |     8  |     6  |     5  |    40  |
|---------------+-------+--------+--------+--------+--------|
|Jensen         |    21 |     5  |     6  |     6  |    38  |
|---------------+-------+--------+--------+--------+--------|
|Hollingsworth  |    15 |     5  |     6  |     6  |    32  |
|---------------+-------+--------+--------+--------+--------|
|All ❸          |    57 |    18  |    18  |    17  |   110  |
-----------------------------------------------------------------------
```

The numbered items in the previous SAS output correspond to the following:

❶ The order of the values of the class variable Quarter shows that most sales occurred in quarter 3 followed by quarters 1, 2, and then 4.

❷ The order of the values of the class variable SalesRep shows that Garcia made the most sales overall, followed by Jensen and then Hollingsworth.

❸ The universal class variable ALL is included in both dimensions of this example to show the frequency data that SAS used to order the data when creating the summary table.

Review of SAS Tools

Global Statement

TITLE<*n*> <*'title'*>;
> specifies a title. The argument *n* is a number from 1 to 10 that immediately follows the word TITLE, with no intervening blank, and specifies the level of the TITLE. The text of each *title* can be up to 132 characters long (256 characters long in some operating environments) and must be enclosed in single or double quotation marks.

TABULATE Procedure Statements

PROC TABULATE <*option(s)*>;

CLASS *variable(s)</option(s)>*;

VAR *analysis-variable(s)*;

TABLE <<*page-expression,*> *row-expression,*> *column-expression*;

PROC TABULATE <*option(s)*>;
> starts the procedure.
>> You can specify the following *options* in the PROC TABULATE statement:
>
>> DATA=*SAS-data-set*
>>> specifies the *SAS-data-set* to be used by PROC TABULATE. If you omit the DATA= option, then the TABULATE procedure uses the SAS data set that was created most recently in the current job or session.
>
>> FORMAT=*format-name*
>>> specifies a default format for formatting the value in each cell in the table. You can specify any valid SAS numeric format or user-defined format.
>
>> MISSING
>>> considers missing values as valid values to create the combinations of class variables. A heading for each missing value appears in the table.
>
>> ORDER=DATA | FORMATTED | FREQ | UNFORMATTED
>>> specifies the sort order that is used to create the unique combinations of the values of the class variables, which form the headings of the table. A brief description of each sort order follows:
>>
>>> DATA
>>>> orders values according to their order in the input data set.
>>
>>> FORMATTED
>>>> orders values by their ascending formatted values. This order depends on your operating environment.
>>
>>> FREQ
>>>> orders values by descending frequency count.

UNFORMATTED

orders values by their unformatted values, which yields the same order as PROC SORT. This order depends on your operating environment. This sort sequence is particularly useful for displaying dates chronologically.

ORDER= used on a CLASS statement overrides ORDER= used on the PROC TABULATE statement.

CLASS *variable(s)/option(s)*;

identifies class variables for the table. Class variables determine the categories that PROC TABULATE uses to calculate statistics.

MISSING

considers missing values as valid values to create the combinations of class variables. A heading for each missing value appears in the table. If MISSING should apply only to a subset of the class variables, then specify MISSING in a separate CLASS statement with the subset of the class variables.

ORDER=DATA | FORMATTED | FREQ | UNFORMATTED

specifies the sort order used to create the unique combinations of the values of the class variables, which form the headings of the table. If ORDER= should apply only to a subset of the class variables, then specify ORDER= in a separate CLASS statement with the subset of the class variables. In this way, a separate sort order can be specified for each class variable. A brief description of each sort order follows:

DATA

orders values according to their order in the input data set.

FORMATTED

orders values by their ascending formatted values. This order depends on your operating environment.

FREQ

orders values by descending frequency count.

UNFORMATTED

orders values by their unformatted values, which yields the same order as PROC SORT. This order depends on your operating environment. This sort sequence is particularly useful for displaying dates chronologically.

ORDER= used on a CLASS statement overrides ORDER= used on the PROC TABULATE statement.

VAR *analysis-variable(s)*;

identifies analysis variables for the table. Analysis variables contain values for which you want to compute statistics.

TABLE <<*page-expression,* >*row-expression,*> *column-expression*;

defines the table that you want PROC TABULATE to produce. You must specify at least one TABLE statement. In the TABLE statement you specify *page-expressions,* *row-expressions,* and *column-expressions,* all of which are constructed in the same way and are referred to collectively as *dimension expressions.* Use commas to separate dimension expressions from one another. You define relationships among variables, statistics, and other elements within a dimension by combining them with one or more operators. *Operators* are symbols that tell PROC TABULATE what actions to perform on the variables, statistics, and other elements. The table that follows lists the common operators and the actions that they symbolize:

Operator	Action
, comma	separates dimensions of the table
* asterisk	crosses elements within a dimension
blank space	concatenates elements within a dimension
= equal	overrides default cell format or assigns label to an element
( )parentheses	groups elements and associates an operator with each concatenated element in the group
[ ]square brackets	groups the STYLE= option for crossing, and groups style attribute specifications within the STYLE= option
{ } braces	groups the STYLE= option for crossing, and groups style attribute specifications within the STYLE= option

Learning More

Locating procedure output
> See Chapter 31, "Understanding and Customizing SAS Output: The Basics," on page 533.

Missing values
> For a discussion about missing values, see *SAS Language Reference: Concepts*. Information about handling missing values is also in *PROC TABULATE by Example*.

ODS
> For complete documentation on how to use the Output Delivery System, see *The Complete Guide to the SAS Output Delivery System*.

PROC TABULATE
> See the TABULATE procedure in the *SAS Procedures Guide*.
>
> For a detailed discussion and comprehensive examples of the TABULATE procedure, see *PROC TABULATE by Example*.

SAS formats
> See *SAS Language Reference: Dictionary*. Many formats are available with SAS, such as fractions, hexadecimal values, roman numerals, social security numbers, date and time values, and numbers written as words.

Statistics
> For a list of the statistics available in the TABULATE procedure, see the discussion of concepts in the TABULATE procedure in the *SAS Procedures Guide*. For more information about the listed statistics, see the discussion of elementary statistics in the appendix of the *SAS Procedures Guide*.

Style attributes

For information about style attributes that can be set for a style element by using the Output Delivery System, see "Fundamental Concepts for Using Base SAS Procedures" in the *SAS Procedures Guide*.

Summary tables

For additional examples of how to produce a variety of summary tables, see *SAS Guide to Report Writing: Examples*.

For a discussion of how to use the REPORT procedure to create summary tables, see Chapter 27, "Creating Detail and Summary Reports with the REPORT Procedure," on page 431.

Tabular reports

For interactive online examples and discussion, see lessons related to creating tabular reports in *SAS Online Tutor for Version 8: SAS Programming*.

Title statement

See Chapter 25, "Producing Detail Reports with the PRINT Procedure," on page 367.

CHAPTER

27

Creating Detail and Summary Reports with the REPORT Procedure

431

Introduction

Purpose

SAS provides a variety of report writing tools that produce detail and summary reports. The reports enable you to communicate information about your data in a organized, concise manner. The REPORT procedure enables you to create detail and summary reports in a single report writing tool.

In this chapter, you will learn how to use PROC REPORT to

- produce simple detail reports
- produce simple summary reports
- produce enhanced reports by adding additional statements that order and group observations, sum columns, and compute overall totals
- customize the appearance of reports by adding column spacing, column labels, line separators, and formats.

Prerequisites

To understand the examples in this chapter, you should be familiar with the following features and concepts:

- data set options
- the TITLE statement
- the LABEL statement
- WHERE processing
- creating and assigning SAS formats.

Understanding How to Construct a Report

Using the Report Writing Tools

The REPORT procedure combines the features of PROC MEANS, PROC PRINT, and PROC TABULATE along with features of the DATA step report writing into a powerful report writing tool. PROC REPORT enables you to

- create customized, presentation-quality reports
- develop and store report definitions that control the structure and layout
- view previously defined reports
- generate multiple reports from one report definition.

There are three different ways that you can use PROC REPORT to construct reports:

- in a windowing environment with a prompting facility
- in a windowing environment without a prompting facility
- in a nonwindowing environment where you use PROC REPORT to submit a series of statements.

The windowing environment requires minimal SAS programming skills and allows immediate, visual feedback as you develop the report. This chapter explains how you use the nonwindowing environment to create summary and detail reports.

Types of Reports

The REPORT procedure enables you to construct two types of reports:

detail report
> contains one row for every observation that is selected for the report (see Output 27.1 on page 435). Each of these rows is a detail row.

summary report
> consolidates data so that each row represents multiple observations (see Output 27.5 on page 440). Each of these rows is also called a detail row.

Both detail and summary reports can contain summary lines as well as detail rows. A summary line summarizes numerical data for a set of detail rows or for all detail rows. You can use PROC REPORT to provide both default summaries and customized summaries.

Laying Out a Report

Establishing the Layout

If you first decide on the layout of the report, then creating the report is easier. You need to determine

□ which columns to display in the report

□ the order of the columns and rows

□ how to label the rows and columns

□ which statistics to display

□ whether to display a column for each value of a particular variable

□ whether to display a row for every observation, or to consolidate multiple observations in a single row.

Once you establish the layout of the report, use the COLUMN statement and DEFINE statement in the PROC REPORT step to construct the layout.

Constructing the Layout

The COLUMN statement lists the report items to include as columns of the report, describes the arrangement of the columns, and defines headers that span multiple columns. A *report item* is a data set variable, a calculated statistic, or a variable that you compute based on other items in the report.

The DEFINE statement defines the characteristics of an item in the report. These characteristics include how PROC REPORT uses an item in the report, the text of the column header, and the format to display the values.

You control much of a report's layout by the usages that you specify for variables in the DEFINE statements. The types of variable usages are

ACROSS
> creates a column for each value of an ACROSS variable.

ANALYSIS

> computes a statistic from a numeric variable for all the observations represented by a cell of the report. The value of the variable depends on where it appears in the report. By default, PROC REPORT treats all numeric variables as ANALYSIS variables and computes the sum.

COMPUTED

> computes a report item from variables that you define for the report. They are not in the input data set, and PROC REPORT does not add them to the input data set.

DISPLAY

> displays a row for every observation in the input data set. By default, PROC REPORT treats all character variables as DISPLAY variables.

GROUP

> consolidates into one row all of the observations from the data set that have a unique combination of the formatted values for all GROUP variables.

ORDER

> specifies to order the rows for every observation in the input data set according to the ascending, formatted values of the ORDER variable.

The position and usage of each variable in the report determine the report's structure and content. For example, PROC REPORT orders the detail rows of the report according to the values of ORDER and GROUP variables (from left to right). Similarly, PROC REPORT orders columns for an ACROSS variable from top to bottom, according to the values of the variable. For a complete discussion of how PROC REPORT determines the layout of a report, see the *SAS Procedures Guide*.

Input File and SAS Data Set for Examples

The examples in this chapter use one input file* and one SAS data set. The input file contains sales records for a company, TruBlend Coffee Makers, that distributes the coffee machines. The file has the following structure:

```
01     1        Hollingsworth   Deluxe        260      49.50
01     1        Garcia          Standard       41      30.97
01     1        Hollingsworth   Deluxe        330      49.50
01     1        Jensen          Standard     1110      30.97
01     1        Garcia          Standard      715      30.97
01     1        Jensen          Deluxe        675      49.50
02     1        Jensen          Standard       45      30.97
02     1        Garcia          Deluxe         10      49.50


...more data lines...


12     4        Hollingsworth   Deluxe        125      49.50
12     4        Jensen          Standard     1254      30.97
12     4        Hollingsworth   Deluxe        175      49.50
```

The input file contains the following values from left to right:

- □ the month that a sale was made
- □ the quarter of the year that a sale was made

---

* See the "Data Set for Chapters 25, 26, and 27" on page 715 for a complete listing of the input data.

□ the name of the sales representative

□ the type of coffee maker sold (standard or deluxe)

□ the number of units sold

□ the price of each unit in US dollars.

The SAS data set is named YEAR_SALES. This data set contains all the sales data from the input file and a new variable named AmountSold, which is created by multiplying Units by Price.

The following program creates the SAS data set that this chapter uses:

```
data year_sales;
infile 'your-input-file';
input Month $ Quarter $ SalesRep $14. Type $ Units Price;
AmountSold = Units * Price;
run;
```

Creating Simple Reports

Displaying All the Variables

By default, PROC REPORT uses all of the variables in the data set. The layout of the report depends on the type of variables in the data set. If the data set contains any character variables, then PROC REPORT generates a simple detail report that lists the values of all the variables and the observations in the data set. If the data set contains only numeric variables, then PROC REPORT sums the value of each variable over all observations in the data set and produces a one-line summary of the sums. To produce a detail report for a data set with only numeric values, you have to define the columns in the report.

By default, PROC REPORT opens the REPORT window so that you can modify a report repeatedly and see the modifications immediately. To run PROC REPORT without the REPORT window and send your results to the SAS procedure output, you must use the NOWINDOWS option in the PROC REPORT statement.

The following PROC REPORT step creates the default detail report for the first quarter sales:

```
options linesize=80 pageno=1 nodate;

proc report data=year_sales nowindows;
   where quarter='1';
   title1 'TruBlend Coffee Makers, Inc.';
   title2 'First Quarter Sales Report';
run;
```

The WHERE statement specifies a condition that SAS uses to select observations from the YEAR_SALES data set. Before PROC REPORT builds the report, SAS selectively processes observations so that the report contains only data for the observations from the first quarter. For additional information about WHERE processing, see "Selecting Observations" on page 375.

The following detail report shows all the variable values for those observations in YEAR_SALES that contains first quarter sales data:

Output 27.1   The Default Report When the Data Set Contains Character Values

```
                        TruBlend Coffee Makers, Inc.❹                     1
                        First Quarter Sales Report


                                                             AmountSol
     Month❶   Quarter   SalesRep      Type        Units      Price      d❷
     01       1         Hollingsworth Deluxe       260       49.5     12870❸
     01       1         Garcia        Standard       41      30.97     1269.77
     01       1         Hollingsworth Standard      330      30.97    10220.1
     01       1         Jensen        Standard      110      30.97     3406.7
     01       1         Garcia        Deluxe        715      49.5     35392.5
     01       1         Jensen        Standard      675      30.97    20904.75
     02       1         Garcia        Standard     2045      30.97    63333.65
     02       1         Garcia        Deluxe         10      49.5       495
     02       1         Garcia        Standard       40      30.97     1238.8
     02       1         Hollingsworth Standard     1030      30.97    31899.1
     02       1         Jensen        Standard      153      30.97     4738.41
     02       1         Garcia        Standard       98      30.97     3035.06
     03       1         Hollingsworth Standard      125      30.97     3871.25
     03       1         Jensen        Standard      154      30.97     4769.38
     03       1         Garcia        Standard      118      30.97     3654.46
     03       1         Hollingsworth Standard       25      30.97      774.25
     03       1         Jensen        Standard      525      30.97    16259.25
     03       1         Garcia        Standard      310      30.97     9600.7
```

The following list corresponds to the numbered items in the preceding report:

❶ The order of the columns corresponds to the position of the variables in the data set.

❷ The default column width for numeric variables is nine. Therefore, the column label for AmountSold wraps across two lines.

❸ A blank line does not automatically appear between the column labels and the data values.

❹ The top of the report has a title, produced by the TITLE statement.

The following PROC REPORT step produces the default summary report when the YEAR_SALES data set contains only numeric values:

```
options linesize=80 pageno=1 nodate;
proc report data=year_sales (keep=Units AmountSold)
            colwidth=10 nowindows;
   title1 'TruBlend Coffee Makers, Inc.';
   title2 'Total Yearly Sales';
run;
```

The KEEP= data set option specifies to process only the numeric variables Units and Amountsold. PROC REPORT uses these variables to create the report. The COLWIDTH= option increases the column width so that the column label for AmountSold displays on a single line.

The following report displays a one-line summary for the two numeric variables:

Output 27.2   The Default Report When the Data Set Contains Only Numeric Values

```
                    TruBlend Coffee Makers, Inc.                      1
                         Total Yearly Sales

                      Units    AmountSold
                      40989   1320479.48
```

PROC REPORT computed the one-line summary for Units and AmountSold by summing the value of each variable for all the observations in the data set.

Specifying and Ordering the Columns

The first step in constructing a report is to select the columns that you want to appear in the report. By default, the report contains a column for each variable and the order of the columns corresponds to the order of the variables in the data set.

You use the COLUMN statement to specify the variables to use in the report and the arrangement of the columns. In the COLUMN statement you can list data set variables, statistics that are calculated by PROC REPORT, or variables that are computed from other items in the report.

The following program creates a four column sales report for the first quarter:

```
options linesize=80 pageno=1 nodate;

proc report data=year_sales nowindows;
   where Quarter='1';
   column SalesRep Month Type Units;
   title1 'TruBlend Coffee Makers, Inc.';
   title2 'First Quarter Sales Report';
run;
```

The COLUMN statement specifies the order of the items in the report. The first column lists the values in SalesRep, the second column lists the values in Month, and so forth.

The following output shows the report:

Output 27.3 Displaying Selected Columns

```
                    TruBlend Coffee Makers, Inc.                        1
                     First Quarter Sales Report

       SalesRep        Month   Type          Units
       Hollingsworth   01      Deluxe          260
       Garcia          01      Standard         41
       Hollingsworth   01      Standard        330
       Jensen          01      Standard        110
       Garcia          01      Deluxe          715
       Jensen          01      Standard        675
       Garcia          02      Standard       2045
       Garcia          02      Deluxe           10
       Garcia          02      Standard         40
       Hollingsworth   02      Standard       1030
       Jensen          02      Standard        153
       Garcia          02      Standard         98
       Hollingsworth   03      Standard        125
       Jensen          03      Standard        154
       Garcia          03      Standard        118
       Hollingsworth   03      Standard         25
       Jensen          03      Standard        525
       Garcia          03      Standard        310
```

Ordering the Rows

You control much of the layout of a report by deciding how you use the variables. You tell PROC REPORT how to use a variable by specifying a usage option in the DEFINE statement for the variable.

To specify the order of the rows in the report, you can use the ORDER option in one or more DEFINE statements. PROC REPORT orders the rows of the report according to the values of the ORDER variables. If the report contains multiple ORDER variables, then PROC REPORT first orders rows according to the values of the first ORDER variable in the COLUMN statement.* Within each value of the first ORDER variable, the procedure orders rows according to the values of the second ORDER variable in the COLUMN statement, and so forth.

The following program creates a detail report of sales for the first quarter that is ordered by the sales representatives and month:

```
options linesize=80 pageno=1 nodate;

proc report data=year_sales nowindows;
   where Quarter='1';
   column SalesRep Month Type Units;
   define SalesRep / order;
   define Month / order;
   title1 'TruBlend Coffee Makers, Inc.';
   title2 'First Quarter Sales Report';
run;
```

The DEFINE statements specify that SalesRep and Month are the ORDER variables. The COLUMN statement specifies the order of the columns. By default, the rows are ordered by the ascending formatted values of SalesRep. The rows for each sales representative are ordered by the values of Month.

The following output shows the report:

Output 27.4   Ordering the Rows

```
                        TruBlend Coffee Makers, Inc.                       1
                         First Quarter Sales Report

         SalesRep         Month    Type         Units
         Garcia           01       Standard        41
                                   Deluxe         715
                          02       Standard      2045
                                   Deluxe          10
                                   Standard        40
                                   Standard        98
                          03       Standard       118
                                   Standard       310
         Hollingsworth    01       Deluxe         260
                                   Standard       330
                          02       Standard      1030
                          03       Standard       125
                                   Standard        25
         Jensen           01       Standard       110
                                   Standard       675
                          02       Standard       153
                          03       Standard       154
                                   Standard       525
```

PROC REPORT does not repeat the values of the ORDER variables from one row to the next when the values are the same.

---

* If you omit the COLUMN statement, then PROC REPORT processes the ORDER variables according to their position in the input data set.

Consolidating Several Observations into a Single Row

You can create summary reports with PROC REPORT by defining one or more GROUP variables. A *group* is a set of observations that has a unique combination of values for all GROUP variables. PROC REPORT tries to consolidate, or summarize, each group into one row of the report.

To consolidate all columns across a row, you must define all variables in the report as either GROUP, ANALYSIS, COMPUTED, or ACROSS. The GROUP option in one or more DEFINE statements identifies the variables that PROC REPORT uses to form groups. You can define more than one variable as a GROUP variable, but GROUP variables must precede variables of the other types of usage. PROC REPORT determines the nesting by the order of the variables in the COLUMN statement. For more information about defining the usage of a variable, see "Constructing the Layout" on page 433.

The value of an ANALYSIS variable for a group is the value of the statistic that PROC REPORT computes for all observations in a group. For each ANALYSIS variable, you can specify the statistic in the DEFINE statement. By default, PROC REPORT uses all numeric variables as the ANALYSIS variables and computes the SUM statistic. The statistics that you can request in the DEFINE statement are as follows:

Descriptive statistic keywords

CSS	PCTSUM
CV	RANGE
MAX	STD
MEAN	STDERR
MIN	SUM
N	SUMWGT
NMISS	USS
PCTN	VAR

Quantile statistic keywords

MEDIAN|P50	Q3|P75
P1	P90
P5	P95
P10	P99
Q1|P25	QRANGE

Hypothesis testing keyword

PRT	T

For definitions and discussion of these elementary statistics, see the Appendix in the *SAS Procedures Guide.*

The following program creates a summary report that shows the total yearly sales for each sales representative:

```
options linesize=80 pageno=1 nodate;
```

```
proc report data=year_sales nowindows colwidth=10;
   column SalesRep Units AmountSold;
   define SalesRep /group;❶
   define Units / analysis sum;❷
   define AmountSold/ analysis sum;❸
   title1 'TruBlend Coffee Makers Sales Report';
   title2 'Total Yearly Sales';
run;
```

The following list corresponds to the numbered items in the preceding program:

❶ The DEFINE statement specifies that SalesRep is the GROUP variable.

❷ The DEFINE statement specifies that Units is an ANALYSIS variable and specifies that PROC REPORT computes the SUM statistic.

❸ The DEFINE statement specifies that AmountSold is an ANALYSIS variable and specifies that PROC REPORT computes the SUM statistic.

The following output shows the report:

Output 27.5   Grouping Multiple Observations in a Summary Report

```
               TruBlend Coffee Makers Sales Report                1
                     Total Yearly Sales

          SalesRep           Units   AmountSold
          Garcia             15969   512070.78
          Hollingsworth      10620   347246.1
          Jensen             14400   461162.6
```

Each row of the report represents one group and summarizes all observations that have a unique value for SalesRep. PROC REPORT orders these rows in ascending order of the GROUP variable, which in this example is the sales representative ordered alphabetically. The values of the ANALYSIS variables are the sum of Units and AmountSold for all observations in a group, which in this case is the total units and amount sold by each sales representative.

Changing the Default Order of the Rows

You can modify the default ordering sequence for the rows of a report by using the ORDER= or DESCENDING option in the DEFINE statement. The ORDER= option specifies the sort order for a variable. You can order the rows by

DATA   the order of the data in the input data set

FORMATTED   ascending formatted values

FREQ   ascending frequency count

INTERNAL   ascending unformatted or internally stored values

By default, PROC REPORT uses the formatted values of a variable to order the rows. The DESCENDING option reverses the sort sequence so that PROC REPORT uses descending values to order the rows.

The following program creates a detail report of the first quarter sales that is ordered by number of sales:

```
options linesize=80 pageno=1 nodate;

proc report data=year_sales nowindows;
   where Quarter='1';
   column SalesRep Type Units Month;
   define SalesRep / order❶ order=freq;❷
   define Units / order❶ descending;❸
   define Type / order❶;
   title1 'TruBlend Coffee Makers, Inc.';
   title2 'First Quarter Sales Report';
run;
```

The following list corresponds to the numbered items in the preceding program:

❶ The DEFINE statements specify that SalesRep, Units, and Type are ORDER variables that correspond to the number of sales each sales representative made.

❷ The ORDER=FREQ option orders the rows of the report by the frequency of SalesRep.

❸ The DESCENDING option orders the rows for UNITS from the largest to the smallest value.

The following output shows the report:

Output 27.6 Changing the Order Sequence of the Rows

```
                    TruBlend Coffee Makers, Inc.                      1
                     First Quarter Sales Report

           SalesRep          Type          Units  Month❶
           Hollingsworth❷    Deluxe          260   01
                             Standard❸      1030   02
                                        ❹  330   01
                                           125   03
                                            25   03
           Jensen            Standard        675   01
                                             525   03
                                             154   03
                                             153   02
                                             110   01
           Garcia            Deluxe          715   01
                                              10   02
                             Standard        2045   02
                                              310   03
                                              118   03
                                               98   02
                                               41   01
                                               40   02
```

The following list corresponds to the numbered items in the preceding report:

❶ The order of the columns corresponds to the order in which the variables are specified in the COLUMN statement. The order of the DEFINE statements does not affect the order of the columns.

❷ The order of the rows is by ascending frequency of SalesRep so that the sales representative with the least number of sales (observations) appears first while the sales representative with the greatest number of sales appears last.

❸ The order of the rows within SalesRep is by ascending formatted values of Type so that sales information about the deluxe coffee maker occurs before the standard coffee maker.

❹ The order of the rows within Type is by descending formatted values of Units so that the observation with the highest number of units sold appears first.

Creating More Sophisticated Reports

Adjusting the Column Layout

Understanding Column Width and Spacing

You can modify the column spacing and the column width by specifying options in either the PROC REPORT statement or the DEFINE statement. To control the spacing between columns, you can use the SPACING= option in

- [ ] the PROC REPORT statement to specify the default number of blank characters between all columns
- [ ] the DEFINE statement to override the default value and to specify the number of blank characters to the left of a particular column.

By default, PROC REPORT inserts two blank spaces between the columns. To remove space between columns, specify SPACING=0. The maximum space that PROC REPORT allows between columns depends on the number of columns in the report. The sum of all column widths plus the blank characters to left of each column cannot exceed the line size.

To specify the column widths, you can use the following options:

- [ ] the COLWIDTH= option in the PROC REPORT statement to specify the default number of characters for columns that contain computed variables or numeric data set variables
- [ ] the WIDTH= option in the DEFINE statement to specify the width of the column that PROC REPORT uses to display a report item.

By default, the column width is nine characters for numeric values. You can specify the column width as small as one character and as large as the line size. PROC REPORT sets the width of a column by first looking at the WIDTH= option in the DEFINE statement. If you omit WIDTH=, then PROC REPORT uses a column width large enough to accommodate the format for a report item. If you do not assign a format, then the column width is either the length of the character variable or the value of the COLWIDTH= option.

You can adjust the column layout by specifying how to align the formatted values of a report item and the column header with the column width. The following options in the DEFINE statement align the columns:

CENTER   centers the column values and column header.

LEFT   left-aligns the column values and column header.

RIGHT   right-aligns the column values and column header.

Modifying the Column Width and Spacing

The following program modifies column spacing in a summary report that shows the total yearly sales for each sales representative:

```
options linesize=80 pageno=1 nodate;
```

```
proc report data=year_sales nowindows spacing=3;❶
   column SalesRep Units AmountSold;
   define SalesRep /group right;❷
   define Units / analysis sum width=5;❸
   define AmountSold/ analysis sum width=10;❸
   title1 'TruBlend Coffee Makers Sales Report';
   title2 'Total Yearly Sales';
run;
```

The following list corresponds to the numbered items in the preceding program:

❶ The SPACING= option in the PROC REPORT statement inserts three blank characters between all the columns.

❷ The RIGHT option in the DEFINE statement right-aligns the name of the sales representative and the column header in the column.

❸ The WIDTH= options in the DEFINE statements specify enough space to accommodate column headers on one line.

The following output shows the report:

Output 27.7 Adjusting Column Width and Spacing

```
             TruBlend Coffee Makers Sales Report            1
                     Total Yearly Sales


              SalesRep   Units   AmountSold
                 Garcia   15969     512070.78
          Hollingsworth   10620     347246.1
                 Jensen   14400     461162.6
```

The column width for SalesRep is 14 characters wide, which is the length of the variable.

Customizing Column Headers

Understanding the Structure of Column Headers

By default, PROC REPORT does not insert a vertical space beneath column headers to visually separate the detail rows from the headers. To further improve the appearance of a report, you can underline the column headers, insert a blank line beneath column headers, and specify your own column headers. The HEADLINE and HEADSKIP options in the PROC REPORT statement enable you to underline the column headers and insert a blank line after the column headers, respectively.

By default, SAS uses the variable name or the variable label, if the data set variable was previously assigned a label, for the column header. To specify a different column header, place text between single or double quotation marks in the DEFINE statement for the report item.

By default, PROC REPORT produces line breaks in the column header based on the width of the column. When you use multiple sets of quotation marks in the label, each set defines a separate line of the header. If you include split characters in the label, then PROC REPORT breaks the header when it reaches the split character and continues the header on the next line. By default, the split character is the slash (/). Use the SPLIT= option in the PROC REPORT statement to specify an alternative split character.

Modifying the Column Headers

The following program creates a summary report with multiple-line column headers for the variables SalesRep, Units, and AmountSold:

```
options linesize=80 pageno=1 nodate;

proc report data=year_sales nowindows spacing=3 headskip;❶
   column SalesRep Units AmountSold;
   define SalesRep /group 'Sales/Representative';❷
   define Units / analysis sum 'Units Sold' width=5;❷
   define AmountSold/ analysis sum 'Amount' 'Sold';❷
   title1 'TruBlend Coffee Makers Sales Report';
   title2 'Total Yearly Sales';
run;
```

The following list corresponds to the numbered items in the preceding program:

❶ The HEADSKIP option inserts a blank line after the column headers.

❷ The text in quotation marks specifies the column headers.

The SPLIT= option in the PROC REPORT statement is omitted because the label for SalesRep uses the default split character and the label for AmountSold identifies where to split the label by using multiple sets of quotation marks.

The following output shows the report:

Output 27.8   Modifying the Column Headers

```
              TruBlend Coffee Makers Sales Report                   1
                     Total Yearly Sales

              Sales          Units       Amount
              Representative  Sold         Sold

              Garcia         15969     512070.78
              Hollingsworth  10620     347246.1
              Jensen         14400     461162.6
```

The label Units Sold is split between two lines because the column width for this report item is 5 characters wide.

Specifying Formats

Using SAS Formats

A simple and effective way to enhance the readability of your reports is to specify a format for the report items. To assign a format to a column, you can use the FORMAT statement or the FORMAT= option in the DEFINE statement. The FORMAT statement only works for data set variables. The FORMAT= option assigns a SAS format or a user-defined format to any report item.

PROC REPORT determines how to format a report item by searching for the format to use in these places and in this order:

1 the FORMAT= option in the DEFINE statement

2 the FORMAT statement

3 the data set.

PROC REPORT uses the first format that it finds. If you have not assigned a format, then PROC REPORT uses the BEST9. format for numeric variables and the $w.$ format for character variables.

Applying Formats to Report Items

The following program illustrates how to apply formats to the columns of a summary report of total yearly sales for each sales representative:

```
options linesize=80 pageno=1 nodate;

proc report data=year_sales nowindows spacing=3 headskip;
   column SalesRep Units AmountSold;
   define SalesRep / group 'Sales/Representative';
   define Units / analysis sum 'Units Sold' format=comma7.;
   define AmountSold / analysis sum 'Amount' 'Sold' format=dollar14.2;
   title1 'TruBlend Coffee Makers Sales Report';
   title2 'Total Yearly Sales';
run;
```

PROC REPORT applies the COMMA7. format to the values of the variable Units and the DOLLAR14.2 format to the values of the variable AmountSold.

The following output shows the report:

Output 27.9 Formatting the Numeric Columns

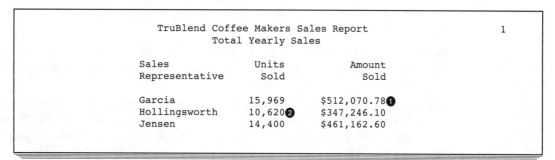

```
                TruBlend Coffee Makers Sales Report                    1
                       Total Yearly Sales

           Sales            Units          Amount
           Representative    Sold           Sold

           Garcia           15,969       $512,070.78❶
           Hollingsworth    10,620❷      $347,246.10
           Jensen           14,400       $461,162.60
```

The following list corresponds to the numbered items in the preceding report:

❶ The variable AmountSold uses the DOLLAR14.2 format for a maximum column width of 14 spaces. Two spaces are reserved for the decimal part of a value. The remaining 12 spaces include the decimal point, whole numbers, the dollar sign, commas, and a minus sign if a value is negative.

❷ The variable Units uses the COMMA7. format for a maximum column width of seven spaces. The column width includes the numeric value, commas, and a minus sign if a value is negative.

These formats do not affect the actual data values that are stored in the SAS data set. That is, the formats only affect the way values appear in a report.

Using Variable Values as Column Headers

Creating the Column Headers

To create column headers from the values of the data set variables and produce cross-tabulations, you can use the ACROSS option in a DEFINE statement. When you define an ACROSS variable, PROC REPORT creates a column for each value of the ACROSS variable.

Columns created by an ACROSS variable contain statistics or computed values. If nothing is above or below an ACROSS variable, then PROC REPORT displays the number of observations in the input data set that belong to a cell of the report (N statistic). A *cell* is a single unit of a report, formed by the intersection of a row and a column.

The examples in this chapter show how to display frequency counts (the N statistic) and statistics that are computed for ANALYSIS variables. For information about placing computed variables in the cells of the report, see the REPORT procedure in *SAS Procedures Guide*.

Creating Frequency Counts

The following program creates a report that tabulates the number of sales for each sales representative:

```
options linesize=84 pageno=1 nodate;

proc report data=year_sales nowindows colwidth=5 headline;❶
   column SalesRep Type N;❷
   define SalesRep / group 'Sales Representative';
   define Type / across 'Coffee Maker';❸
   define N / 'Total';
   title1 'TruBlend Coffee Makers Yearly Sales Report';
   title2 'Number of Sales';
run;
```

The following list corresponds to the numbered items in the preceding program:

❶ The HEADLINE option in the PROC REPORT statement underlines all column headers and the spaces between them.

❷ The COLUMN statement specifies that the report contain two data set variables and a calculated statistic, N. The N statistic causes PROC REPORT to add a third column that displays the number of observations for each sales representative.

❸ The DEFINE statement specifies that Type is an ACROSS variable.

The following output shows the report:

Output 27.10   Showing Frequency Counts

```
               TruBlend Coffee Makers Yearly Sales Report                1
                          Number of Sales


          Sales               Coffee Maker❶
          Representative   Deluxe    Standard   Total❷
          -----------------------------------------------
          Garcia              4         36         40
          Hollingsworth       8         24         32
          Jensen              4         34         38
```

The following list corresponds to the numbered items in the preceding report:

❶ Type is an ACROSS variable with nothing above or below it. Therefore, the report shows how many observations the input data set contains for each sales representative and coffee maker type.

❷ The column for N statistic is labeled Total and contains the total number of observations for each sales representative.

By default, PROC REPORT ordered the columns of the ACROSS variable according to its formatted values. You can use the ORDER= option in the DEFINE statement to alter the sort order for an ACROSS variable. See "Changing the Default Order of the Rows" on page 440 for more information.

Sharing a Column with Multiple Analysis Variables

You can create sophisticated cross-tabulation by having the value of ANALYSIS variables appear in columns that the ACROSS variable creates. When an ACROSS variable shares columns with one or more ANALYSIS variables, PROC REPORT will stack the columns. For example, you can share the columns of the ACROSS variable Type with the ANALYSIS variable Units so that the each column contains the number of units sold for a type of coffee maker.

To stack the value of an ANALYSIS variable in the columns created by the ACROSS variable, place that variable next to the ACROSS variable in the COLUMN statement:

```
column SalesRep Type, Unit;
```

The comma separates the ACROSS variable from the ANALYSIS variable. To specify multiple ANALYSIS variables, list their names in parentheses next to the ACROSS variable in the COLUMN statement:

```
column SalesRep Type,(Unit AmountSold);
```

If you place the ACROSS variable before the ANALYSIS variable, then the name and values of the ACROSS variable are above the name of the ANALYSIS variable in the report. If you place the ACROSS variable after the ANALYSIS variable, then the name and the values of the ACROSS variable are below the name of the ANALYSIS variable.

By default, PROC REPORT calculates the SUM statistic for the ANALYSIS variables. To display another statistic for the column, use the DEFINE statement to specify the statistic that you want computed for the ANALYSIS variable. See the list on page 439 for a list of the available statistics.

The following program creates a report that tabulates the number of coffee makers sold and the average sale in dollars for each sales representative:

```
options linesize=84 pageno=1 nodate;

proc report data=year_sales nowindows headline;
   column SalesRep Type,(Units Amountsold);❶
   define SalesRep / group 'Sales Representative';
   define Type / across '';❷
   define units / analysis sum 'Units Sold' format=comma7.;❸
   define AmountSold /analysis mean 'Average/Sale' format=dollar12.2;❹
   title1 'TruBlend Coffee Makers Yearly Sales Report';
run;
```

The following list corresponds to the numbered items in the preceding program:

❶ The COLUMN statement creates columns for SalesRep and Type. The ACROSS variable Type shares its columns with the ANALYSIS variables Units and Amountsold.

❷ The DEFINE statement uses a blank as the label of Type in the column header.

❸ The DEFINE statement uses the ANALYSIS variable Units to compute a SUM statistic.

❹ The DEFINE statement uses the ANALYSIS variable AmountSold to compute a MEAN statistic.

The following output shows the report:

Output 27.11 Sharing a Column with Multiple Analysis Variables

```
                    TruBlend Coffee Makers Yearly Sales Report                1


                          Deluxe                 Standard
             Sales      Units    Average      Units     Average
             Representative  Sold     Sale       Sold       Sale
             -----------------------------------------------------------------
             Garcia          945   $11,694.38   15,024    $12,924.81
             Hollingsworth   760    $4,702.50    9,860    $12,901.09
             Jensen          820   $10,147.50   13,580    $12,369.78
```

The values in the columns for a particular type of coffee maker are the total units sold and the average dollar sale for each sales representative.

Summarizing Groups of Observations

Using Group Summaries

For some reports, you may want to summarize information about a group of observations and visually separate each group. To do so, you can create a break in the report before or after each group.

To visually separate each group, you insert lines of text, called *break lines*, at a break. Break lines can occur at the beginning or end of a report, at the top or bottom of each page, and whenever the value of a group or order variable changes. The break line can contain

- □ text (including blanks)
- □ summaries of statistics
- □ report variables
- □ computed variables.

To create group summaries, use the BREAK statement. A BREAK statement must include (in this order)

- □ the keyword BREAK
- □ the location of the break (BEFORE or AFTER)
- □ the name of a GROUP variable that is called the *break variable*.

PROC REPORT creates a break each time the value of the break variable changes. If you want summaries to appear before the first row of each group, then use the BEFORE argument. If you want the summaries to appear after the last row of each group, then use the AFTER argument.

To create summary information for the whole report, use the RBREAK statement. A RBREAK statement must include (in this order)

- □ the keyword RBREAK
- □ the location of the break (BEFORE or AFTER).

When you use the RBREAK statement, PROC REPORT inserts text, summary statistics for the entire report, or computed variables at the beginning or end of the detail rows of a report. If you want the summary to appear before the first row of the report, then use the BEFORE argument. If you want the summaries to appear after the last row of each group, then use the AFTER argument.

Both the BREAK and RBREAK statements support options that control the appearance of the group and the report summaries. You can use any combination of options in the statement in any order. For a list of the available options, see the REPORT procedure in *SAS Procedures Guide*.

Creating Group Summaries

The following program creates a summary report that uses break lines to display subtotals with yearly sales for each sales representative, and a yearly grand total for all sales representatives:

```
options linesize=80 pageno=1 nodate linesize=84;

proc report data=year_sales nowindows headskip;
   column Salesrep Quarter Units AmountSold;
   define SalesRep / group 'Sales Representative';
   define Quarter / group center;❶
   define Units / analysis sum 'Units Sold' format=comma7.;
   define AmountSold / analysis sum 'Amount/Sold' format=dollar14.2;
   break after SalesRep / summarize skip ol suppress;❷
   rbreak after / summarize skip dol;❸
   title1 'TruBlend Coffee Makers Sales Report';
   title2 'Total Yearly Sales';
run;
```

The following list corresponds to the numbered items in the preceding program:

❶ The CENTER option in the DEFINE statement centers the values of the variable Quarter and the label of the column header.

❷ The BREAK statement adds break lines after a change in the value of the GROUP variable SalesRep. The SUMMARIZE option writes a summary line to summarize the statistics for each group of break lines. The SKIP option inserts a blank line after each group of break lines. The OL option writes a line of hyphens (-) above each value in the summary line. The SUPPRESS option suppresses printing the value of the break variable and the overlines in the break variable column.

❸ The RBREAK statement adds a break line at the end of the report. The SUMMARIZE option writes a summary line that summarizes the SUM statistics for the ANALYSIS variables Units and AmountSold. The SKIP option inserts a blank line before the break line. The DOL option writes a line of equal signs (=) above each value in the summary line.

The following output shows the report:

Output 27.12 Creating Group Summaries

```
                    TruBlend Coffee Makers Sales Report                    1
                          Total Yearly Sales

            Sales                         Units           Amount
            Representative   Quarter      Sold            Sold

            Garcia           1            3,377       $118,019.94
                             2            3,515       $108,859.55
                             3            7,144       $225,326.28
                             4            1,933        $59,865.01
                                          -------     --------------
                                          15,969❶     $512,070.78❶

            Hollingsworth    1            1,770        $59,634.70
                             2            3,090        $96,160.55
                             3            3,285       $109,704.35
                             4            2,475        $81,746.50
                                          -------     --------------
                                          10,620      $347,246.10

            Jensen           1            1,617        $50,078.49
                             2            2,413        $74,730.61
                             3            6,687       $222,290.99
                             4            3,683       $114,062.51
                                          -------     --------------
                                          14,400      $461,162.60

                                          =======     ==============
                                          40,989❷     $1,320,479.48❷
```

The following list corresponds to the numbered items in the preceding report:

❶ The values of the ANALYSIS variables Units and AmountSold in the group summary lines are sums for all rows in the group (subtotals).

❷ The values of the ANALYSIS variables Units and AmountSold in the report summary line are sums for all rows in the report (grand totals).

In this report, Units and AmountSold are ANALYSIS variables that are used to calculate the SUM statistic. If these variables were defined to calculate a different statistic, then the values in the summary lines would be the value of that statistic for all rows in the group and all rows in the report.

Review of SAS Tools

PROC REPORT Statements

PROC REPORT <**DATA=**_SAS-data-set_><_option(s)_>;

BREAK _location break-variable_ </_option(s)_>;

COLUMN _column-specification(s)_;

DEFINE _report-item_ /<_usage_> <_option(s)_>;

RBREAK _location_</_option(s)_>;

TITLE<_n_> <_'title'_>;

WHERE *where-expression*;

PROC REPORT <DATA=*SAS-data-set*> <*option(s)*>;

starts the procedure. If no other statements are used, then SAS shows all variables in the *SAS-data-set* in a detail report in the REPORT window. If the data set contains only numeric data, then PROC REPORT shows all variables in a summary report. Other statements, listed below, enable you to control the structure of the report.

You can specify the following *options* in the PROC REPORT statement:

COLWIDTH=*column-width*

specifies the default number of characters for columns that contain computed variables or numeric data set variables.

DATA=*SAS-data-set*

names the SAS data set that PROC REPORT uses. If you omit DATA=, then PROC REPORT uses the most recently created data set.

HEADLINE

inserts a line of hyphens (-) under the column headers at the top of each page of the report.

HEADSKIP

inserts a blank line beneath all column headers (or beneath the line that the HEADLINE option inserts) at the top of each page of the report.

SPACING=*space-between-columns*

specifies the number of blank characters between columns. For each column, the sum of its width and the blank characters between it and the column to its left cannot exceed the line size.

SPLIT=*'character'*

specifies the split character. PROC REPORT breaks a column header when it reaches that character and continues the header on the next line. The split character itself is not part of the column header, although each occurrence of the split character is counted toward the 256-character maximum for a label.

WINDOWS | NOWINDOWS

selects a windowing or nonwindowing environment.

When you use WINDOWS, SAS opens the REPORT window, which enables you to modify a report repeatedly and to see the modifications immediately. When you use NOWINDOWS, PROC REPORT runs without the REPORT window and sends its results to the SAS procedure output.

BREAK *location break-variable* <*/option(s)*>;

produces a default summary at a break (a change in the value of a GROUP or ORDER variable). The information in a summary applies to a set of observations. The observations share a unique combination of values for the break variable and all other GROUP or ORDER variables to the left of the break variable in the report.

You must specify the following arguments in the BREAK statement:

location

controls the placement of the break lines, where *location* is

AFTER

places the break lines immediately after the last row of each set of rows that have the same value for the break variable.

BEFORE

places the break lines immediately before the first row of each set of rows that have the same value for the break variable.

break-variable

is a GROUP or ORDER variable. PROC REPORT writes break lines each time the value of this variable changes.

You can specify the following *options* in the BREAK statement:

OL

inserts a line of hyphens (-) above each value that appears in the summary line.

SKIP

writes a blank line for the last break line.

SUMMARIZE

writes a summary line in each group of break lines.

SUPPRESS

suppresses the printing of the value of the break variable in the summary line, and of any underlining or overlining in the break lines.

COLUMN <*column-specification(s)*>;

identifies items that form columns in the report and describes the arrangement of all columns. You can specify the following *column-specification(s)* in the COLUMN statement:

☐ *report-item(s)*

☐ *report-item-1, report-item-2 <. . . , report-item-n>*

where *report-item* identifies items that form columns in the report. A report-item is either the name of a data set variable, a computed variable, or a statistic.

report-item-1, report-item-2 <. . . , report-item-n>

identifies report items that collectively determine the contents of the column or columns. These items are said to be stacked in the report because each item generates a header, and the headers are stacked one above the other. The header for the leftmost item is on top. If one of the items is an ANALYSIS variable, then a computed variable, or a statistic, its values fill the cells in that part of the report. Otherwise, PROC REPORT fills the cells with frequency counts.

DEFINE *report-item* / <*usage*> <*option(s)*>;

describes how to use and display a report item. A report item is either the name or alias (established in the COLUMN statement) of a data set variable, a computed variable, or a statistic. The *usage* of the report item is

☐ ACROSS

☐ ANALYSIS

☐ COMPUTED

☐ DISPLAY

☐ GROUP

☐ ORDER

You can specify the following *options* in the DEFINE statement:

CENTER

centers the formatted values of the report item within the column width, and centers the column header over the values.

column-header

defines the column header for the report item. Enclose each header in single or double quotation marks. When you specify multiple column headers,

PROC REPORT uses a separate line for each one. The split character also splits a column header over multiple lines.

DESCENDING
reverses the order in which PROC REPORT displays rows or values of a GROUP, ORDER, or ACROSS variable.

FORMAT=*format*
assigns a SAS format or a user-defined format to the report item. This format applies to *report-item* as PROC REPORT displays it; the format does not alter the format associated with a variable in the data set.

ORDER=DATA | FORMATTED | FREQ | INTERNAL
orders the values of a GROUP, ORDER, or ACROSS variable according to the specified order, where

DATA
orders values according to their order in the input data set.

FORMATTED
orders values by their formatted (external) values. By default, the order is ascending.

FREQ
orders values by ascending frequency count.

INTERNAL
orders values by their unformatted values, which yields the same order that PROC SORT would yield. This order is operating environment dependent. This sort sequence is particularly useful for displaying dates chronologically.

RIGHT
right-justifies the formatted values of the specified report item within the column width and right-justifies the column headers over the values. If the format width is the same as the width of the column, then RIGHT has no affect on the placement of values.

SPACING=*horizontal-positions*
defines the number of blank characters to leave between the column that is being defined and the column immediately to its left. For each column, the sum of its width and the blank characters between it and the column to its left cannot exceed the line size.

statistic
associates a statistic with an ANALYSIS variable. PROC REPORT uses this statistic to calculate values for the ANALYSIS variable for the observations represented by each cell of the report. If you do not associate a statistic with the variable, then PROC REPORT calculates the SUM statistic. You cannot use *statistic* in the definition of any other kind of variable.

WIDTH=*column-width*
defines the width of the column in which PROC REPORT displays *report-item*.

RBREAK *location <* /option(s)*>*;
produces a default summary at the beginning or end of a report.
You must specify the following argument in the RBREAK statement:

location
controls the placement of the break lines and is either

AFTER
places the break lines at the end of the report.

BEFORE
>   places the break lines at the beginning of the report.
You can specify the following *options* in the RBREAK statement:

DOL
>   specifies to double overline each value that appears in the summary line.

SKIP
>   writes a blank line after the last break line of a break located at the beginning of the report.

SUMMARIZE
>   includes a summary line as one of the break lines. A summary line at the beginning or end of a report contains values for statistics, ANALYSIS variables, or computed variables.

TITLE<*n*> <*'title'*>;
>   specifies a title. The argument *n* is a number from 1 to 10 that immediately follows the word TITLE, with no intervening blank, and it specifies the level of the TITLE. The text of each *title* must be enclosed in single or double quotation marks. The maximum title length depends on your operating environment and the value of the LINESIZE= system option. Refer to the SAS documentation for your operating environment for more information.

WHERE *where-expression*;
>   subsets the input data set by identifying certain conditions that each observation must meet before an observation is available for processing. *Where-expression* defines the condition. The condition is a valid arithmetic or logical expression that generally consists of a sequence of operands and operators.

Learning More

KEEP= data set option
>   For an additional example, see "Reading Selected Variables" on page 85. For a complete documentation about the KEEP= data set option, see the *SAS Language Reference: Dictionary*.

PROC PRINT
>   For a discussion of how to create several types of detail reports, see Chapter 25, "Producing Detail Reports with the PRINT Procedure," on page 367.

PROC REPORT
>   For complete documentation, see *SAS Procedures Guide*.

PROC TABULATE
>   For a discussion of how to create several types of summary reports, see Chapter 26, "Creating Summary Tables with the TABULATE Procedure," on page 403

Report writing examples
>   For step-by-step instructions for creating a variety of reports, see *SAS Guide to Report Writing: Examples*.

SAS formats
>   For complete documentation, see *SAS Language Reference: Dictionary*. Many formats are available with the SAS software, such as fractions, hexadecimal values, roman numerals, social security numbers, date and time values, and numbers written as words.

WHERE statement

For a discussion, see "Understanding the WHERE Statement" on page 375. For complete reference documentation about the WHERE statement, see *SAS Language Reference: Dictionary*. For a complete discussion of WHERE processing, see *SAS Language Reference: Concepts*

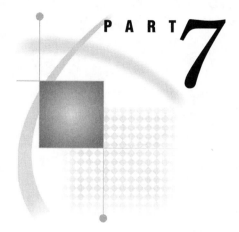

P A R T **7**

Producing Plots and Charts

Plotting the Relationship between Variables

Introduction

An effective way to examine the relationship between variables is to plot their values. You can use the PLOT procedure to display relationships and patterns in the data.

In this chapter, you will learn how to

- □ plot one set of variables
- □ enhance the appearance of a plot
- □ create multiple plots on separate pages
- □ create multiple plots on the same page
- □ plot multiple sets of variables on the same pair of axes.

Prerequisites

To understand the examples in this chapter, you should be familiar with the following features and concepts:

- □ the LOG function
- □ the FORMAT statement
- □ the LABEL statement
- □ the TITLE statement
- □ SAS system options.

Input File and SAS Data Set for Examples

The examples in this chapter use one input file* and one SAS data set. The input file contains information about the high and low values of the Dow Jones Industrial Average from 1954 to 1998. The input file has the following structure:

```
1954   31DEC1954   404.39   11JAN1954   279.87
1955   30DEC1955   488.40   17JAN1955   388.20
1956   06APR1956   521.05   23JAN1956   462.35
1957   12JUL1957   520.77   22OCT1957   419.79
1958   31DEC1958   583.65   25FEB1958   436.89
...more data lines...
1995   13DEC1995 5216.47   30JAN1995 3832.08
1996   27DEC1996 6560.91   10JAN1996 5032.94
1997   06AUG1997 8259.31   11APR1997 6391.69
1998   23NOV1998 9374.27   31AUG1998 7539.07
```

The input file contains the following values from left to right:

□ the year that the observation describes
□ the date of the yearly high for the Dow Jones Industrial Average
□ the yearly high value for the Dow Jones Industrial Average
□ the date of the yearly low for the Dow Jones Industrial Average
□ the yearly low value for the Dow Jones Industrial Average.

The following program creates the SAS data set HIGHLOW:

```
options pagesize=60 linesize=80 pageno=1 nodate;

data highlow;
    infile 'your-input-file';
    input Year @7 DateOfHigh date9. DowJonesHigh @28 DateOfLow date9. DowJonesLow;
    format LogDowHigh LogDowLow 5.2 DateOfHigh DateOfLow date9.;
    LogDowHigh=log(DowJonesHigh);
    LogDowLow=log(DowJonesLow);
run;
```

The computed variables LogDowHigh and LogDowLow contain the log transformation of the yearly high and low values for the Dow Jones Industrial Average.

```
proc print data=highlow;
    title 'Dow Jones Industrial Average Yearly High and Low Values';
run;
```

---

* Refer to Appendix 1, "Additional Data Sets," on page 711 for a complete listing of the input data.

Output 28.1 A Listing of the HIGHLOW Data Set

Dow Jones Industrial Average Yearly High and Low Values   1

Obs	Year	DateOf High	Dow Jones High	DateOfLow	Dow JonesLow	Log Dow High	Log DowLow
1	1954	31DEC1954	404.39	11JAN1954	279.87	6.00	5.63
2	1955	30DEC1955	488.40	17JAN1955	388.20	6.19	5.96
3	1956	06APR1956	521.05	23JAN1956	462.35	6.26	6.14
4	1957	12JUL1957	520.77	22OCT1957	419.79	6.26	6.04
5	1958	31DEC1958	583.65	25FEB1958	436.89	6.37	6.08
6	1959	31DEC1959	679.36	09FEB1959	574.46	6.52	6.35
7	1960	05JAN1960	685.47	25OCT1960	568.05	6.53	6.34
8	1961	13DEC1961	734.91	03JAN1961	610.25	6.60	6.41
9	1962	03JAN1962	726.01	26JUN1962	535.76	6.59	6.28
10	1963	18DEC1963	767.21	02JAN1963	646.79	6.64	6.47
11	1964	18NOV1964	891.71	02JAN1964	768.08	6.79	6.64
12	1965	31DEC1965	969.26	28JUN1965	840.59	6.88	6.73
13	1966	09FEB1966	995.15	07OCT1966	744.32	6.90	6.61
14	1967	25SEP1967	943.08	03JAN1967	786.41	6.85	6.67
15	1968	03DEC1968	985.21	21MAR1968	825.13	6.89	6.72
16	1969	14MAY1969	968.85	17DEC1969	769.93	6.88	6.65
17	1970	29DEC1970	842.00	06MAY1970	631.16	6.74	6.45
18	1971	28APR1971	950.82	23NOV1971	797.97	6.86	6.68
19	1972	11DEC1972	1036.27	26JAN1972	889.15	6.94	6.79
20	1973	11JAN1973	1051.70	05DEC1973	788.31	6.96	6.67
21	1974	13MAR1974	891.66	06DEC1974	577.60	6.79	6.36
22	1975	15JUL1975	881.81	02JAN1975	632.04	6.78	6.45
23	1976	21SEP1976	1014.79	02JAN1976	858.71	6.92	6.76
24	1977	03JAN1977	999.75	02NOV1977	800.85	6.91	6.69
25	1978	08SEP1978	907.74	28FEB1978	742.12	6.81	6.61
26	1979	05OCT1979	897.61	07NOV1979	796.67	6.80	6.68
27	1980	20NOV1980	1000.17	21APR1980	759.13	6.91	6.63
28	1981	27APR1981	1024.05	25SEP1981	824.01	6.93	6.71
29	1982	27DEC1982	1070.55	12AUG1982	776.92	6.98	6.66
30	1983	29NOV1983	1287.20	03JAN1983	1027.04	7.16	6.93
31	1984	06JAN1984	1286.64	24JUL1984	1086.57	7.16	6.99
32	1985	16DEC1985	1553.10	04JAN1985	1184.96	7.35	7.08
33	1986	02DEC1986	1955.57	22JAN1986	1502.29	7.58	7.31
34	1987	25AUG1987	2722.42	19OCT1987	1738.74	7.91	7.46
35	1988	21OCT1988	2183.50	20JAN1988	1879.14	7.69	7.54
36	1989	09OCT1989	2791.41	03JAN1989	2144.64	7.93	7.67
37	1990	16JUL1990	2999.75	11OCT1990	2365.10	8.01	7.77
38	1991	31DEC1991	3168.83	09JAN1991	2470.30	8.06	7.81
39	1992	01JUN1992	3413.21	09OCT1992	3136.58	8.14	8.05
40	1993	29DEC1993	3794.33	20JAN1993	3241.95	8.24	8.08
41	1994	31JAN1994	3978.36	04APR1994	3593.35	8.29	8.19
42	1995	13DEC1995	5216.47	30JAN1995	3832.08	8.56	8.25
43	1996	27DEC1996	6560.91	10JAN1996	5032.94	8.79	8.52
44	1997	06AUG1997	8259.31	11APR1997	6391.69	9.02	8.76
45	1998	23NOV1998	9374.27	31AUG1998	7539.07	9.15	8.93

Note: All graphics output in this chapter uses an OPTIONS statement that specifies PAGESIZE=40 and LINESIZE=76. When the PAGESIZE= and LINESIZE= options are set, they remain in effect until you reset the options with another OPTIONS statement, or you end the SAS session. △

Plotting One Set of Variables

Understanding the PLOT Statement

The PLOT procedure produces two-dimensional graphs that plot one variable against another within a set of coordinate axes. The coordinates of each point on the plot correspond to the values of two variables. Graphs are automatically scaled to the values of your data, although you can control the scale by specifying the coordinate axes.

You can create a simple two-dimensional plot for one set of measures by using the following PLOT statement:

> **PROC PLOT** <DATA=*SAS-data-set*>;
>
>   **PLOT** *vertical*horizontal*;

where *vertical* is the name of the variable to plot on the vertical axis and *horizontal* is the name of the variable to plot on the horizontal axis.

By default, PROC PLOT selects plotting symbols. The data determines the labels for the axes, the values of the axes, and the values of the tick marks. The plot displays the following:

- [ ] the name of the vertical variable that is next to the vertical axis and the name of the horizontal variable that is beneath the horizontal axis
- [ ] the axes and the tick marks that are based on evenly spaced intervals
- [ ] the letter A as the plotting symbol to indicate one observation; the letter B as the plotting symbol if two observations coincide; the letter C if three coincide, and so on
- [ ] a legend with the name of the variables in the plot and meaning of the plotting symbols.

The following display shows the axes, values, and tick marks on a plot.

Display 28.1   Diagram of Axes, Values, and Tick Marks

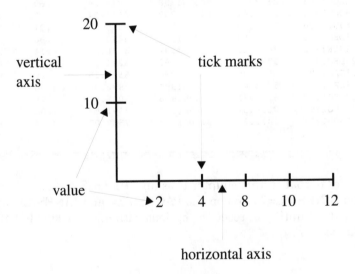

Note: PROC PLOT is an interactive procedure. After you issue the PROC PLOT statement, you can continue to submit any statements that are valid with the procedure without resubmitting the PROC statement. Therefore, you can easily and quickly experiment with changing labels, values for tick marks, and so on. △

Example

The following program uses the PLOT statement to create a simple plot that shows the trend in high Dow Jones values from 1954 to 1998:

```
options pagesize=40 linesize=76 pageno=1 nodate;

proc plot data=highlow;
   plot DowJonesHigh*Year;
   title 'Dow Jones Industrial Average Yearly High';
run;
```

The following output shows the plot:

Output 28.2   Using a Simple Plot to Show Data Trends

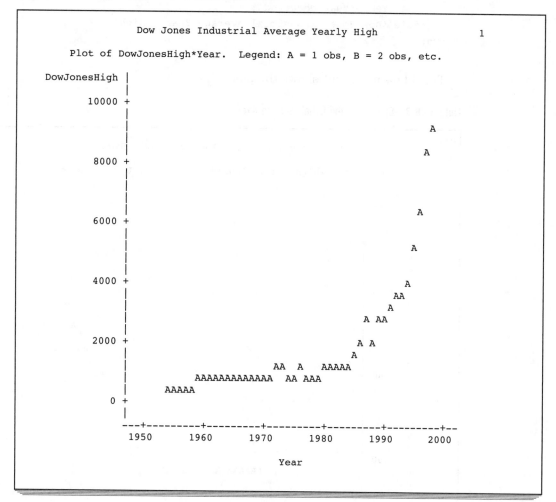

The plot graphically depicts the exponential trend in the high value of the Dow Jones Industrial Average over the last 50 years. The greatest growth has occurred in the last 10 years, increasing by almost 6,000 points.

Enhancing the Plot

Specifying the Axes Labels

Sometimes you might want to supply additional information about the axes. You can enhance the plot by specifying the labels for the vertical and horizontal axes.

The following program plots the log transformation of DowJonesHigh for each year and uses the LABEL statement to change the axes labels:

```
options pagesize=40 linesize=76 pageno=1 nodate;

proc plot data=highlow;
   plot LogDowHigh*Year;
   label LogDowHigh='Log of Highest Value'
         Year='Year Occurred';
   title 'Dow Jones Industrial Average Yearly High';
run;
```

The following output shows the plot:

Output 28.3   Specifying the Labels for the Axes

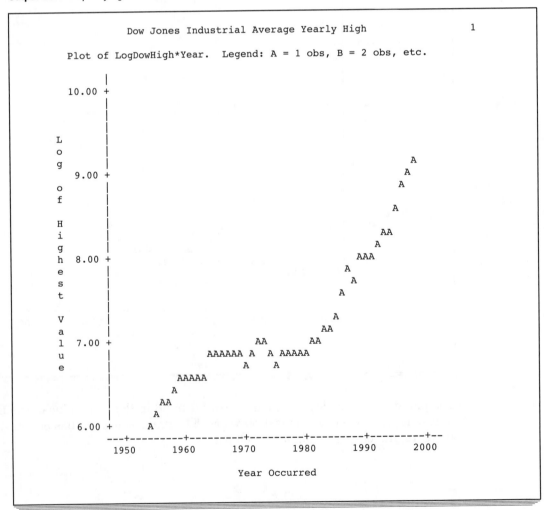

Plotting the log transformation of DowJonesHigh changes the exponential trend to a linear trend. The label for each variable is centered parallel to its axis.

Specifying the Tick Marks Values

In the previous plots, the range on the horizontal axis is from 1950 to 2000. Tick marks and labels representing the years are spaced at intervals of 10. You can control the selection of the range and the interval on the horizontal axis with the HAXIS= option in the PLOT statement. A corresponding PLOT statement option, VAXIS=, controls the values of the tick mark on the vertical axis.

The forms of the HAXIS= and VAXIS= options follow. You must precede the first option in a PLOT statement with a slash.

PLOT *vertical*horizontal* / HAXIS=*tick-value-list*;

PLOT *vertical*horizontal* / VAXIS=*tick-value-list*;

where *tick-value-list* is a list of all values to assign to tick marks.

For example, to specify tick marks every five years from 1950 to 2000, use the following option:

```
haxis=1950 1955 1960 1965 1970 1975 1980 1985 1990 1995 2000
```

Or, you can abbreviate this list of tick marks:

```
haxis=1950 to 2000 by 5
```

The following program uses the HAXIS= option to specify the tick mark values for the horizontal axis:

```
options pagesize=40 linesize=76 pageno=1 nodate;

proc plot data=highlow;
   plot LogDowHigh*Year / haxis=1954 to 1998 by 4;
   label LogDowHigh='Log of Highest Value'
         Year='Year Occurred';
   title 'Dow Jones Industrial Average Yearly High';
run;
```

The following output shows the plot:

Output 28.4   Specifying the Range and the Intervals of the Horizontal Axis

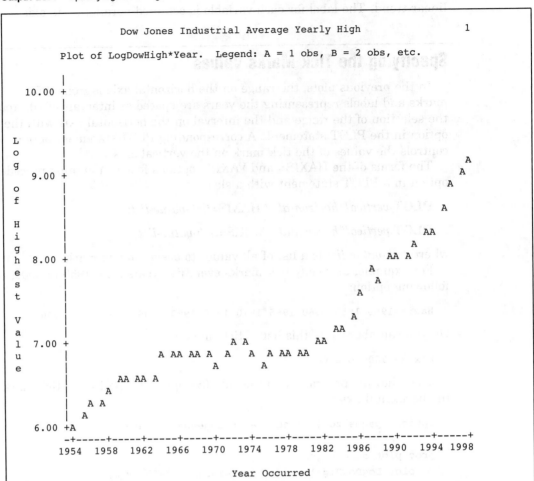

The range of the horizontal axis is from 1954 to 1998, and the tick marks are now
arranged at four-year intervals.

Specifying Plotting Symbols

By default, PROC PLOT uses the letter A as the plotting symbol to indicate one
observation, the letter B as the plotting symbol if two observations coincide, the letter C
if three coincide, and so on. The letter Z represents 26 or more coinciding observations.

In many instances, particularly if you are plotting two sets of data on the same pair
of axes, then you use the following form of the PLOT statement to specify your own
plotting symbols:

PLOT *vertical***horizontal='character'*;

where *character* is a plotting symbol to mark each point on the plot. PROC PLOT uses
this character to represent values from one or more observations.

The following program uses the plus sign (+) as the plotting symbol for the plot:

```
options pagesize=40 linesize=76 pageno=1 nodate;

proc plot data=highlow;
   plot LogDowHigh*Year='+' / haxis=1954 to 1998 by 4;
```

```
      label LogDowHigh='Log of Highest Value'
            Year='Year Occurred';
      title 'Dow Jones Industrial Average Yearly High';
   run;
```

The plotting symbol must be enclosed in either single or double quotation marks. The following output shows the plot:

Output 28.5 Specifying a Plotting Symbol

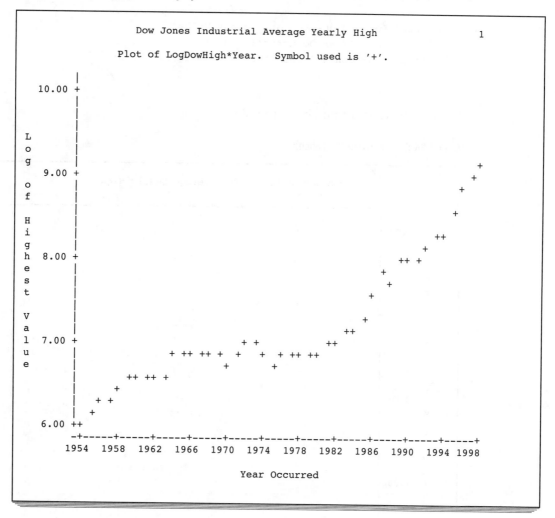

Note: When a plotting symbol is specified, PROC PLOT uses that symbol for all points on the plot regardless of how many observations might coincide. If observations coincide, then a message appears at the bottom of the plot telling how many observations are hidden. △

Removing the Legend

Often, a few simple changes to a plot will improve its appearance. You can draw a frame around the entire plot, rather than just on the left side and bottom. This makes it easier to determine the values that the plotting symbols represent on the left side of the plot. Also, you can suppress the legend when the labels clearly identify the variables in the plot or when the association between the plotting symbols and the variables is clear.

The following program uses the NOLEGEND option in the PROC PLOT statement to suppress the legend and the BOX option in the PLOT statement to box the entire plot:

```
options pagesize=40 linesize=76 pageno=1 nodate;

proc plot data=highlow nolegend;
   plot LogDowHigh*Year='+' / haxis=1954 to 1998 by 4
                             box;
   label LogDowHigh='Log of Highest Value'
         Year='Year Occurred';
   title 'Dow Jones Industrial Average Yearly High';
run;
```

The following output shows the plot:

Output 28.6   Removing the Legend

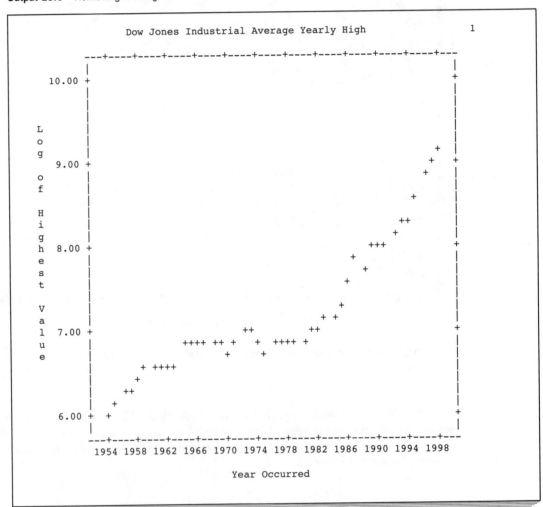

Plotting Multiple Sets of Variables

Creating Multiple Plots on Separate Pages

You can compare trends for different sets of measures by creating multiple plots. To request more than one plot from the same SAS data set, simply specify additional sets of variables in the PLOT statement. The form of the statement is

PLOT *vertical-1*horizontal-1 vertical-2*horizontal-2*;

All the options that you list in a PLOT statement apply to all of the plots that the statement produces.

The following program uses the PLOT statement to produce separate plots of the highest and lowest values of the Dow Jones Industrial Average from 1954 to 1998:

```
options pagesize=40 linesize=76 pageno=1 nodate;

proc plot data=highlow;
   plot LogDowHigh*Year='+' LogDowLow*Year='o'
                         / haxis=1954 to 1998 by 4 box;
   label LogDowHigh='Log of Highest Value'
         LogDowLow='Log of Lowest Value'
         Year='Year Occurred';
   title 'Dow Jones Industrial Average Yearly High';
run;
```

The following output shows the plots:

Output 28.7 Creating Multiple Plots on Separate Pages

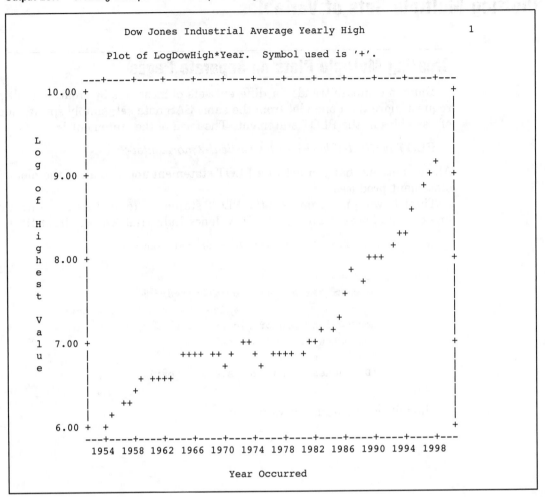

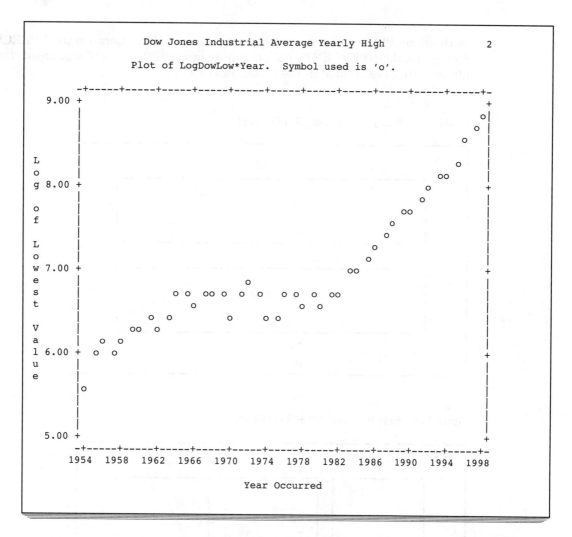

The plots appear on separate pages and use different vertical axes. Different plotting symbols represent the high and low values of the Dow Jones Industrial Average.

Creating Multiple Plots on the Same Page

You can more easily compare the trends in different sets of measures when the plots appear on the same page. PROC PLOT provides two options that display multiple plots on the same page:

the VPERCENT= option

the HPERCENT= option.

You can specify these options in the PROC PLOT statement by using one of the following forms:

PROC PLOT <DATA=*SAS-data-set*> VPERCENT=*number*;

PROC PLOT <DATA=*SAS-data-set*> HPERCENT=*number*;

where *number* is the percent of the vertical or the horizontal space given to each plot. You can substitute the aliases VPCT= and HPCT= for these options.

To fit two plots on a page, one beneath the other, as in Figure 28.1 on page 472, use VPERCENT=50; to fit three plots, use VPERCENT=33; and so on. To fit two plots on a page, side by side, use HPERCENT=50; to fit three plots, as in Figure 28.2 on page 472, use HPERCENT=33; and so on. Figure 28.3 on page 473 combines both of these options in the same PLOT statement to create a matrix of plots. Because the VPERCENT= option and the HPERCENT= option appear in the PROC PLOT statement, they affect all plots that are created in the PROC PLOT step.

Figure 28.1 Plots Produced with VPERCENT=50

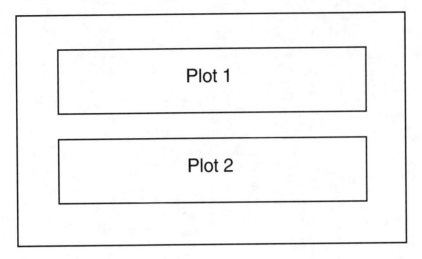

Figure 28.2 Plots Produced with HPERCENT=33

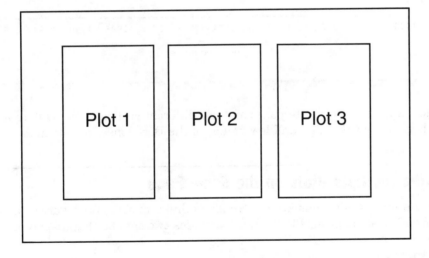

Figure 28.3 Plots Produced with VPERCENT=50 and HPERCENT=33

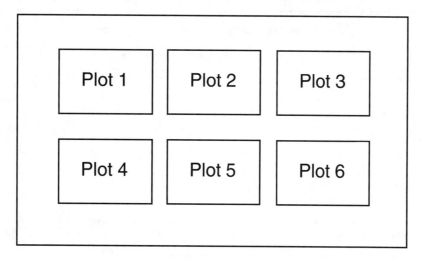

The following program uses the VPERCENT= option to display two plots on the same page so that you can compare the trends for the high and the low Dow Jones values:

```
options pagesize=40 linesize=76 pageno=1 nodate;

proc plot data=highlow vpercent=50;
   plot LogDowHigh*Year='+' LogDowLow*Year='o'
                          / haxis=1954 to 1998 by 4 box;
   label LogDowHigh='Log of High'
         LogDowLow='Log of Low'
         Year='Year Occurred';
   title 'Dow Jones Industrial Average Yearly High';
run;
```

PROC PLOT will use 50% of the vertical space on the page to display each plot. The following output shows the plots:

Output 28.8 Creating Multiple Plots on the Same Page

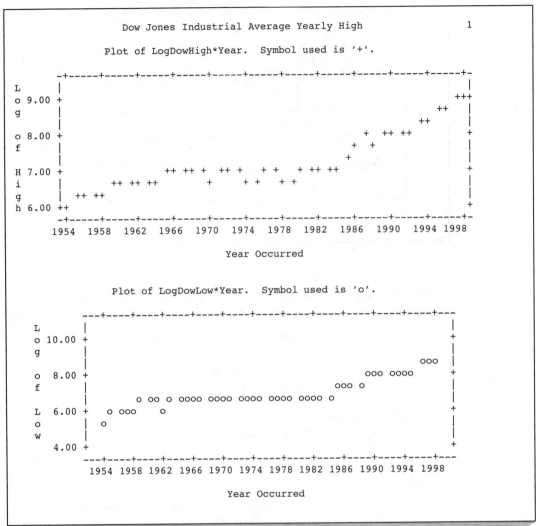

The two plots appear on the same page, one beneath the other.

Plotting Multiple Sets of Variables on the Same Axes

The easiest way to compare trends in multiple sets of measures is to superimpose the plots on one set of axes by using the OVERLAY option in the PLOT statement. The variable names, or variable labels if they exist, from the first plot become the axes labels. Unless you use the HAXIS= option or the VAXIS= option, PROC PLOT automatically scales the axes to best fit all the variables.

The following program uses the OVERLAY option to plot the high and the low Dow Jones Industrial Average values on the same pair of axes:

```
options pagesize=40 linesize=76 pageno=1 nodate;

proc plot data=highlow;
    plot LogDowHigh*Year='+' LogDowLow*Year='o'
                        / haxis=1954 to 1998 by 4
                          overlay box;
    label LogDowHigh='Log of High or Low'
```

```
        Year='Year Occurred';
    title 'Dow Jones Industrial Average';
  run;
```

A new label for the variable LogDowHigh is specified because PROC PLOT uses only this variable to label the vertical axis.

The following output shows the plot:

Output 28.9 Overlaying Two Plots

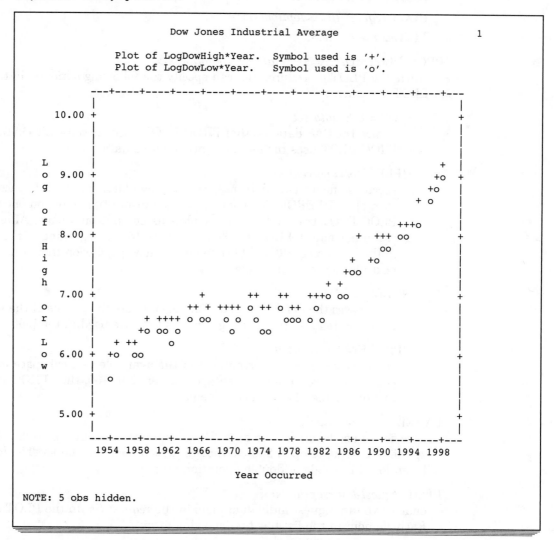

The linear trends in the high and low Dow Jones values over the years from 1954 to 1998 are easily noticed.

Note: When the SAS system option OVP is in effect and overprinting is allowed, the plots are superimposed; otherwise, when NOOVP is in effect, PROC PLOT uses the plotting symbol from the first plot to represent points that appear in more than one plot. In such a case, the output includes a message telling you how many observations are hidden. △

Review of SAS Tools

PROC PLOT Statements

PROC PLOT <DATA=*SAS-data-set*> <*options*>;

LABEL *variable='label'*;

PLOT *request-list* <*/option(s)*>;

TITLE<*n*> <*'title'*>;

PROC PLOT <DATA=*SAS-data-set*> <*option(s)*> ;
  starts the PLOT procedure. You can specify the following *option(s)* in the PROC
  PLOT statement:

  DATA=*SAS-data-set*
    names the SAS data set that PROC PLOT uses. If you omit DATA=, then
    PROC PLOT uses the most recently created data set.

  HPERCENT=*percent(s)*
    specifies one or more percentages of the available horizontal space to use for
    each plot. HPERCENT= enables you to put multiple plots on one page.
    PROC PLOT tries to fit as many plots as possible on a page. After using each
    of the percent(s), PROC PLOT cycles back to the beginning of the list. A zero
    in the list forces PROC PLOT to go to a new page even though it could fit the
    next plot on the same page.

  NOLEGEND
    suppresses the default legend. The legend lists the names of the variables
    being plotted and the plotting symbols that are used in the plot.

  VPERCENT=*percent(s)*
    specifies one or more percentages of the available vertical space to use for
    each plot. If you use a percentage greater than 100, then PROC PLOT prints
    sections of the plot on successive pages.

LABEL *variable='label'*;
  specifies to use labels for the axes. *Variable* names the variable to label and *label*
  specifies a string of up to 256 characters, which includes blanks. The *label* must
  be enclosed in single or double quotation marks.

PLOT *request-list* <*/option(s)*>;
  enables you to request individual plots in the *request-list* in the PLOT statement.
  Each element in the list has the following form:

  *vertical*horizontal*<='symbol'>

  where *vertical* and *horizontal* are the names of the variables that appear on the
  axes and *symbol* is the character to use for all points on the plot.
  You can request any number of plot statements in one PROC PLOT step. A list
  of options pertains to a single plot statement.

  BOX
    draws a box around the entire plot, rather than only on the left side and
    bottom.

  HAXIS=<*tick-value-list*>
    specifies the tick mark values for the horizontal axis. The *tick-value-list*
    consists of a list of values to use for tick marks.

OVERLAY
> superimposes all of the plots that are requested in the PLOT statement on one set of axes. The variable names, or variable labels if they exist, from the first plot are used to label the axes. Unless you use the HAXIS= or the VAXIS= option, PROC PLOT automatically scales the axes in the way that best fits all the variables.

VAXIS=*<tick-value-list>*
> specifies tick mark values for the vertical axis. The *tick-value-list* consists of a list of values to use for tick marks.

TITLE*<n>* *<'title'>*;
> specifies a title. The argument *n* is a number from 1 to 10 that immediately follows the word TITLE, with no intervening blank, and specifies the level of the TITLE. The text of each *title* must be enclosed in single or double quotation marks. The maximum title length that is allowed depends on your operating environment and the value of the LINESIZE= system option. Refer to the SAS documentation for your operating environment for more information.

Learning More

PROC CHART and PROC UNIVARIATE
> When you are preparing graphics presentations, some data lends itself to charts, while other data is better suited for plots. For a discussion about how to make a variety of charts, see Chapter 29, "Producing Charts to Summarize Variables," on page 479.

PROC PLOT
> In addition to the features that are described in this chapter, you can also use PROC PLOT to create contour plots, to draw a reference line at a particular value on a plot, and to change the characters that are used to draw the borders of the plot. For complete documentation, see the *SAS Procedures Guide*.

SAS functions
> SAS provides a wide array of numeric functions that include arithmetic and algebraic expressions, trigonometric and hyperbolic expressions, probability distributions, simple statistics, and random number generation. For complete documentation, see *SAS Language Reference: Dictionary*.

CHAPTER

29

Producing Charts to Summarize Variables

Introduction

Purpose

Charts, like plots, provide a technique to summarize data graphically. You can use a chart to show the values of a single variable or several variables. A bar chart also enables you to graphically examine the distribution of the values of a variable.

In this chapter, you will learn how to create

□ vertical bar charts

□ horizontal bar charts

□ pie charts

□ block charts

□ high-resolution histograms and comparative histograms.

The examples range in complexity from simple frequency bar charts to more complex charts that group variables and include summary statistics.

Prerequisites

To understand the examples in this chapter, you should be familiar with the following features and concepts:

□ the LABEL statement

□ the TITLE statement

□ SAS system options

□ creating and assigning SAS formats.

Understanding the Charting Tools

Base SAS software provides two procedures that produce charts:

□ PROC CHART

□ PROC UNIVARIATE.

PROC CHART produces a variety of charts for character or numeric variables. The charts include vertical and horizontal bar charts, block charts, pie charts, and star charts. These types of charts graphically display the values of a variable or a statistic that are associated with those values. PROC UNIVARIATE produces histograms for continuous numeric variables that enable you to visualize the distribution of your data.

PROC CHART is a useful tool to visualize data quickly. However, you can use PROC GCHART* to produce high-resolution, publication-quality bar charts that include color and various fonts when your site licenses SAS/GRAPH software. You can use PROC UNIVARIATE to customize the histograms by adding tables with summary statistics directly on the graphical display. PROC UNIVARIATE also enables you to overlay the histogram with fitted density curves or kernel density estimates so that you can examine the underlying distribution of your data.

Input File and SAS Data Set for Examples

The examples in this chapter use one input file** and one SAS data set. The input file contains the enrollment and exam grades for an introductory chemistry course. The 50 students enrolled in the course attend several lectures, and a discussion section one day a week. The input file has the following structure:

```
Abdallah      F Mon  46 Anderson    M Wed  75
Aziz          F Wed  67 Bayer       M Wed  77
Bhatt         M Fri  79 Blair       F Fri  70
Bledsoe       F Mon  63 Boone       M Wed  58
Burke         F Mon  63 Chung       M Wed  85
Cohen         F Fri  89 Drew        F Mon  49
Dubos         M Mon  41 Elliott     F Wed  85
...more data lines...
Simonson      M Wed  62 Smith N     M Wed  71
Smith R       M Mon  79 Sullivan    M Fri  77
Swift         M Wed  63 Wolfson     F Fri  79
Wong          F Fri  89 Zabriski    M Fri  89
```

The input file contains the following values from left to right:
- the student's last name (and first initial if necessary)
- the student's gender (F or M)
- the day of the week for the student's discussion section (Mon, Wed, or Fri)
- the student's first exam grade.

The following program creates the GRADES data set that this chapter uses:

```
options pagesize=60 linesize=80 pageno=1 nodate;

data grades;
    infile 'your-input-file';
    input Name & $14. Gender : $2. Section : $3. ExamGrade1 @@;
run;


proc print data=grades;
    title 'Introductory Chemistry Exam Scores';
run;
```

---

* PROC GCHART and PROC CHART produce identical charts.

** See the "Data Set for Chapters 25, 26, and 27" on page 715 for a complete listing of the input data.

Note: Most output in this chapter uses an OPTIONS statement that specifies PAGESIZE=40 and LINESIZE=80. Other examples use an OPTIONS statement with a different line size or page size to make a chart more readable. When the PAGESIZE= and LINESIZE= options are set, they remain in effect until you reset the options with another OPTIONS statement, or you end the SAS session. △

Output 29.1   A Listing of the GRADES Data Set

```
                    Introductory Chemistry Exam Scores                      1

                                                  Exam
          Obs     Name        Gender    Section   Grade1

           1     Abdallah       F        Mon        46
           2     Anderson       M        Wed        75
           3     Aziz           F        Wed        67
           4     Bayer          M        Wed        77
           5     Bhatt          M        Fri        79
           6     Blair          F        Fri        70
           7     Bledsoe        F        Mon        63
           8     Boone          M        Wed        58
           9     Burke          F        Mon        63
          10     Chung          M        Wed        85
          11     Cohen          F        Fri        89
          12     Drew           F        Mon        49
          13     Dubos          M        Mon        41
          14     Elliott        F        Wed        85
          15     Farmer         F        Wed        58
          16     Franklin       F        Wed        59
          17     Freeman        F        Mon        79
          18     Friedman       M        Mon        58
          19     Gabriel        M        Fri        75
          20     Garcia         M        Mon        79
          21     Harding        M        Mon        49
          22     Hazelton       M        Mon        55
          23     Hinton         M        Fri        85
          24     Hung           F        Fri        98
          25     Jacob          F        Wed        64
          26     Janeway        F        Wed        51
          27     Jones          F        Mon        39
          28     Jorgensen      M        Mon        63
          29     Judson         F        Fri        89
          30     Kuhn           F        Mon        89
          31     LeBlanc        F        Fri        70
          32     Lee            M        Fri        48
          33     Litowski       M        Fri        85
          34     Malloy         M        Wed        79
          35     Meyer          F        Fri        85
          36     Nichols        M        Mon        58
          37     Oliver         F        Mon        41
          38     Park           F        Mon        77
          39     Patel          M        Wed        73
          40     Randleman      F        Wed        46
          41     Robinson       M        Fri        64
          42     Shien          M        Wed        55
          43     Simonson       M        Wed        62
          44     Smith N        M        Wed        71
          45     Smith R        M        Mon        79
          46     Sullivan       M        Fri        77
          47     Swift          M        Wed        63
          48     Wolfson        F        Fri        79
          49     Wong           F        Fri        89
          50     Zabriski       M        Fri        89
```

You can create bar charts with this data set to

□ examine the distribution of grades

□ determine a letter grade for each student

□ compare the number of students in each section

□ compare the number of males and females in each section

□ compare the performance of the students in different sections.

Charting Frequencies with the CHART Procedure

Types of Frequency Charts

By default, PROC CHART creates a frequency chart in which each bar, section, or block in the chart represents a range of values. By default, PROC CHART selects ranges based on the values of the chart variable. At the center of each range is a *midpoint*. A midpoint does not always correspond to an actual value of the chart variable. The size of each bar, block, or section represents the number of observations that fall in that range.

PROC CHART makes several different types of charts:

vertical and horizontal bar charts
  display the magnitude of data with the length or height of bars.

block charts
  display the relative magnitude of data with blocks of varying size.

pie charts
  display data as wedge-shaped sections of a circle that represent the relative contribution of each section to the whole circle.

star charts
  display data as bars that radiate from a center point, like spokes in a wheel.

The shape of each type of chart emphasizes a certain aspect of the data. The chart that you choose depends on the nature of your data and the aspect that you want to emphasize.

Creating Vertical Bar Charts

Understanding Vertical Bar Charts

A vertical bar chart emphasizes individual ranges. The horizontal, or midpoint, axis shows the values of the variable divided into ranges. By default, the vertical axis shows the frequency of values for a given range. The differences in bar heights enables you to quickly determine which ranges contain many observations and which contain few observations.

The VBAR statement in a PROC CHART step produces vertical bar charts. If you use the VBAR statement without any options, then PROC CHART automatically

□ scales the vertical axis

□ determines the bar width

□ selects the spacing between bars

□ labels the axes.

For continuous numeric data, PROC CHART determines the number of bars and the midpoint for each bar from the minimum and maximum value of the chart variable. For character variables or discrete numeric variables, PROC CHART creates a bar for each value of the chart variable. However, you can change how PROC CHART determines the axes by using options.

Note: If the number of characters per line (LINESIZE=) is not sufficient to display vertical bars, then PROC CHART automatically produces a horizontal bar chart. △

The Program

The following program uses the VBAR statement to create a vertical bar chart of frequencies for the numeric variable ExamGrade1:

```
options pagesize=40 linesize=80 pageno=1 nodate;

proc chart data=grades;
   vbar ExamGrade1;
   title 'Grades for First Chemistry Exam';
run;
```

The following output shows the bar chart:

Output 29.2 Using a Vertical Bar Chart to Show Frequencies

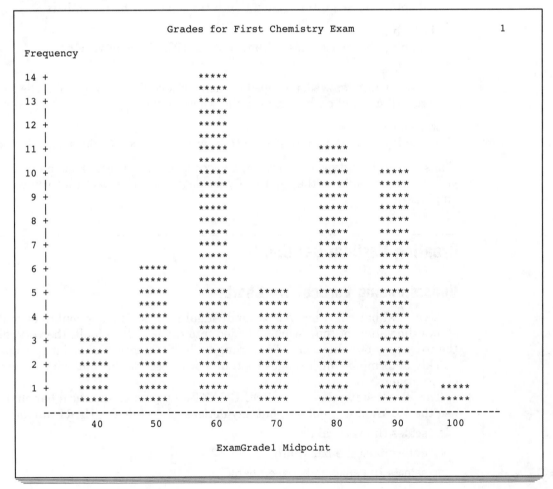

The midpoint axis for the above chart ranges from 40 to 100 and is incremented in intervals of 10. The following table shows the values and frequency of each bar:

Range	Midpoint	Frequency
35 to 44	40	3
45 to 54	50	6
55 to 64	60	14
65 to 74	70	5
75 to 84	80	11
85 to 94	90	10
95 to 104	10	1

Note: Because PROC CHART selects the size of the ranges and the location of their midpoints based on all values of the numeric variable, the highest and lowest ranges can extend beyond the values in the data. In this example the lowest grade is 39 while the lowest range extends from 35 to 44. Similarly, the highest grade is 98 while the highest range extends from 95 to 104. △

Creating a Horizontal Bar Chart

Understanding Horizontal Bar Charts

A horizontal bar chart has essentially the same characteristics as a vertical bar chart. Both charts emphasize individual ranges. However, a horizontal bar chart rotates the bars so that the horizontal axis shows frequency and the vertical axis shows the values of the chart variable. To the right of the horizontal bars, PROC CHART displays a table of statistics that summarizes the data.

The HBAR statement in a PROC CHART step produces horizontal bar charts. By default, the table of statistics includes frequency, cumulative frequency, percentage, and cumulative percentage. You can request specific statistics so that the table contains only these statistics and the frequency.

Understanding HBAR Statistics

The default horizontal bar chart uses less space than charts of other shapes. PROC CHART takes advantage of the small size of horizontal bar charts and displays statistics to the right of the chart. The statistics include

Frequency
  is the number of observations in a given range.

Cumulative Frequency
  is the number of observations in all ranges up to and including a given range. The cumulative frequency for the last range is equal to the number of observations in the data set.

Percent
  is the percentage of observations in a given range.

Cumulative Percent
  is the percentage of observations in all ranges up to and including a given range.
  The cumulative percentage for the last range is always 100.

Various options enable you to control the statistics that appear in the table. You can select the statistics by using the following options: FREQ, CFREQ, PERCENT, and CPERCENT. To suppress the table of statistics, use the NOSTAT option.

The Programs

The following program uses the HBAR statement to create a horizontal bar chart of the frequency for the variable ExamGrade1:

```
options pagesize=40 linesize=80 pageno=1 nodate;

proc chart data=grades;
   hbar Examgrade1;
   title 'Grades for First Chemistry Exam';
run;
```

The following output shows the bar chart:

Output 29.3   Using a Horizontal Bar Chart to Show Frequencies

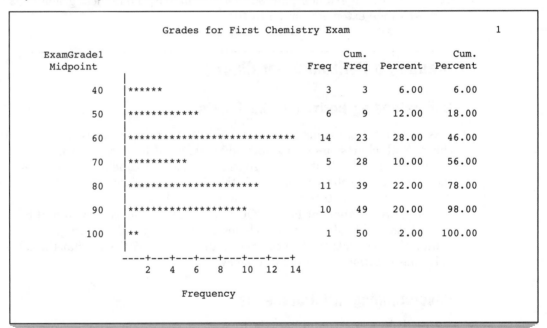

The cumulative percent shows that the median grade for the exam (the grade that 50% of observations lie above and 50% below) lies within the midpoint of 70.

The next example produces the same horizontal bar chart as above, but the program uses the NOSTAT option to eliminate the table of statistics.

```
options pagesize=40 linesize=80 pageno=1 nodate;

proc chart data=grades;
   hbar Examgrade1 / nostat;
   title 'Grades for First Chemistry Exam';
run;
```

The following output shows the bar chart:

Output 29.4 Removing Statistics from a Horizontal Bar Chart

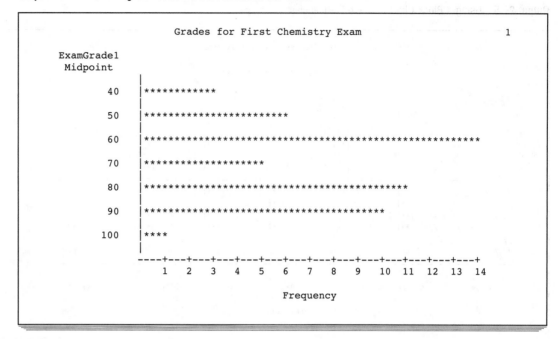

Creating Block Charts

Understanding Block Charts

A block chart displays the relative magnitude of data by using blocks of varying height. Each block in a square represents a category of data. A block chart is similar to a vertical bar chart. It uses a more sophisticated presentation of the data to emphasize the individual ranges. However, a block chart is less precise than a bar chart because the maximum height of a block is 10 lines.

The BLOCK statement in a PROC CHART step produces a block chart. You can also use the BLOCK statement to create three-dimensional frequency charts. For an example, see "Creating a Three-Dimensional Chart" on page 497. If you create block charts with a large number of charted values, then you might have to adjust the SAS system options LINESIZE= and PAGESIZE= so that the block chart fits on one page.

Note: If the line size or page size is not sufficient to display all the bars, then PROC CHART automatically produces a horizontal bar chart. △

The Program

The following program uses the BLOCK statement to create a block frequency chart for the numeric variable ExamGrade1:

```
options linesize=120 pagesize=40 pageno=1 nodate;

proc chart data=grades;
   block Examgrade1;
   title 'Grades for First Chemistry Exam';
run;
```

The OPTIONS statement increases the line size to 120.

The following output shows the block chart:

Output 29.5   Using a Block Chart to Show Frequencies

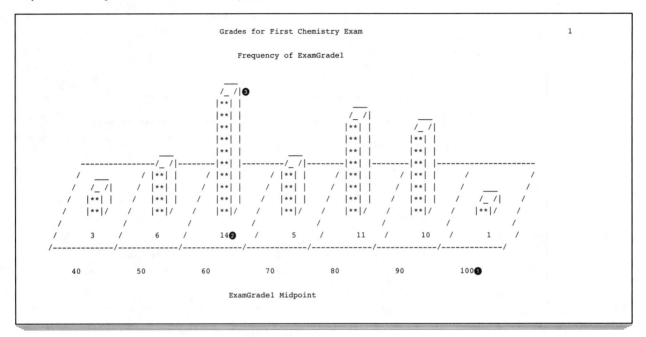

The chart shows the effects of using the BLOCK statement.

❶ PROC CHART uses the same midpoints for both the bar chart and block chart. The midpoints appear beneath the chart.

❷ The number of observations represented by each block appear beneath the block.

❸ The height of a block is proportional to the number of observations in a block.

Creating Pie Charts

Understanding Pie Charts

A pie chart emphasizes the relative contribution of parts (a range of values) to the whole. Graphing the distribution of grades as a pie chart shows you the size of each range relative to the others just as the vertical bar chart does. However, the pie chart also enables you to visually compare the number of grades in a range to the total number of grades.

The PIE statement in a PROC CHART step produces a pie chart. PROC CHART determines the number of sections for the pie chart the same way it determines the number of bars for a vertical chart, with one exception: if any slices of the pie account for fewer than three print positions, then PROC CHART groups them into a category called "Other."

PROC CHART displays the values of the midpoints around the perimeter of the pie chart. Inside each section of the chart, PROC CHART displays the number of observations in the range and the percentage of observations that the number represents.

The SAS system options LINESIZE= and PAGESIZE= determine the size of the pie. If your printer does not print 6 lines per inch and 10 columns per inch, then the pie looks elliptical. To make a circular pie chart, you must use the LPI= option in the

PROC CHART statement. For more information, see the CHART procedure in the *SAS Procedures Guide*.

The Program

The following program uses the PIE statement to create a pie chart of frequencies for the numeric variable ExamGrade1:

```
options pagesize=40 linesize=80 pageno=1 nodate;

proc chart data=grades;
   pie ExamGrade1;
      title 'Grades for First Chemistry Exam';
run;
```

The following output shows the pie chart:

Output 29.6 Using a Pie Chart to Show Frequencies

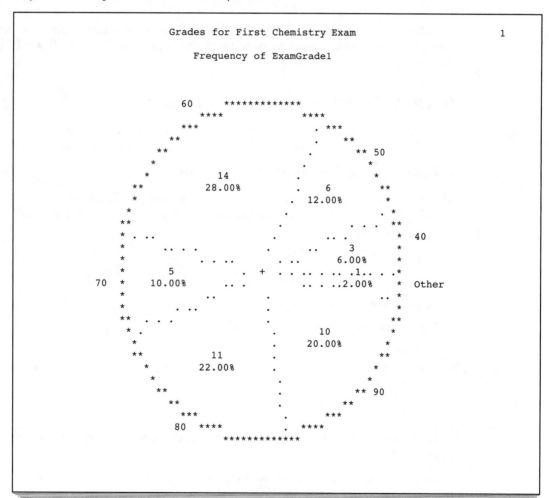

In this pie chart the **Other** section represents the one grade in the range with a midpoint of 100. The size of a section corresponds to the number of observations that fall in its range.

Customizing Frequency Charts

Changing the Number of Ranges

You can change the appearance of the charts in the following ways:

To specify...	Use this option
midpoints that define the range of values that each bar, block, or section represents	MIDPOINTS= option
the number of bars on the chart and let PROC CHART compute the midpoints	LEVELS= option
a variable that contains discrete numeric values. PROC CHART will produce a bar chart with a bar for each distinct value	DISCRETE option

Note: Most examples in this section use vertical bar charts. However, unless documented otherwise, you can use any of the options in the PIE, BLOCK, or HBAR statements. △

Specifying Midpoints for a Numeric Variable

You can specify midpoints for a continuous numeric variable by using the MIDPOINTS= option in the VBAR statement. The form of this option is

VBAR *variable* / MIDPOINTS=*midpoints-list*;

where *midpoints-list* is a list of the numbers to use as midpoints.

For example, to specify the traditional grading ranges with midpoints from 55 to 95, use the following option:

```
midpoints=55 65 75 85 95
```

Or, you can abbreviate the list of midpoints:

```
midpoints=55 to 95 by 10
```

The corresponding ranges are as follows:

```
50 to 59
60 to 69
70 to 79
80 to 89
90 to 99
```

The following program uses the MIDPOINTS= option to create a bar chart for ExamGrade1:

```
options pagesize=40 linesize=80 pageno=1 nodate;

proc chart data=grades;
   vbar Examgrade1 / midpoints=55 to 95 by 10;
   title 'Assigning Grades for First Chemistry Exam';
run;
```

The MIDPOINTS= option forces PROC CHART to center the five bars around the traditional midpoints for exam grades.

The following output shows the bar chart:

Output 29.7 Specifying the Midpoints for a Vertical Bar Chart

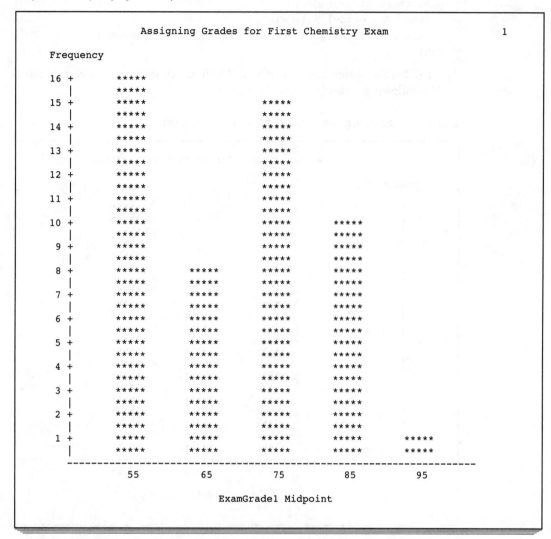

A traditional method to assign grades assumes the data is normally distributed. However, the bars do not appear as a normal (bell-shaped) curve. If grades are assigned based on these midpoints and the traditional pass/fail boundary of 60, then a substantial portion of the class will fail the exam because more observations fall in the bar around the midpoint of 55 than in any other bar.

Specifying the Number of Midpoints in a Chart

You can specify the number of midpoints in the chart rather than the values of the midpoints by using the LEVELS= option. The procedure selects the midpoints.

The form of the option is

VBAR *variable* / LEVELS=*number-of-midpoints*;

where *number-of-midpoints* specifies the number of midpoints.

The following program uses the LEVELS= option to create a bar chart with five bars:*

```
options pagesize=40 linesize=80 pageno=1 nodate;

proc chart data=grades;
    vbar Examgrade1 / levels=5;
    title 'Assigning Grades for First Chemistry Exam';
run;
```

The LEVELS= option forces PROC CHART to compute only five midpoints.

The following output shows the bar chart:

Output 29.8 Specifying Five Midpoints for a Vertical Bar Chart

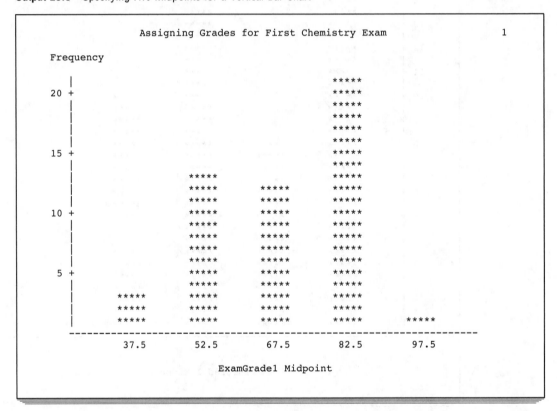

Assigning grades for these midpoints results in three students with exam grades in the lowest range.

Charting Every Value

By default, PROC CHART assumes that all numeric variables are continuous and automatically chooses intervals for them unless you use MIDPOINTS= or LEVELS=. You can specify that a numeric variable is discrete rather than continuous by using the DISCRETE option. PROC CHART will create a frequency chart with bars for each distinct value of the discrete numeric variable.

The following program uses the DISCRETE option to create a bar chart with a bar for each value of ExamGrade1:

---

* You can use SAS to normalize the data before the chart is created.

```
options pagesize=40 linesize=80 pageno=1 nodate;

proc chart data=grades;
   vbar Examgrade1 / discrete;
   title 'Grades for First Chemistry Exam';
run;
```

The following output shows the bar chart:

Output 29.9 Specifying a Bar for Each Exam Grade

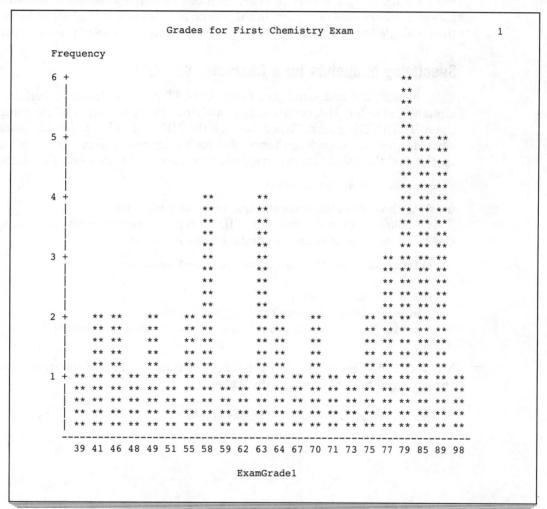

The chart shows that in most cases only one or two students earned a given grade. However, clusters of three or more students earned grades of 58, 63, 77, 79, 85, and 89. The mode for this exam (most frequently earned exam grade) is 79.

Note: PROC CHART does not proportionally space the values of a discrete numeric variable on the horizontal axis. △

Charting the Frequency of a Character Variable

You can create charts of a character variable as well as a numeric variable. For instance, to compare enrollment among sections, PROC CHART creates a chart that shows the number of students in each section.

Creating a frequency chart of a character variable is the same as creating a frequency chart of a numeric variable. However, the main difference between charting a numeric variable and charting a character variable is how PROC CHART selects the midpoints. By default, PROC CHART uses each value of a character variable as a midpoint, as if the DISCRETE option were in effect. You can limit the selection of midpoints to a subset of the variable's values, but if you do not define a format for the chart variable, then a single bar, block, or section represents a single value of the variable.

Specifying Midpoints for a Character Variable

By default, the midpoints that PROC CHART uses for character variables are in alphabetical order. However, you can easily rearrange the order of the midpoints with the MIDPOINTS= option. When you use the MIDPOINTS= option for character variables, you must enclose the value of each midpoint in single or double quotation marks, and the values must correspond to values in the data set. For example,

```
midpoints='Mon' 'Wed' 'Fri'
```

uses the three days the class sections meet as midpoints.

The following program uses the MIDPOINTS= option to create a bar chart that shows the number of students enrolled in each section:

```
options pagesize=40 linesize=80 pageno=1 nodate;

proc chart data=grades;
    vbar Section / midpoints='Mon' 'Wed' 'Fri';
    title 'Enrollment for an Introductory Chemistry Course';
run;
```

The MIDPOINTS= option alters the chart so that the days of the week appear in chronological rather than alphabetical order.

The following output shows the bar chart:

Output 29.10 Ordering Character Midpoints Chronologically

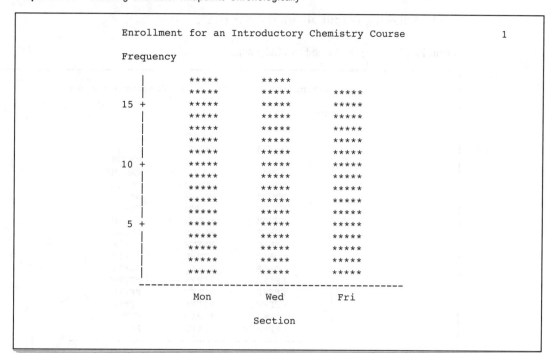

The chart shows that the Monday and Wednesday sections have the same number of students; the Friday section has one fewer student.

Creating Subgroups within a Range

You can show how a subgroup contributes to each bar or block by using the SUBGROUP= option in the BLOCK statement, HBAR statement, or VBAR statement. For example, you can use the SUBGROUP= option to explore patterns within a population (gender differences).

The SUBGROUP= option defines a variable called the *subgroup variable*. PROC CHART uses the first character of each value to fill in the portion of the bar or block that corresponds to that value, unless more than one value begins with the same first character. In that case, PROC CHART uses the letters A, B, C, and so on to fill in the bars or blocks.

If you assign a format to the variable, then PROC CHART uses the first character of the formatted value. The characters that PROC CHART uses in the chart and the values that they represent are shown in a legend at the bottom of the chart.

PROC CHART orders the subgroup symbols as A through Z, and as 0 through 9, with the characters in ascending order. PROC CHART calculates the height of a bar or block for each subgroup individually and rounds the percentage of the total bar up or down. So the total height of the bar might be greater or less than the height of the same bar without the SUBGROUP= option.

The following program uses GENDER as the subgroup variable to show how many members in each section are male and female:

```
options pagesize=40 linesize=80 pageno=1 nodate;

proc chart data=grades;
   vbar Section / midpoints='Mon' 'Wed' 'Fri'
                  subgroup=Gender;
      title 'Enrollment for an Introductory Chemistry Course';
```

```
run;
```

The following output shows the bar chart:

Output 29.11 Using Gender to Form Subgroups

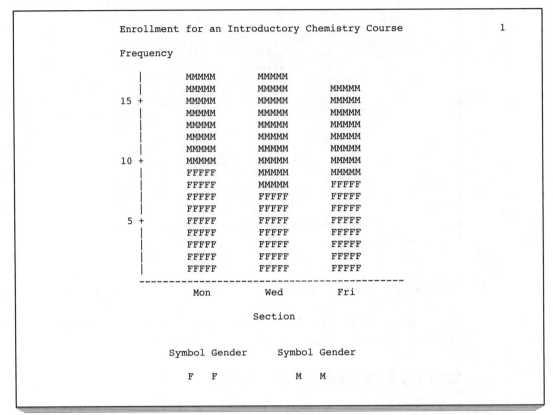

PROC CHART fills each bar in the chart with the characters that represent the value of the variable GENDER. The portion of the bar that is filled with Fs represents the number of observations that correspond to females; the portion that is filled with Ms represents the number of observations that correspond to males. Because the value of Gender contains a single character (F or M), the symbol that PROC CHART uses as the fill character is identical to the value of the variable.

Charting Mean Values

PROC CHART enables you to specify what the bars or sections in the chart represent. By default, each bar, block, or section represents the frequency of the chart variable. You can also identify a variable whose values determine the sizes of the bars, blocks, or sections in the chart.

You define a variable called the *sumvar variable* by using the SUMVAR= option. With the SUMVAR= option, you can also use the TYPE= option to specify whether the sum of the Sumvar variable or the mean of the Sumvar variable determines the size of the bars or sections. The available types are

SUM

> sums the values of the Sumvar variable in each range. Then PROC CHART uses the sums to determine the size of each bar, block, or section. SUM is the default type.

MEAN

> determines the mean value of the Sumvar variable in each range. Then PROC CHART uses the means to determine the size of each bar, block, or section.

The following program creates a bar chart grouped by gender to compare the mean value of all grades in each section:

```
options pagesize=40 linesize=80 pageno=1 nodate;


proc chart data=grades;
    vbar Section / midpoints='Mon' 'Wed' 'Fri' group=Gender
                   sumvar=Examgrade1 type=mean;
        title 'Mean Exam Grade for Introductory Chemistry Sections';
    run;
```

The SUMVAR= option specifies that the values of ExamGrade1 determine the size of the bars. The TYPE=MEAN option specifies to compare the mean grade for each group. The following output shows the bar chart:

Output 29.12   Using the SUMVAR= Option to Compare Mean Values

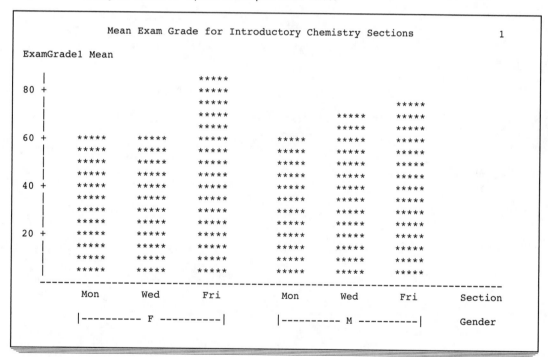

The chart shows that the females in the Friday section achieved the highest mean grade, followed by the males in the same section.

Creating a Three-Dimensional Chart

Complicated relationships such as the ones charted with the GROUP= option might be easier to understand if you present them as three-dimensional block charts. The following program uses the BLOCK statement to create a block chart for the numeric variable ExamGrade1:

```
options linesize=120 pagesize=40 pageno=1 nodate;
proc chart data=grades;
```

```
block Section / midpoints='Mon' 'Wed' 'Fri'
                sumvar=Examgrade1 type=mean
                group=Gender;
format Examgrade1 4.1;
title 'Mean Exam Grade for Introductory Chemistry Sections';
run;
```

The FORMAT statement specifies the number of decimals that PROC CHART uses to report the mean value of ExamGrade1 beneath each block.

Note: If the line size or page size is not sufficient to display all the bars, then PROC CHART produces a horizontal bar chart. △

The following output shows the block chart:

Output 29.13   Using a Block Chart to Compare Group Means

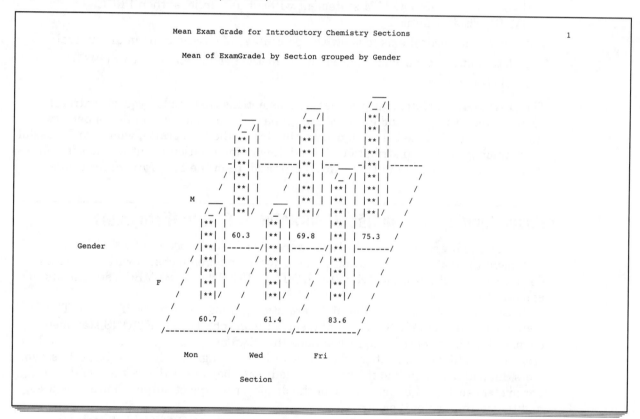

The value that is shown beneath each block is the mean of ExamGrade1 for that combination of Section and Gender. You can easily see that both females and males in the Friday section earned higher grades than their counterparts in the other sections.

Creating High-Resolution Histograms

Understanding How to Use the HISTOGRAM Statement

A histogram is similar to a vertical bar chart. This type of bar chart emphasizes the individual ranges of continuous numeric variables and enables you to examine the distribution of your data.

The HISTOGRAM statement in a PROC UNIVARIATE step produces histograms and comparative histograms. PROC UNIVARIATE creates a histogram by dividing the data into intervals of equal length, counting the number of observations in each interval, and plotting the counts as vertical bars that are centered around the midpoint of each interval.

If you use the HISTOGRAM statement without any options, then PROC UNIVARIATE automatically

- □ scales the vertical axis to show the percentage of observations in an interval
- □ determines the bar width based on the method of Terrell and Scott (1985)
- □ labels the axes.

The HISTOGRAM statement provides various options that enable you to control the layout of the histogram and enhance the graph. You can also fit families of density curves and superimpose kernel density estimates on the histograms, which can be useful in examining the data distribution. For additional information about the density curves that SAS computes, see the UNIVARIATE procedure in the *SAS Procedures Guide*.

Understanding How to Use SAS/GRAPH to Create Histograms

If your site licenses SAS/GRAPH software, then you can use the HISTOGRAM statement to create high-resolution graphs. When you create charts with a graphics device, you can also use the AXIS, LEGEND, PATTERN, and SYMBOL statements to enhance your plots.

To control the appearance of a high-resolution graph, you can specify a GOPTIONS statement before the PROC step that creates the graph. The GOPTIONS statement changes the values of the graphics options that SAS uses when graphics output is created. Graphics options affect the characteristics of a graph, such as size, colors, type fonts, fill patterns, and line thickness. In addition, they affect the settings of device parameters such as the appearance of the display, the type of output that is produced, and the destination of the output.

Most of the examples in this chapter use the following GOPTIONS statement:

```
goptions reset=global
         gunit=pct
         hsize= 5.625 in
         vsize= 3.5 in
         htitle=4
         htext=3
         vorigin=0 in
         horigin= 0 in
         cback=white border
         ctext=black
         colors=(black blue green red yellow)
         ftext=swiss
         lfactor=3;
```

For additional information about how to modify the appearance of your graphics output, see *SAS/GRAPH Software: Reference, Volumes 1 and 2*.

Creating a Simple Histogram

The following program uses the HISTOGRAM statement to create a histogram for the numeric variable ExamGrade1:

```
proc univariate data=grades noprint;
   histogram ExamGrade1;
   title 'Grades for First Chemistry Exam';
run;
```

The NOPRINT option suppresses the tables of statistics that the PROC UNIVARIATE statement creates.

The following figure shows the histogram:

Figure 29.1 Using a Histogram to Show Percentages

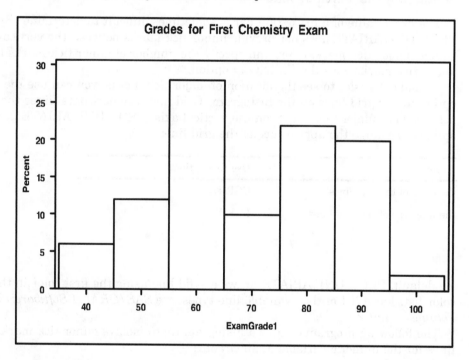

The midpoint axis for the above histogram goes from 40 to 100 and is incremented in intervals of 10. The following table shows the values:

Interval	Midpoint
35 to 44	40
45 to 54	50
55 to 64	60
65 to 74	70
75 to 84	80

Interval	Midpoint
85 to 94	90
95 to 104	10

Note: Because PROC UNIVARIATE selects the size of the intervals and the location of their midpoints based on all values of the numeric variable, the highest and lowest intervals can extend beyond the values in the data. In this example the lowest grade is 39 while the lowest interval extends from 35 to 44. Similarly, the highest grade is 98 while the highest interval extends from 95 to 104. △

Changing the Axes of a Histogram

Enhancing the Vertical Axis

The exact value of a histogram bar is sometimes difficult to determine. By default, PROC UNIVARIATE does not provide minor tick marks between the vertical axis values (major tick marks). You can specify the number of minor tick marks between major tick marks with the VMINOR= option.

To make it easier to see the location of major tick marks, you can use the GRID option to add grid lines on the histogram. Grid lines are horizontal lines that are positioned at major tick marks on the vertical axis. PROC UNIVARIATE provides two options to change the appearance of the grid line:

To set	Use this option
the color of the grid lines	CGRID=
the line type of the grid lines	LGRID=

By default, PROC UNIVARIATE draws a solid line using the first color in the device color list. For a list of the available line types, see *SAS/GRAPH Software: Reference, Volumes 1 and 2.*

The following program creates a histogram that displays minor tick marks and grid lines for the numeric variable ExamGrade1:

```
proc univariate data=grades noprint;
   histogram Examgrade1 / vminor=4 grid lgrid=34;
   title 'Grades for First Chemistry Exam';
run;
```

Four minor tick marks are inserted between each major tick mark. Narrowly spaced dots are used to draw the grid lines.

The following figure shows the histogram:

Figure 29.2 Specifying Grid Lines for a Histogram

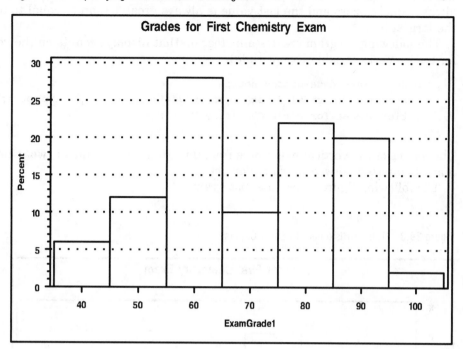

Now, the height of each histogram bar is easily determined from the chart. The following table shows the percentage each interval represents:

Interval	Percent
35 to 44	6
45 to 54	12
55 to 64	28
65 to 74	10
75 to 84	22
85 to 94	20
95 to 104	2

Specifying the Vertical Axis Values

PROC UNIVARIATE enables you to specify what the bars in the histogram represent, and the values of the vertical axis. By default, each bar represents the percentage of observations that fall into the given interval.

The VSCALE= option enables you to specify the following scales for the vertical axis:

- □ COUNT
- □ PERCENT
- □ PROPORTION.

The VAXIS= option enables you to specify evenly spaced tick mark values for the vertical axis. The form of this option is

HISTOGRAM *variable* / VAXIS=*value-list*;

where *value-list* is a list of numbers to use as major tick mark values. The first value is always equal to zero and the last value is always greater than or equal to the height of the largest bar.

The following program creates a histogram that displays counts on the vertical axis for the numeric variable ExamGrade1:

```
proc univariate data=grades noprint;
    histogram Examgrade1 / vscale=count vaxis=0 to 16 by 2 vminor=1;
    title 'Grades for First Chemistry Exam';
run;
```

The values of the vertical axis range from 0 to 16 in increments of two. One minor tick mark is inserted between each major tick mark.

The following figure shows the histogram:

Figure 29.3 Using a Histogram to Show Counts

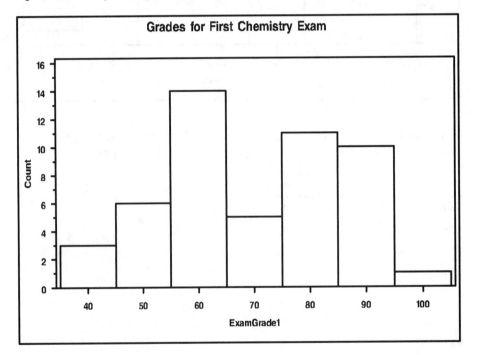

Specifying the Midpoints of a Histogram

You can control the width of the histogram bars by using the MIDPOINTS= option. PROC UNIVARIATE uses the value of the midpoints to determine the width of the histogram bars. The difference between consecutive midpoints is the bar width.

To specify midpoints, use the MIDPOINTS= option in the HISTOGRAM statement. The form of the MIDPOINTS= option is

HISTOGRAM *variable* / MIDPOINTS=*midpoint-list*;

where *midpoint-list* is a list of numbers to use as midpoints. You must use evenly spaced midpoints that are listed in increasing order.

For example, to specify the traditional grading ranges with midpoints from 55 to 95, use the following option:

```
midpoints=55 65 75 85 95
```

Or, you can abbreviate this list of midpoints:

```
midpoints=55 to 95 by 10
```

The following program uses the MIDPOINTS= option to create a histogram for the numeric variable ExamGrade1:

```
proc univariate data=grades noprint;
    histogram Examgrade1 / vscale=count vaxis=0 to 16 by 2 vminor=1
                        midpoints=55 65 75 85 95❶ hoffset=10❷
                        vaxislabel='Frequency'❸;
    title 'Grades for First Chemistry Exam';
run;
```

The following list corresponds to the numbered items in the preceding program:

❶ The MIDPOINTS= option forces PROC UNIVARIATE to center the five bars around the traditional midpoints for exam grades.

❷ The HOFFSET= option uses a 10 percent offset at both ends of the horizontal axis.

❸ The VAXISLABEL= option uses Frequency as the label for the vertical axis. The default label is Count.

The following figure shows the histogram:

Figure 29.4 Specifying Five Midpoints for a Histogram

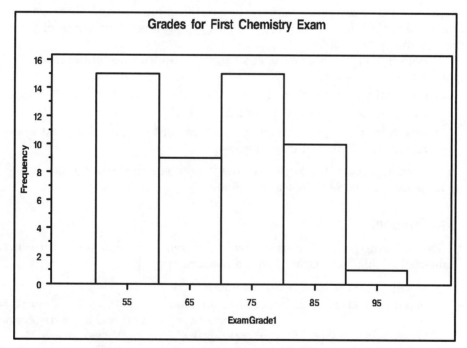

The midpoint axis for the above histogram goes from 55 to 95 and is incremented in intervals of 10. The histogram excludes any exam scores that are below 50.

Displaying Summary Statistics in a Histogram

Understanding How to Use the INSET Statement

PROC UNIVARIATE enables you to add a box or table of summary statistics, called an *inset*, directly in the histogram. Typically, an inset displays statistics that PROC

UNIVARIATE has calculated, but an inset can also display values that you provide in a SAS data set.

To add a table of summary statistics, use the INSET statement. You can use multiple INSET statements in the UNIVARIATE procedure to add more than one table to a histogram. The INSET statements must follow the HISTOGRAM statement that creates the plot that you want augmented. The inset appears in all the graphs that the preceding HISTOGRAM statement produces.

The form of the INSET statement is

INSET<*keyword(s)*> </ *option(s)*>

You specify the keywords for inset statistics (such as N, MIN, MAX, MEAN, and STD) immediately after the word INSET. You can also specify the keyword DATA= followed by the name of a SAS data set to display customized statistics that are stored in a SAS data set. The statistics will appear in the order in which you specify the keywords.

By default, PROC UNIVARIATE uses appropriate labels and appropriate formats to display the statistics in the inset. To customize a label, specify the keyword followed by an equal sign (=) and the desired label in quotation marks. To customize the format, specify a numeric format in parentheses after the keyword. You can assign labels that are up to 24 characters. If you specify both a label and a format for a keyword, then the label must appear before the format. For example,

```
inset n='Sample Size' std='Std Dev' (5.2);
```

requests customized labels for two statistics (sample size and standard deviation). The standard deviation is also assigned a format that has a field width of five and includes two decimal places.

Various options enable you to customize the appearance of the inset. For example, you can

- specify the position of the inset
- specify a heading for the inset table
- specify graphical enhancements, such as background colors, text colors, text height, text font, and drop shadows.

For a complete list of the keywords and the options that you can use in the INSET statement, see the *SAS Procedures Guide*.

The Program

The following program uses the INSET statement to add summary statistics for the numeric variable ExamGrade1 to the histogram:

```
proc univariate data=grades noprint;
    histogram Examgrade1 /vscale=count vaxis=0 to 16 by 2 vminor=1 hoffset=10
                          midpoints=55 65 75 85 95 vaxislabel='Frequency';
    inset n='No. Students' mean='Mean Grade' min='Lowest Grade'❶
          max='Highest Grade' / header='Summary Statistics'❷ position=ne❸
                          format=3.❹;
    title 'Grade Distribution for the First Chemistry Exam';
run;
```

The following list corresponds to the numbered items in the preceding program:

❶ The statistical keywords N, MEAN, MIN, and MAX specify that the number of observations, the mean exam grade, the minimum exam grade, and the maximum exam grade appear in the inset. Each keyword is assigned a customized label to identify the statistic in the inset.

❷ The HEADER= option specifies the heading text that appears at the top of the inset.

❸ The POSITION= option uses a compass point to position the inset. The table will appear at the northeast corner of the histogram.

❹ The FORMAT= option requests a format with a field width of three for all the statistics in the inset.

The following figure shows the histogram:

Figure 29.5 Adding an Inset to a Histogram

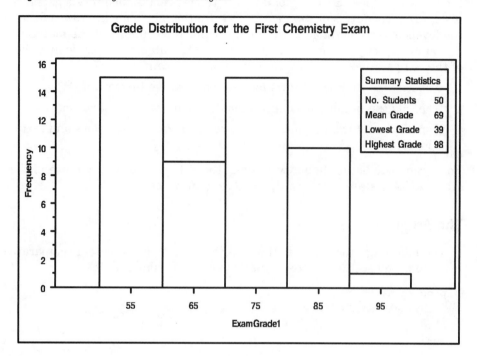

The histogram shows the data distribution. The table of summary statistics in the upper-right corner of the histogram provides information about the sample size, the mean grade, the lowest value, and the highest value.

Creating a Comparative Histogram

Understanding Comparative Histograms

A comparative histogram is a series of component histograms that are arranged as an array or a matrix. PROC UNIVARIATE uses uniform horizontal and vertical axes to display the component histograms. This enables you to use the comparative histogram to visually compare the distribution of a numeric variable across the levels of up to two classification variables.

You use the CLASS statement with a HISTOGRAM statement to create either a one-way or a two-way comparative histogram. The form of the CLASS statement is

CLASS *variable-1<(variable-option(s))> <variable-2<(variable-option(s))>></ options>;*

Class variables can be numeric or character. Class variables can have continuous values, but they typically have a few discrete values that define levels of the variable. You can reduce the number of classification levels by using a FORMAT statement to combine the values of a class variable.

When you specify one class variable, PROC UNIVARIATE displays an array of component histograms (stacked or side-by-side). To create the one-way comparative histogram, PROC UNIVARIATE categorizes the values of the analysis variable by the formatted values (levels) of the class variable. Each classification level generates a separate histogram.

When you specify two class variables, PROC UNIVARIATE displays a matrix of component plots. To create the two-way comparative histogram, PROC UNIVARIATE categorizes the values of the analysis variable by the cross-classified values (levels) of the class variables. Each combination of the cross-classified levels generates a separate histogram. The levels of *class variable-1* are the labels for the rows of the matrix, and the levels of *class variable-2* are the labels for the columns of the matrix.

You can specify options in the HISTOGRAM statement to customize the appearance of the comparative histogram. For example, you can

☐ specify the number of rows for the comparative histogram

☐ specify the number of columns for the comparative histogram

☐ specify graphical enhancements, such as background colors and text colors for the labels.

For a complete list of the keywords and the options that you can use in the HISTOGRAM statement, see the *SAS Procedures Guide*.

The Program

The following program uses the CLASS statement to create a comparative histogram by gender and section for the numeric variable ExamGrade1:

```
proc format;
    value $gendfmt 'M'='Male'
                   'F'='Female'❶;
run;

proc univariate data=grades noprint;
    class Gender❷ Section(order=data)❸;
    histogram Examgrade1 / midpoints=45 to 95 by 10 vscale=count vaxis=0 to 6 by 2
                        vaxislabel='Frequency' turnvlabels❹ nrows=2 ncols=3❺
                        cframe=ligr❻ cframeside=gwh cframetop=gwh cfill=gwh❼;
    inset mean(4.1) n / noframe❽ position=(2,65)❾;
    format Gender $gendfmt.❶;
    title 'Grade Distribution for the First Chemistry Exam';
run;
```

The following list corresponds to the numbered items in the preceding program:

❶ PROC FORMAT creates a user-written format that will label Gender with a character string. The FORMAT statement assigns the format to Gender.

❷ The CLASS statement creates a two-way comparative histogram that uses Gender and Section as the classification variables. PROC UNIVARIATE produces a component histogram for each level (a distinct combination of values) of these variables.

❸ The ORDER= option positions the values of Section according to their order in the input data set. The comparative histogram displays the levels of Section according to the days of the week (Mon, Wed, and Fri). The default order of the levels is determined by sorting the internal values of Section (Fri, Mon, and Wed).

❹ The TURNVLABELS option turns the characters in the vertical axis labels so that they display vertically instead of horizontally.

⑤ The NROWS= option and the NCOLS= option specify a 2 × 3 arrangement for the component histograms.

⑥ The CFRAME= option specifies the color that fills the area of each component histogram that is enclosed by the axes and the frame. The CFRAMESIDE= option and the CFRAMETOP= option specify the color to fill the frame area for the column labels and the row labels that appear down the side and across the top of the comparative histogram. By default, these areas are not filled.

⑦ The CFILL= option specifies the color to fill the bars of each component histogram. By default, the bars are not filled.

⑧ The NOFRAME option suppresses the frame around the inset table.

⑨ The POSITION= option uses axis percentage coordinates to position the inset. The position of the bottom-left corner of the inset is 2% of the way across the horizontal axis and 65% of the way up the vertical axis.

The following figure shows the comparative histogram:

Figure 29.6 Using a Comparative Histogram to Examine Exam Grades by Gender and Section

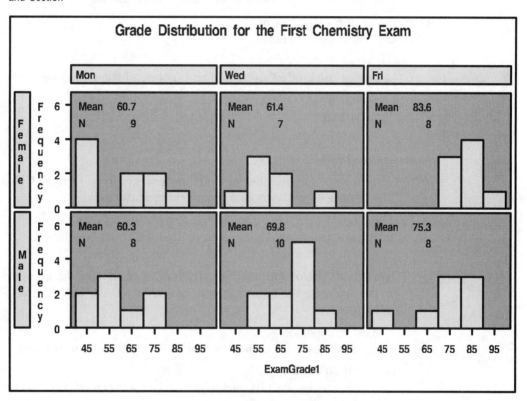

The comparative histogram is a 2 × 3 matrix of component histograms for each combination of Section and Gender. Each component histogram displays a table of statistics that reports the mean of ExamGrade1 and the number of students. You can easily see that both females and males in the Friday section earned higher grades than their counterparts in the other sections.

Review of SAS Tools

PROC CHART Statements

PROC CHART <DATA=*SAS-data-set* > <*options*>;

  chart-type variable(s) <*/options*>;

PROC CHART <DATA=*SAS-data-set*> <*options*> ;
  starts the CHART procedure. You can specify the following *options* in the PROC CHART statement:

    DATA=*SAS-data-set*
      names the SAS data set that PROC CHART uses. If you omit DATA=, then PROC CHART uses the most recently created data set.

    LPI=*value*
      specifies the proportions of PIE and STAR charts.

chart-type variable(s) < */options*>;
  is a chart statement where

    chart-type
      specifies the kind of chart and can be any of the following:

        □ BLOCK

        □ HBAR

        □ PIE

        □ VBAR.

      You can use any number of chart statements in one PROC CHART step. A list of options pertains to a single chart statement.

    variable(s)
      identifies the variables to chart (called the *chart variables*).

    options
      specifies a list of options. Not all types of chart support all options.
      You can use the following options in the VBAR, HBAR, and BLOCK statements:

        GROUP=*variable*
          produces a set of bars or blocks for each value of *variable*.

        SUBGROUP=*variable*
          proportionally fills each block or bar with characters that represent different values of *variable*.

      You can use the following options in the VBAR, HBAR, BLOCK, and PIE statements:

        DISCRETE
          creates a bar, block, or section for every value of the chart variable.

        LEVELS=*number-of-midpoints*
          specifies the *number-of-midpoints*. The procedure selects the midpoints.

        MIDPOINTS=*midpoints-list*
          specifies the values of the midpoints.

SUMVAR=*variable*
> specifies the *variable* to use to determine the size of the bars, blocks, or sections.

TYPE=SUM | MEAN
> specifies the type of chart to create, where

SUM
>> sums the values of the Sumvar variable in each range. Then PROC CHART uses the sums to determine the size of each bar, block, or section.

MEAN
>> determines the mean value of the Sumvar variable in each range. Then PROC CHART uses the means to determine the size of each bar, block, or section.

You can use the following options in the HBAR statement:

NOSTAT
> suppresses the printing of the statistics that accompany the chart by default.

FREQ
> requests frequency statistics.

CFREQ
> requests cumulative frequency statistics.

PERCENT
> requests percentage statistics.

CPERCENT
> requests cumulative percentage statistics.

PROC UNIVARIATE Statements

PROC UNIVARIATE <*option(s)*>;

CLASS *variable-1*<(*variable-option(s)*))>
  <*variable-2*<(*variable-option(s)*))>> </*option(s)*>;

HISTOGRAM <*variable(s)*> </*option(s)*>;

INSET <*keyword(s)* > </*option(s)*>;

PROC UNIVARIATE *option(s)*;
> starts the UNIVARIATE procedure. You can specify the following *options* in the PROC UNIVARIATE statement:

DATA=*SAS-data-set*
> names the SAS data set that PROC UNIVARIATE uses. If you omit DATA=, then PROC UNIVARIATE uses the most recently created data set.

NOPRINT
> suppresses the descriptive statistics that the PROC UNIVARIATE statement creates.

CLASS *variable-1*<(*variable-option(s)*)> <*variable-2*<(*variable-option(s)*)>>
</ *option(s)*>;
> specifies up to two variables whose values determine the classification levels for the component histograms. Variables in a CLASS statement are referred to as *class variables*.
> You can specify the following *option(s)* in the CLASS statement:

ORDER=DATA | FORMATTED | FREQ | INTERNAL
specifies the display order for the class variable values, where

DATA
orders values according to their order in the input data set.

FORMATTED
orders values by their ascending formatted values. This order depends on your operating environment.

FREQ
orders values by descending frequency count so that levels with the most observations are listed first.

INTERNAL
orders values by their unformatted values, which yields the same order as PROC SORT. This order depends on your operating environment.

HISTOGRAM *<variable(s)> </option(s)>;*
creates histograms and comparative histograms using high-resolution graphics for the analysis variables that are specified. If you omit *variable(s)* in the HISTOGRAM statement, then the procedure creates a histogram for each variable that you list in the VAR statement, or for each numeric variable in the DATA= data set if you omit a VAR statement.

You can specify the following *options* in the PROC UNIVARIATE statement:

CGRID=*color*
specifies the color for grid lines when a grid displays on the histogram.

GRID
specifies to display a grid on the histogram. Grid lines are horizontal lines that are positioned at major tick marks on the vertical axis.

HOFFSET=*value*
specifies the offset in percentage screen units at both ends of the horizontal axis.

GRID
specifies to display a grid on the histogram. Grid lines are horizontal lines that are positioned at major tick marks on the vertical axis.

LGRID=*linetype*
specifies the line type for the grid when a grid displays on the histogram. The default is a solid line.

MIDPOINTS=*value(s)*
determines the width of the histogram bars as the difference between consecutive midpoints. PROC UNIVARIATE uses the same *value(s)* for all variables. You must use evenly spaced midpoints that are listed in increasing order.

VAXIS=*value(s)*
specifies tick mark values for the vertical axis. Use evenly spaced values that are listed in increasing order. The first value must be zero and the last value must be greater than or equal to the height of the largest bar. You must scale the values in the same units as the bars.

VMINOR=*n*
specifies the number of minor tick marks between each major tick mark on the vertical axis. PROC UNIVARIATE does not label minor tick marks.

VSCALE=*scale*
specifies the scale of the vertical axis, where *scale* is

COUNT
scales the data in units of the number of observations per data unit.

PERCENT
scales the data in units of percentage of observations per data unit.

PROPORTION
scales the data in units of proportion of observations per data unit.

INSET *<keyword(s)> </option(s)>*;
places a box or table of summary statistics, called an *inset*, directly in the histogram.
You can specify the following *options* in the PROC UNIVARIATE statement:

keyword(s)
specifies one or more keywords that identify the information to display in the inset. PROC UNIVARIATE displays the information in the order that you request the keywords. For a complete list of keywords, see the INSET statement in *SAS/GRAPH Software: Reference, Volumes 1 and 2*.

FORMAT=*format*
specifies a format for all the values in the inset. If you specify a format for a particular statistic, then this format overrides FORMAT=*format*.

HEADER=*string*
specifies the heading text where *string* cannot exceed 40 characters.

NOFRAME
suppresses the frame drawn around the text.

POSITION=*position*
determines the position of the inset. The *position* is a compass point keyword, a margin keyword, or a pair of coordinates (x, y). The default position is NW, which positions the inset in the upper-left (northwest) corner of the display.

GOPTIONS Statement

GOPTIONS *options-list*;
specifies values for graphics options. Graphics options control characteristics of the graph, such as size, colors, type fonts, fill patterns, and symbols. In addition, they affect the settings of device parameters, which are defined in the device entry. Device parameters control such characteristics as the appearance of the display, the type of output that is produced, and the destination of the output.

FORMAT Statement

FORMAT *variable format-name*;
enables you to display the value of a *variable* by using a special pattern that you specify as *format-name*.

Learning More

PROC CHART
For complete documentation, see the *SAS Procedures Guide*. In addition to the features that are described in this chapter, you can also use PROC CHART to create star charts, to draw a reference line at a particular value on a bar chart, and to change the symbol that is used to draw charts. You can also create charts based, not only on frequency, sum, and mean, but also on cumulative frequency, percent, and cumulative percent.

PROC UNIVARIATE
For complete documentation, see the *SAS Procedures Guide*.

PROC PLOT
For a discussion about how to plot the relationship between variables, see Chapter 28, "Plotting the Relationship between Variables," on page 459. When you are preparing graphics presentations, some data lends itself to charts, while other data is better suited for plots.

SAS formats
For complete documentation, see *SAS Language Reference: Dictionary*. Many formats are available with SAS, including fractions, hexadecimal values, roman numerals, social security numbers, date and time values, and numbers written as words.

PROC FORMAT
For complete documentation about how to create your own formats, see the *SAS Procedures Guide*.

SAS/GRAPH software
For complete documentation, see *SAS/GRAPH Software: Reference, Volumes 1 and 2*. If your site has SAS/GRAPH software, then you can use the GCHART procedure to take advantage of the high-resolution graphics capabilities of output devices and produce charts that include color, different fonts, and text.

TITLE and FOOTNOTE statements
For a discussion about using titles and footnotes in a report, see "Understanding Titles and Footnotes" on page 388.

PART 8

Designing Your Own Output

30

Writing Lines to the SAS Log or to an Output File

Introduction

Purpose

In previous chapters you learned how to store data values in a SAS data set and to use SAS procedures to produce a report that is based on these data values. In this chapter, you will learn how to

- design output by positioning data values and character strings in an output file
- prevent SAS from creating a data set by using the DATA _NULL_ statement
- produce reports by using the DATA step instead of using a procedure
- direct data to an output file by using a FILE statement.

Prerequisites

Before proceeding with this chapter, you should be familiar with the concepts presented in

□ Chapter 1, "What Is the SAS System?," on page 3

□ Chapter 2, "Introduction to DATA Step Processing," on page 19.

Understanding the PUT Statement

When you create output using the DATA step, you can customize that output by using the PUT statement to write text to the SAS log or to another output file. The PUT statement has the following form:

PUT<*variable*<*format*>><*'character-string'*>;

where

variable
    names the variable that you want to write.

format
    specifies a format to use when you write variable values.

'character-string'
    specifies a string of text to write. Be sure to enclose the string in quotation marks.

Writing Output without Creating a Data Set

In many cases, when you use a DATA step to write a report, you do not need to create an additional data set. When you use the DATA _NULL_ statement, SAS processes the DATA step without writing observations to a data set. Using the DATA _NULL_ statement can increase program efficiency considerably.

The following is an example of a DATA _NULL_ statement:

```
data _null_;
```

The following program uses a PUT statement to write newspaper circulation values to the SAS log. Because the program uses a DATA _NULL_ statement, SAS does not create a data set.

```
data _null_;
    length state $ 15;
    input state $ morning_copies evening_copies year;
    put state morning_copies evening_copies year;
    datalines;
Massachusetts 798.4 984.7 1999
Massachusetts 834.2 793.6 1998
Massachusetts 750.3 .     1997
Alabama       .     698.4 1999
Alabama       463.8 522.0 1998
Alabama       583.2 234.9 1997
Alabama       .     339.6 1996
;
```

The following output shows the results:

Output 30.1 Writing to the SAS Log

```
184   data _null_;
185      length state $ 15;
186      input state $ morning_copies evening_copies year;
187      put state morning_copies evening_copies year;
188      datalines;
Massachusetts 798.4 984.7 1999
Massachusetts 834.2 793.6 1998
Massachusetts 750.3 . 1997
Alabama . 698.4 1999
Alabama 463.8 522 1998
Alabama 583.2 234.9 1997
Alabama . 339.6 1996

196  ;
```

SAS indicates missing numeric values with a period. Note that the log contains three missing values.

Writing Simple Text

Writing a Character String

In its simplest form, the PUT statement writes the character string that you specify to the SAS log, to a procedure output file, or to an external file. If you omit the destination (as in this example), then SAS writes the string to the log. In the following example, SAS executes the PUT statement once during each iteration of the DATA step. When SAS encounters missing values for MORNING_VALUES or EVENING_COPIES, the PUT statement writes a message to the log.

```
data _null_;
   length state $ 15;
   infile 'your-input-file';
   input state $ morning_copies evening_copies year;
   if morning_copies=. then put '** Morning Circulation Figures Missing';
   else
   if evening_copies=. then put '** Evening Circulation Figures Missing';
run;
```

The following output shows the results:

Output 30.2 Writing a Character String to the SAS Log

```
93   data _null_;
94      length state $ 15;
95      infile 'your-input-file';
96      input state $ morning_copies evening_copies year;
97      if morning_copies =. then put '** Morning Circulation Figures Missing';
98      else
99      if evening_copies =. then put '** Evening Circulation Figures Missing';
100  run;
NOTE: The infile 'your-input-file' is:
      File Name=file-name,
      Owner Name=xxxxxx,Group Name=xxxx,
      Access Permission=rw-r--r--,
      File Size (bytes)=223

** Evening Circulation Figures Missing
** Morning Circulation Figures Missing
** Morning Circulation Figures Missing
NOTE: 7 records were read from the infile 'your-input-file'.
      The minimum record length was 30.
      The maximum record length was 31.
```

Writing Variable Values

Output 30.2 on page 519 shows that the value for MORNING_COPIES is missing for two observations in the data set, and the value for EVENING_COPIES is missing for one observation. To identify which observations have the missing values, write the value of one or more variables along with the character string. The following program writes the value of YEAR and STATE, as well as the character string:

```
data _null_;
   length state $ 15;
   infile 'your-input-file';
   input state $ morning_copies evening_copies year;
   if morning_copies =. then put
      '** Morning Circulation Figures Missing: ' year state;
   else
   if evening_copies =. then put
      '** Evening Circulation Figures Missing: ' year state;
   run;
```

Notice that the last character in each of the strings is blank. This is an example of list output. In list output, SAS automatically moves one column to the right after writing a variable value, but not after writing a character string. The simplest way to include the required space is to include it in the character string.

SAS keeps track of its position in the output line with a pointer. Another way to describe the action in this PUT statement is to say that in list output, the pointer moves one column to the right after writing a variable value, but not after writing a character string. In later sections of this chapter, you will learn ways to move the pointer to control where the next piece of text is written.

The following output shows the results:

Output 30.3 Writing a Character String and Variable Values

```
164  data _null_;
165     length state $ 15;
166     infile 'your-input-file';
167     input state $ morning_copies evening_copies year;
168     if morning_copies =. then put
169        '** Morning Circulation Figures Missing: ' year state;
170     else
171     if evening_copies =. then put
172        '** Evening Circulation Figures Missing: ' year state;
173     run;
NOTE: The infile 'your-file-name' is:
     File Name=file-name,
     Owner Name=xxxxxx,Group Name=xxxx,
     Access Permission=rw-r--r--,
     File Size (bytes)=223

** Evening Circulation Figures Missing: 1997 Massachusetts
** Morning Circulation Figures Missing: 1999 Alabama
** Morning Circulation Figures Missing: 1996 Alabama
NOTE: 7 records were read from the infile 'your-input-file'.
     The minimum record length was 30.
     The maximum record length was 31.
```

Writing on the Same Line More than Once

By default, each PUT statement begins on a new line. However, you can write on the same line if you use more than one PUT statement and at least one trailing @ ("at" sign).

The trailing @ is a type of *pointer control* called a line-hold specifier. Pointer controls are one way to specify where SAS writes text. In the following example, using the trailing @ causes SAS to write the item in the second PUT statement on the same line rather than on a new line. The execution of either PUT statement holds the output line for further writing because each PUT statement has a trailing @. SAS continues to write on that line when a later PUT statement in the same iteration of the DATA step is executed and also when a PUT statement in a later iteration is executed.

```
options linesize=80 pagesize=60;

data _null_;
   length state $ 15;
   infile 'your-input-file';
   input state $ morning_copies evening_copies year;
   if morning_copies =. then put
      '** Morning Tot Missing: ' year state @;
   if evening_copies =. then put
      '** Evening Tot Missing: ' year state @;
   run;
```

The following output shows the results:

Output 30.4   Writing on the Same Line More than Once

```
157   options linesize=80 pagesize=60;
158
159   data _null_;
160      length state $ 15;
161      infile 'your-input-file';
162      input state $ morning_copies evening_copies year;
163      if morning_copies =. then put
164         '** Morning Tot Missing: ' year state @;
165      if evening_copies =. then put
166         '** Evening Tot Missing: ' year state @;
167      run;
NOTE: The infile 'your-input-file' is:
      File Name=file-name,
      Owner Name=xxxxxx,Group Name=xxxx,
      Access Permission=rw-r--r--,
      File Size (bytes)=223

** Evening Tot Missing: 1997 Massachusetts ** Morning Tot Missing: 1999 Alabama
** Morning Tot Missing: 1996 Alabama
NOTE: 7 records were read from the infile 'your-input-file'.
      The minimum record length was 30.
      The maximum record length was 31.
```

If the output line were long enough, then SAS would write all three messages about missing data on a single line. Because the line is not long enough, SAS continues writing on the next line. When it determines that an individual data value or character string does not fit on a line, SAS brings the entire item down to the next line. SAS does not split a data value or character string.

Releasing a Held Line

In the following example, the input file has five missing values. One record has missing values for both the MORNING_COPIES and EVENING_COPIES variables. Three other records have missing values for either the MORNING_COPIES or the EVENING_COPIES variable.

To improve the appearance of your report, you can write all the missing variables for each observation on a separate line. When values for the two variables MORNING_COPIES and EVENING_COPIES are missing, two PUT statements write to the same line. When either MORNING_COPIES or EVENING_COPIES is missing, only one PUT statement writes to that line.

SAS determines where to write the output by the presence of the trailing @ sign in the PUT statement and the presence of a null PUT statement that releases the hold on the line. Executing a PUT statement with a trailing @ causes SAS to hold the current output line for further writing, either in the current iteration of the DATA step or in a future iteration. Executing a PUT statement without a trailing @ releases the held line.

To release a line without writing a message, use a null PUT statement:

```
put;
```

A null PUT statement has the same characteristics of other PUT statements: by default, it writes output to a new line, writes what you specify in the statement (nothing in this case), and releases the line when it finishes executing. If a trailing @ is in effect, then the null PUT statement begins on the current line, writes nothing, and releases the line.

The following program shows how to write one or more items to the same line:

- If a value for MORNING_COPIES is missing, then the first PUT statement holds the line in case EVENING_COPIES is missing a value for that observation.
- If a value for EVENING_COPIES is missing, then the next PUT statement writes a message and releases the line.
- If EVENING_COPIES does not have a missing value, but if a message has been written for MORNING_COPIES (MORNING_COPIES=.), then the null PUT statement releases the line.
- If neither EVENING_COPIES nor MORNING_COPIES has missing values, then the line is not released and no PUT statement is executed.

```
options linesize=80 pagesize=60;

data _null_;
   length state $ 15;
   infile 'your-input-file';
   input state $ morning_copies evening_copies year;
   if morning_copies=. then put
      '** Morning Tot Missing: ' year state @;
   if evening_copies=. then put
      '** Evening Tot Missing: ' year state;
   else if morning_copies=. then put;
run;
```

The following output shows the results:

Output 30.5   Writing One or More Times to a Line and Releasing the Line

```
7    data _null_;
8       length state $ 15;
9       infile 'your-input-file';
10      input state $ morning_copies evening_copies year;
11      if morning_copies=. then put
12         '** Morning Tot Missing: ' year state @;
13      if evening_copies=. then put
14         '** Evening Tot Missing: ' year state;
15      else if morning_copies=. then put;
16   run;
NOTE: The infile 'your-input-file' is:
      File Name=your-input-file,
      Owner Name=xxxxxx,Group Name=xxxx,
      Access Permission=rw-r--r--,
      File Size (bytes)=223

** Evening Tot Missing: 1997 Massachusetts
** Morning Tot Missing: 1999 Alabama
** Morning Tot Missing: 1998 Alabama ** Evening Tot Missing: 1998 Alabama
** Morning Tot Missing: 1996 Alabama
NOTE: 7 records were read from the infile 'your-input-file'.
      The minimum record length was 30.
      The maximum record length was 31.
```

Writing a Report

Writing to an Output File

The PUT statement writes lines of text to the SAS log. However, the SAS log is not usually a good destination for a formal report because it also contains the source statements for the program and messages from SAS.

The simplest destination for a printed report is the SAS output file, which is the same place SAS writes output from procedures. SAS automatically defines various characteristics such as page numbers for the procedure output file, and you can take advantage of them instead of defining all the characteristics yourself.

To route lines to the procedure output file, use the FILE statement. The FILE statement has the following form:

FILE PRINT <*options*>;

PRINT is a reserved fileref that directs output that is produced by PUT statements to the same print file as the output that is produced by SAS procedures.

Note: Be sure that the FILE statement precedes the PUT statement in the program code. △

FILE statement *options* specify options that you can use to customize output. The report that is produced in this section uses the following options:

NOTITLES
   eliminates the default title line and makes that line available for writing. By default, the procedure output file contains the title "The SAS System." Because the report creates another title that is descriptive, you can remove the default title by specifying the NOTITLES option.

FOOTNOTES
   controls whether currently defined footnotes are written to the report.

   Note: When you use the FILE statement to include footnotes in a report, you must use the FOOTNOTES option in the FILE statement and include a FOOTNOTE statement in your program. The FOOTNOTE statement contains the text of the footnote. △

Note: You can also remove the default title with a null TITLE statement: `title;`. In this case, SAS writes a line that contains only the date and page number in place of the default title, and the line is not available for writing other text. △

Designing the Report

After choosing a destination for your report, the next step in producing a report is to decide how you want it to look. You create the design and determine which lines and columns the text will occupy. Planning how you want your final report to look helps you write the necessary PUT statements to produce the report. The rest of the examples in this section show how to modify a program to produce a final report that resembles the one shown here.

```
    ----+----1----+----2----+----3----+----4----+----5----+----6----+----7--
  1                  Morning and Evening Newspaper Circulation
  2
  3      State                Year                  Thousands of Copies
  4                                                 Morning      Evening
  5
  6      Alabama              1984                    256.3        480.5
  7                           1985                    291.5        454.3
  8                           1986                    303.6        454.7
  9                           1987                        .        454.5
 10                                                   ------      --------
 11                           Total for each category  851.4       1844.0
 12                                  Combined total          2695.4
 13
 14
 15      Massachusetts        1984                        .            .
 16                           1985                        .         68.0
 17                           1986                    222.7         68.6
 18                           1987                    224.1         66.7
 19                                                   ------       ------
 20                           Total for each category  446.8        203.3
 21                                  Combined total          650.1
 22
 23
 24
 25
 26
 27
 28
 29
 30                              Preliminary Report
    ----+----1----+----2----+----3----+----4----+----5----+----6----+----7--
```

Writing Data Values

After you design your report, you can begin to write the program that will create it. The following program shows how to display the data values for the YEAR, MORNING_COPIES, and EVENING_COPIES variables in specific positions.

In a PUT statement, the @ followed by a number is a pointer control, but it is different from the trailing @ described earlier. The @*n* argument is a column-pointer control. It tells SAS to move to column *n*. In this example the pointer moves to the specified locations, and the PUT statement writes values at those points using list output. Combining list output with pointer controls is a simple but useful way of writing data values in columns.

```
options pagesize=30 linesize=80 pageno=1 nodate;

data _null_;
   infile 'your-input-file';
   input state $ morning_copies evening_copies year;
   file print notitles;
   put @26 year @53 morning_copies @66 evening_copies;
run;
```

The following output shows the results:

Output 30.6   Data Values in Specific Locations in the Output

```
                              1999              798.4      984.7
                              1998              834.2      793.6
                              1997              750.3      .
                              1999              .          698.4
                              1998              463.8      522
                              1997              583.2      234.9
                              1996              .          339.6
```

Improving the Appearance of Numeric Data Values

In the design for your report, all numeric values are aligned on the decimal point (see Output 30.6 on page 526). To achieve this result, you have to alter the appearance of the numeric data values by using SAS formats. In the input data all values for MORNING_COPIES and EVENING_COPIES contain one decimal place, except in one case where the decimal value is 0. In list output SAS writes values in the simplest way, that is, by omitting the 0s in the decimal portion of a value. In formatted output, you can show one decimal place for every value by associating a format with a variable in the PUT statement. Using a format can also align your output values.

The format that is used in the program is called the *w.d* format. The *w.d* format specifies the number of columns to be used for writing the entire value, including the decimal point. It also specifies the number of columns to be used for writing the decimal portion of each value. In this example the format 5.1 causes SAS to use five columns, including one decimal place, for writing each value. Therefore, SAS prints the 0s in the decimal portion as necessary. The format also aligns the periods that SAS uses to indicate missing values with the decimal points.

```
options pagesize=30 linesize=80 pageno=1 nodate;

data _null_;
   infile 'your-input-file';
   input state $ morning_copies evening_copies year;
   file print notitles;
   put @26 year @53 morning_copies 5.1 @66 evening_copies 5.1;
run;
```

The following output shows the results:

Output 30.7   Formatted Numeric Output

```
                              1999              798.4      984.7
                              1998              834.2      793.6
                              1997              750.3      .
                              1999              .          698.4
                              1998              463.8      522.0
                              1997              583.2      234.9
                              1996              .          339.6
```

Writing a Value at the Beginning of Each BY Group

The next step in creating your report is to add the name of the state to your output. If you include the name of the state in the PUT statement with other data values, then the state will appear on every line. However, remembering what you want your final report to look like, you need to write the name of the state only for the first observation of a particular state. Performing a task once for a group of observations requires the use of the BY statement for BY-group processing. The BY statement has the following form:

BY *by-variable(s)*<NOTSORTED>;

The *by-variable* names the variable by which the data set is sorted. The optional NOTSORTED option specifies that observations with the same BY value are grouped together but are not necessarily sorted in alphabetical or numerical order.

For BY-group processing,

☐ ensure that observations come from a SAS data set, not an external file.

☐ when the data is grouped in BY groups but the groups are not necessarily in alphabetical order, use the NOTSORTED option in the BY statement. For example, use

```
by state notsorted;
```

The following program creates a permanent SAS data set named NEWS.CIRCULATION, and writes the name of the state on the first line of the report for each BY group.

```
options pagesize=30 linesize=80 pageno=1 nodate;

libname news 'SAS-data-library';
data news.circulation;
   length state $ 15;
   input state $ morning_copies evening_copies year;
   datalines;
Massachusetts 798.4 984.7 1999
Massachusetts 834.2 793.6 1998
Massachusetts 750.3 .     1997
Alabama       .     698.4 1999
Alabama       463.8 522.0 1998
Alabama       583.2 234.9 1997
Alabama       .     339.6 1996
;

data _null_;
   set news.circulation;
   by state notsorted;
   file print notitles;
   if first.state then put / @7 state @;
   put @26 year @53 morning_copies 5.1 @66 evening_copies 5.1;
run;
```

During the first observation for a given state, a PUT statement writes the name of the state and holds the line for further writing (the year and circulation figures). The next PUT statement writes the year and circulation figures and releases the held line.

In observations after the first, only the second PUT statement is processed. It writes the year and circulation figures and releases the line as usual.

The first PUT statement contains a slash (/), a pointer control that moves the pointer to the beginning of the next line. In this example, the PUT statement prepares to write on a new line (the default action). Then the slash moves the pointer to the beginning of the next line. As a result, SAS skips a line before writing the value of STATE. In the output, a blank line separates the data for Massachusetts from the data for Alabama. The output for Massachusetts also begins one line farther down the page than it would have otherwise. (That blank line is used later in the development of the report.)

The following output shows the results:

Output 30.8   Effect of BY-Group Processing

```
        Massachusetts    1999                 798.4       984.7
                         1998                 834.2       793.6
                         1997                 750.3         .

        Alabama          1999                   .         698.4
                         1998                 463.8       522.0
                         1997                 583.2       234.9
                         1996                   .         339.6
```

Calculating Totals

The next step is to calculate the total morning circulation figures, total evening circulation figures, and total overall circulation figures for each state. Sum statements accumulate the totals, and assignment statements start the accumulation at 0 for each state. When the last observation for a given state is being processed, an assignment statement calculates the overall total, and a PUT statement writes the totals and additional descriptive text.

```
options pagesize=30 linesize=80 pageno=1 nodate;
libname news 'SAS-data-library';

data _null_;
   set news.circulation;
   by state notsorted;
   file print notitles;
      /* Set values of accumulator variables to 0 */
      /* at beginning of each BY group.           */
      if first.state then
         do;
            morning_total=0;
            evening_total=0;
            put / @7 state @;
         end;
   put @26 year @53 morning_copies 5.1 @66 evening_copies 5.1;

      /* Accumulate separate totals for morning and */
      /* evening circulations.                       */
   morning_total+morning_copies;
   evening_total+evening_copies;
```

```
                /* Calculate total circulation at the end of  */
                /* each BY group.                             */

        if last.state then
           do;
               all_totals=morning_total+evening_total;
               put @52 '------' @65 '------' /
                   @26 'Total for each category'
                   @52 morning_total 6.1 @65 evening_total 6.1 /
                   @35 'Combined total' @59 all_totals 6.1;
           end;
    run;
```

The following output shows the results:

Output 30.9 Calculating and Writing Totals for Each BY Group

```
        Massachusetts     1999                  798.4        984.7
                          1998                  834.2        793.6
                          1997                  750.3           .
                                               ------       ------
                          Total for each category 2382.9    1778.3
                                   Combined total       4161.2

        Alabama           1999                     .         698.4
                          1998                  463.8        522.0
                          1997                  583.2        234.9
                          1996                     .         339.6
                                               ------       ------
                          Total for each category 1047.0    1794.9
                                   Combined total       2841.9
```

Notice that Sum statements ignore missing values when they accumulate totals. Also, by default, Sum statements assign the accumulator variables (in this case, MORNING_TOTAL and EVENING_TOTAL) an initial value of 0. Therefore, although the assignment statements in the DO group are executed for the first observation for both states, you need them only for the second state.

Writing Headings and Footnotes for a One-Page Report

The report is complete except for the title lines, column headings, and footnote. Because this is a simple, one-page report, you can write the heading with a PUT statement that is executed only during the first iteration of the DATA step. The automatic variable _N_ counts the number of times the DATA step has iterated or looped, and the PUT statement is executed when the value of _N_ is 1.

The FOOTNOTES option on the FILE statement and the FOOTNOTE statement create the footnote. The following program is complete:

```
options pagesize=30 linesize=80 pageno=1 nodate;
libname news 'SAS-data-library';

data _null_;
   set news.circulation;
   by state notsorted;
```

```
file print notitles footnotes;
if _n_=1 then put @16 'Morning and Evening Newspaper Circulation' //
                  @7  'State' @26 'Year' @51 'Thousands of Copies' /
                  @51 'Morning      Evening';
if first.state then
   do;
      morning_total=0;
      evening_total=0;
      put / @7 state @;
   end;
put @26 year @53 morning_copies 5.1 @66 evening_copies 5.1;
morning_total+morning_copies;
evening_total+evening_copies;
if last.state then
   do;
      all_totals=morning_total+evening_total;
      put @52 '------' @65 '------' /
          @26 'Total for each category'
          @52 morning_total 6.1 @65 evening_total 6.1 /
          @35 'Combined total' @59 all_totals 6.1;
   end;
   footnote 'Preliminary Report';
run;
```

The following output shows the results:

Output 30.10   The Final Report

```
            Morning and Evening Newspaper Circulation

     State              Year              Thousands of Copies
                                          Morning      Evening


     Massachusetts      1999               798.4        984.7
                        1998               834.2        793.6
                        1997               750.3          .
                                          ------       ------
                        Total for each category 2382.9   1778.3
                                Combined total         4161.2

     Alabama            1999                 .           698.4
                        1998               463.8        522.0
                        1997               583.2        234.9
                        1996                 .           339.6
                                          ------       ------
                        Total for each category 1047.0   1794.9
                                Combined total         2841.9




            
            
            
            
                        Preliminary Report
```

Notice that a blank line appears between the last line of the heading and the first data for Massachusets although the PUT statement for the heading does not write a blank line. The line comes from the slash (/) in the PUT statement that writes the value of STATE in the first observation of each BY group.

Executing a PUT statement during the first iteration of the DATA step is a simple way to produce headings, especially when a report is only one page long.

Review of SAS Tools

Statements

BY *variable-1* <. . . *variable-n* > <NOTSORTED>;
indicates that all observations with common values of the BY *variables* are grouped together. The NOTSORTED option indicates that the *variables* are grouped but that the groups are not necessarily in alphabetical or numerical order.

DATA _NULL_;
specifies that SAS will not create an output data set.

FILE PRINT <NOTITLES> <FOOTNOTES>;
directs output to the SAS procedure output file. Place the FILE statement before the PUT statements that write to that file. The NOTITLES option suppresses titles that are currently in effect, and makes the lines unavailable for writing other text. The FOOTNOTES option, along with the FOOTNOTE statement, writes a footnote to the file.

PUT;
by default, begins a new line and releases a previously held line. A PUT statement that does not write any text is known as a null PUT statement.

PUT <*variable* <*format*>> <*character string*>;
writes lines to the destination that is specified in the FILE statement; if no FILE statement is present, then the PUT statement writes to the SAS log. By default, each PUT statement begins on a new line, writes what is specified, and releases the line. A DATA step can contain any number of PUT statements.

By default, SAS writes a *variable* or *character-string* at the current position in the line. SAS automatically moves the pointer one column to the right after writing a variable value but not after writing a character string; that is, SAS places a blank after a variable value but not after a character string. This form of output is called list output. If you place a *format* after a variable name, then SAS writes the value of the *variable* beginning at its current position in the line and using the *format* that you specify. The position of the pointer after a formatted value is the following column; that is, SAS does not automatically skip a column. Using a format in a PUT statement is called formatted output. You can combine list and formatted output in a single PUT statement.

PUT<@*n*> <*variable* <*format*>> <*character-string*> </> <@>;
writes lines to the destination that is specified in the FILE statement; if no FILE statement is present, then the PUT statement writes to the SAS log. The @*n* pointer control moves the pointer to column *n* in the current line. The / moves the pointer to the beginning of a new line. (You can use slashes anywhere in the PUT statement to skip lines.) Multiple slashes skip multiple lines. The trailing @, if present, must be the last item in the PUT statement. Executing a PUT statement with a trailing @ holds the current line for use by a later PUT statement either in

the same iteration of the DATA step or a later iteration. Executing a PUT
statement without a trailing @ releases a held line.

TITLE;
specifies title lines for SAS output.

Learning More

Pointer controls
For more information about pointer controls, see the PUT statement in the
Statements section of *SAS Language Reference: Dictionary*.

Statements
For more information about the statements that are described in this chapter, see
the Statements section of *SAS Language Reference: Dictionary*.

CHAPTER

31

Understanding and Customizing SAS Output: The Basics

Introduction

Purpose

In this chapter you will learn to understand your output so that you can enhance its appearance and make it more informative. It discusses DATA step and PROC step output.

This chapter describes how to enhance the appearance of your output by

☐ adding titles, column headings, footnotes, and labels

☐ customizing headings

☐ changing a portion of a heading

☐ numbering pages and controlling page divisions

☐ printing date and time values

☐ representing missing numeric values with a character.

Prerequisites

Before proceeding with this chapter, you should understand the concepts that are presented in:

☐ Chapter 2, "Introduction to DATA Step Processing," on page 19

☐ Chapter 30, "Writing Lines to the SAS Log or to an Output File," on page 517.

Understanding Output

Output from Procedures

When you invoke a SAS procedure, SAS analyzes or processes your data. You can read a SAS data set, compute statistics, print results, or create a new data set. One of the results of executing a SAS procedure is creating procedure output. The destination of procedure output varies with the method of running SAS, the operating environment, and the options that you use. The form and content of the output varies with each procedure. Some procedures, such as the SORT procedure, do not produce printed output.

SAS has numerous procedures that you can use to process your data. For example, you can use the PRINT procedure to print a report that lists the values of each variable in your SAS data set. You can use the MEANS procedure to compute descriptive statistics for variables across all observations and within groups of observations. You can use the UNIVARIATE procedure to produce information on the distribution of numeric variables. For a graphic representation of your data, you can use the CHART procedure. Many other procedures are available through SAS.

Output from DATA Step Applications

Although output is usually generated by a procedure, you can also generate output by using a DATA step application. Using the DATA step, you can

☐ create a SAS data set

- □ write to an external file
- □ produce a report.

To generate output, you can use the FILE and PUT statements together within the DATA step. Use the FILE statement to identify your current output file. Then use the PUT statement to write lines that contain variable values or text strings to the output file. You can write the values in column, list, or formatted style.

You can use the FILE and PUT statements to target a subset of data. If you have a large data set that includes unnecessary information, this kind of DATA step processing can save time and computer resources. Write your code so that the FILE statement executes before a PUT statement in the current execution of a DATA step. Otherwise, your data will be written to the SAS log.

If you have a SAS data set, you can use the FILE and PUT statements to create an external file that another computer language can process. For example, you can create a SAS data set that lists the test scores for high school students. You can then use this file as input to a FORTRAN program that analyzes test scores. The following table lists the variables and the column positions that an existing FORTRAN program expects to find in the input SAS data set:

Variable	Column location
YEAR	10-13
TEST	15-25
GENDER	30
SCORE	35-37

You can use the FILE and PUT statements in the DATA step to create the data set that the FORTRAN program reads:

```
data _null_;
   set out.sats1;
   file 'your-output-file';
   put @10 year @15 test
       @30 gender @35 score;
run;
```

Output from the Output Delivery System (ODS)

Beginning with Version 7, procedure output is much more flexible because of the Output Delivery System (ODS). ODS is a method of delivering output in a variety of formats and of making the formatted output easy to access. Important features of ODS include the following:

- □ ODS combines raw data with one or more table definitions to produce one or more output objects. When you send these objects to any or all ODS destinations, your output is formatted according to the instructions in the table definition. ODS destinations can produce an output data set, traditional monospace output, output that is formatted for a high-resolution printer, output that is formatted in HyperText Markup Language (HTML), and so on.
- □ ODS provides table definitions that define the structure of the output from procedures and from the DATA step. You can customize the output by modifying these definitions or by creating your own definitions.

□ ODS provides a way for you to choose individual output objects to send to ODS destinations. For example, PROC UNIVARIATE produces five output objects. You can easily create HTML output, an output data set, traditional Listing output, or Printer output from any or all of these output objects. You can send different output objects to different destinations.

□ ODS stores a link to each output object in the Results folder in the Results window.

In addition, ODS removes responsibility for formatting output from individual procedures and from the DATA step. The procedure or DATA step supplies raw data and the name of the table definition that contains the formatting instructions; then ODS formats the output. Because formatting is now centralized in ODS, the addition of a new ODS destination does not affect any procedures or the DATA step. As future destinations are added to ODS, they will automatically become available to the DATA step and to all procedures that support ODS.

For more information and examples, see Chapter 32, "Understanding and Customizing SAS Output: The Output Delivery System (ODS)," on page 561.

Input SAS Data Set for Examples

The following program creates a SAS data set that contains Scholastic Aptitude Test (SAT) information for university-bound high school seniors from 1972 through 1998. (To view the entire DATA step, see "DATA Step to Create the Data Set SAT_SCORES" on page 714.) The data set in this example is stored in a SAS data library that is referenced by the libref ADMIN. For selected years between 1972 and 1998, the data set shows estimated scores that are based on the total number of students nationwide taking the test. Scores are estimated for male (m) and female (f) students, for both the verbal and math portions of the test.

```
options pagesize=60 linesize=80 pageno=1 nodate;
libname admin 'your-data-library';

data admin.sat_scores;
   input Test $ Gender $ Year SATscore @@;
   datalines;
Verbal m 1972 531   Verbal f 1972 529
Verbal m 1973 523   Verbal f 1973 521
Verbal m 1974 524   Verbal f 1974 520
   ...more SAS data lines...
Math   m 1996 527   Math   f 1996 492
Math   m 1997 530   Math   f 1997 494
Math   m 1998 531   Math   f 1998 496
;

proc print data=admin.sat_scores;
run;
```

The following output shows a partial list of the results:

Output 31.1 The ADMIN.SAT_SCORES Data Set: Partial List of Output

```
                        The SAS System                              1

          Obs     Test     Gender    Year    SATscore

           1     Verbal      m       1972      531
           2     Verbal      f       1972      529
           3     Verbal      m       1973      523
           4     Verbal      f       1973      521
           5     Verbal      m       1974      524
           6     Verbal      f       1974      520
           7     Verbal      m       1975      515
           8     Verbal      f       1975      509
           9     Verbal      m       1976      511
          10     Verbal      f       1976      508
          11     Verbal      m       1977      509
          12     Verbal      f       1977      505
          13     Verbal      m       1978      511
          14     Verbal      f       1978      503
          15     Verbal      m       1979      509
          16     Verbal      f       1979      501
          17     Verbal      m       1980      506
          18     Verbal      f       1980      498
          19     Verbal      m       1981      508
          20     Verbal      f       1981      496
          21     Verbal      m       1982      509
          22     Verbal      f       1982      499
          23     Verbal      m       1983      508
          24     Verbal      f       1983      498
          25     Verbal      m       1984      511
          26     Verbal      f       1984      498
          27     Verbal      m       1985      514
          28     Verbal      f       1985      503
          29     Verbal      m       1986      515
          30     Verbal      f       1986      504
```

Locating Procedure Output

The destination of your procedure output depends on the method that you use to start, run, and exit SAS. It also depends on your operating environment and on the settings of SAS system options. The following table shows the default destination for each method of operation.

Method of Operation	Destination of Procedure Output
windowing environment	OUTPUT and RESULTS windows
interactive line mode	on the terminal display, as each step executes
noninteractive SAS programs	depends on the operating environment
batch jobs	line printer or disk file

Making Output Informative

Adding Titles

At the top of each page of output, SAS automatically writes the following title:

```
The SAS System
```

You can make output more informative by using the TITLE statement to specify your own title. A TITLE statement writes the title you specify at the top of every page. The form of the TITLE statement is

TITLE<*n*><*'text'*>;

where *n* specifies the relative line that contains the title, and *text* specifies the text of the title. The value of *n* can be 1 to 10. If you omit *n*, SAS assumes a value of 1. Therefore, you can specify TITLE or TITLE1 for the first title line. By default, SAS centers a title.

To add the title 'SAT Scores by Year, 1972-1998' to your output, use the following TITLE statement:

```
title 'SAT Scores by Year, 1972-1998';
```

The TITLE statement is a global statement. This means that within a SAS session, SAS continues to use the most recently created title until you change or eliminate it, even if you generate different output later. You can use the TITLE statement anywhere in your program.

You can specify up to ten titles per page by numbering them in ascending order. If you want to add a subtitle to your previous title, for example, the subtitle 'Separate Statistics by Test Type,' then number your titles by the order in which you want them to appear. To add a blank line between titles, skip a number as you number your TITLE statements. Your TITLE statements now become

```
title1 'SAT Scores by Year, 1972-1998';
title3 'Separate Statistics by Test Type';
```

To modify a title line, you change the text in the title and resubmit your program, including all of the TITLE statements. Be aware that a TITLE statement for a given line cancels the previous TITLE statement for that line and for all lines with higher-numbered titles.

To eliminate all titles including the default title, specify

```
title;
```

or

```
title1;
```

The following example shows how to use multiple TITLE statements.

```
options linesize=80 pagesize=60 pageno=1 nodate;
libname admin 'SAS-data-library';

data report;
   set admin.sat_scores;
   if year ge 1995 then output;
```

```
   title1 'SAT Scores by Year, 1995-1998';
   title3 'Separate Statistics by Test Type';
run;


proc print data=report;
run;
```

The following output shows the results:

Output 31.2   Report Showing Multiple TITLE Statements

```
                    SAT Scores by Year, 1995-1998                    1

                  Separate Statistics by Test Type

          Obs     Test      Gender    Year    SATscore

           1      Verbal      m        1995      505
           2      Verbal      f        1995      502
           3      Verbal      m        1996      507
           4      Verbal      f        1996      503
           5      Verbal      m        1997      507
           6      Verbal      f        1997      503
           7      Verbal      m        1998      509
           8      Verbal      f        1998      502
           9      Math        m        1995      525
          10      Math        f        1995      490
          11      Math        m        1996      527
          12      Math        f        1996      492
          13      Math        m        1997      530
          14      Math        f        1997      494
          15      Math        m        1998      531
          16      Math        f        1998      496
```

Although the TITLE statement can appear anywhere in your program, you can associate it with a particular procedure step by positioning it

- □ before the step that produces the output
- □ after the procedure statement but before the next DATA or RUN statement, or the next procedure.

Remember that the TITLE statement applies globally until you change or eliminate it.

Adding Footnotes

The FOOTNOTE statement follows the same guidelines as the TITLE statement. The FOOTNOTE statement is a global statement. This means that within a SAS session, SAS continues to use the most recently created footnote until you change or eliminate it, even if you generate different output later. You can use the FOOTNOTE statement anywhere in your program.

A footnote writes up to ten lines of text at the bottom of the procedure output or DATA step output. The form of the FOOTNOTE statement is

FOOTNOTE<*n*><*'text'*>;

where *n* specifies the relative line to be occupied by the footnote, and *text* specifies the text of the footnote. The value of *n* can be 1 to 10. If you omit *n*, SAS assumes a value of 1.

To add the footnote '1967 and 1970 SAT scores estimated based on total number of people taking the SAT,' specify the following statements anywhere in your program:

```
footnote1 '1967 and 1970 SAT scores estimated based on total number';
footnote2 'of people taking the SAT';
```

You can specify up to ten lines of footnotes per page by numbering them in ascending order. When you alter the text of one footnote in a series and execute your program again, SAS changes the text of that footnote. However, if you execute your program with numbered FOOTNOTE statements, SAS eliminates all higher-numbered footnotes.

```
footnote;
```

or

```
footnote1;
```

The following example shows how to use multiple FOOTNOTE statements.

```
options linesize=80 pagesize=30 pageno=1 nodate;
libname admin 'SAS-data-library';

data report;
   set admin.sat_scores;
   if year ge 1996 then output;
   title1 'SAT Scores by Year, 1996-1998';
   title3 'Separate Statistics by Test Type';
   footnote1 '1996 through 1998 SAT scores estimated based on total number';
   footnote2 'of people taking the SAT';
run;

proc print data=report;
run;
```

The following output shows the results:

Output 31.3 Report Showing a Footnote

```
                    SAT Scores by Year, 1996-1998                      1

                 Separate Statistics by Test Type

          Obs      Test     Gender     Year     SATscore

           1      Verbal       m       1996        507
           2      Verbal       f       1996        503
           3      Verbal       m       1997        507
           4      Verbal       f       1997        503
           5      Verbal       m       1998        509
           6      Verbal       f       1998        502
           7      Math         m       1996        527
           8      Math         f       1996        492
           9      Math         m       1997        530
          10      Math         f       1997        494
          11      Math         m       1998        531
          12      Math         f       1998        496




             1996 through 1998 SAT scores estimated based on total number
                           of people taking the SAT
```

Although the FOOTNOTE statement can appear anywhere in your program, you can associate it with a particular procedure step by positioning it

☐ after the RUN statement for the previous step

☐ after the procedure statement but before the next DATA or RUN statement, or before the next procedure.

Remember that the FOOTNOTE statement applies globally until you change or eliminate it.

Labeling Variables

In procedure output, SAS automatically writes the variables with the names that you specify. However, you can designate a label for some or all of your variables by specifying a LABEL statement either in the DATA step or, with some procedures, in the PROC step of your program. Your label can be up to 256 characters long, including blanks.

For example, to describe the variable SATscore with the phrase 'SAT Score,' specify

```
label SATscore ='SAT Score';
```

If you specify the LABEL statement in the DATA step, the label is permanently stored in the data set. If you specify the LABEL statement in the PROC step, the label is associated with the variable only for the duration of the PROC step. In either case, when a label is assigned, it is written with almost all SAS procedures. The exception is the PRINT procedure. Whether you put the LABEL statement in the DATA step or in the PROC step, with the PRINT procedure you must specify the LABEL option as follows:

```
proc print data=report label;
run;
```

The following example shows how to use a label statement.

```
options linesize=80 pagesize=30 pageno=1 nodate;
libname admin 'SAS-data-library';

data report;
   set admin.sat_scores;
   if year ge 1996 then output;
   label Test='Test Type'
         SATscore='SAT Score';
   title1 'SAT Scores by Year, 1996-1998';
   title3 'Separate Statistics by Test Type';
run;

proc print data=report label;
run;
```

The following output shows the results:

Output 31.4   Variable Labels in SAS Output

```
                      SAT Scores by Year, 1996-1998                    1

                    Separate Statistics by Test Type

                  Test                        SAT
          Obs     Type     Gender     Year    Score

           1     Verbal       m       1996     507
           2     Verbal       f       1996     503
           3     Verbal       m       1997     507
           4     Verbal       f       1997     503
           5     Verbal       m       1998     509
           6     Verbal       f       1998     502
           7      Math        m       1996     527
           8      Math        f       1996     492
           9      Math        m       1997     530
          10      Math        f       1997     494
          11      Math        m       1998     531
          12      Math        f       1998     496
```

Developing Descriptive Output

The following example incorporates the TITLE, LABEL, and FOOTNOTE statements, and produces output.

```
options linesize=80 pagesize=40 pageno=1 nodate;
libname admin 'SAS-data-library';

proc sort data=admin.satscores;
   by gender;
run;
```

```
proc means data=admin.satscores maxdec=2 fw=8;
   by gender;
   label SATscore='SAT score';
   title1 'SAT Scores by Year, 1967-1976';
   title3 'Separate Statistics by Test Type';
   footnote1 '1972 and 1976 SAT scores estimated based on the';
   footnote2 'total number of people taking the SAT';
run;
```

The following output shows the results:

Output 31.5 Titles, Labels, and Footnotes in SAS Output

```
                      SAT Scores by Year, 1967-1976                        1

                     Separate Statistics by Test Type

----------------------------------- Gender=f -----------------------------------

                            The MEANS Procedure

    Variable    Label        N        Mean     Std Dev     Minimum     Maximum
    ------------------------------------------------------------------------
    Year                     4     1975.00        2.58     1972.00     1978.00
    SATscore    SAT score    4      515.00       11.75      503.00      529.00
    ------------------------------------------------------------------------


----------------------------------- Gender=m -----------------------------------

    Variable    Label        N        Mean     Std Dev     Minimum     Maximum
    ------------------------------------------------------------------------
    Year                     4     1975.00        2.58     1972.00     1978.00
    SATscore    SAT score    4      519.25        9.95      511.00      531.00
    ------------------------------------------------------------------------









                    1972 and 1976 SAT scores estimated based on the
                         total number of people taking the SAT
```

Controlling Output Appearance

Specifying SAS System Options

You can enhance the appearance of your output by specifying SAS system options on the OPTIONS statement. The changes that result from specifying system options remain in effect for the rest of the job, session, or SAS process, or until you issue another OPTIONS statement to change the options.

You can specify SAS system options through the OPTIONS statement, through the OPTIONS window, at SAS invocation, at the initiation of a SAS process, and in a configuration file. Default option settings can vary among sites. To determine the settings at your site, execute the OPTIONS procedure or browse the OPTIONS window.

The OPTIONS statement has the following form:

OPTIONS *option(s)*;

where *option* specifies one or more SAS options that you want to change.

Note: An OPTIONS statement can appear at any place in a SAS program, except within data lines. △

Numbering Pages

By default, SAS numbers pages of output starting with page 1. However, you can suppress page numbers with the NONUMBER system option. To suppress page numbers, specify the following OPTIONS statement:

```
options nonumber;
```

This option, like all SAS system options, remains in effect for the duration of your session or until you change it. Change the option by specifying

```
options number;
```

You can use the PAGENO= system option to specify a beginning page number for the next page of output that SAS writes. The PAGENO= option enables you to reset page numbering in the middle of a SAS session. For example, the following OPTIONS statement resets the next output page number to 5:

```
options pageno=5;
```

Centering Output

By default, SAS centers both the output and output titles. However, you can left-align your output by specifying the following OPTIONS statement:

```
options nocenter;
```

The NOCENTER option remains in effect for the duration of your SAS session or until you change it. Change the option by specifying

```
options center;
```

Specifying Page and Line Size

Procedure output is scaled automatically to fit the size of the page and line. The number of lines per page and the number of characters per line of printed output are determined by the settings of the PAGESIZE= and LINESIZE= system options. The default settings vary from site to site and are further affected by the machine, operating environment, and method of running SAS. For example, when SAS runs in interactive mode, the PAGESIZE= option by default assumes the size of the device that you specify. You can adjust both your page size and line size by resetting the PAGESIZE= and LINESIZE= options.

For example, you can specify the following OPTIONS statement:

```
options pagesize=40 linesize=64;
```

The PAGESIZE= and LINESIZE= options remain in effect for the duration of your SAS session or until you change them.

Writing Date and Time Values

By default, SAS writes at the top of your output the beginning date and time of the SAS session during which your job executed. This automatic record is especially useful when you execute a program many times. However, you can use the NODATE system option to specify that these values not appear. To do this, specify the following OPTIONS statement:

```
options nodate;
```

The NODATE option remains in effect for the duration of your SAS session or until you change it.

Choosing Options Selectively

Choose the system options that you need to meet your specifications. The following program, which uses the conditional IF-THEN/ELSE statement to subset the data set, includes a number of SAS options. The OPTIONS statement specifies a line size of 64, left-aligns the output, numbers the output pages and supplies the date that the SAS session was started.

```
options linesize=64 nocenter number date;

libname admin '/u/lirezn/saslearnV8';
data high_scores;
   set admin.sat_scores;
   if SATscore < 525 then delete;
run;

proc print data=high_scores;
   title 'SAT Scores: 525 and Above';
run;
```

The following output shows the results:

Output 31.6   Effect of System Options on SAS Output

```
SAT Scores: 525 and Above                                          1
                              10:59 Wednesday, October 11, 2000

Obs     Test      Gender    Year    SATscore

1       Verbal      m       1972      531
2       Verbal      f       1972      529
3       Math        m       1972      527
4       Math        m       1973      525
5       Math        m       1995      525
6       Math        m       1996      527
7       Math        m       1997      530
8       Math        m       1998      531
```

Controlling the Appearance of Pages

Input Data Set for Examples of Multiple-page Reports

In the sections that follow, you learn how to customize multiple-page reports.

The following program creates and prints a SAS data set that contains newspaper circulation figures for morning and evening editions. Each record lists the state, morning circulation figures (in thousands), evening circulation figures (in thousands), and year that the data represents.

```
data circulation_figures;
   length state $ 15;
   input state $ morning_copies evening_copies year;
   datalines;
Colorado   738.6 210.2 1984
Colorado   742.2 212.3 1985
Colorado   731.7 209.7 1986
Colorado   789.2 155.9 1987
Vermont    623.4 566.1 1984
Vermont    533.1 455.9 1985
Vermont    544.2 566.7 1986
Vermont    322.3 423.8 1987
Alaska      51.0  80.7 1984
Alaska      58.7  78.3 1985
Alaska      59.8  70.9 1986
Alaska      64.3  64.6 1987
Alabama    256.3 480.5 1984
Alabama    291.5 454.3 1985
Alabama    303.6 454.7 1986
Alabama      .   454.5 1987
Maine        .     .   1984
Maine        .    68.0 1985
Maine      222.7  68.6 1986
Maine      224.1  66.7 1987
Hawaii     433.5 122.3 1984
Hawaii     455.6 245.1 1985
Hawaii     499.3 355.2 1986
```

```
Hawaii    503.2 488.6 1987
;


proc print data=circulation_figures;
run;
```

The following output shows the results:

Output 31.7 SAS Data Set CIRCULATION_FIGURES

```
                            The SAS System                              1

                           morning_   evening_
              Obs   state    copies     copies    year

               1   Colorado   738.6     210.2     1984
               2   Colorado   742.2     212.3     1985
               3   Colorado   731.7     209.7     1986
               4   Colorado   789.2     155.9     1987
               5   Vermont    623.4     566.1     1984
               6   Vermont    533.1     455.9     1985
               7   Vermont    544.2     566.7     1986
               8   Vermont    322.3     423.8     1987
               9   Alaska      51.0      80.7     1984
              10   Alaska      58.7      78.3     1985
              11   Alaska      59.8      70.9     1986
              12   Alaska      64.3      64.6     1987
              13   Alabama    256.3     480.5     1984
              14   Alabama    291.5     454.3     1985
              15   Alabama    303.6     454.7     1986
```

```
                            The SAS System                              2

                           morning_   evening_
              Obs   state    copies     copies    year

              16   Alabama        .     454.5     1987
              17   Maine          .         .     1984
              18   Maine          .      68.0     1985
              19   Maine      222.7      68.6     1986
              20   Maine      224.1      66.7     1987
              21   Hawaii     433.5     122.3     1984
              22   Hawaii     455.6     245.1     1985
              23   Hawaii     499.3     355.2     1986
              24   Hawaii     503.2     488.6     1987
```

Writing Centered Title and Column Headings

Producing centered titles with TITLE statements is easy, because centering is the default for the TITLE statement. Producing column headings is not so easy. You must insert the correct number of blanks in the TITLE statements so that the entire title, when centered, causes the text to fall in the correct columns. The following example shows how to write centered lines and column headings. The titles and column headings appear at the top of every page of output.

```
options linesize=80 pagesize=20 nodate;

data report1;
   infile 'your-data-file';
   input state $ morning_copies evening_copies year;
run;

title 'Morning and Evening Newspaper Circulation';
title2;
title3        'State           Year                  Thousands of Copies';
title4        '                                         Morning      Evening';

data _null_;
   set report1;
   by state notsorted;
   file print;
   if first.state then
      do;
         morning_total=0;
         evening_total=0;
         put / @7 state @;
      end;
   put @26 year @53 morning_copies 5.1 @66 evening_copies 5.1;
   morning_total+morning_copies;
   evening_total+evening_copies;
   if last.state then
      do;
         all_totals=morning_total+evening_total;
         put @52 '------' @65 '------' /
             @26 'Total for each category'
             @52 morning_total 6.1 @65 evening_total 6.1 /
             @35 'Combined total' @59 all_totals 6.1;
      end;
run;
```

The following output shows the results:

Output 31.8 Centered Lines and Column Headings in SAS Output

```
                    Morning and Evening Newspaper Circulation                    1

           State         Year                       Thousands of Copies
                                                    Morning      Evening

        Colorado         1984                        738.6        210.2
                         1985                         742.2        212.3
                         1986                         731.7        209.7
                         1987                         789.2        155.9
                                                     ------       ------
                         Total for each category     3001.7        788.1
                                   Combined total           3789.8

        Vermont          1984                         623.4        566.1
                         1985                         533.1        455.9
                         1986                         544.2        566.7
                         1987                         322.3        423.8
                                                     ------       ------
                         Total for each category     2023.0       2012.5
                                   Combined total           4035.5
```

```
                    Morning and Evening Newspaper Circulation                    2

           State         Year                       Thousands of Copies
                                                    Morning      Evening

        Alaska           1984                          51.0         80.7
                         1985                          58.7         78.3
                         1986                          59.8         70.9
                         1987                          64.3         64.6
                                                     ------       ------
                         Total for each category      233.8        294.5
                                   Combined total            528.3

        Alabama          1984                         256.3        480.5
                         1985                         291.5        454.3
                         1986                         303.6        454.7
                         1987                           .          454.5
                                                     ------       ------
                         Total for each category      851.4       1844.0
                                   Combined total           2695.4
```

```
                    Morning and Evening Newspaper Circulation                    3

          State         Year                    Thousands of Copies
                                                 Morning      Evening

          Maine         1984                        .             .
                        1985                        .           68.0
                        1986                      222.7         68.6
                        1987                      224.1         66.7
                                                 ------        ------
                        Total for each category  446.8         203.3
                                  Combined total         650.1

          Hawaii        1984                      433.5        122.3
                        1985                      455.6        245.1
                        1986                      499.3        355.2
                        1987                      503.2        488.6
                                                 ------        ------
                        Total for each category  1891.6       1211.2
                                  Combined total        3102.8
```

When you create titles and column headings with TITLE statements, consider the following:

- □ SAS writes page numbers on title lines by default. Therefore, page numbers appear in this report. If you do not want page numbers, specify the NONUMBER system option.

- □ The PUT statement pointer begins on the first line after the last TITLE statement. SAS does not skip a line before beginning the text as it does with procedure output. In this example, the blank line between the TITLE4 statement and the first line of data for each state is produced by the slash (/) in the PUT statement in the FIRST.STATE group.

Writing Titles and Column Headings in Specific Columns

The easiest way to program headings in specific columns is to use a PUT statement. Instead of calculating the exact number of blanks that are required to make text fall in particular columns, you move the pointer to the appropriate column with pointer controls and write the text. To write headings with a PUT statement, you must execute the PUT statement at the beginning of each page, regardless of the observation that is being processed or the iteration of the DATA step. The FILE statement with the HEADER= option specifies the headings you want to write.

Use the following form of the FILE statement to specify column headings.

FILE PRINT HEADER=*label*;

PRINT is a reserved fileref that directs output that is produced by any PUT statements to the same print file as the output that is produced by SAS procedures. The *label* variable defines a statement label that identifies a group of SAS statements that execute each time SAS begins a new output page.

The following program uses the HEADER= option of the FILE statement to add a header routine to the DATA step. The routine uses pointer controls in the PUT statement to write the title, skip two lines, and then write column headings in specific locations.

```
options linesize=80 pagesize=24;
```

```
data _null_;
   set circulation_figures;
   by state notsorted;
   file print notitles header=pagetop; ❶
   if first.state then
         do;
             morning_total=0;
             evening_total=0;
             put / @7 state @;
         end;
   put @26 year @53 morning_copies 5.1 @66 evening_copies 5.1;
   morning_total+morning_copies;
   evening_total+evening_copies;
   if last.state then
      do;
         all_totals=morning_total+evening_total;
         put @52 '------' @65 '------' /
             @26 'Total for each category'
             @52 morning_total 6.1 @65 evening_total 6.1 /
             @35 'Combined total' @59 all_totals 6.1;
      end;
   return; ❷
pagetop: ❸
   put @16 'Morning and Evening Newspaper Circulation' //
       @7 'State' @26 'Year' @51 'Thousands of Copies'/
       @51 'Morning       Evening';
   return; ❹
run;
```

The following list corresponds to the numbered items in the preceding program:

❶ The PRINT fileref in the FILE statement creates Listing output. The NOTITLES option eliminates title lines so that the lines can be used by the PUT statement. The HEADER= option defines a statement label that points to a group of SAS statements that executes each time SAS begins a new output page. (You can use the HEADER= option only for creating print files.)

❷ The RETURN statement that is located before the header routine marks the end of the main part of the DATA step. It causes execution to return to the beginning of the step for another iteration. Without this return statement, the statements in the header routine would be executed during each iteration of the DATA step, as well as at the beginning of each page.

❸ The pagetop: label identifies the header routine. Each time SAS begins a new page, execution moves from its current position to the label pagetop: and continues until SAS encounters the RETURN statement. When execution reaches the RETURN statement at the end of the header routine, execution returns to the statement that was being executed when SAS began a new page.

❹ The RETURN statement ends the header routine. Execution returns to the statement that was being executed when SAS began a new page.

The following output shows the results:

Output 31.9 Title and Column Headings in Specific Locations

```
              Morning and Evening Newspaper Circulation

    State          Year              Thousands of Copies
                                     Morning     Evening

    Colorado       1984               738.6       210.2
                   1985               742.2       212.3
                   1986               731.7       209.7
                   1987               789.2       155.9
                                     ------      ------
                   Total for each category 3001.7    788.1
                          Combined total        3789.8

    Vermont        1984               623.4       566.1
                   1985               533.1       455.9
                   1986               544.2       566.7
                   1987               322.3       423.8
                                     ------      ------
                   Total for each category 2023.0   2012.5
                          Combined total        4035.5

    Alaska         1984                51.0        80.7
                   1985                58.7        78.3
                   1986                59.8        70.9
```

```
              Morning and Evening Newspaper Circulation

    State          Year              Thousands of Copies
                                     Morning     Evening
                   1987                64.3        64.6
                                     ------      ------
                   Total for each category  233.8    294.5
                          Combined total         528.3

    Alabama        1984               256.3       480.5
                   1985               291.5       454.3
                   1986               303.6       454.7
                   1987                 .         454.5
                                     ------      ------
                   Total for each category  851.4   1844.0
                          Combined total        2695.4

    Maine          1984                 .           .
                   1985                 .          68.0
                   1986               222.7        68.6
                   1987               224.1        66.7
                                     ------      ------
                   Total for each category  446.8    203.3
                          Combined total         650.1
```

Changing a Portion of a Heading

You can use variable values to create headings that change on every page. For example, if you eliminate the default page numbers in the procedure output file, you can create your own page numbers as part of the heading. You can also write the numbers differently from the default method. For example, you can write "Page 1" rather than "1." Page numbers are an example of a heading that changes with each new page.

The following program creates page numbers using a Sum statement and writes the numbers as part of the header routine.

```
options linesize=80 pagesize=24;

data _null_;
   set circulation_figures;
   by state notsorted;
   file print notitles header=pagetop;
   if first.state then
        do;
            morning_total=0;
            evening_total=0;
            put / @7 state @;
        end;
   put @26 year @53 morning_copies 5.1 @66 evening_copies 5.1;
   morning_total+morning_copies;
   evening_total+evening_copies;
   if last.state then
      do;
         all_totals=morning_total+evening_total;
         put @52 '------' @65 '------' /
             @26 'Total for each category'
             @52 morning_total 6.1 @65 evening_total 6.1 /
             @35 'Combined total' @59 all_totals 6.1;
      end;
   return;

   pagetop:
     pagenum+1;  ❶
     put @16 'Morning and Evening Newspaper Circulation'
             @67 'Page ' pagenum //  ❷
         @7 'State' @26 'Year' @51 'Thousands of Copies'/
         @51 'Morning        Evening';
   return;
run;
```

The following list corresponds to the numbered items in the preceding program:

❶ In this Sum statement, SAS adds the value 1 to the accumulator variable PAGENUM each time a new page begins.

❷ The literal Page and the current page number print at the top of each new page.

The following output shows the results:

Output 31.10 Changing a Portion of a Heading

```
             Morning and Evening Newspaper Circulation        Page 1

       State          Year              Thousands of Copies
                                         Morning      Evening

       Colorado       1984                 738.6        210.2
                      1985                 742.2        212.3
                      1986                 731.7        209.7
                      1987                 789.2        155.9
                                          ------       ------
                      Total for each category 3001.7    788.1
                               Combined total      3789.8

       Vermont        1984                 623.4        566.1
                      1985                 533.1        455.9
                      1986                 544.2        566.7
                      1987                 322.3        423.8
                                          ------       ------
                      Total for each category 2023.0   2012.5
                               Combined total      4035.5

       Alaska         1984                  51.0         80.7
                      1985                  58.7         78.3
                      1986                  59.8         70.9
```

```
             Morning and Evening Newspaper Circulation        Page 2

       State          Year              Thousands of Copies
                                         Morning      Evening
                      1987                  64.3         64.6
                                          ------       ------
                      Total for each category  233.8     294.5
                               Combined total      528.3

       Alabama        1984                 256.3        480.5
                      1985                 291.5        454.3
                      1986                 303.6        454.7
                      1987                   .          454.5
                                          ------       ------
                      Total for each category  851.4    1844.0
                               Combined total      2695.4

       Maine          1984                   .            .
                      1985                   .          68.0
                      1986                 222.7         68.6
                      1987                 224.1         66.7
                                          ------       ------
                      Total for each category  446.8     203.3
                               Combined total      650.1
```

Controlling Page Divisions

The report in Output 31.10 on page 553 automatically split the data for Alaska over two pages. To make attractive page divisions, you need to know that there is sufficient space on a page to print all the data for a particular state before you print any data for it.

First, you must know how many lines are needed to print a group of data. Then you use the LINESLEFT= option in the FILE statement to create a variable whose value is the number of lines remaining on the current page. Before you begin writing a group of data, compare the number of lines that you need to the value of that variable. If more lines are required than are available, use the _PAGE_ pointer control to advance the pointer to the first line of a new page.

In your report, the maximum number of lines that you need for any state is eight (four years of circulation data for each state plus four lines for the underline, the totals, and the blank line between states). The following program creates a variable named CKLINES and compares its value to eight at the beginning of each BY group. If the value is less than eight, SAS begins a new page before writing that state.

```
options pagesize=24;

data _null_;
   set circulation_figures;
   by state notsorted;
   file print notitles header=pagetop linesleft=cklines;
   if first.state then
        do;
            morning_total=0;
            evening_total=0;
            if cklines<8 then put _page_;
            put / @7 state @;
        end;
   put @26 year @53 morning_copies 5.1 @66 evening_copies 5.1;
   morning_total+morning_copies;
   evening_total+evening_copies;
   if last.state then
      do;
          all_totals=morning_total+evening_total;
          put @52 '------' @65 '------' /
              @26 'Total for each category'
              @52 morning_total 6.1 @65 evening_total 6.1 /
              @35 'Combined total' @59 all_totals 6.1;
      end;
   return;

   pagetop:
      pagenum+1;
      put @16 'Morning and Evening Newspaper Circulation'
              @67 'Page ' pagenum //
          @7 'State' @26 'Year' @51 'Thousands of Copies'/
          @51 'Morning        Evening';
   return;
run;
```

The following output shows the results:

Output 31.11   Output with Specific Page Divisions

```
                  Morning and Evening Newspaper Circulation          Page 1

         State              Year               Thousands of Copies
                                               Morning      Evening

         Colorado           1984                738.6        210.2
                            1985                742.2        212.3
                            1986                731.7        209.7
                            1987                789.2        155.9
                                               ------       ------
                            Total for each category  3001.7       788.1
                                    Combined total          3789.8

         Vermont            1984                623.4        566.1
                            1985                533.1        455.9
                            1986                544.2        566.7
                            1987                322.3        423.8
                                               ------       ------
                            Total for each category  2023.0       2012.5
                                    Combined total        4035.5
```

```
                  Morning and Evening Newspaper Circulation          Page 2

         State              Year               Thousands of Copies
                                               Morning      Evening

         Alaska             1984                 51.0         80.7
                            1985                 58.7         78.3
                            1986                 59.8         70.9
                            1987                 64.3         64.6
                                               ------       ------
                            Total for each category   233.8        294.5
                                    Combined total          528.3

         Alabama            1984                256.3        480.5
                            1985                291.5        454.3
                            1986                303.6        454.7
                            1987                   .         454.5
                                               ------       ------
                            Total for each category   851.4       1844.0
                                    Combined total        2695.4
```

```
                  Morning and Evening Newspaper Circulation          Page 3

         State              Year               Thousands of Copies
                                               Morning      Evening

         Maine              1984                   .            .
                            1985                   .          68.0
                            1986                222.7         68.6
                            1987                224.1         66.7
                                               ------       ------
                            Total for each category   446.8        203.3
                                    Combined total          650.1
```

Representing Missing Values

Recognizing Default Values

In the following example, numeric data for male verbal and math scores is missing for 1972. Character data for gender is missing for math scores in 1975. By default, SAS replaces a missing numeric value with a period, and a missing character value with a blank when it creates the data set.

```
options pagesize=60 linesize=80 pageno=1 nodate;

libname admin 'SAS-data-library';
data admin.sat_scores2;
   input Test $ 1-8 Gender $ 10 Year 12-15 SATscore 17-19;
   datalines;
verbal   m 1972 .
verbal   f 1972 529
verbal   m 1975 515
verbal   f 1975 509
math     m 1972 .
math     f 1972 489
math       1975 518
math       1975 479
;
run;

proc print data=admin.sat_scores2;
   title 'SAT Scores for Years 1972 and 1975';
run;
```

The following output shows the results:

Output 31.12 Default Display of Missing Values

```
                SAT Scores for Years 1972 and 1975                    1

        Obs     Test     Gender    Year    SATscore

         1      verbal      m      1972        .
         2      verbal      f      1972       529
         3      verbal      m      1975       515
         4      verbal      f      1975       509
         5      math        m      1972        .
         6      math        f      1972       489
         7      math               1975       518
         8      math               1975       479
```

Customizing Output of Missing Values by Using a System Option

If your data set contains missing numeric values, you can use the MISSING= system option to display the missing values as a single character rather than as the default period. You specify the character you want to use as the value of the MISSING= option. You can specify any single character.

In the following program, the MISSING= option in the OPTIONS statement causes the PRINT procedure to display the letter M, rather than a period, for each numeric missing value.

```
options missing='M' pageno=1;

libname admin 'SAS-data-library';
data admin.sat_scores2;
    input Test $ 1-8 Gender $ 10 Year 12-15 SATscore 17-19;
    datalines;
verbal    m 1972
verbal    f 1972 529
verbal    m 1975 515
verbal    f 1975 509
math      m 1972
math      f 1972 489
math        1975 518
math        1975 479
;

proc print data=admin.sat_scores2;
    title 'SAT Scores for Years 1972 and 1975';
run;
```

The following output shows the results:

Output 31.13   Customized Output of Missing Numeric Values

```
                    SAT Scores for Years 1972 and 1975                    1

        Obs      Test      Gender      Year      SATscore

         1       verbal       m        1972         M
         2       verbal       f        1972        529
         3       verbal       m        1975        515
         4       verbal       f        1975        509
         5       math         m        1972         M
         6       math         f        1972        489
         7       math                  1975        518
         8       math                  1975        479
```

Customizing Output of Missing Values by Using a Procedure

Using the FORMAT procedure is another way to represent missing numeric values. It enables you to customize missing values by formatting them. You first use the FORMAT procedure to define a format, and then use a FORMAT statement in a PROC or DATA step to associate the format with a variable.

The following program uses the FORMAT procedure to define a format, and then uses a FORMAT statement in the PROC step to associate the format with the variable SCORE. Note that you do not follow the format name with a period in the VALUE statement but a period always accompanies the format when you use it in a FORMAT statement.

```
options pageno=1;
libname admin 'SAS-data-library';

proc format;
   value xscore .='score unavailable';
run;

proc print data=admin.sat_scores2;
   format SATscore xscore.;
   title 'SAT Scores for Years 1972 and 1975';
run;
```

The following output shows the results:

Output 31.14 Numeric Missing Values Replaced by a Format

```
              SAT Scores for Years 1972 and 1975                    1

        Obs      Test      Gender    Year      SATscore

         1       verbal      m       1972    score unavailable
         2       verbal      f       1972             529
         3       verbal      m       1975             515
         4       verbal      f       1975             509
         5       math        m       1972    score unavailable
         6       math        f       1972             489
         7       math                1975             518
         8       math                1975             479
```

Review of SAS Tools

Statements

FILE *file-specification*;
> identifies an external file that the DATA step uses to write output from a PUT statement.

FILE PRINT <HEADER=*label*> <LINESLEFT=*number-of-lines*>;
> directs the output that is produced by any PUT statements to the same print file as the output that is produced by SAS procedures. The HEADER option defines a statement label that identifies a group of SAS statements that you want to execute each time SAS begins a new output page. The LINESLEFT= option defines a variable whose value is the number of lines left on the current page.

FOOTNOTE <*n*> <'*text*'>;
> specifies up to ten footnote lines to be printed at the bottom of a page of output. The variable *n* specifies the relative line to be occupied by the footnote, and *text* specifies the text of the footnote.

LABEL *variable='label'*;
> associates the variable that you specify with the descriptive text that you specify as the label. Your label can be up to 256 characters long, including blanks. You can use the LABEL statement in either the DATA step or the PROC step.

OPTIONS *option(s)*;
> changes the value of one or more SAS system options.

TITLE *<n> <'text'>*;
> specifies up to ten title lines to be printed on each page of the SAS print file and other SAS output. The variable *n* specifies the relative line that contains the title line, and *text* specifies the text of the title.

SAS System Options

NUMBER | NONUMBER
> controls whether the page number prints on the first title line of each page of output.

PAGENO=*n*
> resets the page number for the next page of output.

CENTER | NOCENTER
> controls whether SAS procedure output is centered.

PAGESIZE=*n*
> specifies the number of lines that can be printed per page of output.

LINESIZE=*n*
> specifies the printer line width for the SAS log and the standard SAS print file used by the DATA step and procedures.

DATE | NODATE
> controls whether the date and time are printed at the top of each page of the SAS log, the standard print file, or any file with the PRINT attribute.

MISSING=*'character'*
> specifies the character to be printed for missing numeric variable values.

Learning More

SAS output
> □ Chapter 30, "Writing Lines to the SAS Log or to an Output File," on page 517
> □ Chapter 32, "Understanding and Customizing SAS Output: The Output Delivery System (ODS)," on page 561

CHAPTER

32

Understanding and Customizing SAS Output: The Output Delivery System (ODS)

Introduction

Purpose

The Output Delivery System (ODS) enables you to produce output in a variety of formats, such as

- [ ] an HTML file
- [ ] a traditional SAS Listing
- [ ] a PostScript file
- [ ] an RTF file (for use with Microsoft Word)
- [ ] an output data set.

In this chapter, you will learn how to create ODS output for the formats that are listed above.

Prerequisites

Before using this chapter, you should be familiar with the concepts presented in:

□ Chapter 1, "What Is the SAS System?," on page 3

□ Chapter 23, "Directing SAS Output and the SAS Log," on page 347

You should also be familiar with DATA step processing, and creating procedure output.

Input Data Set for Examples

The examples in this chapter are based on data from a college entrance exam called the Scholastic Aptitude Test, or SAT. The data is provided in one input file that contains the average SAT scores of students that are entering the university from 1972 to 1998. The input file has the following structure:

```
Verbal m 1972 531
Verbal f 1972 529
Verbal m 1973 523
Verbal f 1973 521
Math   m 1972 527
Math   f 1972 489
Math   m 1973 525
Math   f 1973 489
```

The input file contains the following kinds of values:

□ type of SAT test

□ gender of the student

□ year the test was given

□ average test score of the entering first-year college class.

The following program creates the data set that this chapter uses. (For a complete listing of the input data, see "Data Set for Chapter 22" on page 714.)

```
data sat_scores;
   input Test $ Gender $ Year SATscore @@;
   datalines;
Verbal m 1972 531  Verbal f 1972 529
Verbal m 1973 523  Verbal f 1973 521
Verbal m 1974 524  Verbal f 1974 520
...more data lines...
Math   m 1996 527  Math   f 1996 492
Math   m 1997 530  Math   f 1997 494
Math   m 1998 531  Math   f 1998 496
;
```

Note: The examples use file names that may not be valid in all operating environments. For information about how your operating environment uses file specifications, see the documentation for your operating environment. △

Understanding ODS Output Formats and Destinations

The Output Delivery System (ODS) enables you to produce output in a variety of formats that you can easily access. ODS removes responsibility for formatting output from individual procedures and from the DATA step. The procedure or DATA step supplies the data and the *table definition*, which contains formatting instructions for the output.

The following figure illustrates the concept of output for SAS Version 8. The data and the table definition form an *output object*, which creates the type of ODS output that you specified in the table definition.

Figure 32.1 Model of the Production of ODS Output

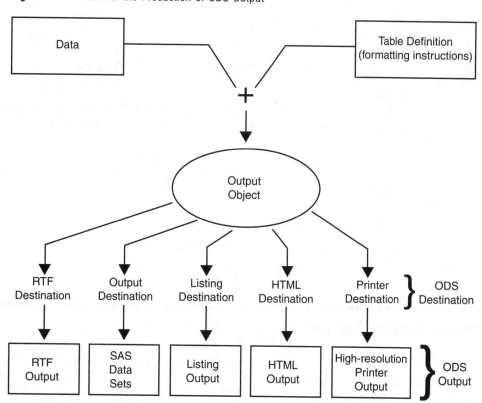

The following definitions describe the terms in the preceding figure:

data

> Each procedure that supports ODS and each DATA step produces data, which contains the results (numbers and characters) of the step in a form similar to a SAS data set.

table definition

> The table definition is a set of instructions that describes how to format the data. This description includes but is not limited to

> > □ the order of the columns

> > □ text and order of column headings

> > □ formats for data

> > □ font sizes and font faces.

output object
ODS combines formatting instructions with the data to produce an output object. The output object, therefore, contains both the results of the procedure or DATA step and information about how to format the results. An output object has a name, a label, and a path.

Note: Although many output objects include formatting instructions, not all of them do. In some cases the output object consists of only the data. △

ODS destinations
An ODS destination specifies a specific type of output. ODS supports a number of destinations, including the following:

RTF
produces output that is formatted for use with Microsoft-Word.

Output
produces a SAS data set.

Listing
produces traditional SAS output (monospace format).

HTML
produces output that is formatted in Hyper Text Markup Language (HTML). You can access the output on the web with your web browser.

Printer
produces output that is formatted for a high-resolution printer. An example of this type of output is a PostScript file.

ODS output
ODS output consists of formatted output from any of the ODS destinations.

For detailed information about ODS, see *The Complete Guide to the SAS Output Delivery System*.

Selecting an Output Format

You select the format for your output by opening and closing ODS destinations in your program. When one or more destinations are open, ODS can send output objects to them and produce formatted output. When a destination is closed, ODS does not send an output object to it and no output is produced.

By default, all programs automatically produce Listing output along with output for other destinations that you specifically open. Therefore, by default, the Listing destination is open, and all other destinations are closed.

To create formatted output, open one or more destinations by using the following ODS statements:

ODS HTML *file-specification(s)*;

ODS OUTPUT *data-set-definition*;

ODS PRINTER *file-specification*;

ODS RTF *file-specification*;

The argument *file-specification* opens the destination and specifies one or more files to write to. The argument *data-set-definition* opens the Output destination and enables SAS to create a data set from an output object.

To view or print the ODS output that you have selected, you need to close all the destinations that you opened, except for the Listing destination. You can use separate statements to close individual destinations, or use one statement to close all destinations (including the Listing destination). To close ODS destinations, use the following statements:

ODS HTML CLOSE;

ODS OUTPUT CLOSE;

ODS PRINTER CLOSE;

ODS RTF CLOSE;

ODS _ALL_ CLOSE;

Note: The ODS _ALL_ CLOSE statement, which closes all open destinations, is available with SAS Release 8.2 and higher. △

In some cases you might not want to create Listing output. Use the `ODS LISTING CLOSE;` statement at the beginning of your program to close the Listing destination and prevent SAS from producing Listing output. Closing unnecessary destinations conserves system resources.

Note: Because ODS statements are global statements, it is good practice to open the Listing destination at the end of your program. If you execute other programs in your current SAS session, Listing output is then available. To open the Listing destination, use the `ODS LISTING;` statement at the end of your program. △

Creating Formatted Output

Creating HTML Output for a Web Browser

Understanding the Four Types of HTML Output Files

When you use the ODS HTML statement, you can create output that is formatted in HTML. You can browse the output files with Internet Explorer, Netscape, or any other browser that fully supports the HTML 3.2 tag set.

The ODS HTML statement can create four types of HTML files:

- □ a body file that contains the results of the DATA step or procedure
- □ a table of contents that links to items in the body file
- □ a table of pages that links to items in the body file
- □ a frame file that displays the results of the procedure or DATA step, the table of contents, and the table of pages.

The body file is required with all ODS HTML output. If you do not want to link to your output, then creating a table of contents, a table of pages, and a frame file is not necessary.

Creating HTML Output: The Simplest Case

To produce the simplest kind of HTML output, the only file you need to create is a body file.

The following example executes the MEANS procedure and creates an HTML body file and the default Listing file. These files contain summary statistics for the average

SAT scores of entering first-year college students. The output is grouped by the CLASS variables Test and Gender.

```
options pageno=1 nodate pagesize=30 linesize=78;
ods html file='summary-results.htm';  ❶

proc means data=sat_scores fw=8;  ❷
   var SATscore;
   class Test Gender;
   title1 'Average SAT Scores Entering College Classes, 1972-1998*';
   footnote1 '* Recentered Scale for 1987-1995';
run;

ods html close;  ❸
```

The following list corresponds to the numbered items in the preceding program:

❶ The ODS HTML statement opens the HTML destination and creates the body file SUMMARY-RESULTS.HTM.

❷ The MEANS procedure produces summary statistics for the average SAT scores of entering first-year college students. The output is grouped by the CLASS variables Test and Gender.

❸ The ODS HTML CLOSE statement closes the HTML destination to make output available for viewing.

The following output shows the results in HTML format:

Display 32.1   ODS Output: HTML Format

Average SAT Scores Entering College Classes, 1972-1998*

The MEANS Procedure

Analysis Variable : SATscore							
Test	Gender	N Obs	N	Mean	Std Dev	Minimum	Maximum
Math	f	27	27	481.8	7.0057	473.0	496.0
	m	27	27	521.6	4.3175	515.0	531.0
Verbal	f	27	27	503.0	8.2671	495.0	529.0
	m	27	27	510.5	6.7218	501.0	531.0

* Recentered Scale for 1987-1995

The following output shows the results in the Listing format:

Output 32.1 ODS Output: Listing Format

```
          Average SAT Scores Entering College Classes, 1972-1998*              1

                             The MEANS Procedure

                        Analysis Variable : SATscore

                       N
Test      Gender      Obs      N      Mean    Std Dev    Minimum    Maximum
-----------------------------------------------------------------------------
Math      f            27     27     481.8     7.0057      473.0      496.0

          m            27     27     521.6     4.3175      515.0      531.0

Verbal    f            27     27     503.0     8.2671      495.0      529.0

          m            27     27     510.5     6.7218      501.0      531.0
-----------------------------------------------------------------------------




                         * Recentered Scale for 1987-1995
```

Creating HTML Output: Linking Results with a Table of Contents

The ODS HTML destination enables you to link to your results from a table of contents and a table of pages. To do this, you need to create the following HTML files: a body file, a frame file, a table of contents, and a table of pages (see "Understanding the Four Types of HTML Output Files" on page 565). When you view the frame file and select a link in the table of contents or the table of pages, the HTML table that contains the selected part of the procedure results appears at the top of your browser.

The following example creates multiple pages of output from the UNIVARIATE procedure. You can access specific output results (tables) from links in the table of contents or the table of pages. The results contain statistics for the average SAT scores of entering first-year college classes. The output is grouped by the value of Gender in the CLASS statement and by the value of Test in the BY statement.

```
proc sort data=sat_scores out=sorted_scores;
   by Test;
run;



options pageno=1 nodate;

ods listing close; ❶
ods html file='odshtml-body.htm' ❷
         contents='odshtml-contents.htm'
         page='odshtml-page.htm'
         frame='odshtml-frame.htm';
```

```
proc univariate data=sorted_scores;  ❸
   var SATscore;
   class Gender;
   by Test;
   title1 'Average SAT Scores Entering College Classes, 1972-1998*';
   footnote1 '* Recentered Scale for 1987-1995';
run;

ods html close;  ❹
ods listing;  ❺
```

The following list corresponds to the numbered items in the preceding program:

❶ By default, the Listing destination is open. To conserve resources, the ODS LISTING CLOSE statement closes this destination.

❷ The ODS HTML statement opens the HTML destination and creates four types of files:

   □ the body file (created with the FILE= option), which contains the formatted data

   □ the contents file, which is a table of contents with links to items in the body file

   □ the page file, which is a table of pages with links to items in the body file

   □ the frame file, which displays the table of contents, the table of pages, and the body file.

❸ The UNIVARIATE procedure produces statistics for the average SAT scores of entering first-year college students. The output is grouped by the value of Gender in the CLASS statement and the value of Test in the BY statement.

❹ The ODS HTML CLOSE statement closes the HTML destination to make output available for viewing.

❺ The ODS LISTING statement reopens the Listing destination so that the next program that you run can produce Listing output.

The following SAS log shows that four HTML files are created with the ODS HTML statement:

Output 32.2   Partial SAS Log: HTML File Creation

```
489  ods listing close;
490  ods html file='odshtml-body.htm'
491          contents='odshtml-contents.htm'
492          page='odshtml-page.htm'
493          frame='odshtml-frame.htm';
NOTE: Writing HTML Body file: odshtml-body.htm
NOTE: Writing HTML Contents file: odshtml-contents.htm
NOTE: Writing HTML Pages file: odshtml-page.htm
NOTE: Writing HTML Frames file: odshtml-frame.htm
494
495  proc univariate data=sorted_scores;
496    var SATscore;
497    class Gender;
498     by Test;
499    title1 'Average SAT Scores Entering College Classes, 1972-1998*';
500    footnote1 '* Recentered Scale for 1987-1995';
501  run;
```

The following output shows the frame file, which displays the table of contents (upper left side), the table of pages (lower left side), and the body file (right side).

Display 32.2 View of the HTML Frame File

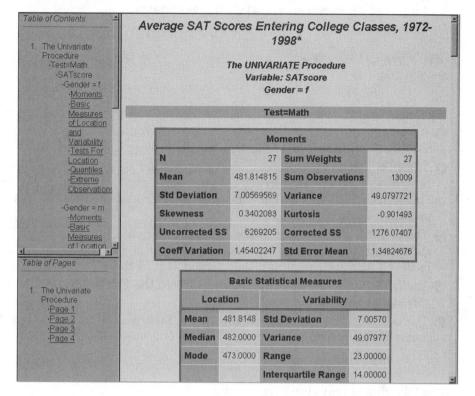

Both the Table of Contents and the Table of Pages contain links to the results in the body file. If you click on a link in the Table of Contents or the Table of Pages, SAS displays the corresponding results at the top of the browser.

Creating PostScript Output for a High-Resolution Printer

You can create output that is formatted for a high-resolution printer if you open the Printer destination. Before you can access the file, however, you must close the Printer destination.

The following example executes the MEANS procedure and creates a PostScript file which contains summary statistics for the average SAT scores of entering first-year college students. The output is grouped by the value of Gender in the CLASS statement and the value of Test in the BY statement.

```
proc sort data=sat_scores out=sorted_scores;
   by Test;
run;

options pageno=1 nodate;

ods listing close; ❶
ods printer ps file='odsprinter_output.ps'; ❷
```

```
proc means data=sorted_scores fw=8; ❸
    var SATscore;
    class Gender ;
    by Test;
    title1 'Average SAT Scores Entering College Classes, 1972-1998*';
    footnote1 '* Recentered Scale for 1987-1995';
run;

ods printer close; ❹
ods listing; ❺
```

The following list corresponds to the numbered items in the preceding program:

❶ By default, the Listing destination is open. To conserve resources, the program uses the ODS LISTING CLOSE statement to close this destination.

❷ The ODS PRINTER statement opens the Printer destination and specifies the file to write to. The PS (PostScript) option ensures that you create a generic PostScript file. If this option is missing, ODS produces output for your current printer, if possible.

❸ The MEANS procedure produces summary statistics for the average SAT scores of entering first-year college students. The output is grouped by the value of Gender in the CLASS statement and the value of Test in the BY statement.

❹ The ODS PRINTER CLOSE statement closes the Printer destination to make output available for printing.

❺ The ODS LISTING statement reopens the Listing destination so that the next program that you run can produce Listing output.

The following output shows the results:

Display 32.3   ODS Output: PostScript Format

Creating RTF Output for Microsoft Word

You can create output that is formatted for use with Microsoft Word if you open the RTF destination. Before you can access the file, you must close the RTF destination.

The following example executes the UNIVARIATE procedure and creates an RTF file that contains summary statistics for the average SAT scores of entering first-year college students. The output is grouped by the CLASS variable Gender.

```
ods listing close; ❶
ods rtf file='odsrtf_output.rtf'; ❷

proc univariate data=sat_scores; ❸
    var SATscore;
    class Gender;
    title1 'Average SAT Scores Entering College Classes, 1972-1998*';
    footnote1 '* Recentered Scale for 1987-1995';
run;

ods rtf close; ❹
ods listing; ❺
```

The following list corresponds to the numbered items in the preceding program:

❶ By default, the Listing destination is open. To conserve resources, the ODS LISTING CLOSE statement closes this destination.

❷ The ODS RTF statement opens the RTF destination and specifies the file to write to.

❸ The UNIVARIATE procedure produces summary statistics for the average SAT scores of entering first-year college students. The output is grouped by the CLASS variable Gender.

❹ The ODS RTF CLOSE statement closes the RTF destination to make output available.

❺ The ODS LISTING statement reopens the Listing destination so that the next program that you run can produce Listing output.

The following output shows the first page of the RTF output:

Display 32.4   ODS Output: RTF Format

1

Average SAT Scores Entering College Classes, 1972–1998*

The UNIVARIATE Procedure
Variable: SATscore
Gender=f

Moments			
N	54	Sum Weights	54
Mean	492.425926	Sum Observations	26591
Std Deviation	13.1272464	Varience	172.324598
Skewness	0.38649931	Kurtosis	0.03082111
Uncorrected SS	13103231	Corrected SS	9133.2037
Coeff Variation	2.66588169	Std Error Mean	1.78639197

Basic Statistical Measures			
Location		Variability	
Mean	492.4259	Std Deviation	13.12725
Median	495.5000	Variance	172.32460
Mode	473.0000	Range	56.00000
		Interquartile Range	20.00000

NOTE: The mode displayed is the smallest of 4 modes with a count of 4.

Tests for Location: Mu0=0				
Test		Statistic	p Value	
Student's t	t	275.6539	Pr > |t|	<.0001
Sign	M	27	Pr >= |M|	<.0001
Signed Rank	S	7425	Pr >= |S|	<.0001

Quantiles (Definition 5)	
Quantile	Estimate
100% Max	529.0
99%	529.0
95%	520.0
90%	505.0
75% Q3	502.0
50% Median	495.5

* Recentered Scale for 1987–1995

Selecting the Output That You Want to Format

Identifying Output

Program output, in the form of output objects, contain both the results of a procedure or DATA step and information about how to format the results. To select an output object for formatting, you need to know which output objects your program creates. To identify the output objects, use the ODS TRACE statement. The simplest form of the ODS TRACE statement is as follows:

ODS TRACE ON|OFF;

ODS TRACE determines whether to write to the SAS log a record of each output object that a program creates. The ON option writes the trace record to the log, and the OFF option supresses the writing of the trace record.

The trace record has the following components:

Name is the name of the output object.

Label is the label that briefly describes the contents of the output object.

Template is the name of the table definition that ODS used to format the output object.

Path shows the location of the output object.

In the ODS SELECT statement in your program, you can refer to an output object by name, label, or path.

The following program executes the UNIVARIATE procedure and writes a trace record to the SAS log.

```
ods trace on;
```

```
proc univariate data=sat_scores;
   var SATscore;
   class Gender;
   title1 'Average SAT Scores Entering College Classes, 1972-1998*';
   footnote1 '* Recentered Scale for 1987-1995';
run;
```

```
ods trace off;
```

The following output shows the results of ODS TRACE. Two sets of output objects are listed because the program uses the class variable Gender to separate male and female results. The path component of the output objects identifies the female (f) and male (m) objects.

Output 32.3 ODS TRACE Output in the Log

```
403  ods trace on;
404
405  proc univariate data=sat_scores;
406     var SATscore;
407     class Gender;
408     title1 'Average SAT Scores Entering College Classes, 1972-1998*';
409     footnote1 '* Recentered Scale for 1987-1995';
410  run;

Output Added:
-------------

Name:       Moments
Label:      Moments
Template:   base.univariate.Moments
Path:       Univariate.SATscore.f.Moments

Output Added:
-------------

Name:       BasicMeasures
Label:      Basic Measures of Location and Variability
Template:   base.univariate.Measures
Path:       Univariate.SATscore.f.BasicMeasures
-------------

Output Added:
-------------

Name:       TestsForLocation
Label:      Tests For Location
Template:   base.univariate.Location
Path:       Univariate.SATscore.f.TestsForLocation
-------------

Output Added:
-------------

Name:       Quantiles
Label:      Quantiles
Template:   base.univariate.Quantiles
Path:       Univariate.SATscore.f.Quantiles
-------------

Output Added:
-------------

Name:       ExtremeObs
Label:      Extreme Observations
Template:   base.univariate.ExtObs
Path:       Univariate.SATscore.f.ExtremeObs
-------------

Output Added:
-------------

Name:       Moments
Label:      Moments
Template:   base.univariate.Moments
Path:       Univariate.SATscore.m.Moments
-------------

Output Added:
-------------

Name:       BasicMeasures
Label:      Basic Measures of Location and Variability
Template:   base.univariate.Measures
Path:       Univariate.SATscore.m.BasicMeasures
-------------
```

```
Output Added:
-------------
Name:        TestsForLocation
Label:       Tests For Location
Template:    base.univariate.Location
Path:        Univariate.SATscore.m.TestsForLocation
-------------

Output Added:
-------------
Name:        Quantiles
Label:       Quantiles
Template:    base.univariate.Quantiles
Path:        Univariate.SATscore.m.Quantiles
-------------

Output Added:
-------------
Name:        ExtremeObs
Label:       Extreme Observations
Template:    base.univariate.ExtObs
Path:        Univariate.SATscore.m.ExtremeObs
-------------
411
412   ods trace off;
```

Selecting and Excluding Program Output

For each destination, ODS maintains a selection list or an exclusion list. The selection list is a list of output objects that produce formatted output. The exclusion list is a list of output objects for which no output is produced.

You can select and exclude output objects by specifying the destination in an ODS SELECT or ODS EXCLUDE statement. If you do not specify a destination, ODS sends output to all open destinations.

Selection and exclusion lists can be modified and reset at different points in a SAS session, such as at procedure boundaries. If you end each procedure with an explicit QUIT statement, rather than waiting for the next PROC or DATA step to end it for you, the QUIT statement resets the selection list.

To choose one or more output objects and send them to open ODS destinations, use the ODS SELECT statement. The simplest form of the ODS SELECT statement is as follows:

ODS SELECT *<ODS-destination> output-object(s)*;

The argument *ODS-destination* identifies the output format, and *output-object* specifies one or more output objects to add to a selection list.

To exclude one or more output objects from being sent to open destinations, use the ODS EXCLUDE statement. The simplest form of the ODS EXCLUDE statement is as follows:

ODS EXCLUDE *<ODS-destination> output-object(s)*;

The argument *ODS-destination* identifies the output format, and *output-object* specifies one or more output objects to add to an exclusion list.

The following example executes the UNIVARIATE procedure and creates 10 output objects. The ODS SELECT statement uses the name component in the trace records to select only the BasicMeasures and the TestsForLocation output objects. Because the HTML and Printer destinations are open, ODS creates HTML and Printer output from the output objects.

```
options nodate pageno=1;

ods listing close;
ods html file='odsselect-body.htm'
         contents='odsselect-contents.htm'
         page='odsselect-page.htm'
         frame='odsselect-frame.htm';
ods printer file='odsprinter-select.ps';

ods select BasicMeasures TestsForLocation;
proc univariate data=sat_scores;
   var SATscore;
   class Gender;
   title1 'Average SAT Scores Entering College Classes, 1972-1998*';
   footnote1 '* Recentered Scale for 1987-1995';
run;

ods html close;
ods printer close;
ods listing;
```

The following two displays show the results in Printer format. They show the Basic Statistical Measures and Tests for Location tables based on gender.

Display 32.5 ODS SELECT Statement: Printer Format (females)

Average SAT Scores Entering College Classes, 1972–1998*   1

The UNIVARIATE Procedure
Variable: SATscore
Gender = f

Basic Statistical Measures			
Location		**Variability**	
Mean	492.4259	Std Deviation	13.12725
Median	495.5000	Variance	172.32460
Mode	473.0000	Range	56.00000
		Interquartile Range	20.00000

NOTE: The mode displayed is the smallest of 4 modes with a count of 4.

Tests for Location: Mu0=0				
Test	**Statistic**		**p Value**	
Student's t	t	275.6539	Pr > |t|	< .0001
Sign	M	27	Pr > = |M|	< .0001
Signed Rank	S	742.5	Pr >= |S|	< .0001

* Recentered Scale for 1987–1995

Display 32.6 ODS SELECT Statement: Printer Format (males)

Average SAT Scores Entering College Classes, 1972–1998* 2

The UNIVARIATE Procedure
Variable: SATscore
Gender = m

Basic Statistical Measures			
Location		Variability	
Mean	516.0185	Std Deviation	7.90865
Median	516.0000	Variance	62.54682
Mode	523.0000	Range	30.00000
		Interquartile Range	14.00000

Tests for Location: Mu0=0				
Test	Statistic		p Value	
Student's t	t	479.4679	Pr > |t|	< .0001
Sign	M	27	Pr > = |M|	< .0001
Signed Rank	S	742.5	Pr >= |S|	< .0001

* Recentered Scale for 1987–1995

The following two displays show the results in HTML format. They, too, show the Basic Statistical Measures and Tests for Location tables based on gender.

Display 32.7 ODS SELECT Statement: HTML Format (females)

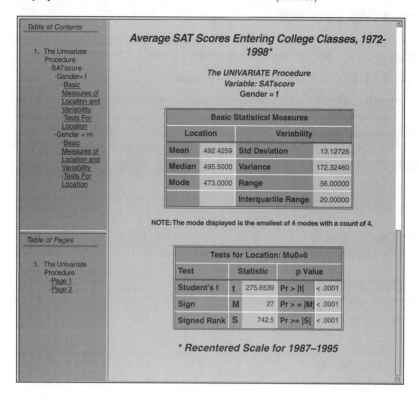

Display 32.8 ODS SELECT Statement: HTML Format (males)

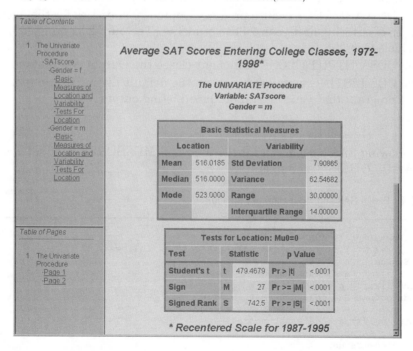

Creating a SAS Data Set

ODS enables you to create a SAS data set from an output object. To create a single output data set, use the following form of the ODS OUTPUT statement:

ODS OUTPUT *output-object(s)=SAS-data-set*;

The argument *output-object* specifies one or more output objects to turn into a SAS data set, and *SAS-data-set* specifies the data set that you want to create.

In the following program, ODS opens the Output destination and creates the SAS data set MYFILE.MEASURES from the output object BasicMeasures. ODS then closes the Output destination.

```
libname myfile 'SAS-data-library';

ods listing close; ❶
ods output BasicMeasures=myfile.measures; ❷

proc univariate data=sat_scores; ❸
   var SATscore;
   class Gender;
run;

ods output close; ❹
ods listing; ❺
```

The following list corresponds to the numbered items in the preceding program:

❶ By default, the Listing destination is open. To conserve resources, the ODS LISTING CLOSE statement closes this destination.

❷ The ODS OUTPUT statement opens the Output destination and specifies the permanent data set to create from the output object BasicMeasures.

❸ The UNIVARIATE procedure produces summary statistics for the average SAT scores of entering first-year college students. The output is grouped by the CLASS variable Gender.

❹ The ODS OUTPUT CLOSE statement closes the Output destination.

❺ The ODS LISTING statement reopens the default Listing destination so that the next program that you run can produce Listing output.

The following SAS log shows that the MYFILE.MEASURES data set was created with the ODS OUTPUT statement:

Output 32.4   Partial SAS Log: SAS Data Set Creation

```
404  libname myfile 'SAS-data-library';
NOTE: Libref MYFILE was successfully assigned as follows:
      Engine:        V8
      Physical Name: path-name
405  ods listing close;
406  ods output BasicMeasures=myfile.measures;
407
408  proc univariate data=sat_scores;
409     var SATscore;
410     class Gender;
411  run;
NOTE: The data set MYFILE.MEASURES has 8 observations and 6 variables.
```

Customizing ODS Output

Customizing ODS Output at the Level of a SAS Job

ODS provides a way for you to customize output at the level of the SAS job. To do this, you use a *style definition*, which describes how to show such items as color, font face, font size, and so on. The style definition determines the appearance of the output. The fancyprinter style definition is one of several that is available with SAS.

The following example uses the fancyprinter style definiton to customize program output. The output consists of two output objects, Moments and BasicMeasures, that the UNIVARIATE procedure creates. The STYLE= option on the ODS PRINTER statement specifies that the program use the fancyprinter style.

```
options nodate pageno=1;


ods listing close;
ods printer ps file='style_job.ps' style=fancyprinter;
ods select Moments BasicMeasures;


proc univariate data=sat_scores;
   var SATscore;
   title 'Average SAT Scores for Entering College Classes, 1972-1982*';
   footnote1 '* Recentered Scale for 1987-1995';
run;


ods printer close;
ods listing;
```

The following output shows the results:

Display 32.9 Printer Output: Titles, Footnote, and Variables Printed in Italics

For detailed information about style and table definitions, as well as the TEMPLATE procedure, see *The Complete Guide to the SAS Output Delivery System*.

Customizing ODS Output by Using a Template

Another way to customize ODS output is by using a template. In ODS, templates are called *table definitions*. A table definition describes how to format the output. It can determine the order of table headings and footnotes, the order of columns, and the appearance of the output. A table definition can contain one or more columns, headings, or footnotes.

Many procedures that fully support ODS provide table definitions that you can customize. You can also create your own table definition by using the TEMPLATE procedure. The following is a simplified form of the TEMPLATE procedure:

PROC TEMPLATE;
     DEFINE *table-definition*;
     HEADER *header(s)*;

COLUMN *column(s)*;
END;

The DEFINE statement creates the table definition that serves as the template for writing the output. The HEADER statement specifies the order of the headings, and the COLUMN statement specifies the order of the columns. The arguments in each of these statements point to routines in the program that format the output. The END statement ends the table definition.

The following example shows how to use PROC TEMPLATE to create customized HTML and printer output. In the example, the SAS program creates a customized table definition for the Basic Measures output table from PROC UNIVARIATE. The following customized version shows that

☐ the "Measures of Variability" section precedes the "Measures of Location" section

☐ column headings are modified

☐ statistics are displayed in a bold, italic font with a 7.3 format.

```
options nodate nonumber linesize=80 pagesize=60; ❶

proc template; ❷
   define table base.univariate.Measures; ❸
   header h1 h2 h3; ❹
   column VarMeasure VarValue LocMeasure LocValue; ❺

   define h1; ❻
      text "Basic Statistical Measures";
      spill_margin=on;
      space=1;
   end;
   define h2; ❻
      text "Measures of Variability";
      start=VarMeasure;
      end=VarValue;
   end;
   define h3; ❻
      text "Measures of Location";
      start=LocMeasure;
      end=LocValue;
   end;

   define LocMeasure; ❼
      print_headers=off;
      glue=2;
      space=3;
      style=rowheader;
   end;
   define LocValue; ❼
      print_headers=off;
      space=5;
      format=7.3;
      style=data{font_style=italic font_weight=bold};
   end;
   define VarMeasure; ❼
      print_headers=off;
      glue=2;
```

```
            space=3;
            style=rowheader;
         end;
      define VarValue; ❼
         print_headers=off;
         format=7.3;
         style=data{font_style=italic font_weight=bold};
      end;
   end; ❽
run; ❾


ods listing close;
ods html file='scores-body.htm' ❿
      contents='scores-contents.htm'
         page='scores-page.htm'
         frame='scores-frame.htm';
ods printer file='scores.ps'; ⓫
ods select BasicMeasures; ⓬


title;
proc univariate data=sorted_scores mu0=3.5; ⓭
   var SATscore;
run;


ods html close; ⓮
ods printer close; ⓮
ods listing; ⓯
```

The following list corresponds to the numbered items in the preceding program:

❶ All four options affect the Listing output. The NODATE and NONUMBER options affect the Printer output. None of the options affects the HTML output.

❷ PROC TEMPLATE begins the procedure for creating a table.

❸ The DEFINE statement creates the table definition base.univariate.Measures in SASUSER.

❹ The HEADER statement determines the order in which the table definition uses the headings, which are defined later in the program.

❺ The COLUMN statement determines the order in which the variables appear. PROC UNIVARIATE names the variables.

❻ These DEFINE blocks define the three headings and specify the text to use for each heading. By default, a heading spans all columns. This is the case for H1. H2 spans the variables VarMeasure and VarValue. H3 spans LocMeasure and LocValue.

❼ These DEFINE blocks specify characteristics for each of the four variables. They use FORMAT= to specify a format of 7.3 for LocValue and VarValue. They also use STYLE= to specify a bold, italic font for these two variables. The STYLE= option does not affect the Listing output.

❽ The END statement ends the table definition.

❾ The RUN statement executes the procedure.

❿ The ODS HTML statement begins the program that uses the customized table definition. It opens the HTML destination and identifies the files to write to.

⓫ The ODS PRINTER statement opens the Printer destination and identifies the file to write to.

⓬ The ODS SELECT statement selects the output object that contains the basic measures.

⓭ PROC UNIVARIATE produces one object for each variable. It uses the customized table definition to format the data.

⓮ The ODS statements close the HTML and the PRINTER destinations.

⓯ The ODS LISTING statement opens the listing destination for output.

The following display shows the printer output:

Display 32.10   Customized Printer Output from the TEMPLATE Procedure

The UNIVARIATE Procedure
Variable: SATscore

Basic Statistical Measures			
Measures of Variability		**Measures of Location**	
Std Deviation	*16.025*	**Mean**	*504.222*
Variance	*256.791*	**Median**	*505.000*
Range	*58.000*	**Mode**	*503.000*
Interquartile Range	*22.000*		—

NOTE: The mode displayed is the smallest of 3 modes with a count of 5.

The following display shows the HTML output:

Display 32.11   Customized HTML Output from the TEMPLATE Procedure

Storing Links to ODS Output

When you run a procedure that supports ODS, SAS automatically stores a link to each piece of ODS output in the Results folder in the Results window. It marks the link with an icon that identifies the output destination that created the output.

In the following example, SAS executes the UNIVARIATE procedure and generates Listing, HTML, Printer, and Rich Text Format (RTF) output as well as a SAS data set (Output output). The output contains statistics for the average SAT scores of entering first-year college students. The output is grouped by the CLASS variable Gender.

```
ods listing close;
ods html file='store-links.htm';
ods printer file='store-links.ps';
ods rtf file='store-links.rtf';
ods output basicmeasures=measures;

proc univariate data=sat_scores;
   var SATscore;
   class Gender;
   title;
run;

ods _all_ close;
ods listing;
```

PROC UNIVARIATE generates a folder called Univariate in the Results folder. Within this folder is another folder (SAT score) for the variable in the VAR statement. This folder contains two folders (Gender=f and Gender=m), one for each variable in the CLASS statement. The Gender=f and Gender=m folders each contain a folder for each output object. Within the folder for each output object is a link to each piece of output. The icon next to the link indicates which ODS destination created the output. In this example, the Moments output was sent to the Listing, HTML, Printer, and RTF destinations. The Basic Measures of Location and Variability output was sent to the Listing, HTML, Printer, RTF, and Output destinations.

The Results folder in the display that follows shows the folders and output objects that the UNIVARIATE procedure creates.

Display 32.12   View of the Results Folder

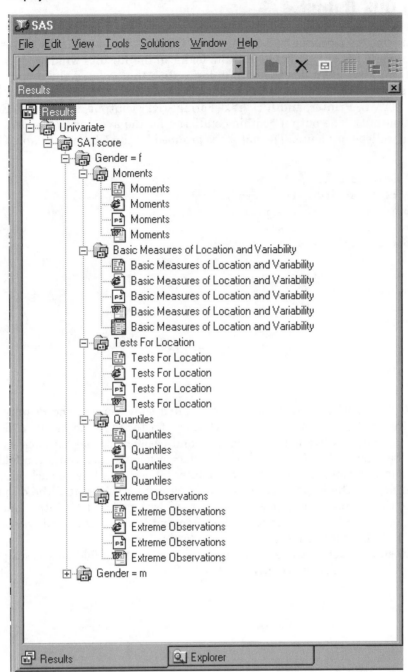

Review of SAS Tools

ODS Statements

ODS EXCLUDE <*ODS-destination*> *output-object(s)*;
    specifies one or more output objects to add to an exclusion list.

ODS HTML*HTML-file-specification(s)* <STYLE='*style-definition*'>;
opens the HTML destination and specifies the HTML file or files to write to. After the destination is open, you can create output that is written in Hyper Text Markup Language (HTML).

You can specify up to four HTML files to write to. The specifications for these files have the following form:

BODY='*body-file-name*'
identifies the file that contains the HTML output.

Alias: FILE=

CONTENTS='*contents-file-name*'
identifies the file that contains a table of contents for the HTML output. The contents file has links to the body file.

FRAME='*frame-file-name*'
identifies the file that integrates the table of contents, the page contents, and the body file. If you open the frame file, you see a table of contents, a table of pages, or both, as well as the body file. If you specify FRAME=, you must also specify CONTENTS= or PAGE= or both.

PAGE='*page-file-name*'
identifies the file that contains a description of each page of the body file and links to the body file. ODS produces a new page of output whenever a procedure explicitly asks for a new page. The SAS system option PAGESIZE= has no effect on pages in HTML output.

The STYLE= option enables you to choose HTML presentation styles.

ODS LISTING;
opens the Listing destination.

Note: The Listing destination is open by default. △

ODS LISTING CLOSE;
closes the Listing destination so that no Listing output is created.

ODS OUTPUT *output-object(s)=SAS-data-set*;
opens the Output destination and converts one or more output objects to a SAS data set.

ODS PRINTER PS *file-specification*;
opens the Printer destination and specifies the file to write to. The PS (PostScript) option ensures that you create a generic PostScript file. If this option is missing, ODS produces output for your current printer.

ODS RTF *file-specification*;
opens the RTF destination and specifies the file to write to. After the destination is open, you can create RTF output.

ODS HTML CLOSE;
ODS OUTPUT CLOSE;
ODS PRINTER CLOSE;
ODS RTF CLOSE;
closes the specific destination and enables you to view the output.

ODS _ALL_ CLOSE;
closes all open destinations.

ODS SELECT <*ODS-destination*> *output-object(s)*;
specifies one or more output objects to add to a selection list.

ODS TRACE ON | OFF;

> turns the writing of the trace record on or off. Turning trace on is useful because the results list the output objects that your program creates.

Procedures

PROC MEANS DATA=*SAS-data-set* <FW=>;

CLASS *variable(s)*;
VAR *variable(s)*;

> provides data summarization tools to compute descriptive statistics for variables across all observations and within groups of observations. The DATA= option specifies the input SAS data set, and FW= specifies the field width for statistics.
>
> The CLASS statement specifies the variables whose values define the subgroup combinatins for the analysis.
>
> The VAR statement identifies the analysis variables and determines their order in the output.

PROC TEMPLATE;

DEFINE *table-definition*;
COLUMN *header(s)*;
HEADER *column(s)*;
END;

> creates an ODS table definition. The DEFINE statement uses the COLUMN and HEADER statements to create column and table headings.

PROC UNIVARIATE DATA=*SAS-data-set*;

VAR *variable(s)*;
CLASS *variable(s)*;
BY *variable(s)*;

> provides data summarization tools and information about the distribution of numeric variables. The DATA= option specifies the input SAS data set.
>
> The VAR statement identifies the analysis variables and determines their order in the output.
>
> The CLASS statement specifies up to two variables whose values define the classification levels for the analysis.
>
> The BY statement calculates separate statistics for each BY group.

Learning More

ODS output

> For detailed information about the Output Delivery System, see *The Complete Guide to the SAS Output Delivery System*.

SAS procedures

> For information about procedures, see the *SAS Procedures Guide*.

PART *9*

Storing and Managing Data in SAS Files

33

Understanding SAS Data Libraries

Introduction

Purpose

The way in which SAS handles data libraries is different from one operating environment to another. In this chapter, you will learn basic concepts about the SAS data library and how to use libraries in SAS programs. For more detailed information, see the SAS documentation for your operating environment.

Prerequisites

Before proceeding with this chapter, you should understand the concepts presented in

☐ Chapter 1, "What Is the SAS System?," on page 3

☐ Chapter 2, "Introduction to DATA Step Processing," on page 19.

What Is a SAS Data Library?

A *SAS data library* is a collection of one or more SAS files that are recognized by SAS and can be referenced and stored as a unit. Each file is a member of the library. SAS data libraries help to organize your work. For example, if a SAS program uses more than one SAS file, then you can keep all the files in the same library. Organizing files in libraries makes it easier to locate the files and reference them in a program.

Under most operating environments, a SAS data library roughly corresponds to the level of organization that the operating environment uses to organize files. For example, in directory-based operating environments, a SAS data library is a group of SAS files in the same directory. The directory might contain other files, but only the SAS files are part of the SAS data library.

Operating Environment Information: Under the CMS operating environment, a SAS data library is a group of SAS files with the same filetype. Under the OS/390 operating environment, a SAS data library is a specially formatted OS/390 data set. This kind of data set can contain only SAS files. △

Accessing a SAS Data Library

Telling SAS Where the SAS Data Library Is Located

No matter which operating environment you are using, to access a SAS data library, you must tell SAS where it is. To do so, you can either

- □ directly specify the operating environment's physical name for the location of the SAS data library. The physical name must conform to the naming conventions of your operating environment, and it must be in single quotation marks. For example, in the SAS windowing environment, the following DATA statement creates a data set named MYFILE:

  ```
  data 'c:\my documents\sasfiles\myfile';
  ```

- □ assign a SAS *libref* (library reference), which is a SAS name that is temporarily associated with the physical location name of the SAS data library.

Assigning a Libref

After you assign a libref to the location of a SAS data library, then in your SAS program you can reference files in the library by using the libref instead of using the long physical name that the operating environment uses. The libref is a SAS name that is temporarily associated with the physical location of the SAS data library. There are several ways to assign a libref:

- □ LIBNAME statement
- □ LIBNAME function
- □ New Library window from the SAS Explorer window
- □ for some operating environments, operating environment commands

A common method for assigning a libref is to use the LIBNAME statement to associate a name with a SAS data library. Here is the simplest form of the LIBNAME statement.

    LIBNAME *libref* '*SAS-data-library*' ;

where

libref	is a shortcut name to associate with the SAS data library. This name must conform to the rules for SAS names. A libref cannot exceed eight characters.

    Operating Environment Information: Under the OS/390 operating environment, the libref must also conform to the rules for operating environment names. △

    Think of the libref as an abbreviation for the operating environment's name for the library. Because the libref endures only for the duration of the SAS session, you do not have to use the same libref for a particular SAS data library each time you use SAS.

    Operating Environment Information: Under the CMS operating environment, the libref typically specifies the filetype of all files in the library. In this case, you must always use the same libref for a SAS data library because the filetype does not change. △

SAS-data-library	is the physical name for the SAS data library. The physical name is the name that is recognized by your operating environment. Enclose the physical name in single or double quotation marks.

Operating Environment Information: Here are examples of the LIBNAME statement for different operating environments. For more examples, see the SAS documentation for your operating environment.

Windows	`libname mydata 'c:\my documents\sasfiles';`
UNIX	`libname mydata '/u/myid/sasfiles';`
OS/390	`libname mydata 'edc.company.sasfiles';`

△

    When you assign a libref with the LIBNAME statement, SAS writes a note to the SAS log confirming the assignment. This note also includes the operating environment's physical name for the SAS data library.

Using Librefs for Temporary and Permanent Libraries

    When a libref is assigned to a SAS data library, you can use the libref throughout the SAS session to access the SAS files that are stored in that library or to create new files.

    When you start a SAS session, SAS automatically assigns the libref WORK to a special SAS data library. Normally, the files in the WORK library are *temporary files*; that is, usually SAS initializes the WORK library when you begin a SAS session, and deletes all files in the WORK library when you end the session. Therefore, the WORK library is a useful place to store SAS files that you do not need to save for a subsequent SAS session. The automatic deletion of the WORK library files at the end of the session prevents you from wasting disk space.

    Files that are stored in any SAS data library other than the WORK library are usually *permanent files*; that is, they endure from one SAS session to the next. Store SAS files in a permanent library if you plan to use them in multiple SAS sessions.

Storing Files in a SAS Data Library

What Is a SAS File?

You store all SAS files in a SAS data library. A *SAS file* is a specially structured file that is created, organized, and maintained by SAS. The files reside in SAS data libraries as members with specific types. Examples of SAS files are as follows:

- □ SAS data sets (which can be SAS data files or SAS data views)
- □ SAS catalogs
- □ SAS/ACCESS descriptor files
- □ stored compiled DATA step programs

Note: A file that contains SAS statements, even one that is created during a SAS session, is usually not considered a SAS file. For example, in directory-based operating environments, a .sas file is a text file that typically contains a program and is not considered a SAS file. △

Understanding SAS Data Sets

A *SAS data set* is a SAS file that is stored in a SAS data library that consists of descriptor information. Descriptor information identifies the attributes of a SAS data set and its contents, and data values that are organized as a table of observations (rows) and variables (columns). A SAS data set can be either a SAS data file or a SAS data view.

If the descriptor information and the observations are in the same physical location, then the data set is a *SAS data file*, which has a member type DATA. A SAS data file can have an index associated with it. One purpose of an index is to optimize the performance of WHERE processing. Basically, an index contains values in ascending order for a specific variable or variables. The index also includes information about the location of those values within observations in the SAS data file.

If the descriptor and the observations are stored separately, then they form a *SAS data view*, which has a member type VIEW. The observations in a SAS data view might be stored in a SAS data file, an external database, or an external file. The descriptor contains information about where the data is located and which observations and variables to process. You use a view like a SAS data file. You might use a view when you need only a subset of a large amount of data. In addition to saving storage space, views simplify maintenance because they automatically reflect any changes to the data. There are three types of SAS data views:

- □ DATA step views
- □ SAS/ACCESS views
- □ PROC SQL views.

Note: SAS data views usually behave like SAS data files. Other chapters in this book do not distinguish between the two types of SAS data sets. △

Understanding Other SAS Files

In addition to SAS data sets, a SAS data library can contain the following types of SAS files:

SAS catalog

is a SAS file that stores many kinds of information, in separate units called *catalog entries*. Each entry is distinguished by an *entry name* and an *entry type*. Some catalog entries contain system information such as key definitions. Other catalog entries contain application information about window definitions, help windows, formats, informats, macros, or graphics output. A SAS catalog has a member type CATALOG.

SAS/ACCESS descriptor

is a SAS file that contains information about the layout of an external database. SAS uses this information in order to build a SAS data view in which the observations are stored in an external database. An access descriptor has a member type ACCESS.

stored compiled DATA step program

is a SAS file that contains a DATA step, which has been compiled and stored in a SAS data library. A stored compiled DATA step program has a member type PROGRAM.

Complete discussion of all SAS files except SAS data sets is beyond the scope of this chapter. For more information about SAS files, see *SAS Language Reference: Concepts*.

Referencing SAS Data Sets in a SAS Data Library

Understanding Data Set Names

Every SAS data set has a two-level name of the form *libref.filename*. You can always reference a file with its two-level name. However, you can also use a one-level name (just *filename*) to reference a file. By default, a one-level name references a file that uses the libref WORK for the temporary SAS data library.

Note: This chapter separates the issues of permanent versus temporary files and one-level versus two-level names. Other chapters in this book and most SAS documentation assume typical use of the WORK libref and refer to files that are referenced with a one-level name as temporary and to files that are referenced with a two-level name as permanent. △

Operating Environment Information: The documentation that is provided by the vendor for your operating environment provides information about how to create temporary and permanent files. From the point of view of SAS, files in the WORK library are temporary unless you specify the NOWORKINIT and NOWORKTERM options and the files in all other SAS data libraries are permanent. However, your operating environment's point of view might be different. For example, the operating environment might enable you to create a temporary directory or OS/390 data set, that is, one that is deleted when you log off. Because all files in a SAS data library are deleted if the underlying operating environment structure is deleted, the way the operating environment views the SAS data library determines whether the library endures from one session to the next. △

Using a One-Level Name

Typically, when you reference a SAS data set with a one-level name, SAS by default uses the libref WORK for the temporary library. For example, the following program creates a temporary SAS data set named WORK.GRADES:

```
data grades;
   infile 'file-specification';
   input Name $ 1-14 Gender $ 15-20 Section $ 22-24 Grade;
run;
```

However, if you want to use a one-level name to reference a permanent SAS data set, you can assign the reserved libref USER. When USER is assigned and you reference a SAS data set with a one-level name, SAS by default uses the libref USER for a permanent SAS data library. For example, the following program creates a permanent SAS data set named USER.GRADES. Note that you assign the libref USER as you do any other libref.

```
libname user 'SAS-data-library';
```

```
data grades;
   infile 'file-specification';
   input Name $ 1-14 Gender $ 15-20 Section $ 22-24 Grade;
run;
```

Therefore, when you reference a SAS data set with a one-level name, SAS

1 looks for the libref USER. If it is assigned to a SAS data library, then USER becomes the default libref for one-level names.

2 uses WORK as the default libref for one-level names if the libref USER has not been assigned.

If USER is assigned, then you must use a two-level name (for example, WORK.TEST) to access a temporary data set in the WORK library. For example, if USER is assigned, then to print the data set WORK.GRADES requires a two-level name in the PROC PRINT statement:

```
proc print data=work.grades;
run;
```

If USER is assigned, then you need to make only one change in order to use the same program with files of the same name in different SAS data libraries. Instead of specifying two-level names, simply assign USER differently in each case. For example, the following program concatenates five SAS data sets in *SAS-data-library-1* and puts them in a new SAS data set, WEEK, in the same library:

```
libname user 'SAS-data-library-1';
```

```
data week;
   set mon tues wed thurs fri;
run;
```

By changing just the name of the library in the LIBNAME statement, you can combine files with the same names in another library, *SAS-data-library-2*:

```
libname user 'SAS-data-library-2';
```

```
data week;
   set mon tues wed thurs fri;
run;
```

Note: At your site, the libref USER might be assigned for you when you start a SAS session. Your SAS Support Consultant will know whether the libref is assigned. △

Using a Two-Level Name

You can always reference a SAS data set with a two-level name, whether the libref you use is WORK, USER, or some other libref that you have assigned. Usually, any two-level name with a libref other than WORK references a permanent SAS data set.

In the following program, the LIBNAME statement establishes a connection between the SAS name INTRCHEM and *SAS-data-library*, which is the physical name for the location of an existing OS/390 data set or a directory, for example. The DATA step creates the SAS data set GRADES in the SAS data library INTRCHEM. SAS uses the INPUT statement to construct the data set from the raw data in *file-specification*.

```
libname intrchem 'SAS-data-library';

data intrchem.grades;
    infile 'file-specification';
    input Name $ 1-14 Gender $ 15-20 Section $ 22-24 Grade;
run;
```

When the SAS data set INTRCHEM.GRADES is created, you can read from it by using its two-level name. The following program reads the file INTRCHEM.GRADES and creates a new SAS data set named INTRCHEM.FRIDAY, which is a subset of the original data set:

```
data intrchem.friday;
   set intrchem.grades;
      if Section='Fri';
run;
```

The following program displays the SAS data set INTRCHEM.FRIDAY:

```
proc print data=intrchem.friday;
run;
```

Review of SAS Tools

Statements

LIBNAME *libref* '*SAS-data-library*';
  on most operating environments, associates a *libref* with a SAS data library.
  Enclose the name of the SAS data library in single or double quotation marks.

SAS Data Set Reference

You can reference any SAS data set with a two-level name of the form *libref.filename*. By default, if you use a one-level name to reference a SAS data set, then SAS uses the libref USER if it is assigned. If USER is not assigned, then SAS uses the libref WORK.

Learning More

LIBNAME statement
For more information about the LIBNAME statement, including options for the statement and information about specifying an engine other than the default engine, see "Statements" in *SAS Language Reference: Dictionary*.

Operating environment
For operating environment specifics, see the SAS documentation for your operating environment.

SAS files
Detailed information about SAS files can be found in Part 3, "SAS Files Concepts," in *SAS Language Reference: Concepts*.
For detailed information about PROC SQL views, see the *SAS Procedures Guide*.

SAS tools
To learn about the tools that are available for managing SAS data libraries, including the DATASETS procedure, see Chapter 34, "Managing SAS Data Libraries," on page 599.

USER libref
For information about the USER= system option, which you can use instead of the LIBNAME statement to assign the USER libref, see "SAS System Options" in *SAS Language Reference: Dictionary*. Note that if you assign the libref both ways or if you assign it more than once with either method, then the last definition holds.

WORK library
For more information about the WORKINIT and NOWORKINIT and the WORKTERM and NOWORKTERM system options, which control when SAS initializes the WORK library, see "SAS System Options" in *SAS Language Reference: Dictionary*.

Operating Environment Information: These options are implemented slightly differently on the VMS operating environment. For details, see the *SAS Companion for the OpenVMS Operating Environment.* △

CHAPTER

34

Managing SAS Data Libraries

Introduction

Purpose

In this chapter, you will learn about the tools that are available for managing SAS data libraries, including the DATASETS procedure. Subsequent chapters describe how to use the DATASETS procedure.

Prerequisites

Before using this chapter, you should understand the concepts presented in Chapter 33, "Understanding SAS Data Libraries," on page 591.

Choosing Your Tools

As you accumulate more SAS files, you will need to manage the SAS data libraries. Managing libraries generally involves using SAS procedures or operating environment commands to perform routine tasks such as

☐ getting information about the contents of libraries and individual SAS files

☐ renaming, deleting, and moving files

☐ renaming variables

☐ copying libraries and files.

You can use operating environment commands to manage SAS files, but for the most part, their use is restricted to the library level. To delete or copy individual SAS files, such as a SAS data set, it is necessary to use SAS utility procedures.

Operating Environment Information: For SAS files that are stored on directory-based computers or in the CMS operating environment and that do not have auxiliary files (such as a SAS data set without an index or audit trail file), you can use operating environment utilities at both the library and file level. If a SAS data set has either an index file or an audit trail file, then you must use SAS utility procedures to delete the file. △

One advantage of SAS utility procedures is that you can use them in any operating environment at any level. If you learn SAS procedures, then you can handle any file management task for your SAS data libraries without knowing the corresponding operating environment commands.

There are several SAS tools that are available for basic file management. You can use these features alone or in combination.

SAS Explorer   includes windows that enable you to perform most file management tasks without submitting SAS program statements. For example, you can create new libraries and SAS files, open existing SAS files, and perform most file management tasks such as moving, copying, and deleting files. To use SAS Explorer windows, type `libname`, `catalog`, or `dir` in the command bar, or select the Explorer icon from the Toolbar menu.

CATALOG procedure   provides catalog management utilities with the COPY and CONTENTS statements.

COPY procedure   copies all members of a library or individual files within the library.

CONTENTS procedure   lists the contents of libraries and provides general information about characteristics of library members.

DATASETS procedure   combines all library management functions into one procedure. If you do not use SAS Explorer or if SAS executes in a batch or interactive line mode, then using this procedure can save you time and resources.

Understanding the DATASETS Procedure

The DATASETS procedure is an interactive procedure; that is, the procedure remains active after a RUN statement is executed. After you start the procedure, you can continue to manipulate files within a SAS data library until you have finished all the tasks that you have planned. This capability can save time and resources when you have a number of tasks for one session.

Here are some important features to know about the DATASETS procedure:

□ You can specify the input library in the PROC DATASETS statement.

When you start the DATASETS procedure, you can also specify the input library, which is referred to as the procedure input library. If you do not specify a library as the source of files, then SAS uses the default library, which could be the temporary library WORK or the USER library. To specify a different input library, you must start the procedure again.

□ Statements execute in the order in which they are written.

For example, to see the contents of a SAS data set, to copy a data set from another library, and then to see the contents of the second data set so that you can visually compare with the first data set, the SAS statements that perform those tasks must be specified in that order so that they execute correctly.

□ Groups of statements can execute without a RUN statement.

For the DATASETS procedure *only*, SAS recognizes these statements as implied RUN statements and therefore executes them immediately when you submit them:

- □ APPEND statement
- □ CONTENTS statement
- □ MODIFY statement
- □ COPY statement
- □ PROC DATASETS statement.

SAS reads the statements that are associated with one task until it reaches one of the above statements. SAS executes all of the preceding statements immediately and then continues reading until it reaches another of the above statements. To cause the last task to execute, you must submit a RUN or QUIT statement.

Note: If you are running in interactive line mode, then this feature enables you to receive messages that statements have already executed before you submit a RUN statement. △

□ The RUN statement does not stop a PROC DATASETS step.

You must submit a QUIT statement, a new PROC statement, or a DATA step. Submitting a QUIT statement executes any statements that have not executed and ends the procedure.

Looking at a PROC DATASETS Session

The following example illustrates how PROC DATASETS behaves in a typical session. In the example, a file from one SAS data library is used to create a test file in another SAS data library. A data set is copied and its contents are described so that the output can be visually checked in order to be sure that the variables are compatible with an existing file in the test library.

The following program is arranged in groups to show which statements are executed as one task. The tasks and the action by SAS are numbered in the order in which they occur in the program.

```
proc datasets library=test89; ❶

   copy in=realdata out=test89; ❷
      select income88;

   contents data=income88; ❸
run;

   modify income88; ❹
      rename Sales=Sales88;

quit; ❺
```

The following list corresponds to the numbered items in the preceding program:

❶ Starts the DATASETS procedure and specifies the procedure input library TEST89.

❷ Copies the data set INCOME88 from the SAS data library REALDATA. SAS recognizes these statements as one task. When SAS reads the CONTENTS statement, it immediately copies INCOME88 into the library TEST89. The CONTENTS statement acts as an implied RUN statement, which causes the

COPY statement to execute. This action is more noticeable if you are running SAS in the windowing environment.

❸ Describes the contents of the data set. Visually checking the output can verify that the variables are compatible with an existing SAS data set. When SAS receives the RUN statement, it describes the contents of INCOME88. Because the previous task has executed, it finds the data set in the procedure input library TEST89.

   After visually checking the contents, you determine that it is necessary to rename the variable Sales. Because the DATASETS procedure is still active, you can submit more statements.

❹ Renames the variable Sales to Sales88.

❺ Stops the DATASETS procedure. SAS executes the last two statements and ends the DATASETS procedure.

Review of SAS Tools

Procedures

PROC DATASETS <LIBRARY=*libref*>;
   starts the procedure and specifies the library that the procedure processes, that is, the procedure input library. If you do not specify the LIBRARY= option, then the default is the WORK or USER library. PROC DATASETS automatically sends a directory listing to the SAS log when it is submitted.

Statements

QUIT;
   executes any preceding statements that have not run and stops the procedure.

RUN;
   executes the preceding group of statements that have not run without ending the procedure.

Learning More

DATASETS procedure
   To learn about using the DATASETS procedure to manage SAS data libraries whose members are primarily data sets, see
      □ Chapter 35, "Getting Information about Your SAS Data Sets," on page 603
      □ Chapter 36, "Modifying SAS Data Set Names and Variable Attributes," on page 613
      □ Chapter 37, "Copying, Moving, and Deleting SAS Data Sets," on page 625.

SAS windowing environment
   For information about managing SAS files through the SAS windowing environment, see Chapter 39, "Using the SAS Windowing Environment," on page 651.

Operating environment commands
   For information about managing SAS files using operating environment commands, see the SAS documentation for your operating environment.

Getting Information about Your SAS Data Sets

Introduction

Purpose

As you create libraries of SAS data sets, SAS generates and maintains information about where the library is stored in your operating environment, how and when the data sets were created, and how their contents are defined. Using the DATASETS procedure, you can view this information without displaying the contents of the data set or referring to additional documentation.

In this chapter, you will learn how to get the following information about SAS data libraries and SAS data sets:

- □ names and types of SAS files that are included in a SAS data library
- □ names and attributes for variables in SAS data sets
- □ summary information about storage parameters for the operating environment
- □ summary information about the history and structure of SAS data sets.

Prerequisites

Before using this chapter, you should understand the concepts presented in

□ Chapter 33, "Understanding SAS Data Libraries," on page 591
□ Chapter 34, "Managing SAS Data Libraries," on page 599.

Input Data Library for Examples

The examples in this chapter use a SAS data library that contains information about the climate of the United States. The DATA steps that create the data sets are shown in "Data Sets for Chapters 35 and 36" on page 718.

Requesting a Directory Listing for a SAS Data Library

Understanding a Directory Listing

A *directory listing* is a list of files in a SAS data library. Each file is called a member, and each member has a member type that is assigned to it by SAS. The member type indicates the type of SAS file, such as DATA or CATALOG. When SAS processes statements, SAS not only looks for the specified file, it verifies that the file has a member type that can be processed by the statement.

The directory listing contains two parts:

□ heading
□ list of library member names and their member types.

Listing All Files in a Library

To obtain a directory listing of all members in a library, you need only the PROC DATASETS statement and the LIBRARY= option. For example, the following statements send a directory listing to the SAS log for a library that contains climate information. The LIBNAME statement assigns the libref USCLIM to this library.

```
options pagesize=60 linesize=80 nonumber nodate;
libname usclim 'SAS-data-library';

proc datasets library=usclim;
```

The following output shows the resulting SAS log, which contains the directory listing:

Output 35.1   Directory Listing for the Library USCLIM

```
22    options pagesize=60 linesize=80 nonumber nodate;
23    libname usclim 'SAS-data-library';
NOTE: Libref USCLIM was successfully assigned as follows:
      Engine:        V8
      Physical Name: external-file
24
25    proc datasets library=usclim;
                           -----Directory----- ❶

              Libref:           USCLIM
              Engine:           V8
              Physical Name:    external-file
              File Name:        external-file
              Inode Number:     1864992
              Access Permission: rwxr-xr-x
              Owner Name:        userid
              File Size (bytes): 4096


                                      File
          #   Name ❷     Memtype ❸   Size    Last Modified
          --------------------------------------------------
          1   BASETEMP   CATALOG    20480   15NOV2000:14:38:35
          2   HIGHTEMP   DATA       16384   15NOV2000:14:26:48
          3   HURRICANE  DATA       16384   15NOV2000:14:29:11
          4   LOWTEMP    DATA       16384   15NOV2000:14:30:08
          5   REPORT     CATALOG    20480   15NOV2000:14:39:02
          6   TEMPCHNG   DATA       16384   15NOV2000:14:30:41
```

The following list corresponds to the numbered items in the preceding output:

❶ Heading   gives the physical name as well as the libref for the library. Note that some operating environments provide additional and different information. For example, not all operating environments have an inode number.

❷ Name   contains the second-level SAS member name that is assigned to the file. If the files are different member types, then you can have two files of the same name in one library.

❸ Memtype   indicates the SAS file member type. The most common member types are DATA and CATALOG. For example, the library USCLIM contains two catalogs of type CATALOG and four data sets of type DATA.

Listing Files That Have the Same Member Type

To show only certain types of SAS files in the directory listing, use the MEMTYPE= option in the PROC DATASETS statement. The following statement produces a listing for USCLIM that contains only the information about data sets:

```
proc datasets library=usclim memtype=data;
```

The following output shows the SAS log, which lists only the data sets that are stored in USCLIM:

Output 35.2 Directory Listing of Data Sets Only for the Library USCLIM

```
7     options pagesize=60 linesize=80 nonumber nodate;
8     libname usclim 'SAS-data-library';
NOTE: Libref USCLIM was successfully assigned as follows:
      Engine:        V8
      Physical Name: external-file
9
10    proc datasets library=usclim memtype=data;
                          -----Directory-----

                  Libref:           USCLIM
                  Engine:           V8
                  Physical Name:    external-file
                  File Name:        external-file
                  Inode Number:     1864992
                  Access Permission: rwxr-xr-x
                  Owner Name:       userid
                  File Size (bytes): 4096


                                   File
         #  Name       Memtype   Size  Last Modified
         -----------------------------------------------------
         1  HIGHTEMP   DATA     16384   15NOV2000:14:26:48
         2  HURRICANE  DATA     16384   15NOV2000:14:29:11
         3  LOWTEMP    DATA     16384   15NOV2000:14:30:08
         4  TEMPCHNG   DATA     16384   15NOV2000:14:30:41
```

Note: Examples in this book focus on using PROC DATASETS to manage only SAS data sets; you can also list other member types by specifying MEMTYPE=. For example, MEMTYPE=CATALOG lists only SAS catalogs. △

Requesting Contents Information about SAS Data Sets

Using the DATASETS Procedure for SAS Data Sets

To look at the contents of a SAS data set without displaying the observations, use the CONTENTS statement in the DATASETS procedure. The CONTENTS statement and its options provide descriptive information about data sets and a list of variables and their attributes.

Listing the Contents of One Data Set

The SAS data library USCLIM contains four data sets, with the data set TEMPCHNG containing data for extreme changes in temperature. The following program displays the variables in the data set TEMPCHNG:

```
proc datasets library=usclim memtype=data;
   contents data=tempchng;
run;
```

The CONTENTS statement produces a contents listing, and the DATA= option specifies the name of the data set. The following output shows the results from the CONTENTS statement, which are sent to SAS output rather than to the SAS log. Note that output from the CONTENTS statement varies for different operating environments.

Output 35.3   Contents Listing for the Data Set TEMPCHNG

```
                                The SAS System

                            The DATASETS Procedure  ❶

Data Set Name: USCLIM.TEMPCHNG                         Observations:           5
Member Type:   DATA                                    Variables:              6
Engine:        V8                                      Indexes:                0
Created:       14:32 Wednesday, November 15, 2000      Observation Length:     56
Last Modified: 14:32 Wednesday, November 15, 2000      Deleted Observations:   0
Protection:                                            Compressed:             NO
Data Set Type:                                         Sorted:                 NO
Label:


                     -----Engine/Host Dependent Information-----  ❷

         Data Set Page Size:          8192
         Number of Data Set Pages:    1
         First Data Page:             1
         Max Obs per Page:            145
         Obs in First Data Page:      5
         Number of Data Set Repairs:  0
         File Name:                   /u/userid/usclim/tempchng.sas7bdat
         Release Created:             8.0202M0
         Host Created:                HP-UX
         Inode Number:                14595
         Access Permission:           rw-r--r--
         Owner Name:                  userid
         File Size (bytes):           16384


                 -----Alphabetic List of Variables and Attributes-----  ❸

         #    Variable    Type    Len    Pos    Format     Informat
         ---------------------------------------------------------------
         2    Date        Num      8      0     DATE9.     DATE7.
         6    Diff        Num      8     32
         4    End_f       Num      8     16
         5    Minutes     Num      8     24
         3    Start_f     Num      8      8
         1    State       Char    13     40                $CHAR13.
```

The following list describes information that you might find in contents listing and corresponds to the numbered items in the preceding output:

❶ Heading   contains field names. Fields are empty if they do not apply to the data set. Field names are listed below:

Data Set Name	is the two-level name that is assigned to the data set.
Member Type	is the type of library member.
Engine	is the access method that SAS uses to read from or write to the data set.
Created	is the date that the data set was created.
Last Modified	is the last date that the data set was modified.

Protection	indicates whether the data set is password protected for READ, WRITE, or ALTER operations.
Data Set Type	applies only to files with the member type DATA. Information in this field indicates that the data set contains special observations and variables for use with SAS statistical procedures.
Label	is the descriptive information that you supply in a LABEL= data set option to identify the data set.
Observations	is the total number of observations currently in the data set.
Variables	is the number of variables in the data set.
Indexes	is the number of indexes for the data set.
Observation Length	is the length of each observation in bytes.
Deleted Observations	is the number of observations marked for deletion, if applicable.
Compressed	indicates whether the data is in fixed-length or variable-length records. If the data set is compressed, then additional fields indicate whether new observations are added to the end of the data set or written to unused space within the data set and whether the data set can be randomly accessed by observation number rather than sequential access only.
Sorted	indicates whether the data set has been sorted.
❷ Engine/Host Dependent Information	lists information about the engine, which is the mechanism for reading from and writing to files, and about how the data set is stored by the operating environment. Depending on the engine, the output in this section might differ. For more information, see the SAS documentation for your operating environment.
❸ Alphabetical List of Variables and Attributes	lists all the variable names in the data set in alphabetical order and describes the attributes that are assigned to the variable when it is defined. The attributes are described below:
#	is the logical position of the variable in the observation. This is the number that is assigned to the variable when it is defined.
Variable	is the name of the variable.
Type	indicates whether the variable is character or numeric.
Len	is the length of the variable in bytes.
Pos	is the physical position in the observation buffer of the first byte of the variable's associated value.
Format	is the format of the variable.
Informat	is the informat of the variable.

In addition, if applicable, the output also displays a table that describes

□ indexes for indexed variable(s)

□ any defined integrity constraints

□ sort information.

Listing the Contents of All Data Sets in a Library

You can list the contents of all the data sets in a library by specifying the keyword _ALL_ with the DATA= option. The following statements produce a directory listing in SAS output for the library and a contents listing for each data set in the directory:

```
    contents data=_all_;
run;
```

To send only a directory listing to SAS output, add the NODS option. The following statements produce a directory listing but suppress a contents listing for individual data sets. Use this form if you want the directory listing for the procedure input library:

```
    contents data=_all_ nods;
run;
```

Include the libref if you want the directory listing for another library. This example specifies the library STORM:

```
    contents data=storm._all_ nods;
run;
```

Requesting Contents Information in Different Formats

For a variation of the contents listing, use the VARNUM option or the SHORT option in the CONTENTS statement. For example, the following statements produce a list of variable names in the order in which they were defined, which is their logical position in the data set:

```
    contents data=tempchng varnum;
run;
```

The CONTENTS statement specifies the data set TEMPCHNG and includes the VARNUM option to list variables in order of their logical position. (By default, the CONTENTS statement lists variables alphabetically.)

The following output shows the contents in variable number order:

Output 35.4   Listing Contents of the Data Set TEMPCHNG in Variable Number Order

```
                              The SAS System

                          The DATASETS Procedure

Data Set Name: USCLIM.TEMPCHNG                    Observations:          5
Member Type:   DATA                               Variables:             6
Engine:        V8                                 Indexes:               0
Created:       14:32 Wednesday, November 15, 2000 Observation Length:    56
Last Modified: 14:32 Wednesday, November 15, 2000 Deleted Observations:  0
Protection:                                       Compressed:            NO
Data Set Type:                                    Sorted:                NO
Label:


                -----Engine/Host Dependent Information-----

     Data Set Page Size:        8192
     Number of Data Set Pages:  1
     First Data Page:           1
     Max Obs per Page:          145
     Obs in First Data Page:    5
     Number of Data Set Repairs: 0
     File Name:                 /u/userid/usclim/tempchng.sas7bdat
     Release Created:           8.0202M0
     Host Created:              HP-UX
     Inode Number:              14595
     Access Permission:         rw-r--r--
     Owner Name:                userid
     File Size (bytes):         16384


                -----Variables Ordered by Position-----

     #     Variable    Type   Len    Format      Informat
     ----------------------------------------------------------
     1     State       Char    13                $CHAR13.
     2     Date        Num      8    DATE9.       DATE7.
     3     Start_f     Num      8
     4     End_f       Num      8
     5     Minutes     Num      8
     6     Diff        Num      8
```

If you do not need all of the information in the contents listing, then you can request an abbreviated version by using the SHORT option in the CONTENTS statement. The following statements request an abbreviated version and then end the DATASETS procedure by issuing the QUIT statement:

```
    contents data=tempchng short;
run;
quit;
```

The following output lists the variable names for the TEMPCHNG data set:

Output 35.5   Listing Variable Names Only for the Data Set TEMPCHNG

```
                            The SAS System

                         The DATASETS Procedure

            -----Alphabetic List of Variables for USCLIM.TEMPCHNG-----

                    Date Diff End_f Minutes Start_f State
```

Review of SAS Tools

Procedures

PROC DATASETS <LIBRARY=*libref* <MEMTYPE=*mtype(s)*>>;
   The MEMTYPE= option restricts processing to a certain type or types of SAS files
   and restricts the library directory listing to SAS files of the specified member types.

DATASETS Procedure Statements

CONTENTS <DATA=<*libref*>.*SAS-data-set*> <NODS> <SHORT> <VARNUM> ;
   describes the contents of a specific SAS data set in the library. The default data
   set is the most recently created data set for the job or session. For the
   CONTENTS statement in PROC DATASETS, when you specify DATA=, the
   default libref is the procedure input library. However, for the CONTENTS
   procedure, the default libref is either WORK or USER.
      Use the NODS option with the keyword _ALL_ in the DATA= option to produce
   only the directory listing of the library in SAS output. That is, the NODS option
   suppresses the contents of individual files. You cannot use the NODS option when
   you specify only one SAS data set in the DATA= option.
      The SHORT option produces only an alphabetical list of variable names, index
   information, integrity constraint information, and sort information for the SAS
   data set.
      The VARNUM option produces a list of variable names in the order in which
   they were defined, which is their logical position in the data set. By default, the
   CONTENTS statement lists variables alphabetically.

Learning More

CATALOG procedure
   You can use the CATALOG procedure to obtain contents information about
   catalogs. For more information, see the *SAS Procedures Guide*.

DATASETS procedure
   For more information about the DATASETS procedure and the CONTENTS
   statement as well as the CONTENTS procedure, see the *SAS Procedures Guide*.

Windowing environment
For information about using the windowing environment in order to obtain information about SAS data sets, see Chapter 39, "Using the SAS Windowing Environment," on page 651.

CHAPTER

36

Modifying SAS Data Set Names and Variable Attributes

Introduction

Purpose

SAS enables you to modify data set names and variable attributes without creating new data sets. In this chapter, you will learn how to use statements in the DATASETS procedure to

- □ rename data sets
- □ rename variables
- □ modify variable formats
- □ modify variable labels.

This chapter focuses on using the DATASETS procedure to modify data sets. However, you can also use some of the illustrated statements and options to modify other types of SAS files.

Note: You cannot use the DATASETS procedure to change the values of observations, to create or delete variables, or to change the type or length of variables. These modifications are done with DATA step statements and functions. △

Prerequisites

Before using this chapter, you should understand the concepts presented in

- □ Chapter 33, "Understanding SAS Data Libraries," on page 591

□ Chapter 34, "Managing SAS Data Libraries," on page 599
□ Chapter 35, "Getting Information about Your SAS Data Sets," on page 603.

Input Data Library for Examples

The examples in this chapter use a SAS data library that contains information about the climate of the United States. The DATA steps that create the data sets in the SAS data library are shown in "Data Sets for Chapters 35 and 36" on page 718.

Renaming SAS Data Sets

Renaming data sets is often required for effective library management. For example, you might rename a data set when you archive it or when you add new data values.

Use the CHANGE statement in the DATASETS procedure to rename one or more data sets in the same library. Here is the syntax for the CHANGE statement:

CHANGE *old-name=new-name*;

where

old-name   is the current name of the SAS data set.

new-name   is the name that you want to give the data set.

This example renames two data sets in the SAS data library USCLIM, which contains information about the climate of the United States. The following program starts the DATASETS procedure, then changes the name of the data set HIGHTEMP to USHIGH and the name of the data set LOWTEMP to USLOW:

```
options pagesize=60 linesize=80 nonumber nodate;
libname usclim 'SAS-data-library';

proc datasets library=usclim;
   change hightemp=ushigh lowtemp=uslow;
run;
```

As it processes these statements, SAS sends messages to the SAS log, as shown in the following output. The messages verify that the data sets are renamed.

Output 36.1 Renaming Data Sets in the Library USCLIM

```
7     options pagesize=60 linesize=80 nonumber nodate;
8     libname usclim 'SAS-data-library';
NOTE: Libref USCLIM was successfully assigned as follows:
      Engine:        V8
      Physical Name: external-file
9
10    proc datasets library=usclim;
                          -----Directory-----

                  Libref:            USCLIM
                  Engine:            V8
                  Physical Name:     external-file
                  File Name:         external-file
                  Inode Number:      1864992
                  Access Permission: rwxr-xr-x
                  Owner Name:        userid
                  File Size (bytes): 4096


                                      File
              #  Name      Memtype    Size  Last Modified
              ---------------------------------------------------
              1  BASETEMP  CATALOG    20480 15NOV2000:14:38:35
              2  HIGHTEMP  DATA       16384 15NOV2000:14:26:48
              3  HURRICANE DATA       16384 15NOV2000:14:29:11
              4  LOWTEMP   DATA       16384 15NOV2000:14:30:08
              5  REPORT    CATALOG    20480 15NOV2000:14:39:02
              6  TEMPCHNG  DATA       16384 15NOV2000:14:30:41
11    change hightemp=ushigh lowtemp=uslow;
12    run;
NOTE: Changing the name USCLIM.HIGHTEMP to USCLIM.USHIGH (memtype=DATA).
NOTE: Changing the name USCLIM.LOWTEMP to USCLIM.USLOW (memtype=DATA).
```

Modifying Variable Attributes

Understanding How to Modify Variable Attributes

Each variable in a SAS data set has attributes such as name, type, length, format, informat, label, and so on. These attributes enable you to identify a variable as well as define to SAS how the variable can be used.

By using the DATASETS procedure, you can assign, change, or remove certain attributes with the MODIFY statement and subordinate statements. For example, using MODIFY and subordinate statements enables you to

☐ rename variables

☐ assign, change, or remove a format, which changes the way the values are printed or displayed

☐ assign, change, or remove labels.

Note: You cannot use the MODIFY statement to modify fixed attributes such as the type or length of a variable. △

Renaming Variables

You might need to rename variables, for example, before combining data sets that have one or more matching variable names. The DATASETS procedure enables you to rename one or more variables by using the MODIFY statement and its subordinate RENAME statement. Here is the syntax for the statements:

MODIFY *SAS-data-set*;

    RENAME *old-name=new-name*;

where

SAS-data-set   is the name of the SAS data set that contains the variable that you want to rename.

old-name   is the current name of the variable.

new-name   is the name that you want to give the variable.

This example renames two variables in the data set HURRICANE, which is in the SAS data library USCLIM. The following statements change the variable name State to Place and the variable name Deaths to USDeaths. The DATASETS procedure is already active, so the PROC DATASETS statement is not necessary.

```
modify hurricane;
    rename State=Place Deaths=USDeaths;
run;
```

The SAS log messages verify that the variables are renamed to Place and USDeaths as shown in the following output. All other attributes that are assigned to these variables remain unchanged.

Output 36.2   Renaming Variables in the Data Set HURRICANE

```
38      modify hurricane;
39          rename State=Place Deaths=USDeaths;
NOTE: Renaming variable State to Place.
NOTE: Renaming variable Deaths to USDeaths.
40   run;
```

Assigning, Changing, or Removing Formats

SAS enables you to assign and store formats, which are used by many SAS procedures for output. Assigning, changing, or removing a format changes the way the values are printed or displayed. By using the DATASETS procedure, you can change a variable's format with the MODIFY statement and its subordinate FORMAT statement. You can change a variable's format either to a SAS format or to a format that you have defined and stored, or you can remove a format. Here is the syntax for these statements:

MODIFY *SAS-data-set*;

    FORMAT *variable(s) <format>*;

where

SAS-data-set   is the name of the SAS data set that contains the variable whose format you want to modify.

variable(s)   is the name of one or more variables whose format you want to assign, change, or remove.

format   is the format that you want to give the variable(s). If you do not specify a format, then SAS removes any format that is associated with the specified variable(s).

When you assign or change a format, follow these rules:

☐ List the variable name before the format.

☐ List multiple variable names or use an abbreviated variable list if you want to assign the format to more than one variable.

☐ Do not use punctuation to separate items in the list.

The following FORMAT statement illustrates ways to include many variables and formats in the same FORMAT statement:

```
format Date1-Date5 date9. Cost1 Cost2 dollar4.2 Place $char25.;
```

The variables Date1 through Date5 are written in abbreviated list form, and the format DATE9. is assigned to all five variables. The variables Cost1 and Cost2 are listed individually before their format. The format $CHAR25. is assigned to the variable Place.

There are two rules when you are removing formats from variables:

☐ List the variable names only.

☐ Place the variable names last in the list if you are using the same FORMAT statement to assign or change formats.

For example, by using the SAS data set HURRICANE, the following statements change the format for the variable Date from a full spelling of the month, date, and year to an abbreviation of the month and year, remove the format for the variable Millions, and display the contents of the data set HURRICANE before and after the changes. Note that because the FORMAT statement does not send messages to the SAS log, you must use the CONTENTS statement if you want to make sure that the changes were made.

```
contents data=hurricane;
   modify hurricane;
      format Date monyy7. Millions;
   contents data=hurricane;
run;
```

The following output from the two CONTENTS statements displays the contents of the data set before and after the changes. The format for the variable Date is changed from WORDDATE18. to MONYY7., and the format for the variable Millions is removed.

Output 36.3   Modifying Variable Formats in the Data Set HURRICANE

```
                               The SAS System

                           The DATASETS Procedure

Data Set Name: USCLIM.HURRICANE              Observations:            5
Member Type:   DATA                          Variables:               5
Engine:        V8                            Indexes:                 0
Created:       14:31 Wednesday, November 15, 2000   Observation Length: 48
Last Modified: 9:19 Thursday, November 16, 2000     Deleted Observations: 0
Protection:                                  Compressed:             NO
Data Set Type:                               Sorted:                 NO
Label:


                  -----Engine/Host Dependent Information-----

        Data Set Page Size:         8192
        Number of Data Set Pages:   1
        First Data Page:            1
        Max Obs per Page:           169
        Obs in First Data Page:     5
        Number of Data Set Repairs: 0
        File Name:                  /u/userid/usclim/hurricane.sas7bdat
        Release Created:            8.0202M0
        Host Created:               HP-UX
        Inode Number:               14593
        Access Permission:          rw-r--r--
        Owner Name:                 userid
        File Size (bytes):          16384


                -----Alphabetic List of Variables and Attributes-----

    #    Variable    Type    Len    Pos    Format      Informat    Label
    ----------------------------------------------------------------------
    2    Date        Num      8      0     WORDDATE18. DATE9.
    4    Millions    Num      8     16     DOLLAR6.                Damage
    5    Name        Char     8     35
    1    Place       Char    11     24                 $CHAR11.
    3    USDeaths    Num      8      8
```

```
                              The SAS System

                          The DATASETS Procedure

Data Set Name: USCLIM.HURRICANE              Observations:          5
Member Type:   DATA                          Variables:             5
Engine:        V8                            Indexes:               0
Created:       14:31 Wednesday, November 15, 2000   Observation Length: 48
Last Modified: 9:23 Thursday, November 16, 2000     Deleted Observations: 0
Protection:                                  Compressed:            NO
Data Set Type:                               Sorted:                NO
Label:


                 -----Engine/Host Dependent Information-----

        Data Set Page Size:        8192
        Number of Data Set Pages:  1
        First Data Page:           1
        Max Obs per Page:          169
        Obs in First Data Page:    5
        Number of Data Set Repairs: 0
        File Name:                 /u/userid/usclim/hurricane.sas7bdat
        Release Created:           8.0202M0
        Host Created:              HP-UX
        Inode Number:              14593
        Access Permission:         rw-r--r--
        Owner Name:                userid
        File Size (bytes):         16384


             -----Alphabetic List of Variables and Attributes-----

    #    Variable   Type   Len   Pos   Format   Informat   Label
    ------------------------------------------------------------------
    2    Date       Num     8     0    MONYY7.  DATE9.
    4    Millions   Num     8    16                        Damage
    5    Name       Char    8    35
    1    Place      Char   11    24             $CHAR11.
    3    USDeaths   Num     8     8
```

Assigning, Changing, or Removing Labels

A label is the descriptive information that identifies variables in tables, plots, and graphs. You usually assign labels when you create a variable. If you do not assign a label, then SAS uses the variable name as the label. However, in CONTENTS output, if a label is not assigned, then the field is blank. By using the MODIFY statement and its subordinate LABEL statement, you can assign, change, or remove a label. Here is the syntax for these statements:

MODIFY *SAS-data-set*;

    LABEL *variable=<'label'>*;

where

SAS-data-set	is the name of the SAS data set that contains the variable whose label you want to modify.
variable	is the name of the variable whose label you want to assign, change, or remove.
label	is the label, which can be from 1 to 256 characters, that you want to give the variable. If you do not specify a label and one exists, then SAS removes the current label.

When you use the LABEL statement, follow these rules:

□ Enclose the text of the label in single or double quotation marks. If a single quotation mark appears in the label (for example, an apostrophe), then enclose the text with double quotation marks.

□ Limit the label to no more than 256 characters, including blanks.

□ To remove a label, use a blank as the text of the label, that is, *variable*=' '.

For example, by using the SAS data set HURRICANE, the following statements change the label for the variable Millions and assign a label for the variable Place. Because the LABEL statement does not send messages to the SAS log, the CONTENTS statement is specified to verify that the changes were made. The QUIT statement stops the DATASETS procedure.

```
        contents data=hurricane;
            modify hurricane;
                label Millions='Damage in Millions' Place='State Hardest Hit';
        contents data=hurricane;
    run;
    quit;
```

The following output from the two CONTENTS statements displays the contents of the data set before and after the changes:

Output 36.4   Modifying Variable Labels in the Data Set HURRICANE

```
                         The SAS System

                      The DATASETS Procedure

Data Set Name: USCLIM.HURRICANE              Observations:            5
Member Type:   DATA                          Variables:               5
Engine:        V8                            Indexes:                 0
Created:       14:31 Wednesday, November 15, 2000    Observation Length: 48
Last Modified: 9:23 Thursday, November 16, 2000      Deleted Observations: 0
Protection:                                  Compressed:             NO
Data Set Type:                               Sorted:                 NO
Label:


                 -----Engine/Host Dependent Information-----

       Data Set Page Size:          8192
       Number of Data Set Pages:    1
       First Data Page:             1
       Max Obs per Page:            169
       Obs in First Data Page:      5
       Number of Data Set Repairs:  0
       File Name:                   /u/userid/usclim/hurricane.sas7bdat
       Release Created:             8.0202M0
       Host Created:                HP-UX
       Inode Number:                14593
       Access Permission:           rw-r--r--
       Owner Name:                  userid
       File Size (bytes):           16384


             -----Alphabetic List of Variables and Attributes-----

    #    Variable    Type    Len    Pos    Format    Informat    Label
    -----------------------------------------------------------------------
    2    Date        Num      8      0     MONYY7.   DATE9.
    4    Millions    Num      8     16                           Damage
    5    Name        Char     8     35
    1    Place       Char    11     24               $CHAR11.
    3    USDeaths    Num      8      8
```

```
                              The SAS System

                          The DATASETS Procedure

Data Set Name: USCLIM.HURRICANE              Observations:          5
Member Type:   DATA                          Variables:             5
Engine:        V8                            Indexes:               0
Created:       14:31 Wednesday, November 15, 2000    Observation Length:    48
Last Modified: 9:28 Thursday, November 16, 2000      Deleted Observations: 0
Protection:                                  Compressed:           NO
Data Set Type:                               Sorted:               NO
Label:


                  -----Engine/Host Dependent Information-----

       Data Set Page Size:          8192
       Number of Data Set Pages:    2
       First Data Page:             1
       Max Obs per Page:            169
       Obs in First Data Page:      5
       Number of Data Set Repairs:  0
       File Name:                   /u/userid/usclim/hurricane.sas7bdat
       Release Created:             8.0202M0
       Host Created:                HP-UX
       Inode Number:                14593
       Access Permission:           rw-r--r--
       Owner Name:                  userid
       File Size (bytes):           24576


              -----Alphabetic List of Variables and Attributes-----

 #    Variable   Type    Len    Pos    Format     Informat    Label
-------------------------------------------------------------------------------
 2    Date       Num      8      0     MONYY7.    DATE9.
 4    Millions   Num      8     16                            Damage in Millions
 5    Name       Char     8     35
 1    Place      Char    11     24                $CHAR11.    State Hardest Hit
 3    USDeaths   Num      8      8
```

Review of SAS Tools

DATASETS Procedure Statements

CHANGE *old-name=new-name*;
> renames the SAS data set that you specify with *old-name* to the name that you specify with *new-name*. You can rename more than one data set in the same library by using one CHANGE statement. All new names must be valid SAS names.

MODIFY *SAS-data-set*;
> identifies the SAS data set that you want to modify. These are some of the subordinate statements that you can use with the MODIFY statement:

> FORMAT *variable(s) <format>*;
>> assigns, changes, or removes the format for the variable(s) that you specify with *variable(s)* by using the format that you specify with *format*. You can

give more than one variable the same format by listing more than one variable before the format. Do not specify *format* if you want to remove a format.

LABEL *variable=<'label'>*;
assigns, changes, or removes the label for the variable that you specify with *variable*. To remove a label, place a blank space inside the quotation marks.

RENAME *old-name=new-name*;
changes the name of the variable(s) that you specify with *old-name* to the name that you specify with *new-name*. You can rename more than one variable in the same data set by using one RENAME statement. All names must be valid SAS names.

Learning More

Informats and formats
For more information about informats and formats available for reading and displaying data, see *SAS Language Reference: Dictionary*.

LABEL statement
For information about the LABEL statement that is used in the DATA step, see *SAS Language Reference: Dictionary*.

MODIFY statement
The MODIFY statement in the DATASETS procedure has additional statements that change informats and that create and delete indexes for variables. See the *SAS Procedures Guide*.

Renaming variables
You can use the RENAME= data set option and the RENAME statement in the DATA step to rename variables. See *SAS Language Reference: Dictionary*.

Variables
To learn how to create and delete variables in the DATA step, see Chapter 5, "Starting with SAS Data Sets," on page 81.

CHAPTER

37

Copying, Moving, and Deleting SAS Data Sets

Introduction

Purpose

Copying, moving, and deleting SAS data sets are the library management tasks that you will perform most frequently. For example, you perform these tasks to create test files, make backups, archive files, and remove unused files. The DATASETS procedure enables you to work with all the files in a SAS data library or with specific files in the library.

In this chapter, you will learn how to use the DATASETS procedure to

□ copy an entire library

□ copy specific SAS data sets

□ move specific SAS data sets

□ delete specific SAS data sets

□ delete all files in a library.

This chapter focuses on using the DATASETS procedure to copy, move, and delete data sets. You can also use the illustrated statements and options to copy, move, and delete other types of SAS files.

Prerequisites

Before using this chapter, you should understand the concepts presented in

☐ Chapter 33, "Understanding SAS Data Libraries," on page 591

☐ Chapter 34, "Managing SAS Data Libraries," on page 599

☐ Chapter 36, "Modifying SAS Data Set Names and Variable Attributes," on page 613.

Input Data Libraries for Examples

The examples in this chapter use five SAS data libraries that contain sample data sets that are used to collect and store weather statistics for the United States and other countries. The libraries have the librefs PRECIP, USCLIM, CLIMATE, WEATHER, and STORM. The following LIBNAME statements assign the librefs:

```
libname precip 'SAS-data-library-1';
libname usclim 'SAS-data-library-2';
libname climate 'SAS-data-library-3';
libname weather 'SAS-data-library-4';
libname storm 'SAS-data-library-5';
```

Note: For each LIBNAME statement, *SAS-data-library* is a different physical name for the location of the SAS data library. In order to copy all or some SAS data sets from one library to another, the input and output libraries must be in different physical locations. △

The DATA steps that create the data sets in the SAS data libraries CLIMATE, PRECIP, and STORM are shown in "Data Sets for Chapter 36" on page 720. The DATA steps that create the data sets in the SAS data library USCLIM are shown in "Data Sets for Chapters 35 and 36" on page 718.

Copying SAS Data Sets

Copying from the Procedure Input Library

You can use the COPY statement in the DATASETS procedure to copy all or some SAS data sets from one library to another. When copying data sets, SAS duplicates the contents of each file, including the descriptor information, and updates information in the directory for each library.

CAUTION:
During processing, SAS automatically writes the data from the input library into an output data set of the same name. If there are duplicate data set names, then you do not receive a warning message before copying starts. Before you make changes to libraries, it is

important to obtain directory listings of the input and output libraries in order to visually check for duplicate data set names. △

To copy files from the procedure input library (specified in the PROC DATASETS statement), use the COPY statement. Here is the syntax of the COPY statement.

COPY OUT=*libref* <options>;

where

libref   is the libref for the SAS data library to which you want to copy the files. You must specify an output library.

For example, the library PRECIP contains data sets for snowfall and rainfall amounts, and the library CLIMATE contains data sets for temperature. The following program lists the contents so that they can be visually compared before any action is taken:

```
options pagesize=60 linesize=80 nonumber nodate;


proc datasets library=precip;
   contents data=_all_ nods;
   contents data=climate._all_ nods;
run;
```

The PROC DATASETS statement starts the procedure and specifies the procedure input library PRECIP. The first CONTENTS statement produces a directory listing of the library PRECIP. Then, the second CONTENTS statement produces a directory listing of the library CLIMATE.

The following SAS output shows the two directory listings:

Output 37.1   Checking Directories of PRECIP and CLIMATE before Copying

```
                        The SAS System

                    The DATASETS Procedure

                    -----Directory-----

            Libref:             PRECIP
            Engine:             V8
            Physical Name:      external-file
            File Name:          external-file
            Inode Number:       1864994
            Access Permission:  rwxr-xr-x
            Owner Name:         userid
            File Size (bytes):  4096


                              File
         #  Name  Memtype     Size  Last Modified
         -------------------------------------------------
         1  RAIN  DATA       16384  15NOV2000:14:32:09
         2  SNOW  DATA       16384  15NOV2000:14:32:35
```

```
                              The SAS System

                          The DATASETS Procedure

                          -----Directory-----

                Libref:             CLIMATE
                Engine:             V8
                Physical Name:      external-file
                File Name:          external-file
                Inode Number:       1864993
                Access Permission:  rwxr-xr-x
                Owner Name:         userid
                File Size (bytes):  4096


                                   File
            #  Name      Memtype    Size   Last Modified
            -------------------------------------------------
            1  HIGHTEMP  DATA      16384   15NOV2000:14:31:17
            2  LOWTEMP   DATA      16384   15NOV2000:14:31:39
```

There are no duplicate names in the directories, so the COPY statement can be issued to achieve the desired results.

```
copy out=climate;
run;
```

The following SAS log shows the messages as the data sets in the library PRECIP are copied to the library CLIMATE. There are now two copies of the data sets RAIN and SNOW: one in the PRECIP library and one in the CLIMATE library.

Output 37.2   Messages Sent to the SAS Log during Copying

```
35       copy out=climate;
36   run;
NOTE: Copying PRECIP.RAIN to CLIMATE.RAIN (memtype=DATA).
NOTE: There were 5 observations read from the data set PRECIP.RAIN.
NOTE: The data set CLIMATE.RAIN has 5 observations and 4 variables.
NOTE: Copying PRECIP.SNOW to CLIMATE.SNOW (memtype=DATA).
NOTE: There were 3 observations read from the data set PRECIP.SNOW.
NOTE: The data set CLIMATE.SNOW has 3 observations and 4 variables.
```

Copying from Other Libraries

You can copy from a library other than the procedure input library without using another PROC DATASETS statement. To do so, use the IN= option in the COPY statement to override the procedure input library. Here is the syntax for the option.

COPY OUT=*libref-1* IN=*libref-2*;

where

libref-1   is the libref for the SAS data library to which you want to copy files.

libref-2   is the libref for the SAS data library from which you want to copy files.

The IN= option is a useful tool when you want to copy more than one library into the output library. You can use one COPY statement for each input library without repeating the PROC DATASETS statement.

For example, the following statements copy the libraries PRECIP, STORM, CLIMATE, and USCLIM to the library WEATHER. The procedure input library is PRECIP, which was specified in the previous PROC DATASETS statement.

```
copy out=weather;
copy in=storm out=weather;
copy in=climate out=weather;
copy in=usclim out=weather;
run;
```

The following SAS log shows that the data sets from these libraries have been consolidated in the library WEATHER:

Output 37.3   Copying Four Libraries into the Library WEATHER

```
54       copy out=weather;
NOTE: Copying PRECIP.RAIN to WEATHER.RAIN (memtype=DATA).
NOTE: There were 5 observations read from the data set PRECIP.RAIN.
NOTE: The data set WEATHER.RAIN has 5 observations and 4 variables.
NOTE: Copying PRECIP.SNOW to WEATHER.SNOW (memtype=DATA).
NOTE: There were 3 observations read from the data set PRECIP.SNOW.
NOTE: The data set WEATHER.SNOW has 3 observations and 4 variables.
55       copy in=storm out=weather;
NOTE: Copying STORM.TORNADO to WEATHER.TORNADO (memtype=DATA).
NOTE: There were 5 observations read from the data set STORM.TORNADO.
NOTE: The data set WEATHER.TORNADO has 5 observations and 4 variables.
56       copy in=climate out=weather;
NOTE: Copying CLIMATE.HIGHTEMP to WEATHER.HIGHTEMP (memtype=DATA).
NOTE: There were 5 observations read from the data set CLIMATE.HIGHTEMP.
NOTE: The data set WEATHER.HIGHTEMP has 5 observations and 4 variables.
NOTE: Copying CLIMATE.LOWTEMP to WEATHER.LOWTEMP (memtype=DATA).
NOTE: There were 5 observations read from the data set CLIMATE.LOWTEMP.
NOTE: The data set WEATHER.LOWTEMP has 5 observations and 4 variables.
NOTE: Copying CLIMATE.RAIN to WEATHER.RAIN (memtype=DATA).
NOTE: There were 5 observations read from the data set CLIMATE.RAIN.
NOTE: The data set WEATHER.RAIN has 5 observations and 4 variables.
NOTE: Copying CLIMATE.SNOW to WEATHER.SNOW (memtype=DATA).
NOTE: There were 3 observations read from the data set CLIMATE.SNOW.
NOTE: The data set WEATHER.SNOW has 3 observations and 4 variables.
57       copy in=usclim out=weather;
58    run;
NOTE: Copying USCLIM.BASETEMP to WEATHER.BASETEMP (memtype=CATALOG).
NOTE: Copying USCLIM.HURRICANE to WEATHER.HURRICANE (memtype=DATA).
NOTE: There were 5 observations read from the data set USCLIM.HURRICANE.
NOTE: The data set WEATHER.HURRICANE has 5 observations and 5 variables.
NOTE: Copying USCLIM.REPORT to WEATHER.REPORT (memtype=CATALOG).
NOTE: Copying USCLIM.TEMPCHNG to WEATHER.TEMPCHNG (memtype=DATA).
NOTE: There were 5 observations read from the data set USCLIM.TEMPCHNG.
NOTE: The data set WEATHER.TEMPCHNG has 5 observations and 6 variables.
NOTE: Copying USCLIM.USHIGH to WEATHER.USHIGH (memtype=DATA).
NOTE: There were 6 observations read from the data set USCLIM.USHIGH.
NOTE: The data set WEATHER.USHIGH has 6 observations and 5 variables.
NOTE: Copying USCLIM.USLOW to WEATHER.USLOW (memtype=DATA).
NOTE: There were 7 observations read from the data set USCLIM.USLOW.
NOTE: The data set WEATHER.USLOW has 7 observations and 5 variables.
```

Copying Specific SAS Data Sets

Selecting Data Sets to Copy

To copy only a few data sets from a large SAS data library, use the SELECT statement with the COPY statement. After the keyword SELECT, simply list the data set name(s) with a blank space between the names, or use an abbreviated member list (such as YRDATA1-YRDATA5) if applicable.

For example, the following statements copy the data set HURRICANE from the library USCLIM to the library STORM. The input procedure library is PRECIP, so the COPY statement includes the IN= option in order to specify the USCLIM input library.

```
copy in=usclim out=storm;
    select hurricane;
run;
```

The following SAS log shows that only the data set HURRICANE was copied to the library STORM:

Output 37.4   Copying the Data Set HURRICANE to the Library STORM

```
76      copy in=usclim out=storm;
77          select hurricane;
78   run;
NOTE: Copying USCLIM.HURRICANE to STORM.HURRICANE (memtype=DATA).
NOTE: There were 5 observations read from the data set USCLIM.HURRICANE.
NOTE: The data set STORM.HURRICANE has 5 observations and 5 variables.
```

Excluding Data Sets from Copying

To copy an entire library except for a few data sets, use the EXCLUDE statement with the COPY statement. After the keyword EXCLUDE, simply list the data set name(s) that you want to exclude with a blank space between the names, or use an abbreviated member list (such as YRDATA1-YRDATA5) if applicable.

The following statements copy the files in the library PRECIP to USCLIM except for the data set SNOW. The procedure input library is PRECIP, so the IN= option is not needed.

```
copy out=usclim;
    exclude snow;
run;
```

The following SAS log shows that the data set RAIN was copied to USCLIM and that the data set SNOW remains only in the library PRECIP:

Output 37.5 Excluding the Data Set SNOW from Copying to the Library USCLIM

```
96       copy out=usclim;
97          exclude snow;
98   run;
NOTE: Copying PRECIP.RAIN to USCLIM.RAIN (memtype=DATA).
NOTE: There were 5 observations read from the data set PRECIP.RAIN.
NOTE: The data set USCLIM.RAIN has 5 observations and 4 variables.
```

Moving SAS Data Libraries and SAS Data Sets

Moving Libraries

The COPY statement provides the MOVE option to move SAS data sets from the input library (either the procedure input library or the input library named with the IN= option) to the output library (named with the OUT= option). Note that with the MOVE option, SAS first copies the files to the output library, then deletes them from the input library.

The following statements move all the data sets in the library PRECIP to the library CLIMATE:

```
    copy out=climate move;
run;
```

The following SAS log shows that the data sets in PRECIP were moved to CLIMATE:

Output 37.6 Moving Data Sets in the Library PRECIP to the Library CLIMATE

```
116      copy out=climate move;
117  run;
NOTE: Moving PRECIP.RAIN to CLIMATE.RAIN (memtype=DATA).
NOTE: There were 5 observations read from the data set PRECIP.RAIN.
NOTE: The data set CLIMATE.RAIN has 5 observations and 4 variables.
NOTE: Moving PRECIP.SNOW to CLIMATE.SNOW (memtype=DATA).
NOTE: There were 3 observations read from the data set PRECIP.SNOW.
NOTE: The data set CLIMATE.SNOW has 3 observations and 4 variables.
```

After moving files with the MOVE option, a directory listing of PRECIP from the CONTENTS statement confirms that there are no members in the library. As the output from the following statements illustrates, the library PRECIP no longer contains any data sets; therefore, the library CLIMATE contains the only copy of the data sets RAIN and SNOW.

```
    contents data=_all_ nods;
run;
```

The following outputs show the SAS log, then the directory listing for the library PRECIP:

Output 37.7 SAS Log from the CONTENTS Statement

```
135      contents data=_all_ nods;
136  run;
WARNING: No matching members in directory.
```

Output 37.8 Directory Listing of the Library PRECIP Showing No Data Sets

```
                    The SAS System

                 The DATASETS Procedure

                  -----Directory-----

          Libref:           PRECIP
          Engine:           V8
          Physical Name:    external-file
          File Name:        external-file
          Inode Number:     1864994
          Access Permission: rwxr-xr-x
          Owner Name:       userid
          File Size (bytes): 4096
```

Note: The data sets are deleted from the SAS data library PRECIP, but the libref is still assigned. The name that is assigned to the library in your operating environment is not removed when you move all files from one library to another. △

Moving Specific Data Sets

You can use the SELECT and EXCLUDE statements to move one or more SAS data sets. For example, the following statements move the data set HURRICANE from the library USCLIM to the library STORM:

```
copy in=usclim out=storm move;
   select hurricane;
run;
```

Output 37.9 Moving the Data Set HURRICANE from the Library USCLIM to the Library STORM

```
173      copy in=usclim out=storm move;
174          select hurricane;
175  run;
NOTE: Moving USCLIM.HURRICANE to STORM.HURRICANE (memtype=DATA).
NOTE: There were 5 observations read from the data set USCLIM.HURRICANE.
NOTE: The data set STORM.HURRICANE has 5 observations and 5 variables.
```

Similarly, the following code uses the EXCLUDE statement to move all files except the data set SNOW from the library CLIMATE to the library USCLIM:

```
copy in=climate out=usclim move;
   exclude snow;
run;
```

Output 37.10 Moving All Data Sets Except SNOW from the Library CLIMATE to the Library USCLIM

```
193      copy in=climate out=usclim move;
194        exclude snow;
195  run;
NOTE: Moving CLIMATE.HIGHTEMP to USCLIM.HIGHTEMP (memtype=DATA).
NOTE: There were 5 observations read from the data set CLIMATE.HIGHTEMP.
NOTE: The data set USCLIM.HIGHTEMP has 5 observations and 4 variables.
NOTE: Moving CLIMATE.LOWTEMP to USCLIM.LOWTEMP (memtype=DATA).
NOTE: There were 5 observations read from the data set CLIMATE.LOWTEMP.
NOTE: The data set USCLIM.LOWTEMP has 5 observations and 4 variables.
NOTE: Moving CLIMATE.RAIN to USCLIM.RAIN (memtype=DATA).
NOTE: There were 5 observations read from the data set CLIMATE.RAIN.
```

Deleting SAS Data Sets

Specifying Data Sets to Delete

Use the DELETE statement to delete one or more data sets from a SAS data library. If you want to delete more than one data set, then simply list the names after the DELETE keyword with a blank space between the names, or use an abbreviated member list if applicable (such as YRDATA1-YRDATA5).

CAUTION:

SAS immediately deletes the files in a SAS data library when the program statements are submitted. You are not asked to verify the delete operation before it begins, so be sure that you intend to delete the files before submitting the program. △

For example, the following program specifies USCLIM as the procedure input library, then deletes the data set RAIN from the library:

```
proc datasets library=usclim;
   delete rain;
run;
```

The following output shows that SAS sends messages to the SAS log when it processes the DELETE statement:

Output 37.11   Deleting the Data Set RAIN from the Library USCLIM

```
212  proc datasets library=usclim;
                        -----Directory-----

                 Libref:            USCLIM
                 Engine:            V8
                 Physical Name:     external-file
                 File Name:         external-file
                 Inode Number:      1864992
                 Access Permission: rwxr-xr-x
                 Owner Name:        userid
                 File Size (bytes): 4096


                                        File
             #  Name      Memtype     Size  Last Modified
             --------------------------------------------------
             1  BASETEMP  CATALOG     20480  15NOV2000:14:38:35
             2  HIGHTEMP  DATA        16384  16NOV2000:12:14:50
             3  LOWTEMP   DATA        16384  16NOV2000:12:14:54
             4  RAIN      DATA        16384  16NOV2000:12:14:59
             5  REPORT    CATALOG     20480  15NOV2000:14:39:02
             6  TEMPCHNG  DATA        16384  15NOV2000:14:30:41
             7  USHIGH    DATA        16384  15NOV2000:14:26:48
             8  USLOW     DATA        16384  15NOV2000:14:30:08
213     delete rain;
214  run;
NOTE: Deleting USCLIM.RAIN (memtype=DATA).
```

Specifying Data Sets to Save

To delete all data sets but a few, you can use the SAVE statement to list the names of the data sets that you want to keep. List the data set names with a blank space between the names, or use an abbreviated member list (such as YRDATA1-YRDATA5) if applicable.

The following statements delete all the data sets except TEMPCHNG from the library USCLIM:

```
save tempchng;
run;
```

The following output shows the SAS log from the delete operation. SAS sends messages to the SAS log, verifying that it has kept the data sets that you specified in the SAVE statement and deleted all other members of the library.

Output 37.12   Deleting All Members of the Library USCLIM Except the Data Set TEMPCHNG

```
232     save tempchng;
233  run;
NOTE: Saving USCLIM.TEMPCHNG (memtype=DATA).
NOTE: Deleting USCLIM.BASETEMP (memtype=CATALOG).
NOTE: Deleting USCLIM.HIGHTEMP (memtype=DATA).
NOTE: Deleting USCLIM.LOWTEMP (memtype=DATA).
NOTE: Deleting USCLIM.REPORT (memtype=CATALOG).
NOTE: Deleting USCLIM.USHIGH (memtype=DATA).
NOTE: Deleting USCLIM.USLOW (memtype=DATA).
```

Deleting All Files in a SAS Data Library

To delete all files in a SAS data library at one time, use the KILL option in the PROC DATASETS statement.

CAUTION:

> **The KILL option deletes all members of the library immediately after the statement is submitted.** You are not asked to verify the delete operation, so be sure that you intend to delete the files before submitting the program. △

For example, the following program deletes all data sets in the library WEATHER and stops the DATASETS procedure:

```
proc datasets library=weather kill;
run;
quit;
```

The following output shows the SAS log:

Output 37.13   Deleting All Members of the Library WEATHER

```
250   proc datasets library=weather kill;
                        -----Directory-----

                Libref:            WEATHER
                Engine:            V8
                Physical Name:     external-file
                File Name:         external-file
                Inode Number:      1864996
                Access Permission: rwxr-xr-x
                Owner Name:        userid
                File Size (bytes): 4096


                                     File
          #  Name        Memtype    Size  Last Modified
          ------------------------------------------------------
          1  BASETEMP    CATALOG    20480  16NOV2000:11:15:14
          2  HIGHTEMP    DATA       16384  16NOV2000:11:14:50
          3  HURRICANE   DATA       16384  16NOV2000:11:15:19
          4  LOWTEMP     DATA       16384  16NOV2000:11:14:53
          5  RAIN        DATA       16384  16NOV2000:11:15:00
          6  REPORT      CATALOG    20480  16NOV2000:11:15:30
          7  SNOW        DATA       16384  16NOV2000:11:15:06
          8  TEMPCHNG    DATA       16384  16NOV2000:11:15:36
          9  TORNADO     DATA       16384  16NOV2000:11:14:46
         10  USHIGH      DATA       16384  16NOV2000:11:15:40
         11  USLOW       DATA       16384  16NOV2000:11:15:46
NOTE: Deleting WEATHER.BASETEMP (memtype=CATALOG).
NOTE: Deleting WEATHER.HIGHTEMP (memtype=DATA).
NOTE: Deleting WEATHER.HURRICANE (memtype=DATA).
NOTE: Deleting WEATHER.LOWTEMP (memtype=DATA).
NOTE: Deleting WEATHER.RAIN (memtype=DATA).
NOTE: Deleting WEATHER.REPORT (memtype=CATALOG).
NOTE: Deleting WEATHER.SNOW (memtype=DATA).
NOTE: Deleting WEATHER.TEMPCHNG (memtype=DATA).
NOTE: Deleting WEATHER.TORNADO (memtype=DATA).
NOTE: Deleting WEATHER.USHIGH (memtype=DATA).
NOTE: Deleting WEATHER.USLOW (memtype=DATA).
251   run;
252   quit;
```

Note: All data sets and catalogs are deleted from the SAS data library, but the libref is still assigned for the session. The name that is assigned to the library in your operating environment is not removed when you delete the files that are included in the library. △

Review of SAS Tools

Procedures

PROC DATASETS LIBRARY=*libref* <KILL>;
:   starts the procedure and specifies the procedure input library for subsequent statements. The KILL option deletes all members and member types from the library.

DATASETS Procedure Statements

COPY OUT=*libref* <IN=*libref*> <MOVE>;
:   copies files from the procedure input library that is specified in the PROC DATASETS statement to the output library that is specified in the OUT= option. The IN= option specifies a different input library. The MOVE option deletes files from the input library after copying them to the output library.
    You can use the following statements with the COPY statement:

    EXCLUDE *SAS-data-set*;
    :   specifies a SAS data set that you want to exclude from the copy process. Files that you do not list in this statement are copied to the output library.

    SELECT *SAS-data-set*;
    :   specifies a SAS data set that you want to copy to the output library.

DELETE *SAS-data-set*;
:   deletes only the SAS data set that you specify in this statement.

SAVE *SAS-data-set*;
:   deletes all members of the library except those that you specify in this statement.

Learning More

CATALOG procedure
:   You can use the CATALOG procedure to copy, move, and delete entries in SAS catalogs. See the *SAS Procedures Guide*.

DATASETS procedure
:   For more information about the DATASETS procedure, which you use to copy, move, and delete other member types, see the *SAS Procedures Guide*.

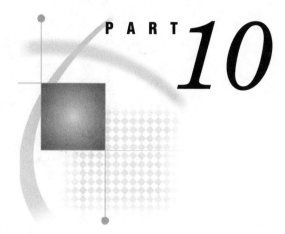

PART *10*

Understanding Your SAS Environment

CHAPTER

38

Introducing the SAS Environment

Introduction

Purpose

In this chapter, you will learn about the various ways that you can run SAS programs. More importantly, it explains the different modes that SAS can run in, and which modes are best, depending on the types of jobs you are doing.

This chapter also introduces the SAS windowing environment, which is the default processing mode.

Even though SAS has a different appearance for each operating environment, most of the actions that are available from the menus are the same.

One of the biggest differences between operating environments is the way that you select menu items. If your workstation is not equipped with a mouse, then here are the keyboard equivalents to mouse actions:

Mouse Action	Keyboard Equivalent
double-click	type an **s** or an **x** in the space next to the item, then press the ENTER or RETURN key.
right-click	instead of right-clicking an item, type **?** in the space next to the item, then press the ENTER or RETURN key.

Examples in this book show SAS windows as they appear in the Microsoft Windows environment. For the most part, corresponding windows in other operating environments will yield similar results. If you do not see the drop-down menus in your operating environment, then enter the global command PMENU at a command prompt.

Prerequisites

To understand the discussions in this chapter, you should be familiar with the basics of DATA step programming in Chapter 6, "Understanding DATA Step Processing," on page 97.

Operating Environment Differences

Even though SAS has a different appearance for each operating environment, most of the actions that are available from the menus are the same.

One of the biggest differences between operating environments is the way that you select menu items. If your workstation is not equipped with a mouse, then here are the keyboard equivalents to mouse actions:

Mouse Action	Keyboard Equivalent
double-click the item	type an **s** or an **x** in the space next to the item, then press the ENTER or RETURN key
right-click the item	type **?** in the space next to the item, then press the ENTER or RETURN key

Examples in this book show SAS windows as they appear in the Microsoft Windows environment. For the most part, corresponding windows in other operating environments will yield similar results. If you do not see the drop-down menus in your operating environment, then enter the global command PMENU at a command prompt.

Starting a SAS Session

To start a SAS session, you must invoke SAS. At the operating environment prompt, execute the SAS command. In most cases, the SAS command is

sas

Note: The SAS command may vary from site to site. Consult your SAS Software Representative if you need more information. △

You can customize your SAS session when it starts by specifying SAS system options, which then remain in effect throughout a session. For example, you can use the LINESIZE= system option to specify a line size for the SAS log and print file. Some system options can be specified only at initialization, and other system options can be specified during a SAS session. For details, see "Customizing SAS Sessions and Programs at Startup" on page 693.

Selecting a SAS Processing Mode

Processing Modes and Categories

All four modes that you can use to run SAS belong to one of two categories:

☐ foreground processing

☐ background processing.

The following figure shows the four different modes and the processing types they belong to. As your processing requirements change, you might find it helpful to change from one processing mode to another.

Figure 38.1   Modes of Running SAS during Foreground or Background Processing

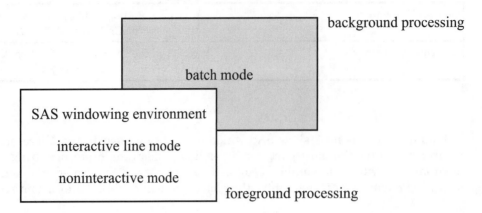

Understanding Foreground Processing

Foreground processing includes all the ways that you can run SAS in except batch mode. Foreground processing begins immediately, but as your program runs, your current workstation session is occupied, so you can not use it to do anything else.* With foreground processing, you can route your output to the workstation display, to a file, to a printer, or to tape.

If you can answer yes to one or more of the following questions, then you might want to consider foreground processing:

- Are you learning SAS programming?
- Are you testing a program to see if it works?
- Do you need fast turnaround?
- Are you processing a fairly small data file?
- Are you using an interactive application?

Understanding Background Processing

Batch processing is the only way to run SAS in the background. Your operating environment coordinates all the work, so you can use your workstation session to do other work at the same time that your program runs. However, because the operating environment also schedules your program for execution and assigns it a priority, the program may have to wait in the input queue (the operating environment's list of jobs to be run) before it is executed. When your program runs to completion, you can browse, delete, or print your output.

Background processing may be required at your site. In addition, consider the following questions:

- Are you an experienced SAS user, likely to make fewer errors than a novice?
- Are you running a program that has already been tested and refined?
- Is fast turnaround less important than minimizing the use of computer resources?
- Are you processing a large data file?
- Will your program run for a long time?
- Are you using a tape?

If you answer yes to one or more of these questions, then you might want to choose background processing.

---

*   In a workstation environment, you can switch to another window and continue working.

Processing in the SAS Windowing Environment

Overview

The SAS windowing environment is a graphical user interface (GUI) that consists of a series of windows with which you can organize files and folders, edit and execute programs, view program output, and view messages about your programs and your SAS session.

Because it is an interactive and graphical facility, you can use a single session to prepare and submit a program and, if necessary, to modify and resubmit the program after browsing the output and messages. You can move from window to window and even interrupt and return to a session at the same point you left it.

General Characteristics

The SAS windowing environment is the default environment for a SAS session (unless your environment is customized at your site).

Note: Because it is the default environment, many topics in this book describe tasks as you would perform them in the SAS windowing environment. △

The five most commonly used windows in the SAS windowing environment are Explorer, Results, Editor, Log, and Output.

Explorer
> is a hierarchical system of folders, subfolders, and individual items. It provides a primary graphical interface to SAS from which you can
>
> □ access and work with data, such as catalogs, tables, libraries, and operating environment files
>
> □ open SAS programming windows
>
> □ access the Output Delivery System (ODS)
>
> □ create and define customized folders.
>
> You can use Explorer to view or set libraries and file shortcuts, view or set library members and catalog entries, or open and edit SAS files.
>
> Note that when you start the SAS windowing environment, the Explorer might appear as a single-paned window that lists libraries that are currently available. You can add a navigational tree to the Explorer window by selecting
>
> 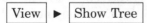 View ► Show Tree
>
> or by issuing the TREE command.

Editor or *Program Editor*□
> provides an area to enter, edit, and submit SAS statements and to save SAS source files.

Log
> enables you to browse and scroll the SAS log. The SAS log provides messages about what is happening in your SAS session.

Output
> enables you to browse and scroll procedure output.

Results
> enables you to browse and manipulate an index of your procedure output.

Display 38.1 SAS Windowing Environment: SAS Explorer, Log and Editor Windows, (Windows Operating System)

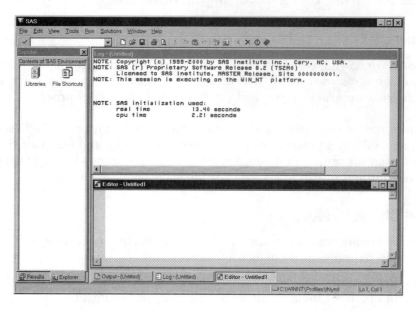

Note: Together, the Program Editor, Log, and Output windows are sometimes referred to as the *programming windows.* △

Additional windows are also available in the SAS windowing environment that enable you to

- access online help
- view and change some SAS system options
- view and change function key settings
- create and store text information.

For more information about these windows and about performing tasks in the windowing environment, see Chapter 39, "Using the SAS Windowing Environment," on page 651.

Invoking the SAS Windowing Environment

To invoke the SAS windowing environment, execute the SAS command followed by any system options that you want to put into effect. The SAS windowing environment is set as the default method of operation for SAS, but it may not be the default setting at your work site.

If the SAS windowing environment is not the default method of operation, you can specify the DMSEXP option in the SAS command. Or, you can include the DMSEXP option in the configuration file, which contains settings for system options. For more information about the configuration file, see "Customizing SAS Sessions and Programs at Startup" on page 693.

You specify options in the SAS command as you do any other command options on your system. The following table shows how you would start the SAS windowing environment and specify the DMSEXP option under various operating environments:

Operating Environment	Command
OS/390	sas options ('dmsexp')
Windows	sas -dmsexp
UNIX	sas -dmsexp
OpenVMS	sas /dmsexp
CMS	sas (dmsexp

For details about how to specify command options on other systems, see the SAS documentation for your operating environment.

Ending a SAS Windowing Environment Session

You can end your SAS windowing environment session with the BYE or ENDSAS command. Specify BYE or ENDSAS on the SAS command line, and then execute the command by pressing ENTER or RETURN (depending on which operating environment you use).

You can also end your session with the ENDSAS statement in the Program Editor window. Type the following statement on a data line and submit it for execution:

```
endsas;
```

Interrupting a SAS Windowing Environment Session

You might occasionally find it necessary to return to your operating environment from a SAS session. If you do not want to end your SAS session, then you can escape to the operating environment by issuing the X command. Simply execute the following command on the command line:

```
x
```

From your operating environment, you can then return to the same SAS session as you left it, by executing the appropriate operating environment command. For example, under the OS/390 operating environment, the operating environment command is RETURN or END; under the OpenVMS operating environment, the command is LOGOFF.

Use this form of the X command to execute a single operating environment command:

X *operating-environment-command*

or, if the command contains embedded blanks,

X *'operating-environment-command'*

For example, on many systems you can display the current time by specifying

```
x time
```

After the command executes, you can take the appropriate action to return to your SAS session.

For information about interrupting a SAS session in other operating environments, see the SAS documentation for your operating environment.

Processing Interactively in Line Mode

General Characteristics

With line mode processing, you enter programming statements one line at a time; DATA and PROC steps are executed after you enter a RUN statement, or after another step boundary. Program messages and output appear on the monitor.

You can modify program statements only when you first enter them, before you press ENTER or RETURN, which means that you must type your entries carefully.

Invoking SAS in Line Mode

To invoke SAS in line mode, execute the SAS command followed by any system options that you want to put into effect. The NODMS system option activates an interactive line mode session. If NODMS is not the default system option at your site, you can either specify the option with the SAS command or include the NODMS specification in the configuration file, the file that contains settings for system options that are put into effect at invocation. The following table shows you how to specify the NODMS system option with the SAS command under various operating environments.

Operating Environment	*Command*
OS/390	sas options ('nodms')
Windows	sas -nodms
UNIX	sas -nodms
OpenVMS	sas /nodms
CMS	sas (nodms

Using the Run Statement to Execute a Program in Line Mode

In line mode, DATA steps are executed only when a new step boundary is encountered. This occurs after you enter a RUN DATA or PROC statement. In other words, if you submit **DATA X; X=1;** in the windowing environment, then you will not see execution until the next RUN DATA or PROC statement is submitted.

At the beginning of each line, SAS prompts you with a number and a question mark to enter more statements. If you use a DATALINES statement, then a greater-than symbol (>) replaces the question mark, indicating that data lines are expected.

When you are using line mode, the log will be easier to read if you follow this programming tip: cause each DATA or PROC step to execute before you begin entering programming statements for the next step. Either an END statement or a semicolon that marks the end of datalines causes a step to execute immediately.

Ending a Line Mode SAS Session

To end your session, type **endsas;** at the SAS prompt, then press ENTER or RETURN. Your session ends, and you are returned to your operating environment.

Interrupting a Line Mode SAS Session

In line mode, you can escape to the operating environment by executing the following statement:

```
x;
```

You can return to your SAS session by executing the appropriate operating environment command. Use this form of the X statement to execute a single operating environment command:

X *operating-environment-command*;

or, if the command contains embedded blanks,

X *'operating-environment-command'*;

For example, on many systems you can display the current time by specifying

```
x time;
```

When you use this form of the X command, the command executes, and you are returned to your SAS session.

Processing in Batch Mode

The first step in executing a program in batch mode is to prepare files that include

- □ any control language statements that are required by the operating environment that you are using to manage the program
- □ the SAS statements necessary to execute the program.

Then you submit your file to the operating environment, and your workstation session is free for other work while the operating environment executes the program. This is called *background processing* because you cannot view or change the program in any way until after it executes. The log and output are routed to the destination that you specify in the operating environment control language; without a specification, they are routed to the default. For examples of batch processing, see the SAS documentation for your operating environment.

Processing Noninteractively

General Characteristics

Noninteractive processing has some characteristics of interactive processing and some of batch processing. When you process noninteractively, you execute SAS program statements that are stored in an external file. You use a SAS command to submit the program statements to your operating environment.

Note: The SAS command is implemented differently under each operating environment. For example, under OS/390 the command is typically a CLIST, and under CMS it is an EXEC. △

As in interactive processing, processing begins immediately, and your current workstation session is occupied. However, as with batch processing, you cannot interact with your program.

Note: For some exceptions to this, see the SAS documentation for your operating environment. △

You can see the log or procedure output immediately after the program has run. Log and listing output are routed to the workstation, unlike the SAS windowing environment, where you must explicitly save output to a file. If you decide that you must correct or modify your program, then you must use an editor to make necessary changes and then resubmit your program.

Executing a Program in Noninteractive Mode

When you run a program in noninteractive mode, you do not enter a SAS session as you do in interactive mode; instead of starting a SAS session, you are executing a SAS program. The first step is to enter the SAS statements in a file, just as you would for a batch job. Then, at the system prompt, you specify the SAS command followed by the complete name of the file and any system options that you want to specify.

The following example executes the SAS statements in the member TEMP in the partitioned data set *your-userid*.UGWRITE.TEXT on the OS/390 operating environment:

```
sas input(ugwrite.text(temp))
```

Note that the INPUT operand points to the file that contains the SAS statements for a noninteractive session.

The next example executes the SAS statements that are stored in the subdirectory [USERID.UGWRITE.TEXT] on the OpenVMS operating environment in the file TEMP.SAS:

```
$ sas [userid.ugwrite.text] temp
```

SAS looks for the file on the current disk.

The following example executes the SAS statements in the CMS file TEMP SAS A:

```
sas temp
```

Note: Note that in CMS, SAS looks for filetype SAS on any accessed disk. CMS executes the first file called temp that it finds on any accessible mini disk. If TEMP SAS lives on disk 'G', then it will still be executed. △

For details about how to use noninteractive mode on other operating environments, see the SAS documentation for your operating environment. Consult your SAS Site Representative for information specific to your site.

Browsing the Log and Output

Log and output information either appears in your workstation display or it is sent to a file. The default action is dependent on your operating environment. In either case, you can browse the information within your display or by opening the appropriate file.

See your operating environment documentation for more information.

Review of SAS Tools

Command

OPTIONS
    view the option settings when you use the windowing environment.

Options

PROC OPTIONS *options*;
  lists the current values of all SAS system options.

System Options

DMS | NODMS
  at invocation, specifies whether the SAS Programming windows are to be active in a SAS session.

LINESIZE=*n*
  specifies the line width for SAS output.

VERBOSE
  at invocation, displays a listing of all options in the configuration file and on the command line.

Statements

DATALINES;
  signals to SAS that the data follows immediately.

ENDSAS
  causes a SAS job or session to terminate at the end of the current DATA or PROC step.

OPTIONS *option*;
  changes one or more system options from the default value set at a site.

RUN
  causes the previously entered SAS step to be executed.

X '*operating-environment-command*';
  is used to issue an operating environment command from within a SAS session. *Operating-environment-command* specifies the command. Omitting the command puts you into the operating environment's submode.

Commands

BYE
  ends a SAS session.

ENDSAS
  ends a SAS session.

EXPLORER
  invokes the Explorer window.

PMENU
  turns on drop-down menus in windows.

X <'*operating-environment-command*'>
  executes the operating environment command and then prompts you to take the appropriate action to return to SAS. Omitting the command puts you into the operating environment's submode.

Learning More

Operating environment information

For information about specific customization options and preferences, see the documentation for your operating environment.

Windowing environment commands

For a list of all the commands that you can use in the SAS windowing environment, see SAS online Help.

| Help | ▶ | SAS System Help |

Select

Base SAS software

. The help topic is called Command Reference.

Books

For more examples of using the SAS windowing environment, see *Getting Started with the SAS System*.

39

Using the SAS Windowing Environment

Introduction

Purpose

In this chapter, you will learn about the SAS windowing environment, including how to get organized, how to access help, and how to find and use appropriate commands.

In addition, you will learn how to use the SAS windowing environment to work with files, SAS programs, and SAS output.

Prerequisites

Before proceeding with this chapter, you should understand the concepts presented in Chapter 38, "Introducing the SAS Environment," on page 639

Operating Environment Differences

Even though SAS has a different appearance for each operating environment, most of the actions that are available from the menus are the same.

One of the biggest differences between operating environments is the way that you select menu items. If your workstation is not equipped with a mouse, then here are the keyboard equivalents to mouse actions:

Mouse Action	Keyboard Equivalent
double-click the item	type an **s** or an **x** in the space next to the item, then press the ENTER or RETURN key
right-click the item	type **?** in the space next to the item, then press the ENTER or RETURN key

Examples in this book show SAS windows as they appear in the Microsoft Windows environment. For the most part, corresponding windows in other operating environments will yield similar results. If you do not see the drop-down menus in your operating environment, then enter the global command PMENU at a command prompt.

Getting Organized

Overview

The SAS windowing environment helps you to organize your data, and to locate and access your files easily. In this section, you learn how to use windows to

☐ explore libraries and library members

☐ assign a library reference

Exploring Libraries and Library Members

The SAS windowing environment opens to the Explorer window by default on many hosts. You can issue the EXPLORER command to invoke this window if it does not appear by default. You can use Explorer to view the libraries that are currently available, as well as to explore their contents.

☐ To list available libraries, select the Libraries folder, and then select **Open** from the pop-up menu.

☐ To explore the contents of a library, select a specific library, and then select **Explore from Here** from the pop-up menu.

☐ To explore the contents of a library member, select a specific library member, and then select **Open** from the pop-up menu.

Note: If the Explorer Tree view is on, then you can explore libraries and library members by expanding and collapsing tree nodes. You can expand or collapse Tree nodes by selecting their expansion icons, which look like + and - symbols. You can toggle the Explorer Tree view by selecting

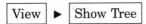

from the Explorer window. △

Display 39.1 SAS Explorer Window with Tree View On

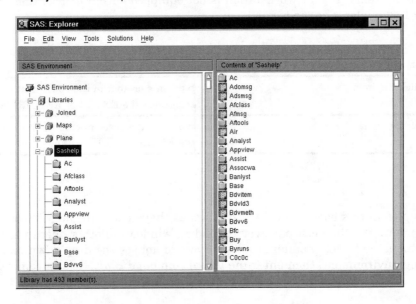

Assigning a Library Reference

Assign a library reference before continuing your work in a SAS session, so that you can have a permanent storage location for your working SAS files.

1 From the Explorer window, select the **Libraries** folder.

2 Select

The New Library window appears.

3 Enter a name for the library.

4 Select an engine type.

5 Enter an operating environment directory pathname or browse to select the directory.

6 Fill in any other fields as necessary for the engine, and enter any options that you want to specify.

   If you are not sure which engine to choose, then use the Default engine (which is selected automatically).

   The Default engine enables SAS to choose which engine to use for any data sets that exist at the given path of your new library. If no data sets exist, then the base SAS engine is assigned.

7 Select OK. The new library will appear under the **Libraries** folder in the Explorer window.

Note: If you want SAS to assign the new library automatically at startup, then select the **Enable at Startup** check box in the New Library window. △

You can use the following ways to assign a library, depending on your operating environment:

Menu

   File ► New

   (from the Explorer window only)

Command   DMLIBASSIGN (from any window)

Pop-up   New (from the Explorer window only)

Toolbar   New Library (from any window)

Managing Library Assignment Problems

If any permanent library assignment that is stored in the SAS Registry fails at startup, then the following note appears in the SAS Log:

NOTE: One or more library startup assignments were not restored.

The following errors are common causes of library assignment problems:

□ library dependencies are missing

□ required field values for library assignment in the SAS Registry are missing

□ required field values for library assignment in the SAS Registry are invalid

   For example, library names are limited to eight characters, and engine values must match actual engine names.

□ encrypted password data for a library reference has changed in the SAS Registry.

CAUTION:

You can correct many library assignment errors in the SAS Registry Editor. If you are unfamiliar with library references or the SAS Registry Editor, ask for assistance. Errors can be made easily in the SAS Registry Editor, and can prevent your libraries from being assigned at startup. △

To correct a library assignment error in the SAS Registry Editor:

1 Select

   Solutions ► Accessories ► Registry Editor

or issue the REGEDIT command.

2 Select one of the following paths, depending on your operating system, and then make modifications to keys and key values as needed:

    `CORE\OPTIONS\LIBNAMES`

or

    `CORE\OPTIONS\LIBNAMES\CONCATENATED`

or

    `CORE\LIBNAMES`

For example, if you determine that a key for a permanent concatenated library has been renamed to something other than a positive whole number, then you can rename that key again so that it is in compliance. Select the key, and then select **Rename** from the pop-up menu to begin the process.

Finding Online Help

Accessing SAS Online Help System

To access the SAS online Help, select

| Help | ▶ | SAS System Help |

Accessing Window Help

You can access help on an individual window in any of the following ways:

☐ Issue the HELP command from the command line of the window.

☐ Select the window's help button, if one exists.

☐ Select the Help icon on the toolbar.

☐ From the window for which you want help, select

| Help | ▶ | Using This Window |

Accessing SAS OnlineDoc and SAS OnlineTutor

SAS OnlineDoc is a CD that provides reference information about SAS software. SAS OnlineDoc has a table of contents, index, and a search engine that enables you to find information quickly. For some operating systems, you can access it by selecting

| Help | ▶ | Books and Training | ▶ | OnlineDoc |

SAS OnlineTutor is an interactive online training application that enables you to learn about the SAS environment, SAS programming, and specific SAS products. SAS OnlineTutor is available on CD and must be licensed. If your site has licensed and installed SAS OnlineTutor, then you can access this product by selecting

| Help | ▶ | Books and Training | ▶ | OnlineTutor |

For more information about configuring the SAS OnlineDoc CD or installing SAS OnlineTutor at your site, contact your SAS Installation Representative.

Using SAS Windowing Environment Command Types

Overview

There are specific types of SAS windowing environment commands. The type of commands that you use might depend on the task that you need to complete, or on your personal preferences. These commands can be in the form of

☐ command line commands

☐ pull-down menu commands

☐ line commands (in text editing windows)

☐ keyboard function keys.

For information about specific commands that can be issued in the SAS windowing environment, see "Working with SAS Windows" on page 659. For information about specific commands that can be used in the SAS text editor, see "Working with Text" on page 664.

Using Command Line Commands

Command line commands can be entered in two places:

☐ on the command line (if it is turned on)

☐ in the Command window (if it is available).

If the command line is turned on, then you can place your cursor on the command line and type commands. You can toggle the command line on or off for a specific window by selecting

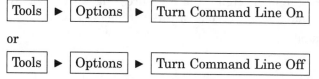

| Tools | ► | Options | ► | Turn Command Line On |

or

| Tools | ► | Options | ► | Turn Command Line Off |

The Command window (if it is available in your operating environment) includes a text area. You can place your cursor in this area and then issue commands.

To execute a command, type the command on the command line and then press the ENTER or RETURN key, depending on which operating environment you are using. You can specify a simple one-word command, multiple commands separated by semicolons, or a command followed by an option.

For example, if you want to move from the Editor window and open both the Log and the Output windows, on the command line of the Editor window, specify

```
log; output
```

Display 39.2 Entering Commands on the Command Line

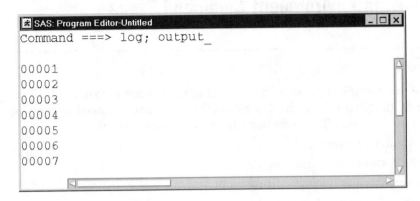

Next, press ENTER or RETURN to execute both commands. The Log and Output windows appear. The Output window is the active window because the command to open this window was executed last.

Using Pull-Down Menus

SAS windowing environment windows can display pull-down menus instead of a command line. You can then make menu selections to do things that you would usually accomplish by typing commands.

If your operating environment does not default to using drop-down menus, then issue the PMENU command at a command line to turn on menus for all windows that support them.

You can point and click menus and menu items with a mouse to make your selections. In some operating environments, you can also make menu selections by moving your cursor over the menu items and then pressing ENTER or RETURN. Depending on the item that you select, one of three things happens:

□ a command executes

□ a pull-down menu appears

□ a dialog box appears.

In many cases, double-clicking on items and right-clicking on items will cause different menus to appear. Sometimes you might want to try one or the other when selecting an item does not give you the expected result.

In other operating environments with workstations that are not equipped with a mouse, here are the keyboard equivalents to mouse actions:

Mouse Action	Keyboard Equivalent
double-click	type an **s** or an **x** in the space next to the item, then press the ENTER or RETURN key.
right-click	instead of right-clicking an item, type **?** in the space next to the item, then press the ENTER or RETURN key.

Using Line Commands

Line commands are one or more letters that copy, move, delete, and otherwise edit text. You can execute line commands by typing them in the numbered part of a text editing window (such as the Editor or the SAS NOTEPAD).

Although line commands are usually executed in the numbered part of the display or with function keys, they can also be executed from the command line if preceded by a colon.

Note: Issue the NUMBERS command to toggle line numbers on or off in text editing windows. △

For more information about line commands, see "Working with Text" on page 664.

Using Function Keys

Your keyboard includes function keys to which default values have already been assigned. You can browse or alter those values in the Keys window. To open the Keys window, select

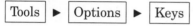

Tools ▶ Options ▶ Keys

or issue the KEYS command.

To change the setting of a key in the Keys window, type the new value over the old value. The new setting takes effect immediately and is saved permanently when you execute the END command to close the Keys window.

Function keys enable you to tailor your key settings to meet your needs in a particular SAS session. For example, If you might need to submit a number of programs and need to move between the Editor window and the Output window. Then each time you finish viewing your output, you must type the PGM and ZOOM commands on the command line and press ENTER or RETURN. As a shortcut, define one of your function keys to perform this action by typing the following commands over an unwanted value or where no value existed before:

```
pgm; zoom
```

Then, each time you press that function key, the commands are executed, saving you time. You can also use function keys to execute line commands. Simply precede the line command with a colon as you would if you were issuing the line command from the command line.

Working with SAS Windows

Overview

This section provides information about some helpful commands that you can use in the SAS windowing environment. For more information about how to execute commands, see "Using SAS Windowing Environment Command Types" on page 657.

Calling Windows

The SAS windowing environment has numerous windows that you can use to complete tasks. You can use the following commands to open a window and make it active.

Window Command	Window Name
AF C=*library.catalog.entry.type*	Build
DMFILEASSIGN	File Shortcut Assignment
DMLIBASSIGN	New Library
EDOP	Editor Options
EXPFIND	Find
EXPLORER	Explorer
FOOTNOTES	Footnotes
FSBROWSE	FSBrowse
FSEDIT	FSEdit
FSFORM *formname*	FSForm
FSVIEW	FSView
HELP	Help
KEYS	Keys
LOG	Log
NOTEPAD, NOTE	Notepad
ODSRESULTS	Results
ODSTEMPLATES	Templates
OPTIONS	Options
OUTPUT, LISTING, LIST, LST	Output
PROGRAM, PGM, PROG	Program Editor
REGEDIT	Registry Editor
REPOSMGR	Repository Manager
SASENV	Explorer (Contents Only view)
SETPASSWORD	Password
TITLES	Titles
VAR	Properties

You can use window commands at any command prompt. You might find it helpful to use multiple window commands together.

For example, from the Log window, the following string of commands changes the active window, maximizes it, and changes the word *paint* to *print*:

```
pgm; zoom; change paint print
```

The following display shows that the cursor immediately moves to the Editor, which has been maximized to fill the entire display (due to the ZOOM command). The word *paint* has been changed to *print*, and the cursor rests after the last character of that text string.

Display 39.3   Executing a Window-Call Command in a Series

Managing Windows

Window management commands enable you to access and use windows more efficiently. The following list includes the commands that you might use most often when managing windows:

BYE   ends a SAS session.

CLEAR   removes all text from an active window.

END   closes a window. In the Editor, this command acts like the SUBMIT command.

NEXT   moves the cursor to the next open window and makes it active.

PREVWIND   moves the cursor to the previous open window and makes it active.

RECALL   returns statements that are submitted from a text editor window (such as the Editor or SAS NOTEPAD) to the text editor.

ZOOM   enlarges a window to occupy the entire display. Execute it again to return a window to its previous size. This command is not available in all operating environments.

Scrolling Windows

Scrolling commands enable you to maneuver within text, and the command names indicate what they do. They include

BACKWARD	moves the contents of a window backward.
FORWARD	moves the contents of a window forward.
LEFT	moves the contents of a window to the left.
RIGHT	moves the contents of a window to the right.
TOP	moves the cursor to the first character of the first line in a window.
BOTTOM	displays the last line of text.
HSCROLL, VSCROLL	HSCROLL determines the amount that you move to the left or right when using the LEFT or RIGHT commands. VSCROLL determines the amount that you move forward or backward when using the FORWARD or BACKWARD commands.

Use the following options with the HSCROLL and VSCROLL commands as needed. HALF is the default scroll amount.

PAGE	is the entire amount that shows in the window.
HALF	is half the amount that shows in the window.
MAX	is the maximum portion to the left or right or to the top or bottom that shows in the window.
n	is *n* lines or columns, where *n* is the number that you specify.
CURSOR	When used with HSCROLL, the cursor moves to the left or right of the display, when the LEFT or RIGHT command is executed.
	Note: This option is valid only in windows that allow editing. △
	When used with VSCROLL, the cursor moves up and down when the FORWARD and BACKWARD command is executed.

Example: Scrolling Windows

To set the automatic horizontal scrolling value to five character spaces, then specify

```
hscroll 5
```

Now, when you execute the LEFT or RIGHT command, you move five character spaces in the appropriate direction. If you want to set the automatic vertical scrolling value to half a page, then specify

```
vscroll half
```

Then, when you execute the FORWARD command, half of the previous page remains on the display and half of a new page is scrolled into view.

If you need to scroll a specific number of lines forward or backward, then use the scroll amount on the FORWARD command to temporarily override the default scrolling

value. You can specify scrolling values with the BACKWARD and FORWARD
commands and the LEFT and RIGHT commands.

Changing Colors and Highlighting in Windows

SAS gives you a simple way to customize your environment if your display supports
color. You can change SAS windowing environment colors with the COLOR command.
You can also change SAS code color schemes by using the SYNCONFIG command. To
change windowing environment colors, simply specify the COLOR command followed by
the field or window element that you want changed, and the desired color. You might
also be able to change highlighting attributes, such as blinking and reverse video.

For example, to change the border of a window to red, specify

```
color border red
```

This changes the border to red.

Other available colors are blue, green, cyan, pink, yellow, white, black, magenta,
gray, brown, and orange. If the color that you specify is not available, then SAS
attempts to match the color to its closest counterpart.

Some color selections are valid only for certain windows.

For more information, see the online help for the SASColor window. You can access
the SASColor window with the SASCOLOR command.

You can also change the color scheme of text in the windows in which you enter code,
such as the Editor window and NOTEPAD. This is useful, because you can make
different elements of the SAS language appear in different colors, which makes it easier
to parse code. To change the color scheme for code, use the SYNCONFIG command.
The SYNCOLOR command toggles color coding off and on in these windows.

For more information about changing the color schemes for windows in which you
create and edit code, see the online help that is available when you issue the
SYNCONFIG command.

Finding and Changing Text

Often, you might want to search for a character string and change it. You can locate
the character string by specifying the FIND command and then the character string.
Then the cursor moves to the first occurrence of the string that you want to locate.
Remember to enclose a string in quotation marks if CAPS ON is in effect.

You can change a string by specifying the CHANGE command, then a space and the
current character string, and then a space and the new character string. Remember to
enclose in quotation marks any string that contains an embedded blank or special
characters. For both the FIND and CHANGE commands, the character string can be
any length.

With both the FIND and CHANGE commands, you can specify the following options
to locate or change a particular occurrence of a string:

ALL

FIRST

ICASE

LAST

NEXT

PREFIX

PREV

SUFFIX
WORD

For details about which options you can use together, see the *SAS Language
Reference: Dictionary*. Note that the option ALL finds or changes all occurrences of the
specified string. In the following example, all occurrences of *host* are changed to
operating environment:

```
change host 'operating environment' all
```

To resume the search for a string that was previously specified with the FIND
command, specify the RFIND command. To continue changing a string that was
previously specified with the CHANGE command, specify the RCHANGE command. To
find the previous occurrence of a string, specify the BFIND or FIND PREV command;
you can use the PREFIX, SUFFIX, and WORD options with the BFIND command.

Cutting, Pasting, and Storing Text

With the cut and paste facility, you can
- □ identify the text that you want to manipulate
- □ store a copy of the text in a temporary storage place called a paste buffer
- □ insert text
- □ list the names of all current paste buffers or delete them.

You can manipulate and store text by using the following commands:

MARK	identifies the text that you want to cut or paste.
CUT	removes the marked text from the display and stores it in the paste buffer.
STORE	copies the marked text and stores it in the paste buffer.
PASTE	inserts the text that you have stored in the paste buffer at the cursor location.

Working with Text

The SAS Text Editor

The SAS text editor is an editing facility that is available in the Editor and SAS
NOTEPAD windows of base SAS software, SAS/FSP, and SAS/AF software. You can edit
text from the command line and from any line on which code appears in an edit window.

This section provides information about commands that you can use to perform
common text editing tasks by using the SAS text editor. For more information about all
SAS windowing environment commands, see "Using SAS Windowing Environment
Command Types" on page 657.

Moving and Rearranging Text

Some of the basics of moving, deleting, inserting, and copying single lines of text
have already been reviewed. The rules are similar for working with a block of text;
simply use double letters on the beginning and ending lines that you want to edit.

For example, alphabetizing the following list requires that you move a block of text. Note the MM (move) block command on lines 5 and 6 and the B line command on line 1 of the example.

```
b 001  c signifies the line command copy
00002  d signifies the line command delete
00003  i signifies the line command insert
00004  m signifies the line command move
mm 05  a signifies the line command after
mm 06  b signifies the line command before
00007  r signifies the line command repeat
```

Press the ENTER or RETURN key to execute the changes. Here are the results:

```
00001  a signifies the line command after
00002  b signifies the line command before
00003  c signifies the line command copy
00004  d signifies the line command delete
00005  i signifies the line command insert
00006  m signifies the line command move
00007  r signifies the line command repeat
```

Mastering a few more commands greatly increases the complexity of what you can do within the text editor. Several commands enable you to justify text. Specify the JL (justify left) command to left justify, the JR (justify right) command to right justify, and the JC (justify center) command to center text. To justify blocks of text, use the JJL, JJR, and JJC commands. For example, if you want to center the following text,

```
00001 Study of Advertising Responses
00002 Topnotch Hotel Website
00003 Conducted by Global Information, Inc.
```

then simply add the JJC block command on the first and last lines and press ENTER or RETURN.

You can also shift text right or left the number of spaces that you choose by executing the following set of line commands:

>[n]   shifts text to the right the number of spaces that you specify; the default is one space.

<[n]   shifts text to the left the number of spaces that you specify; the default is one space.

To shift a block of text left, specify the following command on the beginning and ending line numbers of the block:

<<[n]

Specify the following command to shift a block of text to the right:

>>[n]

Displaying Columns and Line Numbers

To display column numbers in the text editor, specify the COLS line command. This command is especially useful if you are writing an INPUT statement in column mode, as shown in the following figure:

Display 39.4   Executing the COLS Command

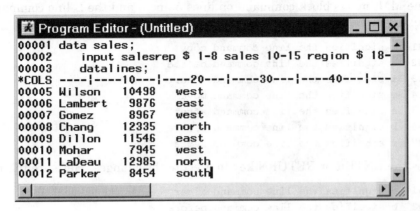

To remove the COLS line command or any other pending line command, execute the RESET command on the command line. You can also execute the D (delete) line command on the line where you have specified the COLS command to achieve the same results.

The NUMBERS command numbers the data lines in the Editor and SAS NOTEPAD windows. Specify the following command to add numbers to the data lines:

```
numbers on
```

To remove the numbers, specify

```
numbers off
```

You can also use the NUMBERS command without an argument, executing the command once to turn numbers on, and again to turn them off.

Uppercasing and Lowercasing Text

Overview

Uppercasing and lowercasing text involves two sets of commands to accomplish two kinds of tasks:

Command	Action
CAPS	changes the default
CU, CL line commands	change the case of existing text

Changing the Default

To change the default case of text as you enter it, use the CAPS command. After you execute the CAPS command, the text that you enter is uppercased as soon as you press ENTER or RETURN. Under some operating systems, with CAPS ON, characters that are entered or modified are translated into uppercase when you move the cursor from the line. Character strings that you specify with a FIND, RFIND, or BFIND command are interpreted as having been entered in uppercase unless you enclose the character strings in quotation marks.

For example, if you want to find the word *value* in the Log window, then on the command line, specify

```
find value
```

If the CAPS command has already been specified, then SAS searches for the word *VALUE* instead of *value*. You receive a message indicating that no occurrences of *VALUE* have been found, as shown in the following display:

Display 39.5   The Results of the FIND Command with CAPS ON

```
SAS: Log-Untitled                                    _ □ ×
Command ===>
WARNING: No occurrences of "VALUE" found.
8    ;
9    run;
10   proc print;
11   run;

NOTE: There were 4 observations read from the datase
NOTE: PROCEDURE PRINT used:
      real time            0.26 seconds
      cpu time             0.08 seconds
```

However, specify the following command and SAS searches for the word *value*, and finds it:

```
find 'value'
```

Setting CAPS ON remains in effect until the end of your session or until you turn it off. You can execute the CAPS command by specifying

```
caps on
```

To discontinue the automatic uppercasing of text, specify

```
caps off
```

You can also use the CAPS command like a toggle switch, executing it once to turn the command on, and again to turn it off.

Changing the Case of Existing Text

To uppercase or lowercase text that has already been entered, use the line commands CU and CL. Execute the CU (case upper) command to uppercase a line of text and the CL (case lower) command to lowercase a line of text.

In the following example, the CU and CL line commands each mark a line of text that will be uppercased and lowercased, respectively.

```
00001 Study of Gifted Seventh Graders
cu002 Burns County Schools, North Carolina
cl003 Conducted by Educomp, Inc.
```

Press ENTER or RETURN to execute the commands. The lines of text are converted as follows:

```
00001 Study of Gifted Seventh Graders
00002 BURNS COUNTY SCHOOLS, NORTH CAROLINA
00003 conducted by educomp, inc.
```

For a block of text, you have two choices. First, you can execute the CCU block command to uppercase a block of text and the CCL block command to lowercase a block of text. Position the block command on both the first and last lines of text that you want to convert. Second, you can designate a number of lines to be uppercased or lowercased by specifying a numeric *argument*, as shown below:

```
cu3 1 Study of Gifted Seventh Graders
00002 Burns County Schools, North Carolina
00003 Conducted by Educomp, Inc.
```

Press ENTER or RETURN to execute the command. The three lines of text are converted to uppercase, as shown below:

```
00001 STUDY OF GIFTED SEVENTH GRADERS
00002 BURNS COUNTY SCHOOLS, NORTH CAROLINA
00003 CONDUCTED BY EDUCOMP, INC.
```

Combining and Separating Text

You can combine and separate pieces of text with a number of line commands. With the TC (text connect) command, you can connect two lines of text. For example, if you want to join the following lines, then type the TC line command as shown below. Note that the second line is deliberately started in column 2 to create a space between the last word of the first line and the first word of the second line.

```
tc001 This study was conducted by
00002  Educomp, Inc., of Annapolis, Md.
```

Press ENTER or RETURN to execute the command. The lines appear as shown below:

```
00001 This study was conducted by Educomp, Inc., of Annapolis, Md.
```

Conversely, the TS (text split) command shifts text after the cursor's current position to the beginning of a new line.

Remember that you can also use a function key to execute the TC line command, the TS line command, or any other line command as long as you precede it with a colon.

Working with Files

Ways to Find a File

There are a number of ways in which you can find a file or library member in the SAS windowing environment, including

☐ using the Explorer window

☐ using the Find window.

Using Explorer to Find a File

When the SAS windowing environment opens, the Explorer window also opens by default in many operating environments. You can issue the EXPLORER command to open the Explorer window if it does not open by default.

☐ To find a file in the Contents Only view of the Explorer window, select the **Libraries** folder or the **File Shortcuts** folder, and then select **Open** from the pop-up menu. You can continue this process with subfolders until you locate the appropriate file.

☐ To find a file in the Tree view of the Explorer window, use the expansion icons (+ and – icons) located in the tree until the appropriate file appears in the window.

Note: You might find it useful to use specific navigational tools to move through the different levels of the Explorer window:

Menu

> | View | ▶ | Up One Level |

Command   UPLEVEL

△

For more information about selecting an Explorer window view, see "Customizing the Explorer Window" on page 701.

Using the Find Window to Find a File

The Find window enables you to search for an expression (such as a text string or a library member) that exists in a SAS library. The default search looks at everything in the library, except catalogs, but you can click the check box for the search to include the catalogs in the library as well.

Display 39.6 The Find Window

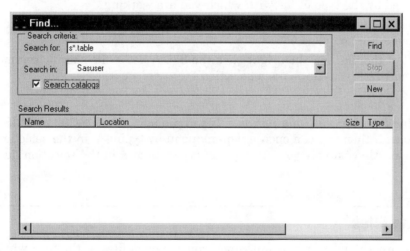

To search for a file:

1 Select

> | Tools | ▶ | Find |

from the Explorer window to open the Find window.

    Alternatively, issue the EXPFIND or EXPFIND *<library-name>* command. If you issue the EXPFIND command, then SASUSER is the default library. If you issue the EXPFIND WORK command, then WORK is the default library.

2   In the Search For field, enter the expression that you want to find. Wildcard characters are acceptable.

3   From the **Search In** drop-down list, select the library in which you want to search.

4   Click **Search Catalogs** to expand the search to include the catalogs of the library that you have selected.

Searching catalogs can lengthen search time considerably depending on the size and number of catalogs in the library.

5   Click Find.

Example: Finding Files with the Find Window

You can find TABLE files that begin with a specific letter and exist in a specific library. For a file that starts with the letter *S* and which exists in the SASHELP library

1   Select

Tools ▶ Find

to open the Find window.

2   Type **s*.table** in the Search For field.

3   Select **SASHELP** from the **Search In** drop-down list.

4   Click Find.

Issuing File-Specific Commands

There are a number of commands that you can issue against a file after you find the file in the SAS windowing environment. The commands that are available are determined by the type of file with which you are working.

1   Find the file with which you want to work. For more information, see "Ways to Find a File" on page 668.

2   Select the file, and then right-click the file. A list of file-specific commands appears from which you can make a selection.

Operating Environment Information: If you are using the OS/390 or CMS operating environment, then you can open a pop-up menu by typing **?** in the selection field next to an item. Alternatively you can type an type an**s** or **x** in the selection field next to an item. △

Opening Files

There are a number of ways in which you can open files in the SAS windowing environment.

To open a SAS file from Explorer:

1   Open a library and appropriate library members until you see the file that you want to open.

2   Select the file, then select **Open** from the pop-up menu.

Depending on the file type, you might also be able to select **Open in Editor**.

Note: In some cases, the pop-up menu also enables you to select **Browse in SAS Notepad**, which enables you to open a file in the SAS NOTEPAD window. △

To open a file that has a file shortcut:

1 Open the `File Shortcuts` folder.

2 Select a file shortcut, and then select **Open** from the pop-up menu.

Assigning a File Shortcut

File shortcut references provide aliases to external files (such as a .sas program file or a .dat text file). A file shortcut is the same as a file reference or fileref. In operating environments that support drag and drop functionality, you can drag file shortcuts from the Explorer window to the Editor window to display their contents.

To assign a file shortcut

1 From the Explorer window, select the `File Shortcuts` folder.

2 Select

3 In the Name field of the File Shortcut Assignment window, enter a name for the file shortcut.

4 Select the method or device that you want to use for the file shortcut.

The methods or devices that are available from the **Method** drop-down list depend on your operating environment. The DISK method is the default method (if it is available for your operating environment).

5 Select the **Enable at Startup** check box if you want SAS to automatically assign the file shortcut each time SAS starts. This option is not available for all the file shortcut methods.

If you want to stop a file shortcut from being enabled at startup, then select the file shortcut in the SAS Explorer window, and then select **Delete** from the pop-up menu.

6 Fill in the fields of the Method Information area, including the name and location of the file for which you want to create a file shortcut. You can select Browse to locate the actual file. The fields that are available in this area depend on the type of method or device that you select.

Note: Selecting a new method type erases any entries that you might have made in the Method Information fields. △

7 Select OK to create the new file shortcut. The file shortcut appears in the File Shortcut folder of the SAS Explorer window.

You can use the following ways to create a file shortcut, depending on your operating environment:

Menus

while your mouse is positioned on `File Shortcuts` in the Explorer window.

Command

DMFILEASSIGN<file-shortcut-name><METHOD=><AUTO=>

file-shortcut-name	specifies an existing file shortcut reference.
METHOD= method-name	specifies which method to use when the File Shortcut Assignment window opens.

AUTO= Yes|No   sets the state of the File Shortcut Assignment window's **Enable at Startup** check box when the window opens.

Pop-up
New File Shortcut if you have opened the **File Shortcut** folder in the Explorer window.

Toolbar
New (while your mouse is positioned on **File Shortcuts** in the Explorer window.)

Modifying an Existing File Shortcut

You can modify existing file shortcut references, if needed.
From the command line:

1 Issue the following command:

DMFILEASSIGN *file-shortcut-name*

The File Shortcut Assignment window appears. Its fields include information that is specific to the chosen file shortcut.

2 Edit the fields of the File Shortcut Assignment window as needed.

From the SAS Explorer:

1 Right-click the **File Shortcuts** folder and select **Open**. Alternatively, you can double-click the folder to open it.

2 Right-click the file shortcut reference that you want to change, and then select **Modify**.

3 Edit the fields of the File Shortcut Assignment window as needed.

Operating Environment Information: If you are using the OS/390 or CMS operating environment, then you can open a pop-up menu by typing **?** in the selection field next to an item. Alternatively you can type an type an**s** or **x** in the selection field next to an item. △

Printing Files

There are a number of ways in which you can print files. Often, printing capabilities depend on the type of file with which you are working, as well as your operating environment.

Nonetheless, the following lists common ways in which you might be able to print a file.

Printing from Explorer   Find the appropriate file in the SAS Explorer window. Right-click over the file, and then select **Print**.

Printing from a Text Editor   Open your file into a text editor such as the Editor or the SAS NOTEPAD. Use the text editor's printing commands.

Refer to your operating environment documentation for information about printing files.

Working with SAS Programs

Overview

SAS programs are specific types of files. When you work with SAS programs, you typically use the SAS programming windows (the Editor, Log, and Output windows).

Editor Window

Of all the programming windows, the Editor is the window that you might use most often. It enables you to

☐ enter and submit the program statements that define a SAS program

☐ edit text

☐ store your program in a file

☐ copy contents from an already-created file

☐ copy contents into another file.

Display 39.7 The Editor Window with Line Numbers Turned On

```
┌──────────────────────────────────────────────────────┐
│ 🏃 Program Editor - (Untitled)          _ □ ✕        │
│ Command ===>                                      ▲   │
│ 00001 data scores;                                    │
│ 00002    input name $ 1-8 score 10-12;                │
│ 00003 datalines;                                      │
│ 00004                                                 │
│ 00005 Jones      85                                   │
│ 00006 Potter     90                                   │
│ 00007 Chang      87                                   │
│ 00008 Gomez      89                                   │
│ 00009 ;                                               │
│ 00010                                                 │
│ 00011 proc print;                                     │
│ 00012 run;│                                           │
│ 00013                                                 │
│ 00014                                                 │
│ 00015                                                 │
│ 00016                                                 │
│ 00017                                                 │
│ 00018                                             ▼   │
│ ◄                                                 ►   │
└──────────────────────────────────────────────────────┘
```

Note: The Editor window shown here includes line numbers. You might find line numbers helpful when creating or editing programs. To toggle line numbers on or off, issue the NUMBERS command. △

Command Line Commands and the Editor

There are a number of commands that you might find useful while working on programs in the Editor. You can execute these commands from the command line.

TOP	scrolls to the beginning of the Editor.
BOTTOM	scrolls to the last line of text.
BACKWARD	scrolls back toward the beginning of the text.
FORWARD	scrolls forward toward the end of the text.
LEFT	scrolls to the left of the window.
RIGHT	scrolls to the right of the window.
ZOOM	increases the size of the window. You can issue this command again to return the window to its previous size.
UNDO	cancels the effect of the most recently submitted text editing command. Continuing to execute the UNDO command undoes previous commands, starting with the most recent and moving backward.
SUBMIT	submits the block of statements in your current SAS windowing environment session.
RECALL	returns to the Editor window the most recently submitted block of statements in your current SAS windowing environment session. Continuing to execute the RECALL command recalls previous statements, starting with the most recent and moving backward.
CLEAR	clears a window as specified. You can clear the Editor, Log, or Output windows from another window by executing the CLEAR command with the appropriate option as shown in the following examples:

```
clear pgm
clear log
clear output
```

CAPS	converts everything that you type to uppercase.
FIND	searches for a specified string of characters. Enclose the string in quotation marks if it contains embedded blanks or special characters.
CHANGE	changes a specified string of characters to another. Follow the command keyword with the first string, a space, and then the second string. The rules for embedded blanks and special characters apply. For example, you might specify

```
change 'operating system' platform
```

This CHANGE command replaces the first occurrence of *operating system* with the word *platform*. Note that the first string must be enclosed in quotation marks because it contains an embedded blank.

Note: Some of the more useful command line commands have been listed here. Almost all SAS commands are valid in the Editor window. For more information about other command line commands, see "Working with SAS Windows" on page 659. △

Line Commands and the Editor

The left-most portion of the Editor window includes a numbered field. This field is where you enter line commands. These commands are denoted by one or more letters, and can move, copy, delete, justify, or insert lines.

Some common line commands include

- □ M — moves a line of text
- □ C — copies a line of text
- □ D — deletes a line of text
- □ I — inserts a line of text.

When you use some line commands, you also need to specify a location. For example, if you type an *M* in the numbered field for a line in the Editor, then you must specify where you want the line of text to be moved. You can use the *A* (after) and *B* (before) line commands to specify a location.

If you type an **A** in the numbered field for a line, then the line of text that you want to move will be placed after the line marked with an A after you press the ENTER or RETURN key. If you type a **B** in the numbered field for a line, then the line of text that you want to move will be placed before the line marked with a B after you press the ENTER or RETURN key.

The following examples show how to use line commands to move a line of text in the Editor window to a new location. To make the following lines alphabetical, place the first line after the last line. To do this, use the M and A line commands:

```
m 001 Lincoln f Wake Ligon  135
00002 Andrews f Wake Martin 140
00003 Black   m Wake Martin 149
a 004 Jones   m Wake Ligon  142
```

After pressing the ENTER or RETURN key, your Editor window lines appear as follows:

```
00001 Andrews f Wake Martin 140
00002 Black   m Wake Martin 149
00003 Jones   m Wake Ligon  142
00004 Lincoln f Wake Martin 135
```

There are many other line commands and combinations of line commands that you can use to edit the statements of a program in the Editor window. For more information, see "Working with Text" on page 664.

Output Window

You can browse and scroll procedure output from your current SAS session with the Output window. The results of submitting a program, if it contains a PROC step that produces output, are usually displayed in the Output window.

Display 39.8   The Output Window Showing the Results of a Submitted Procedure

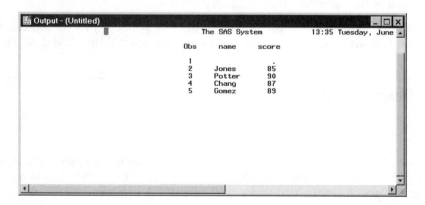

Most of the command line commands described earlier for the Editor window can be used in the Output window. The CLEAR command is particularly useful in the Output window because all output is appended to the previous output within a SAS session. If you want to avoid accumulating output, then execute the CLEAR command before you submit your next program. From any other window, you can clear the Output window by specifying

```
clear output
```

Log Window

The Log window enables you to

☐ recognize when you have made programming errors

☐ understand what is necessary to correct those errors

☐ receive feedback on the steps that you take to correct errors.

Display 39.9 The Log Window Showing Information about a SAS Session

The Log window shows the SAS statements that you have submitted as well as messages from SAS concerning your program. Under most operating environments, it tells you

☐ when the program was executed

☐ the release of SAS under which the program was run

☐ details about the computer installation and its site number

☐ the number of observations and variables for a given output data set

☐ the computer resources that each step used.

You can use command line commands in the Log window, just as you can in the Editor and Output windows. For more information, see " Editor Window" on page 673.

Using Other Editors

NOTEPAD Window

Although the Editor was designed for writing SAS programs, you can also use the NOTEPAD window to create and edit SAS programs. The NOTEPAD is a text editor that you can use to create, edit, save, and submit SAS programs. You might find

NOTEPAD useful as a separate place to work on code. To open NOTEPAD, issue the NOTEPAD or NOTES command.

Display 39.10 The SAS NOTEPAD Window with Line Numbers Turned On

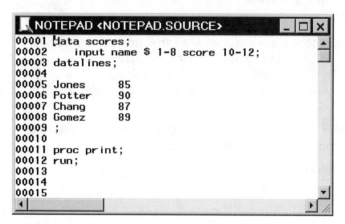

Note: The SAS NOTEPAD window shown here includes line numbers. You might find line numbers helpful when you create or edit programs. To toggle line numbers on or off in NOTEPAD, issue the NUMBERS command. △

If you open multiple NOTEPADS, then you can cut, copy, and paste text between NOTEPAD windows and the Editor window, multiple SAS sessions, and other applications.

Note: To submit a program from NOTEPAD, you must either select

or issue the NOTESUBMIT command. △

Note: The program information that is presented in this book uses the Editor windows as the default editor. △

Creating and Submitting a Program

To create and submit a SAS program:

1 Type the text of your program in the Editor.
2 Type **submit** on the command line, and then press ENTER or RETURN.

   You can also use the function key, menu command, or toolbar item that is assigned to submit programs in your environment.

   Note: If you are submitting a program from the SAS NOTEPAD window, then you must use the NOTESUBMIT command instead of the SUBMIT command. △

Storing a Program

To store a program:

1 In the Editor window, create or edit a program.
2 On the command line, issue the FILE command followed by a fileref or an actual filename. If you use an actual filename, then enclose it in quotation marks.

The FILE command does not clear the contents of the Editor window. You can store one copy of a program and then continue working in the Editor window.

If you try to store a program with a fileref or filename that already exists, then SAS displays a requestor window. The requestor window enables you to choose to

☐ overwrite the contents of the existing file with the new file

☐ append the new file to the existing file

☐ cancel the FILE command.

Often you will want to replace a file with an updated version. To suppress the requestor window, add the REPLACE option to the FILE command after the fileref or complete filename. To add the text in the Editor window to the end of an existing file, specify the APPEND option with the FILE command after the fileref or complete filename.

Note: You can also store a program as a SAS object or as a file that is specific to your operating environment. After you have created or edited a program, select

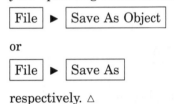

| File | ▶ | Save As Object |

or

| File | ▶ | Save As |

respectively. △

Debugging a Program

You or someone in your organization might be able to help debug a program with the information that appears in the Log window after a program is submitted. If you are having problems with your program, save the contents of the Log window to an external file, if you need to study it after your SAS session has ended.

To save the contents of the Log window to an external file:

1 Open the Log window if it is not already open.

2 From the command line, execute the FILE command followed by a fileref or an actual filename. If you use a filename, then enclose the name in quotation marks.

The FILE command stores a copy of the information in the Log window without removing what is currently displayed. If you specify the name of an existing fileref or file, then a requestor window appears and offers you three choices: overwriting the contents of the existing file with the new file, appending the new file to the existing file, or canceling the command.

Opening a Program

There is more than one way to open a SAS program. Two of the most popular methods are listed in this section.

To open a SAS program from the Editor window:

1 Select:

| File | ▶ | Open |

2 Use the Open window to locate the appropriate SAS program file.

To open a SAS program with commands:

1 Open the Editor window if it is not already open.

2 On the command line, specify the INCLUDE command followed by an assigned fileref or an actual filename. Remember to enclose an actual filename in single or double quotation marks.

By default, a program is appended to the end of any existing program statements.

Note: If program statements already exist in the Editor, then you can determine where your program is appended by using the B (before) or A (after) line commands. For more information about line commands, see Line Commands"Using Line Commands" on page 659. △

If you want to replace the text that is already in the Editor window with the program that you open, then specify the REPLACE option with the INCLUDE command after the fileref or filename.

Editing a Program

To edit a program:

1 Open an existing program in the Editor window.

2 Edit existing program statements or append new statements to the program.

Use command line commands and line commands as needed.

3 Store the program.

Assigning a Program to a File Shortcut

You can assign a program to a file shortcut to make it easier to find and work with the file in the future. For more information about file shortcuts, see "Assigning a File Shortcut" on page 671.

Working with Output

Overview

You can manage your SAS procedure output with the SAS Output Delivery System (ODS). Procedures that fully support ODS

- □ combine the raw data that they produce with one or more table definitions to produce one or more output objects that contain formatted results
- □ store a link to each output object in the Results folder in the Results window
- □ can generate various types of file output, such as HTML, Listing, and in some cases, SAS/Graph output
- □ can generate output data sets from procedure output
- □ provide a way for you to customize the procedure output by creating table definitions that you can use whenever you run the procedure.

The SAS windowing environment enables you to use many features of ODS through the Results, Templates, Preferences, and SAS Registry Editor windows. The Results window provides pointers to the procedure output that is produced by SAS. The Templates window provides a way to manage all the table, column header, and style definitions (sometimes called templates) that can be associated with procedure output.

Finally, the Preferences window and the SAS Registry Editor can be used to set the type(s) of procedure output that you want SAS to produce.

This section details only those portions of ODS that are related to the SAS windowing environment. For more information about ODS, see Chapter 23, "Directing

SAS Output and the SAS Log," on page 347 and *The Complete Guide to the SAS Output Delivery System.*

Setting Output Format

Depending on your operating environment, SAS output can be produced in one or more formats (or types). Listing output is the default type. Other output types include HTML, Output Data Sets, and PostScript. Pointers to procedure output appear in the Results window.

To set your output type, use either the Preferences window (if available in your operating environment), the SAS Registry Editor, or both.

Setting Output Type with the Preferences Window

If your operating environment supports the Preferences window, you can set output type as follows:

1 Select

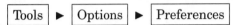

or issue the DLGPREF command to open the Preferences window.

2 Select the **Results** tab.

3 Select or deselect the check boxes that match the output types that you want to produce.

If you choose to produce HTML output, then you can further define the output by selecting

□ an HTML style

Click the **Style** box and highlight a style. Styles among other things, define output colors and fonts.

□ the folder to which the output is saved

Select **Use WORK folder** to save HTML output only for the duration of the current session. Your output is deleted when your current SAS session ends.

Enter a path in the **Folder** text box to save HTML output to a folder that is not deleted when your SAS session ends.

□ the **View Results as they are Generated** check box.

If selected, then each time HTML output is produced, your browser automatically opens and loads the output.

Setting Output Type with the SAS Registry Editor

To set output type with the SAS Registry Editor:

1 Select

or issue the REGEDIT command to open the SAS Registry Editor.

2 From the tree on the left side, expand the ODS folder.

3 Expand the Preferences folder.

4 Select the appropriate output type.

5 On the right side, select the Value key, and then select **Modify** from the pop-up menu.

6 In the dialog box that appears, edit the Value Data field as needed.

If this field is set to 1, then the output type is produced. If this field is set to 0, then the output type is not produced.

Assigning a Default Viewer to a SAS Output Type

When you produce output in SAS, output pointers appear in the Results window. You can assign a default viewer for each of the types of output that you produce. After a default viewer is assigned, you can double-click an output pointer in the Results window to open output in its default viewer. For example, double-clicking on a PostScript output pointer could open Ghostview with your PostScript output loaded.

Operating Environment Information: In the Windows operating environment, default viewers are established automatically with information from your Windows Registry. △

To assign a default viewer to a SAS Output Type:

1 From the Explorer window, select

| Tools | ► | Options | ► | Explorer |

2 Select **Host Files** from the drop-down menu at the top of the Explorer Options window.

3 Scroll through the registered file types until you find the file type with which you want to work.

4 Select the appropriate file type, and then select Edit .

5 Select Add , and then enter an action name and action command for the file type in the Edit Action window.

For example, add the following action name and action command to set Ghostview as the default viewer for PostScript file types:

Action Name   *&Edit*

Action   *x ghostview '%s' &*
Command

6 Select OK from the Edit Action window.

7 Select the action that you just specified, and then select Set Default .

Operating Environment Information: In the Windows operating environment, default viewers are established automatically with information from your Windows Registry. △

Working with Output in the Results Window

The Results window provides pointers to the procedure or DATA step output that SAS produces. This window might open by default when you start a SAS session. You can also open the Results window by selecting

| View | ► | Results |

or by issuing the ODSRESULTS command.

Display 39.11   The Results Window in Tree View

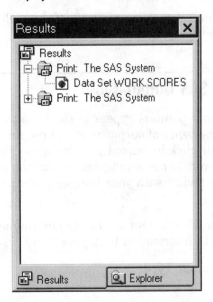

You can use the Results window to
□ navigate pointers to output
□ delete results pointers
□ rename results pointers
□ save listing output to other formats
□ quickly view the first output pointer item
□ view results properties.

Customizing the Results Window View

You can have the Results window display in one of three views:
□ Tree
□ Contents Only
□ Explorer.

In Tree view (the default), only a navigational tree is present. In Contents Only view, the tree is turned off, and contents appear as folders. In Explorer view, the Results window appears with two panes: one for the tree and one for the contents.

To toggle the Tree view pane, issue the TREE command from the Results window. To toggle the Contents pane, issue the CHILD command from the Results window. You can also select commands from the **View** menu of the Results window to perform the same actions, such as **Show Tree**, **Show Contents**, and others.

Note: By default, output pointers are listed by label rather than by name in the Tree pane. Labels are typically more descriptive than output names. You can use the following SAS system option to change this setting: LABEL. △

Using Results Pointers to Navigate Output

When SAS runs a procedure or a DATA step, pointers to the output are placed in the Results window. To use the pointers in the Results window, see "Navigating the Results Window in Tree View" on page 683, "Navigating the Results Window in Contents Only View" on page 683, or "Navigating the Results Window in Explorer View" on page 683.

Navigating the Results Window in Tree View

In Tree view, output pointers appear in a procedural hierarchy. To work with your SAS output:

1 Locate the folder that matches the procedure output that you want to view.

2 Use the expansion icons (+ or – icons) next to the folder to open or hide its contents. You can also

- □ double-click a folder to make it expand or collapse

- □ select a folder, and then select **Open** from the pop-up menu.

3 When you locate the appropriate pointer, double-click the pointer or select the pointer and then select **Open** from the pop-up menu.

The appropriate output appears.

Operating Environment Information: If you are using the OS/390 or CMS operating environment, then you can open a pop-up menu by typing **?** in the selection field next to an item. Alternatively you can type an type an**s** or **x** in the selection field next to an item. △

You can also use the following ways to navigate in the Tree view:

Menu	View ▶ Up One Level
Command	UPLEVEL
Toolbar	Up One Level icon
Key	Depending on your operating environment, you might also use arrow and backspace keys to navigate.

Navigating the Results Window in Contents Only View

In Contents Only view, output pointers appear in a procedural hierarchy, beginning with the top level of the hierarchy. You can drill down or roll up within the hierarchy to find the appropriate output.

When you open a folder, the current window contents are replaced with the contents of the selected folder. To work with your SAS output:

1 Locate the folder that matches the procedure output that you want to view.

2 Select the folder, and then select **Open** from the pop-up menu.

You can also double-click a folder to open it.

3 When you locate the appropriate pointer, double-click the pointer or select the pointer, and then select **Open** from the pop-up menu.

The appropriate output appears.

Operating Environment Information: If you are using the OS/390 or CMS operating environment, then you can open a pop-up menu by typing **?** in the selection field next to an item. Alternatively you can type an type an**s** or **x** in the selection field next to an item. △

Navigating the Results Window in Explorer View

In Explorer view, two window panes exist. The left pane includes a hierarchical view (the Tree view) of the procedure output that you can view. The right pane shows the contents (the Contents view) of the item that is currently in focus.

Deleting Results Pointers

You can delete results pointers by deleting the procedure folder in which the pointers exist. When you delete a procedure folder in the Results window, any output pointer that exists in that folder is removed.

Note: When you delete a procedure folder that contains a listing output pointer, the actual listing output is removed from the Output window. If other output pointers exist in the folder (such as HTML), then only the pointer is removed; the actual output remains available. △

To delete procedure output:

1 In the Results window, select the procedure folder that matches the procedure that you want to delete.

2 Select **Delete** from the pop-up menu.

3 Select **Yes** to confirm the deletion.

Tip

You can also delete output pointers by selecting the procedure folder that you want to delete, and then selecting

| Edit | ▶ | Delete |

Renaming Results Pointers

To rename results pointers:

1 Select the pointer that you want to rename.

2 Select **Rename** from the pop-up menu.

3 Type in a new name and/or a description, and then select OK .

Tip

You can also rename results pointers by selecting the pointer that you want to rename, and then selecting

| Edit | ▶ | Rename |

Saving Listing Output to Other Formats

To save listing output to a file from the Results window:

1 Expand the Results window tree until you find the appropriate listing output pointer.

2 Select the listing output pointer, and then select **Save As** from the pop-up menu.

To save listing output to a file from the Output window:

1 Access the Output window.

2 On the command line, specify the FILE command followed by a fileref or an actual filename. If you use a filename, then surround the filename with quotation marks.

Note: The FILE command stores a copy of the information in the Output window without removing what is currently displayed. △

To save listing output as a catalog object:

1 Expand the Results window tree until you find the appropriate listing output item.

2 Select the listing output item, and then select **Save As Object** from the pop-up menu.

Viewing the First Output Pointer Item

To view the first output pointer item:

1 Select the appropriate results pointer.

2 Select `View` from the pop-up menu.

The first output pointer item listed for the results pointer that you selected appears. For example, if you produced listing and HTML output for a procedure and the listing output was created first, then the listing output would appear.

Viewing Results Properties

You can view the properties of a Results window folder, an output pointer, or an output pointer item (such as listing or HTML output).

1 In the Results window, select the appropriate folder, output pointer, or output pointer item.

2 Select `Properties` from the pop-up menu.

Working with Output Templates

Overview

Templates contain descriptive information that enables the Output Delivery System (ODS) to determine the desired layout of a procedure's results.

The Templates window provides a way to manage all the templates that are currently available to SAS. Specifically, you can use the Templates window to

☐ browse PROC TEMPLATE source code

☐ edit PROC TEMPLATE source code

☐ view template properties.

Display 39.12 The Templates Window in Explorer View

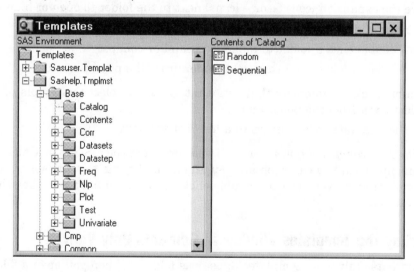

You can open the Templates window by selecting

from the Results window, or by issuing the ODSTEMPLATES command.

You can create or modify templates with PROC TEMPLATE.

Note: Templates that are supplied by SAS are stored in SASHELP. Templates that are created with PROC TEMPLATE are stored in SASUSER or whatever library that you specify in the ODS PATH statement. △

Customizing the Templates Window View

The Templates window appears in one of three views:

□ Explorer

□ Tree

□ Contents Only.

In Explorer view (the default), the Templates window appears with two panes: one for the tree and one for the contents. In Tree view, only a navigational tree is present. In Contents Only view, the tree is turned off.

To toggle the Contents pane, issue the CHILD command from the Templates window. To toggle the Tree pane, issue the TREE command from the Templates window.

For more information, see "Navigating the Templates Window in Explorer View" on page 686, "Navigating the Templates Window in Tree View" on page 686, or "Navigating the Templates Window in Contents Only View" on page 686.

Navigating the Templates Window in Explorer View

In Explorer view, two window panes exist. The left pane includes a hierarchical view (the Tree view) of the templates that you can view. The right pane shows the contents (the Contents view) of the template currently in focus.

You can open additional template windows from the Explorer view by selecting a template, and then selecting **Explore from Here** from the pop-up menu.

Navigating the Templates Window in Tree View

In Tree view, templates appear in a hierarchy. To work with a template:

1 Locate the folder that includes the template that you want to view.

2 Use the expansion icons (+ or – icons) next to the folder to open or hide its contents.

   You can also

   □ double-click a folder to make it expand or collapse

   □ select a folder, and then select **Open** from the pop-up menu.

3 Double-click the template that you want to see, or select the template, and then select **Open** from the pop-up menu.

   The template code appears in a browser window.

Operating Environment Information: If you are using the OS/390 or CMS operating environments, then you can open a pop-up menu by typing **?** in the selection field next to an item. Alternatively, you can double-click by typing an **s** or **x** in the selection field next to an item. △

Navigating the Templates Window in Contents Only View

In Contents Only view, templates appear as folders. When you open a folder, the current window contents are replaced with the contents of the selected folder. To work with your templates in this view:

1 Locate the folder that includes the template that you want to view.

2 Select the folder, and then select **Open** from the pop-up menu.

   You can also double-click on a folder to open it.

3 Double-click on the template that you want to see, or select the template, and then select **Open** from the pop-up menu.

   The template code appears in a browser window.

Operating Environment Information: If you are using the OS/390 or CMS operating environments, then you can open a pop-up menu by typing **?** in the selection field next to an item. alternatively, you can double-click by typing an **s** or **x** in the selection field next to an item. △

Browsing PROC TEMPLATE Source Code

To browse the PROC TEMPLATE source code:

1 Locate the appropriate template in the Templates window.

2 Select the template, and then select **Open** from the pop-up menu.

   Template code appears in a browser window.

Editing PROC TEMPLATE Source Code

To edit the PROC TEMPLATE source code:

1 Locate the appropriate template in the Templates window.

2 Select the template, and then select **Edit** from the pop-up menu. Template code appears in an editor window.

3 Modify the template code as needed.

4 Select

 Run ► Submit

to submit your modified template code.

Note: If syntax errors occur when the code for an edited template is submitted, then the errors appear in the Log window. △

Note: Additional information for PROC TEMPLATE is available in the *SAS Procedures Guide.* △

Viewing Template Properties

To view template properties:

1 Locate the appropriate template in the Templates window.

2 Select the template, and then select **Properties** from the pop-up menu.

The Properties dialog box lists the type, path, size, description, and modification date for the template. You can also view this information by selecting

 View ► Details

when the Templates window is active.

Printing Output

The method that you use to print output depends on the type of output that you produce, as well as your operating environment. SAS windowing environment windows have menus with print options that enable you to print the contents of that particular window. This feature varies from operating system to operating system, but is available in all operating environments.

If you produce HTML output, then you can open the output in a Web browser, and then print the output from the Web browser with the Web browser's printing command.

For more information about printing, refer to your SAS operating environment companion documentation and your operating environment documentation.

Review of SAS Tools

Statements

ODS PATH *location(s)*

specifies which locations to search for definitions that were created by PROC TEMPLATE, as well as the order in which to search for them.

<libname.>item-store <(READ | UPDATE | WRITE)>

item-store
identifies an item store that contains style definitions, table definitions, or both.

Windows

File Shortcut Assignment
enables you to create or edit file shortcut references. To open this window, issue the DMFILEASSIGN command.

Find
enables you to search for an expression that exists in a SAS library. To open this window, select

 Tools ► Find

from Explorer or issue the EXPFIND command.

Log
enables you to review information about the programs that you have run. To open this window, select

View ► Log

or issue the LOG command.

Output
enables you to see listing output. To open this window, select

View ► Output

or issue the OUTPUT command.

Editor
enables you to enter, edit, submit, and save SAS program statements. To open this window, select

 View ► Editor

or issue the PGM command.

Results
provides pointers to the procedure output that you produce with SAS. To open this window, select

View ► Results

or issue the ODSRESULTS command.

SAS NOTEPAD
> enables you to enter, edit, submit, and save SAS program statements. To open this window, issue the NOTEPAD or NOTES command.

SAS Registry Editor
> enables you to edit the SAS Registry and to customize aspects of the SAS windowing environment. To access this window, issue the REGEDIT command.

Templates
> provides a way to manage the output templates that are currently available. To access this window, select

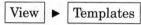 View ▶ Templates

> from within the Results window.

Commands

AUTOEXPAND	automatically expands the tree hierarchy when you select a tree node or when procedure output is produced.
AUTOSYNC	enables you to automatically navigate to the first available output in the Output window by means of a single click.
CHILD	toggles the Contents pane on and off.
CLEAR	removes all the SAS output pointers.
DELETESELS	removes the item currently in focus.
	Note: If the output pointer is associated with listing output, then the listing output is also removed. △
DESELECT_ALL	deselects any items that are selected while the Contents pane is viewable.
DETAILS	toggles the item details on and off while the Contents pane is viewable.
DMOPTLOAD	recalls system option settings saved by DMOPTSAVE.
DMOPTSAVE	saves all system option settings for recall in later SAS sessions
FIND	searches for a match to the string that you provide.
LARGEVIEW	displays large icons (on some operating environments) while the Contents pane is viewable.
PMENU	turns on menus in windows.
PRINT	prints the desired SAS listing output.
REFRESH	refreshes the window's contents.
RENAMESELS	enables you to rename the output pointer that currently has focus.
SELECT_ALL	selects all items while the Contents pane is viewable.
SMALLVIEW	displays small icons (on some operating environments) in a horizontal fashion while the Contents pane is viewable.
TREE	toggles the Tree view (hierarchical view) on and off.
UPLEVEL	moves focus up one level in the hierarchy.

Procedures

Use PROC TEMPLATE to set template information.

Learning More

To learn more about SAS language elements, see
SAS Language Reference: Dictionary.

To learn more about printing and the SAS Output Delivery System, see
The Complete Guide to the SAS Output Delivery System.

To find examples that will help you get started, see
Getting Started with the SAS System.

CHAPTER

40

Customizing the SAS Environment

Introduction

Purpose

In this chapter, you will learn how to make the following types of SAS System customizations:

☐ those that remain in effect for the current session only

☐ those that remain in effect from session to session

☐ those that you can apply to the SAS windowing environment, which is the default SAS environment.

Prerequisites

To use this chapter effectively, you should be familiar with the SAS windowing environment. For more information about the SAS windowing environment, see *Chapter 39, "Using the SAS Windowing Environment," on page 651.*

Operating Environment Differences

Even though SAS has a different appearance for each operating environment, most of the actions that are available from the menus are the same.

One of the biggest differences between operating environments is the way that you select menu items. If your workstation is not equipped with a mouse, then here are the keyboard equivalents to mouse actions:

Mouse Action	Keyboard Equivalent
double-click the item	type an **s** or an **x** in the space next to the item, then press the ENTER or RETURN key
right-click the item	type **?** in the space next to the item, then press the ENTER or RETURN key

Examples in this book show SAS windows as they appear in the Microsoft Windows environment. For the most part, corresponding windows in other operating environments will yield similar results. If you do not see the drop-down menus in your operating environment, then enter the global command PMENU at a command prompt.

Customizing Your Current Session

Ways to Customize

As you become familiar with SAS, you will probably develop preferences for how you want SAS configured. Many options are available to you to make SAS conform to your preferred working style. Some of the things that you can change are

- window color and font attributes
- library and file shortcuts
- output appearance
- file-handling capabilities
- the use of system variables.

You can customize your current SAS session in a number of ways, including

- at the startup of a SAS session or program
- through SAS system options
- with drop-down menu options.

Customizing SAS Sessions and Programs at Startup

Setting Invocation-Only Options Automatically

You can specify some system options only when you invoke SAS. These system options affect

- the way SAS interacts with your operating system
- the hardware that you are using
- the way in which your session or program is configured.

Note: There are other system options that you can specify at any time. For more information, see "Customizing with SAS System Options" on page 694. △

Usually, any invocation-only options are set by default when SAS is installed at your site. However, you can specify invocation-only options on the command line each time you invoke SAS.

To avoid having to specify options that you use every time you run SAS, set the options in a configuration file. Each time you invoke SAS, SAS looks for that file and uses the customized settings it contains. Be sure to examine the default configuration file before creating your own.

Note: If you specify options both in the configuration file and in the SAS command, then the options are concatenated. If you specify an option in the SAS command that also appears in the configuration file, then the setting from the SAS command overrides the setting in the configuration file. △

To display the current settings for all options that are listed in the configuration file and on your command line as you invoke the system, use the VERBOSE system option in the SAS command.

Executing SAS Statements Automatically

Just as you can set SAS system options automatically when you invoke SAS, you can also execute statements automatically when you invoke SAS by creating a special autoexec file. Each time you invoke SAS, it looks for this special file and executes any of the statements it contains.

You can save time by using this file to execute statements that you use routinely. For example, you might add

- ☐ OPTIONS statements that include system options that you use regularly
- ☐ FILENAME and LIBNAME statements to define the file shortcuts and libraries that you use regularly.

Operating Environment Information: In order to execute SAS statements automatically in the CMS operating environment, you must have a file shortcut defined as SASEXEC. △

Customizing with SAS System Options

Using the OPTIONS Statement and the Options Window

SAS system options determine global SAS settings, such as how

- ☐ your SAS output appears
- ☐ files are handled by SAS
- ☐ observations from SAS data sets are processed
- ☐ system variables are used.

The previous section discusses some invocation-only options that must be set at startup. However, there are many system options that can be set at any time. These system options can be set in an OPTIONS statement as well as in the SAS Options window.

It is important to note that system option settings remain in effect until you change them again, or until your current session ends.

There are several ways to view your system option settings. The two most common methods are using

- ☐ the SAS Options window (type OPTIONS at a command line)
- ☐ the OPTIONS procedure.

To obtain a complete list of system option settings using the OPTIONS procedure, submit the following statements:

```
proc options;
run;
```

The SAS Options window groups options by function. The left side of the window includes a tree that lists the available option groups. You can expand option groups to see subgroups.

Operating Environment Information: Mainframe users can expand groups and subgroups by using the mouse or by typing an **s** or an **x** before the group or subgroup name. When you select a subgroup, the individual options of that subgroup appear on the right side of the window. △

Display 40.1 SAS Options Window

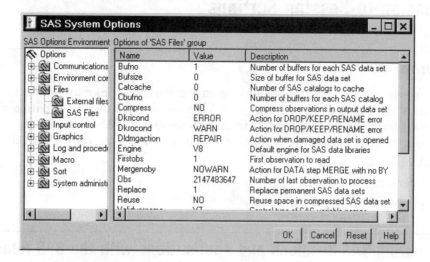

To open the SAS Options window

☐ issue the OPTIONS command

☐ or select

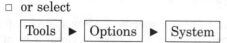

The options in each group or subgroup are listed alphabetically, followed by options that are specific to your operating environment (which are also listed alphabetically).

Finding Options in the SAS Options Window

You can find options in a number of ways

☐ Expand the option groups and subgroups on the left side of the window until the appropriate option appears on the right side of the window.

☐ Select an option group or subgroup, then select **Find Option** from the pop-up menu. In the Find Option window, enter the name of the option that you want to locate, and then select OK.

Setting Options in the SAS Options Window

1 In the SAS Options window, find the option that you want to set.

2 Select the option from the right side of the SAS Options window.

3 Select **Modify Value** or **Set to Default** from the pop-up menu. Mainframe users can type an **S** or an **X** before the option name to access the pop-up menu.

☐ If you choose **Modify Value**, then a dialog box appears that enables you to edit the option value.

☐ If you choose **Set to Default**, then the option value is reset to the default SAS System value.

4 Select OK to save your changes. Select Reset to return all edited options to their previous values.

Note: If all the items on the pop-up menu are grayed out (that is, unavailable), then the options are invocation-only options and can be set only when a SAS session is started. △

Customizing Session-to-Session Settings

Overview

The previous section discusses making customizations that stay in effect for the duration of the current SAS session only. This section provides information about making customizations that remain from SAS session to SAS session.

You can make customizations that remain from session to session with the

☐ SAS Registry Editor

☐ Preferences window

☐ Options window.

Customizing SAS Sessions and Applications with the SAS Registry Editor

Understanding the SAS Registry

The *SAS Registry* stores information about specific SAS sessions and applications. Unlike system options, customizations to the SAS Registry remain in effect for more than one SAS session. You can make SAS Registry customizations by using either PROC REGISTRY or the SAS Registry Editor.

This section shows you how to use the *SAS Registry Editor*, which is a graphical alternative to PROC REGISTRY. For more information about PROC REGISTRY, see the *SAS Procedures Guide*.

CAUTION:
   Changes to SAS Registry should be well planned. In many cases, it is appropriate to have a designated person in charge of SAS Registry edits. Inappropriate SAS Registry edits can adversely affect your SAS session performance.   △

SAS Registry Editor values, which store data, exist in *keys* and *subkeys*. Keys and subkeys, which look like folders, appear in a tree on the left side of the SAS Registry Editor. If a key has subkeys, then you can expand or collapse it with the + and − icons that are found in the tree. If a key or subkey has values, then the values appear on the right side of the window.

Operating Environment Information: In the OS/390 and CMS operating environments, you can select a + or − icon by positioning your cursor on it and then pressing the ENTER key. △

Display 40.2   The SAS Registry Editor

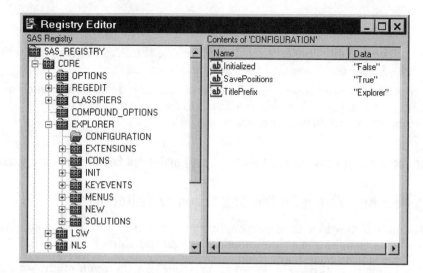

To customize SAS sessions and applications, use the SAS Registry Editor to add, modify, rename, and delete keys and key values.

You can also use the SAS Registry Editor to

☐ import registry files (starting at any key)

☐ export the contents of the registry (starting at any key)

☐ unregister a registry file.

Opening the SAS Registry Editor

To open the SAS Registry Editor, select

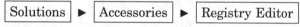

Solutions ▶ Accessories ▶ Registry Editor

or issue the REGEDIT command.

Finding Information in the SAS Registry Editor

You can search for specific information in the SAS Registry Editor, including specific keys, key value names, and key value data.

1 Select the key from which you want to start a search.

2 Open the drop-down menu and select **Find**.

3 In the Registry Editor Find window, type your search string in the Find What field.

4 Check one or more of the Keys, Value Name, or Value Data check boxes, depending on where you want to perform your search.

5 Select ⌷Find⌷ to begin the search.

Setting Keys in the SAS Registry Editor

You can add, modify, rename, or delete keys in the SAS Registry Editor. For example, you might want SAS to be able to work with a new paper type when printing output. Therefore, you might need to create a new key that represents the paper type. Additionally, you would have to create and set key values for this new paper type. For more information, see "Setting New Key Values in the SAS Registry Editor" on page 698.

Note: When you add a key, the new key becomes a subkey of the most recently selected key. △

To set a key in the SAS Registry Editor:

1 Expand or collapse the keys on the left side of the SAS Registry Editor (using the + and − icons) until you find the appropriate key.

2 With a key selected, select an action from the drop-down menu (such as **New Key**, **Rename**, or **Delete**). A dialog box appears that enables you to enter additional information or confirm an action.

CAUTION:
Delete removes all subkeys and values (if any) under the key that you are deleting. △

Setting New Key Values in the SAS Registry Editor

If you create a new key, then you might want to add values to that key. Adding values includes assigning a value name as well as the value data.

Note: If your new key is similar to an existing key, then you might want to review that key's subkeys and key values. The review process might help you determine which subkeys and key values you should have for the new key. △

To add a new key value:

1 Select the new key on the left side of the SAS Registry Editor.

2 Select an action from the pop-up menu (such as **New String Value**, **New Binary Value**, or **New Double Value**).

3 In the dialog box that appears, enter a name and a value for the new key value. Select OK to complete the process.

Editing Existing Key Values in the SAS Registry Editor

1 Select a key on the left side of the SAS Registry Editor.

2 If the key contains subkeys, then continue to expand the key by selecting the + icon.

3 Select the key value that you want to edit on the right side of the SAS Registry Editor.

4 Select the appropriate action from the pop-up menu (such as **Modify**, **Rename**, or **Delete**). A dialog box appears that enables you to enter additional information or confirm an action.

Importing Registry Files

You can import a registry file to populate and modify the SAS Registry quickly. Registry files are text files that you create with a text editor. For information about registry file syntax, see PROC REGISTRY in the *SAS Procedures Guide*.

1 Select

File ► Import Registry File

2 Select the file that you want to import, and then select OK.

If errors occur during the import, then a message appears in the status bar and the errors are reported in the Log window. All registry changes can be sent to the log if you use the SAS Registry Editor option **Output full status to Log**. For more information, see "Setting Registry Editor Options" on page 699.

Exporting Registry Files

You can export (or copy) all or a portion of the SAS Registry to a file:

1 Select the key in the existing registry from where you want to begin exporting the file. Selecting a root key exports the entire tree, beginning at the root key that you select.

2 Select

 File ▶ Export Registry File

3 Enter the full path to the file or browse to select the file to which you want to save the existing registry, and then select OK .

If errors occur during the export, then a message appears in the status bar and the errors are reported in the Log window. All registry changes can be sent to the log if you use the **Output full status to Log** SAS Registry Editor option.

Uninstalling an Imported Registry File

The uninstall function reads an imported registry file and removes the keys found in the file from the registry. If any errors occur during this process, then a message appears in the status bar and errors are reported in the Log window.

Note: SAS ships with a set of ROOT keys. Root keys are not removed during an uninstall process. △

1 Select

 File ▶ Uninstall Registry File

2 Select the external registry file that you want to uninstall from the SAS Registry, and then select OK . A message appears in the message line when the uninstall is complete.

Setting Registry Editor Options

1 Open the SAS Registry Editor if it is not already open.

2 From the Registry Editor window, select

 Tools ▶ Options ▶ Registry Editor

3 In the Select Registry View group box, choose a view for the Registry Editor.

  □ View Overlay mode enables you to modify data anywhere in the registry. The HKEY_USER_ROOT overlays the HKEY_SYSTEM_ROOT. The parent root for overlay view mode is shown as SAS REGISTRY.

  □ In View All mode, the Registry Editor shows all the entries that are contained in the two main entry points into the registry: HKEY_SYSTEM_ROOT and HKEY_USER_ROOT. Typically, the HKEY_SYSTEM_ROOT tree is stored in the SASHELP library and the HKEY_USER_ROOT is stored in the SASUSER library.

4 Select or deselect appropriate check boxes:

Open HKEY_SYSTEM _ROOT for write access — enables you to open the registry for write access if you have write access to SASHELP.

Output full status to Log — writes to the log all changes that were made when the registry file was imported or uninstalled. Usually, only errors appear in the Log window.

View unsigned integers in hexadecimal format
enables you to view unsigned integers in the value list in HEX or DECIMAL format.

You can select Reset all options to return all Registry Editor Options window settings to the default values.

Customizing SAS Sessions with the Preferences Window

The Preferences window includes a series of tabs that you can access to set SAS preferences. Preferences enable you to customize and control your SAS environment. For example, you might use the **General** tab to select a startup logo, or the **Results** tab to control your output preferences, or even the **Editing** tab to set editor preferences, if, for example, your cursor inserts or overtypes text in an editor.

Preference window settings remain in effect from one SAS session to the next.

To access the Preferences window, select

Tools ► Options ► Preferences

or issue the DLGPREF command.

Operating Environment Information: The Preferences window is unavailable in some operating environments. Additionally, some preference settings are specific to your operating environment. Refer to the SAS documentation for your operating environment for more information about setting preferences. △

Saving System Option Settings with the DMOPTSAVE and DMOPTLOAD Commands

Perhaps the easiest way to save your system option settings from one SAS session to another is to use the global commands DMOPTSAVE and DMOPTLOAD. After you set up your system options in a way that best suits your working style, type **DMOPTSAVE** at the comand line and press ENTER. This saves the current system option settings for later use. Later, when you have started another SAS session and would like to retrieve your saved settings, type **DMOPTLOAD** at the comand line and press ENTER. This changes your system option settings back to the system option settings in effect when you issued the DMOPTSAVE command.

The DMOPTSAVE and DMOPTLOAD commands have other useful features:

□ You can issue parameters to name different sets of system option settings and control where they are saved.

□ You can view the saved system option settings by using SAS Explorer, because they are saved by default as a data set.

□ You can also issue parameters to save the system option settings to a registry key.

When you issue a DMOPTSAVE command without parameters, SAS saves a data set (myopts) that contains the system option settings to the default library. The default library is usually the library where the current user profile is. In most cases, this is the SASUSER library.

See SAS online Help for more details about using these commands.

Customizing the SAS Windowing Environment

Customizing the Explorer Window

Ways to Customize the Explorer Window

You can customize the Explorer window in these ways:

- □ select Contents Only view or Explorer view
- □ change how items appear in the contents view
- □ add and remove folders (including one that adds access to files in your operating environment)
- □ enable member, entry, and operating environment file types to appear
- □ add a pop-up menu action
- □ hide member, entry, and operating environment file types.

Selecting Contents Only View or Explorer View

The Explorer window can appear in either *Explorer view* or *Contents Only view*. In Explorer view, the Explorer window includes two sides: a tree view on the left that lists folders, and a contents view on the right that shows the contents of the folder that is selected in the tree view.

Display 40.3 The Explorer Window with Explorer View Enabled

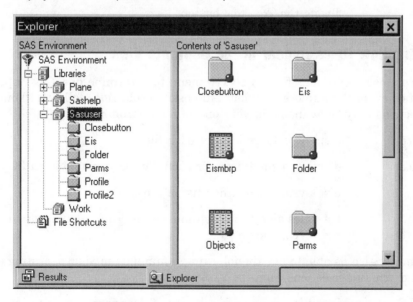

In Contents Only view, the Explorer window is a single-paned window that shows the contents of your SAS environment. As you open folders, the folder contents replace the previous contents in the same window. In Contents Only view, you navigate the Explorer window using pull-down and pop-up menu actions, and toolbar items (if a toolbar is available).

Display 40.4 The Explorer Window with Contents Only View Enabled

Operating Environment Information: In most operating environments, the Explorer appears in Contents Only view by default. △

Depending on your operating environment, you can toggle between the two views in these ways:

Menu:

| View | ► | Show Tree |

Command: TREE

Toolbar   Toggle the Tree tool button

Changing How Items Appear in the Contents View

You can make selections from the **View** menu to determine how files appear in the Contents view of the Explorer window. All possible selections follow, although not all the selections may be available in your operating environment:

Large Icons   displays a large icon for each file.

Small Icons   displays a small icon for each file (only available on PC hosts).

List   displays a left-justified list of files.

Details   lists files along with columns of descriptive information (such as file size, type, and so on).

You might also be able to use the following commands in your operating environment instead of making selections from the **View** menu:

DETAILS   lists files along with columns of descriptive information (such as file size, type, and so on).

LARGEVIEW   displays a large icon for each file.

SMALLVIEW   depending on your operating environment, this command displays either a list of files or a small icon for each file.

Adding and Removing Folders

The Explorer window shows the Libraries and File Shortcuts folders by default in many operating environments. You can turn off these folders, or turn on other folders, including Extensions, My Favorite Folders, and Results.

1 From the Explorer window, select

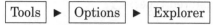
Tools ► Options ► Explorer

2 From the drop-down list at the top of the window, select **Initialization**.

3 Select the folder that you want to add or remove, and then select **Add** or **Remove**. The Description field changes to On or Off to reflect your change.

Operating Environment Information: The My Favorite Folders window enables you to access operating environment-specific files from the Explorer. This feature is not available in CMS and OS/390 operating environments. △

Enabling Member, Entry, and Operating Environment File Types to Appear

Commonly used members, catalog entries, and operating environment files are registered and appear in the Explorer window. Registered types must have at least an icon defined and might also have pop-up menu actions defined. Undefined types do not appear in the Explorer window and have no actions associated with them.

To add (register) an undefined type:

1 From the Explorer window, select

Tools ► Options ► Explorer

2 From the drop-down list at the top of the window, select a category (such as Members, Catalog Entries, or Host Files). The registered types are displayed in the window.

3 Select the **View Undefined Types** check box to see the undefined types for the category.

4 Select a type and then select Edit.

5 Select Select Icon.

6 In the Select Icon dialog box, choose a category from the drop-down list at the top, select an icon, and then select OK to close the dialog box.

7 Add actions for the type (if desired) and then select OK. For more information about adding actions to a type, see "Adding a Pop-Up Menu Action to a Member, Entry, or Operating Environment File Type" on page 703. The type is added to the Registered Types list.

Adding a Pop-Up Menu Action to a Member, Entry, or Operating Environment File Type

You can add a pop-up menu action to any catalog entry, member, or operating environment file type.

1 From the Explorer window, select

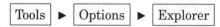
Tools ► Options ► Explorer

2 From the drop-down list at the top of the window, select a category (such as Members, Catalog Entries, or Host Files). The registered types are displayed in the window.

3 Select the registered type that you want to edit.

4 Select ⌈Edit⌉.

5 In the Options dialog box for that entry, select ⌈Add⌉.

6 Enter a name for the action (this is the action that will appear on the pop-up menu for the item), and an action command. To see examples of action commands, look at the commands for registered types.

7 Select ⌈OK⌉.

Note: The letter immediately after the ampersand (&) in the Action section denotes the shortcut key that can be used to perform that action. △

Hiding Member, Entry, and Host File Types

You can hide members, catalog entries, and host files so that they do not appear in the Explorer window.

1 From the Explorer window, select

| Tools | ▶ | Options | ▶ | Explorer |

2 From the drop-down list at the top of the window, select a category (such as Members, Catalog Entries, or Host Files). The registered types are displayed in the window.

3 Select the registered type that you want to remove from view.

4 Select ⌈Remove⌉. Confirm the removal by selecting ⌈OK⌉ when prompted.

When you remove a registered type, it is moved to the View Undefined Types view. To add the registered type back, you must redefine its icon.

Customizing an Editor

You can customize general and text editing options for your editor. For example, if you use line commands when you edit programs, then you might always want the Program Editor to appear with line numbers.

To customize your editor:

1 Select a SAS programming window (such as the Program Editor, Log, Output, or SAS Notepad window).

2 Select

| Tools | ▶ | Options | ▶ | Editor |

3 From the drop-down list, select the category of options that you want to edit.

4 In the Options group box, select an option, and then select **Modify** from the pop-up menu.

5 In the dialog box that appears, edit the option name, value, or both.

Customizing Fonts

You can set default font information for the SAS windowing environment with the Font window. To access the Font window, issue the DLGFONT command or select

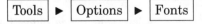

| Tools | ▶ | Options | ▶ | Fonts |

The Font window is host-specific. Refer to your host documentation for more information.

Customizing Colors

Note: Changes made with the SASColor window are visible only after affected SAS windows are closed and then reopened. △

You can also change the default colors in edit windows, such as the Notepad and the Program Editor by using the SYNCONFIG command. This command controls the color of SAS language and programming elements, which makes it easier to parse through a SAS program and understand how it works. SYNCONFIG opens the Edit Scheme window, which gives you several different color schemes to select. You can also modify the provided color schemes.

Setting SAS Windowing Environment Preferences

You can use the Preferences window to customize portions of the SAS windowing environment to your liking. For more information, see "Customizing SAS Sessions with the Preferences Window" on page 700.

Review of SAS Tools

Commands

DLGFONT
> opens the Font window, which is used to control the fonts in the SAS windowing environment.

DLGPREF
> opens the Preferences window, in some operating environments.

OPTIONS
> opens the SAS System Options window.

PMENU
> turns on the menu bar in the windowing environment.

REGEDIT
> opens the Registry Editor window.

SASCOLOR
> opens the SASCOLOR window, which is used to change the color of window elements, such as backgrounds and borders.

SYNCONFIG
> opens the Edit Scheme window, which is used to edit color schemes in the Editor, NOTEPAD, or Program Editor windows.

Procedures

PROC OPTIONS <SHORT|LONG>;

lists the current values of all SAS system options. The SHORT and LONG options determine the format in which you want SAS system options listed.

Note: You can also use the SAS Options window to see the current values of all SAS system options. △

PROC REGISTRY <options>;

maintains the SAS Registry.

Note: You can also use the SAS Registry Editor to maintain the SAS Registry. △

Statements

OPTIONS *option-1<... option-n>*;

changes the value of one or more SAS system options.

System Options

VERBOSE | NOVERBOSE

controls whether SAS writes the settings of all the system options that are specified in the configuration file to either the workstation or batch log.

Windows

Editor Options window
  enables you to set options for specific SAS windowing environment windows, such as the Program Editor. To open the Editor Options window, go to the window that you want to change, and then select

  | Tools | ▶ | Options | ▶ | Editor |

  or issue the EDOPT command.

Explorer Options window
  enables you to set Explorer window options. To open this window, select

  | Tools | ▶ | Options | ▶ | Explorer Options |

  or issue the EXPOPTS command.

Fonts window
  enables you to select the default font that you want to use in the SAS windowing environment. To access this window, issue the DLGFONT command.

  Note: This window is specific to your operating environment. △

Preferences window
  enables you to set SAS system preferences. To access this window, issue the DLGPREF command.

  Note: This window is specific to your operating environment. △

SASColor window
  enables you to change the default colors for the different window elements in your SAS windows. To access this window, issue the SASCOLOR command.

SAS Registry Editor
    enables you to edit the SAS Registry and to customize aspects of the SAS
    windowing environment. To access this window, issue the REGEDIT command.

SAS System Options window
    enables you to view or change current SAS system options. To access this window,
    issue the OPTIONS command.

Learning More

☐ For information about operating environment-specific customization options and
   preferences, refer to the SAS documentation for your operating environment.

☐ For more information about SAS procedures, see the *SAS Procedures Guide*.

☐ For more information about the statements and options that are discussed in this
   chapter, see *SAS Language Reference: Dictionary*.

☐ For more tips and examples on using the SAS windowing environment, see *Getting
   Started with the SAS System*.

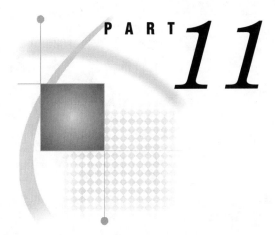

P A R T *11*

Appendix

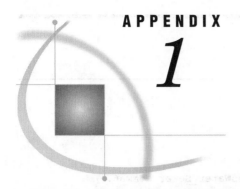

APPENDIX

1

Additional Data Sets

Introduction

This book shows how to create the data sets that are used in each chapter. However, when the input data are lengthy or the actual contents of the data set are not crucial to the chapter, the DATA steps or raw data to create data sets are listed in this appendix instead of within the chapter.

This appendix is organized by chapter number; only the raw data or DATA steps that are not provided in detail in the chapter are included here.

Data Sets for Chapter 5

DATA Step to Create the Data Set CITY

```
data city;
    input Year 4. @7 ServicesPolice comma6.
          @15 ServicesFire comma6. @22 ServicesWater_Sewer comma6.
          @30 AdminLabor comma6. @39 AdminSupplies comma6.
          @45 AdminUtilities comma6.;
    ServicesTotal=ServicesPolice+ServicesFire+ServicesWater_Sewer;
    AdminTotal=AdminLabor+AdminSupplies+AdminUtilities;
    Total=ServicesTotal+AdminTotal;
    label                 Total='Total Outlays'
                  ServicesTotal='Services: Total'
                 ServicesPolice='Services: Police'
                   ServicesFire='Services: Fire'
            ServicesWater_Sewer='Services: Water & Sewer'
                     AdminTotal='Administration: Total'
                     AdminLabor='Administration: Labor'
                  AdminSupplies='Administration: Supplies'
                 AdminUtilities='Administration: Utilities' ;
    datalines;
1980   2,819   1,120     422    391        63      98
1981   2,477   1,160     500    172        47      70
1982   2,028   1,061     510    269        29      79
1983   2,754     893     540    227        21      67
1984   2,195     963     541    214        21      59
1985   1,877     926     535    198        16      80
1986   1,727   1,111     535    213        27      70
1987   1,532   1,220     519    195        11      69
1988   1,448   1,156     577    225        12      58
1989   1,500   1,076     606    235        19      62
1990   1,934     969     646    266        11      63
1991   2,195   1,002     643    256        24      55
1992   2,204     964     692    256        28      70
1993   2,175   1,144     735    241        19      83
1994   2,556   1,341     813    238        25      97
1995   2,026   1,380     868    226        24      97
1996   2,526   1,454     946    317        13      89
1997   2,027   1,486   1,043    226         .      82
1998   2,037   1,667   1,152    244        20      88
1999   2,852   1,834   1,318    270        23      74
2000   2,787   1,701   1,317    307        26      66
;
```

Raw Data for Chapters 23 and 24

Raw Data for OUT.SAT_SCORES3, OUT.SAT_SCORES4, OUT.SAT_SCORES5, OUT.ERROR1, OUT.ERROR2, OUT.ERROR3

```
Verbal m 1972 531   Verbal f 1972 529
Verbal m 1973 523   Verbal f 1973 521
Verbal m 1974 524   Verbal f 1974 520
Verbal m 1975 515   Verbal f 1975 509
Verbal m 1976 511   Verbal f 1976 508
Verbal m 1977 509   Verbal f 1977 505
Verbal m 1978 511   Verbal f 1978 503
Verbal m 1979 509   Verbal f 1979 501
Verbal m 1980 506   Verbal f 1980 498
Verbal m 1981 508   Verbal f 1981 496
Verbal m 1982 509   Verbal f 1982 499
Verbal m 1983 508   Verbal f 1983 498
Verbal m 1984 511   Verbal f 1984 498
Verbal m 1985 514   Verbal f 1985 503
Verbal m 1986 515   Verbal f 1986 504
Verbal m 1987 512   Verbal f 1987 502
Verbal m 1988 512   Verbal f 1988 499
Verbal m 1989 510   Verbal f 1989 498
Verbal m 1990 505   Verbal f 1990 496
Verbal m 1991 503   Verbal f 1991 495
Verbal m 1992 504   Verbal f 1992 496
Verbal m 1993 504   Verbal f 1993 497
Verbal m 1994 501   Verbal f 1994 497
Verbal m 1995 505   Verbal f 1995 502
Verbal m 1996 507   Verbal f 1996 503
Verbal m 1997 507   Verbal f 1997 503
Verbal m 1998 509   Verbal f 1998 502
Math   m 1972 527   Math   f 1972 489
Math   m 1973 525   Math   f 1973 489
Math   m 1974 524   Math   f 1974 488
Math   m 1975 518   Math   f 1975 479
Math   m 1976 520   Math   f 1976 475
Math   m 1977 520   Math   f 1977 474
Math   m 1978 517   Math   f 1978 474
Math   m 1979 516   Math   f 1979 473
Math   m 1980 515   Math   f 1980 473
Math   m 1981 516   Math   f 1981 473
Math   m 1982 516   Math   f 1982 473
Math   m 1983 516   Math   f 1983 474
Math   m 1984 518   Math   f 1984 478
Math   m 1985 522   Math   f 1985 480
Math   m 1986 523   Math   f 1986 479
Math   m 1987 523   Math   f 1987 481
Math   m 1988 521   Math   f 1988 483
Math   m 1989 523   Math   f 1989 482
Math   m 1990 521   Math   f 1990 483
```

```
Math     m 1991 520    Math    f 1991 482
Math     m 1992 521    Math    f 1992 484
Math     m 1993 524    Math    f 1993 484
Math     m 1994 523    Math    f 1994 487
Math     m 1995 525    Math    f 1995 490
Math     m 1996 527    Math    f 1996 492
Math     m 1997 530    Math    f 1997 494
Math     m 1998 531    Math    f 1998 496
```

Data Set for Chapter 22

DATA Step to Create the Data Set SAT_SCORES

```
data sat_scores;
   input Test $ Gender $ Year SATscore @@;
   datalines;
Verbal m 1972 531   Verbal f 1972 529
Verbal m 1973 523   Verbal f 1973 521
Verbal m 1974 524   Verbal f 1974 520
Verbal m 1975 515   Verbal f 1975 509
Verbal m 1976 511   Verbal f 1976 508
Verbal m 1977 509   Verbal f 1977 505
Verbal m 1978 511   Verbal f 1978 503
Verbal m 1979 509   Verbal f 1979 501
Verbal m 1980 506   Verbal f 1980 498
Verbal m 1981 508   Verbal f 1981 496
Verbal m 1982 509   Verbal f 1982 499
Verbal m 1983 508   Verbal f 1983 498
Verbal m 1984 511   Verbal f 1984 498
Verbal m 1985 514   Verbal f 1985 503
Verbal m 1986 515   Verbal f 1986 504
Verbal m 1987 512   Verbal f 1987 502
Verbal m 1988 512   Verbal f 1988 499
Verbal m 1989 510   Verbal f 1989 498
Verbal m 1990 505   Verbal f 1990 496
Verbal m 1991 503   Verbal f 1991 495
Verbal m 1992 504   Verbal f 1992 496
Verbal m 1993 504   Verbal f 1993 497
Verbal m 1994 501   Verbal f 1994 497
Verbal m 1995 505   Verbal f 1995 502
Verbal m 1996 507   Verbal f 1996 503
Verbal m 1997 507   Verbal f 1997 503
Verbal m 1998 509   Verbal f 1998 502
Math   m 1972 527   Math   f 1972 489
Math   m 1973 525   Math   f 1973 489
Math   m 1974 524   Math   f 1974 488
Math   m 1975 518   Math   f 1975 479
Math   m 1976 520   Math   f 1976 475
Math   m 1977 520   Math   f 1977 474
Math   m 1978 517   Math   f 1978 474
```

```
Math    m 1979 516   Math    f 1979 473
Math    m 1980 515   Math    f 1980 473
Math    m 1981 516   Math    f 1981 473
Math    m 1982 516   Math    f 1982 473
Math    m 1983 516   Math    f 1983 474
Math    m 1984 518   Math    f 1984 478
Math    m 1985 522   Math    f 1985 480
Math    m 1986 523   Math    f 1986 479
Math    m 1987 523   Math    f 1987 481
Math    m 1988 521   Math    f 1988 483
Math    m 1989 523   Math    f 1989 482
Math    m 1990 521   Math    f 1990 483
Math    m 1991 520   Math    f 1991 482
Math    m 1992 521   Math    f 1992 484
Math    m 1993 524   Math    f 1993 484
Math    m 1994 523   Math    f 1994 487
Math    m 1995 525   Math    f 1995 490
Math    m 1996 527   Math    f 1996 492
Math    m 1997 530   Math    f 1997 494
Math    m 1998 531   Math    f 1998 496
;
```

Data Set for Chapters 25, 26, and 27

DATA Step to Create the Data Set YEAR_SALES

```
data year_sales;
   input Month $ Quarter $ SalesRep $14. Type $ Units Price @@;
   AmountSold=Units*price;
   datalines;
01 1 Hollingsworth Deluxe    260 49.50 01 1 Garcia        Standard   41 30.97
01 1 Hollingsworth Standard  330 30.97 01 1 Jensen        Standard  110 30.97
01 1 Garcia        Deluxe    715 49.50 01 1 Jensen        Standard  675 30.97
02 1 Garcia        Standard 2045 30.97 02 1 Garcia        Deluxe     10 49.50
02 1 Garcia        Standard   40 30.97 02 1 Hollingsworth Standard 1030 30.97
02 1 Jensen        Standard  153 30.97 02 1 Garcia        Standard   98 30.97
03 1 Hollingsworth Standard  125 30.97 03 1 Jensen        Standard  154 30.97
03 1 Garcia        Standard  118 30.97 03 1 Hollingsworth Standard   25 30.97
03 1 Jensen        Standard  525 30.97 03 1 Garcia        Standard  310 30.97
04 2 Garcia        Standard  150 30.97 04 2 Hollingsworth Standard  260 30.97
04 2 Hollingsworth Standard  530 30.97 04 2 Jensen        Standard 1110 30.97
04 2 Garcia        Standard 1715 30.97 04 2 Jensen        Standard  675 30.97
05 2 Jensen        Standard   45 30.97 05 2 Hollingsworth Standard 1120 30.97
05 2 Garcia        Standard   40 30.97 05 2 Hollingsworth Standard 1030 30.97
05 2 Jensen        Standard  153 30.97 05 2 Garcia        Standard   98 30.97
06 2 Jensen        Standard  154 30.97 06 2 Hollingsworth Deluxe     25 49.50
06 2 Jensen        Standard  276 30.97 06 2 Hollingsworth Standard  125 30.97
06 2 Garcia        Standard  512 30.97 06 2 Garcia        Standard 1000 30.97
07 3 Garcia        Standard  250 30.97 07 3 Hollingsworth Deluxe     60 49.50
07 3 Garcia        Standard   90 30.97 07 3 Hollingsworth Deluxe     30 49.50
```

```
07 3 Jensen        Standard  110 30.97 07 3 Garcia        Standard    90 30.97
07 3 Hollingsworth Standard  130 30.97 07 3 Jensen        Standard   110 30.97
07 3 Garcia        Standard  265 30.97 07 3 Jensen        Standard   275 30.97
07 3 Garcia        Standard 1250 30.97 07 3 Hollingsworth Deluxe      60 49.50
07 3 Garcia        Standard   90 30.97 07 3 Jensen        Standard   110 30.97
07 3 Garcia        Standard   90 30.97 07 3 Hollingsworth Standard   330 30.97
07 3 Jensen        Standard  110 30.97 07 3 Garcia        Standard   465 30.97
07 3 Jensen        Standard  675 30.97 08 3 Jensen        Standard   145 30.97
08 3 Garcia        Deluxe    110 49.50 08 3 Hollingsworth Standard   120 30.97
08 3 Hollingsworth Standard  230 30.97 08 3 Jensen        Standard   453 30.97
08 3 Garcia        Standard  240 30.97 08 3 Hollingsworth Standard   230 49.50
08 3 Jensen        Standard  453 30.97 08 3 Garcia        Standard   198 30.97
08 3 Hollingsworth Standard  290 30.97 08 3 Garcia        Standard  1198 30.97
08 3 Jensen        Deluxe     45 49.50 08 3 Jensen        Standard   145 30.97
08 3 Garcia        Deluxe    110 49.50 08 3 Hollingsworth Standard   330 30.97
08 3 Garcia        Standard  240 30.97 08 3 Hollingsworth Deluxe      50 49.50
08 3 Jensen        Standard  453 30.97 08 3 Garcia        Standard   198 30.97
08 3 Jensen        Deluxe    225 49.50 09 3 Hollingsworth Standard   125 30.97
09 3 Jensen        Standard  254 30.97 09 3 Garcia        Standard   118 30.97
09 3 Hollingsworth Standard 1000 30.97 09 3 Jensen        Standard   284 30.97
09 3 Garcia        Standard  412 30.97 09 3 Jensen        Deluxe     275 49.50
09 3 Garcia        Standard  100 30.97 09 3 Jensen        Standard   876 30.97
09 3 Hollingsworth Standard  125 30.97 09 3 Jensen        Standard   254 30.97
09 3 Garcia        Standard 1118 30.97 09 3 Hollingsworth Standard   175 30.97
09 3 Jensen        Standard  284 30.97 09 3 Garcia        Standard   412 30.97
09 3 Jensen        Deluxe    275 49.50 09 3 Garcia        Standard   100 30.97
09 3 Jensen        Standard  876 30.97 10 4 Garcia        Standard   250 30.97
10 4 Hollingsworth Standard  530 30.97 10 4 Jensen        Standard   975 30.97
10 4 Hollingsworth Standard  265 30.97 10 4 Jensen        Standard    55 30.97
10 4 Garcia        Standard  365 30.97 11 4 Hollingsworth Standard  1230 30.97
11 4 Jensen        Standard  453 30.97 11 4 Garcia        Standard   198 30.97
11 4 Jensen        Standard   70 30.97 11 4 Garcia        Standard   120 30.97
11 4 Hollingsworth Deluxe    150 49.50 12 4 Garcia        Standard  1000 30.97
12 4 Jensen        Standard  876 30.97 12 4 Hollingsworth Deluxe     125 49.50
12 4 Jensen        Standard 1254 30.97 12 4 Hollingsworth Standard   175 30.97
;
```

Data Set for Chapter 28

DATA Step to Create the Data Set HIGHLOW

```
data highlow;
   input Year @7 DateOfHigh:date9. DowJonesHigh @26 DateOfLow:date9. DowJonesLow;
   format LogDowHigh LogDowLow 5.2 DateOfHigh DateOfLow date9.;
   LogDowHigh=log(DowJonesHigh);
   LogDowLow=log(DowJonesLow);
datalines;
1954   31DEC1954   404.39   11JAN1954   279.87
1955   30DEC1955   488.40   17JAN1955   388.20
1956   06APR1956   521.05   23JAN1956   462.35
```

```
1957   12JUL1957   520.77   22OCT1957   419.79
1958   31DEC1958   583.65   25FEB1958   436.89
1959   31DEC1959   679.36   09FEB1959   574.46
1960   05JAN1960   685.47   25OCT1960   568.05
1961   13DEC1961   734.91   03JAN1961   610.25
1962   03JAN1962   726.01   26JUN1962   535.76
1963   18DEC1963   767.21   02JAN1963   646.79
1964   18NOV1964   891.71   02JAN1964   768.08
1965   31DEC1965   969.26   28JUN1965   840.59
1966   09FEB1966   995.15   07OCT1966   744.32
1967   25SEP1967   943.08   03JAN1967   786.41
1968   03DEC1968   985.21   21MAR1968   825.13
1969   14MAY1969   968.85   17DEC1969   769.93
1970   29DEC1970   842.00   06MAY1970   631.16
1971   28APR1971   950.82   23NOV1971   797.97
1972   11DEC1972  1036.27   26JAN1972   889.15
1973   11JAN1973  1051.70   05DEC1973   788.31
1974   13MAR1974   891.66   06DEC1974   577.60
1975   15JUL1975   881.81   02JAN1975   632.04
1976   21SEP1976  1014.79   02JAN1976   858.71
1977   03JAN1977   999.75   02NOV1977   800.85
1978   08SEP1978   907.74   28FEB1978   742.12
1979   05OCT1979   897.61   07NOV1979   796.67
1980   20NOV1980  1000.17   21APR1980   759.13
1981   27APR1981  1024.05   25SEP1981   824.01
1982   27DEC1982  1070.55   12AUG1982   776.92
1983   29NOV1983  1287.20   03JAN1983  1027.04
1984   06JAN1984  1286.64   24JUL1984  1086.57
1985   16DEC1985  1553.10   04JAN1985  1184.96
1986   02DEC1986  1955.57   22JAN1986  1502.29
1987   25AUG1987  2722.42   19OCT1987  1738.74
1988   21OCT1988  2183.50   20JAN1988  1879.14
1989   09OCT1989  2791.41   03JAN1989  2144.64
1990   16JUL1990  2999.75   11OCT1990  2365.10
1991   31DEC1991  3168.83   09JAN1991  2470.30
1992   01JUN1992  3413.21   09OCT1992  3136.58
1993   29DEC1993  3794.33   20JAN1993  3241.95
1994   31JAN1994  3978.36   04APR1994  3593.35
1995   13DEC1995  5216.47   30JAN1995  3832.08
1996   27DEC1996  6560.91   10JAN1996  5032.94
1997   06AUG1997  8259.31   11APR1997  6391.69
1998   23NOV1998  9374.27   31AUG1998  7539.07
;
```

Data Set for Chapter 29

DATA Step to Create the Data Set GRADES

```
data grades;
    input Name &$14. Gender :$2. Section :$3. ExamGrade1 @@;
```

```
          datalines;
Abdallah        F Mon  46 Anderson     M Wed  75
Aziz            F Wed  67 Bayer        M Wed  77
Bhatt           M Fri  79 Blair        F Fri  70
Bledsoe         F Mon  63 Boone        M Wed  58
Burke           F Mon  63 Chung        M Wed  85
Cohen           F Fri  89 Drew         F Mon  49
Dubos           M Mon  41 Elliott      F Wed  85
Farmer          F Wed  58 Franklin     F Wed  59
Freeman         F Mon  79 Friedman     M Mon  58
Gabriel         M Fri  75 Garcia       M Mon  79
Harding         M Mon  49 Hazelton     M Mon  55
Hinton          M Fri  85 Hung         F Fri  98
Jacob           F Wed  64 Janeway      F Wed  51
Jones           F Mon  39 Jorgensen    M Mon  63
Judson          F Fri  89 Kuhn         F Mon  89
LeBlanc         F Fri  70 Lee          M Fri  48
Litowski        M Fri  85 Malloy       M Wed  79
Meyer           F Fri  85 Nichols      M Mon  58
Oliver          F Mon  41 Park         F Mon  77
Patel           M Wed  73 Randleman    F Wed  46
Robinson        M Fri  64 Shien        M Wed  55
Simonson        M Wed  62 Smith N      M Wed  71
Smith R         M Mon  79 Sullivan     M Fri  77
Swift           M Wed  63 Wolfson      F Fri  79
Wong            F Fri  89 Zabriski     M Fri  89
;
```

Data Sets for Chapters 35 and 36

DATA Step to Create the Data Set USCLIM.HIGHTEMP

```
libname usclim 'SAS-data-library';

data usclim.hightemp;
   input State $char14. City $char14. Temp_f Date $ Elevation;
   datalines;
Arizona       Parker          127 07jul05 345
Kansas        Alton           121 25jul36 1651
Nevada        Overton         122 23jun54 1240
North Dakota  Steele          121 06jul36 1857
Oklahoma      Tishomingo      120 26jul43 6709
Texas         Seymour         120 12aug36 1291
;
```

DATA Step to Create the Data Set USCLIM.HURRICANE

```
libname usclim 'SAS-data-library';

data usclim.hurricane;
    input @1 State $char11. @13 Date date7. Deaths Millions Name $;
    format Date worddate18. Millions dollar6.;
    informat State $char11. Date date9.;
    label Millions='Damage';
    datalines;
Mississippi 14aug69 256 1420 Camille
Florida     14jun72 117 2100 Agnes
Alabama     29aug79 5   2300 Frederick
Texas       15aug83 21  2000 Alicia
Texas       03aug80 28  300  Allen
;
```

DATA Step to Create the Data Set USCLIM.LOWTEMP

```
libname usclim 'SAS-data-library';

data usclim.lowtemp;
    input State $char14. City $char14. Temp_f Date $ Elevation;
    datalines;
Alaska        Prospect Creek -80 23jan71 1100
Colorado      Maybell        -60 01jan79 5920
Idaho         Island Prk Dam -60 18jan43 6285
Minnesota     Pokegama Dam   -59 16feb03 1280
North Dakota  Parshall       -60 15feb36 1929
South Dakota  McIntosh       -58 17feb36 2277
Wyoming       Moran          -63 09feb33 6770
;
```

DATA Step to Create the Data Set USCLIM.TEMPCHNG

```
libname usclim 'SAS-data-library';

data usclim.tempchng;
    input @1 State $char13. @15 Date date7. Start_f End_f Minutes;
    Diff=End_f-Start_f;
    informat State $char13. Date date7.;
    format Date date9.;
    datalines;
North Dakota  21feb18 -33 50  720
South Dakota  22jan43 -4  45  2
South Dakota  12jan11 49  -13 120
South Dakota  22jan43 54  -4  27
South Dakota  10jan11 55  8   15
```

```
;
```

Note on Catalogs USCLIM.BASETEMP and USCLIM.REPORT

The catalogs USCLIM.BASETEMP and USCLIM.REPORT are used to show how the DATASETS procedure processes both SAS data sets and catalogs. The contents of these catalogs are not important in the context of this book. In most cases, you would use SAS/AF, SAS/FSP, or other SAS products to create catalog entries. You can test the examples in this chapter without having these catalogs.

Data Sets for Chapter 36

DATA Step to Create the Data Set CLIMATE.HIGHTEMP

```
libname climate 'SAS-data-library';

data climate.hightemp;
   input Place $ 1-13 Date $ Degree_f Degree_c;
   datalines;
Libya         13sep22 136 58
California    10jul13 134 57
Israel        21jun42 129 54
Argentina     11dec05 120 49
Saskatchewan  05jul37 113 45
;
```

DATA Step to Create the Data Set CLIMATE.LOWTEMP

```
libname climate 'SAS-data-library';

data climate.lowtemp;
   input Place $ 1-13 Date $ Degree_f Degree_c;
   datalines;
Antarctica    21jul83 -129 -89
Siberia       06feb33 -90  -68
Greenland     09jan54 -87  -66
Yukon         03feb47 -81  -63
Alaska        23jan71 -80  -67
;
```

DATA Step to Create the Data Set PRECIP.RAIN

```
libname precip 'SAS-data-library';
```

```
data precip.rain;
   input Place $ 1-12 @13 Date date7. Inches Cms;
   format Date date9.;
   datalines;
La Reunion  15mar52 74 188
Taiwan      10sep63 49 125
Australia   04jan79 44 114
Texas       25jul79 43 109
Canada      06oct64 19 49
;
```

DATA Step to Create the Data Set PRECIP.SNOW

```
libname precip 'SAS-data-library';

data precip.snow;
   input Place $ 1-12 @13 Date date7. Inches Cms;
   format Date date9.;
   datalines;
Colorado    14apr21 76 193
Alaska      29dec55 62 158
France      05apr69 68 173
;
```

DATA Step to Create the Data Set STORM.TORNADO

```
libname storm 'SAS-data-library';

data storm.tornado;
   input State $ 1-12 @13 Date date7. Deaths Millions;
   format Date date9. Millions dollar6.;
   label Millions='Damage in Millions';
   datalines;
Iowa         11apr65 257 200
Texas        11may70 26  135
Nebraska     06may75 3   400
Connecticut  03oct79 3   200
Georgia      31mar73 9   115
;
```

Glossary

across variable
in the REPORT procedure, a variable used so that each formatted value of the variable forms a column in the report. If the variable does not have a format, each value forms a column.

active data set
the SAS data set specified in the current analysis.

active window
a window that is open, displayed, and to which keyboard input is directed. Only one window can be active at a time.

alphanumeric characters
a string of characters that can include alphabetic letters, numerals, and special characters or blanks. Most computer systems store strictly numeric data differently from alphanumeric or textual data.

analysis variable

1 (1) a numeric variable used to calculate statistics. Usually an analysis variable contains quantitative or continuous values, but this is not required.
2 in the REPORT procedure, you must associate a statistic with an analysis variable. By default, the REPORT procedure treats a numeric variable as an analysis variable that is used to calculate the SUM statistic.

argument

1 in a SAS function or CALL routine, the values or expressions a user supplies within parentheses on which the function or CALL routine performs the indicated operation.
2 in syntax descriptions, any word that follows the keyword in a SAS statement.

arithmetic expression
see SAS expression.

arithmetic operators
the symbols (+, -, /, *, and **) used to perform addition, subtraction, division, multiplication, and exponentiation in SAS expressions.

array
a group of variables of the same type available for processing under a single name.

array name

a name selected to identify a group of variables or temporary data objects. It must be a valid SAS name that is not the name of a variable in the same DATA step. See also array.

array reference

a reference to the object to be processed in an array. See also array.

ASCII

an acronym for the American Standard Code for Information Interchange. ASCII is a 7-bit character coding scheme (8 bits when a parity check bit is included) including graphic (printable) and control (nonprintable) codes.

ASCII collating sequence

an ordering of characters that follows the order of the characters in the American Standard Code for Information Interchange (ASCII) character coding scheme. SAS uses the same collating sequence as its host operating environment. See also EBCDIC collating sequence.

assignment statement

a DATA step statement that evaluates an expression and stores the result in a variable. An assignment statement has the following form: *variable=expression*;

attributes

See variable attributes.

autocall facility

a feature of SAS that enables you to store the source statements that define a macro and invoke the macro as needed, without having to include the definition in your program.

autoexec file

a file containing SAS statements that are executed automatically when SAS is invoked. The autoexec file can be used to specify some SAS system options, as well as librefs and filerefs that are commonly used.

automatic macro variable

a macro variable defined by SAS rather than by the user.

automatic variable

a variable that is created automatically by the DATA step, some DATA step statements, some SAS procedures, and the SAS macro facility.

background processing

processing in which you cannot interact with the computer. Background sessions may run somewhat slower than foreground sessions because this type of session executes as processor time becomes available. See also foreground processing.

base SAS software

software that includes a programming language that manages your data, procedures for data analysis and reporting, procedures for managing SAS files, a macro facility, help menus, and a windowing environment for text editing and file management.

batch job

a job submitted to the operating environment for batch processing.

batch mode

a method of executing SAS programs in which you prepare a file containing SAS statements and any necessary operating environment commands and submit the program to the computer's batch queue. While the program executes, control returns to your terminal or workstation environment where you can perform other tasks.

Batch mode is sometimes referred to as running in the background. The job output can be written to files or printed on an output device.

Boolean operator

See logical operator.

break

in the REPORT procedure, a section of the report that does one or more of the following: visually separates parts of the report; summarizes statistics and computed variables; displays text, values calculated for a set of rows of the report, or both; executes DATA step statements. You can create breaks when the value of a selected variable changes or at the beginning or end of a report. See also break variable.

break line

in the REPORT procedure, a line of a report that contains one of the following: characters that visually separate parts of the report; summaries of statistics and computed variables (called a summary line); text, values calculated for a set of rows of the report, or both.

break variable

in the REPORT procedure, a group or order variable you select to determine the location of break lines. The REPORT procedure performs the actions you specify for the break each time the value of this variable changes.

BY group

all observations with the same values for all BY variables.

BY value

the value of a BY variable.

BY variable

a variable named in a BY statement whose values define groups of observations to process.

BY-group processing

the process of using the BY statement to process observations that are ordered, grouped, or indexed according to the values of one or more variables. Many SAS procedures and the DATA step support BY-group processing. For example, you can use BY-group processing with the PRINT procedure to print separate reports for different groups of observations in a single SAS data set.

CALL routine

a program that can be called in a DATA step by issuing a CALL statement. A CALL routine may change the value of some of the arguments passed to it, but it does not return a value as a function does.

calling a macro

See macro invocation.

carriage-control character

a specific symbol that tells the printer how many lines to advance the paper, when to begin a new page, when to skip a line, and when to hold the current line for overprint.

catalog

See SAS catalog.

catalog directory

in SAS, a part of a SAS catalog that stores and maintains information about the name, type, description, and update status of each member of the catalog.

catalog entry

See entry type and SAS catalog entry.

category

in the TABULATE procedure, the combination of unique values of class variables. The TABULATE procedure creates a separate category for each unique combination of values that exists in the observations of the data set. Each category created by PROC TABULATE is represented by one or more cells in the table where the pages, rows, and columns that describe the category intersect.

cell

a single unit of a table produced by a SAS procedure, such as the TABULATE or FREQ procedure. The value contained in the cell is a summary statistic for the input data set. The contents of the cell are described by the page, row, and column that contain the cell.

character constant

one or more characters enclosed in quotes in a SAS statement (sometimes called a character literal). The maximum number of characters allowed is 200. See also character string.

character format

instructions to SAS to write character data values using a specific pattern.

character function

a function that enables you to perform character string manipulations, comparisons, evaluations, or analyses.

character informat

instructions to SAS to read character data values into character variables using a specific pattern.

character literal

See character constant.

character string

one or more alphanumeric or other keyboard characters or both. See also character constant.

character value

a value that can contain alphabetic characters, numeric characters 0 through 9, and other special characters. See also character variable.

character variable

a variable whose values can consist of alphabetic and special characters as well as numeric characters.

chart

a graph in which graphics objects (bars, pie slices, and so on) show the magnitude of a statistic. The graphics objects can represent one data value or a range of data values.

chart statistic

the statistical value calculated for the chart variable: frequency, cumulative frequency, percentage, cumulative percentage, sum, or mean.

chart variable

a variable in the input data set whose values are categories of data represented by bars, blocks, slices, or spines.

check box

an item in a window that you can select without affecting any other items. You can deactivate a check box by selecting it again.

class variable

in some SAS procedures, a variable used to group, or classify, data. Class variables can be character or numeric. Class variables can have continuous values, but they typically have a few discrete values that define the classifications of the variable.

collating sequence
See ASCII collating sequence and EBCDIC collating sequence.

column concatenation
in TABULATE procedure output, two or more tables produced by one TABLE statement and placed side by side.

column input
in the DATA step, a style of input that gives column specifications in the INPUT statement for reading data in fixed columns.

command
a keyword that gives directions to the host operating environment or to the SAS windowing environment.

command bar
a row of push buttons at the bottom of a window. The push buttons represent actions or classes of actions that can be executed in that window.

comment
text that provides additional information in a SAS program. SAS ignores comments during processing but writes them to the SAS log. Comments have two forms. A comment can appear as a statement that begins with an asterisk and ends with a semicolon:* *message*; A comment can also appear as text that begins with a forward slash and an asterisk and ends with an asterisk and a forward slash:*/* *message* */*

comment statement
See comment.

comparison operator
a symbolic or mnemonic instruction that tests for a particular relationship between two values. If the comparison is true, the result of executing the instruction is the value 1; if the comparison is false, the result is the value 0.

compilation
the process of checking syntax and translating a portion of a program into a form that the computer can execute.

composite index
an index that locates observations in a SAS data set by the values of two or more key variables. See also index and simple index.

compound expression
an expression containing more than one operator.

computed variable
in the REPORT procedure, a variable whose value is calculated by statements entered in the COMPUTE window.

concatenating

1 for character values, a process in which SAS combines two or more character values, one after the other, into a single character value.
2 for SAS data sets, a process in which SAS combines two or more SAS data sets, one after the other, into a single data set.
3 for external files, the process that enables SAS to access two or more files as if they were one by specifying the filenames one after another in the same SAS statement.
4 in the TABULATE procedure, the operation that instructs the procedure to join information for two or more table objects by placing the output for the second object immediately after the output for the first object. Concatenated objects

produce tables consisting of two or more subtables. See also column concatenation.

condition

in a SAS program, one or more numeric or character expressions that result in a value upon which some decision depends.

configuration file

an external file containing SAS system options that are put into effect when SAS is invoked.

configuration option

a SAS option that can be specified in the SAS command or in a configuration file. Configuration options affect how SAS interfaces with the computer hardware and operating environment.

constant

a number or a character string that indicates a fixed value. Character constants must be enclosed in quotation marks.

constant text

in the SAS macro facility, the strings stored as part of a macro or as a macro variable's value in open code, from which the macro processor generates text to be used as SAS statements, display manager commands, or other macro program statements. Constant text is also called model text.

crossing

in the TABULATE procedure, the process that combines the effects of two or more objects.

data error

a type of execution error that occurs when a SAS program analyzes data containing invalid values. For example, a data error occurs if you specify numeric variables in the INPUT statement for character data. By default, data errors do not cause a program to stop but, instead, to generate notes in the SAS log. See also programming error and syntax error.

data file

See SAS data file.

data lines

lines of unprocessed (raw) data. In a SAS program, data lines follow a CARDS or DATALINES statement.

data set label

in a SAS data set, a user-defined attribute of up to 40 characters used for documenting the SAS data set.

data set option

See SAS data set option.

data set reference

a SAS argument that specifies a SAS data set similar to DATA= *libref.member* or OUT=*libref.member*.

DATA step

a group of statements in a SAS program that begins with a DATA statement and ends with either a RUN statement, another DATA statement, a PROC statement, the end of the job, or the semicolon that immediately follows instream data lines. The DATA step enables you to read raw data or other SAS data sets and use programming logic to create a SAS data set, write a report, or write to an external file.

data value

    1 in SAS, a unit of character or numeric information in a SAS data set. A data value represents one variable in an observation.

    2 in the rectangular structure of a SAS data set, intersection of a row and a column.

date and time format

the instructions that tell SAS how to write numeric values as dates, times, and datetimes.

date and time informat

the instructions that tell SAS how to read numeric values represented as dates, times, and datetimes.

date value

See SAS date value.

declarative statement

a statement that supplies information to SAS and that takes effect when SAS compiles program statements, rather than when it executes them. See also executable statement.

default directory

the directory you are working in at any given time. When you log in, your default directory is usually your home directory.

delimiter

a character that serves as a boundary separating the objects of a character string, programming statement, data line, or list of arguments.

descriptor information

the information SAS creates and maintains identifying the attributes of a SAS data set and its contents.

destination

a specific type of output from the Output Delivery System. Types of output include HTML, Listing, PostScript, RTF, and SAS data sets.

detail row

in the REPORT procedure, a row of a report that either contains information from a single observation in the data set or consolidates the information for a group of observations that have a unique combination of values for all group variables.

dialog box

a type of window that opens to prompt you for additional information, provide additional information, or ask you to confirm a request.

dialog window

a window that prompts a user for additional information in order to perform a specified action.

dimension

in the TABULATE procedure, the page, row, or column portion of a table. PROC TABULATE can produce tables that have one, two, or three dimensions.

dimension expression

in the TABULATE procedure, the portion of the TABLE statement that defines what variables and statistics make up a single dimension of the table. The format of a dimension expression is the same for any of the three dimensions page, row, and column.

DO group

a sequence of statements headed by a simple DO statement and ended by a corresponding END statement. See also DO loop.

DO loop

a sequence of statements headed by an iterative DO, DO WHILE, or DO UNTIL statement; ended by a corresponding END statement; and executed (usually repeatedly) according to directions in the DO statement. See also DO group.

double trailing at sign (@@)

a special symbol used to hold a line in the input buffer across iterations of the DATA step. See also trailing at sign (@).

EBCDIC

an acronym for Extended Binary Coded Decimal Interchange Code. EBCDIC is an 8-bit character coding scheme including graphic (printable) and control (nonprintable) codes.

EBCDIC collating sequence

an ordering of characters that follows the order in the Extended Binary Coded Decimal Interchange Code (EBCDIC) character coding scheme. SAS uses the same collating sequence as its host operating environment. See also ASCII collating sequence.

entry

a unit of information stored in a SAS catalog. Catalog entries differ widely in content and purpose. See also entry type.

entry type

a characteristic of a SAS catalog entry that identifies its structure and attributes to SAS. When you create an entry, SAS automatically assigns the entry type as part of the name.

error message

a message in the SAS log or Message window that indicates that SAS was not able to continue processing the program

executable statement

in the DATA step, a SAS statement that causes some action to occur while the DATA step executes rather than when SAS compiles the DATA step. See also declarative statement.

execution

1 in the DATA step, the process in which SAS carries out statements for each observation or record in the file. See also compilation.

2 in contexts other than the DATA step, such as SAS macros, procedures, and global statements, the process in which SAS performs the actions indicated

explicit array

an array that consists of a valid SAS name, reference to the number of variables or temporary data elements, and an optional list of the array elements. In an explicit array, you must explicitly specify the subscript in the reference when referring to an element. See also explicit array reference.

explicit array reference

a description of the element to be processed in an explicit array. See also explicit array.

exponent

in a mathematical expression, the number or expression that indicates the power to which you raise a base number or expression.

expression
　　See SAS expression.

external file

　　1 a file maintained by the host operating environment that SAS can read data from and route output to. External files can contain raw data, SAS programming statements, procedure output, or output created by the PUT statement. An external file is not a SAS data set. See also fileref.

　　2 in a DATA step, a file that SAS can use the INFILE and INPUT statements to read or a file that SAS can use the FILE and PUT statements to write.

field

　　1 in a hierarchical database, the smallest unit of data storage.

　　2 in an external file, the smallest logical unit of data. See also file and record.

　　3 in windowing environments, a window area that is defined to contain a value that users usually can view, enter, or modify.

file

　　1 a collection of related records treated as a unit. SAS files are processed and controlled through the SAS System and are stored in a SAS data library.

　　2 A Prime INFORMATION file is made up of two parts, a data part and a dictionary part.

　　3 An ADABAS file can contain from 0 to 16,777,215 records. The records are physically stored in compressed form in Data Storage. File control information, field definitions, and inverted list entries are contained in the Associator.

　　4 In CA-DATACOM/DB, each database contains one or more FILE entity-occurrences that comprise specific records, fields, and elements. Each FILE entity-occurrence requires a unique name and specific attributes in the CA-DATADICTIONARY database.

　　5 In SYSTEM 2000 software, each database contains six database files, which together hold the definition, the indexes, the values, and the hierarchical structure of the database. Database files 7 and 8 are optional files for the Update Log and Rollback Log.

file pathname
　　a pathname that identifies a specific file. A file pathname includes a filename, filename extension, and whatever partition and directory specification is necessary.

file reference
　　See fileref.

file specification

　　1 the name of an external file. This name is the name by which the host operating environment recognizes the file. On directory-based systems, the file specification can be either the complete pathname or the relative pathname from the current working directory.

　　2 the pathname or fileref required to identify a file in a SAS command or statement. See also file pathname and fileref.

fileref
　　a name temporarily assigned to an external file or to an aggregate storage location that identifies it to SAS. You assign a fileref with a FILENAME statement or with an operating environment command. Do not confuse filerefs with librefs. Filerefs are used for external files; librefs are used for SAS data libraries. See also libref.

first-level name
　　See libref.

FIRST.*variable*

a temporary variable that SAS creates to identify the first observation of each BY group. The variable is not added to the SAS data set. See also LAST.*variable*.

foreground processing

a type of processing in which you interact with the computer while the process is executing. See also background processing.

format

an instruction SAS uses to display or write each value of a variable. Some formats are supplied by SAS software. Other formats can be written by the user with the FORMAT procedure in base SAS software. See also user-written format.

format modifier

1 a special symbol used in the INPUT and PUT statements that enables you to control the way SAS reads input data and writes output data
2 in the TABULATE procedure, an element of the form F=*format* that can be crossed in a dimension expression to indicate how the values in cells should be formatted.

format, variable

See format.

formatted input

a style of input that uses special instructions called informats in the INPUT statement to determine how values entered in data fields should be interpreted. See also informat.

formatted output

a style of output that uses special instructions called formats in the PUT statement to determine how to write variable values. See also format.

function

in base SAS software, a routine that can accept arguments, perform an operation, and return a value. For example, the ABS function returns the absolute value of a numeric argument. Functions can return either numeric or character results. Some functions are included with SAS.

global command

a command valid in all windows for a given SAS software product.

global macro variable

a macro variable that, once created, can be referenced in any referencing environment in a SAS program, except where blocked by a local macro variable of the same name. A global macro variable exists until the end of the session or program. See also macro variable.

global option

See system option.

group

in Program Manager, a collection of applications, such as Main or Accessories. You can run SAS by adding it to a group.

group variable

1 in the REPORT procedure, a variable that orders the detail rows in a report according to their formatted values and consolidates multiple observations that have a unique combination of values for all group variables into one row.
2 a variable in the input data set that is used to categorize chart variable values into groups

header

in the REPORT procedure, a string of characters that spans the top of one or more columns in the report. A header can occupy multiple lines. See also heading and split character.

header routine

a group of DATA step statements that produces page headers in print files. You identify with the HEADER= option in the FILE statement. A header routine begins with a statement label and ends with a RETURN statement.

heading

1 in reporting procedures, a label that describes the contents of some portion of the table. This includes page, row, and column headings in the TABULATE procedure and column headings in many other procedures. See also header.

2 in SAS output, the text located near the beginning of each page of output. This includes text produced by a HEADER= option in a FILE statement, titles written with a TITLE statement, and default information such as date and page numbers.

host

the operating environment that provides facilities, computer services, and the environment for software applications.

identification variable

in Proc GMAP, a variable common to both the map data set and the response data set that the procedure uses to associate each pair of map coordinates and each response value with a unique map area.

index

1 a component of a SAS data set that enables SAS to access observations in the SAS data set quickly and efficiently. The purpose of SAS indexes is to optimize WHERE-clause processing and facilitate BY-group processing.

2 a component of a SAS data set that contains the data values of a key variable or variables paired with a location identifier for the observation containing the value. The value/identifier pairs are ordered in a structure that enables SAS to search by a value of a variable. See also composite index and simple index.

informat

an instruction that SAS uses to read raw data values to create variable values. Some informats are supplied by SAS software. Other informats can be written by the user with the FORMAT procedure in base SAS software. See also user-written informat.

informat, variable

See informat.

input buffer

the temporary area of memory into which each record of data is read when the INPUT statement executes. Note that the input buffer is a logical concept independent of physical implementation.

interactive line mode

a method of running SAS programs in which you enter one line of a SAS program at a time at the SAS session prompt. SAS processes each line immediately after you press the ENTER or RETURN key. Procedure output and informative messages are returned directly to the display monitor.

interleaving

a process in which SAS combines two or more sorted SAS data sets into one sorted SAS data set based on the values of the BY variables. See also merging and concatenating.

item

in the REPORT procedure, a data set variable, a statistic, or a computed variable. An item can occupy one or more columns in a report. Under some circumstances, multiple items can share a column.

label

in base SAS software, data set label, statement label, label, and variable.

label assignment

in the TABULATE procedure, a method of changing the default heading for a page, row, or column by assigning the new heading in the TABLE statement. A label assignment can change the name of a class or analysis variable or the name of a statistic, but it cannot change the values of a class variable. You use the LABEL statement to assign labels.

label, variable

a descriptive label of up to 40 characters that can be printed in the output by certain procedures instead of, or in addition to, the variable name.

LAST. *variable*

a temporary variable that SAS creates to identify the last observation of each BY group. This variable is not added to the SAS data set. See also FIRST.*variable*.

length, variable

the number of bytes used to store each of a variable's values in a SAS data set.

library reference

See libref.

libref

the name temporarily associated with a SAS data library. For example, in the name SASUSERS.ACCOUNTS, the name SASUSER is the libref. You assign a libref with a LIBNAME statement or with operating environment control language. See also first-level name.

line mode

See interactive line mode.

line-hold specifier

a special symbol used in INPUT and PUT statements that enables you to hold a record in the input or output buffer for further processing. Line-hold specifiers include the trailing at sign (@) and the double trailing at sign (@@).

list input

a style that supplies variable names, not column locations, in the INPUT statement to scan input records for data values separated by at least one blank or other delimiter.

list input, modified

a style that uses special instructions called informats and format modifiers in the INPUT statement to scan input records for data values that are separated by at least one blank or other delimiter, and in some cases, by two blanks.

list input, simple

a style that gives only variable names and dollar signs ($) in the INPUT statement to scan input records for data values that are separated by at least one blank or other delimiter.

list output

a style in which a character string or variable is specified in a PUT statement without explicit directions that specify where SAS should place the string or value.

literal

any character or numeric value in a SAS program that is not the value of a variable, but the literal value of numbers or characters representing it. Character literals are usually enclosed in quotes. See also numeric constant.

logical operator

an operator used in expressions to link sequences of comparisons. The logical operators are AND, OR, and NOT.

macro facility

a portion of base SAS software that you can use for extending and customizing your SAS programs and for reducing the amount of text that must be entered to do common tasks. It consists of the macro processor and the macro language.

macro invocation

an instruction to the macro processor to execute a macro; it is also known as a macro call. A macro invocation can be either name-style (*%name*) or statement-style (*name;*)depending on how the macro was defined.

macro language

the programming language used to communicate with the macro processor.

macro variable

a variable belonging to the macro language whose value is a string that remains constant until you change it. A macro variable is also called a symbolic variable.

macro variable reference

the name of a macro variable preceded by an ampersand (&) that the macro processor replaces with the value of the macro variable named.

master data set

in an update operation, the data set containing the information you want to update. See also transaction data set.

match-merging

a process in which SAS joins observations from two or more SAS data sets according to the values of the BY variables. See also one-to-one merging.

member

a SAS file in a SAS library.

member type

a name assigned by SAS that identifies the type of information stored in a SAS file. Member types include ACCESS, DATA, CATALOG, PROGRAM, and VIEW.

merging

the process of combining observations from two or more SAS data sets into a single observation in a new SAS data set. See also match-merging and one-to-one merging.

methods of running the SAS System

standard methods of operation used to run SAS System programs. These methods are the SAS windowing environment, SAS/ASSIST software, interactive line mode, noninteractive mode, and batch mode.

missing value

a value that indicates that no data are stored for the variable in the current observation. By default, SAS prints a missing numeric value as a single period (.) and a missing character value as a blank space.

mnemonic operator

an arithmetic or logical (Boolean) operator composed of letters rather than symbols (for example, EQ rather than =).

multi-panel report

output that uses sets of columns on a page to display the values of variables. For example, telephone books are usually arranged in multi-panels of names, addresses, and phone numbers on a single page.

name, variable

the identifying attribute of a variable. A variable name must conform to SAS naming rules.

named input

a style in which equal signs appear in the INPUT statement to read data values in the for *variable=data-value*.

named output

a style in which equal signs appear in the PUT statement to write variable values in the form *variable=data-value*.

noninteractive mode

a method of running SAS programs in which you prepare a file of SAS statements and submit the program to the operating environment. The program runs immediately and occupies your current session.

nonstandard data

data that SAS can read or write only with the aid of informats or formats. Examples of nonstandard data are hexadecimal or binary values.

null statement

a statement consisting of a single semicolon or four semicolons, most commonly used to designate the end of instream data in a DATA step.

null value

1 a special value that means absence of information. It is analogous to a SAS missing value.

2 in the SAS macro language, a value consisting of zero characters.

numeric constant

a number that appears in a SAS expression. See also literal.

numeric format

an instruction to SAS to write numeric variable values using a specific pattern.

numeric informat

an instruction to SAS to read numeric data values using a specific pattern.

numeric value

a value that usually contains only numbers, including numbers in E-notation and hexadecimal notation. A numeric value can sometimes contain a decimal point, plus sign, or minus sign. Numeric values are stored in numeric variables.

numeric variable

a variable that can contain only numeric values. By default, SAS stores all numeric variables in floating-point representation.

observation

1 a row in a SAS data set. An observation is a collection of data values associated with a single entity, such as a customer or state. Each observation contains one data value for each variable.

2 the horizontal component of a SAS data file. An observation is a collection of data values associated with a single entity, such as a customer or state. Each observation contains one data value for each variable in the data file.

observation number

a number indicating the relative position of an observation in a SAS data set when you read the entire data set sequentially. This number is not stored internally. See also record ID.

ODS

See Output Delivery System.

one-to-one matching

the process of combining observations from two or more data sets into one observation using two or more SET statements to read observations independently from each data set. See also match-merging.

one-to-one merging

the process of using the MERGE statement (without a BY statement) to combine observations from two or more data sets based on the observations' positions in the data sets. See also match-merging.

output buffer

in the DATA step, the area of memory to which a PUT statement writes before writing to a designated file or output device.

Output Delivery System (ODS)

a system that can produce output in a variety of formats such as HTML, PDF, Listing, PostScript, and a SAS data set.

output object

a combination of procedure or DATA step output and a table definition. An output object tells the Output Delivery System how to format the output.

padding a value with blanks

in SAS, a process in which the software adds blanks to the end of a character value that is shorter than the length of the variable.

period

the default character that SAS uses to print or display a missing value for a numeric variable.

permanent SAS data library

a library that is not deleted when the SAS session terminates; it is available for subsequent SAS sessions. Unless the USER libref is defined, you use a two-level name to access a file in a permanent library. The first-level name is the libref, and the second-level name is the member name.

permanent SAS data set

a data set that remains after the current program or interactive SAS session terminates. Permanent SAS data sets are available for future SAS sessions.

permanent SAS file

a file in a SAS data library that is not deleted when the SAS session or job terminates.

physical filename

the name that the operating environment uses to identify a file.

pointer

in the DATA step, a programming tool that SAS uses to keep track of its position in the input or output buffer.

pointer control

the process of instructing SAS to move the pointer before reading or writing data.

print file

an external file containing carriage-control (printer-control) information. See also carriage-control character and external file.

PROC step

a group of SAS statements that call and execute a procedure, usually with a SAS data set as input.

procedure

See SAS procedure.

PROFILE catalog

a SAS catalog in a special SAS data library that contains information used by the SAS System to control various aspects of your display manager session. See also SASUSER library.

program data vector

the temporary area of memory, or storage area, where SAS builds a SAS data set, one observation at a time. Note that the program data vector is a logical concept that is independent of physical implementation.

programming error

a flaw in the logic of a SAS program that can cause it to fail or to perform differently than the programmer intended. See also syntax error.

propagation of missing values

a consequence of using missing values in which a missing value in an arithmetic expression causes SAS to set the result of the expression to missing. Using that result in another expression causes the next result to be missing, and so on.

raw data

data that have not been read into a SAS data set. See also data lines and raw data file.

raw data file

an external file whose records contain data values in fields. A DATA step can read a raw data file by using the INFILE and INPUT statements.

record

a logical unit of information consisting of fields of related data. A collection of records makes up a file. A record is analogous to a SAS observation or a row in a SAS data set.

requestor window

a window that SAS displays that either provides information only or enables you to confirm, cancel, or modify an action.

SAS catalog

a SAS file that stores many different kinds of information in smaller units called catalog entries. A single SAS catalog can contain several different types of catalog entries.

SAS catalog entry

a separate storage unit within a SAS catalog. Each entry has an entry type that identifies its purpose to SAS. Some catalog entries contain system information such as key definitions. Other catalog entries contain application information such as window definitions, help windows, formats, informats, macros, or graphics output.See also entry type.

SAS command

a command that invokes SAS software. This command may vary depending on operating environment and site. See also SAS invocation.

SAS compilation

the process of converting statements in the SAS language from the form in which you enter them into a form ready for SAS software to use.

SAS data file

a SAS data set that contains both data values and descriptor information associated with the data, such as the variable attributes. SAS data files have the type DATA. See also SAS data set and SAS data view.

SAS data library

a collection of one or more SAS files that are recognized by SAS software and that are referenced and stored as a unit. Each file is a member of the library.

SAS data set

descriptor information and its related data values organized as a table of observations and variables that can be processed by SAS. A SAS data set can be either a SAS data file or a SAS data view.

SAS data set option

an option that appears in parentheses after a SAS data set name. Data set options specify actions that apply only to the processing of that SAS data set. See also SAS system option.

SAS data view

a SAS data set in which the descriptor information and the observations are obtained from other files. A SAS data view contains only the descriptor and other information required to retrieve the data values from other SAS files. Both PROC SQL views and SAS/ACCESS views are considered SAS data views. SAS data views are of member type VIEW. See also SAS data set and SAS data file.

SAS date constant

a string in the form '*ddMMMyy*'d or '*ddMMMyyyy*'d representing a date in a SAS statement. The string should be enclosed in quotes and followed by the character *d* (for example '06JUL2001'd).

SAS date value

an integer representing a date in SAS software. The integer represents the number of days between January 1, 1960, and another specified date. (For example, the SAS date value 366 represents the calendar date January 1, 2001.)

SAS datetime constant

a string in the form '*ddMMMyy*: *hh:mm*: *ss*'dt or or '*ddMMMyyyy* : *hh* : *mm* : *ss*'dt representing a date and time in SAS. The string should be enclosed in quotes and followed by the characters *dt* (for example, '06JUL2001:09:53:22'dt).

SAS datetime value

an integer representing a date and time in SAS. The integer represents the number of seconds between midnight, January 1, 1960, and another specified date and time. (For example, the SAS datetime value for 9:30 a.m., June 5, 2000, is 928661400.)

SAS Display Manager System

an interactive, windowing interface to SAS System software. Display manager commands can be issued by typing them on the command line, pressing function keys, or selecting items from the PMENU facility. Within one session, many different tasks can be accomplished, including preparing and submitting programs, viewing and printing results, and debugging and resubmitting programs.

SAS Editor

a text-editing facility available in some windows of the SAS windowing environment, as well as in windows of SAS/AF, SAS/FSP, and SAS/GRAPH software.

SAS execution

the process in which SAS follows the instructions given by SAS statements to perform an action.

SAS expression

a sequence of operands and operators forming a set of instructions that SAS performs to produce a result value. A single variable name, constant, or function is also a SAS expression.

SAS file

a specially structured file that is created, organized, and, optionally, maintained by SAS. A SAS file can be a SAS data set, a catalog, a stored program, or an access descriptor.

SAS initialization

the setting of global characteristics that must be in place at start-up for a SAS programming environment. SAS performs initialization by setting certain SAS system options called initialization options. Invoking SAS software initiates SAS initialization. See also SAS invocation.

SAS invocation

the process of calling or starting up SAS software by an individual user through execution of the SAS command. Invoking SAS initiates SAS initialization. See also SAS initialization.

SAS keyword

a literal that is a primary part of the SAS language. Keywords are statement names, function names, command names, macro statement names, and macro function names.

SAS language

> 1 a programming language used to manage data.
> 2 as a grouping in SAS documentation, all parts of base SAS software except procedures and the windowing environment.

SAS log

a file that contains the SAS statements you have submitted, messages about the execution of your program, and in some cases, output from the DATA step and from certain procedures.

SAS name

a name whose construction follows certain rules and that can appear in a SAS statement (for example, names of variables and SAS data sets).

SAS print file

an obsolete term that refers to an external file to which a DATA step or a SAS procedure writes output that contains, by default, carriage-control characters, titles, footnotes, and page numbers. Do not use this term. It blurs the distinction between SAS files and external files. Instead, use the term "procedure output file."

SAS procedure

a program accessed with a PROC statement that produces reports, manages files, or analyzes data. Many procedures are included in SAS software.

SAS procedure output file

an obsolete term that makes an external file sound like a SAS file. Use the term "procedure output file" when you need to refer to the destination instead of to the procedure output itself.

SAS program

a group of SAS statements that guide SAS through a process or series of processes.

SAS session

an environment created by invoking SAS in which you can give commands, submit SAS statements, receive responses to the commands, and receive results of the SAS statements until you exit the environment or until the environment is terminated.

SAS Software Consultant

an individual at your computing installation who is designated as a support person for SAS software users at the installation. The consultant can help you with questions about using SAS software.

SAS Software Representative

an individual at your computing installation who is designated as SAS Institute's contact for information on new and existing software. The representative receives any distribution package of software from SAS.

SAS statement

a string of SAS keywords, SAS names, and special characters and operators ending in a semicolon that instructs SAS to perform an operation or that gives information to SAS.

SAS system option

an option that affects processing the entire SAS program or interactive SAS session from the time the option is specified until it is changed. Examples of items controlled by SAS system options include appearance of SAS output, handling of some files used by SAS, use of system variables, processing observations in SAS data sets, features of SAS System initialization, and the way SAS interacts with your computer hardware and with the host operating environment.

SAS time constant

a string in the form 'hh: mm : ss't representing a time in a SAS statement. The string should be enclosed in quotes and followed by the character t (for example, '09:53:22't).

SAS time value

an integer representing a time in SAS software. The integer represents the number of seconds between midnight of the current day and another specified time value. (For example, the SAS time value for 9:30 a.m. is 34200.)

SAS windowing environment

See SAS Display Manager System.

SASUSER library

a default permanent SAS data library that is created at the beginning of your first SAS session. It contains a PROFILE catalog that stores the tailoring features you specify for SAS. You can also store other SAS files in this library. See also PROFILE catalog and SAS data library.

selection field

the portion of a window (shown on the display as an underscore) where you can enter a short command to perform an action, such as B for browse.

selection-field command

a command that enables you to perform actions from a selection field in a SAS windowing environment. For example, entering D in the selection field beside the name of a SAS data set in the DIRECTORY window enables you to delete that SAS data set.

simple expression

a SAS expression that uses only one operator.

simple index

an index that locates observations by the values of one variable. See also composite index and index.

site number

the number used by SAS to identify the site to which SAS software is licensed. The site number appears near the top of the log in every SAS session.

split character

in some SAS procedures, a character that splits headers across multiple lines. If you use the split character in a column header, the procedure breaks the header when it reaches that character and continues the header on the next line. The split character itself is not part of the column header.

standard data

data that are stored with one digit or character per byte.

statement label

a SAS name followed by a colon that prefixes a statement in a DATA step so that other statements can direct execution to that statement as necessary, bypassing other statements in the step.

statement option

a word you specify in a given SAS statement that affects only the processing that statement performs.

step boundary

a point in a SAS program when SAS recognizes that a DATA step or PROC step is complete.

sum statement

a DATA step statement that adds the result of the expression on the right side of the plus sign to the accumulator variable on the left side of the plus sign. A sum statement has the following form: *variable + expression*;

summary table

output that provides a concise overview of the information in a data set.

syntax checking

the process by which SAS checks each SAS statement for proper usage, correct spelling, proper SAS naming conventions, and so on.

syntax error

an error in the spelling or grammar of a SAS statement. SAS finds syntax errors as it compiles each SAS step before execution.

system option

See SAS system option.

table definition

a set of instructions that describes how to format output in the Output Delivery System.

temporary SAS data library

a library that exists only for the current SAS session or job. The most common temporary library is the WORK library. See also WORK data library.

temporary SAS data set

a data set that exists only for the duration of the current program or interactive SAS session. Temporary SAS data sets are not available for future SAS sessions.

temporary SAS file

a SAS file in a SAS data library (usually the WORK data library) that is deleted at the end of the SAS session or job.

text-editing command

a command specific to the text editor.

title
in SAS, a heading printed at the top of each page of SAS output or of the SAS log.

toggle
an option, parameter, or other mechanism that enables you to turn on or turn off a processing feature.

trailing at sign (@)
a special symbol used to hold a line so that you can read from it or write to it with another INPUT or PUT statement.

transaction data set
in an update operation, the data set containing the information needed to update the master data set. See also master data set.

type, variable
See variable type.

updating
a process in which SAS replaces the values of variables in the master data set with values from observations in the transaction data set.

USER data library
a SAS data library defined with the libref USER. When the libref USER is defined, SAS uses it as the default libref for one-level names.

user-written format
a format you define with the FORMAT procedure. See also format.

user-written informat
an informat you define with the FORMAT procedure. See also informat.

variable
a column in a SAS data set. A variable is a set of data values that describe a given characteristic across all observations. See also macro variable.

variable attributes
the name, label, format, informat, type, and length associated with a particular variable.

variable list
a list of variables. You can use abbreviated variable lists in many SAS statements instead of listing all the variable names.

variable type
the classification of a variable as either numeric or character. Type is an attribute of SAS variables.

WHERE expression
a type of SAS expression used to specify a condition for selecting observations for processing by a DATA or PROC step. WHERE expressions can contain special operators not available in other SAS expressions. WHERE expressions can appear in a WHERE statement, a WHERE= data set option, a WHERE clause, or a WHERE command. See also SAS expression and WHERE processing.

WHERE processing
a method of conditionally selecting observations for processing in a DATA or PROC step. WHERE processing involves using a WHERE expression in a WHERE statement, a WHERE= data set option, a WHERE clause, or a WHERE command. See also WHERE expression.

WORK data library
the SAS data library automatically defined by SAS at the beginning of each SAS session or SAS job. It contains SAS files that are temporary by default. When the

libref USER is not defined, SAS uses WORK as the default library for SAS files created with one-level names.

WORK library
See WORK data library.

Index

Your Turn

If you have comments or suggestions about *Step-by-Step Programming with Base SAS, Version 9*, please send them to us on a photocopy of this page or send us electronic mail.

Send comments about this book to

SAS Publishing
Publications Division
SAS Campus Drive
Cary, NC 27513
email: yourturn@unx.sas.com

Send suggestions about the software to

SAS Institute Inc.
Technical Support Division
SAS Campus Drive
Cary, NC 27513
email: suggest@unx.sas.com